The Eighteenth Century
in Indian History

OXFORD IN INDIA READINGS

Themes in Indian History

The Eighteenth Century in Indian History

EVOLUTION OR REVOLUTION?

Edited by

P.J. MARSHALL

OXFORD
UNIVERSITY PRESS

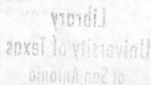

OXFORD
UNIVERSITY PRESS

YMCA Library Building, Jai Singh Road, New Delhi 110001

Oxford University Press is a department of the University of Oxford. It
furthers the University's objective of excellence in research, scholarship, and
education by publishing worldwide in

Oxford New York
Auckland   Cape Town   Dar es Salaam   Hong Kong   Karachi
Kuala Lumpur   Madrid   Melbourne   Mexico City   Nairobi
New Delhi   Shanghai   Taipei   Toronto

With offices in
Argentina   Austria   Brazil   Chile   Czech Republic   France   Greece
Guatemala   Hungary   Italy   Japan   Poland   Portugal   Singapore
South Korea   Switzerland   Thailand   Turkey   Ukraine   Vietnam

Oxford is a registered trade mark of Oxford University Press
in the UK and in certain other countries

Published in India
by Oxford University Press, New Delhi

© Oxford University Press 2003

The moral rights of the author have been asserted
Database right Oxford University Press (maker)

First published 2003
Oxford India Paperbacks 2005

ISBN-13: 978-0-19-567814-7
ISBN-10: 0-19-567814-1

Typeset by Guru Typograph Technology, New Delhi 110045
Printed in India at Roopak Printers, Delhi 110 032
Published by Manzar Khan, Oxford University Press
YMCA Library Building, Jai Singh Road, New Delhi 110 001

Contents

Acknowledgements

The editor and the publisher are happy to acknowledge the generous permission granted to them by the authors to reproduce the essays and articles in this volume. They are particularly grateful to Mrs M. Athar Ali and Mrs Dorothy Stein for their generosity in permitting us to reproduce the work of their late husbands, Professor M. Athar Ali and Professor Burton Stein. Professor Irfan Habib has been kind enough to supply a revised version of his essay on 'The Eighteenth Century in Indian Economic History'.

Items 1 and 4 are reproduced by permission of Ashgate Publishing Ltd; item 3 has been reproduced by permission of the Indian Council for Historical Research; items 2, 7, 9 and 11 by permission of Sage Publications India Private Ltd; items 8 and 13 by permission of Cambridge University Press; item 10 by permission of Oxford University Press, India; item 12 by permission of Princeton University Press; item 14 by permission of Pearson Education; item 15 by permission of Manohar Publishers and Distributors. The copyrights for items 5 and 6 are vested in the authors, Professor C.A. Bayly and Bernard S. Cohn. We acknowledge with gratitude permission given to us to publish this material. The editor would like to thank Professor C.A. Bayly for his valuable suggestions for the contents of this volume.

P.J. Marshall

Introduction

In 1700 the Mughal emperor Aurangzeb ruled over an empire that extended across the north of the Indian subcontinent from Kabul to Assam and whose southern frontier he had recently carried almost to the tip of peninsular India. By 1750, however, Mughal territorial power had shrunk to virtually nothing. Everywhere it had been replaced by a wide variety of autonomous political entities that are usually called 'successor states'. Fifty years later, at the end of the eighteenth century, the political configuration of India was clearly taking on a new shape: a European power, the British East India Company, now dominated both eastern India and the peninsula, while its influence extended far up the Ganges valley and its armies were shortly to coerce the Marathas, the only Indian power that might have replaced Mughal hegemony. A further fifty years was to see British domination over the whole of South Asia.

The British in India immediately began to refer to the battle of Plassey in 1757 and the events following it that first gave them territorial power as a 'revolution' that had led to further revolutions.[1] By the later eighteenth century, Indians who had been brought up in the traditions of Mughal rule were seeing the changes that they associated with the fall of that empire and the unmistakable rise of a new one as an *inqilab*; a world turned upside down.[2]

It is therefore hardly surprising that historians should long have endorsed contemporaries' verdicts that the eighteenth century had been a period of revolutionary change. To many British writers of the age of empire there had been a decline from order into 'the great anarchy, which is only another name for the history of the Mughal empire in its last days', before the foundations were laid for a new British order.[3] Others with different views saw the emergence of an entirely new pattern of economic relations in which foreign domination was to begin the 'perpetual Economic Drain from India', which has ever since made it 'a land of poverty and famine'.[4] Another point of view saw from the mid-eighteenth century the sowing of the seeds of a cultural revolution, in which 'the blight of medieval theocratic rule' would yield to the 'revivifying touch of the new impetus from the west'.[5]

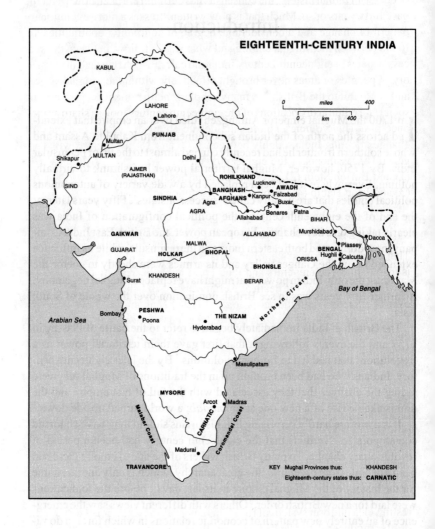

EIGHTEENTH-CENTURY INDIA

KABUL

LAHORE
Lahore
PUNJAB
Multan
Shikapur   MULTAN
Delhi
AJMER
(RAJASTHAN)
SIND   ROHILKHAND
BANGHASH   Lucknow
SINDHIA   AFGHANS   Kanpur Faizabad
Agra   Buxar
AGRA   Benares Patna
Allahabad   BIHAR
GAIKWAR   ALLAHABAD   Murshidabad   Dacca
GUJARAT   MALWA   Plassey
HOLKAR   BHOPAL   BENGAL   Hughli Calcutta
ORISSA
KHANDESH   BHONSLE
Surat   BERAR
Bay of Bengal
PESHWA   Northern Circars
Arabian Sea   Bombay   Poona   THE NIZAM
Hyderabad

Masulipatam

MYSORE
Arcot   Madras
CARNATIC
Madurai

TRAVANCORE   KEY Mughal Provinces thus: KHANDESH
Eighteenth-century states thus: CARNATIC

0   miles   400
0   km   400

Malabar Coast   Coromandel Coast

Although, as the selections that follow will show, there are distinguished historians who still depict the eighteenth century as marking a drastic change of course in Indian history, the consensus has definitely broken down over the past thirty years or so. Much that is now written stresses a more evolutionary pattern of change and a considerable degree of continuity: continuities are found between the Mughal empire and what was to follow, between the successor states of eighteenth-century India and early British rule, and in the history of peoples or areas never brought effectively within the Mughal system and yet to fall to the British. To many scholars, neither the economic nor the social and cultural dislocations of the eighteenth century look as sharp as they once did. This volume explores the debate about the nature and pace of change affecting India roughly between 1700 and 1800. It begins with four general assessments of the eighteenth century, two, those of Frank Perlin (1) and Burton Stein (2), stressing continuities, two, those of M. Athar Ali (3) and Irfan Habib (4), emphasizing disruption.

SUCCESSORS TO THE MUGHAL EMPIRE

That a great imperial system had collapsed by the mid-eighteenth century is irrefutable. The emperors and their court at Delhi were by then virtually powerless. Following the death of Aurangzeb in 1707, there was a rapid turnover of emperors until the accession in 1719 of Muhammad Shah, who was to reign until 1748. He, like his predecessors, had however fallen under the domination of rival factions of court nobility who competed for influence over him. Resources were dissipated, policy initiatives were not carried through and, most portentously for the future of the empire, control over the provinces atrophied.[6] In 1739 the imperial armies were defeated by the invading forces of Nadir Shah, who had seized power in Iran. Delhi was subsequently sacked and a huge indemnity was carried off by the invaders. Afghan invaders broke into northern India four times in mid-century. In 1757 they captured the emperor whose suzerain they claimed to be.[7] For most of the later eighteenth century the emperor lived at Delhi under the protection of the Marathas. From 1803 the British became his protectors.

The ideal of Mughal governance had been a closely integrated empire resting on a uniform system of rule. This rule was to be sustained by taxation on the produce of the land, levied on the same principles throughout the empire. The revenue thus generated was allocated either to an aristocracy who were bound in return to raise and maintain most of the imperial army, or was used to provide the resources needed by the government. Imperial officials maintained order and law officers administered justice. The structure of offices in each province was in theory much the same; office holders served wherever they were appointed and were directly responsible to the emperor, not to the governor of the province. By the middle of the eighteenth century, however, the empire had fragmented into autonomous units ruled without reference to Delhi.

At first sight, the case for cataclysmic change with the disintegration of a great centralized empire seems clear. There is, however, room for debate both about how far a system of centralized imperial administration had ever operated effectively, even in the heyday of Mughal rule, and also about the extent to which Mughal ideals and practices were in fact able to survive the withering of imperial power in the eighteenth century.

The debate about the nature of the Mughal state before the eighteenth century is the theme of a volume by Muzaffar Alam and Sanjay Subrahmanyam in the same series as this book. The editors stress that the empire at any time was always a 'patchwork quilt' of areas over which imperial control operated at very uneven levels, rather than 'a wall-to-wall carpet' of uniform rule. As the empire expanded, the system of taxation and of a service nobility of *mansabdars* could rarely be applied with full rigour to the newly acquired provinces.[8]

Resistance to Mughal authority was widespread well before Aurangzeb's death. By then Mughal attempts to absorb what the Marathas claimed as their homeland in the western Deccan, either by conquest or by incorporating individual Maratha leaders into the imperial system, had failed. Rajput chiefs had long been generally reliable allies of the empire, but attempts to bring their territory more closely under imperial authority provoked fierce resistance during Aurangzeb's reign. In the Punjab, the writ of the Mughal governor was being contested at the end of the seventeenth century by communities of Sikhs. South of Delhi imperial communications were blocked by Jat insurgency, which had not been brought under control by the end of Aurangzeb's reign. Afghan groups constantly challenged Mughal rule in the province of Kabul and they were migrating into India in increasing numbers as traders or as soldiers, nominally in Mughal service but often with ambitions of their own.

The new political order that had emerged by the middle of the eighteenth century in some respects reflected the strengths and weaknesses of the later Mughal empire. Effective Mughal rule had required the subordination of what in the essay by Bernard S. Cohn (5) are called 'regional' or 'local' powers, that is a wide variety of chiefs, rajas, or clan leaders. Subordination had been more complete in some areas than in others. Similarly, as the imperial ties relaxed, the governors of some of the old imperial provinces were able to maintain an effective domination over the regional and local powers within the province and turn it into a new state under their rule. In other provinces authority fragmented and a variety of claimants were able to carve out their own domains.

Nizam al-Mulk, Asaf Jah, set the trend for governors to detach provinces from the empire when he claimed the eastern Deccan as his personal dominion after 1724. Within a few years the southern districts of his jurisdiction were passing under the autonomous rule of officials who styled themselves nawabs of Arcot or of the Carnatic. In the early eighteenth century Murshid Kuli Khan founded a dynasty of rulers in Bengal, and later in Bihar, who asserted increasing autonomy until they unmistakably displayed their independence from Delhi after 1740. In the 1750s, Awadh emerged as an effectively independent state under its governor Safdar Jang. A number of provinces passed into the hands not of Mughal noblemen but of Maratha generals. From the 1720s the Marathas drove northward to bring the provinces of Khandesh, Gujarat, Malwa, Berar, Agra, and most of Orissa under their control. These spoils were divided between the successful Sardars or leaders and became their own domains under the loose suzerainty of the Peshwa, the chief minister of the now powerless Maratha royal house. Afghan leaders incorporated the province of Kabul and Sind into a new kingdom and for a time also ruled in the name of the Mughals in the Punjab.

By the 1750s, however, both Mughal and Afghan claims in the Punjab were being successfully defied by the Sikhs. Following a long period of separate Sikh principalities, a unitary Sikh state was created after 1799 through the ascendancy of a single clan leader, Ranjit Singh. The chiefs of Rajasthan gradually subverted Mughal authority throughout the eighteenth century as they established their own domains. The Jats raided over a wide area, at times occupying Delhi and Agra, until they were penned into states of their own by the Maratha advance. Small Rajput states also survived on the Maratha frontier in Bundelkhand. To the east of Awadh, Rajput and Bhumihar chiefs sought to wrest concessions from the nawabs of Awadh and of Bengal and Bihar. Groups of Afghan migrants asserted their independence in northern India in the eighteenth century. Two considerable and wealthy polities, those of the Rohillas and the Bangash Afghans, were established in the Ganges–Jumna valley.[9] An Afghan polity was also created in the 1720s in Bhopal in central India.

If the exercise of Mughal authority had never constituted a uniform system even in the seventeenth century, the breaking of the links between Delhi and the provinces in the eighteenth century need not necessarily be seen as a political revolution on the scale that it is often assumed to have been. It in no

way marked the end either of the ideals or of the practice of Mughal governance. Both survived into the nineteenth century to influence even the British.
Alternative sources of legitimacy to the endorsement of the emperor, however
nominal, were very slow to emerge. It has been suggested that the cultural
dominance of the Mughal court may actually have become more pervasive as
its political power waned. The later emperors, no doubt in tacit recognition
of their weakness, became more inclusive of Hindus and Shi'ite Muslims and
more ecumenical in their cultural patronage.[10]

The rulers of successor states, the nawabs of the Deccan, Awadh, and Bengal, who were nominal Mughal governors, naturally transplanted the culture
of the imperial court to their new cities: Hyderabad in the eastern Deccan,
Faizabad or Lucknow in Awadh, and Murshidabad in Bengal. Although there
were also significant new trends in their administrative systems, which will
be discussed shortly, the regimes of the former Mughal governors tended to
perpetuate Mughal forms and practices. The hierarchies of officials bore the
same titles, and revenue was assessed and collected on the same essential
principles. The vitality of Mughal institutions is strongly suggested by the
way in which what has been called 'the ideological and bureaucratic structure
of Mughal imperialism' was being adopted throughout the first half of the
eighteenth century by new communities, who, at a great distance in every
sense from Delhi, were colonizing the eastern delta of Bengal.[11] During the
eighteenth century Mughal principles of governance were also being established for the first time in new territory by the nawabs of Arcot in the far
south.[12]

The willingness of regimes that had taken power out of conflict with the
Mughals, and were asserting an ethnic identity of their own also to preserve
Mughal forms, is further evidence of their vitality. The Marathas maintained
sovereign claims on their own behalf without denying the sovereign claims
of the Mughal emperor.[13] In areas where their rule became firmly established,
as Stewart Gordon and John F. Richards show (9), they collected revenue
on Mughal principles, even if they used different names for their officials.[14]
Although the Sikhs developed distinctive community institutions like the
khalsa, which were eventually strongly to oppose Mughal claims, they too
still collected revenue on Mughal principles and alienated large blocks of
land to notables in Mughal-style *jagirs*.[15] Even in the nineteenth century,
qazis throughout the Punjab continued to administer the shariat law as in
Mughal times.[16] Persian remained the official language of diplomacy and of
high-level administration in all those states that had once been part of the
Mughal empire, even when these came under the British. Abdul Majed Khan
(13) describes how an experienced Indian administrator tried to educate the

British in Bengal about the ideals of Mughal statecraft.[17] At least until the 1780s, the British were trying to inform themselves about what they called 'the original constitution of the Mogul empire', thought by them to have been established by Akbar, and to model their government on that.[18]

Notwithstanding the persistence of Mughal ideals and forms of governance throughout the eighteenth century, new trends have been detected in the successor states. These trends appear to have their roots in developments during the seventeenth century. Economic expansion that carried on at least into the first half of the eighteenth century is seen as crucial to them. Over much of India there appears to have been an increase in agricultural output with the extension of the area under cultivation and a growing volume of trade, both internal and by land and sea, with other parts of Asia and with Europe. The chief beneficiaries of economic expansion seem to have been groups between the imperial nobility or their successors, on the one hand, and the vast mass of those who cultivated the land or worked in the towns, on the other. C.A. Bayly, whose analysis of them in northern India is included in this volume (6), describes them as 'a range of intermediate entities' who were situated between 'the revenue-based state and the mass of agrarian society'.[19] 'Regional gentry' is a term sometimes applied to them.[20]

Prominent among such groups were the zamindars, a flexible category with an enormous range from great rajas controlling large blocks of territory and people, to village peasant élites. They held rights to appropriate a portion of the produce of the land. The claims of many of them pre-dated Mughal rule and the Mughals had of necessity to reach accommodations with them, using intimidation and armed coercion as well as the rewards from incorporation into the new order to serve the empire in return for guaranteed income and privileges. Zamindari resistance was, however, more or less endemic whenever the opportunity to rebel presented itself. The Marathas prosecuted their claims as zamindars.[21] The Sikhs had 'a strong social base among the zamindars', particularly among the Jats of the Punjab.[22] Through their control over peasant cultivators, zamindars were able to appropriate for themselves rather than for the Mughal tax system much of the wealth being created by increased agricultural production, and they profited from investments in agricultural improvements and the extension of cultivation.

Other important intermediate groups were the merchant communities, whose operations ranged from stalls in village markets to bulk trading in local towns, banking businesses in the capitals of provinces, export and import from the seaports. Both C.A. Bayly for North India (6) and Rajat Datta for Bengal (15) give accounts of merchant communities in this volume.

Also gaining in importance in the eighteenth century were those who held civil and military office or were supported by grants of revenue as rewards for their piety and learning: people who have been described as 'a locally resident gentry of literate service families'.[23] They too were able to exploit the wealth being generated in the countryside and benefited from the increased flows of trade that enriched the local towns or *qasba*s where many of them lived.[24]

It is the theme of much recent writing that the successor states proved to be more adept than the Mughal empire at gaining the acquiescence of these intermediate groups and thus in rooting their regimes in local support that was to sustain them as the centralizing ambitions and coercive power of the empire decayed. Local gentry with military or administrative skills, merchants and financiers were all given opportunities to profit from the new states' needs, to obtain employment for themselves under them, and to enjoy the patronage that they offered.

A study of Awadh has shown how the new ruler came to terms with zamindars who had a long history of opposition to Mughal government in the past and succeeded in binding them into 'a very loosely organized ruling group' who supported his regime. Hindus held high office in the nawabs of Awadh's government and Hindu ascetics made an important contribution to their forces under their leader, the warlord Anupgira or 'Himmat Bahadur'.[25] The nawabs of Bengal also based their rule on the support of zamindars, made extensive use of local Hindus in high administrative offices formerly filled by Muslims appointed in Delhi, and allowed merchants and bankers to profit from the government in return for their services.[26] The Brahmin Peshwas became the chief ministers of the Maratha kings with an extensive domain of their own, while all the other Maratha rulers recruited Brahmin administrators, especially the Chitpavan sub-caste. Bankers had an important role in the revenue administration and military finance of all the Maratha states.[27] Throughout eighteenth-century India, 'As they struggled to consolidate their increasingly complex armies, tax-farming networks and commercial systems, the new dynasts . . . found an ever-growing need for men of piety and learning to maximize their revenue, to maintain their records and intelligence networks, and grace their courts and sacred foundations with the civilities expected of an established royal dominion'.[28]

The rewards of service to the new states went beyond the strictly material. New rulers everywhere sought legitimacy for themselves in religious terms. The eighteenth century has been seen as an important phase in the formalizing of caste ideals. New rulers, assuming the kingly role of Kshatriyas, extended their patronage to Brahmins and their shrines.[29] The religious endowments of previous regimes were strictly maintained: Sikhs for instance, respecting those of Muslims in the Punjab. While the nawabs of Awadh were assiduous in their patronage of fellow Shi'ite Muslims, they honoured other traditions.[30] As Susan Bayly's chapter, reprinted in this collection (8) shows, the nawab of the Carnatic was munificent to Hindu temples as well as to Muslim holy places.[31] Through such acts of patronage rulers identified themselves with the local cultural traditions of the regions over which they were trying to consolidate new states as well as with norms of kingship thought to have universal authority.

While preserving Mughal forms, the regimes in the new eighteenth-century states tended to inject fresh elements into them or at least to intensify trends apparent in later Mughal rule. The reach of the state was generally extended by a more intrusive administration and its operations became increasingly commercialized. Wherever possible, revenues allocated in the past to *jagirs* for the support of imperial *mansabdars* were put under the direct management of the state as *khalisah* land, or at least the successor state took over the awarding of jagirs. The state's administrators, *amils*, *diwans*, or *kamavisdars* in Maratha usage, supervised the assessment and collection of revenue more closely and generated an ever 'greater quantity, quality and frequency of information' for their rulers.[32] *Ijara*, that is farming out blocks of revenue effectively to the highest bidder for limited periods, spread very widely. Such practices were not approved of in high Mughal statecraft, as they weakened imperial control and were likely to lead to excessive exactions from the countryside without regard to its long-term prosperity. Nevertheless, what amounted to the sale of contracts to raise revenue usually ensured a higher return for the state and gave opportunities for successful zamindars to extend their holdings by farming the revenue of extra land and for moneyed men to develop an interest in the land, either by taking on revenue farms themselves or, as was the general practice, by advancing money to those who did.

Throughout India the richest merchants and bankers were gaining a stake in the new political order. The analysis in C.A. Bayly's chapter (6) of how this was being brought about in northern India has strong affinities elsewhere. The services of bankers meant that the state could rely on prompt cash payment of the revenue which the farmer or zamindar had undertaken to pay. Underwriting the revenue system by enabling the renters to pay on time, and the money to be remitted by bill from where it had been collected to the ruler's capital or wherever else it was needed was one of the essential services of bankers to the new states. Rulers themselves borrowed in advance of their revenue, above all for their military needs, from the most substantial bankers. To British observers, the Jagat Seth Marwari family, bankers to the nawabs of Bengal, seemed to be as rich as the Bank of England. They received the zamindars' revenue payments, managed the Bengal mints, and remitted the tribute due to the emperors to Delhi. In return for their invaluable services, moneyed men could extract concessions from the state. What might be involved has again been revealed from studies of Bengal, where individual merchants were given monopoly grants over commodities like salt and saltpetre and wielded political authority in the saltpetre districts.[33]

Eighteenth-century rulers needed the liquid funds which merchants could provide primarily for the upkeep of their armies. A large part of the Mughal armies had been raised by commanders from their assignments of revenue. The forces of the new states were generally paid for directly by the state in cash from the taxation that it collected itself. Armies were becoming increasingly expensive. The Mughals had maintained a formidable artillery train, employing a large number of foreign artificers, but in addition to expanding their artillery, the new states increasingly imitated the European East India companies in recruiting and drilling to a high standard infantry regiments armed with muskets. In the 1760s the nawab of Awadh was thought to have 268 artillery pieces in addition to his regiments of infantry that were part of the 50,000 men he kept under arms.[34]

The historiography of political change in eighteenth-century India has been dominated by the transition of Mughal provinces into successor states or by the carving out of new domains in the former provinces by rebellious groups. Large areas, however, remained either outside Mughal rule altogether or on the fringes of its effective administrative reach. Mughal governance might still be an influence, but there was no direct Mughal inheritance and different patterns of rule had evolved. Even in the heartlands of Mughal rule in northern and central India, large tracts remained in the eighteenth century beyond the pale of fixed cultivation and village settlement, on which direct Mughal administration was based. Forest or scrub land, often on hilly or other marginal terrain, was inhabited by people who practised shifting cultivation or pastoralism.[35] They had their own political systems and at the most rendered tribute to the Mughals rather than being subject to direct rule and taxation. Recent studies, such as that of Ajay Skaria in this book (11), stress that their relations with the peoples of the plains were not those of backward, 'tribal' outsiders, as they were to become from the nineteenth century onwards, but were marked by mutual dependence with exchange of produce and services (the military qualities of the hill peoples being especially valued) as well as periodic raiding and violence. With the decline of the empire during the eighteenth century the peoples of the hills and the forests became the concern of the rulers of the new states. The Marathas, for instance, fitfully tried to encourage disarming and settled agriculture among the Gonds and Bhils of western and central India, without effectively curbing their autonomy.[36]

In the far south of the Indian peninsula, Mughal rule had either never penetrated at all or had been transient, leaving only a limited impact. Political entities that had emerged from the fall of an earlier imperial system, that of Vijayanagar in the sixteenth century, survived into the eighteenth century. One of them, Mysore, developed on a scale to challenge any of the successor states of northern India. It evolved from the seventeenth century under the Hindu Wodeyar dynasty and then under the usurpations of the military commander Haidar Ali from 1761 and of his son, Tipu Sultan, who succeeded him in 1782. Haidar and Tipu built up a formidable state, maximizing its revenue by direct administration that cut out most intermediaries and by an unusual degree of regulation over certain trades for the benefit of the state. The pepper of the newly acquired Malabar territory was, for instance, placed under state control and was exported overseas in state merchant ships. Enhanced revenue was applied to the most potent and professionalized Indian army of the century. Like other new rulers of the eighteenth century, Haidar Ali sought recognition from the Mughal emperor Tipu, however, as is explained in Kate Brittlebank's chapter (10),[37] claimed himself to be a *padshah*, or emperor, independent of the Mughals. He sought confirmation from the Ottoman sultan at Constantinople.[38] In the manner of the successor states of the north, Mysore expanded at the expense of its neighbours. Small trading states along the Malabar coast of the Arabian Sea were absorbed, leaving only the largest of them, Travancore, also a 'modernizing' successor state, to be preserved by British intervention.

Small kingdoms also survived into the eighteenth century on the eastern coast of the Bay of Bengal. The extract from David Ludden's *Peasant History* describes them (12). They originated in the mostly Telugu *nayaka*s, who had been subordinate to Vijayanagar and had established their autonomy on its downfall, or from *palayakkaran*s or 'poligars', who carved out small domains from the territory of the *nayaka*s, based on temples and a highly militarized population. The effective independence of the small polities of the Coromandel Coast lasted until the mid-eighteenth century, when they began to fall victim to an expanding new state, that of the nawabs of the Carnatic, who with British support competed with Mysore for mastery over the peninsula.[39] On the north-east frontier of India Mughal expansion was halted and rolled back in the 1680s by the Ahom dynasty who maintained an independent Assam under a Hindu tradition of kingship until it was annexed by the British in the early nineteenth century.

The creation of a post-Mughal political order at times entailed serious disruption in some areas, but it cannot be described as a lapse into general anarchy. The transition from Mughal province to successor state was generally peaceful in Bengal or in the heartland of Awadh. It was less so in the eastern Deccan where the Mughals had been unable to create an effective administration in the wake of their conquest at the end of the seventeenth century and where the nizams had difficulty in asserting their authority over what they claimed after 1724.[40] With the weakening of Mughal government in the 1720s, the Punjab, once one of the richest provinces of the empire, went into steep decline before recovering later in the century.[41] The Marathas, who extended their control over so much of northern and central India and raided even further afield, have traditionally been seen as a force of disruption on a large scale. Recent research has, however, radically changed the picture for those provinces that came under their full control. As Stewart Gordon's and John F. Richards' study of a district in Khandesh (9) shows, once conquest had been completed and Maratha rule was secure, effective administration and a regulated revenue demand on Mughal principles was installed. Agriculture was encouraged and trade revived. By the late eighteenth century the domains of leaders like Sindhia, the Gaikwad, or the Bhonsles supported powerful armies sustained by effectively administered revenue systems. In the early stages of expansion, however, when raids enforced demands for contributions, much damage was done, notably to the rich commercial province of Gujarat, which began to recover later in the century. Right through the eighteenth century the Marathas continued to make plundering forays beyond their established frontiers, devastating parts of western Bengal in the 1740s and preying on the states of Rajasthan in the later eighteenth century.[42]

A considerable price in terms of disruption was paid for the fall of an imperial system that had spanned most of India. It is, moreover, likely that an effectively functioning Mughal empire would have been able to prevent Iranian and Afghan incursions from the west and might perhaps even have contained the Europeans on the coast. Attempted British raids in western India and Bengal were easily beaten off by the Mughals in the 1680s.

A new order with considerable potential for stability was, however, coming into existence in the eighteenth century. New states, Bengal, Awadh, Mysore, the Carnatic, the Maratha domains and in the early nineteenth century the Sikh state of the Punjab, were developing effective administrative systems with strong armed forces and consolidating their hold on their populations. They were also expanding to incorporate smaller entities. The Afghans of north India were subjugated by Awadh, Mysore took most of the Malabar states, and the nawabs of Arcot imposed their rule on the southern *nayaka*s. Expansion was producing armed conflicts, but these were usually limited both in their scope and objectives; the new states were not embroiling themselves in mutually destructive, uncontrolled warfare. They were able to survive the invasions of Nadir Shah and the Afghans, but an invasion from the sea by Europeans posed severe new problems for them. Some of the successor states succumbed early, while others tried, in some cases with a degree of success, to adapt to the new threat, above all by reforming their armed forces. By the mid-nineteenth century all such efforts had, however, proved to be vain.

THE INDIAN ECONOMY IN THE EIGHTEENTH CENTURY

Until recent years, it has generally been assumed that India's political history has determined its economic history. The commonly accepted version for this period was that there had been economic expansion under the Mughals because of the regime's capacity to maintain law and order over a huge area. According to one very influential interpretation, the Mughal system had eventually become too burdensome for the Indian economy to support. The regime's ever-increasing demands for revenue to sustain its nobility, its army, and its wars led to spiralling taxes that forced the peasants either to abandon the land or to resort to desperate rebellion.[43] The presumed collapse of law and order in the eighteenth century made any recovery impossible: invaders from outside, warring armies and plundering bands of Sikhs, Jats, or Marathas disrupted trade, sacked towns, and pillaged the countryside. Early British rule meant new wars of conquest and, according to different versions, either plunder of a new kind, as wealth was siphoned out of India, or a long *pax Britannica* in which economic recovery at last became possible.

Setting aside the British for the moment, the previous section of this Introduction indicated that simple propositions about the way in which a stable Mughal peace gave way to eighteenth-century chaos now look dubious. Important parts of India largely escaped upheavals, and elsewhere the incidence of war and disorder may have been less intense than was once supposed. This blurring of the previously stark outlines of political history has coincided with a tendency to write economic history in which the role of the state and its revenue extraction or the consequences of state failure in war and disorder, while certainly not excluded, are kept in proportion.[44] As has already been suggested, political disruption had important economic effects, for a time in Gujarat, in the Punjab, and in Rajasthan, to give obvious examples. In general, however, economic activity in India seems to have been much more robust and deep rooted than used to be supposed. The Mughals, the successor states and the early British all did their best to maximize the wealth they extracted in taxation, but their capacities were limited and much probably escaped them. Grievous as the immediate effects of war, rebellion, or Iranian and Afghan raids might be, recovery seems to have been quick.[45]

Most of the sources which historians have used in writing about eighteenth-century economic history before the dominance of the East India Company have been European ones: material largely derived from the operations of the companies on the coast and therefore inevitably focused on trade or from early British administrative records, notably those for Bengal, as skilfully interpreted by Rajat Datta (15). Rich indigenous sources do, however, survive for the Maratha Deccan, and in particular profusion for parts of Rajasthan. These have been put to very good use in recent studies.[46]

For all the huge regional variations, it is possible to offer some generalizations about an eighteenth-century Indian economy that was loosely integrated by long-distance trade even in cheap bulk commodities, by a common monetary system over much of India, albeit with many local variations, and by links between the financial centres of the subcontinent that enabled credit to be extended and money to be remitted over great distances.

Eighteenth-century India was predominantly an agricultural society, but with a very wide variety of manufacturing and service occupations that probably meant that a smaller proportion of the population was directly dependent on the land than would have been the case in the later nineteenth century under British rule. Datta's chapter (15) provides striking examples of the diversity of occupations within Bengal villages. The agrarian population did not constitute a homogeneous peasantry: it was stratified between the prosperous with large holdings, those who cultivated with their own labour and that of their families, and landless labourers or virtually landless sharecroppers. Ludden's chapter (12) describes a high degree of stratification in the wet lands of the south-east. The use of money was spreading very widely during the century. Wages were being paid in cash. Even small cultivators in many areas paid their taxes in cash, which they acquired by selling a portion of their crop.[47] There was a huge trade in basic food grains, often over long distances, as well as in crops grown specifically for the market, such as sugarcane, raw cotton or oil seeds. Textiles for local consumption were manufactured all over India, certain areas, usually coastal ones, specializing in high quality cloth to be carried overland for consumption in the main cities or to Iran and central Asia and by sea to western and south-east Asia and, through the foreign companies, to Europe, west Africa, and the Americas. Manufacturing and much agricultural production depended on the availability of credit. Raw materials, seed, or the wherewithal to pay tax demands were advanced to weavers and cultivators by their richer neighbours or by the agents of merchants, who received the crops or finished products in repayment. Merchants, including the foreign companies, who operated on a large scale at the ports or at the main inland commercial centres, obtained commodities for long distance trade by advancing money to local merchants. What they were able to advance had often been borrowed from bankers. There was much manufacturing in the countryside, especially of textiles. The distinction between town and countryside was indeed a blurred one. 'Urbanism lay inside agriculture rather than being set apart' from it.[48] Except perhaps for those who specialized in high quality cloth, many weavers and other artisans also cultivated land. Towns acted as market-places and as the centres for long-distance trade; they could also be seats of government and of the office holders involved in it or of local élites; and some had grown round places of pilgrimage. As well as their more prosperous inhabitants, towns attracted masses of servants, labourers, and artisans who worked on luxury goods. At the beginning of the century, the great cities of the Mughal empire, like Delhi, Lahore or Agra, were thought to have had up to 400,000 people in them.[49] The population of large ports, such as Surat,[50] Masulipatam, or the British cities of Madras and Calcutta, might have been about 100,000, while 'hundreds of prosperous market towns (qasbas) had proliferated in northern India'[51] and there had been a similar development of small towns in other regions.

If the framework within which economic activity took place is relatively clear, patterns of change within this framework during the century are much less so. Suggestions that the Mughal regime had provoked a deep economic crisis by the relentless increase of its demands on an economy that could not expand enough to meet them now seem generally to be discounted. Economic expansion appears to have continued right through the seventeenth century.[52] There are strong indications that this growth was maintained over much of India in the first half of the eighteenth century as well.

Growth in the first half of the century in Rajasthan has been clearly documented. Prices rose faster than the level of revenue demand. This provided the incentive for increasing the area under cultivation and for growing more valuable crops. Both grain, taken by the state as taxation, and cash crops were traded out of the province in large quantities.[53] In the Maratha Deccan prices, population, and the area under cultivation all increased.[54] In Bengal there was a marked extension of cultivation in response to the shift eastward of the course of the rivers in the Ganges delta, which had created favourable conditions for opening up new rice lands, whose produce went to feed the growing city of Calcutta and the textile manufacturing districts of the west. The annual transfer of Bengal's surplus taxation in specie by road and river to Delhi in most years up tó the 1740s made it by far the most reliable prop for imperial finances. Murshid Kuli Khan's new city of Murshidabad grew quickly.

For some provinces, such as the Punjab, the case for temporary economic decline by the mid-eighteenth century seems clear. For the great belt of northern India from Delhi to Patna in Bihar and for the eastern Deccan and the Coromandel Coast, the balance between expansion or decline is more difficult to determine. The sufferings of Delhi, as power and wealth left the imperial court, disorder came ever closer, cutting the city's commercial links to the south and west, and Nadir Shah devastated it, were graphically recorded by its poets, even if historians urge some caution in using their evidence.[55] The countryside around Delhi and Agra also went into decline as the Mughal canals were neglected.[56] Further to the east, however, in Awadh and the province of Allahabad, there is evidence of increasing prosperity in both country and towns. Higher revenue yields and the creation of new market centres have been used as evidence for the flourishing condition of agriculture in Awadh and the districts adjacent to it,[57] extending even as far to the east as Bihar, as Muzaffar Alam argues (7). Migrants were drawn to these areas from the unstable western districts. Towns grew vigorously. The nawabs of Awadh attracted large populations to their new cities of Fyzabad and Lucknow. Benares flourished as the capital of a new dynasty of local rulers, as a great commercial and financial centre and as a place of exceptional sanctity attracting many pilgrims. Setting regions of northern India that gained against those that lost, a verdict on the eighteenth century as a whole is that 'growth and decline . . . may have been more nearly balanced out than has usually been appreciated'.[58] Evidence for the south-east is scantier. For a time the eastern Deccan was spared the incursions of the Marathas, as they turned their attentions northwards. On the coast the ports of the British, the Dutch, and the French tended to do well, while some but by no means all, of the Indian ports suffered. There again appear to have been regional shifts: the ports of the northern Coromandel declined as their hinterlands were disrupted, while those further south did better. The judgement of the leading scholar of the region's maritime trade is that during the first half of the eighteenth century there was 'a downturn in economic activity and therefore in commerce. However, the downturn was neither absolute nor uniform.'[59]

If the overall balance for India as a whole suggests that the economic expansion of the seventeenth century continued through the first half of the next century, the impulses behind this continued expansion are not easy to identify. Population growth is unlikely to have been a significant influence. There is much evidence of ingenuity being applied to improve existing crops and practices of husbandry, but little to suggest major innovations in agriculture.[60] This also seems to have been the case with manufacturing. Where textile output increased, it seems essentially to have been due to more people taking up spinning and weaving as a part-time or full-time occupation and to closer control of the weavers and spinners being exercised by merchants and their agents, rather than to technological innovations.[61] Demand from countries outside India for textiles and commodities like raw silk, sugar, opium, or pepper had important consequences for coastal areas such as Gujarat, the Malabar and Coromandel Coasts, and Bengal, and for the often distant hinterlands which supplied the raw materials. The records of the British and Dutch companies show a great regional shift in textile exports to Europe from western India and to a lesser extent from the south-east to Bengal, and there was marked overall growth from the 1720s in the quantities shipped.[62] By the 1740s the French had also become major exporters, although not on the same scale. Trends in India's seaborne trade with other parts of Asia are less clear. Major outlets for Indian exports in western Asia, that is in Iran and around the Persian Gulf and the Red Sea were becoming increasingly disrupted, and compensating flows eastward to the Malay world and to China were as yet to develop fully. An increasing proportion of the trade was being handled by European ships. The great seventeenth-century ports, Surat, Hughli, and Masulipatam, were losing to European and, above all, to British-controlled ports, Madras and Calcutta, if not as yet Bombay. How trade fared overland out of India to the west is even more obscure. 'Long-distance Eurasian trade', according to a recent account, 'could still function on equal terms with overseas trade'. The Afghans developed the route to central Asia via Multan and Shikapur. They supplied India with huge numbers of horses and the caravans of the Indian merchants passed westward through their territory. That trade is said to have remained 'in a flourishing condition' until 'far into the eighteenth century'.[63] Nevertheless, if the overland trade may have been written off prematurely, expansion seems unlikely. Instability in Iran and in the western Mughal provinces of Kabul, Lahore, and Multan was a serious constraint.[64]

If it is unlikely that for the first half of the eighteenth century, with the exception of Bengal, external demand increased on a scale to be an important stimulus, the explanation for such overall growth as may have taken place has therefore to be sought within India. The evident prosperity of a broad band of what have already been identified as 'intermediate' sections of society in town and country appears to be the most probable candidate. Although they were able to batten on a high proportion of the taxes extracted from cultivators, they evidently passed back much of what they extracted through their consumption of higher quality food grains and other foodstuffs, their purchases of cloth and their demand for services of all sorts, including household servants and military retainers. This probably more than made up for any slackening in the demand from the Mughal court and the imperial aristocracy.

'Eighteenth-century north India', Bayly has written, 'possessed what might be called an "intermediate economy". . . . Its products were medium quality cloths, specialist fruit and vegetables and milk products; its services provisioning and carrying for local magnates and moving armies.'[65] Perlin's work on the Maratha Deccan describes how civil and military office-holders increasingly took up residence in small towns and villages, levying their shares in taxes and dues from the rural population, but returning much of what they collected in wages and what they paid for food and cloth for their households.[66] In the territory of the *nayakas* of Madurai in the far south, Ludden (12) shows how the demand of 'burgeoning towns housing state officials, traders, and temples' was sustained by the capacity of intermediaries to siphon off much of the rulers' revenue and to return it by their consumption to the countryside.[67]

If a clear case can be established for continuing economic growth over large parts of India during the first half of the eighteenth century, optimism about the second half of the century is more questionable. There were serious regional famines, notably in Bengal in 1769–70 and in the eastern tracts of northern India in 1783. From 1765, the British were in effective control in Bengal and Bihar, and it is conventionally assumed that both provinces immediately suffered. Although developments in Bengal are likely to have had wider consequences, assessment of them will be left to a later section. Elsewhere, for the two areas where indigenous records have been most extensively exploited, the trends seem to be contradictory. Perlin's findings for the Maratha Deccan suggest that the extension of cultivation, growing use of money, and expanding trade all continued until late in the century.[68] As the great Maratha leaders consolidated their hold on the territory that they claimed, they were able to maintain stable conditions at least into the 1790s. Huge quantities of cotton were exported from the Deccan to the west coast and Bengal.[69] Towns like Poona continued to grow. By contrast, the evidence from Rajasthan, badly affected by famine and the demands of the Marathas, clearly indicates decline in the later eighteenth century. Population fell, trade was disrupted, output declined, and prices were markedly lower.[70]

British influence became intrusive in northern India as Benares was directly incorporated into the East India Company's provinces after 1781 and the Awadh nawabs' revenues were burdened with a large subsidy to be paid for the services of British troops. The rulers of Awadh, however, became adept at protecting their resources from British demands,[71] and although there were many contemporary comments about the apparent decline of the province from the 1770s, and a devastating famine occurred in 1783, decline seems to have been selective. The revenue yield of Rohilkhand fell sharply,[72] but the city of Lucknow was magnificently embellished by the nawabs and new towns like Kanpur were growing rich on supplying the British garrisons.[73] Late eighteenth-century Benares continued to profit both from a prosperous countryside and from trade and financial dealing on a very large scale. Its bankers supported British operations all over India. They made extensive loans to the Company in times of need and transferred the money from Bengal to pay the British armies in the field via their correspondents in western and southern India. Further west, in areas that had languished earlier, there is evidence of recovery late in the eighteenth century. The Sikhs re-established stability, and with it a rising prosperity in the Punjab, and agriculture began to revive in the western Ganges–Jumna valley.[74]

Late eighteenth-century southern India was dominated by the rivalry of two powers, the rulers of Mysore, briefly supported by the French, and the nawab of the Carnatic, consistently backed by the British who fought his wars for him. Both succeeded in expanding the area under their control. The rulers of Mysore were initially successful in exporting war into the Carnatic, on which they inflicted serious damage from 1780 to 1782. In 1791–2 and 1799, however, their territory was invaded by the British and their Indian allies. These wars were notoriously destructive, but the movements of huge armies created many opportunities for the enrichment of the Indians who supplied them, especially the *banjaras* who followed the armies with their stocks of grain and other supplies.[75] Overall, however, military employment and higher wages seem to have been limited compensation for the disruption of agriculture and manufacturing by war and serious famine in the Carnatic from 1781 to 1783.[76] Overseas trade to Europe and south-east Asia seems to have held up well, although the role of the British and the Indian merchants associated with them became very dominant.[77]

Setting Bengal aside for further discussion, the most realistic verdict on the later eighteenth century for the rest of India would probably be that the long phase of expansion from the seventeenth century was running down, but there is no evidence that there had been as yet a dramatic turn for the worse.

THE EUROPEAN INTRUSION

The outline of the events through which two European powers, the French and the British, became a political force in eastern India from the mid-eighteenth century and through which one of them, the British, established a dominance that at the end of the century was about to engulf a vast further extent of territory is very well known indeed; it requires only the briefest of recapitulations. Explanation of these events is, however, highly contentious. By the end of the seventeenth century almost all of India's trade with

Europe and a part of its seaborne trade with the rest of Asia was in the hands of the Dutch and the English East India companies, who operated either from establishments within major Indian ports or from their own autonomous enclaves. By 1740 the situation had changed somewhat in that the British stake in inter-Asian trade had grown greatly and the French had become serious competitors in both European and Asian trade. There were still, however, no obvious intimations that Europeans were likely to assume a major political role. Yet, within a few years, this was precisely what the British and French did. A successful French attack was launched in 1746 on the British settlement of Madras. Over the next few years the British and French were to fight one another in south-eastern India and to back contestants for the succession both of the nawabs of the Carnatic and of the nizams of the Deccan. The British were victorious by 1761, the nawab of the Carnatic effectively becoming their satellite. By then British troops had also intervened in Bengal. Their principal settlement of Calcutta had been taken by the nawab's forces in 1756. The following year a British army and fleet recovered Calcutta and the British won the battle of Plassey on behalf of a rival to the nawab, who then ruled under their protection. He and subsequent British-appointed candidates were reduced to nullities by unremitting intervention and the reality of British rule over Bengal was confirmed by the imperial grant of the *diwani* to them in 1765. In the previous year an attempt by the nawab of Awadh to intervene in Bengal was defeated at the battle of Buxar and Awadh became to some degree a dependent ally of the British. Only in western India and in the western half of the peninsula were the Marathas and Mysore able to hold British expansion in check for a time. In 1799, however, Mysore was overrun and by then, what was to be irresistible pressure, was mounting on the Marathas.

For most British participants these events were indeed revolutionary. Their predominant explanation of them was that up to the 1740s and 1750s the British had existed in India as outsiders, detached from developments in the subcontinent, pursuing their own peaceful commercial objectives within their coastal enclaves. Military and political intervention had been forced upon them, first of all by French aggression and then by the breakdown of stable relations with Indian states, especially in Bengal. British responses had exposed the abject state of post-Mughal India. Neither in the Carnatic nor in Bengal, in spite of the great disproportion of numbers, could Indian armed forces withstand the military expertise of contemporary Europe. Attempts to maintain stable alliances with Indian states from a position of military supremacy had subsequently foundered on the incapacity of Indian rulers and the factiousness and corruption of their governments. New British systems of rule had eventually been imposed. While these might preserve Indian forms, they were totally alien to them in spirit, being based on concepts of legality, security of property and concern for the well-being of the mass of the population. John Bruce, historiographer to the East India Company, wrote in 1793 of an eighteenth-century India 'reduced by perpetual civil wars to perpetual misery'. This 'scene of political anarchy . . . threatened with ruin' the trade of the Company and forced it to take power. The consequence was that indigenous rule that even under the Mughals had been 'founded on violence and persecution' was replaced by 'a milder system under the British government, laws and police'.[78] This was an interpretation of the rise of British power that was frequently to be restated by historians and publicists well affected to the Raj in the nineteenth and twentieth centuries.[79]

Its celebratory tone did not go uncontested at the time. Edmund Burke felt that the origins of British rule in Bengal 'had as good be covered in obscurity' and that British rule, instead of proving a blessing to the Company's provinces, had been a disaster for them.[80] Many have agreed with Burke. Initial intervention in Indian politics has been interpreted as acts of aggression rather than as self-defence and the idealized view of the intentions of early colonial rule has been seen as an apologia for a new order based on Britain's economic advantage. Nevertheless, critics of what might be called the official version of the Raj's origins still tended to preserve the essential arguments underlying that version. They saw, and indeed still see, the British as a marginal presence in India until Indian weakness and Western military strength enabled them to impose their will on some of the most vulnerable of the successor states. They agree that the new British regimes were fundamentally different from what had gone before, but usually attribute the difference to their predatory nature in creating a new system of economic exploitation rather than to their spirit of benevolent concern for the mass of the ruled. What both versions have in common is an interpretation of the rise of the British in terms of a sharp break with the Indian past: conquest by an alien outside force was followed by new regimes quite different in character and purposes from those of their Indian predecessors.

Over the last twenty-five years there has been a marked tendency to seek to place the rise of British power and the new East India Company regimes that followed into their Indian context, rather than stressing the European intentions behind them. Historians are now trying to understand 'the way in which conditions in Indian society determined the emergence and form of British India'.[81] Most attention is given to the successor states to the Mughal empire. The way in which these states had developed both made it possible for Europeans to become political participants in them and provided the structures for early British rule. The arguments most commonly deployed are that these states' dependence on men who could command ready money and mercenary soldiers was making them accessible to Europeans. Rulers or would-be rulers were selling rights to collect revenue and buying military services. Europeans, acting for themselves or in the name of the British or French companies, were willing to undertake revenue farms, to organize loans, and to sell their military expertise and the use of their armies. The eventual outcome of such intervention was to put Europeans in control of more and more of the resources of the state, as was to be the case in the south, or to give them formal authority over it, as in Bengal. The early Company regimes that emerged from these processes of infiltration or takeover are depicted as essentially similar to those of the successor states that they had supplanted. They too paid lip-service to Mughal ideals. They too collected revenue through tax farmers, supplemented the landed revenue by state monopolies of commodities like salt or opium, borrowed from bankers in advance of their revenues, utilized the skills of established administrative cadres and recruited sepoy armies. As soldiers, financiers, or administrators, Indians were, it is argued, indispensable partners both in the seizure of power and in the creation of the new regime.

The way in which Europeans became participants in Indian states can be most clearly demonstrated by the role played by the French in the south. Involvement in Indian political affairs was not a sudden development triggered by European rivalries. In the early 1740s, individual Frenchmen began to make contacts with notables at the court of the nawabs of the Carnatic, and through them sought revenue farms as an alternative investment to trade by sea. After 1746, when the French army demonstrated its prowess in taking Madras, it was obvious to aspiring contenders playing for very high stakes at Arcot or Hyderabad that it was an incomparable asset available for hire. The price was huge grants of revenue rights to the individual French commanders, Dupleix and Bussy. Aspiring *subahdar*s of the Deccan at one time gave Dupleix authority over the whole of the south-east coast below the Kistna river, while Bussy was allocated a large strip of coastal lands called the Northern Circars as a *jagir*. The French had, however, neither the means nor the time to establish effective control over what remained paper grants.[82]

By contrast, the British who pursued similar tactics were able to realize much of what they were promised. They hired out their forces to rivals to the French claimants in the south from 1749, committing themselves above all to the success of Muhammad Ali, Walajah, as nawab of the Carnatic, and taking mortgages on his revenue to repay their efforts. The strength of the British presence in the Carnatic ensured that these mortgages would largely be paid off. The Company's army continued to be hired out to the nawab as he tried to incorporate further territory from the southern *nayaka*s or from Mysore after the end of the French war. Private British people also invested heavily in Muhammad Ali's state, providing him with the funds to pay off the Company's old debts and the new ones that he was incurring for his wars of expansion. They too were eventually repaid out of his revenues.

Until 1757 Europeans had little direct access to the court of the nawabs of Bengal, although they had close links with some of the great financiers and merchants who played an important role in the government. The famous 'Omichund' (Amirchand) was, for instance, deeply involved both with the East India Company, in whose settlement at Calcutta he maintained a palatial house, and with the nawabs' government. Through him and others like him, including the great banking business of the house of Jagat Seth, a deal was worked out for hiring the Company's army to the notables who plotted to depose the nawab before Plassey. The price for the use of the army on that and on subsequent occasions was to be the mortgaging of more and more of the revenues of Bengal to the British, until they were all made over to the Company in the grant of the *diwani* in 1765. Although regulations soon compelled them to act clandestinely, private Europeans competed with Indians or acted as their partners in farming the revenue from the Company's grants.

If the first assertions of European military and political power need to be put into the Indian context that made them possible, this in no way renders obsolete the old debates about motivation. In the first place, it is clear that Indians were not hapless victims in these processes. They had motives of their own. In providing armed men or raising money, Europeans were rendering services that Indians wanted. Muhammad Ali or his French-supported rival in the Carnatic, Chanda Sahib, Mir Jafar, the new nawab of Bengal in 1757, and those who conspired with him before Plassey, short-sighted as they may now seem to have been, were not simply the dupes of wily Europeans. If anything, the French in particular, were often duped by the Indians who gave them unredeemable promises of wealth in return for their military support.

If Europeans often acted on behalf of Indians, they were of course pursuing agendas of their own in doing so. It has long been assumed that these agendas were the national ones of Britain and France. As the British and French in India were to some degree the agents of rival states fighting out a global struggle for supremacy, the extension of this struggle to India has therefore often been seen as the immediate stimulus for the rise of the British empire in India. An alternative and more recent hypothesis for a national British agenda is the assumed compulsion to conquer territory in order to enhance the economic value of India for Britain.[83]

State involvement was certainly important. What distinguished the French and the British from the Dutch in this period is the willingness of both states to support their nationals in India with warships and detachments of regular troops which had a powerful impact on warfare in India. Due to distance and the slowness of communications, the control of governments or of the directors of both companies over their servants in India was inevitably tenuous, so that their role was largely to react to events rather than to try to shape them; but by withholding resources or dismissing servants they could still check the ambitions of men in India, as Dupleix was to find when he was recalled in 1754.

At least at a superficial level, the national agendas of both Britain and France can be described as defensive. For Britain, the trade that had been built up by the East India Company was a part, albeit a subordinate part by comparison with the trade of the Americas, of Britain's worldwide commerce. The preservation of these trades was a matter of great importance to the state, not only because of the contribution that they made in general terms to the national wealth, but because of their particular contribution to Britain's power and her capacity to keep her European rivals in check. Indeed, the similarities between the British 'fiscal–military' organization, that is the link between taxes, borrowing, and military power, and that of Indian states are evident.[84] Overseas trade provided the seamen needed for the British navy; it was an important source of revenue through the customs duties collected on imported commodities, and the richer overseas merchants were extensively involved in lending money to the government or in underwriting the loans that it floated. The East India Company did not contribute significantly to the pool of seamen, but its trade was heavily taxed and it had an important role in the British credit system. The Company fitted easily into the alliance of finance and the landed aristocracy who governed eighteenth-century Britain, described as 'gentlemanly capitalism' in the section from *British Imperialism* by Cain and Hopkins in this volume (14). The directors of the East India Company told ministers in 1756 that their trade was 'a National Trade' because of the revenue that it yielded to government and because of the 'General Distress upon Public Credit' that would be the consequence of the loss of its Indian settlements.[85] British ministers hardly needed such reminders. In times of danger the East India Company's position in India would have to be reinforced.

Neither the British government nor the directors of the East India Company seem to have envisaged expansion of the British stake in India as an objective, at least until very late in the eighteenth century. In the 1750s, the Company's servants were constantly warned against involvement with Indian powers or military adventures. These could have no commercial benefit. Military success did in fact lead to a major expansion of exports of raw silk and cotton cloth from Bengal and the Coromandel Coast, for which the worldwide market held up well until about 1815; but the directors generally regarded increased exports as a means of remitting the profits of territorial empire as a form of tribute to Britain, rather than seeing territorial empire as the basis for an expanded trade. Connections between empire in India and the early stages of industrialization are not easy to make. In the later eighteenth century India neither provided raw materials on any large scale nor market outlets for the industries undergoing rapid expansion. Empire in India did, however, make a significant contribution to Britain's overall balance of payments, as Britain no longer had to pay through her exports to Europe for large quantities of Spanish American bullion to ship to India or China, but was able to use the resources of Bengal to meet much of the cost of the Indian textiles or the Chinese tea imported into London. Britain thus faced the massive expenditures overseas required to fight the long wars against France that began in 1792 relatively unencumbered with existing foreign debts. Without the Indian transfers, Britain's foreign borrowing might have risen to 'seemingly unsustainable levels' in the later stages of the war.[86] There is, however, no evidence that policy-makers in Britain took account of such considerations. Their calculations seem to have been dominated by fear of the consequences of the loss of the existing trade.

The role of Indian trade in France's economy or in its system of public finance was less prominent than it was for Britain. The French company and French ministers appear to have been at least as sceptical as their British counterparts about any possible benefits for trade from political involvement. Their military efforts were limited in the 1750s to vain attempts to protect their trade.[87] British victories produced a change of policy. Were Britain to be deprived of the wealth derived from India, its capacity to assert itself in Europe would be correspondingly weakened. From the 1760s the French therefore cultivated Indian allies who might pose a threat to the British. They dispatched forces to India to support their allies between 1778 and 1783, and threatened to do so again after 1798. Expanded French territorial possessions in India seem to have had no part in government calculations.

While recognizing the importance of national governments in providing some of the essential sinews of war in India, historians seeking explanations of why Europeans took the opportunities for political involvement that the new Indian order offered them now focus for the most part on the motives of men actually in India. Obvious motives are not far to seek. Most British and French people, whether they were employed by the companies or not, were there to make fortunes for themselves. These fortunes had traditionally been made by trading at sea. Private European ships sailed from Indian ports all round the Indian Ocean and the South China Sea. There is clear evidence that by the 1740s trading conditions at sea were less buoyant than they had been earlier in the century.[88] In such circumstances, ambitious European business-men might well seek compensation in political profits on land. Even if they remained interested in shipping, they still needed little incentive, once condi-tions were propitious, to diversify their activities in the way that Indian 'port-folio capitalists' (described as men who 'farmed revenue, engaged in local agricultural trade, commanded military resources', and traded by sea) had long been doing.[89] Conditions for such diversification became propitious in south India as Indian potentates offered valuable concessions in return for cash and troops and in Bengal when the conspirators against Siraj al-Daula turned to the British in 1757. Conditions became more propitious still when the European entrepreneurs could operate in the shadow of the East India Company's protection or even held office under it.

Political profits could take many forms, the simplest of which were the famous 'presents' given by those who had acquired thrones to the Europeans who had backed them, as Mir Jafar was to do for Robert Clive. Soldiers who fought for Indians expected much more than their normal pay in return. Pro-fits could be made from revenue farms, from loans, or from the perquisites of offices held under the government. A most important by-product of political intervention was the opening up of internal trade on conditions highly favour-able to those Europeans who wielded political influence. This was the basis of many fortunes made in Bengal in the 1760s after the previous restraints on European participation in inland trade were swept away.[90]

Since political intervention paid so well and men in India acted under few restraints from home, is it not reasonable to conclude that private interest was the driving force behind such intervention? Changes of nawab in Bengal or wars of conquest on behalf of Muhammad Ali Khan in the Carnatic can indeed hardly be understood in any other terms. Huge rewards were reaped by those involved. Even so, it is not a complete explanation. As well as the pursuit of private gain, there were ideological assumptions behind British intervention in particular, which made it especially potent.[91]

The ideological assumptions of the eighteenth-century British in India were not the imperial ones of their Victorian successors, but they still con-cerned sovereign rights and 'dominion'. Grants were sought from Indians not just for corporate or private profit, but also to give lasting security to the Company's position in India. Grants in Mughal or post-Mughal India were generally temporary, conditional, and might have other grants overlapping them. For the British they must be made permanent and unconditional, whether they were nominally zamindari tenures, *jagirs*, farmans conveying trading privileges or the office of imperial *diwan* for Bengal, Bihar, and Orissa. In 1765 Clive's Bengal Select Committee reflected that the British in Bengal could not have remained any longer as 'Merchants, subjected to the jurisdiction, encroachments and insults of the Country Government'. Fortunately they had been able to 'support your privileges and possessions by the sword' and thus to give 'stability and permanency to your government'. The Company had thus now become 'the Sovereigns of a rich and potent Kingdom'.[92] Like other successor states, the British professed to derive their legitimacy from Mughal grants, but they interpreted these grants in a way that was totally contrary to Mughal traditions. Even the Marathas accepted a shared sovereignty with the emperor. The British still struck coins in the name of the emperor, but they claimed a sovereignty that excluded any Indian authority whatsoever, and it was a sovereignty, as leading Company servants began to anticipate, that would ultimately be exercised by the British crown.[93]

The ability of the British Company servants to give effect by their military power to their assumptions that their grants had conveyed an absolute sovereignty to them meant that they would not constitute yet another successor state to the Mughal empire. They might have won power by taking over existing states from within and they might rule through the existing state apparatus and through alliances with most of the governing élites, but territory under the British was ceasing to be the provinces of a nominal Mughal empire and becoming the possessions of a worldwide British empire.

In practical respects, however, the British were still very much the Indian power that their Indian allies seem to have taken them to be. As Abdul Majed Khan suggests (13), the Muslim grandees at the time of Plassey were in 'absolute ignorance of English attitudes and objectives' and hoped that they could establish with them 'a sort of Anglo–Mughal rule within the framework of Timurid sovereignty'. In this spirit they awarded Mughal titles to British commanders and expected them to behave appropriately.[94] This was perhaps not quite the delusion that it now appears. Indians had good reason for not regarding the European intrusion in the mid-eighteenth century as something qualitatively different from other intrusions. The British and their French rivals had demonstrated a formidable military capacity which had given them an ascendancy both in the Deccan and in Bengal. They were, however, using a military technology and patterns of organization that were in essentials common throughout Eurasia and were employing more and more Indian soldiers. Within a few years the rulers of Mysore in particular were able to put into the field forces that would test those of the Company to the utmost. Behind the Company's armies were structures of command, linked ultimately to Britain, with a local hierarchy of offices, record-keeping and accounting of a higher order, contemporaries thought, than in the British state. This might in theory give the British advantages over Indian competitors in planning and executing objectives and in effectively utilizing resources. Mughal governance was, however, also based on bureaucratic rules and a high standard of account-keeping, and for much of the eighteenth century for the British in India and for the Company at home the pursuit of coherent policies was paralysed by factional disputes and by the unbridled pursuit of personal interest. In this respect, the British may have resembled the Afghan or Iranian invaders of eighteenth-century India. Like them, albeit with relatively little of the violence that they used, great sums had been levied for the Company and for themselves by a host of individuals, Indians as well as British. The British invasion was not, however, to be a transitory raid nor were the British to be absorbed into the post-Mughal Indian order.

THE NEW COLONIAL ORDER

The rationale, both in Britain and in India, for political intervention had been the need to secure the Company's commercial stake on the Coromandel Coast and in Bengal from French threats and from the supposed captiousness of Indian rulers. The Company's trading privileges were to be reformulated in terms of absolute right; limited territorial grants were to become its outright property and it was to maintain armed forces at a level that would guarantee its security. A huge new Fort William at Calcutta symbolized an official policy of standing on the defensive against all potential enemies.

A policy of standing on the defensive and consolidating gains was, however, to prove to be totally impractical. The expansionist forces within the British presence and the willingness of Indians to try to turn these forces to their own purposes continued to drive the British forward at an accelerated pace. Repeated efforts were made to contain territorial expansion and to fix new limits to it, but at best they only produced short periods of relative stability.

Indian rulers continued to hire the Company's troops to fulfil their own ambitions and were increasingly compelled to hire them for British purposes. The hiring of troops for whatever reason required the surrender of revenue on a temporary or permanent basis to support them. In Bengal, British needs for security after Plassey were set at the province's boundaries, and it was immediately decided that security could only be provided by the Company's army, of course at the nawab's expense. The nawab's army was therefore disbanded, while the Company's forces grew to a peacetime establishment by 1784 of 40,000 sepoys as well as contingents of European soldiers. After his disastrous intervention that culminated in defeat at Buxar in 1764, the territory of the nawab of Awadh was included in the Company's security screen. British troops were stationed there and revenue had to be allocated to support them. The Coromandel Coast was seen as their Achilles' heel by the British because of its vulnerability to invasion from Mysore and to seaborne French attacks. The nawab's troops were mostly disbanded and British forces, comparable to the Bengal army, were maintained there as well. Although the nawabs of the Carnatic preserved a nominal autonomy until 1801, most of their revenues were appropriated. The ultimate guarantee of security seemed to be to eliminate Mysore, which was achieved in two stages in 1792 and 1799, large tranches of territory passing under direct British rule on each occasion.

The Company's trade also became a charge on the revenues it collected. The sums spent on exports to Britain, primarily of cotton cloth and raw silk from Bengal, greatly increased after the acquisition of the *diwani*. Large sums were sent from Bengal to China to purchase tea there for Britain.

The need for the Company to maximize what it obtained from grants of revenue was the greatest single motive for the British to become directly involved in the administration of Indian territory. Initial preferences had been for any involvement to be indirect: when it was given assignments on specific territories, the Company expected that Indian revenue farmers and collectors would render to it what was due. Deeper involvement reflected frustrated expectations. Initial estimates of the yields of newly acquired territory were often wildly over-optimistic. When they were not realized, Indian corruption and inefficiency were blamed, leading to the appointment of Europeans as administrators and eventually to intervention to regulate the revenue systems. European involvement in revenue collection was limited in the Carnatic until the acquisition of territory from Mysore after 1792.[95] In Bengal, by contrast, the Company assumed full responsibility from 1772, when the first of many new systems for 'settling' the revenues of Bengal under rules devised by the British was introduced. By the 1780s leading Company servants were coming to believe that to ensure an adequate flow of revenue they must intervene to define the rights of those who paid it. In 1793 the Permanent Settlement was enacted laying down rights and obligations for landholders throughout the whole province of Bengal. Close involvement with revenue also meant close involvement with the administration of justice. The civil courts under the *diwani* became the Company's responsibility, and these too were regulated as were police and criminal justice, which had formally remained within the jurisdiction of the nawabs of Bengal after 1765.

If the need to raise more money was the underlying motive in all the Company's revenue policies, they were also expressions of ideological conviction. Some British administrators had highly sophisticated beliefs in doctrines about political economy;[96] virtually all subscribed to certain general maxims. Indian provinces were naturally fertile and their populations were skilled and industrious, but they had suffered grievously from despotic government. Prosperity would be restored by giving the people security for their persons and property according to due process of law and by enforcing what the directors of the Company called 'the fundamental principles of commerce'; that is, a free market that rewarded the industry of the producer with a fair price.[97]

The East India Company's early regime can be characterized as a very ambitious one. It believed that it had an exclusive sovereignty over the territories that it had acquired. Furthermore, most Company servants considered that a sovereign state must exercise the duties of government, as they understood them, directly through its own agents. Where these duties were being performed by private individuals, usually in Bengal by zamindars, this was a usurpation that must be brought to an end; law and order were matters for the Company's magistrates and police, not for private justice,[98] and the regulation of markets was to be the concern of the Company's customs administration, not of the individuals to whom market rights had been granted.[99] The British also believed that it was their duty to define rights to the produce of the land, and thus by implication to the land itself, in the interests of a more efficient revenue system. The power of the new state was used to support the commercial interests of the East India Company. Finally, the strength of its army gave the Company a coercive power to enforce its will far more effectively than any of its predecessors had ever been able to do.

All this would suggest a formidable foreign intrusion producing a very sharp break in continuity in eighteenth-century India, at least for Bengal and for other areas dominated by the British. Yet, self-confidence about the powers of government was to a considerable degree nullified by caution in using these powers, which inclined the British to non-intervention and to conserving Indian systems as they understood them. Moreover, whatever the Company's servants might intend, there were very severe practical restrictions on what a foreign regime, even with a monopoly of overt force, could achieve in conditions in which it had only limited contact with the mass of the population.

While few British people doubted the abstract truth of their own maxims about government and society, they also believed that Indian societies were different in important respects from European ones, and that laws and institutions appropriate to these societies had evolved over long periods. Sovereign power must therefore be used with caution and discretion. Undue innovations that would not be suited to Indian conditions must be avoided. It was therefore the duty of Bengal's new rulers to restore its 'ancient constitution' to the extent that this was possible. The law they enforced must be what Europeans conceived to be that of Hindus and of Islam. Learned Indians must be encouraged to offer texts for translation to guide the new rulers. The rights to shares in the revenue that the British tried to define must be based on existing customary rights, not on European concepts.[100] Early British governors evidently also felt that they must imitate the nawabs of the successor states in their religious patronage. Warren Hastings had very strong views about the sovereign powers of the new British state in India, but he was also utterly opposed to innovation in forms of government and was lavish in his patronage. He founded a madrasa in Calcutta. An inscription in three languages proudly proclaimed that he had endowed a 'Nobut Khanah' or 'music house' at the Bisheshur temple at Benares.[101]

The practical limitations on the new regime's capacity to bring about change were most marked in Awadh and in the Carnatic. Beyond the directly administered coastal strips, the British presence was essentially a military one with a degree of commercial penetration. The military presence entailed heavy demands on the rulers' revenue resources and periodic British intervention in revenue administration as well as the dismantling of the ruler's own forces. Even so, the nawabs of Awadh and the Carnatic retained much of their autonomy and even showed skill in manipulating the British to support their expansionist aims. The coup pulled off by Shuja al-Daula of Awadh in persuading the British to conquer Rohilkhand for him in 1774 was the most notable example. Until the end of the eighteenth century, in spite of intrusive British intervention, Awadh and the Carnatic continued to develop as successor states of the Mughal empire rather than as components of a British one.[102]

There could be no doubt that Bengal was a British dominion after 1765. Its nawabs were of no account, and from 1772 the apparatus of its central government was placed firmly in the British city of Calcutta, while British officials as collectors of revenue, judges, and magistrates were posted throughout the provinces. However, the structure of the successor state that the nawabs of Bengal had created remained essentially intact. British officials were still heavily dependent on the élites who had served the nawabs. The British could complete the work of the nawabs in dispensing with the Mughal nobility, who had no military role in the new order, but they still needed the experienced revenue administrators to act as the *diwans* and *saristadars*, effectively running both the central *khalsa* revenue office and the new district collectorates. Muslim law officers and Hindu pandits staffed the new courts. Such men were not necessarily merely subservient servants of their new master. Some of them had strong views about principles of good governance and freely engaged in debate to persuade British officials to their point of view.[103] Above all, the Company needed the local authority of the zamindars through whom it continued to obtain most of its revenue. In Bihar, British control was 'more shadow than substance' and large zamindars defied the Company in periodic armed resistance, otherwise largely managing their own affairs.[104] In Bengal itself the Company was able to intervene more effectively in local government and to collect a considerably enhanced revenue, although one that was markedly lower than over-optimistic assessments.[105] The British were still, however, unable to collect revenue effectively without going through a layer of zamindars or other intermediaries. The could neither assess what was due from a mass of small revenue payers nor collect it from them. The indispensability of the zamindars was confirmed with the making of the Permanent Settlement with them, albeit very much on British terms. Zamindars ceased in theory to be the 'little kings' of their localities with authority over the people of the countryside and became landlords with contractual obligations to pay the government's revenue.[106]

The great merchants and bankers who had been props of the nawabs' regime were rapidly displaced under the new one,[107] but the services of Indian commercial men remained essential to it. The bankers of Benares replaced the Jagat Seths of Murshidabad in handling the Company's financial business, especially its need to transfer money from Bengal to other parts of India to support the presidencies of Madras and Bombay in their wars.[108] Advances by bankers to the zamindars or farmers remained the means by which the Company realized its revenue in cash. Even before Plassey, the East India Company was ceasing to purchase its textiles through Indian merchants, but it still needed a hierarchy of Indian intermediaries, gumasthas, dalals, and pykars, to organize production for it.[109] Until the creation of European banking businesses and the private companies called houses of agency, European merchants were dependent on their 'banians', effectively their Indian commercial partners, who provided them with the capital and expertise to carry on their trade.[110]

Any attempt to assess the effect of early British rule on Bengal has to take account of the practical weaknesses that distorted the execution of what was intended as well as of the contradictions in the aims behind policy-making: the Company wished to assert its sovereignty, but also to preserve existing institutions; it wanted to create prosperity through secure rights and free trade, but also to maintain a high level of revenue, to augment that revenue by monopolies of commodities like salt and opium and to keep a substantial portion of Bengal's silk and cloth production under its own control in order to protect its export shipments to London.

Whatever the early propagandists for the Company's rule may have asserted, the blessings of security for person and property and of free trade are only likely to have been extended to small sections of the population. In the early years of the Permanent Settlement many zamindaris were broken up and sold as their holders failed to pay the revenue demand, but thereafter secure property in revenue rights provided an income for a wide range of people who invested in them. The activities of Indian merchants were to some degree constricted as the Company established monopolies or brought weavers and spinners under its control. However, a large part of Bengal's commerce remained beyond the reach of the Company or of private British merchants. This was the case with almost all the huge volume of trade in agricultural produce. It was also true of a considerable proportion of the trade in silk and textiles. Indian merchants were still taking Bengal textiles to the cities of northern India and beyond at the end of the eighteenth century.[111] Estimates for certain districts suggest that the Company then only controlled about a third of the weavers.[112] The prosperity of the Indian commercial communities in Calcutta was spectacularly evident, while the decline of older cities, like Dacca and Murshidabad, lay largely in the next century and country market towns were flourishing.

There can be little optimism about the condition of the mass of the Bengal population in the later eighteenth century. Rather than feeling any beneficial effect from policies aimed at their prosperity, they were exposed to the drive for a higher revenue and for control over part of the labour force. Studies of those weavers who were brought under full Company supervision suggest that their living standard, thought at least in south India to have been higher than that of textile workers in England for much of the eighteenth century,[113] deteriorated as they lost their bargaining power and had to work.for fixed wages.[114] There is clear evidence that population rose and that the area under cultivation increased markedly, but for the mass of the agrarian population, the later eighteenth century appears to have been a period of acute insecurity. Agricultural production, including basic food grains, was already highly commercialized and becoming much more so under Company rule. As Rajat Datta demonstrates in the chapter reproduced in this book (15), even small cultivators depended on the market and on credit. Most were more or less permanently in debt. They were thus extremely vulnerable to rigorously exacted revenue collections and to a succession of natural disasters, notably the famines produced by drought in the west in 1769–70 and by flooding in the east in 1787–8.[115]

At the highest levels of Bengal society, British conquest had produced some spectacular winners and losers. The great fortunes made by 'banians' who had worked as the business agents of prominent British people and profited greatly thereby, have, for instance, to be set against the fall of the Armenian merchant princes, who had flourished under the nawabs. For middling people, who depended on what they derived from revenue tenures, from office or from trade, the new order probably did not as yet require significant adjustments, while opportunities remained plentiful. Conditions for the mass of the population below them were generally harsh and precarious.

CONCLUSION

Assessments of the early British period, even in Bengal, tend to support interpretations of eighteenth-century Indian history in terms of continuity. A foreign regime with an obvious potential for bringing about change through its claims to a sovereignty far more absolute than that of Mughal provincial governors and through the overwhelming force at its disposal appears to have made no deep impact as yet, even on Bengal, where it was firmly entrenched. The British used their powers through the structure of offices that they had inherited from the nawabs and with the mediation of local élites who had served them. They intensified certain trends becoming apparent in the early part of the century: a more rigorously exacted revenue, an increasing volume of overseas trade, and the growing commercialization of agricultural production.

Faced with strong evidence of continuities throughout the eighteenth century, a number of historians have begun to focus on the 1820s or 1830s, rather than on 'the blood-red field of Plassey on that fateful evening of June' 1757,[116] as a clear point of departure from the past. By the 1830s, foreign domination, now spreading far beyond Bengal and the south-east coast, was producing unmistakable effects. As the new empire expanded, the peoples of the hills, forests, and frontiers, who had kept the Mughals, the successor states and the early British, at arm's length, were being subjected to new pressures. The British made war in Nepal in 1813–15 and Assam was conquered in 1826.

Although deficiencies in communications remained a serious constraint at any distance from the coast or from the Ganges, India was becoming more closely integrated into a pattern of worldwide trade dominated by an industrializing Britain in the early nineteenth century. Exports of manufactured textiles, which had remained the staple of overseas trade right through the eighteenth century, began to decline sharply after 1815 and to be replaced by greatly increased shipments of agricultural produce, not only to Britain but also to China. British manufacturers were beginning to find an outlet in India. British banks and business houses in Indian cities were increasingly able to stand on their own without Indian finance or commercial expertise. The Company no longer needed the services of the Indian bankers to remit money or underwrite the collection of the revenue.

In other respects too the British became less dependent on Indian élites. In Bengal by the 1793 Permanent Settlement the Company had entrenched intermediaries between itself and those who cultivated the land. In its later conquests, especially in the south, it tried to cut out such people and deal directly with the rural population. In revenue and judicial administration the British became less reliant on Indian informants and more confident of their own accumulated knowledge.[117] Indians served the Company now on its own terms as junior officials under white command, rather than as repositories of a knowledge that was inaccessible to Europeans. British people began actively to propagate their own values and knowledge through Christian missions and the first wave of new schools and colleges. Some of these initiatives began to evoke significant if still very limited indigenous responses, as in the founding in 1816 in Calcutta of Hindu College, soon to be a hothouse of 'the Bengal renaissance'.

Periods delineated according to centuries based on a European calendar are an entirely artificial construction. For most historians of the past and for some now, the hundred years in Indian history between 1700 and 1800 have no overall coherence. They are years marked by great disruptions and dis-continuities: the fall of the Mughals, the transitory life of the successor states, and the rise of the British. Political failure and economic decline are their only only common features. Much of the material that follows in this book chal-lenges interpretations in terms of decline, and suggests that there were clear continuities to the eighteenth century, whether strictly interpreted as a hund-red years or as a 'long' century, perhaps from about 1680 to about 1830. A recent interpretations argues that the early British period must be seen as part of an even longer 'early modern' continuum, stretching back to the Mughals and only ending in the mid-nineteenth century[118]

However defined, the eighteenth century was a period of decentralization and of the rise of regional polities, Indian and later British, marked by much diversity within the framework of Mughal ideals of government. It was also a period of generally buoyant economic conditions. By the 1830s, however, centralization was replacing the wide diffusion of power, Mughal ideals seemed to be irrelevant and outmoded, and at least modest economic growth was giving way to stagnation.

The British empire in India in the 1830s, or even at later dates, was never a tightly centralized structure nor could it check the continuing rise of regional identities that had been developing during the eighteenth century. Nevertheless, for all the divisions into presidencies and provinces, British India, outside the princely states, embodied British ideals of a unitary sovereign state under a single authority; ideals especially reflected in the charter act of 1833.[119] British provinces were losing any resemblance to eighteenth-century successor states. Although pragmatic caution was still to be a marked feature of British rule, so too was intellectual self-confidence in government as an agent of improvement and willingness to dispense with Indian precedent, most provocatively in those who were influenced by utilitarian doctrines. Economically, the long phase of expansion from the seventeenth into the eighteenth century may have lost some of its momentum in mid-century, but a 'prolonged and widespread depression' does not seem to have set in until the second quarter of the nineteenth century.[120] The material assembled by Rajat Datta (15) indicate that prices in Bengal continued to rise into the nineteenth century. Deflation did not become marked until the later 1820.

By the mid-nineteenth century, when prices began to rise again and economic expansion resumed, India was being governed in ways that were very different from those of the eighteenth century and Indian society was evolving in new directions.[121] Such changes were may or may not have marked the onset of something that can be called a 'revolution' or even the beginnings of 'modernity' (what some historians see is a new 'traditionalism'), but they certainly marked a break with the continuities that had prevailed throughout the eighteenth century.

NOTES AND REFERENCES

1. E.g. letter from Bengal Select Committee, 14 July 1757, S.C. Hill (ed.), *Bengal in 1756–57*, 3 vols, 1905–6, II. 451. Luke Scrafton described his widely-read *Reflections on the Government of Indostan*, London, 1770, as 'an account of the revolutions in Bengal' (p. 1).

2. Rajat Kanta Ray, 'Indian Society and the Establishment of British Supremacy, 1765–1818', in P.J. Marshall (ed.), *The Oxford History of the British Empire*, II, *The Eighteenth Century*, Oxford, 1998, p. 508.

3. William Irvine, edited and augmented by Jadunath Sarkar, *The Later Mughals*, 2 vols, Calcutta, 1922, II. p. 379.

4. R.C. Dutt, *The Economic History of British India*, 1902, p. 51.

5. Sir Jadu-Nath Sarkar (ed.), *The History of Bengal*, II, *Muslim Period 1200–1757*, Dacca, 1948, p. 498.

6. The problems of the centre are analysed in Satish Chandra, *Parties and Politics at the Mughal Court, 1707–40*, 3rd edn, Delhi, 1982; Muzaffar Alam, *The Crisis of Empire in Mughal North India: Awadh and the Punjab, 1707–1748*, Delhi, 1986,

pp. 18–55; Zahir Uddin Malik, *The Reign of Muhammad Shah, 1719–1748*, Bombay, 1977.

7. Jos J.L. Gommans, *The Rise of the Indo-Afghan Empire, c. 1710–1780*, Leiden, 1995, p. 55.

8. Muzaffar Alam and Sanjay Subrahmanyam, 'Introduction', *The Mughal State 1526–1750*, Delhi, 1998, pp. 1–71, especially, p. 57. For a recent statement insisting on the essential 'elements of centralization and systemization in the Mughal polity', see M. Athar Ali, 'The Mughal Polity: A Critique of Revisionist Approaches', *Modern Asian Studies*, xxvii, 1993, p. 706.

9. Gommans, *Indo-Afghan Empire*; Iqbal Husain, *The Ruhela Chieftaincies: The Rise and Decline of Ruhela Power in the Eighteenth Century*, Delhi, 1994.

10. Chandra, *Parties and Politics*, pp. 183–4.

11. Richard Eaton, *The Rise of Islam and the Bengal Frontier 1204–1760*, Berkeley, 1993, p. 312.

12. See below, pp. 347–9 and Muzaffar Alam and Sanjay Subrahmanyam, 'Exploring the Hinterland: Trade and Politics in the Arcot Nizamat (1700–1732)' in Rudrangshu Mukherjee and Lakshmi Subramanian (eds), *Politics and Trade in the Indian Ocean World. Essays in Honour of Ashin Das Gupta*, Delhi, 1998, pp. 113–64.

13. André Wink, *Land and Sovereignty in India: Agrarian Society and Politics under the Eighteenth-century Maratha Svarajya*, Cambridge, 1986, pp. 32–3.

14. Stewart Gordon, *The New Cambridge History of India*, ii, 4, *The Marathas 1680–1818*, Cambridge, 1993, pp. 140–4.

15. Indu Banga, *The Agrarian System of the Sikhs: Late Eighteenth and Early Nineteenth Century*, Delhi, 1978.

16. ———, 'Formation of the Sikh State, 1765–1845', in Indu Banga (ed.), *Five Punjabi Centuries: Polity, Economy, History and Culture, c. 1500–1990. Essays for J.S. Grewal*, Delhi, 1997. p. 93.

17. See below, pp. 367–70.

18. See Warren Hastings's minute in Francis Gladwin, trans., *Ayeen Akbery or the Institutes of the Emperor Akbar*, 3 vols, Calcutta, 1783–6, i, p. ix. This theme is developed in Robert Travers, 'Contested Notions of Sovereignty in Bengal under the British, 1765–1785', Cambridge, Ph D thesis, 2001.

19. *Rulers, Townsmen and Bazaars: North Indian Society in the Age of British Expansion, 1770–1870*, Cambridge, 1983, p. 6.

20. John R. McLane, *Land and Local Kingship in Eighteenth-Century Bengal*, Cambridge, 1993, p. 5.

21. Wink, *Land and Sovereignty*, pp. 33, 46, 154.

22. M. Alam, *Crisis of Empire*, p. 134.

23. See below, p. 138.

24. Bayly, *Rulers, Townsmen and Bazaars*, pp. 52–7; see also the very detailed studies of a similar phenomenon in the Maratha Deccan in Frank Perlin, 'Of White Whale and Countrymen in the Eighteenth-century Maratha Deccan: Extended Class Relations, Rights and the Problem of Rural Autonomy under the Old Regime', *Journal of Peasant Studies*, v, 1978, pp. 172–237, and 'Money-Use in Late Precolonial India and International Trade in Currency Media', in John F. Richards (ed.), *The Imperial Monetary System of Mughal India*, Delhi, 1987, pp. 232–373.

25. M. Alam, *Crisis of Empire*, pp. 212–42; Richard B. Barnett, *North India between Empires: Awadh, the Mughals and the British, 1720–1801*, Berkeley, 1980, pp. 245–7; William R. Pinch, 'Who was Himmat Bahadur? Gosains, Rajputs and the British in Bundelkhand c. 1800', *Indian Economic and Social History Review*, xxxv, 1998, pp. 293–335.

26. McLane, *Land and Local Kingship*, pp. 27–44; A. Rahim, 'The Rise of a Hindu Aristocracy under Bengal Nawabs', *Journal of the Asiatic Society of Pakistan*, vi, 1961, pp. 104–18; Kumkum Chatterjee, *Merchants, Politics and Society in Early Modern India: Bihar 1733–1820*, Leiden, 1996.

27. Wink, *Land and Sovereignty*, pp. 303, 335–8.

28. Susan Bayly, *The New Cambridge History of India*, IV, 3, *Caste, Society and Politics in India from the Eighteenth Century to the Modern Age*, Cambridge, 1999, p. 66.

29. Ibid., Ch. 1 and 2.

30. J.R.I. Cole, *The Roots of North Indian Shi'ism in Iran and Iraq: Religion and State in Awadh, 1722–1859*, Berkeley, 1988.

31. See below, pp. 215–18.

32. Gordon, *Marathas*, p. 188.

33. Chatterjee, *Merchants, Politics and Society*, pp. 71–100.

34. Barnett, *North India between Empires*, pp. 75–83; Seema Alavi, *The Sepoys and the Company: Tradition and Transition in Northern India 1770–1830*, Delhi, 1995, pp. 19–25.

35. Chetan Singh, 'Forests, Pastoralists and Agrarian Society in Mughal India', in David Arnold and Ramachandra Guha (eds), *Nature, Culture and Imperialism: Essays on the Environmental History of South Asia*, Delhi, 1995, pp. 21–48.

36. See also Sumit Guha, *Environment and Ethnicity in India 1200–1999*, Cambridge, 1999, pp. 108–30.

37. See below, pp. 268–92.

38. See below, pp. 277–8; Asok Sen, 'A Pre-British Economic Formation in India of the Late Eighteenth Century: Tipu Sultan's Mysore', in B. De (ed.), *Perspectives in Social Science, I, Historical Dimensions*, Calcutta, 1977, pp. 46–119.

39. See also Nicholas B. Dirks, *The Hollow Crown: Ethnohistory of an Indian Kingdom*, Cambridge, 1987.

40. J.F. Richards, *Mughal Administration in Golconda*, Oxford, 1975; S. Chander, 'From a Pre-colonial Order to a Princely State: Hyderabad in Transition, c. 1748–1865', Cambridge, Ph D thesis, 1987.

41. M. Alam, *Crisis of Empire*, pp. 181–5.

42. Dilbagh Singh, *The State, Landlords and Peasants: Eastern Rajasthan in the 18th Century*, Delhi, 1990, pp. 92–3.

43. Irfan Habib, *The Agrarian System of Mughal India. 1556–1707*, Bombay, 1963, pp. 317–51.

44. Sanjay Subrahmanyam, 'Introduction', in Subrahmanyam (ed.), *Merchants, Markets and the State in Early Modern India*, Delhi, 1990, p. 17.

45. Bayly, *Rulers, Townsmen and Bazaars*, pp. 68–73.

46. For the Deccan, see the essays of Frank Perlin, cited in note 24 and those of Stewart

Gordon collected as *Marathas, Marauders and State-Formation in Eighteenth-century India*, Delhi, 1994; for Rajasthan, see S.P. Gupta, *The Agrarian System of Eastern Rajasthan (c. 1650–c. 1750)*, Delhi, 1986; Dilbagh Singh, *State, Landlords and Peasants*; Madhavi Bajekal, 'Agricultural Production in Six Selected Qasbas in Eastern Rajasthan (c. 1700–1780)', London Ph D thesis, 1991.

47. See below, p. 47; Perlin, 'Money Use in Pre-colonial India', in Richards (ed.), *Imperial Monetary System*.

48. David Ludden, *New Cambridge History of India*, IV, 4, *An Agrarian History of South Asia*, Cambridge, 1999, p. 168; see also below, p. 48.

49. Bayly, *Rulers, Townsmen and Bazaars*, p. 112.

50. On its population, see B.G. Gokhale, *Surat in the Seventeenth Century: A Study of Urban History in Pre-Modern India*, Copenhagen, 1979, pp. 10–11.

51. John F. Richards, *The New Cambridge History of India*, I, 5, *The Mughal Empire*, Cambridge, 1993, p. 194.

52. Ibid., pp. 204, 285, 291–2; M. Alam, *Crisis*, pp. 12–16.

53. See sources in note 46.

54. Frank Perlin, 'Of White Whale and Countrymen'; 'Money-Use in Pre-colonial India' in Richards (ed.), *Imperial Monetary System*.

55. See below, pp. 194–5.

56. Bayly, *Rulers, Townsmen and Bazaars*, p. 87.

57. M. Alam, *Crisis*, pp. 247–55.

58. Bayly, *Rulers, Townsmen and Bazaars*, p. 108.

59. S. Arasaratnam, *Merchants, Companies and Commerce on the Coromandel Coast 1650–1740*, Delhi, 1986, p. 211; see also Bhaswati Bhattacharya, 'The Hinterland and the Coast: The Pattern of Interaction on the Coromandel Coast in the late Eighteenth Century', in Mukherjee and Subramanian (eds), *Politics and Trade in the Indian Ocean World*, pp. 19–51.

60. I.G. Khan, 'Revenue, Agriculture and Warfare in North India: Technical Knowledge and the Mughal Elites from the mid Eighteenth to the Early Nineteenth Century', London Ph D thesis, 1990. On technology in general, see Irfan Habib, 'Technology and Economy in Mughal India', *Indian Economic and Social History Review*, XVII, 1980, pp. 1–34.

61. F. Perlin, 'Proto-Industrialization and Pre-colonial South Asia', *Past and Present*, XCVIII, 1993, p. 86.

62. Niels Steensgaard, 'The Growth and Composition of the Long-distance Trade of England and the Dutch Republic before 1750', in James D. Tracy (ed.), *The Rise of Merchant Empires: Long-Distance Trade in the Early Modern World 1350–1750*, Cambridge, 1990, table on p. 126. See also Om Prakash, *The New Cambridge History of India*, II, 5, *European Commercial Enterprise in Pre-colonial India 1500–1800*, Cambridge, 1997, pp. 211–67.

63. Gommans, *Indo-Afghan Empire*, pp. 37–43, 90.

64. For a less optimistic version, see Stephen Frederic Dale, *Indian Merchants and Eurasian Trade 1600–1750*, Cambridge, 1994, pp. 128–38.

65. *Rulers, Townsmen and Bazaars*, p. 52, see also pp. 62–3.

66. 'Money-Use in Pre-Colonial India', in Richards (ed.), *Imperial Monetary System*.

67. See below, p. 325.

68. See sources in note 24.

69. Lakshmi Subramanian, *Indigenous Capital and Imperial Expansion, Bombay, Surat and the West Coast*, Delhi, 1996, p. 181.

70. Dilbagh Singh, *State, Landlords and Peasants*, p. 91.

71. Barnett, *North India between Empires*, pp. 212–22.

72. Gommans, *Indo-Afghan Empire*, p. 148.

73. Bayly, *Rulers, Townsmen and Bazaars*, pp. 214–15.

74. Ibid., pp. 202–5.

75. Asiya Siddiqi, 'Introduction: Trade and Finance 1750–1860', in Siddiqi (ed.), *Trade and Finance in Colonial India, 1750–1860*, Delhi, 1995, pp. 40–2.

76. Ravi Ahuja, 'Labour Unsettled: Mobility and Protest in the Madras Region 1750–1800', *Indian Economic and Social History Review*, xxxv, 1998, pp. 381–404.

77. S. Arasaratnam, 'Trade and Political Dominion in South India, 1750–1790', *Modern Asian Studies*, xiii, 1979, pp. 19–40.

78. *An Historical View of the Plans for the Government of British India*, London, 1793, pp. 32–3, 38–9.

79. The 1919 edition of the *Oxford History of India*, edited by Vincent Smith, depicted the British as following 'the humble policy' of peaceful merchants until 1756, when 'a marvellous change' followed the outbreak of the French war and the loss of Calcutta. 'The traders who fled in terror to Fulta in June 1756 were the masters of a rich kingdom exactly twelve months later' (p. 466).

80. P.J. Marshall (ed.), *The Writings and Speeches of Edmund Burke*, vi, *The Launching of the Hastings Impeachment 1786–1788*, Oxford, 1991, pp. 315, 317.

81. Bayly, *Rulers, Townsmen and Bazaars*, p. 2.

82. See the interpretation in Catherine Manning, *Fortunes à faire: The French in Asian Trade 1719–48*, Aldershot, 1996, pp. 195–220.

83. André Gundar Frank, *World Accumulation 1492–1789*, London, 1978, p. 153. See also Irfan Habib, below, p. 110. Although Immanuel Wallerstein sees the later eighteenth century as the period in which India began to be 'incorporated' into a European-dominated world economy, he is generally cautious about economically deterministic explantions of the first stages of British conquest (*The Modern World System*, iii: *The Second Era of the Great Expansion of the Capitalist World-Economy, 1730–1840s*, New York, 1989, pp. 179–82).

84. The comparison is made in P.J. Cain and A. G. Hopkins, *British Imperialism: Innovation and Expansion 1688–1914*, London, 1993; see below, pp. 391–2.

85. Cited in P.J. Marshall, 'The British in Asia: Trade to Dominion 1700–1765', in Marshall (ed.), *The Oxford History of the British Empire*, ii, *The Eighteenth Century*, Oxford, 1998, pp. 505–6.

86. On the balance of payments, see Ralph Davis, *The Industrial Revolution and British Overseas Trade*, Leicester, 1979, pp. 53–61 and Javier Cuenca Estaban, 'The British Balance of Payments, 1772–1820: India Transfers and War Finance', *Economic History Review*, 2nd ser., liv, 2001, pp. 58–86, especially, pp. 67–8: for a debate on links between territorial expansion and industrialization, see P.J. Marshall and Rudrangshu Mukherjee, 'Early British Imperialism in India', *Past and Present*, cvi,

1985, pp. 164–73; J.R. Ward, 'The Industrial Revolution and British Imperialism, 1750–1850', *Economic History Review*, 2nd ser., XLVII, 1994, pp. 44–65.

87. Philippe Haudrère, *La Compagnie française des Indes au xviiie siècle (1719–1795)*, 4 vols, Paris, 1989, III, pp. 1000–12.

88. Manning, *Fortunes à faire*, pp. 208–18; P.J. Marshall, *East Indian Fortunes: The British in Bengal in the Eighteenth Century*, Oxford, 1976, pp. 91–6.

89. Sanjay Subrahmanyam and C.A. Bayly, 'Portfolio Capitalists and the Political Economy of Early Modern India', *Indian Economic and Social History Review*, XXV, 1988, p. 418.

90. Marshall, *East Indian Fortunes*, ch. V.

91. I accept C.A. Bayly's criticism of my work for ignoring this. See his 'The British Military–Fiscal State and Indigenous Resistance: India 1750–1820' and 'Returning the British to South Asian History: The Limits of Colonial Hegemony', in *The Origins of Nationality in South Asia: Patriotism and Ethical Government in the Making of Modern India*, Delhi, 1998, pp. 245–51, 287.

92. Amba Prasad (ed.), *Fort William–India House Correspondence*, XIV, *Secret and Select Committee 1750–1781*, Delhi, 1985, pp. 173–7.

93. In a famous letter to William Pitt of 1759, Clive anticipated that the national government would have to take the new 'dominion' in Bengal 'in hand' (G.W. Forrest, *Life of Lord Clive*, 2 vols, London, 1918, II. p. 176). On his return to India in 1764 he speculated on a future 'national jurisdiction' (letter to George Grenville, 14 Oct. 1764, Huntington Library, San Marino, California, MS HM 31637).

94. See below, p. 367.

95. Burton Stein, *Thomas Munro: The Origins of the Colonial State and his Vision of Empire*, Delhi, 1989, pp. 24–30.

96. Ranajit Guha, *A Rule of Property for Bengal: An Essay on the Idea of Permanent Settlement*, Paris, 1963.

97. Cited in P.J. Marshall, *Problems of Empire: Britain and India 1757–1813*, London, 1968, p. 65.

98. Radhika Singha, *A Despotism of Law: Crime and Justice in Early Colonial India*, Delhi, 1998, especially pp. 20–7.

99. See below, pp. 419–26 and Sudipta Sen, *Empire of Free Trade: The East India Company and the Making of the Colonial Market Place*, Philadelphia, 1998.

100. This point is strongly made in Jon Wilson, 'Governing Property, Making Law, Land, Local Society and Colonial Discourse in Agrarian Bengal, *c.* 1785–1830', Oxford DPhil, thesis, 2000.

101. Letter to him from Ali Ibrahim Khan, Sept. 1786, British Library, Add MS 29202, ff. 85–6 (I owe this reference to Dr Natasha Eaton).

102. Barnett, *North India between Empires*; Susan Bayly, see below, p. 220; for a more pessimistic interpretation of the Carnatic, see Jim Phillips, 'A Successor to the Moguls: The Nawab of the Carnatic and the East India Company, 1763–1785', *International History Review*, VII, 1985, pp. 364–89.

103. On this, see Robert Travers, 'Contested Notions of Sovereignty'.

104. Anand A. Yang, *The Limited Raj: Agrarian Relations in Colonial India, Saran District, 1793–1920*, Berkeley, 1989, p. 62.

105. Rajat Datta, *Society, Economy and the Market: Commercialization in Rural Bengal, c. 1760–1800*, Delhi, 2000, pp. 333–41.

106. Cf. McLane, *Land and Local Kingship*, pp. 306–12 and Wilson, 'Governing Property and Making Law'.

107. Chatterjee, *Merchants, Politics and Society*.

108. Subramanian, *Indigenous Capital and Imperial Expansion*.

109. Shubhra Chakrabarti, 'Collaboration and Resistance: Bengal Merchants and the English East India Company, 1757–1833', *Studies in History*, x, 1994, pp. 105–29.

110. P.J. Marshall, 'Masters and Banians in Eighteenth-century Calcutta', in B.B. Kling and M.N. Pearson (eds), *The Age of Partnership: Europeans in Asia before Dominion*, Honolulu, 1979, pp. 191–214.

111. Bayly, *Rulers, Townsmen and Bazaars*, pp. 150–1.

112. D.B. Mitra, *The Cotton Weavers of Bengal 1757–1833*, Calcutta, 1978, pp. 107–8.

113. Prasannan Parthasarathi, 'Rethinking Wages and Competitiveness in the Eighteenth Century: Britain and South India', *Past and Present*, CLVIII, 1998, pp. 79–109.

114. Hameeda Hossain, *The Company Weavers of Bengal: The East India Company and the Organization of Textile Production in Bengal, 1750–1813*, Delhi, 1988.

115. See below, p. 418.

116. Sarkar (ed.), *History of Bengal*, II, p. 497.

117. C.A. Bayly, *Empire and Information: Intelligence Gathering and Social Communication in India 1780–1870*, Cambridge, 1996.

118. This theme is expounded in Ludden, *Agrarian History*.

119. Eric Stokes, *English Utilitarians and India*, Oxford, 1959, pp. 168–83.

120. Siddiqi, 'Introduction' in *Trade and Finance*, p. 22.

121. David Washbrook, 'Economic Depression and the Making of "Traditional" Society in Colonial India 1820–1855', *Transactions of the Royal Historical Society*, 6th ser., III, 1993, pp. 261–3.

BIBLIOGRAPHY

*indicates an item reproduced in whole or in part in this volume.

General Interpretations of the Eighteenth Century

Athar Ali, M., 'The Eighteenth Century: An Interpretation', *The Indian Historical Review*, v, 1978–9, 175–86.

*———, 'Recent Theories of Eighteenth-century India', *The Indian Historical Review*, XIII, 1986–7, 102–10.

Bayly, C.A., *The New Cambridge History of India*, II, 1, *Indian Society and the Making of the British Empire*, Cambridge, 1987, chs. 1–3.

Bayly, Susan, *The New Cambridge History of India*, IV, 3, *Caste, Society and Politics in India from the Eighteenth Century to the Modern Age*, Cambridge, 1999, chs. 1–2.

Chandra, Satish, *The Eighteenth Century in India: Its Economy and the Role of the Marathas, the Jats, the Sikhs and the Afghans*, 2nd edn, Calcutta, 1991.

Chaudhuri, Binay Bhushan, 'Characterizing the Polity and Economy of late Pre-colonial

India: The Revisionist Position in the Debate over "the Eighteenth Century in Indian History" ', *The Calcutta Historical Journal*, xix and xx, 1997–8, 35–92.

De, Barun, 'Problems of the Study of Indian History: With Parlicular Reference to Interpretations of the Eighteenth Century', *Proceedings of the Indian History Congress*, xlix, 1989, 1–56.

Malik, Z.U., 'Core and Periphery: A Contribution to the Debate on the Eighteenth Century', *Proceedings of the Indian History Congress*, li, 1990, 167–99.

Perlin, Frank, 'State Formation Reconsidered, Part II', *Modern Asian Studies*, xix, 1985, 415–80.

*Stein, Burton, 'Eighteenth-century India: Another View', *Studies in History*, v, 1989, 1–27.

————, 'State Formation and Economy Reconsidered', *Modern Asian Studies*, xix, 1985, 387–413.

Washbrook, D.A., 'Progress and Problems: South Asian Economic and Social History, c. 1720–1860', *Modern Asian Studies*, xxii, 1988, 57–96.

The Late Mughal Empire

Alam, Muzaffar and Sanjay Subrahmanyam (eds), *The Mughal State 1526–1750*, Delhi, 1998.

Athar Ali, M., 'The Passing of Empire: The Mughal Case', *Modern Asian Studies*, ix, 1975, 385–96.

Chandra, Satish, *Parties and Politics at the Mughal Court, 1707–40*, 3rd edn, Delhi, 1982.

Habib, Irfan, *The Agrarian System of Mughal India, 1556–1707*, Bombay, 1963.

Hintze, Andrea, *The Mughal Empire and its Decline: An Interpretation of the Sources of Social Power*, Aldershot, 1997.

Malik, Zahir Uddin, *The Reign of Muhammad Shah: 1719–1748*, Bombay, 1977.

Richards, J.F., *The New Cambridge History of India*, i, 5, *The Mughal Empire*, Cambridge, 1993.

Sarkar, Jadunath, *The Fall of the Mughal Empire*, 4 vols, Calcutta, 1912–30; Bombay, 1971–5.

Spear, Percival, *Twilight of the Mughals: Studies in Late Mughal Delhi*, Cambridge, 1951.

Regional Polities

The'Afghans

Gommans, Jos J.L., *The Rise of the Indo-Afghan Empire, 1710–1780*, Leiden, 1995; Delhi, 1999.

Husain, Iqbal, *The Ruhela Chieftains: The Rise and Decline of Ruhela Power in the Eighteenth Century*, Delhi, 1994.

Awadh and North India

Alam, Muzaffar, *The Crisis of Empire in Mughal North India: Awadh and the Punjab, 1707–1748*, Delhi, 1986.

Barnett, Richard B., *North India between Empires: Awadh, the Mughals and the British, 1720–1801*, Berkeley, 1980.

*Bayly, C.A., *Rulers, Townsmen and Bazaars: North Indian Society in the Age of British Expansion, 1770–1870*, Cambridge, 1983.

Cohn, Bernard S., 'The Initial British Impact on India: A Case Study of the Benares Region', *Journal of Asian Studies*, xix, 1960, 418–31; reprinted in Bernard S. Cohn, *An Anthropologist among the Historians and Other Essays*, Delhi, 1987, pp. 320–42.

*————, 'Political Systems in Eighteenth-Century India: The Banaras Region', *Journal of the American Oriental Society*, LXXXII, 1962, 312–19; reprinted in Bernard S. Cohn, *An Anthropologist among the Historians and Other Essays*, Delhi, 1987, pp. 483–99.

Cole, J.R.I., *The Roots of North Indian Shi'ism in Iran and Iraq: Religion and State in Awadh, 1722–1859*, Berkeley, 1988.

Fisher, Michael H., *A Clash of Cultures: Awadh, the British and the Mughals*, Delhi, 1988.

Kolff, Dirk H.A., *Naukar, Rajput and Sepoy: The Ethnohistory of the Military Labour Market in Hindustan, 1450–1850*, Cambridge, 1990.

Pinch, William R., 'Who was Himmat Bahadur? Gosains, Rajputs and the British in Bundelkhand, c. 1800', *Indian Economic and Social History Review*, xxxv, 1998, 293–335.

Bengal (pre 1757)

*Alam, Muzaffar, 'Eastern India in the Early Eighteenth-century "Crisis": Some Evidence from Bihar', *Indian Economic and Social History Review*, xxviii, 1991, 43–71.

Calkins, Philip B., 'The Formation of a Regionally-oriented Ruling Group in Bengal, 1700–1740', *The Journal of Asian Studies*, xxix, 1970, 799–806.

Chatterjee, Kumkum, *Merchants, Politics and Society in Early Modern India: Bihar 1733–1820*, Leiden, 1996.

Chaudhuri, Sushil, *Trade and Commercial Organization in Bengal, 1650–1720*, Calcutta, 1975.

————, *From Prosperity to Decline: Bengal in the Eighteenth Century*, Delhi, 1995.

————, *Prelude to Empire: Plassey Revolution of 1757*, Delhi, 2000.

Eaton, Richard M., *The Rise of Islam and the Bengal Frontier, 1204–1760*, Berkeley, 1993; Delhi, 1994.

Gupta, Brijen K., *Sirajuddaulah and the East India Company, 1756–1757: Background to the Foundation of British Power in India*, Leiden, 1962.

McLane, John R., *Land and Local Kingship in Eighteenth-century Bengal*, Cambridge, 1993.

Prakash, Om, *The Dutch East India Company and the Economy of Bengal, 1630–1720*, Princeton, 1985.

Rahim, A., 'The Rise of a Hindu Aristocracy Under Bengal Nawabs', *Journal of the Asiatic Society of Pakistan*, vi, 1961, 104–18.

Bengal (post 1757)

*Datta, Rajat, *Society, Economy and Market: Commercialization in Rural Bengal, c. 1760–1800*, Delhi, 2000.

Fisch, Jörg, *Cheap Lives and Dear Limbs: The British Transformation of the Bengal Criminal Law, 1769–1817*, Wiesbaden, 1983.

Guha, Ranajit, *A Rule of Property for Bengal: An Essay on the Idea of Permanent Settlement*, Paris and The Hague, 1963; Durham, NC, 1996.

Hossain, Hameeda, *The Company Weavers of Bengal: The East India Company and the Organization of Textile Production in Bengal, 1750–1813*, Delhi, 1988.

Islam, Siraj, *The Permanent Settlement in Bengal: A Study of its Operation, 1790–1819*, Dacca, 1979.

*Khan, Abdul Majed, *The Transition in Bengal, 1756–1775: A Study of Saiyid Muhammad Reza Khan,* Cambridge, 1969.

Kopf, David, *British Orientalism and the Bengal Renaissance: The Dynamics of Indian Modernization, 1773–1835*, Princeton, 1969.

Marshall, P.J., *East India Fortunes: The British in Bengal in the Eighteenth Century*, Oxford, 1976.

———, *The New Cambridge History of India*, ii, 2, *Bengal: The British Bridgehead, Eastern India, 1740–1828*, Cambridge, 1987.

———, 'The Making of an Imperial Icon: The Case of Warren Hastings', *Journal of Imperial and Commonwealth History*, xxvii, 1999, 1–16.

McLane, John R., *Land and Local Kingship in Eighteenth-century Bengal*, Cambridge, 1993.

Ray, Rajat Kanta, 'Colonial Penetration and Initial Resistance: The Mughal Ruling Class, the English East India Company and the Struggle for Bengal, 1756–1800', *Indian Historical Review*, xii, 1985, 1–105.

Ray, Ratnalekha, *Change in Bengal Agrarian Society, c. 1760–1860*, Calcutta, 1979.

Sen, Sudipta, *Empire of Free Trade: The East India Company and the Making of the Colonial Market Place*, Philadelphia, 1998.

Sinha, N.K., *The Economic History of Bengal from Plassey to the Permanent Settlement*, 2 vols, Calcutta, 1956–62.

Yang, Anand A., *The Limited Raj: Agrarian Relations in Colonial Saran District, 1793–1920*, Berkeley, 1989.

'Forest Polities'

Guha, Sumit, *Environment and Ethnicity in India 1200–1999*, Cambridge, 1999.

———, 'Forest Polities and Agrarian Empires: The Khandesh Bhils, c. 1750–1850', *Indian Economic and Social History Review*, xxxiii, 1996, 133–53.

Singh, Chetan, 'Forests, Pastoralists and Agrarian Society in Mughal India', in David Arnold and Ramachandra Guha (eds), *Nature, Culture, Imperialism: Essays on the Environmental History of South Asia*, Delhi, 1995, pp. 21–48.

*Skaria, Ajay, 'Being *Jangli*: The Politics of Wildness', *Studies in History*, xiv, 1998, 193–215.

———, *Hybrid Histories: Forests, Frontiers and Wilderness in Western India*, Delhi, 1999.

The Marathas

Gordon, Stewart, *The New Cambridge History of India*, ii, 4, *The Marathas, 1680–1818*, Cambridge, 1993.

———, *Marathas, Marauders and State-Formation in Eighteen-century India*, Delhi, 1994.

*Gordon, Stewart and John F. Richards, 'Kinship and Pargana in Eighteenth-century Khandesh', *Indian Economic and Social History Review*, xxii, 1985, 371–97.

Guha, Sumit, 'An Indian Penal Regime: Maharashtra in the Eighteenth Century', *Past and Present*, cxlvii, 1998, 101–26.

Perlin, Frank, 'Of White Whale and Countrymen in the Eighteenth-century Maratha Deccan: Extended Class Relations, Rights and the Problem of Rural Autonomy under the Ancien Regime', *Journal of Peasant Studies*, v, 1978, 172–237.

Sardesai, Govind Sakharam, *New History of the Marathas*, 3 vols, Bombay, 1946–8; Delhi, 1986.

Wink, André, *Land and Sovereignty in India: Agrarian Society and Politics under the Eighteenth-century Maratha Svarajya*, Cambridge, 1986.

Mysore

*Brittlebank, Kate, *Tipu Sultan's Quest for Legitimacy: Islam and Kingship in a Hindu Domain*, Delhi, 1997.

Gopal, M.H., *Tipu Sultan's Mysore*, Bombay, 1971.

Guha, Nikhiles, *Pre-British State System in South India: Mysore 1761–1799*, Calcutta, 1981.

Habib, Irfan (ed.), *Confronting Colonialism: Resistance and Modernization Under Haidar Ali and Tipu Sultan*, Delhi, 1999.

Hasan, Mohibbul, *History of Tipu Sultan*, 2nd edn, Calcutta, 1971.

Sen, Asok, 'A Pre-British Economic Formation in India of the Late Eighteenth Century: Tipu Sultan's Mysore', in B. De (ed.), *Perspectives in Social Science*, i, *Historical Dimensions*, Calcutta, 1977, 46–119.

Punjab

Alam, Muzaffar, *The Crisis of Empire in Mughal North India: Awadh and the Punjab, 1707–1748*, Delhi, 1986.

Banga, Indu, *The Agrarian System of the Sikhs, Late Eighteenth and Early Nineteenth Century*, Delhi, 1978.

Grewal, J.S., *New Cambridge History of India*, ii, 3, *The Sikhs of the Punjab*, Cambridge, 1990.

McLeod, W.H., *Evolution of the Sikh Community: Five Essays*, Oxford 1976; Delhi, 1996.

Sachdeva, Veena, *Polity and Economy of the Punjab During the Late Eighteenth Century*, New Delhi, 1993.

Rajasthan

Bajekal, Madhavi, 'The State and the Rural Grain Market in Eighteenth-century Eastern Rajasthan', *Indian Economic and Social History Review*, xxv, 1988, 443–73; reprinted in Sanjay Subrahmanyam (ed.), *Merchants, Markets and the State in Early Modern India*, Delhi, 1990, pp. 90–120.

Gupta, S.P., *The Agrarian System of Eastern Rajasthan, (c. 1650–c. 1750)*, Delhi, 1986.

Singh, Dilbagh, *The State, Landlords and Peasants: Eastern Rajasthan in the 18th Century*, Delhi, 1990.

The South-East

Alam, Muzaffar and Sanjay Subrahmanyam, 'Exploring the Hinterland: Trade and Politics in the Arcot Nizamat (1700–1732)', in Rudrangshu Mukherjee and Lakshmi Subramanian (eds), *Politics and Trade in the Indian Ocean World, Essays in Honour of Ashin Das Gupta*, Delhi, 1998, pp. 113–64.

Arasaratnam, S., *Merchants, Companies and Commerce on the Coromandel Coast, 1650– 1740*, Delhi, 1986.

Arasaratnam, S., *Maritime Trade, Society and European Influence in Southern Asia, 1600–1800*, Aldershot, 1995.

————, *Maritime Commerce and English Power (Southeast India 1750–1800)*, Delhi, 1996.

*Bayly, Susan, *Saints, Goddesses and Kings: Muslims and Christians in South Indian Society, 1700–1900*, Cambridge, 1989.

Dirks, Nicholas B., *The Hollow Crown: Ethnohistory of an Indian Kingdom*, Cambridge, 1987; 2nd edn, Ann Arbor, 1993.

Irschick, Eugene F., *Dialogue and History: Constructing South India, 1795–1896*, Berkeley, 1994.

Leonard, Karen, 'The Hyderabad Political System and its Participants', *Journal of Asian Studies*, xxx, 1971, 569–82.

*Ludden, David, *Peasant History in South India*, Princeton, 1985; Delhi, 1989.

Parthasarathi, Prasannan, *The Transition to a Colonial Economy: Weavers, Merchants and Kings in South Asia 1720–1800*, Cambridge, 2001.

Phillips, Jim, 'A Successor to the Moguls: The Nawab of the Carnatic and East India Company, 1763–1785', *International History Review*, vii, 1985, 364–89.

Richards, J.F., *Mughal Administration in Golconda*, Oxford, 1975.

Stein, Burton, *Thomas Munro: The Origins of the Colonial State and His Vision of Empire*, Delhi, 1989.

Subrahmanyam, Sanjay, 'The Politics of Fiscal Decline: A Reconsideration of Maratha Tanjavur 1676–1799', *Indian Economic and Social History Review*, xxxii, 1995, 177– 217.

Economy

Bayly C.A. and Sanjay Subrahmanyam, 'Portfolio Capitalists and the Political Economy of Early Modern India', *Indian Economic and Social History Review*, xxv, 1988, 401– 24.

Chaudhuri, K.N., *The Trading World of Asia and the English East India Company, 1660– 1760*, Cambridge, 1978.

Das Gupta, Ashin, *Indian Merchants and the Decline of Surat, c. 1700–1750*, Wiesbaden, 1979.

————, *Merchants of Maritime India, 1500–1800*, Aldershot, 1994.

Das Gupta, Ashin and M.N. Pearson (eds), *India and the Indian Ocean, 1500–1800*, Calcutta, 1987; 2nd edn, Delhi, 2000.

Frank, André Gunder, *ReOrient: Global Economy in the Asian Age*, Berkeley, 1998.

Habib, Irfan, 'The Technology and Economy of Mughal India', *Indian Economic and Social History Review*, XVII, 1980, 1–34.

*————, 'The Eighteenth century in Indian Economic History', in Leonard Blussé and Femme Gaastra (eds), *On the Eighteenth Century as a Category in Asian History*, Aldershot, 1998, pp. 217–36.

Kumar, Dharma with Meghnad Desai (eds), *The Cambridge Economic History of India*, II, *c. 1757–c. 1970*, Cambridge, 1983.

Ludden, David, *The New Cambridge History of India*, IV, 4, *An Agrarian History of South Asia*, Cambridge, 1999.

Mukherjee, Rudrangshu and Lakshmi Subramanian (eds), *Politics and Trade in the Indian Ocean World, Essays in Honour of Ashin Das Gupta*, Delhi, 1998.

*Perlin, Frank, 'The Problem of the Eighteenth Century', in 'Commercial Manufacture and the "Protoindustrialisation" Thesis, *Unbroken Landscapes: Commodity, Category, Sign and Identity: Their Production as Myth and Knowledge from 1500*, Aldershot, 1994, pp. 74–81.

————, 'Money Use in Late Pre-colonial India and International Trade in Currency Media', in John F. Richards (ed.), *The Imperial Monetary System of Mughal India*, Delhi, 1987, pp. 232–373.

Prakash, Om, *The New Cambridge History of India*, II, 5, *European Commercial Enterprise in Pre-Colonial India 1500–1800*, Cambridge, 1997.

Raychaudhuri, Tapan and Irfan Habib (eds), *The Cambridge Economic History of India*, I *(c. 1200–c. 1750)*, Cambridge, 1982.

Subrahmanyam, Sanjay (ed.), *Merchants, Markets and the State in Early Modern India*, Delhi, 1990.

The European Intrusion and British Rule

Alavi, Seema, *The Sepoys and the Company: Tradition and Transition in Northern India, 1770–1830*, Delhi, 1995.

Bayly, C.A., *Empire and Information: Intelligence Gathering and Social Communication in India, 1780–1870*, Cambridge, 1996.

————, 'The British Fiscal Military State and Indigenous Resistance: India 1750 to 1820', in *The Origins of Nationality in South Asia: Patriotism and Ethical Government in the Making of Modern India*, Delhi, 1998, pp. 238–75.

Bowen, H.V., *Revenue and Reform: The Indian Problem in British Politics, 1757–1773*, Cambridge, 1991.

*Cain, P.J. and A.G. Hopkins, *British Imperialism: Innovation and Expansion 1688–1914*, London, 1993.

Dodwell, Henry, *Dupleix and Clive: The Beginnings of Empire*, London, 1920.

Edney, Matthew, *Mapping an Empire: The Geographical Construction of British India 1765–1843*, Chicago, 1997.

Furber, Holden, *John Company at Work: A Study of European Expansion in India in the Late Eighteenth Century*, Cambridge, MA, 1951.

————, *Rival Empires of Trade in the Orient. 1600–1800*, Minneapolis, 1976.

————, Rosane Rocher (ed.), *Private Fortunes and Company Profits in the India Trade in the Eighteenth Century*, Aldershot, 1997.

Manning, Catherine, *Fortunes à faire: The French in Asian Trade, 1719–48*, Aldershot, 1996.

Marshall, P.J., *Trade and Conquest: Studies in the Rise of British Dominance in India*, Aldershot, 1993.

———, 'The British in Asia: Trade to Dominion, 1700–1765' in P.J. Marshall, ed., *The Oxford History of the British Empire*, ɪɪ, *The Eighteenth Century*, Oxford, 1998, pp. 487–507.

———, 'Britain and the World in the Eighteenth Century, ɪɪɪ, Britain and India', *Transactions of the Royal Historical Society*, 6th ser., x, 2000, 1–16.

Metcalf, T.R., *The New Cambridge History of India*, ɪɪɪ, 4, *Ideologies of the Raj*, Cambridge, 1994.

Nightingale, Pamela, *Trade and Empire in Western India, 1784–1806*, Cambridge, 1970.

Parker, Geoffrey, *The Military Revolution: Military Innovation and the Rise of the West, 1500–1800*, 2nd edn., Cambridge, 1988, Chap. 4.

Ray, Rajat Kanta, 'Indian Society and the Establishment of British Supremacy, 1765-1818' in P.J. Marshall (ed.), *The Oxford History of the British Empire*, ɪɪ, *The Eighteenth Century*, Oxford, 1998, pp. 508–29.

Siddiqi, Asiya (ed.), *Trade and Finance in Colonial India, 1750–1860*, Delhi, 1995.

Singha, Radhika, *A Despotism of Law: Crime and Justice in Early Colonial India*, Delhi, 1988.

Subramanian, Lakshmi, *Indigenous Capital and Imperial Expansion: Bombay, Surat and the West Coast*, Delhi, 1996.

Sutherland, L.S., *The East India Company in Eighteenth-Century Politics*, Oxford, 1952.

Wallerstein, Immanuel, *The Modern World System*, ɪɪɪ: *The Second Era of the Great Expansion of the Capitalist World-Economy, 1730–1840s*, New York, 1989.

PART I
GENERAL ASSESSMENTS OF THE EIGHTEENTH CENTURY

1

The Problem of the Eighteenth Century*

FRANK PERLIN

This characterization of the last centuries of precolonial history conflicts sharply with time-hallowed images of old-order South Asia, the dominant perception being that South Asian history is a story of repeated decline, the last example of which took place in the late seventeenth and eighteenth centuries, when one region after another apparently succumbed to warfare and banditry (from 'chaos to chaos' in Morris's suggestive phrase).[1] Was not the eighteenth century the period when the Mughal empire, and thus 'the Mughal economy', so called, was effectively dismantled, long before colonial occupation, the trough from which the new colonial world would be born anew?[2] The developments of which we have spoken would thus seem to be merely of a cyclical, fluctuational, or even random character, occurring within given (could they be 'homeostatic'?) limits, and in this respect it is important to note that even modern works of economic history betray a fundamental agnosticism in relation to this problem.[3]

The reasons are clear: they reside in the conundrum, discussed above, concerning the extent to which India's history (i.e. South Asia's) should be considered simply an 'Indian history', that is to say, as an autonomous collectivity of evidence abraded here and there by contacts with European companies and commerce. If it can be considered so, then although the course of the eighteenth century will remain disputable, it will also remain part of that long and separate entity (the history of South Asia) abruptly broken into by the colonial conquests of the late eighteenth and early nineteenth centuries, and

*Frank Perlin, 'The Problem of the Eighteenth Century', in 'Commercial Manufacture and the "Protoindustrialization" Thesis', in *Unbroken Landscapes: Commodity, Category, Sign and Identity; Their Production as Myth and Knowledge from 1500*, Aldershot, 1994, pp. 74–81.

thus always tending to be seen as the final tide of a history that, at base, never changed its fundamental character or, at the least, belonged to a different epoch of history to that which followed under colonial rule—in short, an involuted history. Here, then; our hypothesis needs to be led an essential stage further, the question of the eighteenth century to be confronted, certain connections to be made, and an alternative solution worked out which dispenses, as far as possible, with all 'special (that is to say, substantive) logics'.[4] In particular, various problems were treated in the above section largely as structural features representing a 'kind' of economy, and these will now have to be filled out further as a real history, subject to changes of a particular kind.

It would be wrong to see the problem of the eighteenth century as merely 'economic', even in the larger sense of the term. It has long been established orthodoxy to write of political decentralization in the eighteenth century (thus of imperial decline) as if it were synonymous with decline as such. As the imperial armies fell back and local élites switched their allegiances, we are told, new polities came into being of an apparently less centralized and ordered character than the empire they replaced. Their establishment and stabilization entailed a good deal of military conflict, plunder, and extraordinary exactions, thereby leading to de-urbanization, impoverishment, and a decline in indigenous trade and commerce.

An adequate treatment of the question of decline would require a separate essay, but it remains important to point out that even in the limited terms in which it is customarily discussed, South Asian historians have become increasingly sceptical.[5] Firstly, a critique must begin with the still-dominant tendency to view economic developments and political order (again, as such) as dependent functions of the strengths and stabilities of particular governmental entities, thus of particular dynasties, regimes, and polities. Instead, it could be argued that political decentralization went hand in hand with a broader process of *localization* in the distribution and organization of power—of its multiplication or complexification. The character of political order, according to this thesis, underwent a transformation together with those changes of society and economy outlined above, that is to say with an increase in the density of economic life. This can be shown on a variety of levels, from the rise of new states in Rajasthan, Maharashtra, and Hyderabad, to name some notable examples, to the dispersal of small lordly courts and ostensibly urban functions—mentioned above—within the small towns and villages of the countryside. Manufacturing and cash-cropping for distant markets would in some regions have formed part of this 'rurban'-type economy. At a first view, 'rurbanization' can be observed in the southern Deccan, Bihar, and Bengal, and in Gujarat, as well as in Maharashtra.[6]

Although political changes can be connected with changes of other kinds, it is advisable to cease laying one particular feature before the door of another equally specific. Ziegler's study of Rajput state formation in Mewar exemplifies a more long-term and generalized process; it shows a continuous development of state forms from the fifteenth century, in which Mughal conquest and control would take on a formative role, although eventually providing Rajputs with the institutional means to repudiate that control.[7] Underlying a change towards locally autonomous administrations, and significant shifts in the infrastructural character of the systems of rights concerning these territories, local élites became increasingly sedentarized. This can be seen in Maharashtra over a very long period, the heartland of which was never properly controlled by the Mughals, and where property (both patrimonial and prebendal) and the administrative system can be seen evolving well into the eighteenth century, in a way that enabled local potentate and the state to increase controls over the countryside. No doubt this was a paradoxical development since each political order, as indeed the Mughal empire itself, was thereby subject to fissiparous tendencies on a variety of scales and levels; however, the substantial structural linkages connecting such differentiated scales of political order have been little studied, the main emphasis having been upon growing disorder. In fact, new administrative developments occurred on many levels and were highly dispersed, involving a more complex distribution of power and organization than had existed previously. It is in the eighteenth century that the accounts of income and expenditure of Maratha lords and villages become superabundant, and in the same period that the more powerful of the former manage to set up their own semi-autonomous administrations. The relationship between political power and economic life alters in the eighteenth century, with distant centralized power becoming balanced and complemented by a more dense nexus of diverse other forces.

Our second point, given the role of military conflict in the interpretation of decline, is that there is little research on the effects of warfare on society in South Asia comparable to that conducted in recent years on The Thirty Years War and Wars of the Roses in Europe, the latter responsible for major demystification about the effects of conflict. However, several studies now show that the periods of disruption following violent conquests could be relatively short and that new regimes were eager to set about constructing their own administrations capable of regenerating regular flows of income. The Marathas exemplify such drives, although presented as the archetypal marauders of the literature.[8]

There are many other reasons for scepticism. It has not been shown that eighteenth-century conflicts were more destructive than those accompanying

Mughal expansion (the 'golden age' of the historiography), nor, for that matter, than the Napoleonic Wars in Europe. The effects of war itself are disputed: financing war through increased taxation and borrowing might have deleterious general effects, whereas routes and battlefields were localized (although not always the diseases that accompanied them). Moreover, peasant recruitment in eighteenth-century armies could be a means of injecting wealth into towns and villages, a source of investment in cloth and weapon production, and part and parcel of the 'rurban' demand structure treated above.[9] This does not imply the absence of large-scale disruption: the point concerns its undifferentiated association with generalized decline. Surat, a particularly notorious example, proved remarkably resilient to repeated attack. Seventeenth and eighteenth-century Europe was hardly without its wars and disruptions, regional economic declines, and political decentralizations.

Nor was eighteenth-century warfare random. It was especially marked by piecemeal intrusion into the subcontinent by the East India Companies, which penetrated along many different regional 'fronts', took over rights, interfered in governments, and conquered one piece of territory after another: thus, the textile manufacturing and cotton-growing regions of Bihar and Bengal by 1765; much of what is now eastern Uttar Pradesh by 1775 (its important market entrepôts); most of southern India south of the Kistna river between 1792 and 1801 (including the textile districts of Coromandel, Malabar and Mysore—marketing and textile towns, ports, cash-cropping districts); important cotton-growing districts and commercial towns in south Gujarat between 1800 and 1805; large areas of Andhra and Orissa, also important for their export-oriented textile production, between 1753 and 1803; then in 1818–19 most of Maharashtra among other territories. The latter were last because, commercially speaking, they were the least interesting for the Company, while the rest had obvious industrial and commercial functions.

If it thus seems reasonable, at first sight, to divide the subcontinent into colonial and pre-colonial regions existing separately but simultaneously alongside one another, it is nonetheless no longer possible by the middle of the eighteenth century to conceive of South Asian states as functioning independently of the effects and forces of European intervention. The Companies were using their armies and treasuries to interfere in a massive way (even in territories not formally conquered before the early nineteenth century); local princelings were able to build up and maintain strength through Company alliances, thus affecting the coherence of larger states; armaments were imported and distributed in the hinterland; and European mercenaries hired themselves out to South Asian rulers. In short, we have all the features of what Martin Klein and Ivor Wilks describe in West Africa as the destabilizing effects of an open and violent frontier with the Europeans.[10] Marshall's description of the course of East India Company penetration of Awadh, in northern India, exemplifies such processes, showing their numerous forms, as much commercial and private as political and institutional.[11] Rather than stepping into a political and military vacuum, colonial conquests followed a long history of pre-colonial disruption brought about by the 'open frontier' with the Companies.

However, although this argument helps to break down the rigidity of the frontiers separating colonial and pre-colonial sectors, and gives to the eighteenth century a shape it too often lacks, it needs to be reformulated in terms of the commercial and intercontinental developments of the period which, in my view, impart to these processes of conquest and transition a quite different texture and meaning. Since it is these aspects which are most relevant to the subject of this essay I shall briefly concentrate on them.

Firstly, let us return to the question of money, a feature already shown to have been subject to powerful developments in the seventeenth and eighteenth centuries. Yet money is one of the many features which the pessimists have automatically cast as evidence of decline: gimcrack coinages, privatization of mints and multiplication of both mints and coin types being seen as marking loss of coherence—an increasing disorder affecting economic life. In contrast, we have argued that these changes were closely related to the contemporary needs of a commercializing economy; an economy in which, in addition, local economic life was becoming more dense and vigorous even in essentially agricultural hinterlands; these developments were paralleled in eighteenth-century Europe and elsewhere where illegal money-making fulfilled a similar role.

Vilar rightly argues that money should not be attributed 'special' significance for an understanding of past economic life.[12] However, in certain historical circumstances, where established viewpoints depend upon the idea of the absence of money or of its socially restricted circuit, money, its very existence, its easy passage across political and geographical frontiers, its role in connecting regions, states, classes, town and country, lord, banker, peasant, and merchant, its ready divisions and subdivisions into portions which allowed values to be attributed to the tiny dealings of poor people in the countryside, all of these features and many others give to money a quite unique interpretational status; it would be no exaggeration to say that it provides a further and necessary dimension to the organization of old-order life essential for its understanding.

Now, simultaneous with the broad processes of 'rurbanization' and increasing local money-use treated above, there is evidence that industrial producers were increasingly caught up in advance-payment relationships. A number of authors suggest that seventeenth-century producers possessed some degree of independence from merchants who sold them raw materials and purchased their products.[13] This is a very difficult theme, because it is quite unclear what and who these 'manufacturers' were, the sociology of manufacture remaining largely undifferentiated in the literature.[14] The question is thus whether industry was so structured that some trades, employers, and middlemen would have possessed this relative independence in contrast to the bulk of the manufacturing populations. Even given this qualification, it is reasonable to point to a considerable extension in the use of advance-payments in the eighteenth century. At this time the Dutch and English East India Companies made strenuous efforts to obtain closer supervisory control over textile spinners and weavers, even to the extent of cutting out various levels of intermediary; this enabled Company merchants to inspect looms and demand technical changes.[15] These events parallel many other features of East India Company activities, and also the actions of English private merchants, who sought to drive other merchants out of competition (be they Armenian, South Asian, or those of another European trading company). As Arasaratnam remarks, they closely correlate with the changing character of the international market for textiles.[16] Textiles in Europe as well as South Asia were becoming more varied both in kind and quality, and consumer expectations and quality controls correspondingly more exacting, not least as relatively less skilled workers were incorporated into the lower end of these production networks.

Such change, including the drive to impose a supervisory control sufficiently sensitive to the market, upon numerous dispersed producers, needs to be seen as response to the increasingly competitive character of intercontinental marketing as more parts of the old and new worlds entered production in the course of the eighteenth century. Thus, in both Bengal and Coromandel, as East India Companies accumulated local political power and commercial monopoly, the managerial links with the producer were tightened, an increasing scale and level of violence characterized treatment of producers, and the costs of labour were driven downwards.[17]

But of course, these developments of the late eighteenth century were part and parcel of a gradual transition to colonial rule, and Hossain and Mohsin have shown that the assumption of political control provided an essential impetus to the exploitational controls exercised by the English Company and merchants. During the eighteenth century, South Asian merchants were driven from independent participation in inter-Asian trade and forced into subsidiary roles within South Asia itself in order to survive. Similarly, Armenian, Persian and South Asian purchasers of textiles within the subcontinent were disadvantaged and either forced from the trade or into intermediary functions for the Europeans.[18] Moreover, some writers argue that eighteenth-century bankers were gradually divorced from commercial operations under early colonial rule.[19]

A useful comparison can be made with events in eastern and central Europe during the same period. Commercial manufactures in Bengal and Coromandel were affected by developments astonishingly similar to those described by Klima in the case of Bohemia, where Dutch and English merchants also gained an increasing stranglehold on local regions and producers.[20] With respect to this comparison, it is only of local significance that this process in South Asia is tied in with the slow extension of control by the European trading Companies. Comparison could also be made with other studies of eastern and central Europe, where despite different local conditions, increasingly organized groups of foreign merchants were moving into more direct control over production by the late eighteenth century.[21] However, this obviously does not imply that colonial occupation is without general significance.

For the present, it is worth noting that the vast expansion of textile output in late eighteenth-century Bengal and Coromandel demanded increasing supplies of cotton, yarn, and foodstuffs from an agricultural hinterland that extended far beyond those regions controlled by the East India Company. Yarn was thus carried down from upland villages to the factories of the English East India Company on the Coromandel coast, while merchants of the Company purchased manufactures from producers living in regions of South India under rulers whom it could barely influence without use of troops. Cotton was grown under different political dispensations, for example in Awadh, the upper Ganges valley, and the central-north Deccan, for export to the markets of East India Company Bengal, while both cultivation and transport were financed by banking establishments with offices scattered across north and peninsular South Asia but whose head offices had come by this period to be relocated in distant, colonial Bengal, a feature witnessed in varied circumstances elsewhere.[22]

In summary, by the late eighteenth century we can no longer properly write of a merely 'Indian history' (i.e. South Asian). Well before the colonial conquests of the early nineteenth century, South Asian history, Company history, and the history of a growing international commerce have become inextricably entangled, even fused. This was partly true in the seventeenth century when a vigorous export and import trade linked South Asia's ports and textile manufacturers with inter-Asian and Atlantic trading. But by the eighteenth century the process of integration is of an altogether different scale and character.[23]

NOTES AND REFERENCES

1. Morris D. Morris, 'Towards a Reinterpretation of Nineteenth-century Indian Economic History', *Indian Economic and Social History Review* (v, 1968), 4.

2. One can see how a scholarship rooted in ancient Greek and Latin literature would develop an imagery and temporal landscape of which we are now the unwitting inheritors—historical myth clothed in fact. The question concerns this too unremarked, too natural and common-sensical passage of a known mythological form into the expressive forms of modernity.

3. See the discussion of the two volumes of the *Cambridge Economic History of India*, in my 'Disarticulation of the World'.

4. For 'special logics', see pp. 40–1 & n. 41.

5. C.A. Bayly's, *Rulers, Townsmen and Bazaars. North Indian Society in the Age of British Expansion, 1770–1870* (Cambridge, 1983), which appeared at almost the same time as this essay, also reinterprets the eighteenth century, although with different results.

6. For more detailed arguments and references, see 'Precolonial Indian State' (1981) and 'State Formation Reconsidered' (1985), the latter in *The Invisible City. Money, Administrative and Popular Infrastructures in Asia and Europe, 1500–1900*, Aldershot, 1994.

7. Norman P. Ziegler, 'Some Notes on Rajput Loyalties during the Mughal Period', in J.F. Richards (ed.), *Kingship and Authority in South Asia* (Madison, 1978), pp. 215–51.

8. E.g. S.N. Gordon, 'The Slow Conquest: Administrative Integration of Malwa into the Maratha Empire, 1720–1760, *Modern Asian Studies* (xi, 1977), pp. 1–40.

9. My documentation includes salary accounts for local garrisons of imported troops and troops with typical local peasant names accompanying armies into distant territories; both brought income into the locality, complicated relationships, and modified the distribution of rights.

10. M.A. Khan, 'Social and Economic factors in the Muslim Revolution in Senegambia', *Jl. African His.* (xii, 1972), pp. 425–6; Ivor Wilks, 'Ashanti Government', D. Forde and P.M. Kaberry (eds), *West African Kingdoms in the Nineteenth Century* (London, 1967), pp. 206, 232–4; Emmanuel Terray, 'Asante au XIXe Siècle', *Annales E.S.C.* (xxxii, 1977), pp. 311–25.

11. P.J. Marshall, 'Economic and Political Expansion: The Case of Oudh', *Mod. Asian Studies* (ix, 1975), pp. 465–82.

12. Pierre Vilar, *A History of Gold and Money*, London, 1976, p. 19.

13. K.N. Chaudhuri, 'The Structure of the Indian Textile Industry in the Seventeenth and Eighteenth Centuries', *Indian Economic and Social History Review* (xi, 1974), 147ff; A. Jan Qaisar, 'The Role of Brokers in Medieval India', *Indian Historical Review* (i, 1974), 242–3; S. Arasaratnam, 'Trade and Political Dominion in South India 1750–1790: Changing British-Indian Relationships', *Modern Asian Studies* (xiii, 1979), 19–40, and his 'Weavers, Merchants and the Company: The Handloom Industry in Southeast India', *Indian Economic and Social History Review* (xvii, 1978).

14. Hameeda Hossain, 'The Alienation of Weavers: Impact of the Conflict between the Revenue and Commercial Interests of the East India Company, 1750–1800', *Indian Economic and Social History Review* (xvi, 1979) is especially valuable on the later period: middlemen traders (*dalals* and *paikars*) 'registered themselves as Company weavers in order to seek protection'; 'Advances were accepted by head weavers' (p. 333), she refers to 'principal weavers' and 'inferior weavers' (p. 335). C.f. Gautam Bhadra 'The Role of Pykars in the Silk Industry of Bengal, 1767–1830', revised paper presented to *Indian History Congress* (36th Session, Aligarh, 1975); Arasaratnam, 'Weavers, Merchants and Company'.

15. Hossain, 'Alienation of Weavers', pp. 327 ff., on the Companies in Bengal; ibid., pp. 329 ff. on the extension of advances and on loom inspection.

16. Arasaratnam, 'Weavers, Merchants and Company', pp. 275–80.

17. P.J. Marshall, *East Indian Fortunes: The British in Bengal in the Eighteenth Century* (Oxford, 1976), gives many instances, especially chs. 2–5, e.g. p. 38; Khan Mohammed Mohsin, *A Bengal District in Transition: Murshidabad 1765–1793* (Dacca, 1973), pp. 63–5; Arasaratnam, 'Trade and Political Dominion in South India', 34 ff, and 'Weavers, Merchants and Company', 271 ff; Bhadra, 'Role of Pykars'.

18. These changes are discussed in 'Financial Institutions and Business Structures', § 4, in *The Invisible City*, and in the works cited supra n. 17.

19. M.J. Mehta, 'Indian Bankers in the Late 18th Century and Early 19th Centuries', *Indian History Congress* (40th Session, 1979, Waltair [M.S. University of Baroda conference volume]); Marshall, *East Indian Fortunes*; Karen Leonard, 'The "Great Firm" Theory of the Decline of the Mughal Empire', *Comparative Studies in Soc. & Hist.* (xxi, 1979), pp. 151–67.

20. Arnost Klima, 'English Mercantile Capital in Bohemia in the Eighteenth Century', *Economic History Review* (2nd Ser., xii, 1954); Herman Feudenberger, 'The Woollen-Goods Industry of the Habsburg Monarchy in the Eighteenth Century', *Journal of Economic History* (xx, 1960).

21. E.G. Kisch, 'Textile Industries in Silesia and the Rhineland: A Comparative Study in Industrialization', sec. 2 on Silesia; Feudenberger, 'Woollen-Goods Industry of the Habsburg Monarchy'.

22. Esp. 'Financial Institutions and Business Practices', in *The Invisible City*; Marshall, *East Indian Fortunes*, pp. 78, 99, 100, 107, 137.

23. In 'World Economic Integration', below, 'Financial Institutions and Business Structures', in *The Invisible City*, the concepts of integration and transition have been radically extended.

2

Eighteenth-century India: Another View*

Burton Stein

What follows are partly musings about what I should have said while presenting a seminar at the Centre for Historical Studies of Jawaharlal Nehru University, and partly the outcome of post-seminar discussions with some of my colleagues at the Centre, where I taught for a semester in 1988. This paper seeks to express gratitude for having had the pleasure of being part of the Centre, its faculty, and its students. My thanks are in the highest form I know: a historical argument, for which, if I have it right, my Centre colleagues share some of the credit, but if I am wrong, they are possibly implicated in some of its errors.

My seminar presentation with the above title proposed a revisionist formulation of India's eighteenth century, something upon which I and David Washbrook have worked for some years together with a group of other scholars from the United States, the United Kingdom, and India. This larger group agreed about the importance of resituating what all were agreed should be called 'the late pre-colonial' period of Indian history, Frank Perlin's apt phrase, and of the rescuing it from its long-standing and persistent characterization as a 'chaotic' or 'black' century. Hence, we seek to historiographically reconstitute this era whose core was the eighteenth century, but whose antecedents were earlier and whose consequences extended well into the nineteenth century.

The present statement of that project is my version of a longer, and somewhat different essay done with Washbrook, which will appear in *Modern Asian Studies*. It should also be said that the present argument carries the endorsement of neither Washbrook nor any other scholars.

*Burton Stein, 'Eighteenth-century India: Another View', *Studies in History, v*, 1989, pp. 1–26.

First, the problem. There is no longer any agreed characterization of India's eighteenth century as might have been found a hundred years ago. Then, there was little difficulty in setting the conditions of India that made British imperial dominance possible, if not inevitable; proponents and critics of late Victorian imperialism, including Marx, were in accord with one another and with James Mill, one of the earliest to state the case in his *History of British India* (1817).[1] Mill described a backward society of the subcontinent plunged into ever deeper chaos following the death of the last great Mughal, Aurangzeb. The disorder attending the partition of the great Mughal state into warring successor regimes threatened the trade of the East India Company and impelled it to assume more direct administrative responsibilities until, almost mindlessly, a great British empire existed. His Victorian successors sought to raise the tone of Mill's disdainful pragmatism. Utilitarian and evangelical writers of a different sort from the elder Mill infused the British colonial state in India with the moral mission of an enlightened Britain bringing order and progress to the benighted subcontinent.

The imperialist explanation of British dominance over India is thus a conjunctural one. It is seen as a single, complex process created from a conjoining, or interaction, of two previously independent historic processes: the simultaneous rise of a world-commanding Britain during the seventeenth and eighteenth centuries and the fall of the Mughals, one of the great empires of Eurasia. What imperial historians saw as a providential conjuncture, later Indian nationalist historians interpreted another way, but still conjuncturally. To the latter, the chance interaction of a waxing Britain and a waning India permitted the imposition of colonial rule in the last half of the eighteenth century.

The creation of the colonial state during the first half of the nineteenth century is a subject which has suffered these and other distortions in most of the existing historiography. Because of the failure to notice the central conjuncturality of both the imperialist and the nationalist interpretations, a paradoxical alliance of the two has existed through most of the present century. For both the imperial apologist and the nationalist critic, the state and the economy mastered by the British by its conquests in the eighteenth and early nineteenth centuries were transformed so utterly as to produce a fundamental historical disjunction, a change of such magnitude as to make both state and economy different from what each had previously been.

For imperial historians, beginning with James Mill, who was a witness to the rise to supremacy of Britain, the assumption of direct political rule in the mid-eighteenth century ended an epoch of chaos and state oppression of the pre-colonial epoch. This was, of course, the ready justification for British conquest and rule in India. But beyond that, imperial historians conceived of the eighteenth century as a dark era awaiting the order and modernisation of British rule. Not even Marx could escape this contemporary teleology: his 'Asiatic mode of production' both caricatured the condition of India before the British and apotheosised European capitalism as the force which would release India from its thralldom and usher it 'into history'.

Nationalist historians perceived the historical moment of the British conquest as similarly disjunctive, but their views were differentially valanced. Conceding a chaotic eighteenth century that attended the dissolution of Mughal order, they saw the British conquest, permitted in a weakened instant, as the beginning of a tragic, irreversible process which closed off the possibility of a return to an older trajectory of order and development. Henceforward, India was to be bent to an imperial will which reduced it to an impoverished source of raw materials, soldiers and treasure thus abetting the British creation of an Asian and African imperial system and massive industrial strength, both of which deepened the subjection of India.

To these two classical positions, another was added in more recent times. This began with Eric Stokes', *The English Utilitarians and India* in 1959, to be refined in his later essay, 'The First Century of British Colonial Rule' (1973).[2] According to Stokes, the perceived task of colonial rulers in India during much of the nineteenth century was the modification of older, pre-colonial systems of administration, and *the*, or *a*, major orienting conception of those in England and India who decided on what legacies of the past to modify and how, was utilitarianism. The specificity of this last element—utilitarian political and social doctrines—receded in Stokes' later work, but not the perception that the salient perceived tasks of the colonial 'founders' was upon changing an inherited system of Indian administration. This view certainly broke the confined frame of imperialists and nationalists, and the process of adaptation was shrewdly and subtly traced in Stokes' later work. Less clearly worked out by him was the time frame of alleged utilitarian influence in India, and whether its intellectual and policy-framing notions extended over the whole of the nineteenth century, or whether the crisis of the Great Mutiny closed further Benthamite influences.

The great merit of Stokes' work was that he constructed a reasoned basis for rejecting the simplicity of both the imperialist and the nationalist conjunctural conceptions about the early nineteenth century. He suggested, instead, that the onset of colonial rule involved an interaction between colonial administrative institutions and a largely intact institutional system which predated the British. There was no question here of one state form replacing another, but rather the continuity of a variety of forms, all subject to manifold influences that arose in India as well as from England.

Stokes substantially modified the historiography he inherited. He changed the terms in which conjuncture could be discussed. He rejected the notion of an oppositional conjuncture in the terms of imperialist and nationalist historians and posited something which can be called 'harmonious conjuncture'. According to his later writings, it was not the conjoining of previously independent and opposed historical processes—a rising Britain, a descending India, fortuitously in the same time/space frame—but the similarity, or congruence, of historical trajectories that accounts for both the ease of the British conquest and the continuity of pre-colonial forms during the first century of the colonial regime in India to about 1850. In his later writings, Stokes outlined another sort of conjunctural thesis for understanding the British colonial state to the time of the Great Mutiny. The structure of that colonial regime was formed by the interaction of complementary, rather than opposing, historical processes that independently arose in Britain during the seventeenth and eighteenth centuries and in India at the same time; paradoxically, these processes were brought together amidst the warfare and violence of British conquest.

While Stokes' later writings implied more than they demonstrated about this harmonious conjuncture across the pre-colonial and colonial divide, others explored the implications of his argument more explicitly and fully. This began with a set of essays published in *Modern Asian Studies* in 1973 dealing with the politics of the mature colonial regime in the late nineteenth and early twentieth centuries.

Several of the writers of these essays were concerned with the interaction of administrative changes of the early nineteenth century—Stokes' concern—and the more explicit political consequences of these changes later. The coherence of these writings was never as marked as the sobriquet, 'Cambridge School', applied to them suggested nor as the lead essay in the set by Anil Seal appeared to promise. Yet, this collective work served to underscore Stokes' repudiation of the conventional historiography on the colonial state as expressed on the imperialist and nationalist premises, and it went far toward providing a more suitably complex approach to the mature colonial state of the later nineteenth and twentieth centuries. At the level of general outline—and we have progressed little beyond that—some of the major processes which created the colonial regime of the later nineteenth century were being clarified.

C.A. Bayly's recently published monograph[3] is extending the temporal range of how the continuity of pre-colonial political and economic structures under colonial rule must be addressed. Bayly rejects what he calls the 'Black Century' conception of the eighteenth century, and he offers a strong counter-argument for the political and economic vigour of that period. Imperial decline of the Mughals was accompanied by several important developments. Formerly peripatetic imperial officers and minor service officials niched themselves in small towns where they constituted the core of a 'gentry', to which others were added, local magnates, who were not previously a formal part of the Mughal regime. An increasingly homogenized merchant class also emerged located in numerous Gangetic towns, made up of formerly great imperial merchants and bankers and smaller, local traders. Between the new gentry and the transformed mercantile groups of the Gangetic area, relations of mutual interest and solidarity were forged, but without blunting certain distinctive characteristics of each. Among such characteristics were the court-centred, martial aspects of the gentry and the religious piety (to which credit worthiness was linked) of the merchants.

The emergence and durability of these new formations depended upon three interlinked and flexible relationships, according to Bayly. These were, first, relations of agrarian dependency and clientage by which local rural élites became bound to the urban service-gentry, thereby adding to the already high degree of social differentiation among rural social groups, nearly half of whom were not engaged in cultivation at all. Secondly, the rural economy became a productive hinterland serving the élite consumption of the towns. Finally, state resources derived from taxation to meet the increased fiscal demands as well as the luxury needs of numerous small states created a nexus of revenue collection and trade in which merchant capital figured prominently as a means of channelling revenue proceeds, in which bankers and their advances were essential in meeting state expenses, and in which trade goods circulated as a transfer medium between tax collections and state receipts.

As to the pervasive warfare and military destruction of the eighteenth century, conventionally seen as the prime cause of the chaotic conditions of the age, Bayly conceded that there was much disruption. Invasions from the north-west by Nadir Shah and Zeman Shah in 1739 and 1797 and warfare attending the formation of the Sikh, Maratha, and Jat states did cause destruction and bore economic costs. However, he considers the consequences of such dislocations to have been exaggerated. Much of the loot seized in these wars was sold in India, and markets quickly recovered, or bazaarmen moved, in an orderly way, to other places. Moreover, the era of state-building of the post-Mughal eighteenth century afforded the compensations of many new markets which the courts of 'compact despotisms' generated. These were markets catering for the consumption needs of its townspeople, based upon small royal courts and the needs of its armies, based upon Turkish ordnance and European infantry forces. Among the examples chosen by Bayly to exemplify these developments was the Karnatik state of Haidar Ali Khan.

Bayly concludes that economic decline was limited during the eighteenth century; losses in one area were recouped elsewhere, and there was a general tendency for those regions with the greatest potential for development to receive new populations of labourers (cultivators and artisans) and new capital and skills as well. Moreover, the 'commercialization of royal power', begun under the Mughals, spread after their time to meet the needs of military organization and growing bureaucratization of the numerous smaller polities that succeeded the Mughals. Certain commodities, such as cotton and indigo, lost the prominence they had enjoyed earlier, but other commodities such as opium arose, and all evidence points to the continued vigour of coastal trading around the subcontinental shelf. Indian merchant capital was redeployed in the search of greater control over labour productivity through control over revenue collections of all sorts, and the new unified merchant class met in the new *qasbah*s and the small, permanent markets attached to them (*ganj*). There, during the 'Black Century', was constructed the infrastructure for European trade in, and ultimately dominion over, India.

Another of the Cambridge group to have sought the pathway of continuity over the purported colonial divide of the mid-eighteenth century is David Washbrook. Following the publication of his *The Emergence of Provincial Politics: The Madras Presidency, 1870–1920*, his papers on the eighteenth century have sought to fill out some of the argumentation of the monograph, especially its assumptions about the early colonial period.[4] In the course of this, his interests and studies have taken him into questions about the late, precolonial political economy of south India.

Washbrook deals with the economic and social restructuring of merchant capital in the Coromandel region from the early eighteenth century to about 1850. The major change which he traces is that of merchant capital from its involvement in the apex fiscal institutions of seventeenth- and eighteenth-century regimes in the south to that of defensive petty usury and local trade by the middle of the nineteenth century. During the eighteenth century, Washbrook finds Indian bankers in the south as in Bengal providing much of the capital required by the East India Company and by private European traders for the conduct of their businesses. Indian financiers did this in their multiple roles of tax farmers and large-scale commercial agents. Through these combined functions, they moved Company and private trade funds from factory to factory as well as to Company armies by means of their bills of exchange. This continued to be the case until 1800. Then and before, Indian merchants were involved in the broadest commodity transactions, handling everything from cloth to copper, and rice to rubies, as Washbrook put it; and Coromandel merchants were drawn from more than traditional mercantile castes, for among them were Brahmans, Vellalas, Telugu Baligas, and Muslim grandees from Hyderabad.

By 1830, this system, pivoting upon Indian agents, had passed. The cloth trade had come completely under Company control, and there were monopolies over the trade in opium, indigo, tobacco, and spirits; much of the trade in these commodities was managed by European agency houses from which Indians were excluded, but, more important changes occurred in the revenue system. By 1830, tax farmers were replaced by Company civil officials under *ryotwari* regulations everywhere. This removed Indian merchants from the nexus of revenue collections, currency operations, and remittance financing. The most serious implication of these changes by the end of the first third of the nineteenth century was the removal of Indian finance from the agrarian productive base and the pressing of Indian capital down to the most riskful levels of village production.

Anglo-Indian law imposed during the middle of the nineteenth century, according to Washbrook, had the effect of freezing previously flexible and changing rights and properties. Thus, sales of corporate, communal entitlements such as *mirasi* were now limited and prohibitions were imposed on the sale or transfer of *inam* rights. However, the Company took care that none of this weakened debt collections and contractual obligations.

The forced retreat of Indian merchant capital under these assaults and the curtailment of state investments (that is, of revenue proceeds) in agricultural production, as had been practised in late pre-colonial times, weakened the Coromandel economy. Areas of high agriculture had always faced labour deficits owing to the vast, neighbouring zones of free land in the interior and the competition there for labour. Productive capital based on the investment of revenue collections had served to fix labour in these best agrarian environments, and with the reduction of the scope of Indian merchant capital and the exclusion of Indians from revenue collections during the first half of the nineteenth century, the encompassing institutional system for the reproduction of these microeconomies was weakened. This resulted not only from the reduction of older investment incentives for Indian bankers, from which they derived benefits as tax farmers as well, but also from the Company's changes in the financial operations of temples and their *inam* and *mirasi* rights which limited the portfolio options of Indian merchants and bankers who had previously purchased these rights.

Because the Company could not, or would not, compete in the existing system of agrarian and trade relationships, it forcibly seized control of that system. By so doing, Washbrook argues, the British, by mid-century destroyed an eighteenth-century economy which had been sustained by the participation of Indian financiers in the fiscal operations of the regimes of the region and the redistribution of state resources through trade and investment in production.

Another historian whose work is important on the late pre-colonial economy and state is Frank Perlin. In several papers he has sought to define and set the political and economic character of the 'old regimes' of India based upon records of seventeenth- and eighteenth-century Maharashtra.[5]

The central process of these old regimes is seen as the complex inter-relationship between two kinds of forces: centralizing, state-building ones and local, communal ones. Prior studies of this period and these processes are seen by him as flawed in the separation between scholars holding opposed conceptions about the polities of the time: one a 'taxation-centric' conception of the state, with the entailed view of the top bearing down upon a passive social base; the other, equally distorting, a conception of these societies from the bottom up, tending to deny any centralizing element.

Perlin describes an 'administrative order' of late pre-colonial regimes drawn from Maharashtra during the time of the rise of Shivaji's kingdom during the seventeenth century and its subsequent transformations. The 'infrastructural underbelly of what we call the state' is discovered by him in the administrative forms adopted by the 'great households' of seventeenth century Maharashtra. They had massed lands under their patrimonial control through the acquisition of prebendal rights. These lands comprised their *khalsa*, or state domains, imitating the sultanate regimes of the Deccan. Such imitation was general in the Deccan and probably elsewhere in India, resulting in a 'library of categories and techniques' that was widespread in the Deccan, which included ideas like *khalsa*, and was used by great Maratha households for their interior administration and for their later state-building. Accounting and record-keeping were another element of this. Scribal specialists, *kulkarni* and *deshpande*, served great households and enhanced other, familistic, administrative mechanisms at their disposal. Measurement and money-use added to this capability, and along with scribal specialization, these spread freely around the Deccan permitting the creation of cash revenue systems based upon land surveys and registers. In the process it became possible, perhaps inevitable, that older forms of rights and properties were transformed into other forms of rights and properties. In particular, resumable and prebendal rights and properties were assimilated to heritable rights and properties through money sales.

These changes were attended by ideological conflicts that reflected (manifested as well as mirrored) tension between centralizing forces of state regimes and older usages of local peasantries; one consequence of this was the convening of local assemblies (*gota*) for the purpose of protecting the latter from state demands. Terms like *watan and saranjam* refer, respectively, to communal and prebendal properties; they also refer to two opposed, yet interacting, notions of rights. Larger and more powerful households operated in both spheres where such rights and properties originated—the royal court and the peasant locality; a major linking of the two spheres was the economic power of great households, based upon landholding, control of labour, capital investment in agrarian production and infrastructure, and often, banking and trade. Such 'right accumulating households' of seventeenth- and eighteenth-century Maharashtra were also strategically positioned to benefit from the development of regional and international trade at this time, when new state forms and expanded areas of agrarian settlement were also forming.

Perspectives on the late pre-colonial era in India are neither unified nor settled. The views of the three writers summarized above are far more nuanced and more shaped by local differences in evidence as well as in historical conditions than can be captured in any summary. Moreover, there are some major differences among them. Thus, there is the suggestion by Perlin that there was a degree of stagnation of the late pre-colonial economy which neither Bayly nor Washbrook appear to find as they survey the changes from pre-colonial India to that of colonialism. Nor, obviously, are these views the only ones that could have been considered even among Anglo-American writers, not to speak of Indian scholars such as Sabyasachi Bhattacharya.[6] In fact, a set of disparate historical perspectives on the Indian eighteenth century have emerged; partly in opposition to older imperialist and nationalist interpretations, and partly in opposition to each other.

Still, these several studies provide the basis for the following extended propositionally-stated hypothesis about the contradictions apparent in eighteenth-century south India.

PROPOSITION 1

Contrary to the prevailing and long-established historiography of eighteenth-century India, the economy was dynamic. There was a relocation and restoration of high production amidst the war-torn economy of the age, as Bayly has shown in challenging older notions about the eighteenth century and its decline in the Mughal heartland. The period is also marked by qualitatively new economic relations involving commercialization of rights previously outside of the commercial nexus; investment of capital from new sources, especially of revenue receipts, and in new ways, dictated by the interests of tax-farmers

and monopoly contractors; increased importance of money-use and its penetration into new relations; intensification of pressure for domination over
labour as seen in the more stringent notions of contract between merchants
and artisans, the greater competition among employers of labour, the greater
use of coercion to capture and hold labour.

The evidence of new and expanded relations of production and exchange
during the eighteenth century directly challenges conventional understanding
of Indian economic history which is based on a model of the predatory
Mughal state, in which exchange relations and money-use were presumed to
be limited to the servicing of the military bureaucracy of the time. In that
'orientalist' model of economy, the relations of production are improbably
seen to have been self-reproduced through isolated 'village communities'
and through caste-based relations of subsistence and non-market exchange
(*jajmani*). In the light of this still-widely regnant model, the weight of evidence about money and markets during the eighteenth century is itself revolutionary.

The Mughal, 'orientalist', model should be directly challenged however.
At least beyond the core of Mughal upper India, the accumulation of evidence, including that in the recent *Cambridge Economic History of India*,
Volume 1[7], provides confirmation neither of jajmani relations nor isolated
village communities; on the contrary, in the *CEHI*, and elsewhere (Perlin on
Maharashtra and Ludden on Tirunelveli[8]), a high volume of internal trade in
non-luxury commodities is indicated and such widespread evidence of
money-forms that it is hard to conceive that only a tiny military–political élite
was involved in, and reproduced by, these exchanges.

Elsewhere in India, away from the Mughal heartland, the situation looks
clearer. In the Coromandel region, at a much earlier time, surplus production
from large locality systems of production were continuously redistributed
and reinvested in further production through temples, and later, through
privileged and communal forms of property which the British later aggregated
under the terms of 'mirasi' and 'inam'. Two implications stem from this point.
The first is that to the extent that this redistribution and reinvestment took
place within the context of communal structures such as the temple, the
nadu,[9] and the 'little kingdom',[10] and had the function of reproducing these
forms; moreover, the concept of community is much wider than that of the
isolated village community of the Mughal and 'orientalist' model. In fact, the
area of exchange and investment was wide enough to contain within itself
relations of extended exchange far more complex than the notion of *jajmani*
allows. Also, responses to ecological risks and uncertainties moulded a south

Indian peasantry that was peripatetic, not village-bound, and environmental variation—wet rice culture, well-irrigated garden production, and dry-cropped cotton production—generated trade in bulk commodities including basic foodstuffs, raw materials, and capital goods (tools, seed, draft animals) reposing within local communities and economies.

PROPOSITION 2

Élite consumption and labour coercion are linked factors to which some scholars of south India, notably Aleyev and Karashima,[11] have drawn attention well before the eighteenth century. However, the pressure for enhanced élite consumption, together with the increased demands of state regimes to meet military costs, placed heavier demands upon labourers, diminishing their consumption and the prospects of their very survival, especially during the later eighteenth century. Then, at all levels of the economy, 'surplus receivers' appear to have been seizing greater control over income from 'surplus producers'. This struggle had two principal manifestations. One was competition among surplus receivers to attract and hold agrarian and artisanal labour, often through the granting of privileges to migrants over those enjoyed by local labouring groups with an attendant degradation of communal entitlements and authority. Another later form of this competition appears to have been more destructive. It included forceful migration of labourers and even the destruction of irrigation works, as apparently practiced by Tipu Sultan in his Karnatik wars against the Nawab of Arcot.[12]

Labourers in eighteenth century south India and earlier were not altogether powerless to resist the increasing demands by an élite empowered by the state with fiscal authority, by the state itself driven by its need for money revenue to meet military costs, and by the growing pressures to meet export production for a world market in Indian commodities. Competition among surplus controllers—the state, the bureaucratic élite and traders—actually diminished the ability of all to act in harmony and thus constituted a contradiction of some importance, especially when the competition among these various powerful hegemonic agencies threatened to damage the productive base itself.

This contradiction generated certain important lines of trajectory into the nineteenth-century rise of the colonial state. The East India Company became involved in the struggle for labour control as early as 1720, and by the 1760s, the Company was mediating labour disputes on behalf of surplus receivers in its growing territory. By the 1770s, its arbitration in disputes changed to interventions with force. Not surprisingly, the Company generally ranged itself against existing patrimonial regimes as well as against producers and labourers, and as its political authority spread during the last quarter of the eighteenth century, the legal principles it imposed and the laws it deployed undermined yet further the customary, communal rights of producers. 'Property right' was defined by the Company exclusively in relation to real property, and customary privileges embedded in the communal base of society were treated as restraints of trade. Criminal law was also brought to bear upon indebtedness. By these measures, the Company put its hegemonic military and political power behind surplus receivers to whom it offered protection from the expropriative demands of the various regimes with which it coexisted, a more stable context for competition, fewer threats to the productive base, and a better coercive apparatus to protect property.

Thus, even though the Company demanded higher levels of revenue from the land under its control than any earlier or other regimes, it won the adherence of major surplus receiving groups, especially of those whose wealth and power were founded upon the old regimes' tax-farming, a method the Company continued to employ in its own territories until the first quarter of the nineteenth century. The Company also encouraged the market acquisition of *mirasi* and *inam* rights, entitlements earlier lodged in a matrix of communal obligations. From the middle of the eighteenth century, the Company was constructing state practices which were of greater benefit to the moneyed groups of the south than any of its rival for political hegemony. With respect to the control and subjugation of labour, the Company regime became the exemplary state for capital, and possessors of indigenous capital—money groups of the élite—allied themselves to the Company with a firmness that survived all manner of violations and uncertainties of Company rule to the middle of the nineteenth century.

PROPOSITION 3

There was a fundamental contradiction between the patrimonial, militarist regimes of south India during the eighteenth century and the mercantilist, state-strengthening programmes they pursued through their fiscal institutions that were dependent upon advanced commerce and banking. Patrimonial regimes are defined as those in which access to core authoritative roles and offices depended upon personal relations to rulers. Relations constituted by kinship or by contract-loyalty sought to limit succession to political roles to appropriate families for lineages, whether at the level of large militaristic state regimes, 'little kingdoms', or at the level of local lordships where most revenue bearing land, some commercial profits, and most human labour were increasingly claimed as the property of great and small patrimonial rulers.

There were at least two levels or kinds of authority extant in patrimonial regimes and, arguably, in the Mughal regime of upper India: state level sultans and local lordships. The first were formed around control of large-scale military organizations and the second around control of communal institutions. These constituted two distinct, but overlapping and interacting forms of authority, and to each was attached a form of property, which may be distinguished by the terms 'prebendal' and 'communal'.

The army was the central institution of India and other patrimonial regimes during the sixteenth to the eighteenth centuries in the sense of being the source of rank and office and in being the major recipient of resources directly commanded by state regimes, including the tribute obtained from lesser lordships. Indian armies, together with military forces of other patrimonial regimes of Eurasia, underwent a basic change from about the beginning of the sixteenth-century owing to the introduction of firearms which added infantry and artillery formations to the older core of heavy cavalry. The manufacture and importation of firearms, and the import of war horses, were strategic requirements for every state and therefore entailed a critical dependence of military regimes upon international trade and the most advanced internal commercial and banking interests.

Military requirements in India, as elsewhere in Eurasia, led to the development of fiscal institutions required for their maintenance. We can regard the economic practice of most eighteenth-century regimes as mercantilist, following the canonical formulation of E.F. Heckscher,[13] though one cannot find in India the extensive debates on economic policy of many European countries during the sixteenth to eighteenth centuries.

The core military formations of all successful patrimonial regimes being based on handguns and artillery, money was required for the purchase of arms and for the payment of full time and trained soldiers who used them. This was achieved by extending the demand for cash revenue over all the arable land under state control (e.g. the Mughal and later the Maratha *khalsa*), by demanding cash payments instead of military contingents from tribute-paying subordinate lordships, by the creation of revenue bureaucracies (scribes, records, standardized measures and accounts), by serious attention to foreign trade and to currency and money management, including minting operations and the supply of media stocks for new issues.

'Military fiscalism', as all this has been called by European historians of the same age,[14] or more comprehensively, mercantilism, depended upon, and therefore controlled, the highest levels of commerce and banking. Manifestations of this are most clearly found in attempts to establish new state monopolies, to intensify customs and excise collections, and even to create state debt funds to attract private wealth.

Under the resource requirements of growing military pressures in the eighteenth century, stemming in good part from the military challenges of Europeans as well as from more rapid changes in military technologies (in which Europeans were also implicated), and from greater internal rivalries, the coherence of patrimonial regimes was shattered. Internal structural contradictions limited the ability of these regimes to meet fiscal imperatives. All had come to depend upon mercantile and banking capital realized through tax-farming and through contracting out state monopolies. Bayly called this 'the commercialization of royal power'. Not only did state regimes become dependent upon indigenous capitalists and their institutions, but the latter found ways to use the political powers acquired under tax-farming contracts to increase their private accumulations of capital to the detriment of state receipts. The new instruments of state authority held by tax farmers and by other fiscal agents permitted merchant and banking capital to break into and out of the community institutional structures that had previously contained them. Still, a dangerous contradiction existed. While commercialized patrimonial authority permitted Indian capital to garner ever larger resources, this same authority posed the threats of confiscation and other forms of arbitrariness that limited capitalists in the fullest use of new opportunities.

This contradiction generated further trajectories into colonialism and the nineteenth century, among which the following were important. First, indigenous capital became attracted to the safeguards against arbitrary confiscations provided by mercantilist European companies; second, a process was begun which permitted the victorious English Company to convert its mercantilism and military fiscalism into full-blown colonial dominance over much of India during the first quarter of the nineteenth century. While this conversion was carried out under the guise of 'free trade' in the apparent manner of post-mercantilist regimes in Europe, the means and ends of this transition in India were quite otherwise, as will be discussed more fully in the conclusion.

To specify certain of the more immediate consequences of these processes further, it is argued that under the press of extractive military fiscalism bent on increasing the professional (mercenary) military formations of patrimonial regimes, on providing wider powers to their bureaucratic and scribal agents so as to improve the centralized management of their resources, pre-colonial regimes of the subcontinent extended their claims over resources which had vested in the control of localized social groups. Even when this was successfully carried out, however, as the work of Stewart Gordon and others in northern India have shown,[15] grave risks to patrimonial authority remained. One source was the very instrument of the military.

In a context where loyalties were, at best, personal, and more usually mercenary: army leaders could easily wrest power from weak rulers (untalented fighters, children). Haidar Ali Khan in Mysore showed that even a humble cavalry officer was no further from the throne than the length of sword, the height of his daring, and the breadth of his genius.

Professionalization of the military had other implications. Less dependence upon the levies of local lordships, always a risky matter, and the successful conversion of obligations from subordinate chiefs to provide military contingents to their provision of cash altered the political relations and bonds between great rulers and lesser ones. This relationship had been expressed in pre-colonial Maharashtra as a conception of shared sovereignty i.e. *dayada*.[16] While it was true that merchants and bankers, acting as the agents of the ruler, could supply money more reliably and with greater ease than local chiefs could, the latter remained menacingly entrenched in local community structures. Their resistance to fiscal centralism and their resort to patrimonial force led to the deeper penetration of the war frontier into the society of the age as beleaguered lesser chiefs sought new alliances for survival. Enemies so ubiquitous and entrenched could not be crushed completely even by the most vigorous of sultanist regimes, such as Haidar Ali and Tipu Sultan; such wars constituted a fatal drain upon centrist regimes, for no sooner were resisting local chiefs subdued and sultanist agents placed in control of their territories, than rebellions were launched, often a concert of disenfranchised chiefs and other chiefs with whom marriage and other alliances existed, necessitating yet further military actions.

In addition, bureaucratic agents of centralization often subverted the purposes of the regimes whom they served. The centralization of resources meant the appropriation of communal wealth, and literate fiscal agents, such as Brahmans in the south, were often participants in and beneficiaries of communal entitlements. Their strategic administrative positions combined with their local, communal interests to frustrate the very centralization process they served. This was evident when Tipu Sultan attacked the immunities and properties enjoyed by Hindu temples and priests only to have his Brahman *amildars* protect such entitlements through falsification of revenue accounts. Moreover, even if Brahman fiscal agents were outsiders to the localities in which they happened to be serving, and were therefore not direct beneficaries of ancient entitlements there, they often deployed the resources privately gained as state agents from one place in communally protected entitlements elsewhere.

But, these very measures for protecting communal rights from the full onslaught of central demands altered communal structures. It permitted some of its members to accumulate vastly greater wealth than others. Well-positioned 'insiders' to the communal structure were able to break the confines of local control and establish new relations of a wider sort through a mixing of communal and state entitlements as portfolios of private wealth. Perlin's 'great households' of Maharashtra battened on the fiscal or military offices they held under the Peshwas' state. As tax-farmers they were strategically placed to increase their holdings of communal entitlements through purchase and, additionally, as merchants and bankers, they were able to amass substantial money wealth. But this was a dangerous form of wealth in two senses: being beyond the control of either the state or communal bodies, it threatened both; and being beyond the protection of either, it was at risk from both.

PROPOSITION 4

These various contradictions can be seen to have generated two distinctive, and themselves contradictory, lines of development into the colonial period. The first of these lines terminated around 1820 and marked the highest point the Company seemed capable of achieving in resolving the problems posed to all patrimonial regimes by the mercantile and bureaucratic élites of the old regime. The second line of development carried further into the nineteenth century and involved the transformation of the Company from being a mercantilist regime safeguarding commerce and private wealth to becoming a colonialist regime which placed all indigenous capital in jeopardy.

The first of these lines of development became clear in the generalized trade crisis of around 1820 which, among other things, confirmed the deep linkages between India and other parts of the world through commerce. Around that time, as recounted by Braudel,[17] a long period of world trade growth entered a downward phase which lasted until the close of the nineteenth century. During the downward phase of this long cycle, contradictions between bureaucratic and mercantile élites, on the one hand, and state regimes, on the other, as outlined above, were resolved. The mature colonial state would brook none of the weakening contradictions of the early colonial state.

From its earliest acquisition of territorial sovereignty in the middle of the eighteenth century, the Company had undertaken to guarantee certain forms of communal rights against state encroachment. 'Religious rights' of temples and priests and rights which could be construed as derived from real property were favoured; other communal rights were condemned by the Company, including chiefly the rights and the customary entitlements of labourers. Rights upheld under the Company Raj were precisely those in which the bureaucratic and mercantile élite of the old regime were most interested, and those rights which the Company determined to end—the rights of communally based chieftainships and those of propertyless labour—fortified the dominance for which the élite strove. In this way, the Company won a high order of support from among the most influential in the old regime society whose allies they became, thus easing the way to Company supremacy and its early rule.

In a similar way, the Company, as merchant capitalist, offered a higher degree of security to Indian capital than its rivals. And once its great rival in the south, Tipu Sutlan, was eliminated in 1799, the Company threw massive support behind its tax gatherers and emergent landlord clients by deploying soldiers to collect taxes and intimidate labour.

Around 1820, this process began to change, and the reasons for the change appear not to have been what Eric Stokes called the reforms of utilitarianism. Rather, with its military dominance firmly established, the Company could turn to the resolution of the long-standing contradiction and conflict between communal property rights and the objectives of a centralizing regime of the sort the Company was as much as Tipu Sultan's had been. The Company had, to a degree risen to power by taking the side of communalism against the appropriations of the sultanist state. But once its hegemony was secure, this position was reversed, and the Company sought to achieve that higher centralization that had eluded Tipu Sultan.

By that time the Company was in a better position than Tipu Sultan had ever been to achieve its centralized hegemony. Having eliminated all serious military opposition by 1820, with the defeat of the Marathas, it could now spend less upon soldiers and more upon administrators—European and Indian—to manage the *ryotwari* revenue system and state monopolies over all of the most valuable commerce and to hasten the more complete commercialisation of communal relations.

Given the interdependence that had come to exist between Indian merchant and banking capital and a regime such as that of Tipu Sultan, the assumption by the Company of all revenue-related activities and monopoly systems was potentially very hazardous to Indian capital. Tipu Sultan's commercial ordinances are the fullest policy statements on pre-colonial mercantilism. These and other evidence of his time make it clear that the logic of this interpenetration led to the state—in the person of the ruler—while encouraging all capitalists, becoming the greatest capitalist of all. Under Company Raj, this commanding position was attained, and with it all the dire implications for Indian and any other capital the Company did not license. For, if the state under mercantilism is meant to develop and reproduce capitalists in general, the state-as-capitalist and colonialist must intend to subjugate and diminish capitalists in general and all others who are rivals and competitors to itself. The force of this logic appears to be clear in the south, but the working of it may have been stronger in the very different context of Bengal where the flourishing Anglo-Indian capitalism of the middle and later eighteenth century appears to have begun dying in the early years of the nineteenth century.[18]

PROPOSITION 5

Three forms of property can be identified during late pre-colonial times: pre-bendal, communal, and personal or private. During the latter period a deepening contradiction between the first two proprietorial forms created the conditions for an expansion of the third. For long, private or personal property was a particularistic form for which brahmans and a few others were eligible. Prebendal rights, dependent upon political or military service, was the form favoured by patrimonial regimes and these rights were substantially expanded under military fiscalism. Confronting prebendal rights were communal ones later glossed as *mirasi, inam, watan*, and so forth. These were protected by communal customs and by institutions with considerable juridical authority. In Maharashtra and in south India there were right-adjudicating and protecting assemblies, called *gota* in the former area and *kuttam* in the latter, consisting of local shareholders and corporate organizations capable of self-regulation and of resisting state demands.

Tensions between patrimonial rulers and communities pushed the frontiers between prebendal and communal rights back and forth: rulers advanced claims over communal rights and distributed them as prebendal entitlements (e.g. *saranjam* in Maharashtra, *pattam* in Tamil country) to office-holders who promptly converted them into communal entitlements (e.g. *watan* and *pangu*).

One consequence of the growing intensity of conflicts between rights was the growing independence of office-holders from the coercive authority of the state, on the one side, and the moral and kinship authority of the communal base of the society, on the other. Office-holders stood between the state and the community, mediating their sharpening conflict during the late eighteenth century. Out of this conflict came the expansion of personal property rights. Advancing behind the shields of *amildars*, tax-farmers, and other state agents, prebendal immunities were used to protect as personal rights their gains as office-holders or to distribute some of these gains as personal rights to kinsmen or supporters.

In eighteenth century Maharashtra, great landed households used their interstitial positions between the local communities to which they belonged and the state to whom they owed service in order to convert prebendal offices obtained from the state into hereditary entitlements protected by the community and to amass landed estates composed of multiple and diverse shareholding rights. These properties consisted of bundles of prebendal and communal entitlements which were now removed from the control and the protection of either the state or communal authorities; added to these were commercial and banking wealth as well. Prebendal rights became hereditary in spite of the state, and communal authorities were hardly in a position to control office-holders who, by virtue of their state functions, protected local communities from the engorging demands of the state.

Once more, the line of historical trajectory forward appears clear. Dependent only on the managerial and political skills of its possessors, personal property lacked the security of legal and institutional supports. The Company's strong aversion to prebendal property and its predilection for personal and private property, however restricted, answered a growing eighteenth-century Indian need for the protection of private wealth. The passage of rights described by Ludden in early nineteenth-century Tirunelveli from *pangu*, or communal shares, to *patta*, or private right,[19] may be taken as very general in peninsular India at least. Moreover, Ludden's argument shows that the transformation from *pangu* to *patta* was as much directed by the logic of indigenous histori-cal development as it was imposed by an alien cultural hegemony, and it was pursued by those large landholders with the most to gain from the changing form of dominant property.

PROPOSITION 6

With respect to the 'external' dimension of late pre-colonial Indian history, it has been conventional in imperialist and nationalist views to regard Europe as of little significance before the middle of the eighteenth century and then, suddenly, as all-important, all-determining. This understanding requires cor-rection. Influences and pressures from Europe upon Indian society appear to have affected the manner in which patrimonial regimes of the subcontinent operated from at least the sixteenth century. The research of Fernand Braudel on the Mediterranean world and its connections with Asia, recently and sympathetically extended by K.N. Chaudhuri[20] on the Indian Ocean world, indicates that relations between Europe and India at an even earlier time were very important.

Much of the new military technology and organization which sustained patrimonial military formations were ultimately of European origin even if filtered through and modified by regimes such as the Safavids in Persia and the Ottomans in Turkey. During the seventeenth century, specie flows from Spanish America via Europe stimulated Indian commodity production and trade, as elsewhere in maritime Asia. By the first quarter of the eighteenth century, European traders had niched themselves into the trade systems of patrimonial regimes, and by the 1740s the trading networks centred on the East India Company's Fort William in Calcutta were so substantial as to make the Company the single most important economic force in Bengal and in the lower Ganges area.[21] This also made vital the Company's tribute payments to the shrinking treasury of the Mughals, thereby broadening even further the Company's growing political sway in the Mughal heartland. Long before Clive and Dupleix, European expansion was felt in the subcontinent and there is, perhaps, something to the case that the decline of the Mughal Empire ought to be seen as linked to the contemporaneous decline and crises of the Islamic polities of western Asia in the face of European-generated pressures.

This implies no affirmation of the Wallerstein hypothesis of a 'world system' dominated by Europe.[22] Wallerstein and his colleagues have been commendably cautious about the extent and way in which India fits into his construed 'world system', and with good reason. On the one hand, there are ways in which India to the end of the eighteenth century would have claims to being a 'core' region in its own right. Its strong manufacturing and mercantile base stretched tentacles of capitalist activities from the Persian Gulf to south-east Asia, and, as K.N. Chaudhuri has recently shown, its trade relations with Europe brought stimulation and development as much to the Indians as to the Europeans. On the other hand, and of more importance here, it is arguable whether, before the age of steamships and railways, Europe— or rather Britain—wholly dictated the terms of trade relations with India as much as it followed, with some deviations, the lines already etched in India, taking advantage of the contradictions encountered there. True, these were exacerbated by the Company's economic power and conquests. Still, the Company did not create the general and fundamental conditions of the encounter with India. Moreover, the early nineteenth-century colonial state grew largely from foundations laid by the Indian patrimonial regimes whose contradictions it resolved and whose tendencies it brought to completion.

Not surprisingly, the East India Company, which, along with its counterpart in Holland, the VOC, was the most advanced capitalist institution in the eighteenth-century world, became embattled with the same forces which frustrated its patrimonial predecessors. Like the latter, it had been undermined, humiliated, and finally succeeded during the eighteenth century. The Company's ruling commercial and political objectives were compromised by resistance from communal institutions, by the independence of Indian capital on which the Company depended for its trade and revenue operations as well as for the private trade and remittances of its European servants, by the sapping military resistance of local chiefs, and by a scribal and bureaucratic elite that had built privilege and autonomy out of its political role as the hinge between centralizing regimes and the communal base.

Not surprisingly, this makes the Company appear, at times, very like the patrimonial regimes it was replacing, and nowhere was this more obvious than in the regime of Tipu Sultan in Mysore. For the latter had not only demonstrated that the technological and organizational edge enjoyed by European soldiers could be imitated, but he went even further by adopting the mercantilist logic of the Company as his state trade ordinances of 1793–94 make clear.[23] It is therefore difficult to specify what advantage it possessed that enabled the Company to attain 'paramountcy' by the first quarter of the nineteenth century. Certainly, its procounsuls of that transitional time—Munro, Malcolm, and Metcalf—seemed unaware of any massive advantage, and they spoke more often about the fragility of the Company's position than its ineluctable strength.

The advantages of the Company were, partly, its ability to hire Indian cavalrymen to augment its infantry forces, but more importantly was its increasing dominance over maritime trade and hence over the bullion and specie upon which mercantilist regimes depended for part of their revenue. Hence, when Tipu Sultan failed to establish Mangalore as an entrepôt capable of displacing Madras, his regime was doomed. But, even more critical was the strength which the East India Company derived from occasional injections of treasure from Europe, which was meant to finance trade, but actually subvented war. For much of the late eighteenth century, the Company traded off the capital of its Indian clients—merchants and bankers—and off the revenues of Bengal. At certain critical points, however, bullion arrived from overseas to finance warfare, something of which none of the enemies of the Company was capable. This treasure ultimately assured the victories to Cornwallis and Wellesley. The timely infusion of treasure also won the Company many adherents among Indian bankers, merchants, and military suppliers.

Taken together with the security which the Company offered to capital in its territories then, and to private wealth and its privileges, many of the patrimonial enemies of the Company collapsed as its moneymen, bureaucrats and, finally, its soldiers deserted to the Company. That the colonial conquest of India was as much bought as fought can be seen from the rapid rise of the Company's Indian debt from £8 million in 1786 to £32 million by 1808. This level of indebtedness could not continue, and, by the 1820s, the great turn occurred: massive retrenchments were initiated in Company territories; the *ryotwari* regime replaced Indian tax-farmers (and their investment and commercial functions) with European collectors; a new assault was launched upon communal privileges; and India's foreign trade was changed to peripheralize Indian merchants.

CONCLUSIONS

The seminar at the Centre for Historical Studies sought clarification on a number of points which were inadequately covered in the oral presentation. Criticism of the formulation were also made. Some attention to both concludes this paper.

One point of clarification pertained to how the late pre-colonial era has been situated by Anglo-Americans as compared to how Indian scholars, such as those at the Centre, looked at the problems of the era. Particularly, this involved the privileging of cultural explanations over materialist ones by British and American scholars. Among the latter, what is being called ethno-history has attained its present standing for several reasons: the place of anthropology in studies of India in the US; the demonstration in several ethno-history publications of having a major methodological and substantive contribution to make to the study of India; and the trenchant anthropological attacks upon the ethno- and class-centric biases of historical social science. Given this prominence, and given the weak position of Marxist or even Annalist studies of India (or any other society) in North America and the UK, the view outlined here can scarcely be regarded as obsessed with the problem of culture as might be thought by scholars at some of the major centres of historical study in India. At such select Indian institutions, questions of culture and ideology have not been permitted to be disconnected from the relations of production and social reproduction, and the problematic of transition to capitalism is seen as fundamental. How the transition question was posed and addressed by me at the seminar was rightly criticized.

Contrarywise, my criticism of Mughal historiography and my agnosticism toward the Aligarh School elicited another sort of response. Criticism of the canonical Mughal historiography of Aligarh is based on empirical and theoretical grounds as well as on how that view has wrongly configured much of late pre-colonial historiography. It was a matter of surprise to me (and I judge to others at the seminar) to have had confirmation of the critique of Aligarh historians from several Mughal specialists at the session, but it was also a matter of some dismay to note that while serious reservations about the Aligarh position have come to be felt, this has not yet been manifested in revisionist writings. Thus, the Aligarh view, though found less satisfactory, has not been explicitly challenged and denied its enormous weight in both medieval historiography and that of the late pre-colonial period.

Perhaps most serious in its implications were the questions raised by the seminar about the status of capitalist relations of production and social reproduction. The historical social science argument of Bayly on the north Indian eighteenth century is that the economy did not decline, as is widely held. This and his other findings justify consideration of some revision of received historiography. However, increased commercialization, urbanization, and monetarization of the age and fiscal measures of money-dependent regimes is not seen by Bayly as implying a capitalist structure in dominance. The seminar appreciated that caution, and deplored the tendency of some historians to make the conceptual leap 'to capitalism' as a result of such particularistic attributes. I believe that the transition question may be raised more seriously about some of the eighteenth-century mercantilist regimes of India, and, or course, it must be raised when one has come to the nineteenth-century colonial regime of the East India Company.

The argument I sketched on this requires much elaboration and refinement to be sure, but the transition formulation is entailed by it. The Aligarh assumption and others who follow it (e.g. *CEHI*), that a 'national economy' and centralized state existed in Mughal times, is rejected. Nonetheless, it is recognized that there were extensive trade systems over continental and peninsular India and that the seaward margins were closely linked to a worldwide trade order. This commercial feature—though uneven spatially and temporally—was centuries old by the eighteenth century. Yet, in itself, this can surely not be taken as capitalism nor as a sufficient condition for its development. Following Bayly and others, serious notice must be taken of the impressive evidence from eighteenth-century India of extended circuits of commodity production and exchange linked closely to the fiscal structures of patrimonial regimes of the age, and especially of the vital participation of merchants and moneymen in both extended exchange and state finance. But, this failed to create the conditions for extensive, self-producing capitalist relations.

Two basic reasons for this failure were offered. One is that much accumulation and investment was deployed in reproducing communally organized social and religious institutions rather than increasing the productive base from which ever larger accumulations could be garnered. A second reason is that all forms of property, whether prebendal, communal, or personal, lacked security from appropriation by patrimonial regimes, and thus was poorly mounted to sustain a system of self-generating capitalist relations. The East India Company resolved many of the contradictions within, or completed the mercantilist practices of, regimes of the eighteenth century under which various classes of surplus receivers—landed, merchant and banking—were nurtured. As a mercantilist regime the Company, until around 1830, encouraged all forms of capitalism for all were seen as useful, if not vital, to the Company state being formed. These included Indian banking interests upon whose loans the Company had long depended, contractors of all sorts that worked the monopolies imposed under the Company, tax farmers and holders of grain surpluses. In less then a century the barriers imposed on capitalist development under previous regimes were lowered by the Company's mercantilist policies and its laws favouring property and opposing the entitlements of communities and labourers alike.

Arguably, then, around the turn of the nineteenth century conditions were favourable for an epoch of capitalist development guided by the new winds of 'free trade' wafting from Europe. For by then, the major impediments to rapid capitalist development, present in the patrimonial regimes of the seventeenth and eighteenth centuries, appeared to have been structurally overcome. All appeared to be ready for the final assault upon the residual stratum of communal entitlements.

At this point, however, the Company regime in Madras and Bombay faltered, and instead of pressing forward it retreated. A new set of legal provisions were introduced that gave enhanced protection to old communal rights. This included the establishment of 'native juries' or panchayats, and village and district Indian *munsifs*, exemplified in Thomas Munro's judicial reforms of 1816 in Madras. Following this were a variety of statutory measures protecting various inheritance and property forms in accordance with religious codes.[24] But, even more fundamentally, by the first quarter of the nineteenth century, the potentiality for state-guided capitalist development under the Company was eschewed, and in its place came a set of new forms and pressures that set India upon its course of distorted development, and served imperial interests rather than either the established interests of Anglo-Indian or indigenous Indian capital.

It is here that the crucial disjuncture of colonial rule in India can be marked, for the measures imposed around 1830 changed the trajectory of the previous century that had been capped by the East India Company's mercantilist phase of the late eighteenth and early nineteenth centuries. The change was striking. In 1800, Indian capital seemed destined to continue its central, albeit dependent, place under the Anglo-Indian capitalism of the time, being involved in commodity production and trade as well as in banking, not only at the lowest and most riskful levels of the economy, but at its pinnacle as well. However, a generation later—less in Bengal according to Bhattacharya's research—the high financial and commercial ground of the Indian economy was denied to

Indian capital, and it was ineluctably driven into real estate, petty usury, and localized exchange. This degradation was not the result of utilitarian doctrine, as Stokes had had it, nor was it the extension to India of the doctrine of free trade. The underdevelopment of Indian capital from the early nineteenth century was, nevertheless, deliberate policy and promulgated at the highest counsels of the Company. Lord Bentinck's commitment to the modernization of India through infrastructural development and a central bank carried with it a favoured and dominating position for British managing agencies as a result of the 1820s domination of the Court of Directors of the East India Company by the 'private interest'. Furthermore, there was the determination by British governments that India should finance and man with its soldiers the growing Empire in Asia, beginning with the Burma War of 1824–6.

The changes first appeared in Bengal, the most commercialized zone of India, where Anglo-Indian capitalist development was most advanced. They followed soon after in other parts of British India by a similar breaching of established circuits of capital mobilization and investments in production involving Indian surplus receivers (including tax farmers). This last was accomplished by replacing Indian tax-farming 'portfolio-capitalists', as Sanjay Subrahmanyam had called them,[25] with British revenue collectors under *ryotwari* regulations and Indian monopoly and state finance contractors with British agency houses and banks. All of this must alter conventional ideas about 'the colonial disjuncture'.

Nationalist historiography has long been configured around the proposition that the Mughal state was the model for the British imperial regime both in its massive political and administrative centralization and in its purpose of massive appropriations of the productive resources. A difference of major significance was that the colonial regime was dedicated to serving the interests of imperial Britain. This difference is seen to constitute a major disjuncture—the primary contradiction—of modern Indian history; one that purportedly occurred in the eighteenth century with the domination of the Indian economy by British imperial interests.

When and how this disjuncture occurred is of importance. Nationalist and imperialist historians insist that the moment of disjuncture was the seizure of political control by Britain in 1757. Thenceforward, a new era is seen to have commenced, one that is dominated—for Indians—by the sole task of ending foreign rule before which all other processes lose their historical significance. Among the distortions engendered by this nationalist configuring of the eighteenth to the twentieth century, especially by neo-nationalist practitioners at JNU, is that pertaining to class relations from the beginning to the end of this extended nationalist era. Of particular relevance for the present argument is the failure to give the same historical weight to the collaborationist development of Indian capital during most of the eighteenth century as to the spoliation of Indian commodity producers.

This notion of a fractured eighteenth century, in being historically rooted in a monolithically construed nationalism that marginalizes and sacrifices class contradictions to the 'primary contradiction' of foreign rule, is rejected here; a different submission is made. It is that the critical disjuncture occurred in the early nineteenth century, and when it came, it was after a century or more of intensive commercial, financial and administrative development under the state building mercantilism of patrimonial regimes in India, including the East India Company. During the late pre-colonial era, covering the entire eighteenth century, we see a structure of commercial and industrial relations emerging that ultimately, and fatally, weakened the patrimonial regimes under which it was nourished. Partly, this resulted from the competition among mercantilist regimes of the time, and the superior position of the Company in this competition. Surplus receiving elements gravitated to the ambit of the Company, whose domination over international and regional trade provided more secure opportunities for private accumulations and whose military and legal apparatuses provided greater security for personal wealth. The Company, having completed the economic transformation initiated by the patrimonial regimes it replaced (by military force in the end), having resolved the economic contradictions within these regimes, and having finally fulfilled the mercantilist destiny promulgated under the Elizabethan charter, now embraced another destiny. This was imperial mastery over all of India, and it began in the first third of the nineteenth century.

The disjuncture postulated in imperialist and nationalist historiographies—and assumed by historical social science—is a weak one because it proceeds from an ahistorical counterfactual question of whether India had the capacity to commence a process leading to capitalism from its Mughal base in the seventeenth century. Leaving aside the increasingly questionable characterizations of the Mughal state and economy, it must surely be preferable to abandon this weak counterfactual formulation and adopt a view for which there is considerable evidence about economic and administrative changes over an extended eighteenth century. Then, a concrete, not conjectural, basis for India's transition to capitalism during the nineteenth century was laid. The economic and social mutilation wrought by imperialism can be fully appreciated only against the background of the great changes of the late precolonial era.

NOTES AND REFERENCES

1. The edition published in 1840–8 in London by J. Madden.
2. *Utilitarians*, Clarendon Press, Oxford; 'The First Century . . .' was published in *Past and Present*, no. 58, Feb. 1973.
3. C.A. Bayly, *Rulers, Townsmen and Bazaars: North Indian Society in the Age of British Expansion, 1770–1870*, Cambridge, 1983.
4. Washbrook's monograph was\published by Cambridge University Press, 1976. His relevant papers include: 'Some Notes on Market Relations and the Development of the Economy of South India, *c.* 1750–1850', presented to the Leiden workshop on Comparative Colonial History, 1981; and 'Commerce and Credit in South India: The Transition to Colonialism, 1770–1830', presented to the South Asia Regional Center, University of Pennsylvania, 1984; 'Law, State and Agrarian Society in Colonial India', *Modern Asian Studies*, vol. 15, 1981; 'Progress and Problems: South Asian Economic and Social History, *c.* 1720–1860', *Modern Asian Studies*, vol. 22, 1988.
5. Frank Perlin: 'The Pre-Colonial State in History and Epistemology: A Reconstruction of Societal Formation in the Western Deccan from the Fifteenth to the early Nineteenth Century', in P.J.M. Claessen and P. Skalnik (eds), *The Study of the State*. The Hague: Mouton, 1981; 'Of White Whale and Countrymen. . . .' *The Journal of Peasant Studies* vol. 5, 1978; 'Proto-industrialization and Pre-colonial South Asia', *Past and Present*, no. 98, 1983; 'Growth of Money Economy and Some Questions of Transition in late Pre-colonial India', *The Journal of Peasant Studies*, vol. 11, 1984; 'State Formation Reconsidered', *Modern Asian Studies*, vol. 19, p. 3, July, 1985, pp. 415–81.
6. His essay 'Inequality and Free trade', in B. De (ed.), *Essays in Honour of S.C. Sarkar*, New Delhi, 1978, pp. 689–99.
7. Published by Cambridge University Press, 1982 and 1983. Henceforth *CEHI*.
8. *Peasant History in South India*, Princeton, New Jersey, 1985.
9. The term and concept of *uunadu* is explored in B. Stein, *Peasant State and Society in Medieval South India*, Delhi, 1980.
10. This is most fully explored in Nicholas B. Dirks, *The Hollow Crown: Ethnohistory of an Indian Kingdom*, Cambridge, 1987. Part IV, or his earlier, 'The Pasts of a Palaiya-karar: The Ethnohistory of a South Indian Little King', *The Journal of Asian Studies*, vol. 41, no. 4, 1982, pp. 655–83.
11. N. Karashima, *South Indian History and Society: Studies from Inscriptions, AD 850–1800*, Delhi, 1984, and L. Aleyev, in *CEHI*.
12. The evidence for this is fragmentary. There is the reference in the Madras section of *The Fifth Report on East India Company Affairs, 1812* (edition edited by Walter K. Firminger, 1917, Calcutta; reprint edition of 1969, New York), vol. 1, p. 252 referring to the forced migration by Tipu Sultan of 60,000 Christians from the Carnatic to his Mysore territory causing the abandonment of much cultivation below the ghats, and similar devastation of irrigation works, of cattle and labourers forced to migrate or dispersed by Tipu Sultan in the southern Carnatic, including Tanjore, according to T. Venkatasami Row, *A Manual of the District of Tanjore in the Madras Presidency*, Madras, 1883, pp. 812–13.

13.. *Mercantilism*, translated by M. Shapiro, rev. edn by E.F. Soderlund, London, 1951; orig. 1931.

14. Martin Wolfe, *The Fiscal System of Renaissance France*, New Haven, 1972.

15. For example, his 'Recovery from Adversity in Eighteenth-Century India: Rethinking "Peasants" and Politics in Pre-Modern Kingdoms', *Peasant Studies*, vol. 8, 1979, pp. 61–80.

16. *Land and Sovereignty in India under the Eighteenth-Century Maratha Svarajya*, Cambridge, 1987. My gratitude to Dr Wink for permission to consult his pre-published work.

17. *Civilization and Capitalism, 15th–18th Century*, vol. 3, 'The Perspective of the World', London, 1984; trans. Sian Reynolds, pp. 76–80.

18. Bhattacharya, 'Inequality and Free Trade'.

19. Ludden, *Peasant History*, pp. 198–9.

20. *Trade and Civilisation in the Indian Ocean: An Economic History From the Rise of Islam to 1750*, Cambridge University Press, 1985.

21. S.K. Bhattacharya, *The East India Company and the Economy of Bengal, 1704–1740*, London, 1954.

22. Immanuel Wallerstein, *The Modern World System*, New York, 1976–80, 2 vols.

23. See: *Select Letters of Tippoo Sultan to Various Public Functionaries: Translated and Edited by William Kirkpatrick, Colonel, East India Company*, London: 1811, App. 'E' 'Commercial Regulations', dated 25 March 1793 and 2 April 1794.

24. Washbrook, 'Law and Society'.

25. In his, as yet, unpublished doctoral thesis, 'Trade and the Regional Economy of South India, *c.* 1550 to 1650', Department of Economics, University of Delhi, 1986.

3

Recent Theories of Eighteenth-century India*

M. ATHAR ALI

Until recently, historians tended to view the eighteenth century in two distinct parts separated by two dates representing two important battles. One was 1761, the year of the third battle of Panipat, which signified both the military irrelevance of the Mughal Empire and the immense setback to the Marathas, who might conceivably have replaced the Mughals. The other landmark was 1757, the year of the battle of Plassey, from which the dominance of the English in India could be conveniently held to begin. Historians concerned with the history of these three empires are generally agreed upon this bifurcation of the eighteenth century. To the historians of the Mughal Empire, the death of Aurangzeb in 1707 marked the beginning of the decline of that empire, which was hastened by Nadir Shah's sack of Delhi (1739). Historians concerned with the Marathas could see the eighteenth century as the Maratha century, but the really great successes seemed to occur before 1761, after which stagnation and divisions tended to set in. To Anglo-Indian historians, 1757 is a very firm benchmark, setting the triumph of Clive as the first step in the realization of the manifest destiny of the British in India.

Along with the bifurcation of the eighteenth century, there has been another view, namely, that it was the 'Dark Century' of modern Indian history. I have not seen the actual use of this term by any historian in so designating that century, but Irfan Habib comes very close to doing so when he describes it as a period of 'reckless rapine, anarchy and foreign conquest'.[1] This is clearly a combination of V.A. Smith's view of Maratha polity as a 'Robber State' and the opposite, nationalist conception of British conquest as the ultimate

*M. Athar Ali, 'Recent Theories of Eighteenth-century India', *Indian Historical Review*, xiii, 1986–7, pp. 102–10.

calamity. In a sense, Irfan Habib's brief aside on the eighteenth century would seem to represent a summary of conventional thinking as it prevailed some twenty-five years ago: the decline of the Mughal Empire in the first half of the eighteenth century marked a setback to the strength of the Indian political, social, and economic structure, enabling the British conquest to take place, and eliminating all such elements of internal growth as the previous regime might have fostered. It was, therefore, yet another, though perhaps a more profound version of the simple textbook bifurcation of the eighteenth century.

This entire conception has been challenged by C.A. Bayly in *Rulers, Townsmen, and Bazars: North Indian Society in the Age of British Expansion, 1770–1870.*[2] It is not easy to summarize his basic arguments because of the numerous qualifications he continuously introduces. But one would not be wrong if one were to say that he believes that the Mughal Empire, by its fall, in fact, rendered a service by letting a large number of indigenous groups develop and so enabled a number of networks—established by local castes and communities and immigrant groups, together with merchants and money-lenders—to flourish. British expansion might, in the beginning, have hurt some of these groups, but, ultimately, represented a compromise with many of them. Thus 1757 (Plassey) or 1764 (Buxar) did not constitute a break: rather, a continuity ought to be discerned.

Bayly's views deserve detailed examination. He is not alone in challenging the older theories of the eighteenth century, though others have not dealt with the issue over such a range. Muzaffar Alam, for example, has been concerned with the first half of the century;[3] and Frank Perlin with Maharashtra.[4] Satish Chandra's essay, though insightful, is brief and concentrates again on Indian politics.[5] In many ways, however, these writings represent departures from the older views, though they do not necessarily agree with Bayly. Recently, André Wink, while totally accepting Bayly's view of the eighteenth century, has sought to offer yet another continuity, that of the Mughal Empire and the Marathas.[6]

At first sight, Muzaffar Alam's work offers much promise. Here is the opportunity to study the nature of transformation in the first half of the eighteenth century in specific terms by appealing to detailed local evidence from Awadh. The effort is, however, marred by a very obvious bias in favour of Mughal administration, to an extent that even the use of the word 'Crisis' in the title of his book seems unwarranted by the text. The Empire in its heyday had contributed to prosperity, and its autonomous segments continued to do so in the eighteenth century. He speaks as if this last is an incontestable fact:

Both the Punjab and Awadh registered unmistakable economic growth in the seventeenth century. In the early eighteenth century in both provinces, politics and administration appear to have moved along similar lines.[7]

Muzaffar Alam's evidence of 'economic growth' is extremely slender. He offers a comparison of *jamadami* (estimated revenue) statistics in the *A 'in-i Akbari* with an 'eighteenth-century revenue roll',[8] to establish that it had 'almost doubled' in the intervening period. He admits that the increase seems cancelled by the much greater rise in prices. Yet, at a later point in his book, he insists that 'the rise in *jama*' had a bearing on the increase in agricultural production', which he now seems to regard as being established by the increase in the *jama*', forgetting altogether the increase in prices.

If the evidence for Muzaffar Alam's basic thesis is so poor, much of what he describes—and it is in the description of various incidents culled from sources that his work attracts the reader's interest—has no relevance to his conclusion, namely, that the first half of the eighteenth century was a period of progress. Thus the supreme illogicality of the last sentence of his book:

The growing tendency among the nobles and officials to hold *jagirs* on a permanent and quasi-permanent basis, the struggle to convert *madad-i-ma'ash* (revenue grant) holding into *milkiyat* (private property), the emergence of the *ta'alluqa, ta'ahhud* and *ijara* contracts as the most acceptable forms of government, and the consensus among the regional powers to maintain the Mughal imperial symbols to obtain legitimacy and thus stability and security of their spoils—all indicated the eighteenth century endeavour to make use of the possibilities for growth within existing social structures.[9]

If one were to adopt this line of argument, the Wars of Roses and The Thirty Years' War could also be proof of an 'endeavour to make use of possibilities for growth', for every potentate was seeking his own 'growth' in those wars just as in eighteenth-century India.

Frank Perlin's position on the Mughal Empire is different from Muzaffar Alam's, though his argument is not easy to understand. He tends to discount the influence of the Empire—as a 'system'—on Indian society and deplores 'Mughal and Maratha-centric treatments of economic history'. He maintains:

It is rather necessary to describe those other aspects of society and state formation which lie beyond and incorporate such system-making and which arguably contradict the latter, lead to their constant mutation and compose a space of events, acts and even structured relationships and consequences which transcend the frontiers within which contemporary attempts at systematization occurred.[10]

He appears to argue that the failures of the Mughals or Marathas as centralizing systems were not of central significance, in view of 'the stubbornness of the intermediary ground', that is, the structures of grass-root political, legal, and social institutions and rights. In that sense, there would appear to be no disaster for the Indian economy in the passing of the Mughal Empire.

Perlin thus dismisses all too easily the significance of an imperial system for the economy, and so seemingly overlooks the implications of the rent-extracting state. Bayly wrote before Perlin, and he too tends to avoid giving the Mughal Empire a central place in the picture of Indian society, say, in 1700. Yet he acknowledges that the Mughal Empire 'was more than a mere umbrella raised over virtually autonomous local groups'.

He observes:

It was more like a grid of imperial towns, roads and markets, which pressed heavily on society and modified it, though only at certain points. The system depended on the ability of the Mughal state to appropriate in cash as much as 40 per cent of the value of the total agricultural product. A sophisticated money and produce market must have existed to make this possible, and men who recognized the supremacy of the Emperor must have had influence in small towns and *bazaars*.[11]

Surely, the extraction of rent (40 per cent of the value of produce), 'grids of imperial towns', and 'a sophisticated money and produce market' could not be unimportant elements in an economy. And if we are looking at the scale of commerce and the size of the urban sector as indicators of economic 'development' (especially keeping the ultimate arrival of capitalism in view), then a decline of the Empire, to which these elements were tied, could well represent an economic decline as well. Indeed, this is supported by Ashin Das Gupta's findings about the contraction of the hinterland of Surat during the first half of the eighteenth century without its displacement by any other port.[12]

Bayly's own position on the Mughal Empire is not very definite. After admitting that the Empire implied a certain amount of development of commerce and markets, he does not draw the conclusion that would seem to be inescapable: such development could be seriously affected by the decay of the Empire. On the other hand, he speaks as if the decay-released forces, presumably so far suppressed, 'benefited and consolidated the intermediate classes of society—townsmen, traders, service gentry—who commanded the skills of the market and the pen'.[13]

This is one of the weak links in Bayly's argument. The point at issue is not whether towns remained (or new ones were established while the old decayed still more) and commerce was conducted and the bureaucracy functioned at some levels, but whether there was a greater efflorescence of these activities than in the Mughal century (the seventeenth). Bayly offers no such comparison.

His narratives of the emergence of the Bhumihar zamindars in Banaras and further east, the Rohilas in the middle Doab and trans-Ganga tract (Rohilkhand), and the Jats and Sikhs, in terms of Hindu and Muslim, 'indigenous' and 'external', are all very interesting, but they really lend little weight to his thesis that the Mughal decline reinforced the position of the urban classes and the bureaucracy.

Once the Hindu–Muslim, indigenous–external categories that Bayly plays with are disregarded, at least for the moment, and we focus on the genesis of the new forces stepping into the vacuum created by the declining fortunes of Mughal power, the zamindari antecedents of the bulk of these become clear enough. One uses the term zamindar here in the sense established by Irfan Habib—the hereditary largely caste-bound rural class with control over part of the produce of land and served by armed retainers.[14]

Bayly's description of the Bhumihar chieftains as zamindars, and Muzaffar Alam's survey of Awadh and Punjab in the first half of the eighteenth century, show how the zamindar clans rose in uprising after uprising. S.P. Gupta, in his recent study, has shown how the Amber ruler strengthened his position in the first half of the eighteenth century by taking revenue-farms in contiguous territories in eastern Rajasthan, and thus essentially converted a zamindari into a local sovereignty.[15] Where, as in the case of the Rohilas, there was an immigrant group, it too tried to sink its roots into the soil by replacing old zamindars (for instance, Rajputs in Rohilkhand, with whom the Rohilas came into persistent conflict).[16] The zamindar origins of the Maratha rulers have been investigated by Satish Chandra.[17]

One may note that the emergence of zamindar power on the ruins of the Mughal Empire was implicit in Irfan Habib's analysis of the crisis of the Mughal Empire,[18] and Harbans Mukhia, who seldom finds himself in agreement with him, has come to the same conclusion:

It is thus that even when the Mughal Empire was collapsing, one gets the impression that the class of *zamindars* at various levels was turning out to be the main beneficiary. It was, in other words, an older form of property that was re-emerging in strength.[19]

Wink concedes the same process, despite his assertive observation of continuity between the Mughals and the Marathas, when he sees the Marathas as representing the 'intermediary gentry or *zamindari* stratum' and the eighteenth century, therefore, as 'the century of the "gentrification of the Muslim Empire" '.[20]

Clearly, a reassertion of the zamindars' power over a large part of the country could not lead to a restoration of conditions that prevailed before the Mughal Empire or the Sultanate. It would not be in the zamindars' own interest to give up the right to collect the bulk of agricultural surplus as land revenue once they stepped into the shoes of the preceding Mughal administration, whether as nominal *jagirdars*, revenue-contractors, *ta'alluqdars* or simply usurpers. What happened now was a great admixture of state rights with hereditary landed rights, seen pre-eminently in a steady decentralization of political authority, which was marked as much in the Mughal polity in the first half of the century as in the Maratha polity in the second.

It would be hard to argue that the mutually conflicting small political units into which India was divided in the eighteenth century were individually stronger than the Empire they had supplanted. Bayly does not take up this point at all: what he suggests is that these units were more strongly based on the soil either because they were composed of local élites or based on compromises with them, as could be illustrated by the liberal policy pursued by the surviving Mughal satrapies towards a wide range of Hindu warriors and administrative groups.[21] But, apart from the fact that the Mughal Empire too had promoted an 'eclectic culture' (witness Akbar and Dara Shukoh),[22] many of the compromises that the Mughal satrapies made with the zamindars were signs of weakness, and not of strength; that a zamindar in his locality was strong is, of course, the reason why he could step into the shoes of the contracting Mughal authority. It did not mean that the sum of zamindar-based powers that now arose could be stronger than the unified Empire they had supplanted.

Yet, because of the very fact that the new political units were admixtures, continuing all the essential features of the Mughal land revenue system, while often combining possession of revenue rights with private zamindari rights, the fundamental nature of the state as a rent-extracting institution was preserved. This necessitated that association of rulers with merchants, which revenue collection on any large scale must demand. As courts on local scale continued, and large armies were maintained, a large portion of the agrarian surplus flowed into towns, and much, though not all, of the urban glory of the past could survive. Faizabad, Farrukhabad, and Lucknow were representatives of this urban survival, when Delhi and Agra were fast declining. While the fact that there was still resilience in the Indian economy should not be forgotten, it is not easy to understand how any important new elements can be discerned in the economy of the first half of the eighteenth century, as Bayly's description would lead one to infer.[23]

There is one further element which tends to be forgotten while looking at the eighteenth century—the cultural. In an essay on the decline of the Mughal Empire, I had commented on the cultural failure of the ruling class in not responding to the European challenge on the plane of technology and science.

The cultural distance between India and Europe continued to lengthen in the eighteenth century; none of the regimes seemed capable of even attempting to bridge it.[24] Potentates like Haidar Ali and Mahadji Sindhia saw the challenge in military terms and tried to organize modern armies with French assistance; only Tipu went a little further by trying to develop commerce and production. But none thought in terms of establishing schools or institutions to absorb Western learning or arranging for translations. In other words, not only did the eighteenth-century regimes continue with the revenue system of the Mughals, they also continued with the same ideological apparatus. It is characteristic that Shah Waliullah (d. 1762), the famous Muslim jurist and thinker, does not even show that recognition of European learning and science which was present a hundred and fifty years before in Abul Fazl.[25] Unaided by any conscious endeavour, Indian crafts remained supremely uninfluenced by the proto-industrialization of Europe.[26]

Little substantial has thus been presented to justify the view that there was an internal momentum towards progress or 'growth' in the first half of the eighteenth century. The picture still remains of a society in decline, despite possible accusation that one is 'Mughal-centric' in saying so.

The second major point about the eighteenth century is whether the second half, encompassing British expansion from 1757 to 1807, can be regarded as a continuum of the first, rather than as part of a separate period. Essentially, it raises the question whether the British regime can be regarded, in its initial phase, at any rate, as one which maintained the traditional institutions and policies of the contemporary Indian states. There has been a strong belief that the '1757 Revolution' was a compromise between the English East India Company and the Hindu bankers and merchants to control the Nizamat for mutual profit.[27] This has been built into a theory of the British conquest as an act of collaboration between the East India Company and the powerful indigenous groups.[28]

Bayly finds this thesis 'cliché-ridden' but then goes on to express considerable sympathy with it.[29] All this finds as echo in Harbans Mukhia's observation:

The view that colonial society was the creation of the colonial state is also being slowly questioned.[30]

Mukhia, probably unconsciously, does us good service by putting the whole matter in such terms as to make the weakness of the position most apparent: colonial society was not the product of colonialism, but rather colonialism was the product of colonial society. How, else, would the society be 'colonial' at all?

From such an extreme statement of the case we may return to the less radical suggestion that English power was dependent on compromise and collaboration with certain indigenous groups ad classes. Even this suggestion is hard to accept. There are two possible kinds of collaboration: (a) where two powers meet on an equal plane; and (b) where one power is dominant and the other collaborates because this is the only opportunity for survival or profit. In history, examples of the first are so rare as to be practically absent, while those of the second abound. Clearly, the collaboration secured by the English from Amin Chand and Nand Kumar was of the second type, and we know what end they came to: one was defrauded, the other was hanged. If the Permanent Settlement is viewed in the light of a political compromise, such a view also needs reconsideration. Cornwallis argued for it not because he felt the zamindars would rebel or overthrow the Company's rule, but because he thought that, without a deal with the zamindars, agriculture would continue to decay and the commerce of Bengal would correspondingly contract, leaving little possibility of further growth of the Company's revenues. There was to be no collaboration between the Company and the zamindars as equals in any sense of the term. This applies to all other 'allies' of the Company as well. The merchants and bankers, whom the Company graciously allowed to continue because revenue collection was helped thereby as well as remittances of funds arranged, found their spheres of activity far more narrow than under the previous regimes. Overseas trade was closed to them, and so also much of the trade in muslin, silk, indigo, and saltpetre in eighteenth-century Bengal. Finally, in the case of Subsidiary Alliances, the collaboration was decidedly one-sided. Awadh was compelled to pay 'a massive annual tribute (more than Rs 50 lakhs)',[31] and in 1801, was to lose more than half of its territory to its protector.[32]

Such weighted 'collaboration' could hardly justify one's designating the British conquest as a joint Anglo-Indian enterprise. If any other view is to be dubbed 'Eurocentric', as Bayly warns us,[33] let it be so dubbed. Colonialism had blue-blooded European ancestry; and it will be wrong to make the ancestry dubious in the interest of international understanding.

One must remember that the expansion of British power in India was not simply the expansion of a politically centralizing system, a mere successor to the Mughals and the Marathas, as a rent extracting state. It was the expansion of a colonial power, essentially different in its nature and objectives from all previous regimes. The Upper Gangetic basin, that is the focus of Bayly's study, had not, unlike Bengal and Bihar, come under British control before 1801–7. Yet, already the effects of the Tribute were manifest in this area. The 'want of specie' felt in Upper India after 1770, with disastrous results for long-distance trade, which Bayly recognizes,[34] was the direct consequence of the Tribute, since it stopped all imports of specie and compelled its export to China. Bayly absolutely fails to see this connection, and thus fails to discern the impact of Colonial Tribute even in areas outside formal British control.

The inherent contradiction in Bayly's approach is, perhaps, brought out best by two passages in André Wink. In his introduction he acclaims Bayly's thesis of 'the indigenous component in European expansion', which brought about 'a balanced redistribution of resources rather than any overall significant corrosion.'[35] His Epilogue, however has a totally different conclusion: 'the Maratha documentation shows that it was not the "rapacity" of revenue farmers but rather the impact of the colonial government which interfered with the circulation and diffusion of money, credit and resources'. If Wink remained unconscious of the implications of his conclusion, while framing his introduction, his reader is under no obligation to do the same.[36]

We must therefore harbour much doubt about any theory which seeks to view the eighteenth century India as a single whole. The conventional bifurcation, as presented in old textbooks, might seem to have been very formalistic, based on mere dates of battles. But it was objectively, perhaps, far closer to the realities of social and economic history of India than the many recent theories endeavouring to present us with vistas of continuity and progress in that troubled century.

NOTES AND REFERENCES

1. *Agrarian System of Mughal India*, Bombay, 1963, p. 351.
2. (Cambridge, 1983). Bayly presents his views on the eighteenth century most conveniently in the Introduction, pp. 1–35.
3. *The Crisis of Empire in Mughal North India: Awadh and the Punjab, 1707–1748*, Oxford University Press, Delhi, 1986.
4. 'State Formation Re-considered', *Modern Asian Studies*, vol. XIX; pt 3 (Cambridge, 1985), pp. 414–80.
5. *The 18th Century in India: Its Economy and the Role of the Marathas, the Jats, the Sikhs and the Afghans*, K.P. Bagchi & Co., Calcutta, 1986, pp. 1–40.
6. *Land and Sovereignty in India—Agrarian Society and Politics under the Eighteenth-Century Maratha Svarajya*, Cambridge, 1986.
7. Muzaffar Alam, op. cit., p. 12.
8. Ibid., pp. 103–4. How Muzaffar Alam obtained figures for 'Moradabad–Bareilly' from the *A'in--i-Akbari* is not at all clear. No such *sarkar* or administrative region existed at that time.
9. Ibid., p. 318 (italics mine).
10. Frank Perlin, *Modern Asian Studies*, vol. 19, pt 3 (1985), p. 429.
11. Bayly, op. cit., p. 10.

12. *Indian Merchants and the Decline of Surat, 1700–1750*, Wiesbaden, 1979, p. 134f.
13. Bayly, op. cit., pp. 14–15.
14. Op. cit., ch. V.
15. *The Agrarian System of Eastern Rajasthan, 1650–1750*, Delhi, 1986, pp. 1–37.
16. Iqbal Husain, 'Rohila Powers in India in the 18th Century', thesis, Aligarh Muslim University.
17. *Medieval India: Society, the Jagirdari Crisis and the Village*, Delhi, 1982, pp. 126–38.
18. *Agrarian System of Mughal India*, pp. 334–8.
19. *Feudalism and Non-European Societies*, ed. T. Byres and H. Mukhia, London, 1985, p. 275.
20. *Land and Sovereignty in India*, p. 8.
21. Op. cit., pp. 26–7.
22. M. Athar Ali, 'The Passing of Empire: The Mughal Case', *Modern Asian Studies*, vol. IX, pt 3, Cambridge, 1985, pp. 385–96. See also my article 'Towards An Interpretation of the Mughal Empire', *JRAS*, London, 1978, no. 1, pp. 38–49.
23. I cannot trace any particular remark in Bayly, where this is stated, but the entire trend in his Introduction is to describe many developments in this period as if they were innovations.
24. M. Athar Ali, 'The Passing of Empire: The Mughal Case', op. cit., pp. 385–96.
25. Abul Fazl was aware of the European discovery of the New World (*Ain-i Akbari*, vol. III) and the achievements of European learning (*Insha-i Abul Fazl, daftar*, i); see also my article, 'Towards An Interpretation of the Mughal Empire', *JRAS* (London, 1978), no. 1, pp. 38–49.
26. See Tapan Raychaudhuri's perceptive remarks in *Cambridge Economic History*, vol. II, pt I, ed. Dharma Kumar, Cambridge, 1982, pp. 1–25.
27. K.M. Panikkar, *Asia and Western Dominance*, New York, 1953, p. 99.
28. Cf. R.E. Robinson in *Studies in the Theory of Imperialism*, ed. R. Owen and B. Sutcliffe, London, 1972, p. 120, quoted by Bayly, op. cit., p. 2.
29. Op. cit., pp. 3–4.
30. *Feudalism and Non-European Societies*, p. 248, fn 13.
31. Bayly, op. cit., p. 27.
32. The relations between the Company and Awadh have been studied by Richard B. Barnett, *North India Between Empires*, Berkeley, 1980, pp. 223–39.
33. Op. cit., pp. 3–4.
34. Op. cit., pp. 65–6.
35. André Wink, op. cit., p. 4.
36. Ibid., p. 388.

4

The Eighteenth Century in Indian Economic History*

IRFAN HABIB

A century is only a conventional period of time: even with the most approximate limits it remains an unsuitable pigeonhole for most historical phenomena. The artificiality of such an approximation would be still more obvious when one remembers that economic and social movements on the supranational scale occur in the form of waves, rather than simultaneously everywhere. It is easy to see how processes like capitalism, colonialism, or socialism cannot be put in neat time-periods, applicable to all zones, despite their worldwide sweep. The eighteenth century may have had a certain significance for England as the classic period of Enclosures and the early phase of the Industrial Revolution, for France (till 1789) as the period of the long crisis of the Ancient Regime, and for colonialism, generally, as the phase when colonial 'primary' accumulation reached very high levels. But it is difficult to see how the century would have a definite significance in the same manner for other countries.

In India, mercantilist colonialism's triumph did not coincide with the earlier seizure and expropriation of the Americas and the establishment of the African slave trade. It came in the middle of the eighteenth century, with the Carnatic wars (1746–63) and the battles of Plassey (1757) and Buxar (1764). To lump the pre-colonial and colonial phases together in a single century is difficult to comprehend, unless one refuses to consider the colonial conquest as a fundamental break at all.[1]

The only way in which it is perhaps legitimate to isolate the eighteenth century in India for purposes of historical debate is to consider developments

*Irfan Habib, 'The Eighteenth Century in Indian Economic History', in Leonard Blussé and Femme Gaastra (eds), *On the Eighteenth Century as a Category of Indian History: Van Leur in Retrospect*, Aldershot, 1998, pp. 217–36, revised by the author.

entirely from the point of view of the Indian regimes. We can then take the years, 1707 to 1805, from the death of Aurangzeb to the final subjugation of the bulk of India by the English East India Company after the Second Anglo–Maratha War, as forming the long period during which the Mughal Empire disintegrated and new states struggled to occupy the space it had vacated.[2] Within this indigenous India, we can ask ourselves what the nature of the political process was, and what its implications for the economy of India were, until the absorption of its various parts in the Company's empire. For the purposes of the present paper, it is mainly the economic implications that need concern us.

I

All theories of the eighteenth century must necessarily start with the problem of the economic role of the Mughal Empire before its decline. The conventional concept of 'empire' in Indian history has generally been challenged with Romila Thapar revisiting the Mauryas[3] and with Gerard Fussman's *Annales* piece on the same Empire.[4] Both tend to emphasize the unevenness in depth of central control, the empire presumably drawing smaller and smaller revenues, and so affecting the economy less and less, as it moved away from the centre towards its frontiers. It may be tempting to apply this formula of core-versus-periphery to the Mughal Empire; and there has, indeed, been a distant, though unspecific, suggestion of this in Frank Perlin's disparaging remarks about the historians' tendency towards 'Mughal-centrism', 'in terms of an organization of things flowing from the capitals of the north.'[5]

The abundant documentary evidence on the functioning of the Mughal Empire tends to discount fairly strongly the applicability of the model of empire suggested by Thapar and Fussman. If the terms of revenue-assignments (*jagirs* and *khalisa*) had an average duration of 2.7 years in *pargana* Mathura, near the capital, Agra, during 1628–58, the average term was just 2.5 years in Sehwan in Sind for the period 1592–93, 3.3 years in Dhar (Malwa) for the period 1653–85, and of 3.67 years in Indur (Telingana) in the Deccan, for the period 1631-53.[6] Chetan Singh's suggestion that there was a tendency to keep certain *jagirdars* within particular regions has been adequately refuted by Athar Ali, through the mere exercise of tracing the full careers of the officers concerned.[7]

The revenue statistics, it is true, show a generally high assessment (*jama'*) in relation to the map area in the 'core' provinces of Agra, Delhi, and Lahore; and, yet, revenue-realization in Gujarat, *c.* 1595, in terms of cultivated area was much higher than in Uttar Pradesh.[8] Khandesh and parts of Berar and

Orissa had extraordinarily high revenue-incidence by map area.[9] Urban taxation again seems to have been the heaviest in Gujarat.[10] Coin output from the Deccan mints of the Empire as a proportion of the entire Imperial coins output expanded as the Empire extended into the Deccan until, during the decade 1696–1705, as many as 238 coins catalogued in important museums come from the Mughal mints in the Deccan as against 686 from the north Indian mints.[11] The quantitative evidence does not, therefore, support the thesis of a density of imperial control at the centre and a thinning of it in the more distant provinces.

Behind the surprising degree of systematized centralization and even spread of Mughal administration was, perhaps, not only the momentum given by Akbar's strong measures, but also the existence of a universal land-tax, which, allowing for different shares of local hereditary right-holders (styled zamindars in the Mughal terminology of the seventeenth century), corresponded to the surplus produced by the peasant.[12] Detailed documentation from Rajasthan and Maharashtra adds specific details to the picture, without, however, affecting the generality of the magnitude and nature of the Mughal land-tax.[13] The Mughal Empire found the tax-rent equation already in existence, though its spokesmen such as Abu'l Fazl never claimed on this basis (contrary to the assumption of many European observers) that the king was the owner of the soil. What the Empire did was to greatly systematize revenue assessment and collection, as also the shares it would allow to the various kinds of local claimants, whom it insisted on viewing as forming a single class, that of zamindars. In recent writings there has been a tendency to overlook the major burden of the land-tax, and emphasize instead the adjustments with, and concessions to the zamindars.[14] But if we bear in mind the fact that, with all the concessions given,[15] the land-tax was still the main external charge on the peasant, it would be hard to disagree with Moreland's dictum that 'next to the weather, the administration was the dominant fact in the economic life of the country'.[16]

Once this dominant fact is acknowledged, one can consider arguments as to whether the Mughal Empire obstructed or promoted economic growth, notably in the form of extension of cultivation. In the 1660s François Bernier observed a process of economic decay in India, which he attributed to the royal ownership of land, as reflected in the unrestrained authority of the 'Timariots' (his term for *jagirdars*) and their unpredictably short terms of assignments set by the King.[17] Essentially accepting Bernier's judgement (and that of some of his Indian contemporaries), I suggested that the increasing pressure of revenue led, on the one hand, to a flight of the peasants from land, thereby having a negative effect upon expansion of peasant settlement, and, on the other, to peasant uprisings, and simultaneously to a breakdown in the collaboration between the *jagirdars* and zamindars, so that the agrarian difficulties led to a crisis for the Empire.[18] The process could be controlled to some extent by administrative measures, such as are set out in Aurangzeb's farmans to Rasikdas and Muhammad Hashim, and by reducing the *jama 'dami* to allow *jagirdars* a larger territory from which to meet their salary-claims.[19] Unluckily, neither demographic data nor other statistics (e.g. of area under cultivation) come to us in a manner that would justify any definite conclusion about the progress of the agricultural sector of the economy over the entire course of the seventeenth century.[20]

In the first quarter of the eighteenth century the major administrative constraints tended to collapse, as may be seen so graphically from a rarely quoted passage from Khafi Khan (1731).[21] The sale of tax-farms (*ijara*) became a more and more general practice. C.A. Bayly has given us a new perception of this institution 'as one which consolidated the intermediate classes of society—townsmen, traders, service gentry—who commanded the skills of the market and the pen'.[22] Muzaffar Alam has been won over so far to this approach that he sees the increasing use of this oppressive device as an index of 'growth'.[23] Ratan Chand, the agent through whom a scandalous system of sales of farms was established by the Sayyid brothers, 1713–19, becomes for him an enlightened policy-maker, who 'appreciated the problem' of the process of 'localization of power', and resolved it by 'institutionalizing the *ijara* practice'. He is supposed thereby to have drawn upon himself the conservative accusation of 'having converted statecraft into shopkeeping (*baqqaliat*)'.[24] The text, however, nowhere refers to either statecraft or *baqqaliat*, a Persian word apparently coined by Alam himself for this occasion. What it says, on the other hand, is that the Sayyid brothers sold away in farm the *khalisa* territories (treasury lands) for lakhs of rupees for their own benefit and that posts were given exclusively to the Barha Sayyids (their own clan) and the Banias (*Baqqals*) (Ratan Chand's caste).[25] There could hardly have been any localization of power through such imposition of one's clan followers over the entire Empire. It is not surprising that when Nizamu'l Mulk suggested a set of reforms to the emperor in 1724, the first one was 'the abolition of *ijara* of the *mahals* [sub-districts] of the *khalisa*, which has become the source of the ruin and devastation of the country.'[26]

If there is a question-mark over the ability of the Mughal Empire to promote agricultural expansion, one can, perhaps, be more positive about its contribution to urban growth and the expansion of trade. The tendency towards cash nexus and, therefore, towards induced trade; the large transfer of rural surplus to the towns and its conversion into craft-commodities and services to meet the demands of an essentially town-based ruling class and its dependants; the provision of some degree of security and control over taxation along the routes: and a metallic currency of uniform standard and purity uttered from mints all over the Empire—all these were factors that should have created the basis for commercial expansion.[27] There could have been a real increase in merchant-capital through its absorption of some of the resources of the Mughal ruling class by an indigenously developed system of deposit-banking, credit, brokerage, and insurance. The larger availability of capital so obtained was possibly connected with the remarkable fall in interest rates about the middle of the seventeenth century, though bullion imports into India uncovered by exports of goods might also have helped.[28]

If some of these factors, closely related as they were to the Mughal Empire as an all-India polity, were to weaken or even whither away with the decline of the Empire, it would be hard to argue that commerce and towns would still not have suffered. Gujarat was a province of the Empire that not only had important textile and other industries catering to the inland markets, but, through the Gulf of Cambay, also maintained a large overseas trade. As Ashin Das Gupta has pointed out, the commercial decline of Surat mirrors fairly accurately the decline of the Empire. The story is partly told in Dutch information on arrivals of Indian ships annually at Surat: 87 in 1693; an average of 32 from 1716 to 1720, largely maintained till 1733; but the number ultimately falling to only 19 in 1741.[29] Das Gupta firmly atributes the port's decline to the conditions in the hinterland consequent upon the increasing weakness of the Empire.[30] There was no rival in the Gulf of Cambay to gain at the expense of Surat; and Bombay had a different hinterland and could hardly supplant Surat as a base of Indian shipping. A similar decline seems to have affected Indian shipping in Bengal.[31]

Quantitative information by which the fortunes of inland trade could be traced is much harder to come by. The only way in which security costs can be measured is by way of comparing insurance rates. For *c.* 1795, a peaceful year, we have a list of rates of indigenous firms collected by John Malcolm. Unfortunately being centred on Malwa, they do not give insurance rates between any two places for which we have rates from the seventeenth century. Nevertheless, the seventeenth-century rates seem to have been generally lower: For Ahmadabad to Thatta the rate in 1647 for commercial goods was 0.5 per cent, but for Jaipur to Indore in 1795 it was 2 per cent. For Surat to Agra, it was 2.5 per cent for cochineal in 1655: for Surat to Indore, a fraction of the distance, it was as high as 1.5 per cent for pearls and precious stones in 1795.[32]

Since movements of interest rates may reflect changes in availability of capital, it is relevant to ask if the decline in the interest rates which is so marked in the mid-seventeenth century continued into the eighteenth. K.N. Chaudhuri offers no serial data on interest rates—which, given his access to the English Company's records, is rather a pity—but he does say that 'there was no long-term downward movement in interest rates in India', presumably between 1660 and 1760.[33] In Bengal the rates of interest at which the Company was able to borrow at Hugli in 1670 and 1679 ranged from 1.38 to 1.5 per cent a month; in 1704 at Calcutta it was quoted at no higher than 1 per cent a month.[34] But in 1810–11 Francis Buchanan found that until a year or two earlier the rate against bullion as security was 15 per cent a year at Patna, and had only recently fallen to 12 per cent.[35] If credence is to be given to Buchanan's information, it would seem that interest rates really did remain stable in eastern India from the first decade of the eighteenth century onwards, possibly suggesting thereby a stagnation in capital supply. But for a firm conclusion one would have to await a far more extensive exploration of credit conditions and of a wider spread of quotations of interest rates in the eighteenth century.

II

The indigenous regimes that arose as the Mughal Empire weakened, retreated, and splintered can be very broadly divided into two groups. The first group consisted of states that were created by Mughal officials turning into local rulers: such were the Nazimates of the Deccan, Bengal, and Awadh. These also included states created or enlarged by a simple acquisition of territory in *jagir* and revenue-farm, as in the cases of Jaipur and the Bangash principality.[36] The second set of states were creations of opponents of the Mughal power, principally the Marathas, Jats, Rohillas, and the Sikhs.

The first group of states maintained a direct continuity with imperial administration, including its personnel. But practically all of them (the Deccan, perhaps, more slowly than the others) gave up the system of *jagir* transfers, since this pillar of all-India centralization was no longer essential for their own existence. One can imagine, therefore, that these states could allow both a long-term view to be taken of land-revenue realization and a greater accommodation made with the local zamindar elements.

Of the Deccan under the Nizams during the eighteenth century, there is yet to be a tolerable economic study, despite the large amount of available documentary material. For the Bengal Nazimate, James Grant's interpretation of Mughal revenue statistics, prepared in 1786, seems yet to dominate the field. Grant's major conclusion was that under the Nazimate 'the whole country remained prodigiously underrated', though this led to the imposition of the *abwab* or irregular exactions. The new system taking 'the room of the equitable mode of Mogul administration' tended to favour 'the new class of officers denominated zemindars'.[37] Essentially, his argument was that the land revenue did not increase in correspondence with the rise in prices caused by the silver influx. The Nazims' dependence on the Jagatseths and other mercantile interests in revenue-collection could be seen as part of a rapprochement with non-bureaucratic classes to secure a moderate level of revenue-collection. The level was still high enough to sustain a considerable degree of urbanization with the capital Murshidabad judged by Clive to be as populous as London in 1764.[38]

Muzaffar Alam offers us a picture of expanding cultivation in Awadh and adjacent regions on the basis of eighteenth-century revenue statistics compared with those of the *A'in-i Akbari* (*c*. 1595); but unadjusted to prices they really carry little or no message.[39]

The only successor state, for which rich data exist and have been partly explored, is the Jaipur principality. No evidence about the pace of growth of population or area under cultivation in the first part of the eighteenth century has, however, yet been presented. A lightening of the tax burden is suggested by the movement of cash-tax (*zabti*) rates on various crops, when adjusted to prices, in a weighted index which is here converted into a decennial statement:[40]

Years	Agriculture Prices (1715=100)	*Zabti* Rates (1715=100)
1661–70 (3 years)*	36.52	106.34
1671–80 (1 year)	50.57	112.16
1681–90 (6 years)	44.30	105.99
1701–10	54.06	39.81
1711–20	122.34	102.93
1721–30	89.82	117.05
1731–40	122.56	109.94
1741–50	96.50	110.44

(*) Prices available for 2 out of the 3 years only.

The *zabti* system, however, covered only a small area, the bulk of the crops being under the *jinsi* (or sharing in kind) arrangements. There was little change in the shares demanded for the tax in kind, and Satya Prakash Gupta suggests a possible tendency on the part of the peasant to shift from *jinsi* to *zabti* arrangements, since the latter tended to be more to his advantage.[41] Moreover, the stability of the taxation system seems to have been shaken by the state's increasing resort to *ijara* (tax-farm), which became marked in the

1730s and all-pervasive in the latter half of the century.[42] The picture of progress in agricultural production during the entire period, 1650–1750, is replaced by one of declining cultivation in the next fifty years, with contraction in the cultivated area in localities for which returns are available.[43]

In the second set of states the pride of place is occupied by the Peshwa's government, with its large areas of control and enormously rich archives. Its ruling elements originated not from within the ranks of the Mughal nobility and bureaucracy, but out of the class the Mughals called zamindars, or hereditary rural potentates. These origins partly explain the state-structure the Marathas built; an internal taxation system within the *swarajya*, supplemented by a zone of extraction of tribute out of revenue collection (*chauth* and *sardeshmukhi*), a tribute whose origins lay in the zamindars' customary shares in tax revenue.[44] Simultaneously, there was a strong proneness to institute hereditary 'fiefs' (*saranjam*s) and offices, in contrast to the transferable *jagir*s and posts of the Empire.[45] Not only was *mulk-giri* (lit. country-seizure, but meaning plunder) a long and self-defeating mechanism for continuous tribute-extraction, but the system of establishing hereditary fiscal rights also led to difficulties in internal taxation and maintenance of soldiery. The Peshwas' regime was thus constantly immersed in financial crises even during moments of military triumph.[46]

The impact of the Maratha regime was doubtless uneven. Within Maharashtra, the Peshwas promoted the transformation of *upari*s (non-hereditary or temporary peasants) into cultivators for fiscal advantage,[47] and it is possible to argue that conditions in the Maratha homeland were fairly stable with a steady pace of increase in cultivation until the last years of the regime (1803–18), when, under constraints from British hegemony, the old system broke down with an ever rising burden of financial bankruptcy and expanding tax-farms.[48] Outside Maharashtra, the view of Maratha expansion as a sheer process of devastation was called into question by Stewart N. Gordon on the basis of a set of documents relating to the Maratha conquest and early administration of Malwa, 1728–60.[49] In Gujarat, Muhammad 'Ali Khan gave a fairly favourable account of the Maratha administration, claiming that by 1754 it had led to a certain amount of economic recovery.[50] The insurance rates on money and goods sent from Malwa to different parts of the Maratha dominions in 1795 were about the same or only slightly higher than in 1820.[51] Clearly, these testify to the maintenance of certain levels of law and order throughout Maratha-controlled territory. And yet one cannot altogether exclude from consideration the disorderliness which was built into the Maratha system, involving not only constant plundering forays, but also the supplanting of local zamindars at the pettiest levels by outsiders, so as to make it seem to an observer in 1762–63, that the Brahmans of Konkan wished to become 'proprietors [not simply rulers] of the whole world'.[52] The significant position occupied by bankers and moneylenders in the Maratha states, notably the Brahmans of Pune, perhaps represented more the malfunctioning of the fiscal system than any positive state support to trade and commerce.[53] The extent of net urban growth seems also to have been limited: even Pune, the capital, is not credited with a population of over 100,000 at the end of the century.[54]

The Jat power near Agra and Mathura arose out of rebellion of peasants under zamindar leadership, attaining the apex of power under Suraj Mal (d. 1763), who, though a 'Sage among his people', spoke the Braj dialect and wore 'the dress of a zamindar'.[55] The internal structure of the Jat kingdom has yet to be studied critically; but its special result seems to have been a replacement of Rajput by Jat zamindars.[56] A similar result was brought about, but in favour of the Rohillas, a set of immigrant soldiers, traders, and rural settlers in the Doab but especially in the trans-Ganga tract of Katehr, now Rohilkand. They here built up a network of clan chieftaincies without attaining a possible degree of centralization or even systematic administration. They seem, however, to have reclaimed land and promoted agriculture.[57]

The Punjab remained, for much of the latter part of the eighteenth century, a battleground between the Afghans and the Sikhs. Initially, in Banda Bahadur's uprising 1710–16, the plebeian character of the Sikh revolt was very marked; a contemporary historian speaks of his following as comprising 'sweepers, tanners, the caste of Banjaras (migrant pastoralists and transporters), and other lowly and wretched people'.[58] Khafi Khan, who too speaks of the mass of 'lowly Hindus' joining Banda's banners, says that he had counsellors also from the 'respectable Hindus' like the Khatris (a mercantile and bureaucratic caste) and the 'warlike Jats' (a peasant and zamindar caste).[59] The peasant and plebeian character of the soldiery and even leadership, combined with a very deep-rooted religious millenarism, delayed the transformation of the Sikh polity into a conventional state. But zamindari aspirations became important with time, and social egalitarianism could not prevent the rise of leaders like 'Nawab' Kanpur Singh.[60] Ultimately, in the nineteenth century, under Ranjit Singh, came the full-blown Raj, that was apparently a continuance of Mughal administration with strong Rajput symbolisms and even rites.

The two sets of polities we have been considering do not include a state which had a short life in the latter half of the eighteenth century, but had remarkable features of its own. This was the Mysore of Haidar Ali and Tipu (1761–99). These rulers, transforming a traditional raj, constructed an administration closely built on Mughal lines. The pressure on zamindars inherent in the administrative tradition, was intensified to the point of Haidar Ali's taking away the ten per cent allowance paid to them and managing the revenue-collection directly.[61] The *jagirs* too were largely (not totally) abolished under Tipu.[62] Mysore was the first Indian state to shift almost entirely to European methods of warfare, depending on firearms and infantry, with cavalry and local militia as supporting arms.[63] It was also the first Indian state to produce modern firearms within its borders by importing foreign workmen as instructors.[64] The most interesting aspect was the state's direct intervention in production and commerce. Watches began to be made, and sericulture was introduced.[65] The establishment of 'factories' of a state trading company in other parts of India, and in the Red Sea and the Persian Gulf ports, was part of an attempt to imitate the East India Company's successful combination of trade with government.[66] The only other notable contemporary ruler who saw the urgent importance of shifting to European methods of warfare was Mahadaji Sindhia,[67] but he did not have a vision going beyond his immediate military needs. In this Mysore stood alone; and this was probably the major factor behind the English making it a primary target and bringing about its destruction (1799).

Insufficient as is our present evidence for the economy under the indigenous eighteenth-century regimes, it is enough to cause us to entertain doubts about their having witnessed any significant measure of economic growth. There is no strong reason to believe that their performance in terms of population increase, extension of cultivation, or expansion of trade was superior to that of the Empire in the seventeenth century. A very modest compound rate of population growth of 0.14 per cent has been suggested for the period 1600–1800, given the most plausible estimates of the total population for 1600 and 1800.[68] It is not likely that within this 200 year period the eighteenth century was able to achieve a higher average rate than the seventeenth. At the same time, the splintering of the Empire into various independent regimes was in itself a political fact that was to have enormous economic consequences. Unless one makes it a matter of faith that whatever has happened must have happened for the best, it is difficult to avoid a comparison with China. The Qing Empire, by remaining unified and strong, delayed for almost a century (until the odious Opium War of 1840–2) the colonial assault on China earlier, and so made the modern history of East Asia so different from that of South Asia. By not letting western powers establish bases in China, it protected Tokugawa Japan, and thereby helped to make the Meiji Restoration of 1868 as well as Japan's evolution into an independent capitalist power ultimately possible.

III

From the middle of the eighteenth century, the Indian states were subjected to an inexorable process of subjugation and annexation by the English
East India Company. During the previous years, the colonial trade between
Europe and the East (principally, India) had grown enormously. The total
invoice values of imports from Asia by the English and Dutch Companies
doubled between 1701–10 and 1751–60, reaching 6.51 million pesos in the
last decade: the sale values tended to be practically double again. To this one
must add the trade of the French East India Company, the sale value of whose
imports from Asia during 1741–50 was equal to 16.89 per cent of that of the
combined imports of the other two Companies. At the same time, there was
a substantial change in the composition of these imports. In 1638–40, spices
and paper constituted 68.19 per cent of the Dutch Company's Asian imports
in invoice value; in 1738–40 only 14.2; in the English East India Company's
trade the percentage was 20.01 in 1664–70 and 4.30 in 1731–40. On the other
hand, textiles and silk advanced from 14.16 per cent in the Dutch Company's
imports in 1648–50 to 41.1 per cent in 1738–40; the percentage in the English
Company's imports was 63.07 and 76.41 respectively (silk accounting for
0.49 and 11.06).[69] This change in composition had its partial source in the
Atlantic slave trade, since 'East India' textiles constituted the single largest
item with which slaves were paid for. These textiles are said to have accounted for 27 per cent of all goods shipped from England to Africa from
1699 to 1800.[70] The major market for Indian calicoes remained western and
north-western Europe; but the pressure for Indian textiles for financing the
Atlantic slave trade during its 'golden age' became an additional factor behind the increase of textile supplies from India. The supplies could only be
obtained by export of treasure. The English East India Company in 1700 exported treasure worth £482,219 constituting 83.3 per cent of its total exports:
in 1750 £1,101,921 constituting 78.4 per cent.[71] The limits to availability of
sheer liquid capital in England thus set an obstacle to further expansion of
supplies from India. The only way this constraint could be overcome was not
to raise capital in India, where interest rates were in any case higher than in
England, but simply to seize it. Dupleix articulated the vision first for the
French Company; but it was Clive who was able to show how it could be successfully done after Plassey in 1757 and with the assumption of the Diwani
in 1765. Out of the expected annual revenues of Rs 25 million from Bengal,
the English Company could simply retain as its annual 'net' profit a sum of
Rs 12.2 million or £1.65 million, far exceeding the maximum annual amount
of treasure that the Company had ever sent to India.[72]

The drive to enlarge revenue and so the Company's 'investment', joined to its servants' ambition of building private fortunes, was the primary motive-force of British colonial expansion in India in the eighteenth century. The results of Plassey are immediately seen in the statistics. The company's export of treasure fell from £797, 167 in 1757 to £143,400 in 1760;[73] and its treasure imports into India, put at Rs 3.1 million in 1757-8, absolutely ceased thereafter.[74] There began that constant feature of India's foreign trade for the next 150 years, namely a huge annual exports surplus without India ever attaining a favourable balance of payments. An estimate of India's average annual trade with Europe, including the trade carried on by the non-English companies, clandestine trade, licensed private trade, the English Company's own trade and privilege goods shipped on its ships during the years 1780–90, presents this picture:[75]

Imports into India	Exports from India	Excess of Exports over Imports
£2,393.610	£7,331,563	£4,937,959

This contemporary estimate puts the non-English companies' trade and clandestine trade (English private merchants' trade under non-English flag) at 64.9 per cent of the whole. This may be an exaggeration, though much of the trade formally under the non-English European auspices was really financed by remittances of the English 'Nabobs'. Even if this estimate of surplus exports has some element of overstatement, it shows clearly that Holden Furber's estimate of the drain at £1.78 million a year for the period 1783–4 to 1792–3 is far too low, even in terms of 'prime costs'.[76] When the revolutionary wars in Europe perforce closed the alternative channels provided by the non-English companies, the English customs records could begin to represent the size of the drain better. These, if one enhances the figures by 25 per cent to allow for smuggling, show a surplus of exports from `East India' to Britain of an order of £3.59 million per annum during the years 1795–9 and £3.62 million per annum during 1800–4.[77] This would still be underestimates of the real proceeds, since 'East India' goods were entered in customs house records merely at the values declared by the merchants.[78] It is then very likely that in the 1780s and 1790s the annual Indian Tribute to Britain approximated to about £4 million or Rs 4 crores.[79]

The extraction of this tribute was what colonialism in its eighteenth-century phase was almost entirely about. Furber's casual dismissal of its effect on employment and commerce is not easy to accept.[80] Ghulam Husain

Tabatabai (1781) drew a convincing picture of large-scale artisanal and service unemployment in Bengal;[81] and Cornwallis (1790) sombrely commented on 'the langour' that the Tribute had thrown 'upon the cultivation and the general commerce of the country'.[82] These contemporary statements were surely not made just for effect.

Tribute extraction forced up revenue-maximization in Bengal and Bihar. The revenue collected rose from £2.26 million in 1765–6 to £3.33 million in 1770–1, the last a famine year. With the Double Government abolished, the revenues climbed from £3.26 million in 1771–2 to £3.38 million in 1778–9. Of this last figure, £2.66 million represented the land-revenue. The Permanent Settlement did not offer any relaxation in land-tax demand: in 1790–1, the amount realized was Rs 2.68 crores or £2.68 million.[83] This increase, and then stability, in total revenue realization is all the more remarkable in view of the behaviour of prices. From Brij Narain's annual series of coarse rice prices in eighteenth-century Bengal one can calculate the average decennial movement (in terms of Rs per maund) as follows:[84]

1710–10	0.58		1751–60	1.47
1711–20	0.71		1761–70	1.85
1721–30	0.97		1771–80	1.55
1731–40	1.05		1781–90	1.55
1741–50	1.48		1791–1800	1.14

We can see from these figures that cessation of treasure imports by the English East India Company after 1757 was sufficient to remove the major inflationary factor.[85] The Company's exports of silver from Bengal[86] to help finance its lucrative China trade caused an absolute contraction of the circulating medium, as was seen as early as 1772. The increase and, then, the enforced stabilization of land-revenue collection in the face of a secular downward movement of prices could only have been at the expense of agriculture and commerce, precisely as Cornwallis had pointed out.

The pressure on peasants extended to other areas, as Indian rulers came under the necessity of meeting the Company's levies and indemnities. At the end of the Third Mysore War (1792), not only was half of Mysore taken away, but from the revenues of the remainder Rs 3.30 crores were to be paid within a year.[87] It is not surprising that the fiscal pressure on the Mysore peasants became extremely severe. Awadh, the friendly ally, was made to pay Rs 87 lakhs annually for the nine years preceding 1785, and then Rs 50 lakhs annually until 1801, when the Company coolly annexed half of its territory.[88]

The economic effects of Tribute were not, however, confined to areas which came under the Company's government or its system of indemnities and subsidies. There was, first, the deflationary tendency stemming from the decline of annual silver replenishment, which affected prices and capital supply everywhere. Unfortunately, price-information for the latter half of the eighteenth century has not been properly collected. Nonetheless, Jevons's prices for wheat at Delhi show a long-term decline (when considered on the basis of annual average by decades), beginning with the 1790s and continuing into the next century.[89] Bayly himself notices that 'a great want of specie' was felt in the Delhi region and the Punjab after 1770 and that towns and trade in the area decayed between 1770 and 1800.[90] The diversion of Bengal's exports in silk and textiles entirely to Europe practically closed the traditional trade with Gujarat, whose famous textile industry depended upon Bengal silk. Under these circumstances, one cannot be sure that what took place was a mere 'redeployment of merchant capital within India, not its destruction'.[91]

The issue of Tribute reminds us that in reconstructing economic history, we may be misled by the assembling of a large number of local details into overlooking the larger factors. Bayly's work on the economy and society of north India, with all its emphasis on the last quarter of the eighteenth and the first of the nineteenth century, does not come to grips with the effects of the Drain, perhaps because the Tribute itself seldom directly appears in the kind of evidence he is dealing with. But, as A.K. Banerji has aptly insisted, both history and economic theory should be concerned with what happens to an economy, when it is called upon constantly to part with a portion of GNP, equal to what in other countries would have been their national savings, not for a short period, as with Germany, burdened with reparations after the First World War, but unrelentingly for one and a half centuries or more.[92] For the reason of the Tribute, if for no other, the eighteenth century can hardly be said to exhibit any substantive economic continuity between its earlier and latter parts; nor could that century have harboured any 'indigenous origins of the colonial economy',[93] for surely there could have been no indigenous urge to transfer wealth to Britain.

NOTES AND REFERENCES

1. Cf. M. Athar Ali, 'Recent Theories of Eighteenth-Century India', see above pp. 90–9, *Indian Historical Review* (ICHR), XIII (nos.1 & 2), pp. 102–8.
2. For such a position and for an extensive survey of literature on eighteenth-century Indian regimes, see Barun De, Presidential Address: *PIHC*, 49th Session, Dharwad, 1989, pp. 1–58.
3. *The Mauryas Revisited*, Calcutta, 1987, pp. 1–31.
4. English translation, 'Control and Provincial Administration in Ancient India: the Problem of the Mauryan Empire', *IHR* XIV (1-2), pp. 43–72.

5. 'State Formation Reconsidered', *Modern Asian Studies (MAS)*, p. 423.
6. Irfan Habib, *Agrarian System of Mughal India, 1556-1707*, 2nd edn, Delhi, 1999, pp. 301-2.
7. Chetan Singh, 'Centre and Periphery in the Mughal State', *MAS*, xxii (27, 1982), pp. 299-318: M. Athar Ali, 'The Mughal Polity: a Critique of 'Revisionist' Approaches', *PIHC*, 52nd (New Delhi) Session, Delhi, 1992, p. 309-10.
8. Cf. Shireen Moosvi, *The Economy of the Mughal Empire, c. 1595: A Statistical Study*, Delhi, 1987, p. 142.
9. Ibid., pp. 145 (table) and 147 (map).
10. Ibid., p. 311 (map).
11. S. Moosvi, 'The Mughal Empire and the Deccan', *PIHC*, 43rd Session (Kurukshetra), 1983, pp. 377-8.
12. Cf. Irfan Habib, *Agrarian System of Mughal India*, pp. 230-97.
13. See Satya Prakash Gupta, *The Agrarian System of Eastern Rajasthan (c. 1650-c. 1750)*, Delhi, 1986, pp. 144-55, for eastern Rajasthan. For Maharashtra, see André Wink, *Land and Sovereignty in India: Agrarian Society and Politics under the Eighteenth-Century Maratha Swarajya*, Cambridge, 1986, pp. 265-8.
14. See, especially, André Wink, op.cit., for such a view, within the framework of what he rather quaintly designates *fitna*.
15. On whose size generally, see Irfan Habib, *Agrarian System*, pp. 136-54: S. Moosvi, *Economy of the Mughal Empire*, pp. 176-89: Satya Prakash Gupta, op.cit., pp. 134-40.
16. W.H. Moreland, *The Agrarian System of Moslem India*, Cambridge, 1929, p. xii.
17. *Travels in the Mogul Empire, 1656-68*, trans. by A. Constable, 2nd edn revised by V.A. Smith, London, 1916, esp. p. 227.
18. *Agrarian System of Mughal India*, pp. 342-405.
19. Cf. S. Moosvi, 'Scarcities, Prices and Exploitation: The Agrarian Crisis, 1658-70', *Studies in History* (1), N.S. (1985), pp. 45-55.
20. The evidence of area statistics is surveyed in Irfan Habib, *Agrarian System of Mughal India*, pp. 1-24, and the revenue statistics in ibid., pp. 375-6, 450-66.
21. *Muntakhabu'l Lubab*, ed. Kabir al-Din Ahmad (and Ghulam Qadir), *Bib. Indica*, Calcutta, 1860-74, I, p. 34; for a translation of the passage, see Irfan Habib, op.cit., pp. 372-3.
22. *Rulers, Townsmen and Bazars: North Indian Society in the Age of British Expansion, 1770-1870*, Cambridge, 1983, pp. 14-15.
23. *The Crisis of Empire in Mughal North India: Awadh and the Punjab, 1707-48*, Delhi, 1986, pp. 41-2, 318.
24. Ibid., pp. 41-2.
25. Khafi Khan: *Muntakhabu'l Lubab*, ii, pp. 773, 902, 941-2. Both the modern works that Alam cites here, Satish Chandra, *Parties and Politics at the Mughal Court, 1707-40*, pp. 108-9, and Noman Ahmad Siddiqui, *Land Revenue Administration Under the Mughals (1700-1750)*, Bombay, 1970, p. 96, give an interpretation opposite to his own and in conformity with the actual text of source—a fact left unindicated by Alam.
26. Khafi Khan, ii, p. 948.
27. For detailed argument on these lines, see Irfan Habib. 'Potentialities of Capitalistic Development in the Economy of Mughal India', in *Essays in Indian History: Towards*

a Marxist Perception, New Delhi, 1995, pp. 180–232 (it may, perhaps, be clarified that, despite the title, the potentialities for true capitalistic development within Mughal India are denied); Tapan Raychaudhuri. 'The State and the Economy: The Mughal Empire', in T. Raychaudhuri and I. Habib (ed.), *Cambridge Economic History of India (CEHI),* I, Cambridge, 1982, pp. 172–93.

28. Cf. Irfan Habib, 'Merchant Communities in Pre-colonial India', in James D. Tracy (ed.), *The Rise of Merchant Empires,* Cambridge, 1990, esp. pp. 388–9.

29. *Indian Merchants and the Decline of Surat, c. 1700–1750,* Wiesbaden, 1979, p.283. In his contribution in *CEHI,* I, p. 433, Das Gupta says the merchant fleet at Surat declined from 112 vessels in 1701 to about 20 in 1750.

30. *Indian Merchants and the Decline of Surat,* pp. 134.ff.

31. Ashin Das Gupta in *CEHI,* I, p. 432. Om Prakash, *The Dutch East India Company and the Economy of Bengal, 1630–1720,* pp. 223–4, however, sees 'no clearly discernible trend' in Bengal shipping at least until 1720.

32. For the seventeenth-century rates, see Irfan Habib, 'Banking in Mughal India', in T. Raychaudhuri (ed.), *Contributions to Indian Economic History, 1,* Calcutta, 1960, p.16. For the rates in 1795 see John Malcolm, *Memoir of Central India,* London, 1824, II, pp. 366–9.

33. *The Trading World of Asia and the English East India Company,* Cambridge, 1978, p. 159.

34. R.C. Temple (ed.), *The Diaries of Streynsham Master, 1676–168, and Other Contemporary Papers Relating Thereto,* London, 1911, I, p. 427, and II, pp. 264–5; C.R. Wilson (ed.), *Early Annals of the English in Bengal,* I, London, 1895, pp. 231, 251. See also Sushil Chaudhuri, *Trade and Commercial Organisation in Bengal, 1655–1720,* Calcutta, 1975, pp. 116–18.

35. *An Account of the Districts of Bihar and Patna in 1811–12 [Patna-Gaya Report],* Patna, n.d., II, p. 699.

36. Cf. S.P. Gupta, *Agrarian System of Eastern Rajasthan,* pp. 5–7, for the creation of the Jaipur state under Sawai Jai Singh (d. 1744).

37. 'Analysis of the Finances of Bengal', *Fifth Report from the Select Committee of the Affairs of the East India Company,* London, 1812–13, London, 1812–13, Irish University Press fascimile ed. of the original printing, pp. 265ff. Grant could not but have in mind also the very great increase in revenue-realization after the Company's seizure of the *diwani* in 1765.

38. Durgaprasad Bhattacharya, *Report on the Population Estimates of India,* VIII (1811–20), part-A, New Delhi, 1978, p. 309.

39. *Crisis of Empire in Mughal North India,* pp. 252–3. Richard R. Barnett, *North India between Empires: Awadh, the Mughals and the British. 1720–1801,* Berkeley, 1980, does not similarly give any hard evidence of economic prosperity.

40. Source: Satya Prakash Gupta and Shireen Moosvi. 'Weighted Price and Revenue Rate Indices of Eastern Rajasthan', *IESHR,* XII (2), pp. 183–93. esp. pp. 190–1.

41. *The Agrarian System of Eastern Rajasthan (c. 1650–c. 1750),* p. 50. The evidence, diagrammatically set out on pp. 94–9, does not show a very firm trend towards an increase in the expansion of *zabti* or cash rates on crops.

42. Ibid., p. 229; Dilbagh Singh, *The State, Landlords and Peasants: [Eastern] Rajasthan in the [latter half of the] 18th Century,* New Delhi, 1990, pp. 138–40.

43. Satya Prakash Gupta, op.cit., p. 63: Dilbagh Singh, op.cit., pp. 64–5, 68–9.
44. Cf. Irfan Habib, *Agrarian System of Mughal India*, pp. 184, 400–5, and André Wink, *Land and Society in India*, esp. pp. 34–51, 153–5.
45. Hiroshi Fukazawa, *The Medieval Deccan: Peasants, Social Systems and States, Sixteenth to Eighteenth Centuries*, Bombay, 1991, pp. 70–90. Cf. Surendra Nath Sen, *The Military System of the Marathas*, 2nd edn, Bombay, 1958, pp. 43–63.
46. V.D. Divekar, 'The Emergence of an Indigenous Business Class in Maharashtra in the Eighteenth Century' (*MAS*), 16(1), (1982), pp. 427–44, esp. pp. 427–36.
47. H. Fukazawa, op.cit., pp. 148–98. See also Wink, op.cit., pp. 272–92.
48. Cf. R.D. Choksey, *Economic History of the Bombay-Deccan and Karnataka (1818–1868)*, Poona, 1945, pp. 85–6.
49. 'The Slow Conquest: Administrative Integration of Malwa into the Maratha Empire', *MAS*, 11 (1977), pp. 1–40.
50. *Mir'at-i Ahmadi*, ed. Syed Nawab Ali, II, Baroda, 1927, p. 462: the author himself was the Mughal *diwan* of the *suba*.
51. See the table in Malcolm, *Memoir of Central India*, II, pp. 366–8.
52. Azad Bilgrami, Khizana-i 'Amira, litho., Kanpur, 1871, p. 47.
53. The nature of this relationship has been explored provocatively by Karen Leonard. 'The "Great Firm" Theory of the Decline of the Mughal Empire', *Comparative Studies in Society and History (CSSH)*, 21 (1979), followed by a controversy on the theme with a contribution J.F. Richards in *CSSH*, 23 (1981). See also Divekar, op.cit., who rightly emphasizes (esp. pp. 441–3) the parasitic and economically restricted nature of the usury to which the financial needs of the Maratha regime gave rise.
54. Divekar, op.cit., p. 442.
55. Saiyid Ghulam 'Ali Naqavi, 'Imadu's Sa'adat, litho., Lucknow, 1897, p. 55.
56. Cf. Irfan Habib, *Agrarian System of Mughal India*, pp. 392–5. The detailed political history of the Jat kingdom has been painstakingly reconstructed by Girish Chandra Dwivedi, *The Jats: Their Role in the Mughal Empire*, Bangalore, 1989.
57. For Rohillas, see Iqbal Husain, *The Rise and Decline of Rohilla Chieftaincies*, Delhi, 1994, pp. 202ff.
58. Muhammad Hadi Kamwar Khan, *Tazkiratu's Salatin Chaghata*, ed. Muzaffar Alam, Bombay, 1980, p. 32. See also Muhammad Shafi Warid, Mir'at-i Waridat, Br. Lib., Add. 5579, ff.117a–118b.
59. Khafi Khan, *Muntakhabu'l Lubab*, II, pp. 651–2, 672. Muzaffar Alam, *Crisis of Empire in North India*, pp. 139–45, tends to overemphasize the *zamindar* component of Banda's following. He speaks of 'Jat zamindars' (p. 139), when the only text he cites (*Muntakhabu'l Lubab*, II, p. 651) does not contain the word *zamindar* at all, saying, in fact, that Banda's followers came 'from the caste of Jats, and the Khatris of the Panjab and other lowly communities of the Hindus'.
60. J.S. Grewal, *The Sikhs of the Punjab (New Cambridge History of India*, II, 3). Cambridge, 1990, p. 89.
61. Francis Buchanan, *A Journey from Madras through the Countries of Mysore, Canara and Malabar, & c.* (1800–1), London, 1807, I, pp. 266–7.
62. Mohibbul Hasan, *History of Tipu Sultan*, Calcutta, 1971, p. 344.
63. Nikhilesh Guha, *Pre-British State System in South India: Mysore, 1751–99*, Calcutta, 1985, p. 73, quoting Clive (1764).

64. Ibid., pp. 74–5, quoting Munro (1791); cf. also Mohibbul Hasan, op.cit., p. 350. The process had begun well before 1761, with Haidar Ali's foundry at Dindigul.

65. Mohibbul Hasan, op.cit., pp. 348–9. For sericulture, see also Buchanan, *Journey from Madras*, I, p. 222.

66. Mohibbul Hasan, pp. 344–8. For an interpretation of the state of Haidar Ali and Tipu Sultan generally, see Irfan Habib (ed.), *Resistance and Modernization Under Haidar Ali and Tipu Sultan*, New Delhi, 1999, pp. xvii–xviii; the industrial, commercial and financial measures (and plans) of Tipu Sultan are dealt with in some detail on pp. xxviii–xxxv.

67. Surendra Nath Sen, *Military System of the Marathas*, pp. 115–24.

68. Irfan Habib in Tapan Raychaudhuri and I. Habib (ed.), *Cambridge Economic History of India*, I, Cambridge, 1982, p. 157. S. Moosvi, *Economy of the Mughal Empire, c. 1595*, pp. 405–6, calculates a compound rate of 0.21 per cent for the longer period, 1601–1871.

69. The data are derived from the contributions of Niels Steensgaard and Paul Butel in James D. Tracy (ed), *The Rise of Merchant Empires*, Cambridge, 1990, pp. 110, 112, 114–15, 148–9, 169.

70. Herbert S. Klein in ibid., pp. 291–2.

71. K.N. Chaudhuri. *The Trading World of Asia*, p. 512.

72. See, for the quotation from Clive and comment, Romesh Dutt, *The Economic History of India under early British Rule*, London, 1906, p. 37.

73. K.N. Chaudhuri, *Trading World of Asia*, p. 512.

74. K.N. Chaudhuri in *Cambridge Economic History of India*, II, p. 819 (table 10.2B).

75. Ibid., pp. 816–7 (table on p. 817).

76. *John Company at Work*, Cambridge (Mass), 1951, pp. 313–16.

77. B.R. Mitchell and Phyllis Deane, *Abstract of British Historical Statistics*, p. 311, for the basic customs-house figures. See Phyllis Deane and W.A. Cole, *British Economic Growth, 1688–1959*, Cambridge, 1962, pp. 44–5, for the allowance to be made for smuggling.

78. Dean and Cole, *British Economic Growth*, pp. 42–3. See also Sayera I. Habib, 'Colonial Exploitation and Capital Formation in England in the Early Stages of the Industrial Revolution', *PIHC*, 36th session, Aligarh, 1975, xxII–xxIII.

79. To appreciate its size in real terms, we should remind ourselves that the total annual capital formation in British was about £10 million in the early 1780s and about £20 million in the early years of the next century (Dean and Cole, op.cit., pp. 261–2).

80. For a criticism of Furber's views, see Irfan Habib, *Essays in Indian History: Towards a Marxist Perception*, pp. 274–7. Attempting an exercise in 'revisionist' historiography, Rajat Datta, *Society, Economy and the Market: Commercialization in Rural Bengal, 1760–1800*, New Delhi, 2000, pp. 355–6, assures us with regard to 'the early colonial mode of utilization of Bengal's surplus' that 'there is very little ground to believe that its impact at this stage(!) was anything more than marginal'. For this re-echoing of Furber (without any reference to him), he gives no reasons, not even those that had been advanced by Furber himself.

Datta also follows the arguments of James Grant & Co. in comparing the Drain of Wealth to Britain with the revenue remittances to the Mughal court and thus making out the Drain to be of indigenous origins (pp. 355–8). He thinks the drain to Delhi continued right up to 1758 (p. 355), and he even produces the figure of 10 million rupees for the Drain to Delhi in 1756 (p. 357, table 73, where 'Rs in lakhs' should be 'Rs in millions'), when no 'tribute' was in fact sent to Delhi. It is also worth remarking that in this table Datta constantly puts the drain to Delhi at Rs 10 million or above until 1756, whereas on p.355 he speaks of it as averaging about Rs 50 lakhs (=5 million) between 1721–58. With 'statistics' of such consistency he goes on to show, on the basis of the same table, that while under the Nazims in 1756 the 'drain' was as high as 17.84 per cent of the 'agricultural product' (as estimated by Datta), it declined under the English from 14.95 per cent in 1768 to a mere 8.07 per cent in 1793. But the figure for the Drain in 1793 is as unreal as the figure for 1756. In 1793–4 the Company's 'Investments' drawn from its revenues and calculated at prime costs only, amounted to £1.22 million (Romesh Dutt, *The Economic History of India under Early British Rule*, p. 263, drawing his table from Minutes of Evidence, & c., on the Affairs of the East India Company, 1813). This figure excluded 'private' drain, since that did not come formally out of the revenues. How, then, could the total drain in 1793 have amounted only to Rs 8.07 million (let us overlook Datta's 'lakhs' here), the equivalent of £0.8 million? Incidentally, Datta makes no attempt to reconcile his figures of the 'drain' with the size of it that the British customs house statistics divulge.

81. Siyaru'l Mutakhirin, litho., Lucknow, 1897, ii, pp. 836–7, 840–1.

82. Minute of 3 February 1790, *Fifth Report*, London, 1712–13, p. 493.

83. The data are taken from Romesh Dutt, *Economic History of India under Early British Rule*, pp. 46, 92–3. Let us now hear Rajat Datta on the subject: The fact that the total revenue did not 'even double' itself between 1755 and 1790, shows that the increase was 'moderate'. More, this 'modest (!) increase' justifies Grant's assertion that Bengal was 'under-assessed' *(Society, Economy and the Market*, pp. 334–5). The logic baffles one. An already over-assessed Bengal could have shown only a 'modest' increase, while an under-assessed Bengal could have better stood a much larger one. Datta does not, for that matter, make any reference to the criticisms of Grant's assertions of under-assessment made in Sir John Shore's minute of June 1789, printed in the *Fifth Report*.

84. Brij Narain, *Indian Economic Life, Past and Present*, Lahore, 1929, pp. 95–7, 100–2. Rajat Datta's treatment of prices, in which he curiously makes no mention of Brij Narain's important study, is biased by his anxiety to show that inflationary trends prevailed throughout the eighteenth century: a goal satisfactorily attained by him though drawing in his price graphs a straight single 'trend line' for the whole century *(Society, Economy and the Market*, pp. 77–9, 220–9). His graphs (based primarily on A.S.M. Akhtar Hussain's unpublished London thesis) actually tell a different story. The prices ascend until the 1760s, and then tend to decline, though there are great annual oscillations throughout. The trend indicated by Brij Narain's series is broadly confirmed here.

85. This too is disputed by Rajat Datta, who claims that the Company's exports of bullion to Bengal did not cease but simply went unreported for the entire period of forty years, 1757–97 *(Society Economy and the Market*, pp. 343–5). But see K.N. Chaudhuri's table 10.2B in *CEHI*, ii, p. 819, based on the Company's own account books, where the totals given prove that the amount of treasure exported to Bengal in 1758–9 and the succeeding two years was nil. The table does not cover subsequent years. No

bullion export to Bengal was reported in the following years as well, for the simple reason that there was none to report. A relative diminution of silver supply, which such a cessation was bound to create, was duly noted by contemporaries, against whose 'general feeling', Datta has nothing more substantial to urge than his own feelings (The *batta* on the Arcot rupee, tabulated on p. 349, is not relevant, since that rupee was also of silver, and silver constriction affected south as well as east India). In June 1789 Sir John Shore recognized in his famous minute that 'since the Company's acquisition of the Diwani (1765), the current specie of this country has been greatly diminished in quantity' and that 'its export [to China by the Company] will continue still further to exhaust the country of its silver' (*Fifth Report*, London, 1812–13, p. 183). Surely, he should have known.

86. Tract by James Steuart, London, 1772, cited by S. Bhattacharya, *CEHI*, II, p. 289. *The Ninth Report of the Select Committee, 1783*, also noted the monetary effects of Bengal's silver exports to China (K.N. Chaudhuri. *CEHI*, II, pp. 814–15).

87. Mohibbul Hasan, *Tipu Sultan*, p. 255.

88. Richard B. Barnett, *North India between Empires*, pp. 231–8.

89. W.S. Jevons's letter to the *Times*, 19 April, published by Sourin Roy in *IESHR*, IX (1), pp. 96–7.

90. *Rulers, Townsmen and Bazaars*, pp. 65–6. He does not, rather surprisingly, relate this 'money famine' to the stoppage of flow of bullion into India, to which he himself refers on p. 28.

91. The quotation is from Bayly, p. 462.

92. *Aspects of Indo–British Economic Relations, 1858–1898*, Bombay, 1982, pp. 207–14. Perhaps the only Asian country where the tribute relationship has had a longer history is Indonesia, from which the Dutch Company drew revenues for its investments from as early as the seventeenth century.

93. Cf. Bayly's chapter heading (*Rulers, Townsmen and Bazaars*, p. 229), with the only difference that he puts 'colonial economy' within single quotation marks.

PART II
THE POST-MUGHAL ORDER

5

Political Systems in Eighteenth-century India: The Banaras Region*

BERNARD S. COHN

The historical writing on the eighteenth century in India is dominated by three themes: the decline and final dissolution of the Mughal political system; the attempts by some of the regional powers to expand their power into imperial states; and the success of the British in becoming the heirs of the Mughal empire. These themes are played against a picture of 'anarchy and confusion, selfishness, cowardice and treachery, unpatriotic betrayals and horrible reigns of terror, the tyranny of the strong, the agony of the weak and the futility of isolated attempts.'[1] There has thus far been little attempt to get behind this sordid record to see how the political system of the period actually worked, what—if any—were the enduring structures of political relationships, how parts of the social systems involved were connected, and what principles guided not just personal endeavours but the organization and utilization of power and authority in the society of the time. In stating things in this fashion I am making a number of assumptions; assumptions which in the first instance are not only based on amassing information about 'politics' in a particular place at a particular time but are based on some general findings of social scientists about the nature of political structures and political activities in a wide range of societies known to us from history and ethnography.

I would state my assumptions as follows:

1. Political activities and political structures not only relate to centralized states with roles recognizable as kings, leaders, legislators, administrators

*B.S. Cohn: 'Political Systems in Eighteenth-century India: The Banaras Region', *Journal of the American Oriental Society*, lxxxii, July–Sept. 1962, pp. 312–19.

and citizens or institutions such as courts, tax offices, etc. but must be conceived in broader terms to encompass the whole process of formulation of demands, the determination of policy for the community, the carrying out of policies, the controlling of disruptive behaviour, and maintenance—through marshalling allegiance and support—of the political order and the identity of the political community. These activities and their associated structures, roles, and functions may be found at different levels of a society, ranging from kin-based villages or bands through associations, territorial organizations, up to readily identifiable states.[2]

2. In pre-modern societies, although some individual, family or group may be conceded absolute authority within the political system, power and authority are most frequently distributed among vertically or hierarchically ordered groups. The integrity of the larger groups, paradoxically, is usually maintained through internal conflict and competition among the groups in the society. No one group or individual, because of the nature of the value systems, the economy, technology, and the social structure, can dispense completely with other groups; and even though the leadership of a group may be destroyed, another competing group is put in its place or quickly arises to take the eliminated one's place. Consensus and balance are achieved through conflict and through the awareness that there are always other groups ready to step in. The systems to which I am referring seem to be perpetually on the verge of breaking apart.

3. Although these societies are segmentary in their structure, culturally there are often rituals, traditions, myths, and histories through which the political order is legitimized and maintained. These system-wide values set the common goals and provide a framework and set of ground rules through which the competing segments, both vertically and horizontally, are integrated into the political system.

LEVELS IN THE EIGHTEENTH-CENTURY POLITICAL SYSTEM

In eighteenth-century India it is possible analytically to differentiate four levels of the political system: the imperial, the secondary, the regional, and the local.

The Imperial

The Mughals, building on their predecessors, attempted in the sixteenth and seventeenth centuries to develop a system which would encompass almost the entire subcontinent. To attain this goal they tried to build an administration and army dependent on the throne. In addition, they were able to monopolize the symbols of legitimacy, so that even those groups at other levels—particularly in the eighteenth century—which were striving to free themselves of actual imperial control, nonetheless turned to the remnants of the imperial authority for legitimizing their power. In northern India at least, older Hindu theories and doctrines of political legitimacy seem to have been superseded by the Mughal doctrines.

The Secondary

With the dissolution of Mughal power, if not authority, there emerged successor states, such as Oudh or Bengal, the leadership of which was to some extent imperial in origin, which tried to exercise suzerainty over a major historical, cultural or linguistic region.

The Regional

The individual secondary systems were made up of groups of regional systems; these regional systems had at their heads individuals or families whose status, either as officials or as rulers, was granted to them by the imperial or secondary authority. These leaders were loosely incorporated through rituals of allegiance and financial obligation to the national power and were in competition with potential regional leaders.

The Local

The smallest political unit was represented by lineages, a successful adventurer, a local tax official turned political leader or indigenous chief. They were subordinate to the regional leader but they often derived their positions from the secondary authority. These lineages, families, or leaders directly controlled the local peasants, merchants, and artisans and collected from them cash or a share of the crop, in return for which they offered some protection from outside interference.

THE BANARAS REGION

The city of Banaras has long been a great shrine and civilizational centre; even during Muslim rule it was 'The chief seat of learning in Hindustan (to which) crowds of people flock from the most distant parts for the purpose of instruction.'[3] The region in which Banaras is found is part of the middle Ganges valley and is rich agricultural land. In the tenth, eleventh and twelfth centuries it was part of the Kanauj kingdom which fell to Sihabuddin. In the fourteenth and fifteenth centuries it was under the Sharqi kings who established their capital at Jaunpur, thirty-five miles north of Banaras. During this time Muslim noblemen and adventurers settled in parts of the rural area but seem never to have completely eliminated the hold on the land of semi-tribal groups of Soeris, Bhars and Cheros, who cleared and irrigated it. In the fifteenth century a new element, the Rajputs, locally termed Thakurs (lords), began to affect the internal structure of the region. The Rajputs gradually filtered into the region from the west. At first they came as individuals or families of adventurers who took service with local chieftains; but as more of their kin were attracted, they were gradually able to supplant the semi-tribal or Muslim local leaders, controllers of the land. These Rajputs grew in numbers and strength until at the time of Akbar (1556–1605), out of sixty-two *parganas* listed in *Ain-i-Akbari* of the Banaras region, over fifty were in the hands of Rajputs and only eight were in Muslim control.[4] The form and theory of Mughal administrative, political, military and judicial institutions have been well described; but little attention has thus far been paid to how these forms and theories worked, particularly at what I am terming the local and regional levels. Akbar and his successors tried to build administrations and armies which were imperial in their character and recruitment, but by the eighteenth century Mughal administration broke down and was replaced by a series of successor states based on different principles.

The remainder of this essay will be a description of what the political system in Banaras was like at the local and regional levels. The materials on which the description is based are largely manuscript records from the first years of British rule in the region, when—particularly in dealing with questions of land revenue—the British collected some materials on pre-British political and economic conditions.

THE RAJA OF BANARAS

The essay takes as its focus the relationships of the Raja of Banaras with his superior, the Nawab of Oudh, and his subordinates, the Rajput lineages (usually called brotherhoods in the documents), local chiefs or rajas, and other groups (such as merchants and bankers), all of whom exercised political functions as defined above.

The rise of the Bhumihar family from whom the Rajas of Banaras come is a typical eighteenth-century story. Mansa Ram, the father of the first raja of Banaras, was one of four brothers whose father controlled a few hundred *bigha*s in a village in Jaunpur district. Mansa Ram worked for the local *amil* (tax collector), gained his confidence, and represented this *amil* at the court

of Mir Rustum Ali, who administered the four districts of the Banaras province under Saadat Khan, Nawab Vazir of Oudh. Here he gained the confidence of Mir Rustum Ali, and Mansa Ram displaced his employer the *amil*
and became, in turn, an *amil*. Mansa Ram proved to be a successful tax farmer.
When Saadat Khan died in 1739 Mansa Ram, through lavish presents and the
promise of paying to Safdar Jang (Saadat Khan's nephew and successor) an
enhanced revenue, obtained a *sanad* (royal grant) for his son Balwant Singh
which made the latter Raja of Banaras and zamindar of the three districts of
Banaras, Jaunpur, and Mirzapur.[5]

There are, of course, few words in use in the literature on India which cause
as much confusion as 'zamindar', which today we usually take to mean landlord; someone who owns the land and may transfer his rights on the land
through sale or inheritance. This meaning of zamindar is largely the result of
administrative and legislative action of the last 150 years. In the eighteenth
century zamindars were, to use Moreland's phrase, intermediaries. They
could be, as was Balwant Singh in 1740, a person charged with collecting and
forwarding a stated amount of revenue from other intermediaries. Balwant
Singh was not a sovereign as we know it in European history. Some phases
of government were in the hands of the nawab, or even still in the hands of
the emperor. There were imperial forts at Chunar and Jaunpur manned by imperial troops and troops of the nawab.[6] Important legal and administrative
officers within the zamindari, such as the *kotwal* and *kazi* of the principal
towns, were appointees of the nawab. The minting of coins was in the hands
of the nawab.

The subordination of the raja can clearly be seen at the succession of Chait
Singh after the death of Balwant Singh. It took the intervention of Warren
Hastings to force Suja-ud-daula, the then Nawab of Oudh, to 'confer upon
Chait Singh the zamindari and honors of the late raja'.[7] Chait Singh 'performed
the duties of vassalage by presents of money, elephants, and clothes'.[8] The
Nawab of Oudh tied his turban on Chait Singh's head and presented him with
a sword,[9] symbolizing his acceptance of Chait Singh as his subordinate. The
raja's obligations to the nawabs were the regular payment of revenue and provision of troops when requested. The Raja of Banaras, at every opportunity,
tried to avoid fulfillment of these obligations; and on several occasions the
nawab sent troops to try to bring his subordinate to terms, if not to capture and
kill him. On these occasions Balwant Singh would retreat with his treasure
and army to the jungles of Mirzapur. After a time the nawab, distracted by
similar behaviour in other parts of his state or by his intervention in imperial
politics, would compromise with Balwant Singh and withdraw, at which time
Balwant Singh would resume his control of the zamindari.

Evidently the nawabs could not replace Balwant Singh as there was no one else in the zamindari or outside strong enough to defeat him and to assure even the irregular payment of the revenue. A balancing of relative weakness appears to have been central to the functioning of the system. The nawab could not afford the complete chaos which would result from the crushing of the raja. On occasion the raja could be forced into paying some revenue and providing some troops to support activities of the nawab.

On the raja's side was the need for legitimacy. Even after crushing the Monas Rajputs, who held their land under a *sanad* from Shahjahan, the raja could not fully appropriate their land until the conquest was legitimized by Suja-ud-daula.[10] Power the raja had; but he needed authority as well. Even though the rajas' goal in relation to the nawabs was a consistent one of independence, they could not afford to ignore the ground rules and had to continue to seek the sanction, even if it was ex post facto, of their superordinates, the nawabs. Another check on the rajas' ambition of independence and sovereignty was their battle against political groups within the zamindari, whom they could not crush completely as the raja's army and treasury depended to some extent on the local groups remaining strong enough to collect taxes from the cultivators.

LOCAL POLITICAL STRUCTURES

There were three main types of political structures or 'little kingdoms': rajadoms, *jagir*s and *taluka*s. The taluka is the territory controlled by a lineage of agnatically related kin of the same *biradari* (exogamous local caste group). In the English documents of the late eighteenth and early nineteenth centuries there is some confusion in terminology, and it would be well to examine the meaning of three words, *taluka, tappa*, and *pargana*. All were used to refer to administrative and revenue subdivisions of *zila* or districts. *Pargana*s were revenue subdivisions, often of some antiquity, but were not based on long-standing sociological grounds. They were units of administration and revenue, the officers of which were appointees by some regional, national, or imperial power. *Tappa*s and *taluka*, on the other hand, represented local sociological and political groupings. When the word *taluka* appears in the original revenue settlement records which have been preserved from Jonathan Duncan's settlement of 1788–9 and when there is any context given of the nature of the unit being discussed, invariable reference is made to descendants of one family, brotherhoods or brethren. For example:

Hunter is a Talookah of seven villages . . . all the zemindars are brethern.[11]

Rissoolpoor was formerly a Talookah comprising sixteen villages . . . The zamindars of this talookah are all brethren being descended from one family.[12]

The word *tappa* is sometimes used for the territory of a lineage and sometimes refers to the home territory of a lineage, as well as the lands which the lineage may have conquered from other lineages and in which the tax structure is different. It sometimes refers to the lands of one lineage plus other lands which for taxation purposes are lumped together into one *tappa*. F. Newnham, a member of the Central Board of Revenue in the North-West Provinces, stated in 1822: 'A tuppeh is an official division of the country which has no allusion to proprietary or zemindary rights.'[13] I take the word *taluka* to mean a unit with a social, economic, and political integrity; one in which a lineage controlled the land. The words 'control the land' mean that all other groups within the territory owed an obligation to the members of the dominant lineage to provide part of the harvest if they were tillers of the soil; pay a cash tax if they were merchants; and to provide goods and services if they were artisans or serving castes. The controlling lineage provided priests and fakirs with *mafi* or revenue-free lands. The controlling lineage in turn was responsible for the payment of revenue to the *amils* (tax collectors) or directly to the raja. The controlling lineage also had a military obligation to provide troops for the raja. These troops appear to have been members of the *biradari* and their followers.

There appears to have been a wide range of internal arrangements of the lineages. Some of the more powerful, controlling upwards of one hundred villages, had all the members of the lineage living in one fortified town (such as Baragoan in Chit–Ferozpur in Ballia) while the villages were occupied by cultivators and artisans. In others the members of the dominant lineage were dispersed among the villages, but even in these instances there was a *taluka* mud fort or fortified town which was the centre of the lineage. Some appear to have been completely acephalous; others had *chaudharis* or leading men of the sections of the lineages. R.M. Bird, who was a judge successively in Benaras, Ghazipur, and Mirzapur from 1812 to 1820, Commissioner of Gorakhpur division from 1829 to 1832, member of the Board of Revenue of the North-West Province from 1833 to 1841 (during which time he supervised the settlement of revenue of the province), and who—more than any official of his time—understood the nature of the social structures in Banaras, commented in 1831:

Originally in the Rajput common tenancies, all matters affecting the general estate were decided upon by the united will of the majority . . . there is every reason to believe that before the British accession, the persons who should engage with the government were chosen by the consent or the vote of the majority of all the brotherhood and were the mere representatives of the federated voice.[14]

Some of the lineages physically divided the lands which were their *taluka*, others divided only their share of the produce, keeping the land together. No matter what was shared, the principle of sharing was based genealogically, each line of descendants from the common ancestor being followed out and each adult male member of the lineage receiving his share on the basis of descent. The lineages often combined to fight off threats from neighbouring lineages, from the Raja of Banaras, or later from the British.[15] Though they were able often to combine for concerted action against outside threats, this does not mean that feud and conflict were not part of the internal political structure. In speaking of the Sengar Rajputs of Lakhnessar, Jonathan Duncan, Resident in Banaras 1788–95, stated:

Each landholder has been in the habit of turning his house into a stronghold, and the animosities that have sprung up among their different families are left to spread and rankle without question or check on the part of government.[16]

Duncan had to investigate feuds, one of which had gone on for at least fifteen years, in which the protagonists were ambushing and killing children and low-caste dependants of the feuding households.[17]

The Raja of Banaras' aim was the downgrading of the brotherhoods from their status as zamindars, i.e. having the right to engage directly with the raja for the payment of revenue, to a status in which their revenue was assessed and paid to his officials and in which the members of the brotherhoods became like other *asamis*, tax payers. The rajas were successful in most of the district of Banaras and parts of Mirzapur and Jaunpur, but had little success in most of Ghazipur Ballia.

Structurally, the degradation or elimination of the lineages was difficult given the numbers of lineage mates and the pre-existing diffusion of power within the *taluka*s. Even though the raja might destroy the forts of the lineages, it was almost impossible to completely destroy the web of allegiances of cultivators to the dominant lineage. The raja's administration and army were not strong enough to collect revenue directly from each cultivator. The success in Banaras and Mirzapur reflects the fact that this was the centre of the raja's own army and he could exert more continuous pressure on the brotherhoods, whereas at best he could only raid other parts of the zamindari. In his efforts to eliminate internal opposition, he could not so weaken his source of local military levies or regularity of income to crush lineages entirely.

THE RAJA OF BANARAS AND
THE RAJADOMS

The rajadoms and the *jagir*s differed from the *taluka*s in one major structural feature; there was an acknowledged head, the raja. Inheritance of control of the land passed on in one family, and in this one family to only one person at a time, usually the eldest son of the previous raja, who was recognised as the raja. The local raja stood in roughly the same relationship to other residents of the small kingdom and to the Raja of Banaras as did the lineage in the *taluka*. The raja paid the revenue due from the small kingdom directly to the Raja of Banaras or sometimes directly to the Nawab of Oudh. Often the raja's right to rule his small kingdom was based on a royal grant from the imperial power. The principal rajadoms were found on the frontier of the Banaras province, to the south in the jungle of Mirzapur, to the east on the border of Bihar, and in the north-west on the border of Oudh. The border in the south in Mirzapur represents a natural boundary between the Ganges valley and the hilly tracts of central India. Here there was a marked difference between a tribal population and their Rajput rulers. The other rajadoms, although founded on what may have been old linguistic and political boundaries, do not have the difference in population between tribal and non-tribal. In several of the rajadoms the lineage of the raja differs from the lineage and clan of the bulk of Rajputs in the kingdom. For example, Saltanat Singh, Raja of Badlapur, was a *rajkumar*, while in his kingdom the bulk of the Rajputs were Bisen, Bachgotis, Bais, and Monas.[18] This leads to the speculation that the rajadoms may represent a conquest state of some type.

The rajas, in addition to their tax collecting activities, had a developmental function as well. The Raja of Bijaighar in Mirzapur directed the clearing of jungle, the settling of new cultivators, the construction of irrigation facilities, and introduced the production of silk.[19] The Raja of Bijaighar had direct judicial functions as well. The *jagir*s, like the rajadoms, often had a single head rather than a corporate body or lineage as the dominant internal political power, but the *jagir* was usually held as a revenue free holding, the state's share of the produce or the revenue going to the *jagirdar*. The *jagir*s were granted by imperial, secondary, or regional power in lieu of pay for officials or as a special mark of reward and favour. For example, Ausan Singh, Balwant Singh's *diwan* (head administrator), received two-thirds of Pargana Saidpur Bhitri as his *jagir*.[20] Allup Singh, who was a high cavalry officer in Balwant Singh's army, had a *jagir* of six large villages in Jaunpur district, which were worth 4627 rupees a year. *Jagir*s were usually not granted in perpetuity, particularly those granted to officials as salaries. For residents in the *jagir*s, the *jagirdar* stood in the same relation as did the raja to his subjects. The *jagirdar* received the revenue from the cultivator or the managers of the cultivators.

Balwant Singh made no direct attack on any of the rajas until 1748, when availing himself of the divisions between the Monas Raja of Bhadohi and his non-royal lineage mates, Balwant Singh was able to take the pargana of

Bhadohi away from the Monas raja. In the next five years he successively eliminated the rajas of Bijaighar, Agori, Kantit, and Haldi.[21] These conquests gave Balwant Singh possession of important forts on the Ganges and in the jungles of Mirzapur. From these he controlled the southern half of the zamindari; and Lutefpur and Bijaighar gave him almost impregnable places of retreat, in which, on several occasions, he held out against the Nawabs of Oudh.[22] In many respects it would have appeared to have been easier to dispossess the rajas and take under direct government the territories of the rajas rather than the lineage dominated talukas. The raja could more easily capitalize on the intrigue in a family of Rajputs than a lineage, with its multiplicity of cross-cutting allegiances.[23] Given the fact that the rajadoms often contained different lineages of Rajputs, some of whom may have been partially dispossessed by the raja's families, there may not have been the solidarity in the face of outside threat which sometimes characterized the talukas. After dispossession of the raja and his family, others in the rajadom could be expected to be easier to control as they essentially had not lost too much by the change of masters. They now paid their revenue to an amil of the Raja of Banaras instead of their former raja.

I have written elsewhere about the officials who were the administrators of the Nawab of Oudh, the Raja of Banaras, and the local rajas.[24] Some of the secondary administrators, kazis, kotwals, pargana sarrishtadars, functioned at the regional and local levels and represented a check that the nawab maintained over the actions of the Raja of Banaras. These officials were hinges by which the levels of the political system were connected. The raja's officials, mainly the amils, tended to be tax farmers whose origins were as local adventurers, bankers, caste-mates of the rajas, or secondary or imperial officials who took service with him as means of making a quick fortune.

The raja's main concern with his domination was the assessment and collection of revenue. The amils (tax farmers) obligated themselves to pay a stipulated amount into the raja's treasury every month which they were to collect from a pargana. The amil did not collect the revenue directly from the actual cultivator but rather from representatives of lineages or from one or two persons in a village who claimed to be superior through wealth, caste, or family to others in the village. The revenue was collected in cash and in kind, the mode of collection depending on the crop, local tradition, and availability of cash and credit. I have found no way of estimating how much of the zamindari was assessed in cash and how much in kind. Payment from the amil into the raja's treasury was in cash. Collection of revenue in cash placed the bankers of Banaras and Mirzapur in an important position politically as well as economically. As Jonathan Duncan commented:

The *schroffs* or bankers could in fact in a great measure command the Raja and the government itself with respect to the realization of revenue. The custom being for *kist* (revenue installment) to be raised not in cash but by their (i.e. the bankers) *dakhillas* or notes payable in a certain number of days from the dates thereof; and as the renters (i.e. the *amils*) are generally in arrears to them, they, of course, exact their own terms from the latter for the dakhillas.[25]

Thus far I have spoken of the society of the Banaras region as if it were composed only of agricultural people and the political leaders who controlled them, but in the eighteenth century Banaras was an important trade region. There were several important cities, not the least of which was Banaras itself. Banaras probably had a population of over 150,000 at this time; and Mirzapur, Jaunpur and Ghazipur had populations of at least 10,000 each. There is little in the records directly about the political structure and government of these towns and cities.

Maintenance of law and order in Banaras itself seems to have been in a very crude state. Hastings believed that the thieves in Banaras were regularly licensed and part of their booty was given to the raja.[26] Francis Fowke remarked that the officers in charge of the Banaras courts 'held the office as a kind of private property'.[27]

The Mughal system of maintaining a clerk of the market who supervised the accuracy of weights and measures and maintained the streets and facilities of the bazaar had almost disappeared.[28] Water supplies were polluted, and there was no municipal system of sewage or garbage removal. Even the great sacred tanks near the temples were the repository for all the filth from nearby sections.[29]

The city of Banaras was divided into *mohulla*s or wards, the populations of which were usually of one caste or trade. These wards had gates which could be shut at night.[30]

It may be conjectured that in the eighteenth century much of what we think of as urban government was in the hands of the castes which made up the population of the city. The 'House Tax Hartal' of 1810 showed the strength of these institutions when all economic activity in the city ceased. J.R. Erskine, who had served in Banaras, described the *hartal* as follows:

Between twenty and thirty thousand of the inhabitants of that city (Banaras) consisting of all ranks and descriptions relinquished their occupations, abandoned their dwellings, and assembled in the open fields. Instead of appearing like a tumultuous and disorderly mob, the vast multitude came forth in a state of perfect organization; each caste, trade and profession occupied a distinct spot of ground, and was regulated in all its acts by the orders of its own punchayet, who invariably punished all instance of misconduct and disobedience on the part of any of its members. This state of things continued for more than a month; and whilst the authority of the British Government was, in a manner, suspended, the influence of the punchayet was sufficient to maintain the greatest order and tranquility.[31]

Unfortunately, I know little of the structure of particular caste panchayats or the interrelations of the caste panchayats. It is significant to note that in this same *hartal* there is evidence of connection between the caste panchayats of the city of Banaras and their caste fellows in the countryside. The Lohars are noted in the documents as having one leader for both urban and rural Lohars.[32] I have no similar evidence from the eighteenth or early nineteenth century on the role of caste panchayats in the local political system in the rural area; but I assume, as I have done elsewhere, that it was of considerable importance in judicial matters.[33]

NOTES AND REFERENCES

1. N.K. Sinha, *Rise of Sikh Power*, Calcutta, 1946, p. 1.
2. David Easton, 'Political Anthropology', in Bernard J. Siegal (ed.), *Biennial Review of Anthropology*, Stanford, 1959, pp. 210–62.
3. Abul Fazl-i-Allami, *Ain-i-Akbari*, vol. II, trans. H.S. Jarrett, 2nd edn, Calcutta, 1949, pp. 169–70.
4. Ibid., pp. 174–6.
5. Wilton Oldham, *Memoir of the Ghazipur District*, pt I, Allahabad, 1870, pp. 88–91, 100–1; A.L. Srivastava, *The First Two Nawabs of Oudh*, 2nd edn, Agra, 1954, p. 42; Allahabad Central Record Office, *Duncan Records*, basta 8, vol. 46, 'The Raja of Banares Family'; Imperial Record office, *Persian Correspondence*, vol. V, Calcutta, 1930, p. 306.
6. A.F.S. de Cosson, 'Chunar', *Bengal Past and Present*, vol. IV, 1909, pp. 413–19; D.L. Drake-Brockman, *Mirzapur: A Gazetteer*, U.P. District Gazetteers, vol. XXVII, Allahabad, 1911, p. 307; India Office Library, *Bengal Civil Judicial Proceedings*, 16 Dec. 1796, #40, 'Representation from the Merchants of Chunar'.
7. India Office Library, *Home Miscellaneous Series*, vol. 201 (1), p. 79, Hastings to Chyte Singh 14 Sept. 1770.
8. Ibid., vol. 202, 'Letter from Chyte Singh received Dec. 1770', p. 139.
9. Ibid., vol. 203, 'Letter from Chyte Singh received 6 Mar. 1771', p. 34.
10. Allahabad Central Record Office, *Records Relating to the Family Domains of the Maharaja of Benares*, 1, I, basta 97c, vol. 190 (4), W.W. Bird's Report on Pergunnah Bhudohee, 25 May 1827.
11. Allahabad Central Record Office, *Benares Commissioner's Office*, Register of Settlement 1197–1206', basta 47, vol. 134, p. 121.
12. Ibid., p. 125. See also, pp. 28, 119, 1569 for similar statements.
13. Quoted in Wilton Oldham, *Tenant Rights and Auction Sales in Benares*, Dublin, 1873, p. 24.

14. Allahabad Central Records Office, *Benares Commissioner's Office, Miscellaneous Revenue Files*, basta 102A, vol. 2, 'Circulars', 'Extract Paragraphs four to fifteen from Commissioner Bird's letter of 4 June 1831 . . .', pp. 84–6, paras 5 and 6.

15. For example, the Sengar Rajputs of Lakhnesar in Ballia. India Office Library. Bengal Revenue Proceedings, vol. 32, Consultation of 18 Feb. 1798, J. Duncan to Cornwallis, LS 1 Feb. 1789; India Office Library, *Bengal Board of Revenue Proceedings*, vol. 52, Consultation of 3 Sept. 1799 #40, Routledge to Cowper, LS 20 Aug. 1799; Allahabad Central Record Office, *Benares Commissioner's Office, Miscellaneous Revenue Series*, Basta 98, vol. i, J. Rider to A. Duncan, 18 Jan. 1796.

16. Duncan to Cornwallis, 1 Feb. 1789.

17. Ibid., Enclosure in letter of 1 Feb. 1789, 'Extract from the Proceedings of the Resident of Benares, 17 Nov. 1788'.

18. Aditya Narain Singh, *Biography of Saltanat Bahadur Singh, Talukadar of Badlapur*, MS 1952–3 (Hindi).

19. Allahabad Central Record Office, *Resident's proceedings*, vol. 29, Mar. 1790, 'Proceedings 25 Mar. 1790, "Translation of a Representation from the Canongoe of the Purgannah of Agoure and Beijur, Together with the Zemindars Answer Thereto".'

20. Allahabad Central Record Office, Ghazipur Collectorate, *Copies of Miscellaneous Correspondence 1825–1831*, 'Petition of the Zamindars of Sydpor Bhitri.'

21. *Benares Commissioner's Office, Resident's Proceedings*, Basta #21, vol. #6. Proceedings of 9 May 1788, 'Translation of Omrow Singh's Report on the Date of Dispossession of Sundry of the farmers and landholders of the Districts now comprising these parts'; *Mirzapur Collectorate, Pre-Mutiny Records*, vol. 228, file #1, 'Papers Relating to the Tenure of the Raja of Bijaighar, 1820–1849'; Oldham, p. 100.

22. William Hodges, *Select Views in India*, London, 1786, 'Views of the Forts of Lutterfpoor and Bidijegur'.

23. Allahabad Central Record Office, *Benares Commissioner's Office, Resident's Proceedings*, basta 37, vol. 72, Oct. 1793. Proceedings 16 Oct. 1793, 'Letter from Capt. Denby'; *Duncan Records*, basta 4, vol. 23, Apr. 1789. Duncan to Gov. Gen., LS, 26 Apr. 1789, for examples of factions in raja of Badlapur's family.

24. Bernard S. Cohn, 'The Initial British Impact on India: A Case Study of the Benares Region'.

25. India Office Library, *Bengal Revenue Proceedings*, vol. 25, Consultation, 3 Oct. 1788, Duncan to Gov. Gen., LS 12 Sept. 1788.

26. India Office Library, *Home Miscellaneous Series*, vol. 201 (1), Hastings to Balwant Singh, 14 July 1770, p. 62.

27. India Office Library, *Bengal Secret Consultations*, vol. 32, Consultation 13 Dec. 1775. Fowke to Hastings 16 Nov. 1775.

28. Allahabad Central Record Office, *Benares Commissioner's Office, Resident's Proceedings*, basta #28, vol. 32 Proceedings, 8 July 1790, 'Reports of the Magistrates about the Weights used in their Jurisdictions.'

29. Ibid., Proceedings, 26 July 1790, 'Remarks on the Town of Benares by F. Wilford, Surveyor.'

30. Allahabad Central Record Office, *Benares Collector's Office, Judicial Letters Issued and Received*, basta ii, vol. 10 to H.C. Tucker from F.B. Gubbins, n.d.

31. *Selections of Papers from the Records of the East India House Relative to Revenue*, Police and Civil and Criminal Justice, vol. II, London, 1820, p. 88.

32. Allahabad Central Record Office, *Benaras Commissioner's Office, Benares Revenue Files*, vol. 118, File #1951. W.O. Solmon to M. Moore, 4 Jan. 1811.

33. See Bernard S. Cohn, 'Some Notes on Law and Change in North India,' *Economic Development and Cultural Change*, vol. VIII, #1, 1959, pp. 79–93.

6

The Rise of the Corporations*

C.A. BAYLY

Indian society is so complex that any unqualified exposition of historical trends must be superficial, and any deeper one will become enmeshed in paradox. The outstanding paradox of the eighteenth century was the coexistence of areas of local prosperity with political turbulence and agricultural decline. This at least is partly resolved by attending carefully to geography, and to different levels of power and production. But there remain the more serious difficulties of understanding the quality of the changes which were taking place. Was there simply a redistribution of men and resources between one place and another, with new actors filling old roles? Or was society undergoing a deeper transformation? With work on indigenous archives only just beginning, it is far too early to say. But in two senses, it already appears that more was going on than the time-honoured ouster of old élites by new men and the perpetual motion of dynast following dynast.

First, money had become a crucial component of agrarian relations in the

*C.A. Bayly, 'The Rise of the Corporations', in *Rulers, Townsmen and Bazaars: North Indian Society in the Age of British Expansion, 1770–1870*, Cambridge, 1983, pp. 163–96.

The word 'corporation' (often translating Hindi *sabha*) is used here to mean an occupational or religious organization which transcended the bounds of 'caste' in the sense of *jati*. It would therefore include commercial or priestly associations (*sarrafas*; *mahajans* in the sense used in Gujerat; Brahmin *sabhas* called 'colleges' by European observers), as well as certain types of ascetic *akharas* and other *sampradayan* which integrated urban or rural society and acted as self-regulating entities *de facto*. My usage differs from that of B. Stein, *Peasant State and Society in Medieval South India* (Delhi, 1980), who applies the term to single-caste groups of rural people. The point that such groups needed to be 'incorporated' through temple ritual before their status was secure (Appadurai and Breckenridge, *IESHR*, xiii, 1976) is well taken. But my concern here is with the fact that Indian society could produce dynamic, multi-caste institutions in the context of growing monetization and the weakening of central state power. It was this tendency which was overlooked by Max Weber and other theorists.

more stable tracts. This does not mean that the free market was breaking down old dominances based on force or caste rank. Rather, relationships of power between man and man, village and village, were reinforced and modified by control of cash. Rulers, warriors, and village headmen needed silver rupees, and this caused them to admit men of commerce to a small share of power or to step into the ring as lenders and traders themselves. In the eastern districts especially, the power of the dominant agricultural castes was supported by networks of trade and credit before the end of the eighteenth century.

Secondly, beneath the flux of the regional courts and the great households of their revenue-farmers, more stable patterns of local power were slowly being precipitated between the state and agrarian society. There emerged a unified merchant class wielding covert political power, and a locally resident gentry of literate service families. The concern of this chapter is with the organization and influence of the merchants. But the Islamic gentry provide a useful comparative example of a pre-colonial class which continued to evolve in colonial north India. Both groups, for instance, tended to benefit from the farming-out to great magnates of the government revenue—a practice which became a pervasive feature of the successor regimes.

REVENUE-FARMERS AND ENTREPRENEURS IN THE AGRARIAN SYSTEM

Money slowly penetrated Indian rural society over many centuries. Even at its height, the Mughal military bureaucracy had always been uncomfortably closely tied into commercial networks and dependent on local gentry managers and chamberlains. High Mughal officials in Bengal and south India during the seventeenth century had owned ships, while 'local governors seem in practice to have been free to enter the market on their own initiative'.[1] Holders of revenue assignments posted at a great distance from their assigned lands could hardly have managed them without leaving a great deal of initiative to local men who were skilled at financial management and understood the marketing of produce.[2] Nevertheless, the breakdown of the system of state revenue assignments after 1707 gave rise to a situation in which more and more of the revenue was being farmed out to notables on the basis of cash payments. The beauty of such a system for the new regional rulers and last Mughal viceroys was that it provided a known and regular source of income without the problems of local collection. This was important at a time when rulers had to employ increasingly expensive armies requiring regular cash payments.

The farming of state revenue on one, two, or three year leases appears to have become common in northern India between Rajasthan and Bengal before 1740.[3] But in Benares and Awadh, it was extended to practically all the ruler's ancient taxation rights between 1740 and 1780. Local enterprise capital was involved in the form of duties on transit, toll, ferry, and bazaar duties,[4] besides those on the trade in betel nuts,[5] dressed stone, wood and bamboo, etc.[6] The Gosain traders paid special rates on their transit goods through Benares; and even this tax was farmed out, possibly as a concession to their religious status,[7] possibly in recognition of the difficulty in collecting it from them.

The men who could mobilize capital on a scale large enough to speculate on farms of revenue or state commercial duties were the century's most obvious entrepreneurs. The greatest of them were few in number: the main revenue-farmers in Awadh in 1770 amounted to some fifteen men;[8] in Benares, around thirty-six.[9] Their manner may have echoed the high officials of Mughal times, but their social origins would not have graced the court of Aurangzeb. The two men who controlled up to 60 per cent of the Awadh revenue were respectively a eunuch of Jat origin (Almas Ali Khan) and a Hindu raja scarcely removed from his rustic background (Bhawani Singh). In Benares, too, the old Muslim revenue-farmers had been ousted by aspiring rural Brahmins connected with the raja along with assorted men of commerce.

These warrior–entrepreneurs worked portfolios of revenue-farms, trading ventures, and military supplies through the mechanism of great households, like the Mughal *mansabdars* before them. Many could raise (or thought they could raise) up to five or ten lakhs of rupees annually to finance their farms. Alongside them there were other less wealthy and prominent operators working quietly in the petty darbar halls. Some of the mercenary captains who fitted out and sold their troops to the highest bidder should really be seen as entrepreneurs. Then there were a variety of monopoly farmers, military contractors, and general factotums, such as Shankar Pandit[10] and Beni Ram Pandit,[11] who worked the Benares opium and sugar monopolies respectively for both raja and English Company. Men like this were found in all the smaller states.

The revenue-farmers and enterprisers were not themselves a social class but a group of over-mighty subjects who reflected the adaptation of governments to the problems of cash flow in an uncertain economic climate. They represented a successful conjunction of agrarian might and capital, often buttressed with military force. But straddling the agrarian and commercial worlds, these colossi were vulnerable to groups better entrenched in both. Few revenue-farmers started with sufficiently detailed control over rural resources or sufficient entrée into the markets to survive the loss of government favour. Some, like Sheo Lal Dube, Bernard Cohn's archetype of a 'new man', were able to transform themselves into local magnates and survive into the British period as zamindars.[12] But many like Mir Amjad of Jaunpur failed to coerce intractable village communities, fell into arrears, and disappeared from the scene;[13] or being fine-weather favourites or eunuchs, failed to father their own lineages.

More significant for the future were the social groups which subsisted beneath and even supported the revenue machinery of the regional rulers and the revenue-farmers. For Awadh, Barnett has argued that revenue-farming benefited 'local networks' of power[14] to whom much of the revenue percolated in the form of fees and expenses. One can point, for instance, to the rich commercial farmers and traders of Baiswara who were able to entrench their position under nawabi management.[15] Similarly, the more obscure Muslim and Kayasth élites of the small towns of the Doab and western Awadh benefited as under-managers and collectors for Almas Ali Khan.[16] Within twenty years of his death, this great revenue-farmer survived only in legend, but his clients among the Kayasths of Hathgaon in Fatehpur or the Sayyids of Unao had perpetuated their influence as local gentry and service people around their small towns.[17]

For Benares, Jonathan Duncan's settlement records, reflecting the working of immediate pre-colonial society, give us a more detailed view of the men of capital and local power who subsisted in fractious alliance with the revenue-farmers in the last few years before the Permanent Settlement was introduced into the tract in 1793. Here also, the revenue-farmers were more successful if they could patronize specialist low caste cultivators, but virtually impotent when they came up against powerful joint bodies of village zamindars who might throw up their cultivation if they could not get the terms they desired. Here, too, gentry under-managers (though often Brahmins and Kayasths rather than Muslims) consolidated local power under the aegis of the revenue-farmers. But what is most notable is the extent to which the revenue system was penetrated and constrained by the commercial classes at every level. Even in the parts of the Benares province where the primitive form of assessment in kind still prevailed, village traders and moneylenders played an important part, and the revenue-farmers needed to keep good relations with them in order to sell their portion of the crop for ready cash.[18] From time to time, there were conflicts between the two parties when the revenue-farmers attempted forced sales of old or bad grain for high cash prices. Cash revenue-payment by the cultivators themselves was, however, becoming the norm. This avoided conflict with the traders, and besides, revenue-farmers could not risk falling into arrears when grain prices were low and they were unable to sell their portion at a profit. Cash revenue, on the other hand, tended to put the village élite into uncomfortable dependence on the merchant-moneylenders. So in 1787, we find the zamindars of Karinda complaining that the revenue-farmers had forced a money settlement on them, 'as by reason of the low price of grain, the value of that produce in all the parts of the pergunneh was less than usual, the amil [farmer] told us to enter into cabooleats (or engagements) for a ready-money settlement'.[19]

The existence of a 'money settlement' tended to drive the tendrils of big urban moneylenders deeper into the countryside and reinforce the connection between them and the village traders and shopkeepers (*bakkals*) who had emerged from general agricultural growth. The urban financiers were the men who advanced money to the revenue-farmers and stood as sureties (*malzamins*), or even double-sureties for them with the rulers for punctual payment.[20] In the case of money settlements, a local agent of the banking house accompanied the agent of the revenue-farmer in making the collections from the village zamindars, for 'It was established custom that the person who issued the revenue advances had his treasurer in the pergunnehs.'[21] These local agents generally appear to have been village shopkeepers linked by trading connection, and sometimes by caste, with the big merchants of the city. For instance, the under-collectors for Sheo Lal Dube, the Jaunpur farmer, carried out money transactions 'through the banker who had the money collections of the village',[22] while in the district of Chunar, villagers had always paid their revenue through the agency of the local shopkeepers.[23]

Besides having a hand in revenue collection at village level, traders and moneylenders also controlled the transactions between the subdivisional headquarters and Benares itself. The commercial families changed local coin into Benares *sicca* rupees and avoided the dangerous business of transporting treasure across open country by drawing credit notes on their correspondents in the city. The added security given by this system encouraged the early British Residents to get the bankers to extend their branch agencies in the countryside as quickly as possible. In the case of the few commercial men who openly became revenue-farmers themselves, the advantage of being able to work through their own system of branch agencies partly outweighed the disadvantage of being involved in an area where prudent bankers did not tread. For instance, Sheo Lal Dube was able to set up local branches of his own firm 'Sheo Lal Dube Bunder Dube' for his revenue-farm of the Jaunpur District.[24]

Finally, and at the very pinnacle of the revenue system, the commercial houses made huge temporary loans against the incoming revenue to the raja himself. These promissory notes or *dakhillas* were considered as good as ready coin in the bazaar. Without them, the raja was unable to pay his troops, remit his tribute to the British, or maintain his ceremonial and religious functions in the realm. Thus, fifteen large Lucknow and Benares banking houses handled the whole 40 lakhs of rupees of the Benares revenue in the years 1760–80, taking on it a service fee which appears to have amounted to 2½ per cent or more.[25] Naturally, this gave them very considerable political power. In 1776 the Resident stated that the great Agarwal house of Bhaiaram provided the main obstacle to the consolidation of his influence in the principality,[26] while in 1787, Jonathan Duncan acknowledged that the bankers could 'in a great measure command the Raja and Government, itself with respect to the realization of the revenue'.[27]

In Benares commercial men appear to have made even deeper inroads into agrarian society from time to time. The machinations of the powerful British Residents evidently encouraged their connections among the Indian trading firms to take a more direct role in revenue management. But it was also in the interest of the banking houses themselves to exert closer control when there was a danger that the revenue-farmers might default. In the late 1770s, the banker Kashmiri Mull appears to have taken the revenue-farm for fourteen *parganas* of the Jaunpur and Ghazipur Districts 'in partnership' with one of the royal princes.[28] Other commercial men were also covertly engaged in direct management. But this was a dangerous business, for a banker's commercial credit might suffer if he was too openly involved in government. When asked to become a revenue-farmer, Kashmiri Mull had represented that,

My business was that of a mehajen or banker and that partnership was not my business in consequence of which the Raja taking the Ganga or Ganges and the Deity Beeshesher [Visheshwar] between us declared that this secret should not be revealed to anyone.[29]

Resistance to the involvement of 'professed bankers' in revenue matters was also found amongst the landed magnates. 'Dobey is a banker, what has he to do with public matters?'[30] complained an outraged Jaunpur Rajput as the great banker wove his net across the district. Again 'what foolish malzamin [surety] would take the balances [of a revenue-farm]?' said the disingenuous master of the Benares mint, Kaun Das, who had been involved in the revenue management of the failed farmer Kulb Ali in 1787.[31] So deeply had the control to the men of commerce penetrated that Kulb Ali repaid his debts to them before he satisfied the state itself;[32] it took all the influence of Jonathan Duncan and the rising power of the East India Company to recover the money from the commercial corporations of the city.[33]

MERCHANTS AND THE POLITICAL ECONOMY

The key advantage possessed by the eighteenth-century commercial groups was their ability to command resources across much greater distances than the smaller states with which they dealt. The formal system of official control over the economy was impressive enough. The ruler set the daily price of commodities (*nikhas*) through his urban executive officer, the *kotwal*, and all other prices and percentages in the bazaar followed this automatically.[34] Competition was restricted by officially appointed bazaar superintendents, and in case of scarcity, a ruler might forbid the export of commodities from his territories and coerce the grain merchants into releasing their stocks. But there was a good deal of bluff in all this. In practice, local economic autarchy was impossible and the markets were run by a process of bargaining between dealers, financiers, and the military rulers. It was the commercial community which decided who should or should not pass his *hundis* in the bazaar, and if the merchants were subjected to unduly savage pressure to release food-grains or provide forced loans, they simply closed the bazaar or abandoned the town.[35]

Tribute, military supply, pilgrimage, and trade were linked together in an all-India network which merchants, bankers, and specialist carriers could manipulate to the financial disadvantage of the regional rulers.[36] Bullion—the key to political success—circulated throughout India with considerable speed. The only major external sources were Central Asia and the trickle of imports through European centres, such as Chandernagore and Calcutta.[37] But considerable quantities of hoarded bullion were spasmodically released by rulers of central and north India to finance their military and ceremonial enterprises. Thus, while 'Bengal' silver was transported as far as Jaipur and Surat when there was a heavy demand during the 1770s and 1780s, the north Indian bankers also brought in gold plate from Rajasthan to cover the Nawab of Awadh's subsidy to the British on a number of occasions when silver was in short supply in the east.[38] As the East India Company became more deeply involved in the financial politics of north India, we begin to see how the firms working the all-India capital and bullion markets could play off one regional ruler against another. In 1789, for instance, the Company wished to reduce the discount they were paying to the Benares bankers to provide their agent at Poona with funds. Normally, the annual demand of Maratha pilgrims for cash at the holy city would have brought down the rate a little. But this year, the 'wants of Raghojee Bhonsla' for cash for his troops was so great that the bankers were able to play Marathas off against the British and keep the rate high.[39] In the same year, the commercial houses raised the rate of discount between Benares and Surat to a high 11 per cent, claiming that this was the result of 'fluctuations' and heavy demand in Lucknow.[40] Should rulers try to tax the bullion trade to their own advantage, it would simply dry up. Later, rates for coining at the Benares mint were raised, so the financial houses redirected the bullion and plate they were bringing up from Bengal to Rajasthan and Lucknow, to the detriment of the city's money supply and credit.[41]

Religious corporations, bodies of merchants and many commercial towns had been tough and resourceful in the face of political change. Rulers needed the services provided by these institutions as the costs of warfare and petty statehood rose, and as the revenue was gradually farmed out to entrepreneurs. Long-distance traders, carriers, and even bodies of pilgrims became brokers for goods and services passing between the many decentralized regimes subsisting on areas of high farming. In the Gangetic cities and large market villages, there was a solid rank of middling merchants standing between the great merchant princes and the petty hucksters of agrarian society. Some scholars have made out the lineaments of an Indian bourgeoisie amidst the bustle of north India's more prosperous bazaars.[42] But evidence that merchant capital was becoming more important in the economy does not necessarily imply that merchants were aspiring to a direct political role or that the indigenous state was undergoing fundamental change during the century. There was, of course, no question of *mahajan*s or despised *bakkal*s widely taking on the ceremonial or military functions of rulers. Even the transition between merchant, revenue-farmer, and zamindar was hazardous in the context of strong notions of the separation between the role of ruler and merchant.

What can be said, however, is that the covert and subtly exercised power of merchant bodies imposed limitations on what eighteenth-century rulers could do, and allowed commerce to achieve a more privileged position in regard to the military aristocracy. Contemporary European observers were aware that the bankers not only operated punitive cartels against them but exercised a delicate political influence. So strongly had the power of the banking fraternity of Bengal and Hyderabad impressed itself on the mind of Law de Lauriston, ex-Governor General of French India, that he saw them in 1777 as a key group in any future alliance of the French and Indian states against the English East India Company:

These are the people to whom the nawabs and the rajas always have recourse; whom they consult willingly about all civil, military and political operations, because to some extent all these matters enter into the sphere of the *sarkars* [bankers] because of the good or evil which such an operation could bring to the country. They appear without pretension at the darbars, but they exercise great influence there; one word of a renowned banker will carry more weight than the most eloquent speech of another, whomsoever he be, because this word holds fast to a chain which extends everywhere [tient a une chaîne qui s'extend partout].[43]

De Lauriston's most telling point was that it was the men of commerce in eastern India who had most to gain from European and specifically from English trade. It was they, therefore, who had constrained the rajas and nawabs to allow foreign commerce a much freer hand in the interior of the country than it had ever had in the days of central Mughal rule.

Contemporary opinion differed from region to region in its assessment of the political power of the commercial classes. As might be expected, it was reckoned least formidable in tracts where trade was backward or in decline. H.T. Prinsep, for instance, could caricature the 'enormously wealthy' bankers of the Maratha territories 'absolutely rolling in wealth . . . occupied in the exclusive pursuit of sordid and selfish gains'.[44] But he added significantly that they might achieve influence where revenue was put out to farm or where there was a fierce factional split among the military élite. In some areas which had suffered sharp local agricultural decline, commercial networks had actually been rolled back. In the Delhi territories, for instance, commercial firms with agencies in the small agricultural towns had given advances on the revenue as they did in Benares, though sometime between 1760 and 1800 this practice had ceased as Delhi lost control over its hinterland.[45] But some well-entrenched commercial groups were difficult to uproot from a position of local political influence even against the background of the near collapse of trade. In Bareilly, for instance, the ancient house of Lacchman Das survived the decline of Mughal power and the rise of the Rohillas, and even remained significant in local Hindu and city politics at the beginning of British rule.[46]

Awadh perhaps represents an example midway between Bengal or Benares and those tracts without strong inland trade. Here, the political situation was even more perilous for the bankers than it was in Bengal, but they were still a force to be reckoned with. In Awadh, the great revenue-farmers such as Almas Ali Khan and Bhawani Singh appear to have organized their own cash and credit transactions between Lucknow and the interior fixed markets where revenue was collected.[47] But in some areas, at least, banking houses must have enacted a role similar to that which they played in Benares. For when the Nawab ceded large tracts of his territory to the British in 1801, incoming British collectors had difficulty in guaranteeing the revenue in the Doab because, it was said, commercial houses had withdrawn their agencies when the revenue-farmers had retired to Awadh.[48] Even if their role in the revenue system was somewhat less developed, Lucknow's banking houses provided a key service for the Nawabi government in remitting the annual tribute to Calcutta every year after 1764.[49] So important was the annual tribute that the bankers gained access to the darbar and to the British Resident and began to take a close interest in court faction as they had done in Bengal, Hyderabad, and Benares before. For instance, a famous Jain banker, Lala Bacchraj, who appeared as a partner of the Benares magnate Lala Kashmiri Mull in transferring tribute all over Hindustan in the 1770s and 1780s, had insinuated himself into the centre of the Lucknow court faction by the 1790s. With the aid of the British Resident, he gained an influence over the treasury and 'began to aspire to the distinction of Naib',[50] a major officer of state. Bacchraj's drive for power foundered and he ended his life in a Nawabi prison, along with most of his family.[51] But it was significant that even in this, the most powerful and most agrarian of the north Indian successor states, Indian financiers could come so near to the sources of power.

THE FORMS OF URBAN ORGANIZATION

The political influence of trader-bankers was a common feature of late eighteenth-century regimes. But was this power wielded simply by a few great magnate families subject to the 'instability of oriental fortunes', or did it have a wider social and institutional base? There is indeed a body of opinion which might concede the political importance of individual capitalists in pre-colonial Indian politics but argues that the culture and political ideas of India made it virtually impossible for merchants and townsmen to achieve any significant degree of autonomy or corporate identity in the face of ruling landed élites. Ultimately, these ideas derive from Max Weber's brilliant generalizations on the religion and institutions of India. According to Weber, occupational specialization based on caste fragmented Indian artisan, merchant and service populations, so inhibiting the development of mercantile trust, let alone political action. Caste restrictions made impossible the civic fraternization out of which emerged Western corporate institutions, while the 'passivity' of Hinduism denied rising groups an ideology which could validate their political independence. Thus, urban centres and states remained dominated by the 'patrimonial' regimes of warrior bureaucrats, and for Weber as for Marx, true social change awaited the impact of colonial rule. These ideas continue to influence more recent work. Trade, it has been asserted, was 'merged into and managed by caste bodies';[52] the Indian city was split into 'self-contained and mutually hostile neighbourhoods';[53] the political role of merchants was limited by their dharma, and they remained of low social status. Such ideas are almost circular since the richest sources relate to revenue administration and the cycle of dynasties, and there is a grave lack of evidence on the behaviour and organization of social groups outside the ruling warrior élites and the literate classes dependent on them.

However, the evidence from several parts of north India suggests not only that the economic and political importance of the great trader-bankers was enhanced in the period of the successor states but that corporations of townsmen, merchants, and religious specialists had developed a new coherence and autonomy which in some cases amounted to a virtual civic self-government. These changes were not frustrated by caste fragmentation or the passivity of Hinduism: on the contrary, caste and religion provided building-blocks out of which mercantile and urban solidarities were perceptibly emerging. The influence of trading corporations over the landholding aristocracy was un-doubtedly enhanced by the growing European presence in India. Merchants were adaptable to the style and requirements of the British and gained from the burgeoning of the export trades to China and Europe after 1770. But the commercialization of politics and the rise of the corporations were by origin intrinsic changes within the economy and culture. War and political change, far from destroying towns and trade, had actually galvanized them into greater independence. To illustrate the potential for such changes, we will take the case of Rajasthan. Not only was this an area removed from direct Western influence, but it was the natural habitat of the haughty Indian aristo-cracy.

As James Tod recognized, a century of war had not destroyed trade or production in Rajasthan; only the Pax Britannica made a desert, and

paradoxical as it may appear, there was tenfold more activity and enterprise in the midst of that predatory warfare, which rendered India one wide arena of conflict, than in these days of universal pacification.[54]

As in eastern India, merchants had strengthened their hold on the working of the revenue system by financing the deficits of the rajas and clan leaders and also by working the *takkavi* advances given to cultivators in the village. Contemporary with these economic changes,[55] the political status of townsmen and merchants was increasing. Political fluidity resulting from the decline of Mughal overlordship and the rise of small, local kingdoms caused what Tod called a 'neglect of legislation' during the eighteenth century.[56] Self-governing multi-caste assemblies had taken over responsibility for many aspects of ad-ministration, especially defence and the upkeep of trade routes and *sarai*s. The influence of Jain merchant people had already secured them a number of special privileges or immunities which had developed around the concept of 'sanctuary' (*ashrama*). In several Rajput states, officers of the raja were ex-cluded from the temples and living quarters of Jain merchants, and the high status they had achieved influenced the standing of other townsmen with whom they had dealings. In some cases indeed the rights and privileges of merchants and towns were set out in documents which reminded Tod of medieval European town charters.[57] Tod's analogy between the emergence of Western representative institutions from feudal privilege and the potential for a kind of representative government based on Indian urban councils is fanciful. But he was sufficiently struck by these developments in Rajasthan to record a significant deviation from his usual picture of oriental feudalism. If he was not witnessing the emergence of parliaments, Tod had certainly seen subtle changes in the relations between constituent elements of the pre-colonial state.

Changes like this were taking place elsewhere in India, but the timing and context were often different. In Rajasthan, always a turbulent frontier of em-pire, the apparatus of Mughal urban government, with its Muslim judicial officers responsible to a governor, had never developed strong roots. The bazaar and the service quarters of the towns bargained with or submitted di-rectly to the raja and the Hindu warriors. 'Want of legislation' would force them directly into self-organization. But in the cities of the plains where up to 40 per cent of the population might be Muslim, the Mughal executive officer (*kotwal*) and 'registrar' (*kazi*) retained varying degrees of influence. In Rohilkhand and Awadh, which retained strong Muslim identities, the power of the Hindu urban and commercial groups was growing, but it re-mained encompassed by city-wide Islamic institutions. There existed formal processes of registration and arbitration by *kotwal* and *kazi* even if effective power was left to heads of the corporations.

In the more commercial south and east, however, the authority of the Mughal officials had been largely eroded before 1770 as chapter 8 will show. Here bodies of traders and service people had also attained a significant degree of independence in matters of police, defence, and arbitration. In Benares and Mirzapur particularly, the word corporation can properly be used to describe trading and religious organizations. People of different caste were tied together in broader communities which received explicit recognition from the rulers. Here monetization of revenue demand, the growth of inland trade, and of the city of Benares itself had put trader-bankers into a strategic position in the new Benares dominion.[58] By the 1770s, the power of the major mercantile houses was similar to that acquired by the Jagat Seths in Bengal in the later days of the Nawabi. They could, to use again the words of the British Resident, 'command the state to a large extent in the matter of revenue'. But how was this power represented in institutions? How coherent were mercantile organizations? The mid-Ganges at least appears to have seen the emergence of powerful mercantile corporations similar to the cross-caste merchant *mahajan*s of Gujerat.[59] At Mirzapur, the fastest growing town, there was a 'Dhurnam Pacham' or 'general body of the trading people' which adjudicated disputes between people of different background according to mercantile custom and also adjusted brokerage fees.[60] Royal authority was not eliminated from the town and its hinterland. The petty local raja of Kantit retained considerable prestige and formally appointed a head or *chaudhuri* of the bazaar. But his wealth and power was dwarfed by that of the leading merchant houses and the religious corporations. It was they who patrolled the gated areas of the town, and it was their levies which policed the key trade route which ran south into central India. As in Rajasthan, the 'want of legislation' and the impotence of small states had forced merchants and other groups with regional interests to take up the role of adjudication and protection which had formerly been the preserve of kings.

In Benares a similar set of relationships developed around the Naupatti Sabha (Society of Nine Sharers) which illustrates how merchant interests could be articulated across the boundaries of caste.[61] This association was a body of nine leading city merchant families which had been brought together by the demand of the ruler of Awadh for a huge forced loan during one of his campaigns against Benares during the 1750s. The nine great burghers had come forward to subscribe a part of the loan and so save the holy city and its environs from sack. Political turbulence had galvanized the community into action which permanently placed the 'bankers' in a strong moral and customal relationship with the raja and the other great land-controlling magnates who had been unable to protect the city themselves. But we do have echoes of earlier cooperation for political purposes by the mercantile élite. A central mercantile organization appears to have existed at least from the beginning of the century, and it is said that they played an important role in helping Balwant Singh's line to power in 1739.[62] The Nawab of Awadh who nominally controlled Benares was looking to renew the revenue-farm of the Benares territories to Mir Rustam Ali. But the story goes that the bankers calculated the greatest extent of their capital in order to put up an even larger bid and stronger security for Mansa Ram, the founder of the Bhumihar dynasty. This was a ploy to reduce Muslim influence in the territory and benefit a local dynasty with whom they were on much more equal terms. Though it seems unverifiable, the story encouraged the commercial community to claim high status in regard to the raja's family and descendants.

The nine families in the Naupatti came from different backgrounds. One was Gujerati Brahmin, one Gujerati Vaishya, one Oswal Jain, and the others Agarwals of various subgroups. In the beginning, there was a mix between old established Gujerati firms and relative newcomers from eastern India. All that mattered was finding enough liquid capital to finance the forced loan.[63] Later, the Naupatti became a self-perpetuating oligarchy of status which no aspiring family could enter.[64] But it did not separate itself off from other merchant people, acting instead as a holding alliance at the top of merchant society which overrode caste and sectarian boundaries. So while merchant people had different interests and statuses, the merchant community did have a distinct autonomous existence and was not irrevocably split by distinctions of ritual or residential area. On the contrary, ties of caste helped bind poorer merchants, brokers, hucksters, and bazaar people into a corporate body of opinion which could make itself heard by both rajas and British residents.[65] Our image of caste is one of fragmentation, but in the pre-colonial period it might sometimes be better to use the image of the fasces in which the binding in of each individual element gives strength to the whole.

Let us set out the variety of these relationships. Direct marriage alliances were the lowest common denominator of both social and commercial life. In the course of the hundred years after 1750, the broad category of Agarwal merchants was drawn closer and closer by dozens of strategic marriages which pooled capital and skills. Rich newcomers like the Shah family were able to ally with more established but poorer families who headed the Purbiye (Eastern) Agarwal caste brotherhood. These links could help maintain relations over a much wider area also. Khattri merchants continued to marry their daughters to aspiring families at the other end of the great east-west trade route in the Punjab. The Dassapurwal Gujerati merchants display an even more interesting pattern. They customarily brought in poor young men from towns in Gujerat and other regions, married them to their daughters, and set them up with houses and capital in Benares.[66]

Caste provided larger building-blocks than extended family groups. But these were not the tight-knit caste institutions which appear in some of the anthropological literature. Instead, they were more like loose bodies of patrons and clients drawn from broadly similar ritual groups which clustered around a few important families wielding ritual authority and economic power. Thus, the famous family of Lala Kashmiri Mull was 'chief' of the city's Khattris and Saraswat Brahmins from the Punjab.[67] The cohesion of the group was enhanced by a relationship with the holy men of the local Nanakpanthi assembly who acted as guru (spiritual advisor) to most of the Punjabi people in the city. Like most other mercantile groups in Benares, the Khattris and their Saraswat Brahmin family priests and business partners had a caste assembly or panchayat. It seems to have met irregularly to deliberate on matters of morality and was, by tradition, quite separate from the multi-caste assemblies of 'respectable merchants' which adjudicated business matters.

While the mercantile population possessed a consciousness of caste and caste institutions which were more or less effective in matters of ritual, this did not preclude the formation of wider merchant organizations and bonds of trust which stretched across the boundaries of caste. In some trades, certain castes—or more properly, extended family groups—were predominant. So the Mehra Khattris dominated the cloth trade;[68] Purbiye Agarwals were strong in the grain trade,[69] Gujerati Banias in fine brocades,[70] and so on. Nevertheless, most trades were multi-caste ventures, and in their dealings with each other or with the authorities, merchants needed common institutions. Sometimes these were based on an interest in the trade of one region. Thus we find that, approaching the authorities in the 1780s, 'the merchants trading to Lahor, Multaun and the west', who included Gosains, Brahmins, Khattris and 'Iraqis'; 'the merchants trading to the Duccin [Deccan] and southwards',[71] including Sipahi Nagars,[72] Maratha Brahmins, and Bundelkhandi Jains, and 'the mahajans and traders ordinarily resident in Benares',[73] including Agarwals, Khattris, and others. Another form of organization was based on the particular function performed by merchants at different levels of the trading system. The wholesale commission agents (*arethias*) trading to particular regions had their own organization and spokesmen, as did the petty bazaar lenders.

Conceptions of status and mercantile honour also overrode caste, for it is evident that trade and credit relations over long distances could not have survived without them. 'Creditworthiness', having one's *hundis* accepted in the bazaar, keeping regular commercial books, being frugal rather than 'expensive': these were the measures of respectability which are mentioned regularly in commercial cases, and they are witness to a consistent mercantile 'public opinion'. At the pinnacle of merchant society stood the members of the Naupatti Sabha themselves who functioned as a final panel of arbitration among merchants on matters such as debt, the division of assets in family partitions, bankruptcy, and the status of mercantile custom on legal instruments. During this period it seems to have been unusual for litigation to go beyond these informal, local forums. Only in the few instances where family, caste, or Naupatti arbitration had failed to impose a settlement would the *kotwali* peon—the runner of the city's police chief—or the ruler's courts be brought into the matter.[74] To all intents and purposes then, an ad hoc 'law merchant' existed. Excommunication remained the usual sanction for caste assemblies, but what were the sanctions available to this wider mercantile opinion? In a tight, face-to-face society, the failure of one's credit in the bazaar was a sentence of commercial and sometimes of physical death. But the sanctions of Hindu religion were also available. Oaths were made in Ganges water and in the name of tutelary deities, or with the witness of a Gosain who was technically above caste and kin since he was dead to the world. The ultimate sanction was to have Brahmins mutilate themselves before the door of a debtor in order to heap spiritual demerit on him (dharna); this was only the most dramatic instance of the role of popular religion in reinforcing mercantile trust.[75]

In Benares at this period there is tantalizing evidence of social conflict based upon wealth. A witness in a case says 'it is not the custom of my caste to take the evidence of poor people at arbitrations'.[76] There is also the fact that members of the lower entrepreneurial castes (Kalwars, Telis, and Kacchis) generally appear to have arbitrated each others' disputes and did not have access to the Naupatti, though they were influenced by their mores and business style. Differences of class and status—*grand peuple* against *menu peuple*—are of course perfectly compatible with common civic or mercantile unity against outsiders. At other times, links of caste and patronage ensured that the complaints and difficulties of the poorer commercial people would reach the ears of the authorities. For instance, the merchant élite spoke up for workers in the Benares mint in 1791 when their livelihood was threatened by official action.[77] Later they fiercely resisted an attempt to bring in a limitation on suits for debt under the Bengal Regulations of 1793 on the grounds, among others, that it would damage the small lenders or *khurdea*s, who often waited for more than a generation for the payment of debts.[78]

If there were many links which bound mercantile people together irrespective of caste in all but the spheres of marriage and formal interdining, there were also subtle ties which bound together different occupations and statuses among the residents as a whole. Religious observance created solidarities here too. Gujerati and local Agarwal families joined together in the veneration of the Krishna temple of Gopal Lalji and were counted as members of the Vallabhacharya sect.[79] But the rajas of Benares and cadets of the ruling family were also closely associated with the shrine. From Mansa Ram onward, they customarily supported Gopal Lalji and other major shrines in the city and at Bindachal, the holy place of Mirzapur. As chief devotees and benefactors of shrines so closely associated with the ruling family, merchant people acquired enhanced status.

Within the city, Gosains and other ascetic orders also acted as a body of brokers between different social groups. They attracted veneration from the mass of the people and also had a close hand in the running of the merchant communities, and had even come to head them in nearby Mirzapur. Brahmins similarly acted as a force of integration. Not only did nobles and commercial notables feed or directly maintain the large Brahmin population, but the commercial houses employed Brahmins as runners and agents whenever possible to avoid problems of caste status with their clients and correspondents. The British Resident was horrified to find that it was customary among the merchants to take several paisa per rupee on every *dakhilla* or *hundi* transaction with the rulers for gifts to the Brahmins.[80] It was a further indication of the manner in which the ritual superiority of priest or ascetic could act as a unifying force in urban society.

Common residential areas also created knowledge and sympathies outside caste and between different occupational groups. Sometimes neighbourhood loyalties centred on the service of shrines, tanks, or ghats. But local defence was also an important spur to organization. Some quarters (*mohullas*) were, of course, single-caste residential areas. But an equally common pattern was the community of the great stone house or *haveli*. Each *haveli* was occupied by a single extended family and their dependants, and these were grouped together into gated areas which provided their own defence and police on the basis of a general levy.[81] Property documents show that many of these gated areas were multi-caste residential areas and the state, whether the raja or the decaying remnants of Mughal central authority, had little role in their organization.

At the widest level then the links between the various élites in the cities created a sense of urban solidarity. This was no doubt weak by comparison with medieval Florence, but it provides evidence of the potential for organization between the state and the mass of agrarian society. Cities such as Allahabad, Benares, or Gaya had a special privileged status as *tirthas* or holy places. In theory, they were the property of the gods and all men could worship there. Out of their religious pre-eminence derived a sense of the 'public'.[82] In practice, of course, private property existed in Benares and other holy cities. Yet the central part of the town north of the Dassasswamedh ghat was commonly regarded as an area of particular reverence. There was considerable concern to keep the 'holy mile' (*pakka mahal*) free from undesirable groups. These included not only the representatives of the earlier Muslim authority but even the raja and his collaterals. Apparent attempts by governments to impinge on this sacred liberty were fought vehemently by the Hindu city as a united corporation—the 'Babus [raja and collaterals], Brahmans and Mahajans of the city assembled'.[83] The first indisputable record of an attempt by the citizens to protect the holy places was the protest in 1725 against the raising of an additional pilgrim tax, though there is an echo of a battle in 1664 over the establishment of a mosque on the site of a temple.[84] The British in turn were faced with a series of popular reactions beginning with the famous strike against the proposed house tax in 1809,[85] and stretching forward to the protest against the construction of a municipal waterworks on the holy Ganges in 1889.[86]

The consolidation of corporate entities was a feature of other smaller cities and areas where bodies of merchants and religious men found themselves at an advantage in the face of the aspiring eighteenth-century states. Above all, it was the ascetic groups which successfully combined religion and commerce, and contributed greatly to the synthesis of wealth and Hindu practice which was emerging under the surface of the Indo-Muslim state.

ASCETIC ORDERS AND URBAN LIFE

The last chapter emphasized how Hindu ascetic orders of Bairagis and Gosains had come to play an important role in the eighteenth-century economy. Their annual cycle of pilgrimage from the borders of the Punjab through the holy cities of the plains to Bihar and Orissa allowed them to move goods, money and military force between stable agricultural tracts. They were the largest owners of urban property in Benares, Allahabad, Mirzapur, and Nagpur in the 1780s, and they also helped supply the large fairs and markets of the countryside which were often unsafe for unarmed merchants of lower status. An open and flexible organization enabled the ascetics to pool resources and talent. They took in as novices young boys from war-torn villages, recruiting from all the higher castes.[87] It seems possible that there were as many as half a million Shaivite and Vaishnavite ascetics in north India in the last decade of the century.

For the ascetic corporations it was their religious status and organization which provided the basic immunities out of which a separate political role could grow. As with the Jains, the concept of sanctuary and immunity from punishment at the hands of the ruler encouraged the development of a strong corporate life. From an early period, the Dasnami Naga ascetics, for instance, enjoyed the privilege of self-government under their 'abbots' and regional controllers along with relative immunity from imposts and interference by the rulers' police officials.[88] Hindu holy men achieved an even higher status during the reign of Emperor Akbar when a clear effort was made to formulate an eclectic royal religion. But as with other corporations, it was Aurangzeb's lurch back towards a state founded on Muslim law which propelled the Dasnamis to a tougher defensive position. Tradition records a battle against Islamic revival in Benares in about 1664 when Gosains 'preserved the honour of Vishwanath's seat',[89] that is, preserved the great Viswanath temple on the Benares ghats from plunder. The Lingayat Math at Madanpura also preserves a tale of successful defiance to a Muslim ruler, though here it was a ghostly tiger which is supposed to have routed the interloper.[90] After 1707 the flux of political power stirred the corporations into more strenuous military activity. When the Afghans invaded southern Awadh in 1751, the Dasnamis who were gathered at Allahabad for the bathing festival offered armed resistance and saved the inner city from sack, for 'Siva gave help and thus saved the honour of the Dasnamis'.[91] Hereafter, powerful Gosain armies stalked the north

Indian countryside, playing the role of Swiss mercenaries in Renaissance Europe. Though their commanders were particularly honoured by the Hindu Jats, their status in the Awadh armies was almost as high. The Nawab invested one Gosain leader with the rank of 'four hundred *hazari*', a high order of Mughal chivalry, and also with the right to raise troops without reference to himself.

During the eighteenth century, then, Gosains, Bairagis and other religious corporations came to play an important role both within states and in directing the diplomatic, commercial, and military relations between them. In some localities they virtually acted as rulers in their own right. Gosain dominance at the great Hardwar fair, for instance, underlines the degree to which the corporations could take on the privileges of protection and punishment which had formerly been the preserve of Kings:

These mehunts [abbots] meet in council daily; hear and decide upon all complaints brought before them, either against individuals, or of a nature tending to disturb the public tranquility, and the well management of this immense multitude.[92]

This observer, Captain Hardwicke, saw two fraudulent Marwari merchants fined and lashed by order of the council.[93] The Marathas, who were nominally rulers of the area in which the fair was located, allowed the Gosains almost total control of relations with the other predatory powers and were either un-willing or unable to claw back much of the huge levy which the corporations amassed from visiting merchants and pilgrims.[94] In the holy cities, too, ascetics achieved a striking degree of self-government. Contemporary Muttra, for instance, was run by a combination of the Chaube Brahmins, who con-trolled local trade and pilgrimage, and Vaishnavite monasteries (*kunjis*) which provided protection and ran longer-distance trade.[95] The heroic and costly defence of the ascetics to the invasion of Ahmed Shah Durrani in 1761, when many thousands of them were slaughtered, permanently enhanced their local importance.[96] On the fringes of other dominions, as in major commercial towns, the Gosains were able to establish a near state of their own. One com-mander, Himmat Bahadur, carved out for himself a small kingdom in the cotton-growing tracts of Bundelkhand,[97] while the so-called Sannyasis of the east had established themselves on the borders of Bengal in the 1740s and 1750s to the discomfiture of its later British rulers.

In small Hindu states which emerged after 1740 the religious corporations also achieved important concessions and influence. In the Jat dominion of Bharatpur, for instance, Vaishnavite orders of Ramawat and Nemawat asce-tics obtained considerable wealth and the honour of conferring benediction and legitimacy on the raja. Obeisance to the *mahants* of the main Bairagi temples, which were set at the centre of the new town of Bharatpur, was an important ritual in all the marriage and other ceremonies performed by the royal house. But the *mahants'* power also had a more tangible aspect.[98] They took a tithe in kind on all sorts of grain exported for sale in the bazaars and secured periodical grants of the whole of the raja's share of the produce of the bazaars. In addition, sect leaders received generous grants of revenue-free land or land at reduced revenue, and an annual cess of 4 annas to Rs 2 on all of the 1,200 villages within the bounds of the dominion. Not surprisingly, 'These mehunts become very powerful, especially when they are also *gurus*', or spiritual preceptors to the rulers.[99]

Other bodies of high status had achieved virtual independence within the smaller dominions. Bodies of river-priests at Allahabad, Hardwar, Gaya and Muttra had existed for centuries. The Mughal peace had enhanced their numbers and wealth as more people came to the great ritual centres in order to perform the ceremony of oblation (*shraddha*) for their ancestors. The priests' success depended on the development of links with lineages of rural magnates whose members would visit and endow them with lands and money generation after generation. The constant reiteration of the merits of holy places in the Puranas kept them in the popular mind of the localities, and it was still possible to slip in new names and attributes as late as the eighteenth century.[100]

There were also groups of teaching holy men at some of these centres. After about 1680 communications with the Deccan improved and a large body of Deccani and western Indian teachers began to gather in Benares.[101] Their organization of preceptors and pupils for the purpose of teaching the classical syllabuses of grammar, astronomy, and the holy books were sufficiently well-developed to be regarded as 'colleges' or even as a 'university' by early European travellers. Nanakpanthi north Indians also had a 'college' in the city of Patna. These institutions with their wide and flexible contacts, were in a good position to brave the political changes of the century and they emerged with enhanced moral and political authority. The new Hindu rulers of Benares, like the Marathas and Jats, lavished donations on them. They used the teaching pandits in arbitration and released the bathing priests from any kind of interference by the officers of the state. In Gaya, the bathing priests and pandits achieved an even higher status. On two occasions, they raised their own military forces to defend the area against marauding Marathas and Muslim mercenaries. As Buchanan noted, 'Many zemindar Brahmans and other warlike persons retiring the town with their families and effects gave great addition to the power of the priests.'[102]

CORPORATIONS AND THE ANALYSIS OF
INDIAN SOCIETY

These subtle changes in power and status have been buried by the more dramatic political annals of Mughal decline. Yet there are parallels here with the rise to power of two much more celebrated groups of Brahmins, the Chitpavans of the Deccan and the 'Sipahi' or military Nagar Brahmins of Gujerat. By the mid-century these two castes had staged a virtual coup throughout central and western India where they held a near monopoly of high offices in the state, and their influence spread with the Maratha armies into the Ganges valley.[103] Their success had something in common with that of the corporate groups which we have been discussing. They had mastered the art of diplomacy between the decentralized polities which emerged out of the second phase of Maratha expansion. Their subcaste groupings and marriage networks expanded over a wide area which gave them leverage in a number of small dominions; at first they were able to move information between one centre and another; later, as they began to amass money and land-rights, wealth could be moved around. A key to influence with the Maratha rulers was also their Brahminical status. They could help to 'transform' peasant Kunbi leaders into kingly Marathas, while their skills of literacy were invaluable in the process of state-formation. Like the corporations, then, these two groups of Brahmin administrators were at both a moral and, as it were, a geographical advantage in dealing with contemporary rulers. One major difference was that their internal organization was quite strictly bounded by caste. But this does not invalidate the comparison. It was Brahmins as a status group which achieved great power within the Maratha polities, symbolized by the great public feedings and distributions of charity to them (*dakshina*). Chitpavan Brahmins rose to prominence within this status group.

The intention in this section has been to take a new look at social and political change within the immediate pre-colonial polities of northern India. In doing this, we have encountered a number of changes which may seem surprising in the light of the still vital tradition of thinking about Indian society which derived from the ideas of Max Weber. This tradition insisted on the low status of merchants in India, and the domination of its cities by warrior or bureaucratic élites, which precluded the emergence of 'civic liberties':

in India—since the victory of the patrimonial kings and the Brahmins—it has been the endogamous caste with its exclusive taboos which has prevented the fusion of city dwellers into a status group enjoying social and legal equality, into a connubium sharing table community and displaying solidarity toward the outgroup. Because of the intensity of exclusive caste taboos this possibility was even more remote in India than in China.[104]

Weber's view depends on a number of assumptions and certain historical conditions. The main condition is the existence of large 'bureaucratic empires' or 'patrimonial states' which are held to prevent the emergence of strong corporate bodies. Where such states did not exist, he is prepared to accept that urban and mercantile solidarity might come into being:

To be sure in India during the period of the great salvation religions, guilds appeared with hereditary elders (*schreschths*) uniting in many cities into an association. As residues from this period there are, at present, some cities (Allahabad) with a mutual urban elder corresponding to the occidental mayor.[105]

The argument of this chapter does not directly contradict Weber since he would have acknowledged that the decline of the Mughal state may have enhanced the possibility of self-organization among the local bodies.

This theme can be usefully applied to other periods of Indian history and to other areas. In medieval south India, for instance, self-regulating bodies of long-distance merchants appear to have had great influence within the petty states which developed in areas of high farming.[106] If the rise of merchant and religious corporations within the fragmented Mughal empire was evidence of social change, it was novel mainly by virtue of the geographical extent of the bodies of merchants, ascetics, and Brahmins involved, and the broader context of commercial agriculture.

Weber's main assumption is that Hinduism and Jainism are essentially passive and therefore could never provide a basis for political action in the manner which conceptions of Roman law, and later revived Christianity, did in the West. The degree to which Indian religious belief inhibited business in India has been severely qualified by Singer[107] and Morris,[108] among others, and the evidence for post-Mughal north India suggests that this passivity can be exaggerated in the political sphere also. As we have seen, the concept of sanctuary (*ashrama*) and withdrawal (*sannyas*) could both, by a splendid paradox, provide the basis for self-government and self-defence. In contrast to Christianity, meekness was never a necessary concomitant of either. The Indian pilgrim's staff could readily be transformed into a symbol of force (*danda*). The view that Hindu religious duty (dharma) excluded merchants from political activity is also simplistic. True, merchants were unwilling to compromise their profession as 'money dealers' and aristocrats were unwilling to deal openly in trade, but clandestine channels of influence and accommodation could always be found if circumstances pressed. Moreover, one of the strengths of Hinduism was its ability to adapt to change without losing its intellectual cohesion. Indian political theory, as set out in classical texts and modified in the Puranas, specifically allows for self-defence and self-government by subjects when the king, through moral degradation, is unable to protect them.[109] Significantly, this line of justification ran parallel to that in classical Islamic theory which restricted the power of the sultan to military protection of the body of the faithful. Evidently this implied a degree of self-organization by society and its learned men, even if guilds and corporations acquired no de jure legal status.

One other qualification of Weber's view of Indian kingship must be made. In theory, it was never as monolithic as he implies. Political relations within a raj were founded on the assumption that there existed bonds of mutual obligation between ruler and subject. These were expressed in the form of alienations to worthy groups of parts of the ruler's sovereignty in the form of grants of revenue and other boons. The army, the priests, and other important service groups could therefore be contracted into alliance with the state for the better preservation of order and religion. Where, as in the small Hindu states of eighteenth-century north India, privileged Brahmins and ascetics were also closely connected with trade and urban life, the raj itself evidently took on a more corporate character.

The final assumption made by Weber, and reiterated unconsciously by more recent writers, is that caste distinctions irreparably fragmented urban and mercantile communities. It may be true that caste did indeed prevent the emergence of common civic or corporate dining relations and tight marriage ties between élites, but this did not rule out the possibility of mercantile or even political solidarity. As we have seen, mercantile and credit organizations, conceptions of credit, local defence associations, and festivals necessarily breached these caste boundaries. There seems no reason why the common table and marriage alliance should be the only basis of corporate activity, as Weber assumes.

A PARALLEL CORPORATE CULTURE:
THE ISLAMIC GENTRY TOWN

Chapter 3 indicated that there were other families of townsmen and service people besides Hindu trading and religious people who tenaciously held on to local power despite the shifting patterns of politics. Groups of service gentry, for instance, maintained patches of land-rights and influence in small towns and the suburban quarters of the cities, even when the great nobles (who often included some of their own members) moved away in the train of the regional rulers. Often too, it was local gentry who benefited, along with the bazaar people, from the high spending of the great revenue-farmers, while serving them as under-managers and gentleman troopers.

A large proportion of these families were Muslim and linked by blood or veneration to the famous religious institutions which subsisted on the revenue-free grants of earlier rulers. Where the rule of Muslim potentates waned, or changed its theological complexion, it was often local religious institutions, such as the 'Shahjehani' Sufi foundations of Allahabad[110] or the Firangi Mahal teaching seminary of Lucknow, which maintained the corporate life of the faithful. Despite occasional tensions, these institutions maintained amicable, if wary, relations with the Hindu religious and trading corporations, receiving honour and worship from the lower classes of both major religions in the cities.

It was in some of the smaller *qasbah* towns, however, that the Islamic service gentry were digging themselves in most successfully between 1690 and 1830, and here they had long been evolving a culture which ran parallel to, though not yet in opposition to, that of the Hindu commercial towns.[111]

The warriors and service lineages of the small Islamic township had something in common with the Hindu trading corporations as far as their mode of operation was concerned. They could both work beyond the boundaries of the smaller states, avoiding the consequences of local political or military decline by having skilled members placed in a number of regional or local court centres. But at the same time, they were also consolidating their hold over resources—credit and marketing in one case; land-rights in the other—in particular areas. In both service and market town also a definite corporate consciousness beyond family and caste had been created. What was different were the religious traditions around which these local powers and liberties coalesced.

The proliferation of mosques, schools, Muslim tombs, and great gentry houses gave small gentry towns quite a different quality to the bustling Hindu bazaars. For even more than the quarters of the great Muslim towns, these *qasbah* societies played a key role in transmitting Islamic learning and providing a local Muslim leadership. Clan groups, such as the Sheikhs of Kakori, the Barah Sayyids, and the Sayyids of Jansath or Kara, served regional rulers as court officers and soldiers and remained well entrenched in the lower levels of the British service during the early nineteenth century. Even later they were the dominant group in the associations in defence of Urdu and the district Muslim Leagues which were among the first forays of Muslims into electoral and pressure-group politics.

Like the mercantile and religious institutions of predominantly Hindu towns, this Islamic gentry was a well-rooted social group which evolved slowly from the days of the early Muslim kingdoms and continued to consolidate its power in the early colonial period. Whereas the Hindu traders and bankers had turned to good advantage their position in relation to the smaller principalities, the gentry could swim with the tide of local political fortune, selling their skills as administrators, soldiers, and literati to one regime and another as the old polities fragmented, fissioned, and later stabilized. It was a period of great opportunity when the pressure of an all-encompassing central state had been removed from them, but the penalties for failure were dire. The Barah Sayyids of Muzaffarnagar and Meerut, for instance, had been kingmakers of all Hindustan in the 1710s and 1720s when they virtually controlled the throne of Delhi.[112] They had used the wealth accumulated from service and warfare to dig themselves deeply into local agrarian society around their north-western *qasbah* towns. But when their star fell in the 1740s and 1750s, many Sayyid colonies were wiped out and their revenue rights forfeited to others. Only those lineages which had expanded so fast that their members had become holders of direct cultivating rights survived the storm. Others fled to the northern hills and into Awadh, to creep back to their small towns when the British provided the opportunity to investigate old claims in the 1820s.[113] However, there were many areas where the gentry remained remarkably resilient. The considerable gains made by Muslim zamindars between the time of the *Ain-i-Akbari* and the early British revenue surveys attest to the slow consolidation of these landed service communities around many of the *qasbah* towns.

As chapter 9 will show, north India was witnessing the emergence of a genuine gentry which was more than a body of rent-takers and had a distinct impact on the agriculture, ecology, and society of the lands surrounding their urban bases. But how far can these societies be seen to have had corporate solidarities? In Muslim law, the *qasbah* had no formal status as a corporation, though the term was applied to a place with a distinct urban status which possessed a mosque, a public bath, and a judicial officer (*kazi*). It was, however, an inward sense of cohesion which was important. Tribal genealogy and association with one of the great Islamic ethnicities (*qam*), such as Iran or Turanistan, had been the original badges of status and lines of faction amongst the soldiers and administrators who served the Mughal empire.[114] But these élites often sought out a more secure base and tradition within India. As they embellished their small rural seats with mosques, wells, and groves, a definite sense of pride in home (*watan*) and urban tradition began to emerge. By the 1750s writers were praising the qualities of these small semi-urban places. Early in the following century, we have Persian histories of places like Bilgram or Kakori which are described in the same format as the famous cities of Baghdad, Cairo, or Isfahan. The corporate status and pride of these communities was enhanced by the residence there of families of the holy men who had been settled on revenue-free grants of land by the Mughals and later regional rulers. Thus a tradition of service, religion, and Islamic learning was developed. The flavour of this developing local pride is caught by Murtaza Husain Bilgrami. Writing in the 1770s, he pours scorn on a rival historian who claims to be a Sheikh of Bilgram, saying that he does not truly come from the famous town of light and learning, but from some miserable village across the river.[115]

The ideal Muslim *qasbah* society was formed by literacy, agrarian dependence, and Islam. Families of Muslim service people from *ashraf* (gentry) families were bound together by tight marriage alliances, which often became cross-cousin arrangements. But people from less grand families—even converted Hindu Kayasths and Khattris—could reinforce the community by building up connections of culture and clientage with the élite. Though there always remained lines of social difference between the landholding Muslim gentry and their Hindu cultivators, and though compulsion played a considerable part in agrarian relations, gentry patronage and Hindu veneration of the shrines of Muslim holy men significantly diminished the scope for conflict and enhanced the solidarity of the *qasbah* as a society until well into the colonial period. Gentry families, both Hindu and Muslim, communed in Indo-Persian literary culture, while peasants and craftsmen participated in the same festivals and feast days.

The significance of Muslim *qasbah* society for this study is that it represented almost a mirror image of the Hindu commercial and Brahminical society in the large towns and spread outward into the rural market villages. Both societies witnessed the slow precipitation of economic power and cultural solidarity between the state and agrarian society. Service *qasbah* and commercial city flourished within the ambit of the great revenue-farmers, but the élites of both survived when these over-mighty subjects had passed away. Neither society excluded altogether locally resident members of the minority faith and culture. Thus Muslim weavers and artisans were uneasily bound into the corporate life of the Hindu commercial cities and Hindu cultivators often found an economic and a religious focus in the Islamic *qasbah*. Nevertheless, it was significant that two aspects of pre-colonial social change expressed themselves in such different cultural idioms. There was little as yet to set *qasbah* against merchant *mohulla*; they ran along parallel rather than antagonistic lines. For conflict, there needed to be some fundamental changes: first, the decline of the regional states and their agents which had provided a common political culture and forms of arbitration to minimize these differences: secondly, a series of changes in outlook which emphasized antagonism rather than diversity in religious practice. Yet some of the preconditions for conflict between the Hindu and Muslim leaderships of the later colonial period were present several generations earlier. These preconditions did not exist in the darbars where Hindu and Muslim soldiers fought and intrigued together, nor in agrarian society, but in the contrasting types of solidarities that had emerged between the two.

CONCLUSION

Earlier chapters have shown that there were great regional differences in late eighteenth-century north India, so it would be inappropriate to generalize too widely. But the evidence—especially from the Benares region—suggests that some lines of approach to the period are more viable than others. For instance, the contention that it is possible to see the 'sprouts of capitalism' arising out of India's mercantile economy in the years 1600–1800 does not seem convincing. There is no evidence of change in the 'putting out' system for artisan production which might have brought the producer's labour and tools more directly under the control of capital. The cheapness of artisan labour and the limitations imposed by the merchants' own conception of their social role made this development unlikely. 'Potentialities' for capitalist development in self-cultivating (*khudkasht*) holdings and garden crops certainly existed, as they had done in the high Mughal period. But the very geographical fluidity of élite demand and protection had ensured that these forms of production could not consolidate themselves in any single area. Fyzabad, Benares, or Lucknow exhibited the same potential for capitalist development in the 1780s as the Agra or Delhi region had shown in the 1680s; but by then high farming had retreated around the old imperial capitals. Merchants and townsmen were powerful enough to protect their own interests and modify the forms of the state, but without a stronger political and legal framework they could not dissolve the dominances of rural society.

An alternative path of development was state entrepreneurship.[116] Perhaps the state monopolies and control of tools and labour pioneered by Tipu Sultan in the south or the Raja of Bundhi and Begum Samru in the north might have led to agricultural transformation had conditions been right. Certainly they were able to give a significant stimulus to local economies. These regimes, along with Farrukhabad and the Rohillas, do seem to have been groping towards a new, more active role for the state in society, based perhaps on revitalized religion, as in Mysore, or on greatly expanded systems of *jajmani* relations, as in the northern principalities. But continuous warfare which was necessary for their expansion also vitiated the control of these regimes over capital and labour. The external conditions within which they sought to establish themselves—the pressure of the British and Marathas—were worse even than those faced by the more successful enlightened despots of the next generation outside India such as Mahomed Ali of Egypt.

On the other hand, the notion that the structure of society in the last two centuries of pre-colonial India was undergoing no significant change is difficult to sustain. All 'structural change' must necessarily originate in relatively slight shifts in the economic organization and ideology of societies. The consolidation of a unified merchant class and a locally based service gentry was much more than a simple change of personnel within a static society, though it is easy to miss those evolving classes for the dust thrown up by conventional political history and the concern with 'land-rights'. Both developments were associated with a more general process. This was the quite rapid commercialization of the perquisites of kingship and local lordship which was gathering pace from the end of the Mughal period. A market was created in 'shares' to rights, honours, and powers which brought about a labile expansion of the money economy. The change was significant enough to push the men who dealt with silver rupees or those who recorded the 'shares' into a more important position in society. But it did not alter the form of peasant and artisan production in the short run. On the contrary, the market value of a 'share' in kingship was formed by the extent to which the purchaser could operate non-market forms of political coercion, or make use of the conceptions of rights and obligations which pervaded rural society. In this way 'commercialization' actually blocked out the possibility of 'capitalism' which presupposes a freeing of the labour market.

The growth of a more commercial and more bureaucratic style of government also had implications for the organization of groups between the state and agrarian society. Iqtidar Alam Khan saw an autonomous 'middle class' in the inferior revenue officials and professional servants of the Mughal nobility.[117] But the crucial change here was the rapid precipitation of members of this group as a petty rural service gentry after the empire had passed its peak. For it was landholding and the right to local dues which gave them their autonomy of regional political authority. In the same way, the weakening of state power in the eighteenth century threw traders into turmoil. Yet it also forced the corporations and towns into the new defensive organizations which provided a much firmer basis for a true merchant class.

These pre-colonial origins are important for understanding the much-examined 'India middle classes' of the years after 1860. To a surprising extent, our general historical literature is still imprisoned by what is in effect a variant of the old modernization theory. After 1830, the argument goes, English education and economic change created a new class, first in Bengal and then elsewhere. Colonial political institutions then 'moulded' or 'oppressed' that class (according to the political predilections of the historian). No one would deny that English education and new forms of communication greatly expanded the organization and self-consciousness of intermediate people situated between state and agrarian society. But it must also be recognized that pre-colonial 'mentalities' and forms of organization, particularly those which became stronger in the eighteenth century, were active forces in the creation of this new class and in directing its links with the colonial state and peasantry. Mukherjee has shown how the multi-caste faction (*dal*) of Bengal underpinned the organization of the Calcutta intelligentsia in the 1820s and 1830s.[118] In the south, as Appadurai has recently pointed out, the ancient division between 'right-' and 'left-handed' castes became a principle of conflict and its resolution for the urban life of colonial Madras.[119] Similarly, in the Punjab it could be shown that the charitable and religious donations of the Sikh state formed moral and material bases for the service and merchant people of the colonial period.

In the Ganges valley, the corporate bodies discussed in the last two chapters also continued to contribute to the organization of urban and rural life through at least to the Great Depression of the 1930s. 'Modern' organization—charitable trusts, political and caste association—emerged as accretions around the core of these still vital solidarities. The specific features of such corporations also informed the relations between the elements of the later middle class. The organization of the pre-colonial Hindu corporation and of the Muslim *dargah* or *qasbah* town, turned out to be a middle stage between the fluid relations of the Mughal court and the organization of communal politics in the late nineteenth century. One stage did not necessarily lead on to the other. But the forces of secular nationalism and economic change in the colonial period would have needed to be vastly more powerful to dissolve the corporations into a unified class.

ABBREVIATIONS

AR	*Asiatic(k) Researches*
COR	*Calendar of Oriental Records*, UP Central Records Office, Allahabad
CPC	*Calendar of Persian Correspondence*, National Archives of India, New Delhi
CPR	Conquered and Ceded Provinces Revenue and Revenue (Customs) Proceedings, India Office Library, London
DG	*District Gazetteers of the United Provinces*, 48 vols, Allahabad, 1903–11
DR	'Duncan Records' (Settlement and Miscellaneous), UP Central Records Office, Allahabad

IA   *Indian Antiquary*

IESHR   *Indian Economic and Social History Review*

IHC   Indian Historical Congress

IOL   India Office Library and Records, London

JASB   *Journal of the Asiatic Society of Bengal*

Magt.   Magistrate (of District)

NAI   National Archives of India, New Delhi

NWP   North-Western Provinces

NWPCJ   North-Western Provinces (Criminal) Judicial Proceedings, India Office Library

PR   Proceedings of the Resident (later Agent to the Governor General, Benares) UP Central Records Office, Allahabad

UPR   Uttar Pradesh Central Records Office, Allahabad

NOTES AND REFERENCES

1. J.C. Heesterman, ' "Was there an Indian reaction?" Western expansion in Indian perspective', in H.L. Wesseling (ed.), *Expansion and Reaction*, Leiden, 1978, p. 41.
2. The change was not welcomed see, e.g. Bhimsen, *c.* 1720, 'In the present age unprofessional men having learnt the art of arithmetic have become masters of authority, and engaged in plundering the public', *Tarikh-i-Dilkasha*, tr. V. Khobrekar, Bombay, 1972, p. 232.
3. N.A. Siddiqi, *Land Revenue Administration under the Mughals 1700–50*, Bombay, 1970, pp. 2–3; W.H. Moreland, *From Akbar to Aurangzeb. A Study in Indian Economic History*, new edn., Delhi, 1975, pp. 235, 239–40, 249–54; Richard B. Barnett, *North India between Empires. Awadh, the Mughals and the British 1720–1801*, Berkeley, 1980, pp. 169–70.
4. 11 Jan. 1788, PR.
5. 15 Jan. 1788, PR.
6. In Muttra and Brindaban under Maratha *amil*s the claims of the state extended to 'nightsoil' collected by hereditary sweepers; under the British it became a perquisite of zamindars—a paradigm of change in the political economy, Magt. Muttra to Commr Agra, 15 Mar. 1839, NWP Judl, June 1839, 231/59.
7. The king's duty to protect Brahmins was also commercialized: see J. Duncan's *perwana* to Mahip Narayan Singh, 11 Nov. 1788, PR.
8. Barnett, *North India*, pp. 180–7.
9. K.P. Mishra, *Banaras in Transition 1740–95*, Delhi, 1975, pp. 78–87; DR, vol. 24, 191–3; UPR.
10. See, e.g., Magistrate Benares to Commercial Resident Ghazipur, 4 Oct. 1796, Benares Collectorate Records (rev.) 79, UPR.
11. Note on Beni Ram Pandit, 11 May 1788, vol. 6, DR.
12. B.S. Cohn, 'The Initial British Impact on India: A Case Study of the Banaras Region', *Journal of Asian Studies*, xix (1960), 418–31; cf. 12 Aug. 1788, PR.

13. 11 Jan. 1788, PR.

14. Barnett, *North India*, pp. 188–9ff.

15. E.g. nawabi Gorakhpur, M. Martin, *The History Topography and Statistics of Eastern India*, 3 vols, London, 1838, 1, p. 573.

16. In Etawah, for instance, the Kunnu Prasad, Udai Charan, and Lal Joda Bali families 'greatly benefited' from the rule of Almas Ali, CPR, 10 Dec. 1805, 95/37; in Bareilly the family of Chutter Bihari Lal had supplied several of his *chakladars*, CPR, 17 Feb. 1824, 95/37; in Maratha areas substantial monied men became *amils*, e.g. Purun Chand Pachcowrie, salt merchant, was *amil* of Farrah until 1802 Collr Customs Agra to Bd, 24 Mar. 1809, CPR, 12 April 1809, 97/31; cf. V.D. Divekar, 'The Emergence of an Indigenous Business Class in Maharashtra in the Eighteenth Century' *Modern Asian Studies*, XVI (1982), pp. 427–44; in Farrukhabad from 1770 to 1798, the Mehtab Rai Jain jeweller family had been treasurers taking a commission of 4 annas per cent on *dakhillas* and two rupees on every village within his own *jagir* and an annual pension of Rs 750: correspondence on petition of Mehtab Rai, CPR, June 1808, 91/21, IOL.

17. For an indication of the way in which revenue-farmers' patronage benefited service gentry, see *mahzar* under seal of Ghulam Kwais (n.d.) of Ghulam Saif and Sayyid Mahomed Ali, Mallawan Papers, UPR, publ. *COR*, 1, 16–17. Here Fath Ali 'with the help of his son's father in law, viz. Nadir-uz Zaman, brother of Almas Ali Khan Bahadur [revenue farmer] brought a harkarah [messenger] from Raja Jhau Lal [the Nawab's favourite, Barnett, *North India*, pp. 110, 113, 135] who compelled the aforesaid Qazi [Abdul Razzaq] to give a statement in writing to the effect that Fath Ali and none else is the owner of the property'.

18. Petition of shopkeepers of bazaar Chunoo, 21 Nov. 1787, PR.

19. Petition of zamindars and tenants of Achayl Roy of Perguneh Kurindeh, 11 Jan. 1788, PR.

20. E.g. note on Ram Dayal, 20 April 1788, DR 5, UPR.

21. 24 Dec. 1788, PR; cf. DR 39, pp. 103ff. Dube combined the role of *amil* and *mahajan* in his *parganas*.

22. *Arzi* of *amil* of Secunderapore, 6 July 1795, PR; *amils* also attempted to settle 'turbulent villages' by persuading them to admit *mahajans* who had previously made heavy losses there, *arzi* of Kilroy, 1 Nov. 1792; PR; cf. Raja's answer to Kashmiri Mull, 17 June 1788, PR.

23. J. Treves to Duncan, 21 June 1792; 8 July 1790, PR.

24. Extract from Kulb Ali Khan's Account, DR 39, p. 93; Neave to Duncan, 5 May 1788, DR 14, pp. 1–3, UPR.

25. 27 June, 4 Aug. 1788, PR; Benares Treasury Accounts, DR 31, UPR.

26. Graham to Anderson, 5 Dec. 1777, cited Mishra, *Banaras*, p. 266.

27. A. Shakespear, *Selections from the Duncan Records*, Benares, 1873, 1, 34; 26 Aug. 1788, PR.

28. *Ikranamah* of Kashi Nath, son of Kashmiri Mull, 9 Mar., 13 June 1788, PR.

29. Answer of Kashmiri Mull, 13 June 1788, PR.

30. S.L. Dube to Duncan, 5 Mar. 1789, PR.

31. 28 April, 27 June 1788, 8 Sept. 1789, PR.

32. 27 Jan., 26 Aug. 1788, PR.

33. 26 Aug. 1788, PR.

34. Ibrahim Ali Khan's Report on Markets, 18 Dec. 1788, PR, cf. *Ain*, 11, tr. Jarrett, 41–3.

35. See D.L. Curley, 'Fair grain markets and Mughal famine policy in late eighteenth century Bengal', *Calcutta Historical Journal*, ii (1977), 1–27; for an example of market closure in Malwa, John Malcolm, *A Memoir of Central India Including Malwa and Adjoining Provinces*, London, 1824, ii, 284.

36. Cf. C.N. Cooke, *The Rise, Progress and Present Condition of Banking in India* (Calcutta, 1863), p. 12.

37. See , e.g., the Representation of Kaun Das, Mintmaster, 4 Dec. 1787, PR.

38. See, e.g. For. Sec. Cons., 27 Oct. 1777, 4, NAI; 26 Feb. 1789, PR.

39. Resident Poona to Resident Benares, 10 Apr. 1789, PR.

40. 5 July 1789, PR.

41. Examination of bankers, 15 Sept. 1790; Report of Mintmaster, 1 May 1791, PR.

42. Gautam Bhadra, 'Some Aspects of the Social Position of Merchants at Murshidabad, 1763–93', paper presented to Indian History Congress, Chandigarh, 1973.

43. Law de Lauriston, Minute 1777, *État Politique de l'Inde en 1777*, Paris, 1913, Société de l'Histoire de l'Inde Française, p. 111.

44. H.T. Prinsep, *History of the Political and Military Transactions in India During the Administration of the Marquis of Hastings 1813–23*, London, 1825, 11, 298; but cf. G.T. Kulkarni, 'Banking in the 18th century: A Case study of a Poona Banker', *Artha Vijnana*, xv (1973), 180–200.

45. Metcalfe's Orders on the Delhi Territories, *Delhi Residency and Agency*, 1, 8, 27.

46. The 'Gulistan-i-Rehmat' records several examples of Rohilla rulers favouring merchant and banking groups in order to encourage their settlement: see above, pp. 22–3.

47. Barnett, *North India*, pp. 172ff.

48. Asst Collr to Collr Allahabad, 26 June 1804, CPR, 16 July 1804, 90/40, IOL.

49. Resident Lucknow to Govt, 14 Sept. 1795, Home Misc. 448, IOL; *CPC*, viii, 30, 183, 198.

50. Abu Talib, *Tafzihul Ghafalin* (*History of Asafu 'ddaulah Nawab Vazir of Oudh*), tr. W. Hoey, new edn, Lucknow, 1971, pp. 53, 91–5; P. Basu, *Oudh and the East India Company 1785–1801*, Lucknow, 1943, p. 110.

51. Note on the Bachraj Family, annex. N.B. Edmonstone to Resident Benares, n.d., Bihar and Benares Revenue Consultation, 1 Dec. 1818, 112/11, IOL.

52. D.R. Gadgil, *Origins of the Modern Indian Business Class; an Interim Report*, New York, 1957, pp. 25–34.

53. R. Fox, 'Pariah Capitalism and Traditional Indian Merchants Past and Present', in M. Singer (ed.), *Entrepreneurship and the Modernisation of Occupational Cultures*, Duke Univ., N.C., 1973, pp. 16–34.

54. James Tod, *Rajasthan Annals and Antiquities of Rajasthan or the Central and the Western Rajput States of India*, ed., W. Crooke, London, 1920, 11, 1, 110.

55. Dilbagh Singh, 'Role of the Mahajan'; S.N. and K.N. Hasan and S.P. Gupta, 'Patterns of Agricultural Production in the Territories to Amber *c.* 1650–1750', *IHC 1966*, pp. 244–8.

56. Tod, *Rajasthan*, 1, 171.

57. Ibid., 11, 606, cf. app. 645, *perwana* of Maharana Sri Raj Singh.

58. For a more detailed discussion of Benares and Mirzapur, see C.A. Bayly, 'Indian Merchants in a "traditional" setting, Benares 1780–1820', in C. Dewey and A.G. Hopkins (eds), *The Imperial Impact*, London, 1978.

59. N.A. Thoothi, *History of the Vaishnavas of Gujerat*, London, 1928.

60. *Roop and Saroop Poori* v. *Badli Gir and Laulji*, Mirzapur Court, 3 April 1791, PR.

61. 'A short account of the Nouputtee Mahajans of Benares', For. Misc. 12, pt 1, NAI.

62. According to the story current among descendants of the Naupatti bankers, Lala Gokul Das, a leading Agarwala and the Gujerati head of the corporation were the prime movers in backing Mansa Ram against the previous farmer of the Benares territories, Mir Rustam Ali; it was also said that the commercial community favoured a Hindu rather than Muslim ruler locally. I have not been able to verify this story from contemporary evidence, but it was certainly part of the Naupatti's claim for high status.

63. 'A short account of the Nouputtee'.

64. Family histories, interviews, Sri Kumud Chandra, Dr Giresh Chandra, Benares, 1972–4.

65. Petition of Bankers and Resident's Reply, 13 Jan. 1795, PR.

66. Family history, papers, *panda* book, in possession of Sri Devi Narayan, Sakshi Binayak, Benares, Jan. 1973; interview Sri Govind Das Kothiwal, Mar. 1974.

67. *Gunga Bye* v. *the Mother of Jwalanath*, 3 Aug. 1792, PR.

68. Bayly, *Imperial Impact*, pp. 178–88.

69. Interviews, Chaukhambha, 1973.

70. Family histories, Sri Govind Das Kothiwal, Mar. 1974.

71. Petition, 4 Dec. 1787, PR.

72. Mehta Baldeo Das Vithal Das Vyasa, *Vanshwali Vadnagara Sipahi Nagar Kashi Nivasi*, Nagar Union, Benares, 1938.

73. 18 Jan. 1788; DR Revenue, vol. 5, UPR.

74. Representation of Ibrahim Ali Khan, 7 Mar. 1788, PR.

75. Sir John Shore, 'On Some Extraordinary Facts, Customs and Practices of the Hindoos', *AR*, lv (1795), 331; 7 Mar. 1788, PR.

76. 31 July 1790, PR.

77. Representation of Bhawani Das and others, 19 Apr. 1791; 'Petition of the Principal Bankers', 13 Jan. 1795, PR.

78. Petition of Naupatti and others, 1797, Agent to GG to Govt, 2 April 1798, PR.

79. Ibid.; for ancient links between the Agarwal headman family and the Bhumihar élite, see *mahzar*, 15 Apr. 1838 of Harrakhchand to District Court, 'Memory Book' (*Yadasht Bahi*), Chaukhambha.

80. 15 Sept. 1790, PR.

81. Police Arrangements, Benares Collr, Records, Misc. Series, vol. 8, UPR.

82. J.D.M. Derrett, *Essays in Classical and Modern Hindu Law*, Leiden, 1975, 11, 25, 45.

83. Petition of Bankers and Resident's Remarks, 13 Jan. 1795, PR.

84. J.N. Sarkar and Nirad Bhushan Roy, *A History of the Dasnamis or Nagar Sanyasis*, Allahabad, 1959, pp. 79–80; for a comparable incident in Delhi, see Shiv Das Lakhnavi, *Shahnama Munnawar Kalam*, tr. S.H. Aksari, Patna, 1980, pp. 112–15.

85. See Below, pp. 320–1.

86. Obit. Babu Bireshwar Mittra, *Tribune*, 25 July 1891. The scheme was ultimately accepted.

87. *Juggernath* v. *Hurrkeshen Gir*, 3 Feb. 1795, PR.

88. Sarkar, *Dasnamis*, p. 79.

89. Ibid., p. 67.

90. See pamphlet, *Kumarswami Veera Saiva Math, Kedar Ghat, Banaras*, Tirupandal, Thanjavur, 1955, p. 6.

91. Sarkar, *Dasnamis*, p. 127.

92. Thomas Hardwicke, 'Narrative of a Journey to Sirinagar', *AR*, vi (1799), 315.

93. Ibid., p. 314.

94. Ibid., cf., William Francklin, *A Military Memoir of Mr George Thomas*, Calcutta, 1803, pp. 41–3.

95. For a general description, F.W. Growse, *Mathura, A District Memoir*, 1882, repr. Delhi, 1979, pp. 189–90; see below, p. 321; interviews, Agra Dist., 1981.

96. Prabhu Dayal Mital, *Braj ke Dharm Sampradaiyon ka Itihas. Braj ka Sanskritik Itihas*, 11, Delhi, 1968, pp. 210–12, Muttra in 1815 retained a panchayat of three Brahmins and seven others, BCJ, 12 July 1816, 132/43, IOL; for a similar and apparently ancient corporation at Hardwar, NWPCJ, June 1855, 234/4, IOL.

97. Growse, *Mathura*, p. 308.

98. For the involvement of Bairagis with court politics and trade in Bharatpur, see Resident Bharatpur to Political Agent Delhi, 8 April 1831, For. Misc., Letters from Bharatpur Agency, NAI.

99. J. Lushington, 'Marriage Customs of Jats of Bhurtpore', *JASB*, ii (1833), 285.

100. Bayly, 'Death ritual', in Whaley, *Mirrors of Mortality*, pp. 163–6.

101. Motichandra, *Kashi ka Itihas*, pp. 236–48.

102. Martin, *Eastern India*, 1, 50.

103. Cf. M.L. Patterson, 'Changing Patterns of Occupation among Chitpavan Brahmans', *IESHR*, vii (1970), 375–96.

104. Max Weber, *The City*, tr. and ed. D. Martindale and G. Neuwirth, New York, 1958, p. 97.

105. Ibid., p. 84.

106. B. Stein, *Peasant, State and Society*, pp. 249–52.

107. M. Singer, *When a Great Tradition Modernises* (Philadelphia, 1973).

108. M.D. Morris, 'Values as an obstacle in growth in South Asia', *Journal of Economic History*, xxvii (1967), 588ff; but see below, ch. 10.

109. U.N. Ghoshal, *A History of Indian Political Ideas*, Oxford, 1966, pp. 425–6.

110. C.A. Bayly, *The Local Roots of Indian Politics*, Oxford, 1975, pp. 79–80; interviews, Diara Shah Hajatullah, Allahabad, 1968.

111. See below, ch. 9.

112. Ghulam Husain Khan Tabatabai, *Seir Mutaqherin*, tr. Haji Mustafa, Calcutta, 1789, 111, 83; *DG Muzaffarnagar*, Allahabad, 1920, pp. 163–74.

113. *DG Muzaffarnagar*, pp. 173–4.

114. Even excellent modern studies have failed to grasp the importance of this locally based gentry. D. Lelyveld, *Aligarh's First Generation* (Princeton, 1978) posits a direct move on the part of the Muslim *ashraf* from centralized Mughal court faction to 'modern' professional and peer-group organization in institutions such as

Aligarh College; Iqtidar Alam Khan, in his *Middle Classes of the Mughal Empire* (Aligarh, 1975), draws attention to the importance of minor revenue officials, but not to their economic base in petty landholding; Satish Chandra, however, briefly anticipates the argument, 'Some Aspects of the Growth of a Money Economy in India During the 17th Century', *IESHR*, iii (1967), 326.

115. W. Irvine, 'Ahmad Shah Abdali', *IA*, xxxvi (1907), 10.

116. Asok Sen, 'A Pre-British Economic Formation in India of the Late Eighteenth Century. Tipu Sultan's Mysore', in Barun De (ed.), *Perspectives in Social Sciences*, i, *Historical Dimensions*, Calcutta, 1977, pp. 46–119.

117. Iqtidar Alam Khan, *Middle Classes*.

118. S.N. Mukherjee, 'Caste, Class and Politics in Calcutta, 1818–38', in E. Leach and S.N. Mukherjee (eds), *Elites in South Asia*, Cambridge, 1970, pp. 33–78.

119. A. Appadurai, 'Right and Left Hand castes in South India', *IESHR*, xi (1974), 216–60.

7

Eastern India in the
Early Eighteenth-century 'Crisis':
Some Evidence from Bihar*

Muzaffar Alam

In recent years there has been a significant shift of emphasis in the study of eighteenth-century India, from the high imperial government and adminis-tration to the regional economy and local social context of politics.[1] Scholars of the Mughal empire now have a far better understanding of the conditions that preceded and accompanied Mughal decline in Delhi and in the different parts of the empire, both independently and in their interactional context. One result of these recent studies is that the validity of explaining Mughal decline in purely economic terms is now open to serious doubts. Many South Asians support the contention of these studies that eighteenth-century Indian history, of which Mughal decline evidently formed an important part, ought to be studied in its own idiom. What has, hence, emerged is a critique and a revision of many of the existing studies of Mughal politics and economy.[2]

However, the purpose of this paper is not as a response to either the positive or the negative reactions of these 'revisionist' studies. It is attempted here to examine some historical materials from yet another region, namely, the

*Muzaffar Alam, 'Eastern India in the Early Eighteenth-century "Crisis": Some Evidence from Bihar', *Indian Economic and Social History Review*, xxviii, 1991, pp. 43–71.

Author's note: A version of this paper was presented at a seminar on 'The State, Decentralization and Tax-Farming (The Ottoman Empire, Iran and India)' held at Munich University in May 1990. Professor S. Nurul Hasan has discussed the theme and the sources with me. He also allowed me free access to his personal collection of relevant materials. Gautam Bhadra and Sanjay Subrahmanyam commented on an earlier draft. I acknowledge their help with gratitude.

Mughal province of Bihar, to see if the questions posed in these studies in general, and in my own earlier study of northern India in particular, could help us comprehend better the history of other parts of Mughal India. Organized in three parts, these data try in the first place to see what early eighteenth-century Bihar politics was like and how it interacted with developments at the Mughal court as well as with the general political and administrative problems of the empire in the period. Internal social turbulence has been examined in the second part by way of delineating the local social context of this politics, while in the third part an effort has been made to understand the trends in revenue with a view to assessing the strength or weakness of the economy of the province. All this is clearly in keeping with the framework of my earlier studies of the period, and it will be seen that many of the earlier conclusions seem to be reinforced here by the evidence from Bihar.

To leave matters at such a stage would amount though to disregarding a crucial aspect of the social history of the period, which, it is difficult to deny, was one of turmoil, even though in absolute terms there was little decline in material production and affluence. The question of how this turmoil was perceived and articulated by different social groups needs careful examination. The conclusion of this paper touches upon the relevance of a study of 'Mughal observations of Mughal decline', with a view to attempt it in some depth in the future. We begin, however, with the perspective of some of the chroniclers and littérateurs and the nature of early eighteenth-century Bihar politics as it emerges from their observations.

I

In Mughal India, in the provinces, the two principal officials, the *subadar* (governor) and the *diwan* (revenue and finance minister), and also some other important local functionaries, had fairly clearly defined spheres of power and authority. Accountable for their working directly to the imperial centre, they acted, in theory and in practice, as checks upon each other in the province. This classical pattern of governors and of the relations between the centre and the province underwent definite changes in parts of the Mughal empire in the early eighteenth century, both because of high Mughal politics and the disturbances at local levels in the province.[3] Developments in Bihar also seem to have traversed a similar trajectory in the period.

Early in the eighteenth century some important steps, still within the classical framework, were taken in regard to the eastern provinces including Bihar. The grandson of the reigning Emperor Aurangzeb, Prince Muhammad Azim, who held Bengal, was also appointed *subadar* of Bihar in 1703, while

Murshid Quli Khan, the *diwan* of Bengal, took over Bihar's revenue and financial departments.[4] The new *subadar* and the *diwan* did not get along well; but the Prince nevertheless left a lasting impact on the cultural life of the province, its capital Patna being renamed after him as Azimabad.[5] The prince did lead some successful campaigns against rebel zamindars, but neither he nor the *diwan* Murshid Quli Khan could effect any change in the provincial administration before their return to the court. The prince was recalled because Murshid Quli, who had earned laurels from the Emperor for his achievements in Bengal, did not want him to stay in the province,[6] and also because his uncle, Prince Muhammad Azam, reportedly instigated his transfer, possibly as part of his preparations for the fight for the throne following the imminent death of the ageing Emperor.[7] But before Azim could reach the court, the Emperor died, and this was followed by the victory of his father, Bahadur Shah, in the ensuing civil war. Azim's treasure, collected in Bengal and Bihar, and his strategic moves, contributed a great deal to the new Emperor's victory.

Prince Muhammad Azim, now Azim-ush-Shan, was the most powerful person at the court of his father, Bahadur Shah (1702–12).[8] The prince was again made the *subadar* of Bihar, but he stayed at the centre and his associate, Saiyid Husain Ali Khan, deputized for him in the province.[9] Murshid Quli was recalled to the court, though, for a very brief period.[10]

Husain Ali Khan was certainly an able administrator, even though in his selection Azim-ush-Shan was principally motivated by considerations of dependability and loyalty. But the fact that he was a mere *naib* with no base in the province imposed serious constraints in the effective discharge of his duties. Azim's son, Farrukh Siyar, based in Dacca, also maintained a presence in Patna and often took the initiative in political and military matters,[11] to the obvious inconvenience of Saiyid Husain Ali Khan.[12] In 1712, when Bahadur Shah died, Prince Farrukh Siyar proclaimed his father, Azim-ush-Shan, as the new emperor without waiting for the outcome of the routine war of succession. Later, when he learnt of his father's defeat and death in the civil war in Lahore he arranged for his own coronation. All this was arranged by the prince at the advice of his favourites, namely, Khwaja Muhammad Asim, Qazi Shariatullah, and Ahmad Beg, better known by their titles respectively as Khan-i-Dauran Samsam-ud-Daulah, Mir Jumla, and Ghazi-ud-Din Ahmad Beg. Saiyid Husain Ali Khan resented both these acts, even though on the intervention of Farrukh Siyar's mother, he and his brother, Saiyid Abdullah Khan, the governor of the neighbouring province of Allahabad (the famous Saiyid brothers of our period) agreed to the prince's principal supporters in his bid to wrest the throne from his uncle, Jahandar Shah (1712–13).[13]

Farrukh Siyar, thus, acquired the throne in a situation fraught with possibilities for Bihar. Among the many who supported him there were nobles like Husain Ali Khan, Samsam-ud-Daulah, and Mir Jumla who had lived in Bihar and would continue to take interest in its politics and administration. On the other hand, it is also known that many decisions at the court of Farrukh Siyar, including appointments to the governorship of provinces like Bihar, were to be compromises, in keeping with the plans and ambitions of one or the other of his supporters. The court was marred by intense rivalry among his nobles, and the emperor, instead of keeping a distance, acted like a mere member of a faction.[14]

In 1712, just before Farrukh Siyar's accession to the throne, Nusrat Khan was the governor of Bihar. He was appointed by Jahandar Shah replacing Saiyid Husain Ali Khan, who still deputized for the deceased Prince Muhammad Azim. Nusrat Khan seems to have appreciated the necessity of reorganizing the local administration. He is reported to have encouraged a certain Surat, son of Jagat, to mediate between the governor and the zamindars.[15] Once Farrukh Siyar came to power, Nusrat Khan was, however, removed from Bihar. The new governor was Saiyid Ghairat Khan, a close relative of the Saiyid brothers.[16] Ghairat Khan was, by any standards, an able administrator, but his appointment in Bihar was solely because of his links with the Saiyids. Still, his appointment guaranteed a measure of continuity from Saiyid Husain Ali Khan's time. But before Ghairat Khan could do anything, he too was transferred. Mir Jumla, a powerful leader of the faction opposed to the Saiyids, was the next governor.[17]

Mir Jumla was sent to Bihar, again in a bid to balance the claims and aspirations of the nobles at the centre. To appreciate this, it is necessary to look more carefully at the details of factional court politics. The Saiyids, who had planned by 1714 to become the supreme power, wished the court to free itself from the influence of any noble close to the emperor. Mir Jumla was then promoted by the emperor to counter the growing power of the Saiyids. He was authorized to sign all papers on the emperor's behalf. Unmindful of the regulations, he entertained proposals directly from officials and from candidates seeking positions and promotions, and set the seal and signature of the emperor upon appointment letters (*parwanas* and *sanads*) by-passing the office of the wazir, Saiyid Abdullah Khan. As the presence of Ghairat Khan—the Saiyids' man—in Bihar meant the strengthening of their hand, Mir Jumla was also made governor of Bengal and Bihar, initially with permission to stay at court.[18]

The arrangement suited Mir Jumla, whose primary concern was to gain control over the offices and affairs of the centre; it also suited Murshid Quli

Khan who had by then established himself firmly in Bengal.[19] The Saiyid brothers' counter-moves, however, upset the calculations of the emperor and Mir Jumla. Having lost his hold over the eastern provinces, Saiyid Husain Ali Khan now secured the viceroyalty of the Deccan provinces, with a plan to rule there through his deputy, Daud Khan Panni, with whom he entered into an alliance stipulating a fixed annual revenue in return for freedom to Daud Khan in local administration.[20] This implied a weakening of the central authority vis-à-vis the Saiyids and their clients. But the emperor could not logically object to it, as Mir Jumla had been allowed a similar arrangement with Murshid Quli Khan. As a measure of compromise then, Mir Jumla was asked to leave for Patna, while Saiyid Husain Ali Khan set off for the Deccan.[21] As the Emperor had promised Mir Jumla that he would recall him as soon as Saiyid Husain Ali Khan had left Delhi, the former proceeded slowly towards Patna. He also feared failing against a turbulent group of Bihar-based zamindars, the Ujjainiyas,[22] and have his prospects for a high office at the centre, jeopardized. The Ujjainiyas, had already rocked the Bihar government. Mir Jumla arrived in Bihar in 1715 with some of the best available forces. But his Mughal army, instead of combating the dreaded rebel zamindars in the countryside, harassed the innocent residents and the traders of Patna.[23] According to plan, he did not stay long in the province. Sarbuland Khan became the next governor.

Thus, if on the hand the centre, bedevilled with its own problems, had little time to attend to the difficulties of the Bihar administration, the governors and the other provincial administrators, on the other hand, always had their eyes directed at a position at the centre. Further, Bengal's relations with the centre had also begun steadily to lead to the 'hijacking' of the Bihar government. This comes out more clearly in the governorships of Sarbuland Khan and Fakhr-ud-Daulah.

Sarbuland Khan had governed Awadh and Allahabad efficiently, and his posting in Bihar promised a stable and strong government.[24] He handled the problems of the countryside deftly, encouraged new contracts with the zamindars, and divested the *diwan* of all powers, so as to have full control over the finance and revenue departments.[25] Soon, however, he was also recalled to the court, again solely because of a new development at the centre. Farrukh Siyar, spoiling now for a showdown with the Saiyids, summoned him along with Ajit Singh and Nizam-ul-Mulk to Delhi. All of them were, however, won over by the Saiyids, whose unchallenged ascendancy was once more reflected, among other things, in the appointments in Bihar and correspondence with Murshid Quli Khan for an uninterrupted and secure flow of revenue to Delhi from Bengal.[26]

Sarbuland Khan's brief tenure inaugurated a new pattern of provincial administration, as he showed interest in controlling, either by himself or through his associates, several important local offices, including the *diwani* and *faujdari*s. Even if his immediate successor did not succeed in ruling with additional powers, the features of new *subadari* (governorship) or nawabi rule are unmistakable in the governorship of Fakhr-ud-Daulah. But before examining the difficulties of Fakhr-ud-Daulah's governorship, it is important to return briefly to the immediate aftermath of Sarbuland Khan's governorship.

Early in Muhammad Shah's reign (1720–48), and following the fall of the Saiyids, one of their senior kinsmen, Saiyid Nusrat Yar Khan[27] who rose to the high *mansab* (rank) of 7000/7000, was appointed governor of Bihar. His appointment, as a mark of compensation to the bruised self-esteem of the clan of the Barha Saiyids, was also in consideration of his remaining neutral in the Battle of Hasanpur which eclipsed forever the position of the Saiyids in Mughal politics.[28] Nusrat Yar Khan, who governed the province through his deputy, Abd-ur-Rahim Khan, died in 1723–4.[29] Thereafter, for about five years there was no governor in Bihar important enough to be recorded consistently in our sources. The author of *Siyar-ul-Muta' akhkhirin* did not know who succeeded Nusrat Yar Khan; he only knew that very probably in 1140 (1727–8) or a year before or after, Fakhr-ud-Daulah, brother of Roshan-ud-Daulah, obtained the *subadari* and held it for five years. But it is likely that during these years Samsam-ud-Daulah, then the Mir Bakshi and a highly influential noble at the centre, virtually ruled Bihar through his henchmen.

Samsam-ud-Daulah had enjoyed a long association with Bengal and Bihar. His father, and his elder brother, the saint Khwaja Muhammad Qasim, lay buried in Bengal. For quite some time he himself looked after the management of this shrine and the *madad-i-ma'ash* (revenue free grant) attached to it.[31] He was prominent among those who lived in Patna with Farrukh Siyar and accompanied him to Agra in 1712 to contest for the throne. More than one member of his family as well as his faction figure in the early eighteenth-century politics and administration of Bihar and Bengal where they also held a significant proportion of the total *jagir*s (revenue assignments). If not as a *subadar*, he certainly acted as a mediator between the centre and the administrators in Bengal and Orissa. Shuja-ud-Din, the deputy of Murshid Quli Khan in Orissa was, for all practical purposes, his protégé, for whom he secured Bengal and Orissa on Murshid Quli Khan's death in 1726, even though the latter had willed his grandson, Sarfaraz Khan, to be his successor.[32] Samsam-ud-Daulah seems to have manoeuvred to get him the *subadari* of Bihar as well. Shuja-ud-Din, however, secured Bihar only in 1733–4. To appreciate the factors that prevented Samsam-ud-Daulah from obtaining for Shuja-ud-Din the governorship of Bihar immediately after Murshid Quli's death, it would be necessary to focus attention on the political alignments at the court, together with some details of the administration in the province.

Early in the 1720s, after Nizam-ul-Mulk had given up the *wizarat* and left for the Deccan, a group of nobles under the leadership of Burhan-ul-Mulk, the governor of Awadh, Muizz-ul-Daulah Haider Quli Khan, and Roshan-ud-Daulah Zafar Khan emerged as a powerful faction at the court. This group, except for a brief spell in 1726–7, generally acted in alliance with Samsam-ud-Daulah's faction. Among them, Burhan-ul-Mulk, because of his marked success in Awadh, occupied a distinct position. He used his position to influence the appointments in the provinces, particularly in Allahabad and Bihar, both being in the neighbourhood of Awadh.[33] He got Bihar, first for Aqidat Khan, and then for Roshan-ud-Daulah's brother, Fakhr-ud-Daulah.

Fakhr-ud-Daulah followed the example of Burhan-ul-Mulk. He dealt with refractory zamindars sternly, but in the campaigns against them he managed to secure the support from one group within the class of zamindars itself. As Sarbuland Khan's immediate successors had rarely been able to collect tributes from the *ghatwals* of Palamau and Chotanagpur, he invaded the area in 1730. He also led expeditions against the Ujjainiyas of Jagdishpur (in Shahabad) with an army which included the local militia of Horil Singh of Mathila, Pahlwan Singh of Nokha, and Tribhuwan Singh of Tikari.[34] He also further promoted and encouraged new arrangements (*ta'ahhud*), which had already been initiated earlier, with the zamindars in general, and while doing so, insisted on dealing directly with them or on choosing the mediator himself.

Fakhr-ud-Daulah also tried to reorganize and control the *jagir* administration in the province. A *jagir* in the Mughal system implied a right over revenue in a district or districts assigned to an official against his pay claim, and calculated according to the numerical value of his *mansab*. The responsibility of collecting the revenue was with the official, which he performed with the help of his own agents (*amils* and *gumashtas*) in his *jagir* districts. The *jagir* was ordinarily transferable and was assigned in an area alien to the *jagirdar* (assignee). The *jagirdar* was seen as an agent of the central government and was not supposed to have or develop permanent links with his *jagir* lands. They could, however, choose local men as their agents. Also, as exceptions to the rule, many indigenous zamindars and chiefs held their *jagirs* within their zamindari territories, while many retired and disabled officials or their dependants were awarded *jagirs* on a permanent basis to reinforce the empire at local levels.[35]

In the early eighteenth century, when widespread disturbances in the countryside dislocated the *jagir*s, the *jagir*-holders, particularly the Indians, endeavoured to have their *jagir*s in or around their home towns, or at least, in places where they were posted at that time. Those based at the centre or at some distance from the assignment preferred to hold them on a permanent basis, or at least for a long period. With this, they thought they would have some links with the local people, be able to mobilize them and, thus, would be in a better position to meet the threat from the zamindars. As the Mughals were no longer powerful enough to guarantee security to their local officials, they bowed to their demands, even if it implied a scaling down of the power and authority of the centre. The modified *jagir* came to prevail in almost the whole of north India. In Bihar, for instance, Khwaja Lutfullah Sadiq, Sher Afgan Khan, Samsam-ud-Daulah, Raja Muhkam Singh, and Ismail Quli Khan, all held their *jagir*s initially for a long term and eventually, almost hereditarily.[36]

This development was, however, to the obvious inconvenience of the governors who sought wide powers eventually to turn their provinces into principalities of their own. In Bengal, Murshid Quli Khan tried to convert the entire province into *khalisa* (crown land). Besides the conditional (*mashrut*) *jagir*s of the local officials, he allowed only a few outsiders.[37] Murshid Quli Khan began to do this late in Aurangzeb's reign and legitimized his action by an imperial order which still carried weight. Further, his action caused no real loss to the outsider *jagir*s, as he adjusted their *jagir*s in Orissa which was also under his control. In the 1720s, Burhan-ul-Mulk, who had only Awadh in his governorship, could not abolish the *jagir*s but he minimized outside interference by bringing all the *jagir*s, and the *amil*s of the *jagirdar*s, under his direct jurisdiction. This has been characterized as an *ijara* (tax-farming) arrangement.[38]

In Bihar a very large part of the revenue was assigned in *jagir*s. According to a revenue roll of Muhammad Shah's time only Rs 6,63,717/1¾ out of the estimated revenue or Rs 95,61,622/2 (*jama*) were in *khalisa*; the remaining Rs 88,97,905¼ were assigned in *jagir*s to sixty-six officials[39] posted both within and outside the province. Any drastic change, like the one of Murshid Quli Khan, in such a situation would have antagonized a very substantial number of important nobles. The act would have been self-defeating, in particular when the governors—as we have seen—needed a strong lobby at the centre. Fakhr-ud-Daulah thus initiated in the twelfth regnal year of Muhammad Shah (1731–2) a process similar to that in Awadh in order eventually to have for himself the *ijara* of the entire province. But before he could complete the process, he lost the *subadari*.

As Fakhr-ud-Daulah tried to strengthen his position by acquiring the whole province on *ijara*, he came into conflict with the powerful erstwhile

Mughal tax-farmers and the intermediaries. Among them was one Shaikh Abdullah who had emerged as a key figure in the Bihar *suba* administration, having often enjoyed the position of a *naib* (deputy and representative) or the sole *muta'ahhid* (contractor on behalf) of the governor. He was thus in touch with the zamindars and the martial group commanders (*jama'a-dars*) and headed a large brigade of the local militia. Khwaja Mutasim, brother of Samsam-ud-Daulah, was the second such magnate in Patna, who pretended to live like a mendicant but was in actuality alleged to be the ruler of the province. Nobody, not even the emperor, could have restrained his influence, even though his presence was a grave threat to the authority of the governor. Shaikh Abdullah and Khwaja Mutasim often acted in unison.[40] Fakhr-ud-Daulah dealt with them sternly. Khwaja Mutasim, on a charge of having misappropriated a huge sum pertaining to the treasury, was imprisoned, his mansion confiscated. Later he was released only to leave for Delhi. Shaikh Abdullah was chased out of the province to take shelter in Ghazipur under the jurisdiction of Burhan-ul-Mulk.[41]

All this proved to be the beginning of the end of Fakhr-ud-Daulah's power in Bihar, which was precipitated by a new development leading to a change in the equations among the nobles at the centre. A factor in this was the Maratha threat.

Early in the eighteenth century, the Maratha policy of northward expansion caused serious concern to the Mughals. Regarding the means to be adopted to checkmate the menace, however, opinion at the imperial centre was divided; the wazir, Muhammad Qamar-ud-Din and his party which included his cousin, Nizam-ul-Mulk, the viceroy of the Deccan (who suffered the most against the Marathas) advocated an all-out war, while many others at the court, under the leadership of Samsam-ud-Daulah, were for a controlled move and negotiated settlement.[42] Burhan-ul-Mulk feigned indifference so long as his power in Awadh was not in danger. He did not even hesitate to support their (the Marathas') ally, the Bundelas of central India, against one or the other Mughal appointee, like Muhammad Khan Bangash who threatened to restrain his unchallenged position in Awadh.[43] But when the Bundela territory began to be used by the Marathas to raid the areas close to Awadh he joined the camp of the wazir and manipulated to secure Agra and Malwa, then in control of Samsam-ud-Daulah's friend Raja Jai Singh, to check the Maratha advance in the south-west of Awadh and Allahabad.[44] To Samsam-ud-Daulah this meant the loss not only of an ally but also of a region in upper India. He had to reinforce his position in the east.

Again, Burhan-ul-Mulk also had to be watchful about the movements in his neighbourhood of the Afghan chiefs, including Muhammad Khan Bangash of Farrukhabad who also held the governorship of Allahabad. He had to get Allahabad for a friend, if not for himself, immediately. Accordingly, he first managed the province for Sarbuland Khan, with *faujdari*s of a large part of it for himself. The entire province was taken over by him in 1736.[45] In the early 1730s, Burhan-ul-Mulk himself confronted too many difficulties to pay full attention to those of his erstwhile allies, like Roshan-ud-Daulah. Further, Burhan-ul-Mulk must have felt uneasy at Fakhr-ud-Daulah's inroads into *sarkar* Ghazipur, on the eastern border of Allahabad, ostensibly in pursuit of the Bihar zamindars and Shaikh Abdullah. Samsam-ud-Daulah, thus, had no difficulty in securing Fakhr-ud-Daulah's transfer from Bihar, which was then added to the governorship of Shuja-ud-Din, his protégé in Bengal.[46]

It is a matter of conjecture how closely the politics and administration of Bihar at this stage had come to be influenced also by the developments in the centre's relations with Bengal. In 1712, when Farrukh Siyar, following the news of the death of his father in Lahore and Jahandar Shah's coronation, proclaimed himself the emperor in Patna, Nawab Murshid Quli Khan, then the *diwan* of Bengal, not only refused to comply with his orders, but killed his man, Ajmeri Khan, in a battle near Murshidabad, the new capital of the province.[47] Later, however, both the new emperor, Farrukh Siyar, and Murshid Quli Khan, each appreciating the other's strength, had to compromise. Farrukh Siyar could not afford to meet the threat of disruption of the flow of the revenue from Bengal, while on the other hand, Murshid Quli Khan needed *sanad*s from the centre to legitimize his power. Murshid Quli Khan accepted the new emperor, and in return he retained not only his existing position, but also got the *subadari* of Orissa and the *niyabat* of Bengal. An infant Prince Farkhunda Siyar, who died soon, was the new absentee governor of the province.[48] In 1715, when Mir Jumla had to leave Delhi as the new governor of Bengal and Bihar, he was—as we saw above—instructed not to proceed beyond Patna.

But the relations between the central authorities and Nawab Murshid Quli Khan were not smooth under Farrukh Siyar, because of, among other things, a sharp difference between them in matters relating to the English East India Company's trade in Bengal. The English made full use of these differences and obtained facilities and privileges through orders from the centre, first in 1714 and then in 1717, to the obvious inconvenience of the nawab who, according to some reports, never allowed their execution in full.[49] The central authorities then seem to become extraordinarily considerate to the nawab, extolling his loyalty excessively, perhaps to ensure it, and promising him full authority in local matters, perhaps to mollify him and compensate for the restrictions which the famous farman of 1717 had imposed on his position.[50]

Around this time Samsam-ud-Daulah emerged as the important link between the centre and the eastern provinces. Bihar was then in virtual control of his agent, his own brother Khwaja Mutasim, while Murshid Quli Khan grew in power and authority in Bengal.[51]

While the provincial administrators' endeavour for additional powers implied modifications in the existing 'rules and regulations' set by the centre, it posed no threat to its overarching position as such. There had to be someone to arbitrate in the event of a clash between the provincial officials and local powermongers, and who could have been a better umpire than the erstwhile powerful imperial centre? In addition, the threats from without, including the Maratha raids, also nourished the necessity of continued bonds with the centre of the empire as well as with its different units. *Mansab* and *jagir*, the symbols of the empire, thus, remained intact, even if not wholly in substance, diluting the local claim of *hukumat* (rulership) and *sardari* (leadership). The major focus of the local powermonger, thus, got diverted to commanding the channels of mediation. With Sarbuland Khan, a move was initiated to favour the governor as the sole mediator between the centre and the province. But the process was disrupted because his weak successors had no such vision or because Samsam-ud-Daulah, the *mir bakshi* and the *amir-ul-umara*, had his own stake in the eastern provinces. Sarbuland's recall, thus, caused major damage to Bihar's government. By Fakhr-ud-Daulah's time it was too late for him to emerge as the principal mediator. When he sought this position, he faced trouble from people like Khwaja Mustasim and Shaikh Abdullah.

Why did the local officials seek additional powers? Why did a noble in Delhi clash with the one in the province and try to control the avenues of the province's mediation with the centre? The answers can be provided by the developments within the province, in particular the turmoil in the countryside and its context.

II

Conflicts and compromises with the zamindars were an integral part of the history of the Mughals in India. The zamindars were hereditarily in control of land and its wealth in the countryside. They were also the local political and administrative élites. No power from outside could have ventured to sustain a claim over the surplus produce without their support, following either an all-out war against them or often a series of diplomatic manoeuvres and bargains.

The Mughals, in a large measure, were able to integrate the zamindars in the imperial edifice and even though they (the zamindars) continued struggling for a greater share, they turned out to be the partners of the Mughals in power

and economic exploitation. The hereditary rulers of the localities, who enjoyed virtually sovereign powers in their territories, were absorbed in administration and in return, like any other ordinary official, were given a *mansab* and
a *jagir*. In all major military campaigns these zamindars with armed contingents
of their kinsfolk played a prominent role. The lesser zamindars, spread all
over the empire, formed its backbone and were also responsible for the maintenance of law and order. Zamindari for them became 'the right of service; a
service obligation', often described as *khidmat*. In return, they were entitled
to various types of perquisites and discounts.[52]

This arrangement was intended to build and reinforce the centre. The
zamindar was intended to depend, for his position, on the goodwill of the
Mughal emperor than on his claim to heredity. If a zamindar incurred the
displeasure of the emperor he lost his zamindari. The Mughal emperor insisted on having a direct pact with the higher zamindars subordinates in his
territory and characterized these zamindaris as his *watan jagirs*.[53]

The arrangement remained largely unimpaired so long as the Mughals, on
the one hand, maintained their military superiority and the zamindars saw the
benefits of the alliance on the other. By the early eighteenth century cracks
had begun to surface in 'the apparatus of the empire'. Stresses and strains in
the emperor's relations with his nobles told heavily on the authority of the
Mughals in the provinces. The Mughals were rarely able to effectively protect
the zamindars against the encroachments of their neighbours of other castes
and clans. Their control over *jagirs* was crippled.[54] Efforts, therefore, had
to be made anew to reinforce this arrangement in order to maintain royal
authority in whatever form. *Ijara* became the corner-stone of the renewed arrangement, which facilitated greater control over power and revenue to the
zamindars. But while this encouraged political and financial decentralization,
it also generated further conflicts at the local plane and, thus, created conditions for the centre's symbols to remain significant and for its intervention to
continue. This *ijara* was in effect a *ta'ahhud* (contract) by the zamindar and
was not only for the revenue; it extended to political power as well. It signified
the *ijaradar's hukumat*. The Mughals' intervention was to be sought and
tolerated only to keep his territory economically integrated with the world
beyond. The transformation in the Mughal's arrangement with the zamindars
is illustrated, among others, from the history of their relations with the
Ujjainiya Rajputs of Bihar.

The Ujjainiyas of *sarkar* Shahabad Bhojpur occupied a pre-eminent position in Bihar. They contributed, in several ways, to the process of expansion
and consolidation of Mughal rule in the region and were, in return, generously
rewarded with reasonably high *mansabs*, *inams* and the titles of raja and

maharaja.[55] They were, thus, regional agents of the Mughal central power, participating conspicuously in 'high politics' and the Mughal princes' wars for the throne. There were, however, also incidents of rebellion by the chieftains in Shahabad region, but during the late seventeenth and early eighteenth centuries, the Ujjainiya uprising constantly posed a serious threat to the Mughal authority.

The principal Ujjainiya chief in Shahabad *sarkar* in the late seventeenth century was Raja Rudra Singh, succeeded for a brief period by his nephew, Raja Mandhata Singh. Both with Rudra and Mandhata, the Mughals had generally peaceful relations. They were satisfied with their positions and extended support to the Mughal officials.[56] Still, a large number of their clansmen were at war with the Mughals in Shahabad, Rohtas, Saran, Champaran, and around Patna, the capital of the province, under the leadership of one Kunwar Dhir, the zamindar of *pargana* Peero in *sarkar* Shahabad. It was to set Bihar affairs right that the emperor entrusted the province to Prince Muhammad Azim-ush-Shan and Murshid Quli Khan, who had steered Bengal out of the difficulties that had accompanied the rise of the Afghans and the revolt of Sobha Singh, zamindar of Bhusana.[57] The prince was given special powers, a rise in *mansab*, and control over several local offices,[58] to deal with the rebels, and, indeed, the prince's army did defeat the turbulent chief, forcing him to flee out of the province towards Allahabad. But this defeat, and also the later reverses at the hands of the prince's successor, meant little check on the rebel's actions.

The Ujjainiyas, thus, continued to defy the Mughals even after Dhir's death in 1712, when their leadership was taken over by Dhir's son, Siddhisht Narayan. Siddhisht Narayan proved a still graver threat, mobilizing about 30,000 horsemen and foot-soldiers from amongst his kinsfolk.[59] Often merchants sought special armed escort from the governor to pass through the territories of Shahabad, which were located on the way from Bengal and Bihar to Agra, Delhi and the other trade centres of upper India. They carried out raids even in the *pargana*s around the capital town of the *suba*, usurped many fertile *jagir mahal*s and threatened to block the despatch of royal treasure to the imperial capital.[60] By 1715, Siddhisht Narayan had become so powerful that Mir Jumla, the newly appointed governor, failed to chastise him even after he had come with an army of about 20,000 which included a special battalion of eight to nine thousand Mughal veterans.[61] The next governor, Sarbuland Khan and his son Khanazad Khan, *faujdar* of Shahabad, however, succeeded in defeating the rebel in 1716 and capturing many of his strongholds following a series of engagements with a force of 20,000 cavalry and 30,000 infantry.[62]

The Mughal victory over the Ujjainiyas, it is true, owed a good deal to Sarbuland Khan's military prowess and skill. Earlier, during his tenure as governor of Allahabad he had led several successful campaigns against the zamindars of Jaunpur. Without losing control over that province, he had also provided reinforcement to the governor of Bihar.[63] But it is notable that in his campaigns against the Ujjainiyas and also against other turbulent zamindars his strength lay principally in the fact that he could requisition the services of the other zamindars for his purposes. This he could achieve by initiating with them a new arrangement, generally described in our sources as *ta'ahhud, muqarrari istimrari*, and *ijara*, which all meant revenue farming, with little detailed yearly *tashkhis* (assessment and fixation).[64] Clearly, the new arrangement was preferred as it guaranteed some sort of regularity in the payment of revenue by the local magnates, even as it also meant disadvantages for the state in that its agents were no longer to enjoy the possible, though risky, additional collection (*taufir*) every year. The state grew 'risk-averse' as the economy and the budget began to slip out of its control following the turbulence all around in the empire.[65]

Towards the last years of Farrukh Siyar's reign (1712–19) the new arrangement with the zamindars began to be encouraged. Horil Singh, for instance, secured *muqarrari istimrari* (fixed permanent) contracts for a number of villages in addition to *jagir*s and *nankar*s in his zamindari in the period between 1716 and 1724.[66] Such agreements seem to have been reached also with the zamindars of the Palamau area, which had not received due attention since the middle of Aurangzeb's reign. In an eighteenth-century account of the Chotanagpur area, prepared for the use of early British administrators, Sarbuland Khan is reported to have

settled the parganas of Sher and Shergauty, below the Hills, with Irja Agoury, son of Sulaiman Qanungo. Again, Raja Nagbunshy Singh, zamindar of Nagpur to whom the *ghatwals* of Palamau Ramgarh and Badamy were subordinate, sent his agent Bedman Das Tacoor through the mediation of Irja Agoury and agreed to pay a *nadhrana* of 100,000, of which 45,000 was to be paid in 'species' and the rest in diamonds. The settlement of Sher and Akowrie, Datars . . . and Koodida, situated below the *ghats*, was made with Mirza Azeez Cawn, a Rohilla, and Agoury Ameen Singh for Rs 35,000 to be paid at Patna.[67]

In many cases the new arrangements were reached through intermediaries. One such intermediary was Abdullah Khan who, as the author of *Siyar-ul-Muta'akkhirin* notes:

was a man of consequence in those parts, who seemed to be the main hinge of all government business in that province, for he had for a length of time been always employed by every governor either as his deputy or as a general farmer of revenue. He had connections with almost all the zamindars . . . and had acquired the goodwill of troops as well as of every individual in the province.[68]

A somewhat clear evidence of *hukumat* with *ijara* comes a little later from the time of the *nizamat* of Fakhr-ud-Daulah, who governed the *suba* during 1727–34, and who chose Horil Singh in 1727 as the *naib faujdar* and *shiqdar* of *pargana* Behea, Shahabad, to maintain peace and order in the region.[69] In 1730, he negotiated fresh terms with the Palamau zamindars.[70]

It was, thus, with the objective of dealing with local problems that the governors sought more powers. Bihar politics seemed to be heading for a kind of transformation, in which everyone from the governor, who had more pronounced links with Delhi, to the zamindar with his base and moorings in the countryside, struggled to extend his power. This created conditions of seeming chaos and conflicts shaking the existing framework of political relations. But the political order as such still promised dividends; the conflicts were for acquiring them. The province, as we shall see below, had enough resources to inspire each to fight in the knowledge that victory would guarantee prosperity. The fact that even administrative offices and positions could be purchased with money was conducive to the arrangement that the governor now tried to make with the local magnates. Besides the zamindars who, confident of their paying capacity, endeavoured to buy a greater share in political power, a number of local urban magnates now held positions in provincial finance and administration on a permanent basis.[71] They all clamoured to share Bihar's wealth and affluence which was illustrated, among other things, in the consistent rise in the revenues in the province for over a century.

III

In Bihar, in the decades following the reign of Akbar (1556–1605), revenue, both the estimated (*jama*) and the actual (*hasil*), rose enormously. The *Ain-i-Akbari*, compiled in 1595, puts the *jama* figure of *suba* at 22,19,19,404 *dams*. By the time Akbar died (1605) the increase in *jama* was by over 4 crores, rising by another five crores during Jahangir's reign (1605–26). The increase was nearly twofold during the period between roughly 1630 and 1670; that is in the time of Shahjahan (1626–56) and the early years of Aurangzeb's reign (1656–1707). *Jama* rose further by about 50 per cent at the time of Alivardi Khan (1732–56) in the eighteenth century (see Table 1).

The actual yield or the *hasil* figures also seem to have generally corresponded to the *jama*. Ahmad Reza Khan has collected some interesting *hasil* figures[72] which are worth considering (see Table 2).

There were, however, some unusually low collections ranging between

Table 1. Jama of Suba Bihar

No.	Date	Jama in dams
1.	1595–6	22,19,19,404
2.	1605	26,27,74,167
3.	1607–27	31,60,33,672
4.	1633–8	36,88,30,000
5.	1642–3	38,09,30,000
6.	1646–7	40,00,00,000
7.	,,	40,00,00,000
8.	1638–56	38,32,00,000
9.	,,	38,32,00,000
10.	,,	40,60,00,000
11.	1642–56	39,46,56,932
12.	1638–56	48,60,00,000
13.	1646–56	38,32,00,000
14.	1656	54,53,00,335
15.	1667	72,17,97,019
16.	1656–87	37,84,13,380
17.	1676	45,71,81,000
18.	1678	46,48,55,000
19.	1680	53,51,65,811
20.	1685	39,43,44,532
21.	1687–91	40,71,81,000
22.	1687–95	40,71,81,000
23.	1687–1707	40,71,81,000
24.	1709	40,71,81,000
25.	1712–19	52,76,69,337
26.	1712–36	52,85,55,358
27.	1735–6	52,19,37,670
28.	1750	53,61,93,190
29.	1750	53,61,93,190
30.	,,	54,53,00,035

Table 2. Some Hasil Figures

Year	Hasil in Rupees	Hasil as % of Jama
1685	85,17,683	86.39
1687–91	93,05,431	91.41
1687–95	93,25,551	91.61
1709	93,05,431	91.41
1750	1,00,79,141	75.93

Source: Based on the tables in Irfan Habib, *The Agrarian System of Mughal India*, Bombay, 1963, pp. 401–2 and Ahmad Reza Khan, 'Revenue Statistics of Bihar', in S.H. Askari and Q. Ahmad (eds), *The Comprehensive History of Bihar*, vol. II, pt II, Patna, 1987, pp. 528–30.

Rs 48,85,571 and Rs 57,14,873 in the early 1670s. A possible explanation could be the reported Bihar famine. Around 1670, according to John Marshall who was present in the province at the time, the whole of the country from Banaras to Rajmahal, which then took three to four days of travel, was in the throes of the worst kind of famine. Marshall first noticed the ravages of the famine in May 1670 in *sarkar* Munger, on his way from Bengal to Patna. The famine was caused due to crop failure and the inundation of the Ganga. Marshall's account is supported by the observations of a Dutch traveller, De Graffie, on the poverty and the misery of the people of Patna at the time. But in none of the contemporary indigenous sources is the famine noticed. Marshall and De Graffie may seem then to have exaggerated its impact.[73]

By 1676, following some reliefs and good harvests, the situation appears to have improved. The revenue in c. 1676 was assessed at 45,71,81,000 dams, and in 1678 at 46,48,55,000 dams. Around the same time, Emperor Aurangzeb is reported to have ordered a full-fledged fresh survey of the province. The survey was, however, left incomplete (only five out of the eight *sarkar*s and a *wilayat* could be measured and assessed anew), possibly because of the emperor's preoccupation with the Jodhpur Rajput rebellion and problems in the Deccan.[74] Again, in the province at the time, political conditions were somewhat fluid. An adventurer, claiming to be the son of Prince Muhammad Shuja, the emperor's brother who had been the governor of Bengal and had contested for the throne in the 1656–8 war of succession, gave a call to local functionaries and armed bands to rise against the governor. In another case, one Ganga Ram, an important local official, faced with the charge of embezzlement and misappropriation, rebelled, plundered the town of Bihar with an army of 4000 horsemen, and advanced towards Patna. The situation was, however, brought under control soon.[75]

By the early eighteenth century both the *jama* and the *hasil* had registered further improvement. According to eighteenth-century reports, the revenues in Bihar generally showed a stable upward trend, and the *hasil* usually approximated the *jama* until about the early 1760s when Mir Qasim precipitated problems for both the government and the zamindars by insisting that they pay even the margin of their profits.[76]

The rise in revenue figures in the seventeenth century has been explained in terms of the silver influx into the Mughal economy and the 'Price Revolution', which, in turn, also figures as a cornerstone in the edifice built for the economic history of Mughal India.[77] Such an explanation, at first sight, appeals as it also helps in placing several issues of the general history of the Mughal empire in a neat model developed conveniently after the debate around the history of the early modern European economy. But it provides little enlightenment when we go into the regions to examine the developments there in some detail. It is true that in the seventeenth century, in the wake of the increase in the volume of foreign trade, there was an unmistakable rise in the flow into India of precious metals in payment for the goods exported by both Asian and European merchants. But as the sources of information about the flow primarily concern its adverse effect on European states and economies, they, as it has been pointed out, have highlighted it in an exaggerated manner. This information should be used with caution by historians of Mughal India.

It is interesting that while the European theorists, on the one hand, drew a link between the volume of currency in circulation and the level of prices and there were writers who predicted that the continued export of silver to the Indies would eventually raise the price of Asian commodities, on the other, 'the members of the East India Directorate, some of whom were expert authorities on monetary and financial matters, failed to see a theoretical connection between the massive export of treasure from Europe and the price level in Asia.'[78] Their silence may have been 'something of a minor mystery' theoretically; but it was grounded in the fact that in real life, as we shall see below, it was not possible to perceive the 'Price Revolution' and, above all, to relate it to an increase in money supply. The connection between the two in the Indian context was far from being clear. This was pointed by Om Prakash and J. Krishnamurty as far back as in 1970.[79] Since then Sanjay Subrahmanyam has shown that the attempt to extend the analogy of the American silver and the European 'Price Revolution' to the Asian context floundered not only because of a lack of adequate quantitative information and contradictory evidence but also because it suffered from certain obvious theoretical flaws.[80]

The contention of the silver influx price-rise protagonists does not stand the scrutiny of the relevant evidence from diverse regions.[81] We have little evidence for prices in Bihar. On the basis of some of the prices which Ahmad Reza Khan has collected it is difficult to speculate any trend.[82] But it is significant for our purpose that in its neighbourhood in Bengal the prices of commodities like rice, wheat, sugar, and ghee seem to be generally stable or, at worst, fluctuating. This seems to be the case even with the seventeenth-century prices of saltpetre, acquired mostly from Bihar. All this, while there was an evident increase in the import of bullion into Bengal in the late seventeenth century.

The average annual value of the treasure imported by the Dutch Company increased from f.1.28 million in the 1660s, to f.2.00 million in the 1690s, f.2.43 million in the 1700s, and f.2.87 million in 1710. In addition, there were substantial bullion imports by the English East India Company, besides the small quantities brought in by the French East India Company.[83]

There is some evidence of sustained and marked increase in the prices of textiles in the years between 1720 and 1760, but it is difficult to relate it to any 'deep-seated monetary changes.'[84] On the other hand, in the latter half of the eighteenth century, when bullion had begun to flow out of the region, the prices of some commodities showed an increase.[85] Irfan Habib cites some prices from Agra to suggest some kind of sustained inflationary trends.[86] But the relationship between his evidence on the movement of prices and the available revenue figures for Bihar is unclear. For one, the Agra prices hardly help us to speculate about the price level in Bihar, considering the distance and the slow medieval means of transport. The Bengal prices could perhaps have been closer, but as there was no sustained rise in Bengal prices, these again are of little use in explaining the 'inflation' in the revenue of the province.

There is, thus, not much justification either in the available evidence or in theory to wish away the rise in revenue figures merely as an adjustment to rising prices. Instead, it would perhaps be more rewarding to examine and put together qualitative information about the local history and economy.

It is not without significance that the increase in *jama* coincided with the extension and consolidation of Mughal authority in the province, in particular, in the hilly and forested region in the south. Khokar and Kharagpur were brought under full control following military expeditions in the times of Jahangir (1605–26) and Shahjahan (1626–56), and during the early years of Aurangzeb (1656–1707). Palamau was conquered by Shaista Khan (1639–43), to be annexed and consolidated later by Daud Khan in the early 1660s.[87] Even though the area was itself not so rich in revenue, control over it implied stability in the settled central and northern regions of the province. Some diamond mines were also located there, earning for the area the name of *wilayat-i-kan-i-almas*.[88]

More important than the conquest of the area was the formation of a new *sarkar*, right in a highly fertile and rich part of the province. Under Akbar, the *suba* was divided into seven *sarkar*s, namely Bihar, Champaran, Hajipur, Munger, Rohtas, Saran, and Tirhut. By Shahjahan's time a new *sarkar* under the name of Shahabad Bhojpur had been created, bifurcating Rohtas into two, the old Rohtas and the new Shahabad. The territory of the new *sarkar* also included, in all probability, the lately claimed lands along the western borders, while *sarkar* Rohtas now possibly extended into the Chero areas in the south.[89] The formation of a new *sarkar* in the lands of the powerful Ujjainiya Rajput zamindars was not meant simply to ensure better political and more efficient administrative control. It also implied extension of cultivation. According to an eighteenth century historical discourse on the origins of zamindaris (with an account of the *sarkar*), 'most of the zamindaris during the reign of Shahjahan originated in *bankatai* or populating land after clearing forests. Those who did so became zamindars and obtained *nankar*s (part of the revenue as zamindari right) for their lifetime. After the death of such zamindars, their sons obtained *sanad*s for the rights held by them on condition of continued service'.[90]

What is notable is that this development was not limited to *sarkar* Shahabad alone. The same report, in a section on *Haqiqat-i-Suba Bihar*, notes:

from the time of Shahjahan, it was customary that wood-cutters and plough-men used to accompany his troops, so that forests may be cleared and land cultivated. Ploughs used to be donated by the government. Short-term *pattas* (documents stating the revenue demand) were given, fixed by government at the rate of 1 anna per *bigha* during the first year. *Chaudharis* (intermediaries) were appointed to keep the *raiya* happy with their considerate behaviour and to populate the country. They were to ensure that the *pattas* were issued in accordance with Imperial orders and the pledged word was kept. There was a general order that whosoever cleared a forest and brought land under cultivation, such land would be his *zamindari*. *Qanungos* were instructed to prepare the settlement regulations with the concurrence of the *chaudharis* in a manner as to contribute to the populousness of the territory. The revenue demand was to be determined accordingly. They were to prepare the papers from harvest to harvest and to deposit these with the *amil* at the end of the year. They were to put forward the claims of *rozina, dastur, nankar* and *in'am* etc., before the *amil* at the time of the settlement of the *pargana*, keeping in view their devoted service to the State and the welfare of the *raiyat*. They (the *qanungos*?) were required to obtain the *qubuliyat* in accordance with the regulations, and deposit these with their own signatures, and to secure for them *pattas*. The state revenue was to be deposited by them in the imperial treasury at each *tahsil* harvest-wise, and instalment-wise.

Further, the report also records official instructions that after allowing one plough per twenty *bighas* of well-cultivated land, the other ploughs should be allotted to virgin land or that which had lain fallow for a long time. Ploughs should also be given on behalf of the State. The price of these ploughs should be realized from the zamindars in two to three years. Every *hal mir* (i.e. one who has four or five ploughs) should be given a *dastar* (turban) so that he may clear the forests and bring land under cultivation. In this manner, the people and the *riaya* would be attracted by good treatment to come from other regions and *suba*s to bring under cultivation wasteland and land under forest.[91]

The number of *pargana*s and *mahal*s (revenue districts and subdivisions of *sarkar*) also increased substantially by this means, from 200 under Akbar to 256 plus a *wilayat* (territory) of the diamond mines under Aurangzeb and his successors.[92]

Table 3. Sarkar-*wise* Jama *Figures and* Parganas

Sarkar	No. of Parganas		Jama in dams	
	Ain	18th century	Ain	18th century
Bihar	46	63 including 2 mints	8,44,65,490	22,77,45,905
Munger	31	40	2,96,22,181	6,23,74,807
Champaran	3	3	55,13,420	1,13,75,920
Hajipur	11	11	2,73,635	5,12,44,470
Saran	17	18	1,61,72,304	4,29,55,045
Tirhut	74	102	1,92,20,82	4,43,97,542
Rohtas	18	7	4,08,79,201	3,60,44,103
Shahabad new sarkar bifurcated from Rohtas in 17th C	–	12	–	4,99,27,091

Source: Ain's figures are based on Ahmad Reza Khan's calculations from MSS. Add. 6552 and Add. 7652. For the eighteenth century figures, see I.O. 4369.

The rate of rise was not uniform throughout the *suba*. Indeed, in some areas, the revenues registered an unmistakable decline, while in some others the increase was nominal. Still, in many other areas the increase was spectacular. In *sarkar* Bihar, for instance, in thirty-seven *pargana*s the *jama* rose by 100 per cent or more in eighteen of them, while in five *mahal*s, on the other hand, there was a sharp fall.[93] I have been able to locate some evidence to explain such differences in terms of possible variations in productivity and production in a region of Awadh.[94] In the case of the rich *pargana*s in *sarkar* Bihar, it is not without significance that they were either located close to a river channel and the villages therein thus had good irrigation facilities, or they contained a market and *mandi* and thus the zamindars and the peasants around had some incentives to produce more and better marketable crops. Villages in Arwal, Atri, Ekil, Pilich, and Telehra, for instance, must have had obvious advantages of good irrigation due to their location in relation to rivers. Arwal was also an important town on the road from Patna to Sahsaram and Rohtas.[95] On the other hand, Ballia, Bihar, Bhimpur, Gaya, Ghiyaspur, Patna, Phulwari, Rajgir, and Somai were industrial, commercial, and cultural centres of different sizes and degrees in the province. Around Ballia and Bhimpur were cultivated indigo, opium, and sugar; Rajgir and Somai were known for their quarries, and Ghiyaspur boasted of striped silk.[96]

Bihar also experienced tremendous growth of trade following the establishment of the European trading factories in Patna by the mid-seventeenth century. The Dutch came to Patna in 1632. Around the same time the English also founded their factories in Bihar. They made concentrated attempts to settle in Bihar following the Gujarat famine which threatened their trade in western India. Saif Khan, the governor of Bihar (1625–32), who had earlier held Gujarat and favoured the English there, facilitated the establishment and success of the English trade in the province.[97] In the mid-seventeenth century the Dutch and the English competed fiercely to control Patna which had become an important centre for the supply of sugar and saltpetre, then in great demand in Europe as the principal ingredient for the manufacture of gunpowder.[98] Bihar was also known as a source of supply of cotton and woollen goods, and was estimated to sell woollen manufactures among other areas to 'the cold countries extending from Tartary in the north to China in the east'. Towards the end of seventeenth century the French too had their factory in Patna and traded in the region in 'cloth, sugar, wax, silk, and saltpetre'.[99]

European commercial activities in the region, one can speculate, must have led to an extension in the cultivation of cash crops like cotton, opium, and sugar. They might have also provided incentives to local artisanal production, and all this contributed a good deal to the rise in revenue figures. This is well illustrated from the case of *sarkar* Saran which ranked next to *sarkar* Bihar in increase in revenue. A large number of production centres for saltpetre were located in Saran. The *pargana*s showing a large increase are notably the ones with the largest saltpetre production.[100]

Thus, we may conclude that no serious economic crisis preceded or accompanied the situation of disturbed agrarian relations and contested factional politics in Bihar. Consistent economic growth and prosperity in the region was, on the contrary, the context of the local political turmoil. Thus, for Bihar also it would be unfair to take the evidence of the imperial Mughal chronicles as testimony for assessment of the nature of Mughal decline in the province. If we extend, for example, the universalized account of either Bhim Sen or Khafi Khan to Bihar, it would appear to be in the throes of a serious financial crisis with a wide gap between the estimated revenue and the actual yield and collections, and, certainly with an acute shortage of the lands to be assigned in *jagir*. A careful scrutiny of the evidence directly pertaining to Bihar little justifies such a dismal portrayal of the situation in the province. It would be unjust to infer or speculate that there was a general scarcity of *ser hasil jagir*s from the reports of shortfalls in income from areas disturbed by zamindar uprisings. *Ser hasil jagir*s and zamindar dissidence were not the same all round the empire. Their meanings diverged in different settings and therefore they must be studied in the context of a detailed history of the concerned regions. This may appear to be stating the obvious, but the current state of the debate requires that this point be reiterated.

It needs to be emphasized that the Mughal imperial histories, more than being a portrayal of the conditions of society in general, are an assessment of them by a section of the ruling class. This section had hitherto enjoyed an almost overwhelming political and economic dominance and staked claim to still more privileges on the ground of their having long been in state service. By the late seventeenth and early eighteenth centuries, however, there had arisen some other sections, mainly of Indian ethnic stock, with equal, if not greater, claims to the resources, who succeeded at times in dislodging members of the erstwhile pre-eminent groups. This has sometimes been presented as *inqilab* (upheaval, reversal), and was manifested in the formation of the factions around *khanazad*s (born in house) and *qadim*s (old, ancient), on the one hand, and non-*khanazad*s and *jadid*s (new and upstarts), on the other.[101] The compilers of these histories voice the view of the *khanazad*s who, in their calculations, no longer received their due because of the rise to power of upstarts.

A review of the literature of the period would perhaps enable us better to appreciate what the eighteenth-century crisis was and how it was articulated. We get the impression that all was in ruins from some of the poems of poets who lived in Delhi and observed the developments both within the city and in the empire in the period under review.[102] But we equally know for certain that while the royal palace and the *haveli*s of certain nobles were wanting in glitter, there were many others in Delhi itself to generously patronize the dancers, musicians, and other artists who had hitherto performed only for the select amongst the royalty and nobility. Unique and precious things from all parts of the world still found their way into the bazaars of Delhi, and a lakh of rupees which a mother gave her son to make purchases were still spent in no time in Chandni Chowk.[103] The *hundi*s from the *jagir*s of some nobles may have lost their value, but a single *mahajan* of the city still had enough money in the 1740s to help the emperor, Muhammad Shah, to meet the claims of the Persian invader, Nadir Shah.[104]

More than the ruin of their class, these poets and their ilk, like the compilers of our histories, bewailed the rise in position of those they characterize as the mean and ignoble (*arazil*). The crisis of the society, as it was presented by an eighteenth-century poet, was that 'the jackals had replaced the lions', 'crows cawed in place of the songs of the nightingale', and 'riches were bestowed on dogs and donkeys'.[105] However, their resentment over the eighteenth-century changes should not be explained merely in terms of their personal loss. They had a definite sense of certain social rules and administrative norms which in their belief sustained a just order. In the rise of 'unworthy people' they saw the neglect and violation of the time-honoured rules. An analysis of the nature of such consciousness, and of the degree of its influence on Mughal historical literature, is still awaited.[106]

The portrayal of such shifts and reversals in the context of Bihar is available, for instance, in the works of Shah Ayatullah, an eighteenth-century writer. Shah Ayatullah came from a Sufi family of Phulwari Sharif, a centre of Muslim education and Sufism, about six miles west of Patna. Ayatullah wrote both in Persian and Urdu, with pen names of Shorish in his Persian poetry and Jauhari in his Urdu compositions. In one of his Urdu poems, he complains about the changed and reversed times primarily in terms of the rise of the Hindus. According to him, the Brahmans had gained in status, the Muslims had turned mere *chakar*s (servants) of the infidels and idolatory in temples was supplanting the Islamic worship of one god in the mosques.[107] The poem relates, as its reference to a Hindu *subadar* and a Hindu *diwan* suggests, to the period between 1748 and 1761 when Janaki Ram and Ram Narayan held the highest offices in Bihar and many of the erstwhile nobles and notables had lost their *in 'am*s, the *jagir*s and the *wazifa*s. As Shah Ayatullah came from a religious background, he feared and presented this picture of the desolation of Islam in the deprivations of Muslim nobles and notables. He complained in the main against the rise of the ignoble and the reversal of the times, in this case illustrated from the way Janaki Ram and Ram Narayan sought to restore administration following Maratha inroads, the English East India Company's involvement in Bihar politics, and subsequent disruptions. The Muslim religion at this juncture, as we know from other accounts, was in no particular danger in the province. Bihar gave shelter and promised protection and promotion of their fortunes to some of the erstwhile Muslim nobles' descendants who had left Delhi because of their sufferings in the wake of what they perceived as the arrogant rise and atrocities of the 'infidels' in that city and in its vicinity.[108]

All this is not intended to delegitimize the use of imperial Mughal chronicles as testimony for the history of the period. The chronicles no doubt form the backbone of our evidence, but they are to be read together with all the other categories of sources, imperial and regional, to consider the particularities of both a geographical area and a social group. Before arriving at any generalizations and imposing a meaning of our own we should therefore examine what eighteenth-century society took to be a 'crisis' and what it meant to its different segments. From such a re-examination, it may well emerge that the eighteenth-century 'crisis' is too complex an issue to be understood through the mere analysis of Mughal revenue administration and finance.

NOTES AND REFERENCES

1. Some such notable attempts are the papers of Bernard Cohn, 'Political Systems in Eighteenth Century India: The Benaras Region', see above pp. 123–36; Philip Calkins, 'The Formation of a Regionally Oriented Ruling Group in Bengal: 1700–1740', *Journal of Asian Studies*, 29, 4, 1970; Stewart Gordon, 'The Slow Conquest: Administrative Integration of Malwa into the Maratha Empire: 1720–1760', *Modern Asian Studies*, 11,1, 1977; Frank Perlin, 'Of White Whale and Countrymen in the Eighteenth Century Maratha Deccan', *Journal of Peasant Studies*, 5, 2, 1978; also see regional histories such as J.F. Richards, *Mughal Administration in Golconda*, Oxford, 1975, Richard Barnett, *North India Between Empires*, Berkeley, 1980; C.A. Bayly, *Rulers, Townsmen and Bazaars*, Cambridge, 1983, and André Wink, *Land and Sovereignty in India*, Cambridge, 1986.

2. See, for instance, the reviews of M. Alam, *The Crisis of Empire in Mughal North India* (Delhi, 1986) by Qeyamuddin Ahmad in *Indian Historical Review (IHR)*, 13, 1–2, 1986–7; S. Arasaratnam in *South Asia*, (New Series), 11, 1, 1988 and Marc Gaborieau in *Annales, Economies, Sociétés, Civilizations*, 43, 6, 1988. For a dismissive reaction to some of these studies, see M. Athar Ali, 'Recent Theories of Eighteenth Century India', *IHR*, 13, 1–2, 1986–7, pp. 102–10.

3. M. Alam, *Crisis of Empire*, pp. 56–91; Richard Barnett, *North India*, pp. 17–23.

4. Syed Hasan Askari and Qeyamuddin Ahmad (eds), *The Comprehensive History of Bihar*, vol. ii, pt ii, Patna, 1987, pp. 193–4.

5. Compare Muhammad Hadi Kamwar Khan, *Tazkirat-us-Salatin Chaghta* (Kamwar), ed., Muzaffar Alam, Bombay, 1980, pp. 163, 185, 214, for instance, for references to Patna as Azimabad Patna.

6. Abdul Karim, *Murshid Quli Khan and His Times*, Dacca, 1963, pp. 19–22, for differences between the Prince and Murshid Quli Khan.

7. Muhammad Hashim Khafi Khan, *Muntakhab-ul-Lubab* (K.K.), K.D. Ahmad and Woseley Haig (eds), Bibl. Ind., Calcutta, 1868, K.K. ii, 546. Murshid Quli Khan was not an Iranian, but was certainly in close association with the Iranians at the Mughal court (*Ma'asir-ul-Umara*, Persian text, iii, for his services with Haji Shafi Isfahani and Haji Abdullah Khurasani; Abdul Karim, op. cit., pp. 15–16). A factor in Prince Muhammad Azam's instigating Azim's transfer could have been Murshid Quli Khan's complaint communicated to Azam through his Iranian associates. Most of the eminent Iranians at Aurangzeb's court appear to be close to Azam. Asad Khan and Zulfiqar Khan supported his cause during the struggle for succession in 1707 (W. Irvine, *Later Mughals*, rpt Delhi, 1971, i, pp. 22–36). The father of Alivardi Khan, an Afshar who later rose to be the nawab of Bengal, was also in Azam's camp. K.K. Datta, *Alivardi Khan and His Times*, Calcutta, 1939, pp. 2–3.

8. Kamwar, op. cit., ff. 314a and 318b for Azim-ush-Shan's office, *mansab*, and influence, especially after the death of Bahadur Shah's *wazir*, Mun'im Khan in 1710. Azim was assigned the task of the office of the wazir and was thus at the centre of politics of the nobles and the other princes who aspired high positions including *wizarat*. Mirza Muhammad (MM), *Ibratnama*, Patna MS, Catalogue, vii, 623; ff. 68; Iradat Khan (?) *Tarikh-i-Mubaraknama*, Aligarh MS 345/11f (Mubarak), f 46b;

Munshi Ghulam Husain Tabatabai *Siyar-ul-Muta'akhkhirin (Siyar)*, Lucknow, n.d., II, p. 382. See also Satish Chandra, *Parties and Politics at the Mughal Court, 1707–1740*, Aligarh, 1959, pp. 53–5 and 64–7.

9. *Akbarat-i-Darbar-i-Mulla*, National Library, Calcutta transcripts (Bahadur Shah), 27 Sept. 1708; Kamwar (Aligarh MS.), ff. 308a and 320a.

10. Abdul Karim, op. cit., pp. 28–9.

11. Kamwar (cf. fn.5), p. 138, K.K., II, pp. 708–10.

12. *Akhbarat* (Bahadur Shah), Sitamau Transcripts, 5th R.Y., p. 477; M.M., op. cit., f. 14a.

13. K.K., II, pp. 710–11; Muhammad Ali Khan Ansari, *Bahr-ul-Mawwaj*, Patna MSS 544 (Farsi no. 87), f. 214a.

14. W. Irvine, op. cit., pp. 327–88; Satish Chandra, op. cit., pp. 86–167.

15. Khwaja Muhammad Khalil, *Tarikh-i-Shahanshahi*, Buhar MSS no. 79, National Library, Calcutta, f. 31a.

16. Kamwar (Aligarh MS) f. 346a.

17. M.M., op. cit., f. 34b; Shivdas Lakhnawi, *Shahnama Munawwar Kalam*, Br. M. Or. 1898 and Asiatic Society Bengal MS., Ivanow 25/1/33 (Shivdas), ff. 5, 6b and 7a; Muhammad Qasim Aurangabadi, *Ahwal-ul-Khawaqin (Ahwal)*, Br. M. Add. 26, 244, ff. 106b–7a; Mubarak, f. 80b.

18. K.K. II, p. 739; Satish Chandra, op. cit., pp. 107–8. Notably Saiyid Husain Ali Khan tried to retain the governorship even after the recall of Saiyid Ghairat Khan. According to Kamwar, Khan Zaman, succeeded Ghairat Khan before Mir Jumla's formal appointment. Kamwar (Aligarh MS) ff. 346; *Akhbarat* (Farrukh Siyar), 3rd R.Y., II, p. 38. The Saiyids, thus, appear to make up for their loss in the east by insisting on having the Deccan under Saiyid Husain Ali Khan's charge.

19. To Murshid Quli Khan, who had his own difficulties with the centre, a governor with lesser military and administrative skill was more acceptable. Mir Jumla was also related to Samsam-ud-Daulah. (Mir Jumla's brother, Sadiq Khan was married to Samsam's sister in Patna, *Risala-i-Khan-i-Dauran and Muhammad Shah*, Br. M. Or. 180, f. 47b) and thus was, perhaps, more amenable to the *diwan* of Bengal.

20. K.K. II, p. 739.

21. *Ahwal*, op. cit., f. 106–7b; Shivdas, op. cit., f. 5a.

22. M.M., op. cit., f. 48a. Since Mir Jumla's principal concern was *wizirat* even later on his return from Patna, he clung to Delhi inspite of an order for his withdrawal to Lahore. M.M. op. cit., f. 51b. See also S.H. Askari, *Proceedings of the Indian History Congress*, 1941, pp. 399 ff.

23. *Ahwal*, op. cit., f. 118a; Mubarak, f. 85b; Shivdas, op. cit., ff. 7a and 8a. As Mir Jumla had to rush back to Delhi, he disbanded the large army he had collected. The disaffected 'Mughals' and the *Jama'at-i-Hindustani* thus turned to the personal possessions and properties of the city dwellers. Shivdas, op. cit., f. 6b.

24. Kamwar (Aligarh, MS.), op. cit., ff. 349b and 352b; *Akhbarat* (Farrukh Siyar), 5th R.Y., II, p. 152. For Sarbuland Khan's governorship in Awadh and Allahabad, see M. Alam, *Crisis of Empire*, op. cit., pp. 66, 95, 109, 110, and 259.

25. *Comprehensive History of Bihar*, op. cit., p. 203.

26. M.M., op. cit., ff. 31a and 95a; *Siyar*, op. cit., II, p. 411. According to Mubarak (f. 95a) the emperor was advised to recall Sarbuland Khan also for consultations

about the deteriorating administration and affairs of Bengal, which suggested the centre's strained relations with the province.

27. Kamwar (Aligarh MS.), op. cit., f. 355b, and 350a for his connection with the Saiyid Brothers; Kamwar, op. cit., p. 323 for his support to the emperor against the Saiyid brothers.

28. Muhammad Ali Khan Ansari, *Bahr-ul-Mawwaj* (Patna MS No. 544 Farsi no. 87), f. 278a; *idem, Tarikh-i-Muzaffari*, Aligarh MS. (Subbanallah 364/134), f. 176a for Saiyid Nusrat Yar Khan's *mansab* and titles. *Siyar*, op. cit., II, p. 453; Kamwar, op. cit., f. 380b for his deputy Abd-ur-Rahim Khan. Abd-ur-Rahim Khan had earlier deputized for Sarbuland Khan. Saiyid Muhammad Bilgrami, *Tabsirat-un-Nazirin (Tabsira)*, Aligarh MS. *(Farsiya Akhbar, 204)*, f. 65a.

29. Kamwar (Aligarh MS.), op. cit., f. 378a. When he died he held a rank of 7000/7000.

30. K.K., II, p. 938; Kamwar, op. cit., f. 379a; *Tarikh-i-Muzaffari*, f. 195b; Mirza Muhammad Bakhsh Ashub, *Tarikh-i-Shahadat-i-Farrukh Siyar wa Julus-i-Muhammad Shah*, Patna MS. no. 2608, (Ashub), ff. 54b.

31. *Haqiqat-i-Jagir Mansabdaran Waghairah Suba Bangala*, Berlin MS. Or. Oct. 209, Pertsch Catalogue no. 499. ff. 106; see also Z.U. Malik, *A Mughal Statesman of the Eighteenth Century*, Bombay, 1973, for some information about Samsam-ud-Daulah's career at the centre.

32. Ghulam Husain Salim, *Riyaz-us-Salatin* (ed), A.H. Abid, Bibl. Indic., Calcutta, 1890, p. 289; Munshi Salimullah, *Tarikh-i-Bangala*, ed. S.M. Imamuddin, Dacca, 1979, pp. 94–5; see also K.K. Datta, op. cit., pp. 7–8.

33. M. Alam, *Crisis of Empire*, pp. 243–5.

34. Q. Ahmad, 'A Historical Account of Chotanagpur in the 18th Century by Raja Shitab Rai', *Journal of Historical Research*, Ranchi, 3, 1, 1960, pp. 1–13; R.N. Prasad, *History of Bhojpur, 1332–1860*, Patna, p. 102.

35. M. Athar Ali, *The Mughal Nobility Under Aurangzeb*, Bombay, 1966, pp. 78–80.

36. M. Alam, *Crisis of Empire*, op. cit., pp. 124–30. See also I.O. 4452 for references to *jagirs* in Bihar.

37. Philip Calkins, 'The Revenue Administration in Bengal' (mimeo.). However, the view that Murshid Quli Khan converted Bengal entirely into *khalisa* needs reconsideration. Over the *jagirs* he seems to have evolved a pattern of control, different from the Burhan-ul-Mulk in Awadh.

38. Saiyid Ghulam Ali Khan Naqawi, *Imad-us-Sa'adat*, Lucknow (n.d.), p. 8.

39. I.O. 4503.

40. *Siyar*, op. cit., II, p. 469; *Tarikh-i-Muzaffari*, f. 201a.

41. Ashub, op. cit., ff. 55.

42. Satish Chandra, op. cit., pp. 125–238.

43. M. Alam, *Crisis of Empire*, op. cit., pp. 263–6.

44. Ibid., pp. 270–1; Satish Chandra, op. cit., pp. 210–17.

45. *Tabsira*, op. cit., f. 89a.

46. Yusuf Ali Khan, *Tarikh-i-Bangala Mahabat Jangi*, ed., Abd-us-Subhan, Calcutta, 1969, pp. 6–8; Karam Ali, *Muzaffar Nama*, ff. 20.

47. Abdul Karim, op. cit., pp. 44–7.

48. Kamwar, op. cit., pp. 173 and 182.

49. Abdul Karim, op. cit., pp. 125–91.

50. Compare Saiyid Abdullah Khan's letters to Murshid Quli Khan in Mehta Balmukand, *Balmukand Nama, Letters of a King Maker of the Eighteenth Century*; ed. and trans. Satish Chandra, Bombay, 1972, pp. 14–15 and 34–5.

51. Compare Kamwar, op. cit., pp. 292 and 299, for instance, for royal gifts to Murshid Quli Khan and his additional title of Ala-ud-Daulah granted by Muhammad Shah in his second regnal year. Murshid Quli Khan was now Mutaman-ul-Mulk Ala-ud-Daulah Jafar Khan Nasiri.

52. For an excellent account of the position of zamindars in Mughal India, see Nurul Hasan, 'Zamindars under Mughals', in R.E. Frykenberg, *Land Control and Social Structure in Indian History*, Madison, 1969, pp. 17–31; see also Irfan Habib, *Agrarian System*, op. cit., pp. 136–89; A.R. Khan, *Chieftains in the Mughal Empire During the Reign of Akbar*, Simla, 1977 passim, particularly Introduction and Conclusion.

53. S. Nurul Hasan, op. cit., A.R. Khan, op. cit.

54. M. Alam, op. cit., *Crisis of Empire*, pp. 24–43.

55. For a detailed and documented history of the Ujjainiyas' relations with the Mughals, see Munshi Binayak Prasad, *Tawarikh-i-Ujjainiya* (Urdu), n.d., vols II and III, Lucknow passim; R.N. Prasad provides a summary in *History of Bhojpur*, op. cit., pp. 48–85. For a useful discussion on the issues involved in these relations, see D.H.A. Kolff, *Naukar, Rajput and Sepoy: The Ethnohistory of the Military Labour Market in Hindustan, 1450–1850*, Cambridge, 1990, pp. 159–76.

56. Ibid., vol. II.

57. Abdul Karim, op. cit., pp. 18–26; Om Prakash, 'The Sobha Singh Revolt: Dutch Policy and Response', *Bengal Past and Present*, 1975, 94, 178.

58. Compare *Akhbarat-i Darbar-i Mualla* (Aurangzeb), Sitamau transcripts, op. cit., p. 21.

59. Murtaza Husain Bilgrami, *Hadiqat-ul-Aqalim*, Lucknow, 1879.

60. Mehta Balmukand, *Balmukand Nama*, p. 15.

61. Muhammad Ahsan Ijad, *Farrukh Siyar Nama*, Br. M. Or. 25, ff. 61a–64a; Shivdas, op. cit., f. 16b.

62. *Akhbarat* (Farrukh Siyar), 3rd and 4th R. Ys., pp. 28, 41.

63. *Akhbarat* (Farrukh Siyar), 5th R.Y. p. 43. For Sarbuland Khan's campaigns against the zamindars in *suba* Allahabad, see *Akhbarat* (Farrukh Siyar), 3rd R.Y., I, p. 192, II, p. 268.

64. R.N. Prasad, op. cit., p. 100. Prasad cites *sanads* and *parwanas* from the Dumraon Raj Collection.

65. Murat Çizakça explains the growth of the fixed and full tenure tax-farming (*iltizam*) in the seventeenth-century Ottoman Empire in terms of the State's 'risk-averseness'. See his paper 'Tax-Farming and Decentralisation in the Ottoman Empire, 1520–1695' (mimeo.) presented at the seminar on 'The State, Decentralisation and Tax-Farming (The Ottoman Empire, Iran and India)' held at Munich University in May 1990.

66. Ibid. Earlier, in 1712, too the governor, Nusrat Khan suggested a new arrangement to be made with the zamindars of the province. See *Akhbarat* (Jahandar Shah).

67. Q. Ahmad, op. cit.

68. *Siyar*, op.cit., II, p. 469.

69. R.N. Prasad, op. cit., p. 102.

70. Q. Ahmad, op. cit.

71. I.O. 4369, for instance, mentions the following: Kharak Sen, Kayastha Karan; Gulab Rai, Kayastha Amat; Patni Mal, Kayastha Sribastab; Muhammad Baqar; Maghu; Hari Singh, Kayastha Karan, Manjhu Mal and Mohan Lal; Ganga Prasad, Kayastha Sribastab; Nathu Mal, Kayastha Sribastab, Taj-ud-Din and Muhammad Raza; Kora Mal, Sitapat Rai, and Khushal Chand, Kayastha Sribastab.

72. *Comprehensive History of Bihar*, op. cit., pp. 529–30.

73. Compare S.A. Khan, *John Marshall in India, Notes and Observations on Bengal, 1669–72*, Oxford, 1927, pp. 149–54.

74. I.O. 4369. According to this report, Khwaja Tara Chand, *diwan of khalisa*, who had been assigned the work, was transferred before he could complete the survey.

75. S.H. Aksari, 'Bihar in the Time of Aurangzeb', *Journal of Bihar Research Society*, 31, 4, 1945, pp. 244–72 and 32, 1 and 2, 1946, 56–72 and 151–81.

76. *Ahwal-i-Sarkar Shahabad wa Rohtas*, Berlin MS. OR. Oct. 103, Catalogue, no. 503. But this is to be accepted with some reservations, for earlier on several occasions the Ujjainiyas clashed with the Mughals. In the early 1740s, according to this report, Ujjainiyas deposited eight lakhs out of the Rs 16 lakhs which they collected from the peasants.

77. Aziza Hasan, 'The Silver Currency Output of the Mughal Empire and Prices in India in the 16th and 17th Centuries', *Indian Economic and Social History Review (IESHR)*, 6, 1, 1969, pp. 85–116; Irfan Habib, 'Monetary System and Prices', in T. Raychaudhuri and Irfan Habib (eds), *The Cambridge Economic History of India*, I, Cambridge, 1982, pp. 360–81. See also, M. Athar Ali, op. cit., pp. 103–4.

78. K.N. Chaudhuri, *The Trading World of Asia and the English East India Company, 1660–1760*, Cambridge, 1978, pp. 99–100.

79. Om Parkash and J. Krisnamurthy, 'Mughal Silver Currency: A Critique', *IESHR*, 7,1, 1970, pp. 139–50. This article was written in response to Aziza Hasan's 'The Silver Currency Output of the Mughal Empire . . .', op. cit.

80. Sanjay Subrahmanyam, 'Precious Metal Flows and Prices in Western and Southern Asia, 1500–1750: Some Comparative and Conjunctural Aspects', *Studies in History* (New Series), 7, 1, 1991 (forthcoming).

81. Ibid.

82. Ahmad Raza Khan, 'Suba of Bihar under the Mughals (1582–1707)', PhD thesis, Aligarh Muslim University, 1985, App. A.

83. Om Prakash, *The Dutch East India Company and the Economy of Bengal, 1630–1720*, Delhi, 1988, p. 249; see also pp. 252–3 for prices. For the prices of saltpetre, see Susil Chaudhury, *Trade and Commercial Organization in Bengal, 1650–1720*, Calcutta, 1975, pp. 251–2.

84. K.N. Chaudhuri, op. cit., p. 102.

85. Sanjay Subrahmanyam, op. cit., citing A.S.M. Akhtar Husain, 'A Quantitative Study of Price Movements in Bengal during the 18th and 19th Centuries', PhD thesis, University of London, 1978.

86. Cf. T. Raychaudhuri and Irfan Habib (eds), *The Cambridge Economic History of India*, I, p. 375.

87. Compare *Tuzuk-i-Jahangiri*, ed. Syud Ahmad Khan, Ghazipur, 1863, pp. 154–5; Mutamad Khan, *Iqbalnama-i-Jahangiri*, Calcutta, 1863, pp. 348–50, 260–1;

Muhammad Kazim, *Alamgirnama*, ed. Khadim Husain and Abd-ul-Hai, Calcutta, 1868, pp. 648 ff.

88. Compare, for instance, I.O. 4369.

89. For some idea of the location and the boundary lines of the *sarkars* see, Irfan Habib, *An Atlas of the Mughal Empire*, Delhi, 1982, sheet 10A and notes pp. 39–40. Habib's map does not show the new *sarkar*, even though he refers to it in the Notes. Creation of a new *sarkar* obviously followed extension of cultivation in the area. In a similar development in upper northern India, the emergence in the early eighteenth century of *chakla* Bareilly and *sarkar* Muradabad within the erstwhile Badaon and Sambhal *sarkars* illustrated the manifest wealth of the region. Cf. M. Alam, *Crisis of Empire*, op. cit., p. 253.

90. Compare S. Nurul Hasan, 'Three Studies of Zamindari System', in *Medieval India: A Miscellany*, vol. I, Delhi, 1969, p. 235. Nurul Hasan in this paper analyses primarily two important sets of Persian documents from Bihar, namely *Ahwal-i-Sarkar Shahabad wa Rohtas* and *Haqiqat-i-Suba Bihar* in the context of the massive material available for the eighteenth century on the origins and the nature of zamindaris.

91. Ibid.

92. I.O. 4369; also see Ahmad Raza Khan, op. cit., ch. II for extension of cultivation and increase in cash crops.

93. *Comprehensive History of Bihar*, op. cit., pp. 535–6.

94. M. Alam, *Crisis of Empire*, op. cit., pp. 100–5.

95. Cf. Irfan Habib, *Atlas*, op. cit., Sheets 10A and 10B.

96. Ibid., Sheet 10B.

97. Shahnawaz Khan, *Ma'athir-ul-Umara*, English trans. by H. Beveridge, vol. II, Calcutta, 1952, pp. 687–92; Peter Mundy, *Travels*, vol. II; *Travels in Asia, 1630–34*, ed. R.C. Temple, London, 1914.

98. J.N. Sarkar, 'The Saltpetre Industry of India with Special Reference to Bihar in the Seventeenth Century', *Journal of Bihar and Orissa Research Society*, 23, 1937, p. 3.

99. J.N. Sarkar, 'Advent of European Companies in Bihar', *Comprehensive History of Bihar*, pp. 602 and 603.

100. Irfan Habib, *Atlas*, op. cit., Sheet 10B; Susil Chaudhuri, op. cit., pp. 269–71.

101. For some evidence, see M. Alam, *Crisis of Empire*, op. cit., ch. I; Satish Chandra, op. cit., pp. 174–6 in the context of Nizam-ul-Mulk's Scheme of Reforms. This dimension of eighteenth-century politics, however, needs a careful and thorough analysis.

102. Compare Naim Ahmad (ed.), *Shahr Ashob* (Urdu), Delhi, 1968, pp. 43–8 and 54–76, for instance, for some such poetic compositions of the eighteenth century. See also Ghulam Husain Zulfiqar, *Urdu Shairi ka Siyasi aur Samaji Pasmanzar*, Punjab University, Lahore, 1966, pp. 145–226. See also Frederick Louis Lehmann, 'The Eighteenth Century Transition in India: Response of Some Bihar Intellectuals', PhD thesis, University of Wisconsin, Madison, 1967, pp. 139–44 for some discussion on *Shahr Ashob*.

103. Dargah Quli Khan, *Muraqqa-i-Dihli*, ed. with Urdu trans. and notes by Nurul Hasan Ansari, Dept. of Urdu, University of Delhi, Delhi, 1982, pp. 39 and 110; see also Chander Shekhar and Shama Mitra Chenoy's Introduction to their English trans. of

the *Muraqqa* for a discussion on the state of art in Delhi in the years of Mughal decline.

104. Anand Ram Mukhlis,, *Tazkira*, Sitamau transcript, pp. 104–6.

105. Naim Ahmad (ed.), *Shahr Ashob*, p. 76; Muhammad Sadiq, *History of Urdu Literature*, 2nd edn, Delhi, 1984, pp. 104–5.

106. For an excellent discussion on such consciousness in a comparable Ottoman context, see Cornell H. Fleischer, *Bureaucrat and Intellectual in the Ottoman Empire: The Historian Mustafa Ali*, Princeton, 1986, pp. 191–231; also Douglas A. Howard, 'Ottoman Historiography and the literature of "Decline",' *Journal of Asian History*, 22, 1, 1988.

107. Ibid., pp. 77–9; S.M. Sadruddin Fida, *Hazrat Shah Ayatullah Jauhari: Un ki Hayat aur Shairi*, Dept. of Urdu, Patna University, Patna, 1964, pp. 527–8; Akhtar Orainawi, *Bihar men Urdu Zuban-o-Adab ka Irtiqa*, Patna, 1957, pp. 264–7; Frederick Louis Lehmann, op. cit., pp. 144–9 and App. 1.

108. Shakir Khan, *Gulshan-i-Sadiq*, Patna MS., ff. 50–8, for the migration to Patna of the author who was a descendant of Khwaja Lutfullah Sadiq of Panipat, an important noble of Farrukh Siyar's time. See also Mir Hasan, *Tazkira-i-Shura-i Urdu*, ed. Habib-ur-Rahman Sherwani, Anjuman-i-Taraqqi Urdu, Delhi 1940, p. 115 and Muhammad Husan Azad, *Aab-e-Hayat*, reprint, Lucknow, 1986, pp. 117–21 for Ashraf Ali Fughan who settled in Patna on Raja Ram Narayan's invitation and died there in 1772. Fughan, a foster brother of the Mughal emperor, Ahmad Shah (1748–56), held a rank of 5000 *zat*. Later, Fughan became disgusted with Ram Narayan, but significantly there is no reference to the desolation of Islam in the *hajw* (calumny, satirical poem) he wrote against the raja. For the text of his *hajw* see Naim Ahmad (ed.), *Shahr Ashob*, pp. 52–3.

8

The South Indian State and the Creation of Muslim Community*

SUSAN BAYLY

NAWABI RULE IN TAMILNAD

Having looked at the traditions of south Indian Muslim worship which came into being by the beginning of the eighteenth century, chapters 4 and 5 will show how the various linguistic and status groups who shared in this tradition began to be reshaped into a more formally defined community of Muslim believers. Although the south was never fully 'Islamised', the creation of this limited sense of community was largely due to the rise of the region's first Muslim-ruled state, the nawabi of Arcot (also known as the Carnatic) with its two successive lines of would-be dynasts.

It will be remembered that the first of these two lines of nawabs belonged to an élite population of Dakhni trading and service people, the Navaiyats. The most powerful members of this group were those who had held high posts under the sultans of Bijapur and the other Deccani Muslim states. When these domains came under Mughal rule at the end of the seventeenth century, many leading Dakhnis were able to seek preferment within the imperial service system. For most of these gentry families the crucial opening came at the beginning of the eighteenth century when the whole of the Tamil country (the Payanghat or 'Lower Carnatic', that is the region 'below the Ghats' from Nellore to Kanniyakumari) was declared a *subah* or province of the Mughal empire. In theory the new subah was subject to the adjacent Mughal province of Hyderabad which had been annexed after the conquest of Golkonda in the

*Susan Bayly, 'The South Indian State and the Creation of Muslim Community', in *Saints, Goddesses and Kings: Muslims and Christians in South Indian Society, 1700–1900*, Cambridge, 1989, pp. 151–86.

1680s. Here, too, a line of imperial office-holders, the Nizams of Hyderabad, had begun to carve out an independent dynastic base.

In 1710, when the Mughals had secured the line of fortress sites which held the key to power in the Tamil country, the post of *subahdar* or chief military and revenue officer of the new Carnatic territory went to a Navaiyat military man named Saadatullah Khan (1651–1732). Six years earlier, Saadatullah Khan's brother had been named *qiladar* (fortress commander) of Vellore, the town whose Maratha-built citadel was known as the strongest fortified site in the Carnatic; his nephew, Baqir Ali Khan (d. 1739), succeeded him in this post in 1716.[1] Saadatullah Khan and his successors had much in common with the other eighteenth-century strongmen who sought to make the leap from provincial office-holding to independent dynastic rule within the Mughal (or nominally Mughal) territories of the subcontinent. It was this process of hard-fought state formation which gave rise to the new regional powers of the eighteenth century. Of these Bengal, Awadh, and Hyderabad are the most familiar examples, but the new southern states of Mysore and Travancore conformed to this pattern as well.[2] In many ways the Carnatic was an ideal setting for the construction of a Mughal 'successor' regime: the subah was a new and unstable frontier zone, and despite the presence of Mughal garrisons and revenue takers in the region, it had never acquired secure links to the imperial centre.

The new lineage employed techniques of statecraft which were much like those being used to launch the new regimes of north India and the Deccan. Saadatullah Khan and his kinsmen intermarried with the region's other powerful Navaiyat settler clans, and this web of family and marital ties served as one of the main cornerstones of Navaiyat power over the next 40 years. In addition, like the aspiring rulers of Awadh, Bengal, and the southern states, the Navaiyats were ambitious town-builders. The aim here was to build up an economic base for the new regime; this in turn would finance the necessary expansion of the nawabi's fortress and market centres. By the 1720s Saadatullah Khan had begun to extend existing citadels and strong-points such as Vellore and Gingi. He recruited new groups of artisans, traders, and military men to these fort towns—his recruits included large numbers of Pathan mercenaries from north India and the Deccan—and he made large-scale expenditures on fortifications and on the building of mosques, *idgahs* (prayer enclosures for the annual id festival) and other pious foundations in these localities. In addition the Navaiyats founded new *ganjs* or market centres, as for example at Saadatnagar (1714), Fattahnagar (1715), and Saadatpattan (1718).[3]

Having been vested with the more prestigious Mughal title 'nawab', the new line also sought to turn their seat at Arcot into a true princely capital. Palatial residences were built: no new line could hope to secure a claim to power and authority without investing in the material trappings of kingship. It was also accepted throughout the Indo-Islamic world that the seat of a true dynastic ruler must possess its own Islamic court culture. This might have seemed an unduly ambitious aim for a rough garrison town like Arcot. In fact, Saadatullah Khan and his successors were surprisingly successful in attracting poets, scholars, and Sufis to their new capital, largely because they were able to benefit from the disruption of patronage at other Muslim court centres. Many of Saadatullah Khan's learned and holy men came from the factional conflicts which overtook Delhi after the death of Emperor Aurangzeb in 1707.[4]

While all of the nawab's power bases received an influx of Deccani and north Indian luminaries in this period, it was the citadel town of Vellore which acquired the most important of these new literary figures. In about 1725 the Bijapuri Qadiri Sufi Saiyid Shah Abdul Lateef (1656–1736) took up residence in Vellore: the *khanaqah* (hospice) which he established grew into that most celebrated of south Indian Sufi institutions, the Lateefia madrasa and dargah complex now known as the Hazarat Makan of Vellore (see above, chapter 3, p. 114). As for the emergence of Arcot as a centre of learning, the nawabs had formed a considerable circle of poets and scholars at their court as early as 1720. By 1722 Saadatullah Khan was able to commission one of these literary men (a Punjabi Hindu named Juswant Rai) to compose a Persian chronicle on the rise of Navaiyat power in the Carnatic. Like the *Anwar-nama* which Muhammad Ali Walahjah commissioned from one of his court literati in 1769, this work, the *Sayeed-nama*, was modelled on Firdausi's classic Persian chronicle the *Shahnama*, and on the great sixteenth-century Mughal dynastic chronicle, the *Akbarnama*. This was a key move in the assertion of independent dynastic authority. A court chronicle set the seal on the would-be ruler's achievement; its formulae were familiar to all who knew the conventions of Mughal court culture, and since it talked in terms of reigns and glorious ruling power, the man it honoured might hope to be identified as a dynast and not a mere adventurer.[5]

There was no real distinction between the political aspirations of these rulers and their attempts to foster a tradition of Islamic high culture within their new realm. This was also true of the building programme which the Navaiyats sponsored in their new towns and strongholds. The fortress town of Vellore became renowned as a resort of Sufis, a repository of sacred *barakat* and a military and strategic base for the nawabi, and so too the domain's capital of Arcot (a town without any natural defences) was adorned with princely residences and dynastic monuments, and also with an impressive array of religious foundations. Saadatullah Khan and his successors endowed Arcot with mosques, dargahs, and family tombs, and with another of the great *idgah*s which were such a feature of the Muslim towns of Tamilnad.[6] It was in this period that the capital acquired the nickname 'Shahjahanabad the small'. (Shahjahanabad was the official name of the Mughal capital at Delhi.) The nickname certainly exaggerates the town's size and grandeur, but it is an accurate reflection of the Navaiyats' dynastic ambitions.[7]

The story of the Navaiyats ends rather anti-climactically. In 1740 Saadatullah Khan's successor Dost Ali Khan was killed in battle, campaigning against a 10,000-man Maratha invasion force. Dost Ali Khan's son was forced to abandon his 'open and defenceless' seat at 'Shahjahanabad the small'; he scrambled to take refuge in Vellore and was murdered there in 1742 by another Navaiyat notable, his cousin and brother-in-law the Vellore fortress *qiladar* (commander).[8] At this point the new lord of Hyderabad took the initiative. In 1743 Nizam-ul-mulk Asaf Jah marched into Arcot with a force of 280,000 men, and the Marathas soon evacuated all their positions in the Carnatic. In theory the nawabi had passed to the young son of the murdered Navaiyat nawab, but the nizam claimed to have found a wild free-for-all with any number of would-be nawabs battling for the succession.

Nizam-al-muluck [*sic*] was struck with amazement at the anarchy which prevailed [in Arcot]. . . . Every governor of a fort, and every commander of a district, had assumed the title of Nabob [nawab], and had given to the officers of his retinue the same names as distinguished the persons who held the most considerable employments in the court of the Soubah.[9]

Faced with this spectacle of 'anarchy' the nizam now had an ideal pretext for stepping in and appointing a retainer of his own as subahdar–nawab. This in itself was an assertion of dominion: it was the sort of move by which all the other would-be dynasts in the subcontinent were seeking to create their own independent networks of alliance and affiliation, and it corresponded to the lines of validation and endorsement which were still being set up between south India's petty warrior chiefs and their self-proclaimed overlords or 'little kings'. As it happened, the nizam's first nominee was poisoned; the next man to hold the post was a north Indian soldier-adventurer named Anwaruddin Khan (c. 1674–1749). This new lord of Arcot succeeded to the nawabi in 1744.[10]

Anwaruddin Khan and his successors survived to found the second of the two lines of nawabs who held power in the Carnatic. This new line—soon to be known as the Walahjahs—was responsible for bringing yet another influx of service people into the Tamil country. This new Urdu-speaking élite included Muslim jurists, mystics, and literary men as well as soldiers and government service people; many of them were north Indian *qasbah* gentry like the Walahjahs themselves. Anwaruddin Khan's army commander, Muhammad Najib Khan, was typical of these migrants. Like other Muslim service people who held posts under the Walahjahs, this key military figure is remembered as an accomplished Sufi poet and scholar as well as a soldier. (He claimed descent from the eminent thirteenth-century Chishti saint Shaikh Hamidu'd-Din whose *khanaqah* was located at Nagaur in Rajasthan.) Muhammad Najib Khan and his descendants patronized shrines and learned foundations in the south, and developed close ties with many of the region's leading Sufi institutions. Élite Muslim literati like the Sufis of Hazarat Makan were fulsome in their tributes to these martial service lineages. As the following chapters will show, this was only one of many ways in which the world of the Sufi and the world of the Muslim military man came to intersect in the nawabi period.[11]

The brief career of Anwaruddin Khan can be seen as a transitional stage in the development of a Muslim political tradition in the Carnatic. The Anglo-French war of 1744–8 brought a massive influx of European troops to the Carnatic. The British and French now held the balance of military power in the region, and this made it vital for the new nawabi regime to establish a presence in Madras. This was all the more important as there was now a sizeable Muslim population in this colonial port city—Pathan military and trading people, Labbais and Maraikkayars from southern Tamilnad acting as agents for the East India Company, weavers and other artisans from the Deccan and the northern Tamil districts. This may explain why much of Anwaruddin Khan's religious patronage was focused on Madras: the Masjid-o-Anwari which he built in the mid-1740s served as the city's congregational mosque until 1847. His son Mahfuz Khan (1714–78) also directed acts of conspicuous piety towards the Muslim commercial and artisan populations of Madras: for example he built the graceful Mahfuz Khan Bagh masjid in the trading quarter of 'Blacktown' (now Georgetown).[12]

Anwaruddin Khan died in 1749 at the fort of Ambur (fifty miles west of Arcot) fighting against the last of south India's great Navaiyat military men. This was the celebrated 'Chanda Sahib' (Shams-ud-daula Husain Dost Khan). Chanda Sahib was another of those larger-than-life warriors who figured so dramatically in the political history of Tamilnad. His enemies reviled him as the 'scourge of the Carnatic'; to his contemporary, the military historian Robert Orme, he was 'the ablest soldier that had of late years appeared in the Carnatic', and before his death in 1752 he came close to founding his own dynastic state in the Tamil country.[13] In 1736 this 'renegade' member of the lineage used his 15,000-man army to take control of the great rock fortress at Trichy, headquarters of the Hindu nayaka lineage who had ruled in southern Tamilnad since the 1560s. Chanda Sahib gave his two brothers command of the key citadels of Madurai and Dindigul; he then proclaimed himself heir and successor to the Hindu *nayaka* regime, and began to carve out an independent domain in defiance of the nawab's claim to suzerainty over these ex-*nayaka* domains.

The Maratha invasion force overran Trichy in 1741; the other two brothers were killed, and the Marathas carried Chanda Sahib off to their Maharashtrian stronghold at Satara. In 1749 Chanda Sahib marched back to the Carnatic at the head of a 40,000-man army: this military confederacy was sponsored by one of the contenders in the other great power struggle of the period, the battle over succession to the nizamate. When Chanda Sahib faced the nawab's force at Ambur, Anwaruddin Khan had a new European-trained army of 20,000 men with sixty European mercenaries to man his artillery. This investment in the new accoutrements of eighteenth-century warfare might have paid off except that Chanda Sahib had been sent a force of French soldiers and sepoys from Pondichery.[14]

In the end it was the British-backed candidate who emerged as the new ruler of Hyderabad. Chanda Sahib lost out too: three years after his victory at Ambur he was defeated at Trichy by a joint force of Company sepoys and troops serving Muhammad Ali and his new-found ally the Maratha raja of Tanjore. Thus the unexpected outcome of all these death struggles was that Anwaruddin Khan's son Muhammad Ali (1722–95), took the title Muhammad Ali Walahjah I and ruled as nawab of Arcot for the next forty-six years. His descendants maintained their status as hereditary nawabs for over a century, although their dependence on British arms and finance soon began to rob the nawabs of their credibility as independent sovereign lords. The domain was transformed into a semi-dependent client of the colonial power long before the state was formally absorbed into the Madras Presidency in 1855.

There are three distinct phases in the development of the nawabi as a political system. First, there is the period from 1749 to 1766 when Muhammad Ali was fighting to establish his authority, and the new regime was based precariously in the military strongholds of southern and central Tamilnad. In this period the high costs of the nawab's military partnership with the East India Company were already pushing him into debt, but the realm was still managing to expand its networks of revenue and alliance. The second stage began in 1766 when the nawab moved his court to Madras and set about the delicate task of creating a Muslim dynastic tradition within the debilitating embrace of his English sponsors.[15] During the third stage, the nawabi began to show signs of the decay which was appearing at other Indian Muslim court centres in the early nineteenth century. This stage can be dated from 1801 when the British overturned the established line of succession to the nawabi and proclaimed as nawab a more pliant and politically acceptable member of the lineage. Paradoxically, this period of political decline was also the era in which the court attained its greatest level of lavishness and princely ceremonial.

THE FIRST PHASE OF WALAHJAH RULE
IN THE CARNATIC

Like most other Indian Muslim 'successor' states, the Carnatic remained a Mughal province throughout the eighteenth century. It is true that imperial rule became little more than a fiction in this period, but even so the attempt to create an independent dynastic state within these provincial domains could still be perceived as an act of sedition, and the nawabs as usurpers in rebellion against their legitimate Mughal overlords. The status of these aspiring rulers was all the more uncertain because they had originally come to power as clients and appointees of the nizams. Since these Hyderabad rulers had also cut themselves adrift from the Mughal centre, the nawabs would have to be seen as 'rebel' dependants of overlords who were 'rebels' themselves: such a situation does not fit into any conventional Western notions of state power and sovereignty.[16]

For the Muslim world at large the whole concept of political legitimacy has always been problematic. Ideally, Muslim are all united within the *umma*, the universal community or 'invisible theocracy' of Islam, and the existence of secular rulers—even if these are Muslims—is necessary only because human society has failed to live up to this ideal of perfection.[17] Furthermore, if Muslim kingship is itself an uncertain and morally ambiguous institution (at least in the 'high' or orthodox Sunni tradition) the practice of statecraft in the Muslim world has also depended upon a much more open-ended concept of sovereignty than can be accommodated within the traditions of European political theory. Throughout India, or at least in any Indian state with experience of Muslim rule, anything from the forging of diplomatic alliances to subversion of a rival's clients and retainers and outright warfare could be seen as part of the same political process. In his account of the emergence of the Maratha states of the Deccan, André Wink has shown that a single Islamic term, *fitna*—'rebellion' (though Wink argues that this is an unsatisfactory translation)—came to be applied to all exercises of state power which the Western tradition would divide into contrasting categories of revolt or sedition and 'legitimate' expressions of sovereignty.[18] This meant that in the scramble for power which followed the decline of Mughal authority, virtually anyone with sufficient military backing could exercise sovereign power in an Indian domain. But the very fluidity of this system meant that military power alone could not guarantee a ruler's survival. Precisely because the concept of sovereignty was so open-ended, it was essential for new dynasts to surround themselves with a convincing aura of kingship. In this way they might hope to amass enough authority to resist the 'fitna' which confronted them at all times.

It was all the more difficult for the nawabs of the Carnatic to create a tradition of Islamic kingship since the south had so little direct experience of Muslim rule, and since Arcot could claim only the most remote 'succession' to the Mughals. As in many other eighteenth-century domains, this process of state-building took place in the face of bitter competition from a multitude of rival powers. In the south the battle for resources and strategic advantage was waged against the French and English East India Companies as well as the major regional powers—Hyderabad, the Maratha powers, and the expanding military domain of Mysore under Haidar Ali and Tipu Sultan. In addition to these great powers, the nawabs had to deal with the many contending rajas and poligar chiefs whose tribute and allegiance they claimed. There was also resistance from a variety of military adventurers, all with armies and fortified bases in the Tamil country.

As in north India, these rival powers had two important characteristics in common. First, as the preceding account of *fitna* and political conflict suggests, they were all highly militarized societies. The main prerequisite for the new eighteenth-century regimes was an expensively equipped European-style army; no aspiring ruler could survive without efficient recruiting techniques and control of enough revenue to finance such a force. Secondly, the new state-builders were assiduous in carrying out acts of religious patronage. In both north and south India, displays of conspicuous piety were as important to the process of political consolidation as the formation of armies and the creation of an effective state revenue apparatus.[19]

These two aspects of state-formation were closely linked. Both can be seen as a response to the ambiguities of sovereignty in eighteenth-century India, and both were perceived as indispensable attributes of kingship. It is easy to see why the possession of military power was considered an essential mark of kingly status for any Hindu or Muslim ruler; the Walahjahs maintained a sizeable army until the last quarter of the eighteenth century.[20] As to the ruler's religious role, it has already been shown that in societies which would now be classed as 'Hindu', the building and embellishment of shrines and the recruitment of priestly specialists were seen as fundamental obligations of kingship. At the same time there was an important practical aspect to these acts: in stimulating the consumption of goods and services, the king promoted the material welfare of his domain, and ultimately this too contributed to the cosmic harmony of which he was guarantor.[21]

Over the centuries since the founding of the first Delhi sultanates, Indo-Muslim society evolved a tradition of political thought which united Muslim—especially Persian—and indigenous Hindu perceptions of power and sovereignty. This tradition derived from a very specific notion of correct 'kingly' behaviour. Again, what was required were continual acts of piety and munificence, and here too these benefactions were not to be confined to shrines and ceremonial. It was expected for example that the lord of a true Muslim domain would surround himself with items of value and refinement, and maintain the wide array of clients and retainers who made up a suitable princely 'establishment'. As in the ideal Hindu domain, the Muslim ruler had an obligation to generate wealth. Both his own spending and the model of aristocratic consumption which he provided for his courtiers secured the livelihoods of artisans, ritualists, and commercial people within his domain. In addition to generating revenue, the ruler's displays of patronage and pious charity also showed that he commanded the style and trappings appropriate to kingship, and thus helped to confirm the legitimacy of his rule.[22]

These features can all be seen in the tradition of princely rule which was established by the nawabs of Arcot. Both the Navaiyats and the Walahjahs sought to create a style of munificence which had much in common with the court culture of the other former Mughal domains. Here the ruler's lavish spending is to be equated with piety and moral worth, as is made clear in the classic chronicle of nawabi rule, Burhan Ibn Hasan's *Tuzak-i-Walajahi*. This work has much in common with the Navaiyats' dynastic chronicle, the *Sayeednamah*. In his character sketch of Muhammad Ali Walahjah, Burhan states: 'His chief traits were to open inns, build mosques, found hospitals for the poor, build bridges, dig wells, improve gardens and rivers, both in his own country and elsewhere,—all these in the way of Allah.'[23] This then was an ideal which conceived of bridge-building and other apparently secular works in much the same terms as the founding of mosques and shrines. In all these acts, the nawab was acting as a moral exemplar to his subjects. These same qualities of pious kingship were also to be displayed through his support for holy men and literati.

The spring showers were but a drizzle when compared with his shower of gems in charity . . . The empty pockets of men from far-off lands became filled (with gold); the shoulders and backs of the learned from every part of the country were made heavy (with presents).[24]

In this period, the Walahjahs' acts of princely benefaction were focused on the localities which served as administrative and military centres for the new regional states. In the early phase of Walahjah rule the old Nayaka capital of Trichy received a particularly large share of this largesse. The reasons for this are quite clear. The four miles of walls, towers, ditches, and ramparts which the Nayakas dug into the famous Trichy Rock site in the seventeenth century had transformed this ancient temple down into the most important military stronghold in south India. As one locally based Jesuit missionary reported in 1718,

Trichy, where the [nayaka] prince lives, is a very populous city and of considerable extent. It is the finest fortress between Cape Comorin [Kanniyakumari] and Golconda. Many armies have besieged it, but always unsuccessfully.[25]

Throughout the eighteenth century the town and its Rock Fort were raided and fought over by almost every would-be ruler and power-broker in south India. When Muhammad Ali Walahjah made his bid for the nawabi in 1749, he staked his claim to the succession on his command of the town and its fortifications. It was from Trichy that the declared himself nawab, and throughout the early period of his reign Muhammad Ali's authority was perceived as emanating directly from the Trichy fortress site. Even when he moved his formal capital from Trichy to Arcot and then to the British-built palace complex at Chepauk in Madras, Trichy continued to be hailed as one of the regime's greatest assets: almost by definition, the man who held Trichy was a south Indian ruler.[26]

This was largely due to the fame and sanctity of Trichy's holy places. Like Madurai, Tirunelveli, Vellore and the other great fortress towns of the region—indeed like most of the smaller fort–mart centres (kottai-pettais) located throughout the Tamil country—the town's main strategic points had great religious significance. The Rock fort itself was a place of shrines and holy places: there were the rock-cut Siva temples dating back to Pallava times, the sacred footprint sites which are associated both with Vishnu and with the great Trichy pir, Nathar Wali, and the massive Sri Thayamunavar temple which was cut deep into the interior of the Rock. The surrounding countryside was also dotted with strategically placed rock formations of which the Golden Rock and the so-called Faqir's Rock were the most celebrated: these too contained important local temple and pir cult sites.

By the beginning of the eighteenth century the Rock fort sites were thought of as part of a single interconnecting cluster of holy places. Like other well-known Tamil shrines and temples, each was a popular pilgrimage site in its own right and was known and venerated very widely in south India. At the same time though, almost all such south Indian sites—dargahs, great temples, shrines of lesser blood-taking power deities and their associated cult objects and symbolic tokens—were perceived as forming part of a localized sacred landscape with each of the individual sites taking on enhanced power and prestige from its bonds and legendary interactions with all the others.[27]

Some of these links have already been described—the tales of marriages and kinship ties between gods and goddesses, the claims of discipleship uniting groups of interrelated Sufis, and the intermingling of motifs and pilgrimage programmes which identified individual *pirs* with the 'high' gods and power divinities of a particular region. Within these webs of devotion and cult affiliation, what counted was the power or sacred energy of the gods and cult figures, and the supernatural links and associations which united them: formal boundaries of sect and communal affiliation were of relatively minor importance at this time.

By the beginning of the eighteenth century the Trichy Rock had come to be identified as part of a network which had been built up around the cults of the town's two most famous sacred personages—the lord of the Srirangam temple (Lord Vishnu as Sri Ranghunathaswami) and the Trichy *pir* Nathar Wali. It has already been seen how closely the Srirangam shrine and the Nathar Wali dargah were related in the pre-colonial period. Their devotional traditions were full of shared motifs and legends, and their chronicles and shrine histories portrayed the two beings as counterparts or divine partners. There were dozens of smaller temples and *pir* cult shrines around Trichy which had been drawn into this same web of affiliation and interaction, and as in several other south Indian shrine towns—Kanchi is one of the most striking examples—the Srirangam temple and the Nathar Wali dargah had come to coordinate the timing of some of their annual festival celebrations. They were even known to share the same elephants and other 'kingly' accoutrements.

The Walahjahs directed many of their most lavish acts of 'kingly' piety towards the Trichy holy places. Dozens of *pir* shrines around the town are known to have been endowed and patronized by the Walahjahs and their retainers, and to have been included in the nawabs' great periodic state pilgrimages (such as the 1823 pilgrimage to Nagore). The Nathar Wali shrine was one of the major beneficiaries of this patronage. The graceful dome and most of the other structures which now make up the dargah date from Muhammad Ali's reign, and the shrine's historical traditions claim the Walahjahs as the greatest of the dargah's many benefactors. There was more to this benefaction though than a wish to associate the new regime with one of the most potent of south India's cult saints. The dargah had also been a place of great importance to the Walahjah's old Navaiyat enemy Chanda Sahib: this so-called usurper is still remembered as another of the shrine's major eighteenth-century donors. This was why the Walahjahs were so eager to establish their own rights of 'princely' benefaction at the site, and the obvious way for Muhammad Ali to make the point was through the all-pervading south Indian symbolism of blood and dismemberment.

When Chanda Sahib was put to death by the Maratha raja of Tanjore, his body was handed over to the new Walahjah nawab. Muhammad Ali is said to have had the severed head tied to a camel and paraded five times round the walls of Trichy, and the dismembered torso was buried inside the precincts of the Nathar Wali dargah.[28] The point of this move was to show that Chanda Sahib's domain had been taken over and absorbed into the realm of the triumphant Walahjahs. By asserting themselves in this way, the new ruling line was invoking one of the key principles of the south Asian Sufi tradition. It has already been seen that, like most other *pir*s in the Muslim world, the cult saints of south India were perceived and venerated as royal beings; such *pir*s were also recognized as precursors of real-life kings. This meant that the realm of the Walahjahs could be portrayed as a fulfilment of the supernatural domain ruled by Nathar Wali. By interring Chanda Sahib inside the grounds of the shrine, the nawab's newly vanquished enemy was transformed into a disciple and subject of the warrior *pir*: like the slaughtered Nandi at the hands of the triumphant Penukonda saint, he too was consumed and assimilated into the realm of the nawabs, and thus into the realm of their *pir* and patron Nathar Wali. At the same time, the move fitted in with the motifs which were used to describe succession and domain-building in the south Indian poligar country. In this context, Chanda Sahib was treated as the demonic enemy who is beheaded and triumphed over by the lord of a newly founded warrior chiefdom.

NAWABI STATECRAFT UNDER THE WALAHJAHS

The most successful feature of Walahjah rule was the fact that the nawabs were able to forge links of this kind with south India's fierce *qalandar pir*s and with the power divinities who were revered by the region's important martial groups. Furthermore, they made these moves while simultaneously creating a recognizably 'Islamic' identity for the new regime. For example, it was this focus on Islamic themes which led Muhammad Ali to assign Muslim place-names to the region's key towns. This was yet another assertion of sovereignty; a demonstration that the major strategic and sacred localities of the region had been absorbed into a new domain ruled by Muslims and endowed with the style and symbolism of a conventional Muslim realm. But while Saadatullah Khan and the other Navaiyats had invented straightforward dynastic names such as Saadatnagar and Saadatpattan for their towns, Trichy did not become 'Muhammad Ali-nagar' or 'Walahjah-nagar' under the second nawabi line. What mattered to the Walahjahs was continuity, and the nawab's claim of succession to the *qalandar*s and *tariqa* Sufis of Tamilnad. As a result, this key power base was renamed 'Nathar-nagar' in honour of the town's most potent reigning saint: the nawabs were making an explicit connection between the political system they were seeking to build and the locally based supernatural domain or *vilayat* of the Trichy *pir*.

Even in the early stages of Walahjah rule, Muhammad Ali and his successors were able to go far beyond the limits of a specifically Muslim form of 'kingly' piety. The incorporative and all-embracing form of statecraft which they established was a feature which Arcot had in common with many of the most successful pre-colonial warrior regimes and post-Mughal 'successor states': Martanda Varma's Travancore and the wide-ranging state system of the Marathas are the obvious parallels here. It was also an asset which compensated to some extent for the regime's well-known military and fiscal weaknesses. This was why, despite their commitment to Islamic forms of statecraft, the nawabs also revered and patronized the region's great Hindu holy places. On this point the Walahjahs were seen by their Hindu subjects as differing quite sharply from the south's other Muslim state-builders. In Malabar and the Tamil country Tipu Sultan of Mysore is remembered as a Brahman-killer and a despoiler of south Indian temples, and although the atrocity stories associated with the late eighteenth-century invasions from Mysore are certainly much exaggerated, the contrast with the prevailing memory of Muhammad Ali Walahjah's reign is very striking.[29]

Unlike his Navaiyat predecessors, Muhammad Ali Walahjah appears in the chronicles of several south Indian temples as a ruler who fulfilled the standard dharmic obligation to protect and endow Hindu holy places. The records of the Tirupati shrine make a clear distinction between the Navaiyat nawab Saadatullah Khan, who is said to have reduced the daily allowances of the temple to a mere one sixteenth of the sums fixed by the former Vijayanagar and Nayaka rulers, and Muhammad Ali Walahjah who is praised as a great benefactor of the temple.[30]

In 1760 Muhammad Ali presided over a great rite of royal 'incorporation' at the Silambar temple near Chidambaram, site of the legendary throne of Sulaiman. He and his successors also made names for themselves as patrons and protectors of shrines in major fortress sites such as Palaiyamkottai and Trichy. Sites with strong nawabi associations include the Sri Nellaiyappa temple in Tirunelveli town and the massive Srirangam temple complex at Trichy. There are records of Muhammad Ali's benefactions to Srirangam, and he is even reported to have arbitrated in disputes over ceremonial 'honours' and precedence at this temple.[31] All this suggests that the Walahjahs were able to identify themselves with some of the south's most active and expansive sacred networks. In key localities such as Trichy they succeeded in mapping themselves on to the localities' pre-existing sacred landscape. They then enlisted this idea of an established and dynamic network of south Indian holy places to give definition and identity to the nawabi realm.

These moves also had important strategic consequences. Many of the nawabi period's most hotly contested military campaigns centred on conflicts for control of the region's formally Hindu holy places. This was partly because so many traders, artisans, ritualists, and even military people tended to cluster in the major temple towns; most would-be rulers concentrated on these localities in their campaigns to build alliances with the region's key specialist groups. The shrine's great hoards of coin and jewels made them obvious targets for looting expeditions, and they also represented important long-term sources of revenue for would-be rulers, most notably from the taxing of devotees along the region's major pilgrimage routes. Beginning in 1755, this system was placed on a commercial footing and the revenues of important Hindu shrines were rented out under much the same system as was used in managing the district land revenue, as well as more specialized local resources such as the region's pearl and chank fisheries (see below, chapter 8).[32]

All this suggests that the power which resides in south India's temples should be understood to include the temple's endowment of strategic and commercial resources as well as the sacred forces residing within it. It is this which made the temples such important political assets in the eighteenth century, and the Walahjahs were well aware of their value. This can be seen from the history of south India's most sought after prize, the Tirupati temple complex. The nawab had claimed the right to receive the Tirupati pilgrim taxes during the early 1750s; he was then forced to sign over his income from Tirupati to the East India Company to help pay for his contingents of Company troops. Once this had happened it was clear that the nawab's claims of suzerainty were open to challenge, and virtually all of his military rivals launched raids on the temple in the hope of winning control of its lucrative pilgrim revenues.

The most successful of these raiders was Muhammad Ali's brother Nazibulla Khan. This would-be dynast was one of two so-called 'rebel' Walahjahs who campaigned during the 1750s to unseat Muhammad Ali and take power as ruling lords of the Carnatic. In 1757–8 the key tactic in this exercise in *fitna* was the setting up of blockades to stop pilgrims travelling to Tirupati. Such moves disrupted the flow of revenue to Muhammad Ali's British patrons, and therefore constituted a challenge to the nawab's own authority.[33] The interruption of the Tirupati pilgrim traffic was an assertion of sovereignty in another sense: for both Hindus and Muslims, and for all those who were still not formally identified with one or other communal group, the control of holy places was universally recognized as a sign of sovereign power. This is why the nawab had made such a point of incorporating both Hindu and Muslim pious foundations into his political networks; anyone who hoped to usurp his authority had no choice but to fight for mastery of the region's key sacred sites.[34]

Two years later the Tirupati temple was the scene of another incident in which strategic and sacred considerations again overlapped. In 1759 a Maratha army seized and occupied the temple, and the British dispatched a force of 300 men to retake the site. It was then discovered that only eighty of these sepoys were Hindus of clean caste. None of the others could be permitted to ascend the sacred hill on which the temple stood, and it was therefore impossible to attack the Maratha positions. There was a farcical interlude during which the leaders of the sepoy detachment appealed repeatedly for reinforcements. The Company authorities in Madras kept sending more Muslim and low-caste or *avarna* Hindu sepoys, none of whom could be used in an assault. Eventually the Madras force gave up and went off instead to overrun the fortress of a nearby poligar: this deprived the Marathas of one their important local allies, and they eventually withdrew from the site.[35]

Two points emerge here. First, Tirupati was situated in an upland poligar area, and had long been a key shrine for the sort of warriors and poligar chiefs for whom Brahmanical ideals of purity and ceremonial precedence were relatively unimportant. Even so, the temple had now become an arena of conflict in which considerations of formal caste rank and hierarchy were applied without question. As of the middle of the eighteenth century, there was a now a complex interplay between the world of the great temple and its schemes of hierarchical rank and precedence, and the world of the unstratified martial predator groups.

The second point is that everyone involved in this conflict—the Marathas, the Company, and the nawab—recognized the vital importance of the great south Indian temples both as sources of revenue and as repositories of sovereign power and authority. The British (or at least their officers at the scene) and their client ruler Muhammad Ali seem to have accepted that this conflict involved rival claims to spiritual dominion as well as a straightforward struggle for military and strategic advantage. The nawab could not compromise his position as patron and protector of Hindu holy places, whatever the immediate military situation might appear to dictate. This is why the forces fighting on his behalf had paradoxically to be even more punctilious than a formally 'Hindu' army would have been in preserving the ritual purity of the Tirupati shrine.

What these events show, then, is that there could be no real separation between the sacred function of the Tamil shrines and their role in the political and military process of nawabi-era state formation. When the Walahjah ruler performed acts of patronage at Srirangam, he was acknowledging the shrine as a place of power within one of the great religious networks which comprised his domain. And in associating himself with these holy places, in incorporating them into his realm and assuming authority over them, the nawab was asserting his authority in a way which fused the concepts of secular and supernatural power.

The nawab's tactics of statecraft transcended communal and religious boundaries because such boundaries had little meaning in terms of the actual operation of the region's religious system. In south India, virtually all great shrines and holy places—Muslim, Hindu and Christian—were perceived as fundamentally similar repositories of divine power and energy: all could be absorbed within a ruler's networks of patronage and benefaction and all were proper recipients of his largesse. This shared conception of the power inherent in shrines and holy places was associated with an equally pervasive set of ideas which conceived of individual shrines and pilgrimage places as belonging to unified religious networks. This web of relationships was maintained through the many pilgrimage routes which criss-crossed the region and through the vast body of oral traditions and *stalapurana* texts which created an overarching grid of mutual reference and affiliation for these sites.

ISLAMIC COURT CULTURE UNDER THE WALAHJAHS

The second stage in the evolution of the Walahjah regime can be dated from about 1765–6. It was at this point that Muhammad Ali received the Mughal *sanad*s granting him the rank of *mansabdar* of 9000 and two prestigious new titles: *Amir al-Hind* and *Walajah*. The other key event of this period was that in 1766 the nawab moved his court from Arcot, which had been his capital since 1755, to his opulent new residence at Chepauk in Madras.[36]

The style and culture of the Chepauk court soon began to show signs of the nawab's growing involvement with the English East India Company. The palace itself was probably designed for Muhammad Ali by the notorious Paul Benefield, a military engineer turned financier who could easily stand as the very model of the rapacious eighteenth-century English 'nabob'. Madras had dozens of such figures: East India Company servants and freelance speculators who profited hugely from the business of supplying and servicing the nawab's establishment. Thanks to them and their European agents, Muhammad Ali filled the vast neo-Palladian *mahal*s of the palace with English furniture, pictures, and 'novelties' (magic lanterns, clockwork toys, and the like). A few remnants of this collection are still on show in 'Amir Mahal', the palatial Madras residence which was built for the Walahjahs in 1875.[37]

Twenty years later the web of indebtedness which bound the nawab to his English creditors became the focus of Britain's greatest eighteenth-century political scandal.[38] One result of this was that it became fashionable to portray Muhammad Ali as a decadent oriental potentate—'suspicious, vain and ambitious'—whose fiscal plight was supposed to have been brought about by the 'Mussulman''s taste for pointless luxury. Today, the opulence of India's eighteenth-century courts is no longer dismissed as an empty extravagance, and the rulers themselves are not seen as mere pawns to be swindled and manipulated by the wily European. It is true that like his contemporaries in Lucknow, Benares, and the other new regional capitals of the north, Muhammad Ali had accepted the view that an Italianate neoclassicism—or at least an exuberant approximation of the neoclassical—was the proper style for a princely residence. Thus in architecture as in military matters, Europeans were now the dominant influence throughout much of India, and both the armies and the architectural traditions of the 'successor states' were shaped to fit these canons.[39]

This does not mean that Muhammad Ali was simply aping European taste in a naive attempt to impress his English creditors. For example the nawab was a great patron of European painters such as the Scottish portrait artist George Willison (1741–97), who worked in Madras between 1774 and 1780. These painters were largely supported by commissions from English 'nabobs' who had amassed great fortunes from their illicit Indian investments and now aspired to the role of cultivated patron and art lover. Willison charged Muhammad Ali twice the going rate for his works and earned enough money to retire to England as a 'nabob' in his own right.[40] But this was not a sign of passivity and fecklessness on the part of the nawab. In all pre-colonial Islamic societies the true prince was a patron of art and learning and an arbiter of taste and refinement in his domain. Therefore, in conferring these commissions, Muhammad Ali was engaging in the kind of lavish spending which identified him as a man of power.

In these terms the more costly the picture the more it served the purpose for which it was intended. It could only reflect well on the nawab to be seen as a dispenser of careless largesse to an Englishman. Anyone who profited from his lavish spending could be seen as a retainer; this meant that the European artists and architects whom he recruited enhanced his standing in much the same way as the European mercenaries and military engineers who served in his army.[41] Willison's work also had political value in its own right.

In the Muslim states of the Deccan and north India the ceremonial presentation of portraits had long served as a means of expressing suzerainty and overlordship. In pictures such as *Muhammad Ali Khan, Nawab of Arcot, with Attendants* (c. 1775), Willison presents the nawab as a study in noble serenity; a majestically bearded prince in pearl-decked silk robes. These portraits too were intended for presentation—one was despatched to George III—or for display in the darbar hall at Chepauk. They served the same basic function as the great works of Mughal court portraiture, but as British royals and the nawab's European creditors were to receive the portraits, he commissioned Western artists to ensure that their political message was conveyed intelligibly.[42]

Despite all these signs of the European impact on the court and its culture, the Arcot domain was far from being a mere appendage of the English East India Company. In this phase of Muhammad Ali's reign the central focus of the nawabi was the development of a tradition of kingship which was authentically Islamic and as broadly-based as possible, with links to shrines and sacred places throughout the Carnatic and the wider Muslim world. It was one of the main aims of the *Tuzak-i-Walajahi* to describe the acts of benefaction and largesse which proved that the Walahjahs were true Islamic rulers. The work places much emphasis on Muhammad Ali's role as a mosque-builder, and it also highlights the many other examples of conspicuous piety which involved the formal side of Muslim faith and worship rather than its mystical and ecstatic aspect.

In his worship of Allah he was not remiss even to the smallest extent, and he took on himself the observances of a devotee . . . He was diligent in repeating *durud* [prayer; praise of the Prophet] and immersed himself in thoughts of Allah.[43]

Most of the elegant mosques, tombs, and public buildings which are such a striking legacy of Walahjah rule date from the period after the move to Madras. Several of the finest of these new structures were located in Trichy. It was here for example, in the regime's original power base with its rich mixture of strategic and sacred associations, that Muhammad Ali built the majestic red sandstone Walahjahi masjid on a site near the base of the Rock, close to the palace and darbar hall of the Nayaka rani Magnammal (1689–1704). In Madras too there were imposing new places of worship. These include the graceful masjid Ma'mur in Angappa Nayaka street in Georgetown, built in 1784, and the great Walahjah mosque in Triplicane, another imposing sandstone masjid with an adjoining cluster of *gunbads*—domed tombs of the Walahjah family and their retainers, together with the shrine of the Lucknavi Sufi master Maulana Abdul Ali Bahr al-Ulum.

As its security and resources increased, the regime began to undertake acts of benefaction which were both more lavish and more conspicuously 'Islamic' than those of the earlier nawabi period. The mere building of all these mosques was one sign of this heightening of 'Islamic' identity; another was the fact that the new dynastic monuments were all built in the classical Persianate style which had now come to be accepted throughout north India and the Deccan. Unlike the mosques and dargahs of Kayalpatanam and other Tamil Muslim towns, these Walahjah foundations contain no *mantapams* (pillared halls) or lotus emblems, that is, none of the Tamil Hindu architectural features which were so common in the region's other Muslim architecture.[44]

In addition to this use of a 'high' Islamic style in architecture, Muhammad Ali also sought to create a broader Islamic identity for the regime by building up contacts with the great centres of authority in the so-called Muslim heartlands. Like other eighteenth-century Muslim rulers, including Tipu Sultan of Mysore and, in southeast Asia, the sultans of the Indonesian port state of Atjeh, Muhammad Ali applied for symbols of endorsement and recognition from the Ottoman sultan. In the 1770s he was vested with Ottoman *sanad*s granting him the right to perform acts of service within the sanctuary of the Kaaba and the Prophet's Mosque at Medina. The deceptively humble entitlements which these *sanad*s conferred, the right to light candles and spread the mats in the great holy places, were cherished marks of rank and honour in the Muslim world.[45]

In the *Tuzak-i-Walajahi*, these acts of formal or 'orthodox' piety are seen as part of the nawab's fulfilment of the ideal of princely munificence.

He [Muhammad Ali I] strove to satisfy the physical needs of the needy, and set at rest the anxieties of the poor. Every year he despatched two ships *Safinatu'llah* and *Safinatu'rrasul* laden with presents and money for the maintenance of the stalls for water-supply and serais and for the award of *nadhr* [*nazar*: ceremonial presentations] to the noble and pious residing in Makka [Mecca] the Exalted, Madina the Illuminated, Najaf the Eminent, Karbala the High, and Mashhad the Glorious . . . He renewed in his name, from the sultan of Rum, the hereditary rights to sweep and light the holy places in Makka and Medina.[46]

The financing of the two ships bearing gifts and pilgrims to Mecca and Medina was one of the best known of the nawab's acts of conspicuous piety. It may come as a surprise to find this nominally Sunni lineage supporting Shia holy places and allowing their official chronicler to give equal prominence to the great Shia and Sunni religious centres in this account. The point, though, is that eighteenth-century rulers had to use every possible strategy to reconcile disparate interest groups and associate valuable allies and client communities with their regimes. Under Muhammad Ali's father Anwaruddin Khan, the appointment of *qazi*s had been used as a means of establishing new lines of clientage and affiliation within the realm. The recruitment of Tamil-speaking Muslims had been achieved in part through the appointment of *qazi*s Anwaruddin Khan appointed a Tamil Muslim named Abu-Bakr as *qazi-ul quzat* of Madras and granted him a *jagir* worth 12,000 rupees a year. This scholar-jurist has been described as 'a great savant of the day belonging to the Lubbai community', though it is more likely that he belonged to a prominent *maraikkayar* lineage.[47]

In addition to their commercial expertise, the *maraikkayar* had a key role to play in the nawabs' campaign to create links of patronage with the Islamic centres of west Asia. The two ships bearing alms, pilgrims, and princely gifts to the great holy places were supplied and manned for the nawab by the Tamil Muslim traders of Porto Novo ('Mahmud Bandar').[48] Muhammad Ali also assigned the Porto Novo revenues as charitable donations for the poor of Mecca and Medina. These services enhanced the political importance of the *maraikkayar* centres, and the Tamil traders' ties to the regime can be observed in the wide range of *maraikkayar khanaqah*s and dargahs which were endowed and often substantially rebuilt with benefactions from Muhammad Ali and his leading courtiers.[49]

Throughout India, marriage provided another means by which rulers set the seal on ties of allegiance and affiliation, and these tactical alliances often marked a new stage in the rise of a parvenu ruling house. In Arcot, as in other eighteenth-century domains, marriages were used to enhance the social standing of the ruler and also to confirm bonds of fealty and alliance within the state. Muhammad Ali was a wily practitioner of this art, though again, it was his father Anwaruddin Khan who paved the way. In 1737 this ruler arranged the marriage of his son and successor to the Shia noblewoman Khadija Begum. By allying the Walahjah house to a family which claimed imperial Safavid blood by way of their descent from the Adil Shahis of Bijapur, the marriage introduced a much-needed element of aristocratic distinction to the regime.[50] Marriage was also important in the competitions for client communities which were being fought out between all the rival powers in the Carnatic. The creation of kinship ties with a leading Shia lineage was a valuable coup in this struggle. The Shia migrants had emerged as a powerful and prestigious Muslim subdivision within the Carnatic, and the alliance would thus help to counterbalance the networks of clientage and affiliation built up by the Navaiyats.[51]

These considerations explain why there was a such a strong Shia presence at the nawabs' court and why the Walahjahs associated themselves with the

Shias' religious foundations and festival celebrations.[52] It was at this time that the line established itself as major patrons of Madras city's great annual Mohurram festival. Even today this ancestral tradition is preserved by Muhammad Ali's lineal descendant, the Prince of Arcot. The family's chief role in the festival is to supply one of the ceremonial hand-shaped *panja* standards which are erected along the procession route used by the celebrants. The parading and veneration of Mohurram *panja*s has been widespread in the nawab's former territories since at least the early nineteenth century: according to 'Mahomed Tippoo' (Muhammad Tipu), Persian interpreter to the Madras Supreme Court in the mid-1830s, the *panja*s used in the Carnatic were 'generally made of metallic substances in the form of a hand with five fingers extended . . . [and] are exhibited in different places that are previously furnished and ornamented according to the circumstances of the parties concerned'.[53] Throughout the festival period these emblems receive veneration from Hindus as well as Shia and Sunni Muslims. There are close parallels with the rites of Hindu puja; 'Mahomed Tippoo' reports that the *panja*s were adorned with flowers and presented with offerings of frankincense and sugar.[54]

The *Tuzak-i-Walajahi* focuses on dynastic considerations in explaining the Walahjahs' sponsorship of these *panja* rites. The custom is said to have begun under Muhammad Ali who gave thanks for the birth of his first son by Khadija Begum by pledging that henceforth he would erect one of the *panja*s used in the Mohurram ceremonies with his own hands.[55] This son of Muhammad Ali, who ruled as the nawab Umdatu'l Umara from 1795 to 1801, was himself a Shia. In this brief period of formal Shia rule the nawab built some of Madras city's most important Shia places of worship, including the elegantly proportioned Thousand Lights mosque and possibly its adjacent *ashurkhana* (the enclosure used by Mohurram celebrants). Even after the Madras government's decision to overturn the succession and replace Umdatu'l Umara's son with a nawab of Sunni affiliation, the Walahjahs retained their close ties to Shia families and continued to act as patrons of Shia institutions and ceremonial throughout the Carnatic.

SUFI FOUNDATIONS AND CULT SAINTS IN THE WALAHJAH DOMAIN

Although Muhammad Ali placed greater emphasis on the regime's Islamic connections after the move to Madras, he continued to act as patron and protector of the region's Hindu temples, and he made no move to denounce the 'syncretism' of the region's Sufi foundations and cult shrines, with their many links to Hindu and Christian traditions of worship. As a result it is hard to see how Walahjah rule might conform to any model which presumes a neat historical progression from 'impure' or 'un-Islamic' styles of worship to a growing 'Islamization' of faith and belief. None of the commonly held assumptions about the incompatability of so-called folk and scriptural forms of Islam can be made to apply to the Carnatic either before or during the period of nawabi rule. There was nothing exclusive in the style of Islamic piety and patronage which these rulers built up: no sign that a commitment to the learned and formal traditions of Muslim worship implied a break with the world of the Sufi adept, the Muslim cult saint, and the warrior clansman's tutelary gods and power divinities.

In the years after the move to Madras, Walahjah court patronage reached new heights of grandeur and munificence. From this point on Muhammad Ali used all the resources he could command to turn his court into a haven for scholars, poets, and mystics so as to create that milieu of culture and piety which was the hallmark of the Islamic capital. The nawab was highly successful in attracting men of learning to the Chepauk court. As early as 1768 he had induced the distinguished literary man Mir Ismail Khan Abjadi (d. c. 1788) to move from Chingleput to Madras. This scholar and poet was descended from a long line of Bijapuri Sufis. Muhammad Ali gave him a post as Persian and Arabic tutor to his sons, and after he had fulfilled his commission to compose the great poetic chronicle of Walahjah rule, the *Anwarnama*, Abjadi was granted the title Malikush Shuara, which translates roughly as poet laureate.[56]

Even before the move to Madras, Muhammad Ali had been associated with prominent Sufis from Hyderabad, Arcot, Chicacole, Medak, and Rajamundry. During this period he recruited Sufi adepts and scholars from as far afield as Alwer and Aurangabad as well as mystics and ulama from his own domains.[57] In 1768 the nawab achieved one of his greatest coups by recruiting Maulana Baqir Agah (1745–1805) to his court and appointing him as another tutor to his sons. Over the next twenty years Baqir Agah became one of the most celebrated Muslim literary personalities in India. His output of scholarly and poetic compositions was prodigious. His poems are widely accepted as amongst the most accomplished of the period's Arabic and Persian verse, and his work in the *mathnawi* verse form—particularly his long devotional poem on the life of Abdul Qadir Jilani—made a major contribution to the development of Dakhni as a literary language. Because of his literary and linguistic skills, Baqir Agah was a crucial figure in the nawab's campaign to broaden the Islamic identity of his regime. He was given charge of Muhammad Ali's Arabic correspondence, and therefore acted as the nawab's intermediary in correspondence with the great personages of the Arab 'heartland' including the *sharif* of Mecca and the leading ulama of the Hijaz.[58]

Apart from being a distinguished literary man and a learned adept of the Qadiriyya Sufi *tariqa*, Baqir Agah belonged to one of the leading Navaiyat lineages of the Carnatic. Thus, in inducing him to take service at Chepauk, the nawab was continuing to secure the networks of affiliation and support through which his regime was constituted. Baqir Agah was also closely connected with that most prestigious of south Indian Sufi lineages, the Qadiriyya scholar–mystics of the Vellore Hazarat Makan. He was a disciple of Saiyid Shah Abdul Hasan Qurbi of Hazarat Makan and a friend and contemporary of Qurbi's celebrated son Saiyid Shah Abdul Lateef Zawqi (1738–89). Thus, through his patronage of Baqir Agah, the nawab was able to identify himself with the prestigious Hazarat Makan establishment just as the Navaiyat nawabs had done.[59]

From this point on, the Vellore Hazarat Makan became a crucial source of legitimacy for the Walahjahs, and Muhammad Ali took pains to associate the institution with the most daring political move of his career. In 1773 a force of nawabi and Company troops invaded the Maratha kingdom of Tanjore and deposed the nawab's nominal feudatory Tulsaji (1763–87). This seizure of south India's most productive rice-belt kingdom was Muhammad Ali's final attempt to make the nawabi a dynamic and financially viable 'successor' realm. In England, the takeover was seen as nothing but a crude attempt to preserve the interests of Muhammad Ali's European creditors, and the ensuing outcry led directly to the scandal of the nawab's debts.

Given the importance of the campaign, it is striking that Muhammad Ali sought 'permission and benefaction' from the Vellore scholar-master Zawqi when the army was sent into Tanjore. Zawqi duly blessed the enterprise; when Muhammad Ali sought to reward him with a *jagir* (a privileged revenue assignment) he thrust the *parwana* (documentary) recording the grant into a candle and burnt it to ashes. 'Neither I nor my children need any *jagir*', he declared: the nawab is reported to have been 'awed and silenced' by Zawqi's action.[60] This was a suitably dramatic reminder of the fact that the model Sufi must scorn the blandishments of princes: nonetheless, Zawqi's scruples permitted him to compose a verse in what is known as the *mathnawi* form, hailing the conquest of Tanjore as a triumph of valour and statecraft. In the short term, then, the invasion was a success for the nawab. Although the British soon ate away his added income with huge tribute demands and claims for debt repayments, the acquisition of the Tanjore revenues allowed Muhammad Ali to acquire more troops and expensive new weaponry.[61] The annexation also induced the Vellore Sufis to confer a powerful stamp of Islamic validation on the regime, and for the next few years Muhammad Ali made unprecedented claims of suzerainty within the Tamil country, treating with the European powers as a co-equal sovereign and asserting new rights of overlordship in Ramnad and the other southern warrior domains.

The case of Baqir Agah demonstrates that the regime's Sufi connections were closely allied to its search for contacts with the great centres of Islamic faith and learning in India and in the Arab world. The interpenetration of the realms of popular devotion, Sufi scholarship and high scriptural Islam is illustrated even more clearly in the case of Muhammad Ali's most distinguished literary lion, the illustrious Bahr al-Ulum of Firangi Mahal (see above, p. 147). Bahr al-Ulum had been forced out of Lucknow by the Sunni-Shia power struggle which engulfed the Awadh court during the 1770s. In 1789 he accepted an invitation to take service under Muhammad Ali. The nawab staged a great ceremony of welcome, and when the scholar and his retinue reached the outskirts of Madras, the Walahjah ruler himself shouldered the great man's palanquin (sedan chair).[62]

Under the patronage of Muhammad Ali and his son and successor the Shia nawab Umdatu'l (b. 1748, ruled 1795–1801), Bahr al-Ulum became a leading figure in the literary and intellectual life of the Walahjah court.[63] He and his son lie buried in places of honour next to the great Walahjah mosque in Triplicane, amongst the tombs of other court luminaries and members of the nawab's family. Yet, for all his eminence as a man of learning and scholarship, it has already been seen that Bahr al-Ulum's tomb soon came to function as a much-frequented cult shrine. Its *santanakuttam* rites were (and still are) just like those which take place at the region's other dargahs, and the site attracts large numbers of Hindus and Muslims. Many of these are afflicted with gastric disorders: they offer up prayers and rub their abdomens against the tomb in the hope of absorbing the healing energy which emanates from the site. They also wrap their ailing parts with red sashes: red is a colour associated with power and energy in the cults of many *pir*s and also in the worship of the south Indian *sakti* goddesses.[64]

Bahr al-Ulum is far from being the only eminent scholar–Sufi who has come to attract veneration as a Tamil cult *pir*. At that most elevated of learned foundations, the Hazarat Makan at Vellore, the tomb of the institution's founder Saiyid Muhammad Shah Abdul Hasan Qurbi is also revered as a repository of *barakat*. It is sometimes argued that when a scholar–Sufi becomes the object of a popular tomb cult his devotees do not comprehend his teachings; such cults are supposed to grow up without reference to the *pir*'s original identity as a man of learning. But in the real world no such arbitrary distinctions exist. At Vellore, the small boys who are in the first stage of the madrasa's rigorous curriculum are encouraged by their teachers to sit on the plinth which surrounds Qurbi's tomb while they study. This close contact with the master's *barakat* is intended to quicken their faculties and help them avoid the cane switches which are in liberal use as aides-memoires at the school. None of the élite men of learning at Hazarat Makan would recognize any conflict between Qurbi's role as a scholar–Sufi and the veneration which is due to him and his descendants as figures of miraculous power. Even in the eyes of the madrasa authorities, these two functions overlap and reinforce one another; this is certainly not a *pir* cult which belongs to the world of 'semi-Islamized' or unlettered 'folk' religion.

THE SUFI AS KING

As has already been seen, Muhammad Ali was a lavish benefactor of dargahs. Throughout their rule the Walahjahs provided support for a wide array of Sufi foundations, and the latter part of the eighteenth century was a period of great expansion for centres of Muslim devotional activity in Tamilnad. Many of these benefactions were made to new Sufi establishments. In some cases the recipients were literati and holy men whom the Walahjahs themselves had recruited to the Carnatic, many of them from the nawab's home territory in Awadh.[65] Often, though, the regime's benefactions went to shrines and teaching institutions of longer standing. Their adepts and *pirzada*s included local Tamil-speaking Sufis as well as Deccanis, Malayalis, and Sufis from Muslim centres outside India. A typical beneficiary of this type was Saiyid Shah Rahmatullah Jafari Suthari (d. 1753–4), a literary Sufi who presided over a *khanaqah* and madrasa in Killai.[66]

The support of centres like this enabled the Walahjahs to associate the domain with a living tradition of Sufism. By supporting their shaikhs and by endowing new dargahs and hospices for their devotees, the nawabs could be seen as a line who were visibly enriching the religious landscape of the Carnatic. This is turn was a means of confirming the vitality and expansiveness of the regime. In the nawabi's dealings with Sufis and Sufi foundations, the interpenetration of formal learned Sufism and the tradition of the *pir* cult is clearly apparent. For example, in the early years of his residence in Madras the nawab arranged to have the body of the renowned Sufi Shaikh Maqdum Abdul Haq Sawi (d. 1751) brought to Madras from its place of burial at Rahmatabad, thirty miles west of Nellore. This Bijapur mystic and literary man is better known by his title 'Dastagir Shah Sawi' or simply 'Dastagir Sahib'. His new grave site was situated in the Mylapore area of Madras city, and the graceful dargah which Muhammad Ali had built over the grave in 1789 is still a place of pilgrimage and cult veneration for large numbers of devotees.

'Dastagir Sahib' was another key figure in the complex networks of disci-pleship and affiliation which linked the institutional *tariqa* Sufis of the Carnatic. He too was associated with Hazarat Makan; Zawqi's father Qurbi was one of his disciples. At the same time 'Dastagir Sahib' was himself a disciple of south India's most eminent Naqshbandiya Sufi, Khawja Rahmatullah (1703–80). Sufis of the Naqshbandiya order are known for their connection with movements of militant Islamic fundamentalism: in the eighteenth-century members of the order were active in many parts of Asia in campaigns of Muslim purification and revival.[67]

At first glance, Khawja Rahmatullah appears a typical product of this fundamentalist tradition. His Dakhni tracts attacking 'agelong innovations' displayed his order's characteristic hostility to traditions of worship which diverged from those sanctioned in the Quran and Hadiths. Like many other Indian Naqshbandiyas, he was particularly vehement in denouncing popular religious practices which appeared to derive from Shia rites and observances. For a time he took up residence at the seat of the Pathan nawabs who ruled Karnul (Kurnool) in northern Andhra Pradesh. This was not a successful stay: Rahmatullah had to flee the town when the local Muslim population—both Sunnis and Shias—rose up in arms because of his attacks on the carrying of *panjas* (hand-shaped cult objects) in Mohurram processions. His effect on the Shias of Madras was much the same. A Shia literature composed a chronogram which rendered the date of Rahmatullah's death as 'a wicked dog', and this deadly insult helped to spark off the Sunni-Shia controversy which preoccupied the city's scholars and literati between 1792 and 1802.[68]

Rahmatullah's brief sojourns in two other Andhra Muslim centres, Cud-dapah and Sidhout, were equally explosive. He finally settled in Nellore, an-other domain with a large Pathan population, and founded a *khanaqah* in the small locality which was renamed Rahmatabad in his honour. Muhammad Ali established strong ties with fierce representative of the puritanical or 'fundamentalist' Sufi tradition.[69] The Walahjah nawab 'sought his prayers and benedictions' when Rahmatullah travelled to Madras, and when he died in 1780 the nawab built the vast five-arched dargah at Rahmatabad in which the saint is entombed.[70]

Rahmatullah's disciple 'Dastagir Sahib' shared many of his master's views; his biographies state that Dastagir Sahib 'checked the rising spirit of Shi'sm [sic] in the Carnatic', and his son was known for his attacks on Sufis who displayed 'the wrong attitude towards Shareeat' [sic].[71] But 'Dastagir Sahib' also became a figure of ardent cult veneration for Hindus and Muslims in the Tamil country. Even though this Sufi scholar was a Naqshbandiya associated with attacks on Shiism, 'innovation' and 'syncretic' cult worship in general, he was a notable Sufi adept and was therefore perceived as a man endowed with potent supernatural energies. He soon became a popular cult saint in his own right, and his Hindu devotees know him as '*gyan bhandari*' (Skt. 'storehouse of wisdom'). Thus, far from being too simple or too ill-instructed to grasp the point of his fundamentalist teachings, the use of the title suggests that Dastagir Sahib's devotees were well aware of the master's fierce Naqshbandiya strictures. His fervour simply made him appear all the more potent as an embodiment of the cult *pir*'s active energies. He was obviously a figure of awesome power and majesty, and local people had no hesitation in assimilating him into the tradition of the *pir* and the power divinity.[72]

There is no reason to take the nawab's contacts with these Naqshbandiya Sufis as a sign that the Walahjahs and their court were becoming fundamentalist or 'purist' in this period. What these associations do show is that Muhammad Ali was continuing to pursue the same strategy of incorporation and network-building which he had already initiated in his Trichy period. Thus even after the move to Madras and the creation of the self-consciously mosque-building and Mecca-facing court culture at Chepauk, the Walahjahs continued to draw Hindu holy places into their regional patronage networks. One of the most important of these was the celebrated Sri Partasaratisvami temple, not far from the great Walahjah masjid in Triplicane. This temple was typical of the many Hindu foundations which the nawab managed to link into his web of ceremonial exchange and affiliation. Under Muhammad Ali it became customary to use the great tank of the Triplicane temple for the ceremonial immersion of the *panja*s (sacred emblems) at the climax of the Madras Mohurram festival. Here too, as at Srirangam and Tirupati, local *stalapurana* traditions portray the Walahjahs as benefactors and protectors of the shrine.

The transfer of the body of 'Dastagir Sahib' from Rahmatabad to Madras should also be seen as part of this broadening of the regime's religious identity. In bringing the saint's remains to Madras the nawab succeeded in endowing his capital with a new and potent source of *barakat*. It was also an act which can be seen as a re-enactment of the epic travels which Sufi biographies conventionally ascribe to Sufi masters. These journeys in quest of knowledge and spiritual illumination had a special significance for eighteenth-century Muslim rulers. It will be remembered that the Sufi's epic journeys have long had a variety of symbolic meanings in Muslim *tazkira* literature. The journey is meant to evoke the saint's inner quest and struggle, but it is also intended as a more-or-less literal account of the coming of the Sufi to his new abode, and of the stages by which his new place of residence is transformed into a centre of teaching and piety.

This is a process which corresponds directly to the creation of a Muslim political domain. The Sufi himself has been perceived as a reigning king. 'Hail to thee king of Nagore', proclaim the devotees of Shahul Hamid in the

Nakaiyantati, and many other saints are addressed as Padshah, lord-emperor. From his *khanaqah* or hospice, the *pir* reaches out to rule over an ever-growing spiritual realm: the term used for this, *vilayat*, also refers to a domain or province in the 'real' world. Similarly, dargah, the tomb shrine of a Sufi (Tamilized as *tarka*) is a word meaning court or seat of authority.[73]

Another convention of south Asian Sufi literature has been to portray the ordeals and conflicts of the saint's journey as a war of conquest. With his army of disciples, the *pir* overcomes and subjugates local potentates; these become the first of his liegemen, his devotees. He then goes on to build a network of subject–adherents in the same way as a conventional ruler creates webs of political alliance and affiliation. In regions such as Tamilnad, where Muslim kingdoms were founded much later than in north India, the Sufi has been widely portrayed as a forerunner of 'real' Muslim rulers, and his domain or *vilayat* precedes and paves the way for their rule. Because he marks the place in which Muslim conquerors and rulers will ultimately hold power, the *pir* too is a king in his own right, and he commands his domain with the same power that will eventually come to be vested in these latter-day reigning lords.

By focusing on the idea of Sufis as precursors of kings, it became possible for newly established ruling lines to claim ties of descent or spiritual kinship to the great saints of the past, and through them to the Prophet himself. Such extended genealogies were particularly important to aspiring rulers with less than illustrious family backgrounds. Also, if Sufis were kings and precursors of kings, then kingship itself became harder to attack as a dubious or 'un-Islamic' institution. This was particularly relevant to the Walahjahs, since their fragile new successor state was particularly vulnerable to charges of *fitna* against the Mughals and their hypothetical overlords the Nizams.

It follows then that in moving the body of the Naqshbandiya Sufi Dastagir Sahib to Madras, the nawab had expanded the zone of dominion which was vested in the saint so that it extended into his own sphere of power in the Carnatic. The conveyance of the corpse could thus be perceived as a kind of beating of boundaries, an act of piety which connected the power and sovereignty of the saint to the political dominion which the Walahjahs were seeking to establish. There is a large body of Tamil *tazkira* literature which describes the coming of the Sufis of Tamilnad in precisely these terms; that is, as the creation of a princely domain. For example, one of the best known Ramnad cult saints, Saiyid Ibrahim Shahid Valiyulla of Eruvadi, is identified as a royal hero and conqueror of the twelfth century. (He is usually said to have been born in Medina in AD 1135–6.) This saint's biographer states,

Saiyid Ibrahim Valiyulla came from Arabia to the southern parts of India. He lit the torch of Islam and established the truth in all lands. He founded his kingdom there [in the Tamil country] . . . his grace is still pouring fourth . . .[74]

As in the case of many other south Indian cult saints, Saiyid Ibrahim's journey to India is identified as the progress of an invading army. The saint's 3000 followers are identified not as disciples or companions but as soldier–heroes (Tam. *virar*) and the conventional account of arduous travel takes the form of a military epic. First in Sindh and then in Gujarat, titanic battles are fought against the armies of non-Muslim kings; the *pir* himself takes up his knife and slaughters whole families of enemy unbeliever princes on the battlefield. In each case the opposing forces are put to flight; after each victory the text declares, 'the majority of the people accepted Islam; Saiyid Ibrahim thought his holy work had been completed . . .' and so he moves his cavalcade on to the next field of battle.[75]

When the saint and his followers reach the Tamil country there is another gory confrontation. Here the story of the saint's conquests is set against the background of a romantically conceived power struggle amongst three rival Hindu princes who are described as sons of one of the mediaeval Pandya kings of southern Tamilnad. Saiyid Ibrahim exploits this rift in the enemy camp, captures the Pandya royal seat of Madurai, and proclaims himself sultan. 'Madurai has now been possessed by Saiyid Ibrahim Valiyulla. Announcing himself as the sultan he took charge of the government. He undertook the preaching of Islam in the country. Because of this Islam spread throughout Madurai.'[76]

The description of the saint as sultan of the Madurai domain is not just poetic hyperbole. The *pir* is a ruler; his authority is to be conceived in terms of kingship and dominion, and his realm corresponds precisely to that of a 'real' reigning sovereign. The text associates the Eruvadi saint with a very specific set of dynastic traditions. His realm is identified with the short-lived mediaeval 'sultanate' of Madurai, and he is also depicted as a precursor to the eighteenth-century nawabs of Arcot: the text and biographical traditions place much emphasis on the dargah's history of benefactions from the Walahjahs. As can be seen from the many references to south Indian Hindu rulers in these biographies, the most powerful of south India's Muslim *pir*s also came to be seen as heirs to the region's Hindu dynastic traditions. Madurai itself was southern Tamilnad's pre-eminent temple town and pre-Walahjah dynastic centre. Thus, just as the Nathar Wali biographies link the Trichy *pir* with the region's mediaeval Chola rulers, so this Eruvadi saint is portrayed as master of Madurai, and as heir and successor to the Pandya rulers who claimed authority over much of southern Tamilnad (including most of the former Chola domains) during the later eleventh and twelfth centuries.[77]

What this means is that in Tamilnad as elsewhere in India political power—the power of the Muslim conqueror and ruler—and the power of the sacred and the divine are to be understood as part of a single continuum. Many of the real and semi-legendary Sufis of north India and the Deccan were perceived as sons of princely houses; some eighteenth-century Muslim rulers carried the tokens of their Sufi *murshid*s into battle with them, and opposing armies sometimes confronted one another with an accompanying Sufi at the head of each force.[78] The dargah of the celebrated cult saint Saiyid Baba Fakiruddin is situated in the old Vijayanagar stronghold of Penukonda (now in Andhra Pradesh). In the Persian biography which was transcribed for Mackenzie in 1803, the story of Baba Fakiruddin's miraculous exploits is interwoven with a chronicle of the Hindu warrior lineages who controlled Penukonda, first as feudatories of Vijayanagar and then as Mughal *jagirdars*.

Even before the assertion of Muslim overlordship in the region, these Hindu potentates are regarded in the text as legitimate and worthy rulers, men of 'good nature', once they have been duly incorporated into the saint's domain. When Baba Fakiruddin and his party first arrive in Penukonda (in the early sixteenth century) there is a great confrontation with the local raja 'Seringa Rayar', and the saint gives a display of his awesome annihilating power.[79] The ruler submits: the saint's *khanaqah* is provided with a lavish endowment, and the king, his descendants, and all his court become the saint's faithful devotees. 'This raja for the rest of his life circumambulated the saint's tomb three times every Friday night after taking his bath', says the text.

It is made clear in this text that the forging of these links between king and *pir* is an act of practical statecraft; a move which allows the ruler to incorporate valuable new clients and allies within his realm. As part of his pledge to the saint the ruler is said to have guaranteed rank, honour, and a 'worthy salary' to any 'true believer' (i.e. Muslim) who comes from outside the region to seek service in his domain. The text identifies these incomers as commercial men, and their origins are similar to those of Baba Fakiruddin himself. The *pir*'s homeland is supposed to have been Sistan in south-eastern Afghanistan, and the merchants who are drawn to Penukonda at this time are described as 'true believers' who ply the rich caravan routes north of the Hindu Kush: they come from 'the Province of Tartery and Cashmeer and Cashghur and Cabul and Khundahar', trading in weapons, war horses, camels and 'rare goods' such as Chinese satin, shawls and 'bladder of musk'. These resident traders form the existing domain or *vilayat* of the *pir*, and they provide indispensable resources and services for the raja's exercise of power in this world. Any newcomers who take up the ruler's offer will come in as new disciples of Baba Fakiruddin. Since the saint had incorporated the Hindu raja into his network of service and affiliation, the two realms will begin to grow in parallel: as the text shows, the 'real' kingdom and the *pir*'s invisible supernatural domain are engaged in the same process of recruitment and expansion. The biography itself is both a description of this process and an account of the formation of a successful Muslim community in the Penukonda kingdom.[80]

The consequence of all this is that Baba Fakiruddin becomes guarantor of the sovereignty of this Hindu lineage, a point which is made quite explicity in this conventionally 'Islamic' Persian chronicle with its fierce account of the slaughter of the divine bull Nandi. What the text says is that two or three generations after this first raja's submission, the realm is invaded by a Muslim ruler, the sultan of Bedar. The saint does not desert his favoured disciple: even though the reigning raja is a Hindu, the dargah's chief *pirzada* soothes the ruler and disperses the Muslim invasion force for him.[81]

ABBREVIATIONS

Bahar	*Bahar-i-A'Zam Jahi of Ghulam' Abdu'l-Qadir Nazir*, Trans. S. Muhammad Husayn Nainar, Madras, 1950.
BC	Board's Collections (Documents prepared for Board of Control, London)
BOR	Board of Revenue (Government of Madras)
IESHR	*Indian Economic and Social History Review*
IOL	India Office Library, London
NAI	National Archives of India, New Delhi
PRO	Public Record Office
TCR	Tirunelveli Collectorate Records
TNA	Tamil Nadu Archives, Madras

NOTES AND REFERENCES

1. When the Mughal forces first moved into the Carnatic a Pathan military man, Daud Khan, was appointed *naib* (1700–8). His headquarters was at Jinji; Saadatullah Khan was his deputy. See Muhammad Husayn Nainar (ed.), *Tuzak-i-Walahjahi of Burhan Ibn Hasan* (hereafter *Tuzak*) pt 1, p. 57, 63–4; N.S. Ramaswami, *Political History of Carnatic Under the Nawabs*, New Delhi, 1984, p. 15; Robert Orme, *A History of the Military Transactions of the British Nation in Indostan*, first pub. 1808; Madras, 1861–2, I, pp. 35–7.

2. C.A. Bayly, *Rulers, Townsmen and Bazaars: North Indian Society in the Age of British Expansion, 1770–1870*, Cambridge, 1983, pp. 25–7, 35–72; Richard Barnett, *North India Between Empires. Awadh, the Mughals and the British 1720–1801*, Berkeley, 1980, pp. 240–52; Karen Leonard, 'The Hyderabad Political System and its Participants', *JAS* 30 (1971), pp. 569–82; P. Calkins, 'The Formation of a Regionally Orientated Ruling Group in Bengal 1700–40', *JAS* 29 (1970), pp. 799–806.

3. Muhammad Yousuf Kokan, *Arabic and Persian in Carnatic*, Madras, 1974, p. 17. On the founding of Saadatnagar and the importance of Hindu Chettiar merchants in its development, see S.A.R. Bukhari, 'The Carnatic under the Nawabs as revealed through the Sayeed Nama of Juswant Rai', M. Litt. thesis, University of Madras, 1965, p. 208.

4. Kokan, *Arabic and Persian in Carnatic*, p. 14. In 1752 at the time of Muhammad Ali's confrontation with Chanda Sahib, Arcot was said to have a sizeable garrison, a population of 100,000, and a thriving textile industry. Ramaswami, *Political History*, p. 157.

5. Kokan, *Arabic and Persian in Carnatic*, pp. 14–31; 115–30; Bukhari, 'The Carnatic under the Nawabs'.

6. Kokan, *Arabic and Persian in Carnatic*, p. 17.

7. *Bahar*, p. 113.

8. Orme, *Indostan*, I, pp. 46–8; *Tuzak*, I, pp. 77, 110–11. The assassins were also backed by the many Pathan military men who had settled in Arcot and Vellore under Daud Khan; their pay was in arrears and the nawab had failed to settle their claims.

9. Orme, *Indostan*, I, pp. 50–1. The Nizam was said to have counted eighteen petty lords and fortress commanders all claiming title to the nawabi; at one point, it is said, he threatened to scourge the next man who presumed to call himself nawab in his presence. Ibid.

10. The last Navaiyat claimant to the nawabi was the child nawab Saiyyid Muhammad Khan. In 1744 he was hacked to death at Arcot in the presence of Anwaruddin Khan; the assassins were Pathan military men from the Arcot garrison. *Tuzak*, I, pp. 110–11.

11. The most distinguished of the Vellore Hazarat Makan literary Sufis (Syed Shah Abdul Lateef Zawqi, 1738–89) composed a grandiloquent Persian *mathnawi* on the life of Muhammad Najib Khan. Kokan, *Arabic and Persian in Carnatic*, pp. 86, 147. Another of these soldier–literati was Saiyid Muhammad Musawi Waleh (d. 1700): this Persian and Arabic Sufi poet was known as the first nawabi officer to wear a European-style army uniform, ibid., p. 163. And see *Tuzak*, I, pp. 108–9; Saiyid Athar Abbas Rizvi, *A History of Sufism in India*, 2 vols, New Delhi, 1978–83, II, pp. 99, 315, 433.

12. On the build-up of European forces, see P.J. Marshall, 'British Expansion in India in the Eighteenth Century: A Historical Revision', *History* 60: 198 (1975), pp. 28–43. One of the mosques which dates from this period is said to have been built by a Hindu Komati named 'Kasi Viranna' who was the Company's chief commercial agent in Madras. M.G. Muhammad Ali Marakkayar, 'A Note on Marakkayars in Madras', in *The Madras Tercentenary Commemoration Volume*, Madras, 1939, pp. 65–6; J.T. Wheeler, *Madras in Olden Time*, Madras, 1962, II, pp. 67, 224–5.

13. Orme, *Indostan*, I, p. 119; *Tuzak*, II, pp. 30–126. Chanda Sahib was a nephew of the first Navaiyat nawab Saadatullah Khan. In 1734 he deposed the ruling Nayaka rani Minaksi (1732–6) and declared himself nawab. K. Rajayyan, *History of Madurai (1736–1801)*, Madurai, 1974, pp. 67–70; *Tuzak*, I, p. 72; Orme, *Indostan*, I, pp. 38–9.

14. *Tuzak*, I, pp. 137–8. See Orme, *Indostan*, I, p. 127, on Anwaruddin Khan's 'reform' of his 'undisciplined rabble' of soldiery: he managed to create a 'well-appointed army' of 12,000 cavalry and 8,000 infantry.

15. In 1757 the nawab was forced to surrender the revenues of a key region, the *jagir* of Chingleput, so that he could meet the costs of the Company's assistance in the campaign against Chanda Sahib. This process was to be repeated many times in the course of Muhammad Ali's relations with the British. K. Rajayyan, *History of Tamil Nadu 1565–1982*, Madurai, 1982, p. 195.

16. Sunil Chander rejects the view of Hyderabad as a cohesive 'successor' regime. See his 'From a pre-colonial order to a princely state: Hyderabad in transition *c.* 1748–1865', PhD dissertation, University of Cambridge, 1987. On the Walahjahs' Claims to be Legitimate Mughal 'Successors' see K. Rajayyan, *Tamil Nadu*, p. 109, note 12.

17. André Wink, *Land and Sovereignty in India, Agrarian Society and Politics Under the Eighteenth-century Maratha Svarajya*, Cambridge, 1986, pp. 21–34.

18. Ibid.

19. Bayly, *Rulers, Townsmen*, pp. 129–39.

20. As of 1761, Muhammad Ali owed the Company 2.5 million pagodas for the troops who campaigned against Mysore and the poligars. To reduce this debt he ceded some of his revenue-bearing districts but still owed 2 million pagodas to private creditors. See N.S. Ramaswami, *Political History of Carnatic*, pp. 306–7.

21. See A.M. Hocart, *Kingship*, Oxford, 1927.

22. Bayly, *Rulers, Townsmen*, pp. 57–68.

23. *Tuzak*, ii, p. 12.

24. Ibid., p. 13. Muhammad Ali made numerous *inam* grants in this period. See TCR 7967/ Collec. to BOR 12 April 1837, 12 May 1837/51, 73/pp. 46–9, 74–81/TNA.

25. Quoted in Lewis Moore, *A Manual of the Trichinopoly District*, Madras, 1878, p. 128. In mid-century there was a garrison of 6,000 men, a double wall with sixty towers, 130 cannon, and a moat stocked with crocodiles. Orme, *Indostan*, i, pp. 138, 180.

26. Lewis Moore, *Trichinopoly*, Madras, 1878, p. 128. Trichy was an important Chola centre, and there are seventh-century Pallava inscriptions on the Rock.

27. See e.g. TCR 7968/Collec. to BOR 17 May 1839/66/pp. 219–20/TNA; H.R. Pate, *Madras District Gazetteers: Tinnevelly*, Madras, 1917, p. 499.

28. Orme, *Indostan*, i, pp. 240–1. The grave is still pointed out to visitors.

29. Tipu did attack temples and Brahmins in areas such as Malabar where he was opposed by local revenue takers, and late in his reign he sought a more exclusively Islamic identity for his regime. Earlier, both he and his father patronized Hindu *maths* and temples. While besieging Trichy in 1781, Haidar 'waited in person on the Bramins of Seringham [Srirangam] Pagoda, with a propitiatory acknowledgment to Vistnou [the god Vishnu]'; Tipu acted as benefactor to several Mysore temples. William Fullarton, *View of the English Interest in India*, 2nd edn, London, 1788, p. 7; Francis Buchanan, *Journey from Madras: Through the Countries of Mysore, Canara and Malabar*, 3 vols, London, 1807, ii, p. 251; Walter Hamilton, *East India Gazetteer*, London, 1815, p. 276.

30. Tamil 'Yadast or Memorandum' on Tirupati finances, 1803, Mackenzie Collection—General, vol. 16, p. 476e–1. IOL.

31. *Tuzak*, ii, p. 244; K.D. Swaminathan, 'Two Nawabs of the Carnatic and the Sri Rangam Temple', in *Medieval India. A Miscellany*, iii, Bombay, 1975, pp. 184–7; H.R. Pate, *Tinnevelly*, vol. 1, Madras, 1917, p. 492. See also BOR vol. 796/29 June 1818/44, pp. 7444–512/TNA

32. Ibid. The massive construction of many south Indian temples made them ideal for use as military strongholds. See Orme, *Indostan*, I, p. 541; K.R. Venkatarama Ayyar, *A Manual of Pudukkottai State*, Pudukkottai, 1921, II, pt 1, p. 798.

33. Although the nawab had made over these dues to the East India Company, it would still be a failure of his authority if the sums were not paid. H.A. Stuart, *North Arcot*, (2 vol., 1st pub. 1887), Madras, 1894–5, I, pp. 71–3.

34. Orme, *Indostan*, II, pp. 317–18.

35. Stuart, *North Arcot*, I, pp. 73–4.

36. S. Muhammad Husayn Nainar, 'Some Madras Monuments', p. 68, in *Madras Tercentenary*, pp. 67–72.

37. Benfield was one of the nawab's chief creditors. See Lucy S. Sutherland, *The English East India Company in Eighteenth-Century Politics*, Oxford, 1952, p. 318, notes 1– 2; and J.D. Gurney, 'Fresh light on the character of the Nawab of Arcot', pp. 222–8, in A. Whiteman, J.S. Bromley, and P.G.M. Dickson (eds), *Statesmen, Scholars and Merchants. Essays Presented to Dame Lucy Sutherland*, Oxford, 1973, pp. 222–41. And see Mildred Archer, *India and British Portraiture 1770–1825*, London, 1979, pp. 54–5; Henry Dodwell, *The Nabobs of Madras*, London, 1926, pp. 27–8; Ramaswami, *Political History*, pp. 317–25; H.D. Love, *Vestiges of Old Madras, 1640–1800* (3 vols and Index), London, 1913, II, pp. 609–12. Following the suppression of the nawabi in 1855, the former Walahjah rulers were granted the title Princes of Arcot.

38. Sutherland, *The East India Company*. The financing of the nawab's debts gave rise to vast frauds. Over £30 million was claimed by Muhammad Ali's private creditors; in 1805 only £2.7 million of these claims were found to be legitimate. Ramaswami, *Political History*, pp. 238–326.

39. Banmali Tandan, 'The Architecture of the Nawabs of Avadh', PhD dissertation, University of Cambridge, 1979.

40. Mildred Archer, *Early Views of India: The Picturesque Journeys of Thomas and William Daniell. 1786–1794*, London, 1980, p. 9; Archer, *India and British Portraiture*, pp. 90–107.

41. Like all eighteenth-century Indian rulers, Muhammad Ali employed a large number of European military men. See, e.g., BOR vol. 3566/29 June 1807/p. 185/TNA.

42. W.G. Archer, *Indian Miniatures*, London, 1960, pp. 7–15. Muhammad Ali's largesse was even directed to the city's European churches. The nawab pledged a subscription to an altar-piece by Willison which had been commissioned for St Mary's Church in Ft St George. Archer, *India and British Portraiture*, p. 106. Willison's portrait of Muhammad Ali is reproduced in ibid., Plate II.

43. *Tuzak*, II, p. 12.

44. Even in 'Islamic' Kayalpatanam there are lotus emblems and other Hindu architectural features in several religious foundations, including the fourteenth-century *periyapalli* or 'great mosque'. Many revenue-free *inam* grants were made to mosques, dargahs, and other religious foundations in this period, as can be seen from the nineteenth-century debates over proposed resumptions of many nawabi *inams*. See, e.g., Report on lapsed inams, 30 Nov. 1852/238/TCR/TNA.

45. Kokan, *Arabic and Persian in Carnatic*, p. 91.

46. *Tuzak*, II, p. 12.

47. Many Tamilnad Dakhnis profess to be unware that Tamil-speaking Muslims possess a system of hierarchical ranking: this allows them to dismiss them all as a socially inferior 'convert' population. (See, e.g., Kokan, *Arabic and Persian in Carnatic*, p. 88.) There were similar tactical appointments in the first period of Mughal expansion into south India. One of the most celebrated Tamil Sufi literati, Shaikh Sadaqatullah of Kayalpatanam (1632–1703: described above, p. 84) refused an appointment as *qazi-ul-quzat* for the southern Carnatic but was content for one of his sons to take the post: this scholar served as *qazi* in Madurai and Kayalpatanam until his death in 1717. Ibid., p. 59.

48. Ibid., p. 263.

49. Suharawady, 'Sufis of Tamilnad', p. 38. The most important of the Porto Novo dargahs was built and endowed by the Walahjah office-holder Abdul Nabi Khan.

50. See Kokan, *Arabic and Persian in Carnatic*, p. 90. Compare Michael H. Fisher, 'Political Marriage Alliances at the Shi'i court of Awadh', *CSSH* 25:4 (1983), pp. 593–616.

51. The Navaiyat ruling lineage had strong Shia connections: Saadatullah Khan's brother and nephew were Shias, though the Navaiayat nawabs themselves were Sunni. Muhammad Ali took this process of alliance-building even further by marrying into the family of his defeated Navaiayat rivals (ibid., p. 43). Another of the key groups whose affiliation was secured through marriage alliances were migrants from Awadh, and particularly men from the Walahjahs' home locality of Gopamau. See, e.g., Nawab to Warren Hastings, 6 rajab 1190 [1776–7] *Copies of Papers Relative to the Restoration of the King of Tanjore*, 2 vols, London, 1777, I, p. 340.

52. Many Walahjah *inam* holders were Shias charged with organizing local Mohurram celebrations. BOR vol. 4709/31 Aug. 1835/pp. 410–14/TNA.

53. Mahomed Tippoo, 'Observations on the origin and ceremonies of the Mohurram', *MJLS* 2:9 (1835), p. 319.

54. Ibid.

55. *Tuzak*, II, pp. 6–8.

56. Kokan, *Arabic and Persian in Carnatic*, p. 91. And see Gurney, 'Fresh light', p. 240.

57. Ibid., pp. 91, 222.

58. Zakira Ghouse, 'Baquir Agah's contribution to Arabic and Persian Literature', M. Litt. dissertation, Madras University, 1973, p. 46.

59. Ibid.; Kokan, *Arabic and Persian in Carnatic*, pp. 115–30; Ghouse 'Baquir Agah's Contribution'; H. Suharwardy, 'The Life and Works of the Past Muslim Sufis of Tamilnad with Special Reference to Urdu Literature', TS, n.d., copy with author, p. 46.

60. From a translation of the *'Matla-al-nur'*, pp. 47, 52–3, in 'Hazarath Sayyed Shah Abdul Latheef Qadiri Bijapuri' (typescript: n.d.; Hazarat Makan Library). Another account quotes him as declaiming: 'Kingship and a kingdom are not equal to a grain of barley', ibid., p. 20.

61. Rajayyan, *Tamil Nadu*, pp. 147–52.

62. N. Ahmed Basha, 'Bahrul Uloom: His life and Works', M. Litt. dissertation, University of Madras. The shouldering of the palanquin was a symbol of submission

and homage and was thus a token of the nawab's acceptance as subject, disciple, and spiritual 'servant' of Bahr al-Ulum.

63. Ibid.; Francis Robinson, 'The Ulama of Firangi Mahall', in Barbara Daly Metcalf (ed.), *Moral Conduct and Authority: The Place of Adab in South Asian Islam*, Berkeley, 1984, p. 154; Kokan, *Arabic and Persian in Carnatic*, pp. 201–9, 227–32.

64. A major annual *kanturi* is still held at the dargah; it is presided over by a descendant of Bahr al-Ulum who travels from the Lucknow Firangi Mahal for the event.

65. Kokan, *Arabic and Persian in Carnatic*, pp. 190–8.

66. Suharwardy, 'Sufis of Tamilnad', pp. 43–4.

67. Francis Robinson, *Atlas of the Islamic World Since 1500*, Oxford, 1982, pp. 118–19.

68. Kokan, *Arabic and Persian in Carnatic*, p. 104.

69. Ibid., p. 99.

70. Interviews Madras, Jan.–March 1983; and ibid., p. 101.

71. Kokan, *Arabic and Persian in Carnatic*, pp. 111–12; similar views were held by the scholars of the Vellore Hazarat Makan: Zawqi's biography of his father Qurbi states that this Sufi too 'shunned all association with the Shias and admonished his followers to avoid their company'. ('Hazarath Sayyed Shah Abdul Latheef', p. 22.) One of Qurbi's miracles was to have brought about the deaths of two 'fanatical Shias' who were said to have plotted his murder: 'Their end was very miserable' says the biographer. Ibid., pp. 26–7.

72. It can not be assumed that those who make contact with the world of 'purist' Islam must inevitably renounce their conceptions of the supernatural and submit to the precepts of fundamentalist reformers. See M.C. Ricklefs, 'Islamization in Java', p. 113, in Nehemia Levtzion, (ed.), *Conversion to Islam*, New York and London, 1979, pp. 100–28. See also Ricklefs, *Jogjakarta Under Sultan Mangkubumi, 1749–1792: A History of the Division of Java*, London, 1974, pp. 288–93.

73. The Trichy *pir* Nathar Wali is widely known as Tablē Alam Pādshā [pātushā]. See Richard Maxwell Eaton, 'The Political and Religious Authority of the Shrine of Baba Farid in Pakpattan, Punjab', in Richard C. Martin, ed., *Contributions to Asian Studies*, vol. 17, Leiden, 1982, p. 348.

74. J.M. Sali, *Tamilakattu Tarkakkal*, Tamil ('Tamil Dargahs'), Madras, 1981, p. 175.

75. Ibid., pp. 178–80.

76. Ibid., pp. 182–4. The story appears to combine fragmentary references to the *Mahabharatha* and the classic Persian romances with a semi-historical account of the reassertion of Pandya power in southern Tamilnad in the twelfth and thirteenth centuries.

77. Ibid.

78. 'Historical Sketch of the Pathan Principality of Kurnool', in William Kirkpatrick, *Select Letters of Tipoo Sultan to Various Public Functionaries*, London, 1811, App. G, p. lx.

79. As in the Shahul Hamid biographies, the *pir* tests his strength against the king's *yogis* (Hindu tantric adepts). Amongst other ordeals, the *pir* and the Hindu holy man are sealed up in sacks full of lime (*chunam*) and thrown into a tank. The yogi drowns and his corpse is found half-devoured by flesh-eating fish; Baba Fakiruddin emerges unscathed and levitates to a nearby hilltop from which he proclaims his triumph. (1804 Penukonda MS, Mackenzie, p. 55, IOL.)

80. 1803 Penukonda MS, Mackenzie, pp. 20–2, IOL.
81. The pretext for the Bedar sultan's invasion in a mass pilgrimage to the Penukonda dargah. This is seen by the Hindu king as a ploy to smuggle the sultan's army across his borders, thus suggesting that here too armies and would-be domain builders follow in the wake of the Sufi; the real-life pilgrim follows the route of the *pir*'s first journey into his new domain, and this in turn is the cover for an aspiring ruler's advance into his rival's territory. Ibid., p. 40.

9

Kinship and Pargana in Eighteenth-century Khandesh*

STEWART GORDON AND JOHN F. RICHARDS

INTRODUCTION

The 'texture' or composition of pre-colonial rural India remains a question central not only to historical research, but to modern policy planning. Throughout this century, for example, planners assumed that the village is—and always has been—the significant social unit in the countryside. Hence, the development of village panchayats, village development schemes, and village-oriented rural credit. More recently, pan-village units, such as block areas, have received attention and funding. They have, however, often been criticized as artificial government impositions, with no local roots.

It is in this context that attention is now focused on parganas, a very old form of supra-village local rural organization. The central question, then, is to what extent India, in the seventeenth and eighteenth centuries, was organized into small supra-village units. How did these units arise and what was their function to the central government, to an élite—if any—within the unit, and to cultivating peasants? The answers to these questions, we believe, are crucial to our 'mental map' of pre-colonial India. Let us begin with a brief history of the term pargana.

HISTORY OF THE TERM PARGANA

Parganas—local, contiguous groupings of ten to 150 villages—were a ubiquitous and long-lived feature of the Mughal Empire. The term is, however, much older than the Empire. Of Persian origin, the original meaning was only

*Stewart Gordon and John F. Richards, 'Kinship and Pargana in Eighteenth-century Khandesh', *Indian Economic and Social History Review*, XXII, 1985, pp. 371–97.

region or district. It was introduced into India possibly as early as 1300 in the north, reaching the Deccan with the Tugluqs in the fourteenth century.[1] The term pargana is common in the Adilshahi records of southern Deccan in the fifteenth and sixteenth centuries.[2]

Parganas have long been thought of a simply *tappas*, a much older Hindu term for a grouping of villages, renamed by the Muslim conquerors. This view began with the earliest British studies of Maratha and Mughal administration, even predating the settlement reports of the 1820s. Typical is Mackenzie's preface to the 1809 translation of the 'Hakikut Hindustan,' an eighteenth-century Mughal revenue register.[3]

Thus we find a Soobah or province formed of what constituted a Dasum in the ancient registers and sometimes Naads comprehending the same purgunnahs or subdivisions under the name of mahals . . . an arrangement which it is apprehended originated in the ancient system peculiar to India, of settling a country by little communities in groups of villages instead of the European mode of subdividing the land into estates and farms occupied by single families. . . .

By 1830, a consensus had emerged among the British administrators. Parganas were seen as 'ancient', probably pre-Muslim, and somehow the geographical expression of 'little communities'.

Elaborating this theme of 'little communities', research in this century on parganas has moved from a static, structural view to a more dynamic one. In the past two decades, the focus has been on the development of parganas. The most articulated of these theories is that of Richard Fox in *Kin, Clan, Raja, and Rule*.[4] In examining Oudh, Fox found, first, a long period of infiltration, colonization, and conquest of local areas by immigrant Rajput groups. The kinship of the Rajput clan defined a local area and became coterminous with a pargana. Thereafter, the boundaries of the pargana depended on the strength of the clan vis-á-vis the central government. It was only if the central government became unusually strong and the clan unusually weak that others (grantees or bureaucrats of the central government) might usurp the lands and rights of the Rajput lineage of a pargana.

Though based on eastern Oudh, these recent studies have outlined the organization of local parganas throughout the Mughal Empire. Before examining the specifics of our data and analysis, it is important that we have a clear picture of this generalized model of a pargana, whose main features were as follows:

1. Parganas were of ancient origin.
2. The village represented the area controlled by a single clan/lineage, generally Rajput.

3. The head of the clan occupied the chief position (*deshmukh* or *desai* in Maharashtra) in the pargana and negotiated pargana affairs with whatever central government stood above them. Thus, parganas were the 'building blocks' of empire.
4. Parganas can be seen as 'segments', the physical manifestation of a model of Rajput kinship on the local terrain.
5. The head of the pargana held court and lived in a fortified town, the largest town in the pargana. His kinsmen attended court.
6. The head of the clan could call on his kinsmen to assemble a local military force, the largest and dominant force of the pargana except for the rare intervention of central government power.
7. Ritual flowed outward from the main pargana town, and was patronized and controlled by the clan.
8. Pargana politics were clan politics; conflict followed fissures in the clan and the jockeying of various lines and relatives.
9. The central government, through alliance and bureaucratic pressure, could strengthen the head of the clan, or undercut his power.
10. During decline or crises, the state would dissolve into these pargana lineage units.

The most important feature of this model is, of course, that lineage was the only basis for pargana organization. This assumption overlooks several questions crucial to our understanding of parganas and the local texture of premodern India. What was the importance of the pargana as an administrative unit, its importance to the *state*, rather than to its inhabitants? How much of the pargana infrastructure—human, physical administrative—survived from one empire to the next? Was it, indeed, possible to build an empire by mobilizing heads of parganas? Can we find parganas that were not clan-based, and, if so, why? Can we trace large-scale trends of the eighteenth century, such as monetization, at the pargana level?

ADILABAD, ON PAPER AND ON
THE GROUND

Two unusual, perhaps unique, sources of documentation allow these questions to be answered for a single pargana through two empires, the Mughal and the Maratha. They both yield detailed data on Adilabad pargana, a region in the Tapti river valley, in what is now the north-east corner of Maharashtra state.

On the Mughal side, the basis of this discussion is a detailed village by village report prepared by the Diwan of Khandesh province for the Mughal diwan of the six Deccan provinces at Aurangabad in AD 1699. This sixty-three page report is part of the Inayat Jang Collection, National Archives of India. As we shall see, the report has a narrow administrative focus, but excellent fine-grid detail on revenue, irrigation, and cultivated land.[5]

On the Maratha side, no one document contains the scope, detail, and organization of the diwan's report. Rather, there are the day-to-day and year-to-year documents of the central administration from the first revenue collections in the 1720s through total Maratha control, in 1760. Housed in the Pune Daftar and part of the Peshwa Khandesh Collection, these include letters from the Peshwa to his agents in the field, appeals from local people, yearly and interim accounts, surveys, and instructions. The record is frustrating and fragmentary, but often gives remarkable glimpses into the 'on-the-ground' workings of the pargana. We have supplemented these two main sources with the British reports of Khandesh in the early 1820s, written soon after the conquest of the Deccan. Particularly useful, we shall see, is John Briggs' map, compiled in 1821, before the parganas were consolidated into large administrative units.

Adilabad is today a small rural town located twenty-three miles to the south-west of Burhanpur city in Khandesh district, in the state of Maharashtra. At the turn of the seventeenth century it was a Mughal petty administrative centre (qasbah) in Asir district, Khandesh province. The name of the town, spelt in Arabic script in the Mughal documents, is clearly Muslim in origin. Adilabad can be translated as the 'Abode of Justice' or even ambiguously as the 'Abode of Idol Worshippers'.[6]

With the aid of the map, let us briefly tour the pargana, on horseback, as Mughal and Maratha officials did every season.[7]

Starting west from the walled town of Adilabad, on the banks of the Purna River, we would ride through a broad cultivated river valley, with villages (like Dudhale) partly irrigated by wells. Typical crops in the irrigated fields might be sugarcane, opium, or fruit trees. The unirrigated fields would have, for example, wheat, *channa* dal, or jowar. Soon we would be near the Tapti, but we would probably ride well back from the river itself. As streams approach the Tapti, they get deeper and deeper, eventually joining the river, which is over 100 feet below the plain.[8] To the west, the pargana narrows to include only the river-irrigated villages along the south bank of the Tapti for a distance of more than thirty miles.

Another tour proceeds south from Adilabad town through the essentially flat Purna River valley past villages like Hartala and Rulkhed to a tributary of the Purna which formed the southern boundary of the pargana. We might follow it downstream to its junction with the Purna. There we would find Bodvad, a substantial market, town. The north side of the Purna was a more

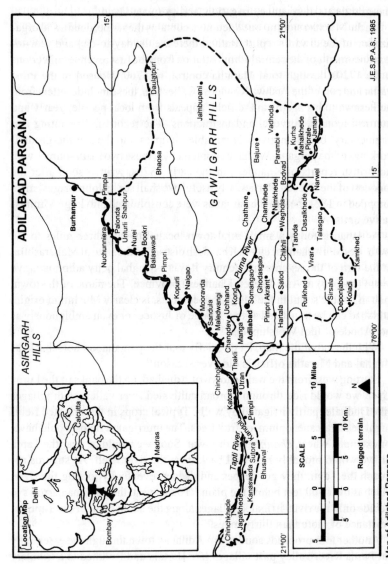

Map of Adilabad Pargana

sparsely populated plain, cut by streams coming from the forested hills arising only five miles north of Bodvad. These steep hills divide the watershed
of the Purna and the Tapti and, considering they were the home of unsubdued
tribal Bhils, we would probably not cross them unless absolutely necessary.

The final tour of the pargana would be north and east along the plateau
overlooking the Tapti. We would find villages regularly, every couple of
miles, all partly irrigated from the Tapti or tributary streams. We would, this
whole tour, be following the old and well-travelled road from Aurangabad to
Burhanpur and would see caravans, grain-carriers, and pilgrims. Returning
from our tour, what sort of a place was Adilabad town?

TAXATION AND SETTLEMENT, 1696

Adilabad town was the last major stopping point for travellers moving north
from Aurangabad to Burhanpur and thence north to Agra along one variant
of the great Mughal north-south routes.[9] In AD 1696 the town lay in the
jurisdiction of Muhammad Afzal, the chief local official (*faujdar*). It was probably his residence and headquarters as well. Local officials included four
town headmen: Ratan Patel, Issa (?) Chaudhuri, Suba (?) Chaudhuri, and Tija
Chaudhuri. The local accountant (*patwari*) was named Narainji. The town's
official revenue figure (*jama*) was set at 648,357 Mughal *dam*s (16,209
rupees). The more meaningful 'established collections' figure (*muqarrar
hasil*) was 8,527 rupees.[10] Receipts (*wasuli*) at the time of the report totaled
4,620 rupees with 3,906 rupees in arrears (*titimmah*). In other words, 54 per
cent of the anticipated revenues had been collected.

These figures refer only to the land taxes imposed on the measured
agricultural area (*raqaba*) of the town. The latter consisted of 3,111 acres of
sown land (*mazrui*) and 2,477 acres of waste or grazing land (*uftada*). The
total also included 470 acres allotted to tax-free grants (*aimma*). Areas in this
category were probably cultivated. The revenue burden on 3,111 acres of
cultivated land subject to taxation in 1696 was 8,527 rupees or 2.74 silver
rupees per acre. Much, if not all, of this land was under irrigation. The water
came either from wells or from the streams flowing from the Purna River
according to the report.[11]

It is interesting that these and only these data were deemed essential
information by the imperial administration at Burhanpur and Aurangabad.
Location, identity of the *jagirdar* and local officials, and revenue assessments
and collections were obviously significant. The surveyed agricultural area of
the town was recorded as well as the source of irrigation for the fields. The
amount of land allotted to holders of tax-free grants was listed. We do not find

population figures, the number of households, or data on crops cultivated, markets held, and so forth. The Mughal system of taxation did not consider population as a variable, but land and its produce.

Looking outward from Adilabad town, the document allows us a limited, economic picture of the whole pargana.

Late seventeenth-century Adilabad pargana consisted of 135 towns and villages (*muwaza*). Of these 124 were classified as 'original' (*asli*) and eleven 'additional' (*dakhili*) village.[12] The latter were relatively newly settled villages whose lands and revenues were treated by the imperial administration as part of one of the older villages. The two settlements together formed a composite revenue unit. Thus, for imperial purposes at least, only 124 villages were listed in series in the documents under consideration.

From the viewpoint of the state, within these boundaries Adilabad pargana constituted a distinct economic unit. The principal determinant of prosperity and production was cultivated land. Adilabad fell within the zone of regulation (*zabt*). This meant that village lands had been subject to a cadastral survey since the mid-seventeenth-century administrative reforms in the Deccan. Under this system of measurement, survey parties (*raqaba*) located and measured cultivated fields and fallow lands. The data thus obtained were used in conjunction with market prices of produce to fix the assessment (*jama*). Let us consider the overall figures from this survey, as follows:[13]

	Sown Area (*mazrui*)	Culturable Fallow and Grazing (*uftada*)	Grants (*aimma*)	Total
Bighas	149,322	98,699	14,643	262,674
(Acres)	(111,999)	(74,024)	(10,982)	(197,005)
(Per cent)	56.9	37.5	5.6	100.0

	Average per village			
Bighas	1204.3	796.0	118.1	2118.3
(Acres)	(903.2)	(597)	(88.6)	(1588.7)

From the total 262,674 bighas of productive land just under 57 per cent were actually cultivated tax-paying lands. Another 37.5 per cent were fallow or grazing lands. The final category, just over 5 per cent of the total, was in the hands of tax-exempt grant-holders (*aimmadars*). The latter could have been either cultivated or fallow lands but was more likely to have been the former. The average village contained just over two thousand bighas (1,500 acres) of productive lands. From this total twelve to thirteen hundred bighas (900 to 1,000 acres) would have been actually sown in any year.

Note two points about the graph on p. 247. First, villages included considerable grazing and common lands (*uftada*).[14] They were used, as they were in Europe at the same period, for a variety of village needs—grazing dairy cattle, firewood, and gathering of flowers and medicinal herbs. Both state and

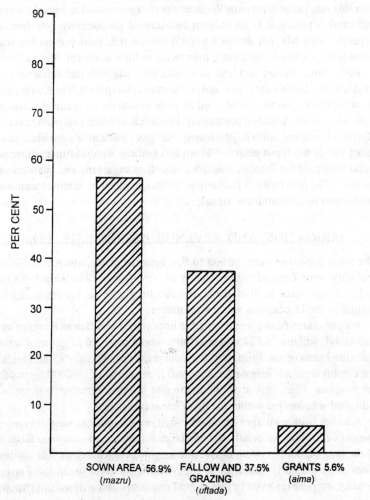

Measured Lands in Adilabad, 1696, by Use.

cultivator recognized that these lands were valuable, but they were not taxed. Second, and not obvious from the graph alone, is that only approximately one-half of the land regularly cultivated was actually cultivated in any year, with the remaining half allowed to lie fallow. This is a high percentage of fallow land for the period, and suggests low population pressure.

In a situation of relatively low population density, we might expect cultivators to choose the most fertile and well-watered tracts. Revenue figures bear this out; because revenue demand per village was tied to annual surveys and market prices, it is an indirect measure of productivity. We find, as expected, that Mughal demand per village on Adilabad was higher than Khandesh as a whole, and more than twice as high as nearby Malwa.[15]

Both contemporary and later evidence, thus, suggests that Adilabad pargana's arable lands were fertile and productive in this period. The Kunbi cultivators of this region were renowned for their industriousness and agricultural skill. The soil in Adilabad comprised 'two kinds of black soil [first] the rich alluvial clay found north of [the town]' that gave place to 'a deep black loam [that] yields the finest crops'.[16] From this soil the Kunbi farmers grew the usual millets of the Deccan, oilseeds, as well as sugarcane and quantities of cotton.[17] The proximity of Burhanpur's urban markets must have stimulated production of commodities for sale.

IRRIGATION AND REVENUE ASSIGNMENT, 1696

The most important contribution to this agrarian productivity in Adilabad probably came from irrigation. Nearly every village within the sub-district had access to some form of artificial water supply. In the uncertain rainfall regime of the Deccan this was a vital matter.

We can quantify, to some extent, the importance of different forms of irrigation. Of Adilabad's 124 villages, thirty-seven received irrigation directly from the Purna or the Tapti. In these villages, approximately 37,805 bighas were cultivated (not irrigated, *cultivated*) from a total of 148,400 bighas for the pargana. Thus, just over one-quarter of all land actually cultivated in Adilabad was located within a mile of these two rivers.

Another twelve villages obtained irrigation waters from watercourses or canals (*nala*). Thus, over half of the villages in the pargana were beneficiaries of the long-standing system of riverine irrigation in Khandesh. This system dates from the early centuries of the Muslim conquest under the Farruqi dynasty, or perhaps even before. Local engineers and masons constructed stone dams or weirs across river courses where rocky ledges made this feasible.[18] A late nineteenth-century gazetteer stressed their importance, as follows:

The weirs, *bandharas*, must, at one time, have been very numerous. In the west there is scarcely a stream of any size without traces of them. Tradition attributes their construction to the Musalman rulers, . . . The sites of these dams were, as a rule, well chosen. Except a few built straight across the stream, the dams are more or less oblique, the watercourse issuing from the lower end. . . . In building a dam, holes were cut in the rock in the proposed line of the wall from six to thirteen inches square, the same or more in depth, and from three to six feet apart. In the holes, stone uprights, sometimes small pillars taken from Hindu temples, were set, and the dam was either built in front of these, or the stones were built into the dam. . . . The materials are common black basalt stone, coarse concrete mixed with small pieces of brick, and the very best cement. . . . While the dams were built with the greatest care, the watercourses, were laid out with the strictest economy, following the lie of the ground and making long bends to avoid cuttings or acqueducts.

These long gently graded watercourses allowed a slow, easily regulated flow of water to the fields. The Farruqi rulers, and presumably the Mughals, appointed channel keepers (*patkaris*) to maintain dams and channels. They were compensated by grants of land.[19]

The report noted another fifty villages in the pargana drew upon wells (*chah*) for irrigation. In the vicinity of Adilabad, in the nineteenth century, wells varied from twenty-two to sixty feet in depth. Most were step-wells. Cultivators worked wells of this type with leather bags to draw water to the surface into earthen channels leading to the plots under irrigation. A good well permitted the use of four leather bags on a daily basis. Each bag irrigated one-quarter acre of land each day. The generally accepted maximum area of irrigation for each well was five acres of land. High yielding garden crops were best served by this type of irrigation according to the nineteenth-century sources.[20] The overall importance of well irrigation obviously depended upon the number of wells in operation. The Mughal record does not provide this information, but we can surmise that the wells were numerous. In 1879, the number of wells was probably around one thousand in the Adilabad section of Bhusaval subdivision .[21] If the same figure held in the seventeenth century the average per village for the pargana might have been eight or nine wells in operation. If the wells were confined to the fifty villages for which they are recorded, this would have been closer to twenty wells per settlement. In short, we might guess that fifty to one hundred acres of prime land might have been watered by well irrigation in these villages.

Management and appropriation of the considerable annual revenue and Adilabad's central location suggest the need for a substantial official presence within the pargana. The summary sheet lists several key figures: first, Muhammad Afzal, the *faujdar*, was an imperial officer (*mansabdar*), responsible for the maintenance of public order and the peaceful collection of revenues. He commanded, recruited, and led a contingent of heavy cavalry. Following the usual practice, his jurisdiction probably extended beyond the boundaries of the subdistrict. Second, the two Islamic judges (*qazi*s), appointed by the regime, enforced both the creedal and commercial provisions of the Muslim holy laws (the shariat). They also provided important legal and social services to the local Muslim community. Qazi Namauddin was attached to the town of Adilabad itself. His jurisdiction extended to 101 surrounding villages. Qazi Bakhityar Badha (?) was responsible for another twenty-three villages in the pargana. Third, the imperial intelligence reporter (*waqi-nigar*) submitted near-daily reports of public events and official news directly to his superior in Ahmadabad. The emperor himself, or one of his highest ranking ministers, scrutinized local reports from all over the empire as a means of obtaining direct, immediate information. Finally, Mahadev Naik, a leading member of the local Maratha aristocracy, not an imperial official per se, filled the joint position of *deshmukh* and *qanungo*. Under these designations he was responsible for ensuring the collection of imperial revenues in the pargana and for keeping accurate local records of tax collections and submissions.

The first three officials were Muslim officers alien to the pargana sent on temporary duty by the imperial administration. The latter, Mahadev Naik, was a local notable whose family undoubtedly had held this position for some time. This cluster of officers, usually acting in concert, carried out vital executive, judicial, revenue, and communication functions in the pargana.

As this official document makes clear, the revenues of each village and town within Adilabad pargana were assigned to an individual or an institution. Under the peculiar Mughal system of revenue assignments, termed *jagir*s, official revenues could be collected directly by individual officers as payment of their salary claims. These *jagirdar*s, as they were termed, did not have to reside within the pargana or in the village they held in *jagir*. But they or their agents would be present in Adilabad to collect regular instalments on the revenues.

In 1696, the largest single *jagirdar* was the *faujdar*, Muhammad Afzal. He held, in addition to Adilabad town itself, another fifteen larger villages for a total grant of 31,816 rupees (18.9 per cent of the total pargana income). Of the individual *jagir* holders listed against each village few others were actually resident in the sub-district. Perhaps fifty officers held one or more villages in Adilabad in this listing. A more precise count is not possible because of the difficulty of deciphering some names and the tendency of the compilers to use varying forms of the same officer's name and titles. A summary report of *jagir*s for 1702, six years later, reveals that Muhammad Afzal was still *faujdar* with a *jagir* valued at 38,905 rupees. Another fifty-six officers, some serving as far away as the Hyderabad Karnatik, held *jagirs* in the pargana in that year.[22]

For the administration, the truly significant fiscal and political unit within the pargana was the village or town. At this level the most important group was not imperial officers per se. Instead, it was the body of village headmen and village accountants who, together with the pargana *deshmukh*, cooperated with the regime in keeping order and collecting taxes. The report lists 304 headmen called *chaudhuri* or *patel* for the 124 villages of the pargana. The average is 2.5 headmen per village. The numbers ranged from one to as many as six in exceptional cases. The report also specified the name and title of each village accountant (*patwari*) as well. The report lists only 133 village accountants. In nearly all the villages only a single account held the post in contrast to the headmen who more often shared their posts.

When the entire list of these 437 men, plus the *deshmukh*, is read, two salient facts are inescapable. First, the empire at this level depended upon Hindu cooperation. Only one recognizably Muslim name appears—and that questionable—for one village accountant (one Shaikh Shakarullah, known as Shankraji). The remainder are all Maratha names ending nearly invariably with the *ji* honorific (Kishnaji, Timaji, etc.). By contrast, the *jagir* holders in Adilabad were nearly all Muslim. Only two recognizably Hindu, not necessarily Maratha, names appeared in the list of *jagir* holders for 1696. The cultural and ethnic divide between the imperial superstructure and local polity is starkly revealed. Second, there is no indication of kinship, caste, or lineage for any of these men. These men were treated singly, individually, as office-holders responsible for land taxes. Caste and lineage, in spite of their local significance, were not important to the imperial administration.

ADILABAD, CONFLICT AND DUAL ADMINISTRATION, 1700–50

It is important to put Adilabad into the context of the political and military events taking place around it. Khandesh, in 1700, was a province at war. Raja Ram, titular head of the Maratha confederacy, led the first major raid into Khandesh the previous year. He joined several commanders, including Nimaji Sindhia, who had been raiding the province for several years. The combined forces attacked the nearby entrepôt of Burhanpur in 1702, almost certainly crossing Adilabad on the way.[23]

Until 1717, Maratha energy was spent in internecine wars. Several leaders had, however, settled in Khandesh, carving out rights and territories. Khan-derao, Dhabade, for example, established a line of posts along the Burhanpur–Surat route and charged one-quarter (*chauth*) on the value of all goods on the road.

Husein Ali Khan and an 8,000-men Mughal army attempted to reopen this road in 1718. The decisive defeat of the Mughal army by the Marathas led to a treaty in 1719, by which emperor Muhammad Shah, in the first year of his reign, conceded one-fourth of the whole revenues of the Deccan to the Marathas.[24] Thus began a new phase in Adilabad's history. Every year thereafter, from 1719 to 1724, the Peshwa led raids into Khandesh.

The Marathas had, at this time, virtually no centralized bureaucracy; it was built through the 1720s. The Peshwa, Baji Rao, as head of the new bureaucracy, began to receive reports and accounts from his Brahmin subordinates in Khandesh in the mid-1720s. These suggest the level of disruption caused by Mughal–Maratha warfare. Of 124 Adilabad villages, eleven were deserted in 1724 and twenty were deserted in 1725. (In nearby Bornar pargana, twelve of the forty-three villages were deserted.) Another indication of disruption is the rare occurrence in forty villages of 'shares' settlement (*battai*), a division of produce at harvest or on the threshing floor.[25] Overall revenue remained low, around Rs 20,000, far below the levels of 1700–1705.[26] The final indi-cation that the administration was struggling in these early years is the rapid change in personnel. In 1724 and 1725, Pushoram Chimnaji was collector; the Peshwa replaced him with Ragho Krishna in 1728, and in 1729 Malhar Baskar was appointed.[27] Narain Dikshit followed him in 1731.[28] The Maratha administration was spread so thin in these early years that the collection area of each of these men included not only Adilabad, but five other parganas clustered some forty miles to the west.

Through the 1730s the pargana appears to have settled into a regular 'dual administration'. The Mughals collected their share, and the Marathas theirs. The documents unfortunately do not give details of Adilabad alone, but con-tinue to lump Adilabad with the earlier group of parganas—Bornar, Lohara, Yaval, Chandsur, and Pachore. Note, in Figure 1, how the collected revenue for the six parganas rose steadily through the 1730s.

It is only in 1739 that we have detailed revenue documents of Adilabad alone. Recovery was largely complete. Of 124 villages, only four were desert-ed.[29] Because Adilabad was still a functioning Mughal pargana, certain vil-lages were excluded from revenue payments to the Marathas, and, thus, disappear from our records. Specifically, ten villages were assigned to the Mughal auditor (*muzmu*) and six more were assigned to unnamed *jagirdars*. The remaining ninety-four villages yielded Rs 96,314 of which Rs 24,078 (one-quarter) went to the Marathas.[30] All but about Rs 4,000 is marked paid

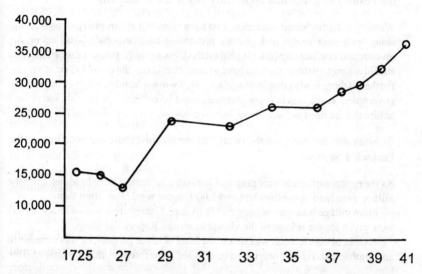

FIGURE 1. ACTUAL COLLECTED REVENUE OF SIX PARGANAS
INCLUDING ADILABAD, 1725–1741

into the government treasury (*vasul*). With the assigned villages, the collection was about three-quarters of the collection of forty years earlier.[31]

The Maratha administrative records suggest the degree of bureaucratic development and penetration. Records from 1748 list each Mughal religious grantee (*aimdar*) and the amount each was taxed. For example, on a grant to Mullah Hazarat Khan worth Rs 200, he paid Rs 19 to the village headman, Rs 41 to the village bookkeeper, Rs 17 to the Maratha regional official (*sardeshmukh*) and Rs 43 directly to the Maratha government.[32] The Marathas even collected a small percentage of the town taxes on commodities coming in for sale to Adilabad, and paid a percentage of the cost of the city's ten watchmen.[33]

At mid-century, political events once more overtook Adilabad. The Maratha central government went to war with the Nizam and his allies, the Gaikwad–Bande coalition of Maratha houses. Warfare raged across Khandesh. The seizure of the estates and towns of Adilabad from Mughal grantees severely disrupted the pargana. In spite of working with administrative documents, one gets a surprisingly graphic picture of the proceedings. Throughout

1751, the Peshwa's day diary has dozens of notations of armed cavalry sent to individual parganas or villages, often following warning letters that the entire revenue should be paid to the Marathas, not the Mughals.

The troops often met resistance. Note, for example, this stern letter from the Peshwa to a Maratha apparently allied to the Mughals:

Warning letter to Pamaji Mahadev. You have remained at Birkul in pargana Leling, along with your troops and you are preventing the Kamavisdar's collecting the revenue and confiscating [the Mughal estates]. Formerly you were informed that you should not remain there. . . . You have written letters to us, but do not expect any reply. Further, if there is any complaint against you, it will not be tolerated. By your actions, government is at a loss because revenue cannot be collected. A letter should be sent to him that he must not stay there, but go away, we give assurance of his safety.[34]

Stray documents give the details of the patrols; these are notations in the Peshwa's daybook:

As the pargana officials were prepared to make a settlement three headmen from the village were held in confinement and 5,000 rupees were taken from them.

From village Nandgav of pargana Manikpunj. Confiscation was taken and orders were given for the release of the village headman. Rupees 701 taken.

A letter of confiscation was sent to the head of Utran pargana; he was summoned and imprisoned. He was ordered to be released. This fine was, therefore, taken from him.[35]

By the end of the year, revenue estimates were in shambles. Appeals for remission came in from all parts of the pargana. Typical is this one with its tacit acceptance of disruption:

Letter of agreement given to government by the headman Baji of village Kotli Pargana Adilabad 1751. Earlier in the year the Peshwa a wrote him and ordered him to pay the revenue which had been fixed. He declared that he was unable to pay the revenue. The government fixed the settlement according to the year's report of actual measurement of land under cultivation. Accordingly the revenue is fixed at Kandesh taka 251.[36]

Other similar documents give the details that the pargana-level officials were directly involved in the report of the land actually remaining in cultivation, from which a new settlement was negotiated. One is perhaps worth quoting, in full:

Letter of agreement. Jahankhan patil and Badghe patil and Sand and Yes Chaudhris of Kasbe Satavgav of pargana Adilabad in 1751 in writing gave a letter of agreement that the Peshwa had called us and ordered us to settle the revenue. We replied that we are unable to pay. Considering future prosperity [or cultivation], Gangapant, representative of the Deshmukh, appealed for a remission of the revenue and Hammat

Khan agreed to stand surety along with the chogule [or *chaudhri*] for the revenue at 'fixed' Kandeshi takas [a monetary unit] 2-0-.5, for the current year. For our share [of the revenue] if there is any alteration, we will be held as outlaws. So this letter of agreement is written.[37]

As the Marathas struggled to take control, we get a most intimate look at Adilabad. The officials seized the *dastur amal*, a crucial Mughal register showing the prevailing rates of taxation in Adilabad.[38] It is worth considering this document in some detail. The first section shows the divisions of the harvest (*battai*), if government and grower were unable to agree on a cash taxation (*battai*). For irrigated garden land (*bagayat*), the division was two shares for the farmer and one for the government on a wide variety of produce, such as ginger, turmeric, vegetables, safflower, tobacco, flowers, opium, sweet potatoes, dal, and irrigated wheat. On unirrigated wheat and coarse grains, the division was equal. The next section has cash amounts for some items (which are largely meaningless since we do not have prevailing market prices). The last two sections were the crucial normative guidelines for the recovery of Adilabad pargana. The first was the payment schedule for bringing uncultivated land into grain production. It consisted of a six-year step-wise division between government and cultivator that began with the five shares to the cultivator and one to the government, and ended with an equal division in the sixth year. Equally important, the *dastur amal* spelt out the pay of the pargana-level officials. The *deshmukh* was to receive 2.5 per cent of the revenue, while the *deshpande* received 1.25 per cent. Finally, pay for the non-cultivating village servants was spelt out. The carpenter, shoemaker, and iron-worker received small shares of the village revenue, while the barber, potter, washerman, and village records-keeper were specifically to receive their shares (probably non-monetized) from the village with no central government involvement.

Supplementing this *dastur amal* were village settlement contracts. We have a complete set for 1752, one for each of Adilabad's 106 inhabited villages. The agreement for Salogav, for example, lists fifty-six cultivators tilling slightly over nine *aut*s (696 acres), and the cash demand. The contract has the sign (the plough) of the headman and the signature of the Maratha *kamavisdar*.[39]

The war ended on 24 November 1752, with the Treaty of Bhalke. Salabat Jung ceded to the Peshwa, among other territories, the *suba* of Burhanpur.[40] The 'dual administration' ended, and Adilabad along with the rest of Khandesh became Maratha. Before we leave this history of Adilabad, let us quote, in full, the Peshwa's instructions in 1753 to his *kamavisdar*, Laxman Bhikaji, working in the pargana.

This year the Mughal share of Adilabad came under the jurisdiction of the Peshwa and its administration was entrusted to you. So you should do the work honestly and pay in advance, as agreed 25,000 rupees, interest at 1 rupee per 100 per month. Interest and advance should be collected from the people [of your district]. Whenever you pay accounts to the government treasury take a receipt. Mushira (fee for conversion of collected coinage to standard rupees) is 3 rupees per one hundred collected. If even the advance is not collectible in the district, government will pay the interest. So a sanad is granted. Gandadar Bhijaji should take up the work of book-keeper (phadnis) for which he will receive 200 rupees per year. After allowable expenses, all remaining revenue should be sent to the government.[41]

ADILABAD'S IMPORTANCE AS AN ADMINISTRATIVE UNIT

Consider the powers vested at the pargana level. Adilabad, throughout the period, was treated as a revenue unit. In Maratha times, it was the pargana-level administrator, the *kamavisdar*, who signed the revenue contracts with individual cultivators and village headmen. These yearly negotiations made the pargana-level administration virtually the only ongoing Maratha presence in the area. Equally important, it was the pargana-level officials who initiated appeals for remission during time of adversity—whether from drought, flood, or invasion. The headmen of villages seeking remission had to come 'face-to-face' with the *kamavisdar*, usually at the head town.[42] The *kamavisdar*'s report was the major evidence on which the Peshwa decided the case. The pargana-level administration also had judicial duties; the *kamavisdar* investigated disputed local rights, such as claims to fill the offices of *deshmukh, qanungo*, and village headmen. These were usually decided right at the pargana level. Each year, also, the *kamavisdar* decided a few dozen criminal and civil cases involving everything from murder to false weights, within his pargana. This would have been an immediate judicial presence for a pargana like Adilabad, because there were no lower courts (except village or caste punchayats). The only appeal from a *kamavisdar*'s decision was to the Peshwa, a costly and difficult venture at Poona some 300 miles away.

The *kamavisdar* reviewed all religious grants (*aima*) in the pargana; he surveyed the land, fixed taxes, and adjudicated disputes. In a similar fashion, the pargana mattered to trade. The *kamavisdar* regulated market towns (*qasbahs*), extracted the transit duties (*zakat*), and, again, adjudicated disputes in the markets. The pargana-level administration could back these decisions with force. A small contingent, fifteen to thirty men, was routinely stationed at a pargana the size of Adilabad. In the case of Adilabad, however, more force was closeby. The major fortress of Asir, with its contingent of several hundred regular soldiers lay only a day's ride away.[43]

Lastly, the pargana administration was responsible for a series of locally important economic decisions. Adilabad's *kamavisdar*, for example, was responsible for offering lightly taxed five-year development loans (*taqavi*) used to open new land, or repopulate villages, or build dams. He also employed and supervised local watchmen (such as the ten at Adilabad city), petty tax collectors on the roads, and all the menials and troops of his establishment. The *kamavisdar* made local purchases of cloth and candles, paper, swords, and food, to stock and supply his office.

ADILABAD ACROSS TWO EMPIRES

Let us return to a related question, raised at the opening of the paper. What were the continuities and discontinuities between the Mughal and Maratha empires in Adilabad pargana? Continuities were many and basic. In administration, for example, the Marathas adopted Mughal terminology wholesale. Documents bristle with Mughal terms like *jama* (settlement), *teriz* (receipts), *izafa* (cultivated). The basis of demand—the maximum expected in the best of times—derived from Mughal figures. More importantly, the method of field assessment and cash commutation was Mughal. Even such basics as the number of villages, that is, what constituted Adilabad, passed directly from Mughal to Maratha. Both empires acknowledged that Adilabad had 124 villages, though at no time during our study were they all inhabited. Possession of critical imperial Mughal documents, such as the settlement rates (*dastur amal*) was important; nearly as important as military might, to the successful Maratha conquest of the pargana. Some of the local personnel remained the same. The Marathas acknowledged and continued all village headmen, record-keepers, and religious grantees (*aima*), as long as their Mughal grant was properly signed and sealed. Finally, the local head of the pargana (*deshmukh*) remained in the Naik family; Mahadev Naik held the office in the early years of the century, with Vasudev Naik replacing him in the mid-century documents.

None of this should surprise us. After all, preceding the Maratha takeover were twenty years of dual Mughal–Maratha administration. Equally significant, and often overlooked, is the long period of Muslim rule in the Deccan. Maharashtra had been familiar with Muslim administration for two hundred years before the Mughal invasion of the south. The conquering Marathas had grown up for generations under a Muslim administrative system.

Thus, what constituted 'Adilabad' was as much an administrative blueprint—a complex of normative settlement and taxation documents, plus village registers and signed contractual obligations—as anything existing on the ground. Even when the area was depopulated (as it was between 1810 and 1818), the pargana could be rebuilt, even with different cultivating peasants, from the pattern contained in the documents.

In spite of these continuities, there were several major discontinuities at the pargana level between the Mughal and Maratha empires. The first change is easy to see in the documents, but difficult to assess. Between the Mughal documents of 1696–1705 and the Maratha village lists of 1755, there is considerable disparity in village names. In fact, less than half the village names correlate, even when using the additional data of geographic coordinates. The disparity is even greater with the first British maps of the 1820s. This contrasts sharply with Rajasthan, for example, where researchers have been able to pinpoint over 90 per cent of all villages mentioned in a seventeenth-century register with the use of modern census data and modern maps.[44] The most likely explanation has to do with Adilabad's extensive periods of adversity, 1700–21, 1750–60, and 1795–1818. We might speculate that depopulated villages were not repopulated on the same site. The continuity of Adilabad's '124 villages' may mask considerably more movement, depopulation, adversity, and colonization than has been recognized. Further research into the village lists is necessary to establish this.

In comparison to this sort of discontinuity, the others seem less significant. First, there were no more Mughal military grants (*jagirs*). Right to the end, the Mughal government persisted in single village grants. After the Maratha conquest, the pargana was granted and treated as a unit; revenue might be divided, but administration was not. Second, the administration, though using Mughal terminology, was Brahmin rather than Muslim and spoke Marathi rather than Persian. The difference may not have been significant to the villagers. Large sections of the Mughal, and even earlier Muslim, financial administrations south of the Narmada had been staffed by Brahmins. For example, both the Qutb Shahi and Adil Shahi revenue departments were run by Brahmins. Kohlapur Brahmins formed the fiscal administration in the Carnatic, especially in the Bangalore area; Brahmins from Ahmadnagar and northern Maharashtra were earlier recruited by the invading Mughals, to administer areas further south.[45] It is at least possible that Adilabad's villagers dealt with Brahmin collectors *both* before and after the Maratha conquest. Third, the credit and economic networks changed. Adilabad's revenue flowed to Poona rather than Delhi. The advance money the collector needed came from a growing banking community in Poona.

All of this suggests that, in Khandesh, parganas had little history of their own. They were on the receiving end of major political and military events.

At the pargana level, raids, wars, and changes of empire meant destroyed and vacant villages, and depopulation, with no evidence of the reassertion of a strong clan/lineage structure at the pargana level.

LINEAGES AND PARGANAS

Adilabad was a pargana without the strong clan/lineage structure we have come to expect from recent studies of Rajput clans in UP. We find numerous markers of the difference, but let us suggest the following: (1) Unlike Rajasthan or the Punjab, the pargana was not named for a dominant clan. (2) The *deshmukh*, the local head of the pargana, held no independent villages. The *deshmukh* was paid a small percentage of the revenue. Thus, even the élite of the 'clan' had no revenue base independent of the central government. (3) Revenue settlements were with cultivators of individual villages, not with a dominant clan. Thus, the central government had full, yearly statistics on actual and expected cultivation. (4) Appeals for remission in bad times came from the village headman and were only secondarily routed to the *deshmukh*. (5) Though the *deshmukh* signed the pargana revenue contract, he was not ultimately responsible for unpaid taxes. Arrears were broken down village by village. (6) In times of serious adversity (1715–20, 1749–55, 1800–18), the *deshmukh*'s troops (if they existed at all, we have no positive evidence) were incapable of keeping local order. If central government forces were occupied in war or revolution, no local force could stop the raids of tribal Bhils, and parganas such as Adilabad went into a downward cycle of devastation and depopulation. These cycles stopped only with the reassertion of strong central government control.[46] It was simply not possible to build or rebuild an empire, in Khandesh, out of negotiations with the pargana leaders.

Why not? First and foremost, the *deshmukhs* of Khandesh were not Rajputs and not heads of Rajput clans. For example, the *deshmukhs* of Raver and Jamner (parganas in central Khandesh) were Reven Kunbis; Chopda's *deshmukh* was a Dore-Gujar. Other Kunbis held the *deshmukhis* of Yaval, Amalner, and Varangao. A Mali family held the office in Erandol. In the area of Adilabad, most of the *deshmukhs* were Marathas.[47]

To see the disappearance of the clan-based pargana as one moves south, consider the crucial area between Rajasthan and Khandesh, the Malwa plateau. Across the plateau, the basis for parganas was mixed. Some were coextensive with Rajput clans. In the sixteenth and seventeenth centuries, many of these clans had been 'planted' by the Mughals to control local populations. Other parganas, however, had no such clan basis. They were the immediate hinterland of small trading and manufacturing towns.[48] However, as one reached south to Khandesh, the Mughal Empire was notably unsuccessful in 'planting' Rajput clans to control or conquer local populations.

Further, the Rajput ideology of lineage loyalty and service (as brilliantly analysed by Norman Ziegler) had little appeal south of the Narmada.[49] Some Maratha houses made half-hearted attempts to assert Rajput status, but few ever married daughters to Rajput houses, and most—such as Sindhia—pursued statehood without ever aspiring to Rajput status. Curiously, the last people to whom the Rajput model appealed were the tribal Bhils of the hill areas surrounding the Khandesh valley. Some of them adopted Rajput names, dress, and a few succeeded in marrying daughters to lesser Rajput lines. Some even succeeded in carving out tiny kingdoms during the chaos of 1800–18, much as Rajputs had in Oudh three centuries earlier.[50] Be that as it may, Khandesh's pargana heads were, on the whole, Kunbis and Marathas, just as were the overwhelming majority of its village headmen and cultivating population.

The final reason that Adilabad did not look like the clan-based model of parganas in the north has to do with economics. Richard Fox is explicit in the dependence of his model on a largely isolated, non-monetized, and self-sufficient region. It was in this sort of arena that Rajput pargana/lineages could prosper, 'segment', and negotiate with the central government. The kinds of goods and services which could be extracted from such an area—fodder, soldiers, grain, and occasional cash tribute—meshed perfectly with the lineage-based pargana structure found in Oudh.

ADILABAD AS A MONETIZED HINTERLAND

Adilabad, in eastern Khandesh, was a different story. As we shall see, it was exactly the reverse, that is, a heavily monetized, market-oriented pargana, close to a major entrepôt.

What were the pressures on Adilabad towards monetization? First and foremost would have to be government land tax. The evidence is highly specific and highly detailed that taxes were paid universally in cash, not in kind. Typical are a set of documents from 1769. Each is a year-end account of a single village showing the receipts and outstanding balance. These were not simply items of account. The finer-grained documents show they are actual cash contracts. Khandesh bundle 128 contains the actual land measurements (*zaminzhada*) and the field-by-field surveys of the fields currently worked by each cultivator in the village; often these documents also record the crops grown on these fields.[51] Attached documents record the type of land and the contract agreement for revenue due.[52] Except for special surveys arising out of disputed land, what we are seeing was described by George Gilberne, one of the British 'men-on-horseback', sixty years later, in 1820.

In a document termed Kowl Katavenee, he [the *kulkarni*] records the engagement made with each individual cultivator or Ryot on taking possession, that he shall pay so much per begah to the Circar [government], etc.[53]

According to Gilberne, the Kulkarni kept a record of actual payments (*tahsil*). Everyone above the cultivator expected that taxes were going to be paid in cash. First, the village headman most often gave the surety (or his guarantee) that the money, in cash, would be paid. The Maratha collector (*kamavisdar*) expected cash. The collector had to pay, in cash, a high percentage of the estimated revenue at the beginning of the revenue year—anywhere from 50 per cent and above. This money, often substantial sums (Rs 25,000 for Adilabad), he got from the Poona banking community. The *kamavisdar* was allowed 1–2 per cent month on the uncollected balance; he certainly expected and regularly collected the cash from his district to pay back the loans. Recall the Peshwa's instructions to Laxman Bhikaji, his *kamavisdar* at Adilabad, in 1753.

Interest and advance should be collected from the people [of your district]. Whenever you pay accounts to the government treasury, take a receipt. Mushira [the charge to convert the currency collected to standard rupees] will be 3 rupees per one hundred collected.

At the top was the central government, which had substantial ongoing cash needs. For example, all civilian officials were paid in cash; religious grants were in cash; supplies, from roof tiles in a fort, to paper, to oil for lamps—were bought with cash; all military supplies—horses, grain, tents, weapons—were bought with cash; finally, all military personnel were paid in cash.

Cash needs of the Marathas, in the eighteenth century, were possibly even greater than the Mughals because a much higher percentage of the army was paid directly in cash. There is no evidence, for example, in Khandesh of soldiers getting small parcels of land in lieu of salary. Even outside the Maratha Empire, soldiers wanted cash on the line, not land. Most military crises throughout the eighteenth century, including European, were, in fact, shortages of cash to pay the troops.

The degree of monetization, in taxation, is so striking that the very few times there was payment in kind, they stand right out. In approximately 250 parganas examined in Malwa and Khandesh, there were only a few cases of settlement in kind. Two were situations in which Maratha officials and the cultivators could not arrive at any settlement. They resorted to division on the threshing floor (*battai*). Another case consisted of the thirty-three villages surrounding Asir fort. They were specifically settled 'in kind' to provide supplies for the fort. The only other time that divisions (*battai*) appears in the documents was during severe political or other disruption. Recall that we found *battai* in Adilabad during the mid-1720s and again in 1750–53, both periods of war and dislocation. A *battai* settlement, in these terms, is understandable, since neither government nor cultivator could sign a cash contract for the coming harvest. The times were just too precarious.

So, if we concede that in normal times cultivators, across the pargana of Adilabad (and across the province of Khandesh) paid taxes in cash, where did the money come from? For McLeod, who examined the countryside on horseback in 1819, this does not seem to have been a problem.

On the Ryots having agreed to pay the specific sum, they repaired home, and set about finding the means of answering the demand. For this purpose, they either sold some of their grain or other articles, or raised money from the Bannian [bankers] or by other means, which they paid, as they could get it, in the hands of the Patells in the presence of the Koolkurnees, Potdars, and Mahar of the Village; the Patell gave the money for examination to the Potdar or Sonar who marked and kept it.[54]

The Maratha materials only corroborate McLeod's statement. The documents have dozens of creative reasons why cultivators could not pay, including plant disease, war, drought, robbery, and so on. No cultivator ever appealed for remission because of the absence or shortage of cash.

So, cultivators raised cash by, as McLeod put it, (1) sale of grain or other articles, (2) raising money from the bania (banker), (3) or other means. Let us look at number one—sale of grain or other articles. Consider the population of Adilabad as *sellers* of goods and services, rather than as tax-payers. The evidence suggests that there was a much wider range of crops grown than has been generally assumed. All the following were listed as regularly grown and taxed in Adilabad: sugarcane, potato, sweet potato, eggplant, other vegetables, ginger, turmeric, opium, wheat, *channa* dal, safflower, flowers (for scents), tobacco, *mogra*, jawar, *rala* (Italian millet), *bhadali* (coarse grain), chaff, and straw.

Although the documents do not directly show that Adilabad's cultivators sold their goods in Burhanpur, the circumstantial evidence is strong. All the commodities Adilabad grew were, in fact, for sale in Burhanpur. The market records of 1756 document them. Also, as you will recall, Burhanpur city was only twenty miles from Adilabad; even with poor roads, this was one day's bullock cart ride.

There were other documented ways that cash entered the Adilabad economy. A major source was the central government. Of all taxes collected, approximately one-fifth was spent locally. These were spent on repair of roads, walls, dams, temples, and government buildings. Over and above these local expenses, the government purchased supplies—paper, candles, food. In Adilabad, this amounted to over Rs 1,000 each year. Around the town of Adilabad, twenty men were hired on monthly salary as guards. Monthly wages were paid to a body of locally recruited soldiers.[55] We should remember that soldiers probably sent money home just as they have in every other war. This would return cash to the countryside. Local officials—*deshmukhs* and *deshpandes*—were paid by the government in cash along with other non-cash perquisites. Finally, the government put cash directly into agriculture in the form of loans given for expansion of agriculture or for recovery from adversity (*tacavi*).

FINAL THOUGHTS ON PARGANAS AND HINTERLAND

The main point suggested by this excursion into eighteenth-century Khandesh is the danger of generalizing from one small region to the whole Mughal Empire. While parganas and Rajput clans might have been coterminous in Oudh, the conjunction was less frequent in Malwa, and largely disappeared as far south as Khandesh. While we indeed found walled towns, and the title of *deshmukh*, these were not markers of strong Rajput-style lineages. Besides conquest, there were various bases of pargana organization in Khandesh, as follows:

1. *The area surrounding a town (qasbah)*. The villages supplying produce and raw materials for the manufacturers of the town might form a pargana.
2. *The area surrounding a fort, especially a large fort*. For example, Asir fort was surrounded by Asir pargana. This was once the territory of an independent chief, but he had been displaced before 1200, and replaced by the bureaucracy of each successive kingdom.
3. *A development grant with attendant rights*. In the two hundred years of Mughal rule, groups had peacefully migrated into areas of Khandesh, and developed (under government patronage) the land. As Kunbis, they worked the land, and it was their leader, likewise a Kunbi, who was the *deshmukh*. This appears to have been the pattern throughout central and eastern Khandesh.

All this suggests that we need to revise our mental map of eighteenth-century Khandesh. Rather than isolated, non-monetized villages or regions, we need to connect villages to cities and towns. Villages, particularly in a paragana like Adilabad, were regularly growing cash crops and finding markets for them. Except in times of severe adversity, they sold their crops and paid taxes in cash.

Cities, like Burhanpur, depended on their hinterlands, like Adilabad, for labour, raw materials, and food. Our research can no longer separate city from hinterland, or city from pargana. They must be treated as one system.

Finally, what of our larger question, the basis and importance of parganas as small regional units in pre-colonial India? Two points emerge from the study. The first is the variety of contexts for parganas in different regions. In Rajasthan and UP, parganas were the result of Rajput immigration and conquest, and the spatial grouping preceded Mughal conquest. In Malwa, the basis of parganas varied. Some were co-extensive with older Rajput settlements, some were more recent Rajput lineages 'planted' to control local populations, and some were simply villages attached to forts or towns. In Khandesh, the pargana appeared largely without strong lineage underpinnings and functioned more as a government unit than as an indigenous 'little kingdom'. We await research that compares these areas to areas further to the south—Maharashtra, Nagpur, or Mysore. Second, parganas were important to local populations, regardless of whether they were Rajput lineages or government groupings. The parganas served as the local focus for tax collection, appeals development loans, and employment. The pargana was, of course, equally important to the central government, with crucial pargana administrative and settlement documents seized by each successive empire—Mughal, Maratha, and British.

Perhaps planners working with 'blocks' of villages can take heart from this study. Governments have been grouping villages for hundreds of years. Such groups, regardless of ethnic or economic base, take on a life of their own as long as they are a conduit to the government for resources and information.

NOTES AND REFERENCES

1. One early reference is in the *Tarikh-i-Firuz Shahi*, dated around 1350. H.M. Elliot and John Dowson, *History of India as Told by its Own Historians*, vol. 3, New Delhi, 1964.

2. Hiroshi Fukuzawa, 'A Study of the Local Administration of Adilshahi Sultanate (AD 1489–1686),' *Hitotsubashi Journal of Economics*, June 1963, p. 41.

3. India Office Library, Mackenzie Collection, General Volume 44, 'Hakeekut Hindustan of Letchmee Narain', trans. supervised by C. Mackenzie, 1809, p. 2.

4. Richard Fox, *Kin, Clan, Raja, and Rule*, Berkeley, 1971. Fox's work follows on Bernard Cohn's two articles on the Benares area, as follows: 'The Initial British Impact on India: A Case Study of the Benares Region', *Journal of Asian Studies*, vol. 19, no. 4, Aug. 1960, pp. 418–31; 'Political Systems of Eighteenth Century India: The Benaras Region', see above, pp. 123–36.

Equally important for his model is the following seminal article: Khashi N. Singh, 'The Territorial base of Medieval Town and Village Settlement in Eastern Uttar Pradesh, India', *Annals of the Association of American Geographers*, 58, 1968, pp. 203–20.

Ifran Habib earlier set out a clear association of Rajput and Jat clans with local territorial divisions within the Mughal Empire in North India. See Irfan Habib, *The Agrarian System of Mughal India*, Aligarh, 1963, pp. 161–9.

5. Documents from the Inayat Jang Collection housed in the National Archives of India, New Delhi, I 11/433–92, 569, 571. 'Details of *pargana Adilabad*, district Burhanpur, *suba* Khandesh in accordance with the *fasli* year 1104.' The 63 page report is stamped with the iron seal of Abdullah dated AH 1099 (his year of appointment). The seal is inscribed *adam tabdil*, indicating that the copies so stamped are copied without modification or alteration.

6. Adil alone means justice or equity. Another meaning offered by Steingass's Persian–English Dictionary is that of 'One who deviates;. . . one who gives partners to God, an idol-worshipper' (p. 829).

7. This map was constructed from the diwan's report, a Maratha village list of 1756, and the following early British map. India Office Library, 'Trigonometrical Survey of the Province of Candeish, divided into Purgunas, completed in 1822, by Messers. Arthur White and Jas Evers, under the direction and superintendence of Captain John Briggs, Political Agent.' The scale of this map is 4.125 mi. to the inch.

8. Pune Daftar, Revenue File No. 3, 'Wingate Report,' 1853, pp. 78–9.

9. Adilabad appears 21'N 76'E in 'The Deccan (West) Political 1707' Map 14A and 'The Deccan (West) Economic' Map 14 B in Irfan Habib, *An Atlas of the Mughal Empire*, Delhi, 1982. The route between Aurangabad and Burhanpur appears on the economic map.

10. The following information is taken from the sheet summarizing Adilabad town, page 2 of the Mughal report. I/11/491.

11. I/11/492.

12. See Irfan Habib, *The Agrarian System of Mughal India*, op. cit, 252 n., for a definition of *dakhili* villages.

13. The measured area figures have been converted to bighas from the units given in the documents. The original listing gives each area in the customary Khandesh units: 1 *aut* = 20 *partan*, 1 *partan* = 4 bighas, 1 bigha = 20 *biswah* (or *pand*). The survey bigha eventually used by the British in Khandesh district was derived from an average of the values for the extant Khandesh bigha. This equivalence was set at 10.33 bighas to 1 acre or 1 bigha equalled 3,739 square yards (0.75 of an acre). James M. Campbell, *Kandesh District Gazetteer*, 1880, p. 205.

See also H.H. Wilson, *A Glossary of Judicial and Revenue Terms*, London, 1868; 1968 reprint edition for definitions of these units. The term *partan* was confined to Kunbi cultivators of the nineteenth century and has since died out in modern usage. The area totals differ slightly from the summary figures given in the report. We have gone through and converted all the numbers on a village by village basis and our own calculations. Thus the total given in the summary is 261,839 bighas instead of 262, 674 given in the text table. Fractional amounts (*biswahs*) have been dropped in making calculations. These values for the Khandesh bigha differ considerably from either the imperial bigha-i *Ilahi* from Akbar's period valued at 0.6 acres or the bigha-i *daftari* of the later seventeenth century valued at 0.4 acres. See Irfan Habib, *The Agrarian System of Mughal India*, op. cit., pp. 353–66, for a full discussion of this question. The justification for using the Khandesh value in this calculation lies in the fact that the bigha values are embedded in land areas using *auts* and *partans*, that is, the original Maratha units of measure—not those of the empire.

14. Crops are not designated in this Mughal record. The nineteenth-century crop pattern is well established. For the seventeenth century we do have scattered references from travellers referring to cotton, sugarcane, and indigo as Khandesh crops. See *Khandesh District Gazetter*, p. 250. Also Irfan Habib, *Atlas of the Mughal Empire*, op. cit., Map 14B, for the economic products of Adilabad and its vicinity noted as cotton and sugarcane.

15. Lands classified as grants were not subject to a revenue demand. Irfan Habib, *The Agrarian System*, op. cit., lists the *hasil-i kamil* for Khandesh at 4,080,019 rupees levied upon 6,339 villages (pp. 21,408). For Malwa the corresponding figures are 8,472,291 rupees levied upon 17,919 villages (pp. 20,408).

Adilabad's annual established collections (*mugarrar hasil*) were 168,539 silver rupees and 11 annas in 1709. The demand for each bigha actually under cultivation in AD 1696 was one and one-third rupees. That this is a relatively high imposition can be shown by several quick calculations. The total *hasil* figure for Khandesh province, *at its highest level*, for the same period reveals an average 643.6 rupees per year per village. For neighbouring Malwa the average *hasil* per village was even lower at 472.8 rupees per year.

16. The term *uftada* is discussed by Irfan Habib, *Agrarian System*, op. cit., pp. 5–6 and 302 n. He equates *uftada* with the 'cultivable waste' category of agricultural land in British period statistics. See Habib as well for a full discussion of subsistence grants, pp. 298–315.

17. *Khandesh District Gazetteer*, p. 349.

18. Ibid., p. 139.

19. Ibid., p. 140.

20. Ibid., p. 143.

21. Ibid., p. 144.

22. I/17/95–96.

23. James Grant Duff, *History of the Maharattas*, New Delhi, rpt, 1971, vol. 1, pp. 223–4. See also, G.T. Kulkarni, *The Mughal–Maratha Relations: Twenty-five Fateful Years (1682–1707)*, Pune, Deccan College, 1983, for details of the military campaigns of this period.

24. Ibid., p. 443.

25. Pune Daftar, Peshwa Khandesh Collections, 38, Hisseb of Babti, 1724, hereafter referred to as P.K.

26. P.K., 38, Hisseb of Babti, 1725.

27. P.K., 198, Hisseb Ismali, 1729.

28. P.K., 236, Hisseb of Babti and Sardeshmukhi, 1731.

29. P.K., 194, Terij, 1739.

30. P.K., 194, Yadidast, 1739.

31. P.K., 194, Terij of jama and vasul, 1739.

32. P.K., 194, Hakikat aima, 1748.
33. P.K., 194, Terij Sair and Rahadari, 1748.
34. P.K., 203, Memorandum of confiscation, 1749.
35. P.K., 30, Rajamandal, Memorandum of warning, 1751.
36. P.K., 128, Letter of agreement, 1751.
37. P.K., 189, Taleband (year-end account), 1753.
38. P.K., 128, Dastur Amal of Adilabad, 1751.
39. P.K., 128, Kaulbandi Zamin, Salogav, 1751.
40. *Selections from the Peshwa Daftar, New Series*, I, Bombay, 1964, Letter 155, p. 140.
41. P.K., 235, Letter from Peshwa to Laxman Bhikaji, 1753.
42. For an extended discussion of this process, see Stewart Gordon, 'Recovery from Adversity in Eighteenth Century India: Rethinking Villages, Peasants, and Politics in Pre-Modern Kingdoms', *Peasant Studies*, VIII, Fall 1979, pp. 61–80.
43. Asir fort, and its influence is discussed in Stewart Gordon, 'Forts and Social Control in the Maratha State', *Modern Asian Studies*, 13 (1979), pp. 1–17.
44. Richard Saran, 'Land Revenue Realization and Irrigation Devices in Merto Pargana, Rajasthan, 1658–1663', unpublished paper presented at the 12th Conference on South Asia, November 1983, Madison, Wisconsin.
45. Op. cit., Mackenzie, introduction, pp. 6–8.
46. Stewart Gordon, op. cit., pp. 1–17.
47. *Khandesh Gazetter*, pp. 62–3.
48. The histories of several of the 'planted' Rajput clans are found in John Malcolm, *A Memoir of Central India*, London, 1832, and Raghubir Sinh, *Malwa in Transition, or A Century of Anarchy and the First Phase 1698–1765*, Bombay, 1936.
49. Note, for example, the differences between Maratha and Rajput military recruitment patterns. Rajputs tended to recruit kinsmen, and could often raise an army of hundreds of armed men, through lineage channels alone. Marathas offered their 'service' to a leader, not necessarily a kinsman, sometimes alone, often with only immediate family, and occasionally as head of a band of non-relatives. Leaders often changed sides in factional disputes, regardless of kin ties. This pattern is illustrated by the lives of some of the well-known Maratha leaders, such as Malhar Rao Holkar. Mahadji Sindhia, and the Pawar brothers.
50. Surajit Sinha, 'State Formation and Rajput Myth in Tribal Central India', *Man in India*, 42, 1 (Jan.–March 1962), pp. 35–79.
51. P.K., 189, Jama vasul.
52. P.K., 184, Kaulbandi, 1963.
53. George Gilberne, *Report on the System of Revenue Management within the Collectorate of Candeish, 1828*. The only known copy of this report is at the British Museum, London. It is catalogued as a printed book, but is, in fact, a MSS, in the hand of the author. B.M. 793 m 17 (11).
54. India Office Library, MSS. European D. 32. (Erskine Collection), 'Account of the Revenue System of the Maratha Country under Nane Furnavese by Lt. John Macleod, 1818', p. 492.
55. P.K., 125, Dastur Amal of Adilabad.

10

Assertion*

KATE BRITTLEBANK

During the first phase of his rule in the 1780s, Tipu Sultan took certain steps which, on the one hand, were aimed at reinforcing his legitimacy as ruler, and, on the other, at loosening ties which bound him to the Mughal emperor. The turbulent political nature of the eighteenth century had provided opportunities for both Haidar and his son to assert themselves and to consolidate their hold on power. It has been seen, for example, how the weakened state of the Wodeyar house had allowed the Muslim parvenus to tighten their grip on the Mysore throne. However, while Haidar's and Tipu's real power in the kingdom was infrequently challenged from within, their neighbours, such as the Nizam of Hyderabad, the Nawab of the Carnatic, and the Maratha chiefs, regarded them as upstarts with ambitions above their station. In addition, the British continually meddled, behind the scenes, in the intrigues of the dowager Rani Lakshmi Ammanni and her plans to bring about their fall.

This chapter, then, will look at the strategies adopted by Tipu (as well as briefly those of his father) in asserting his right to rule and establishing his position and status within the hierarchy of the rulers of the subcontinent. This will be done by looking first at Haidar's—and more specifically Tipu's—relationships with both the Wodeyar dynasty and the Mughal emperor Shah 'Alam. The significance of the assumption of certain titles, their use and meaning will then be examined, followed by a discussion of the importance to aspiring rulers of acceptable genealogies and hereditary rights.

THE WODEYARS

As noted above, to the outside observer, Haidar's relationship with the Wodeyar rulers of Mysore appears to have been somewhat ambiguous.

*Kate Brittlebank, 'Assertion', in *Tipu Sultan's Quest for Legitimacy: Islam and Kingship in a Hindu Domain*, Delhi, 1997, pp. 57–81.

Furthermore, at first glance, this apparent ambiguity seems to have continued into Tipu's reign, only being finally removed with the death of Khasa Chamaraja Wodeyar VIII in 1796. Approved in 1776 as Kartar by Haidar and kept prisoner along with his family at Seringapatnam, Khasa Chamaraja avoided the fate of his predecessors. However, when he eventually died, Tipu did not install a successor.

At the heart of this perceived ambiguity is the continued celebration of the Dasara festival, the public ritual which renewed and reinforced the Wodeyar ruler's kingship.[1] It has been assumed that the performance of this ritual right up to the time of Khasa Chamaraja's death indicated a willingness on Tipu's part to pretend some sort of subservience to the Kartar. Yet, as Colonel Alexander Read noted, the idea of him paying homage at the festival was 'not consistent with either the policy or majesty of Tippoo Sultan'.[2] And looking more closely at the nature of the ritual itself, as well as the few accounts there are of its performance in Mysore during the 1780s, it will be seen why it was that Haidar and Tipu could allow such a festival to occur without it in any way threatening their status or power.

First described as a royal ritual by visitors to Vijayanagara, Mahanavami, Navaratri or Dasara took place over a ten-day period during the month of Asvina, that is mid-September to mid-October.[3] Adopted widely by later south Indian rulers, it had (and still has) great importance in Mysore, where it was instituted in 1610 with the Wodeyars honouring their tutelary goddess Chamundi.[4] A splendid public display of wealth and magnificence, the festival has been described as a combination of a great darbar, *darśan* or viewing, and puja.[5] In addition, there were athletic contests, dancing, and singing processions, at the focus of which were the king's women along with temple dancers from all corners of the realm.[6]

It has been argued that in the Nayaka kingdoms of south India the royal festival was an indication of 'sovereign achievement and "independence" '.[7] However, this was qualified by the fact that its performance was frequently a privilege granted by an overlord.[8] An important part of the festival was the darbar aspect, where homage was paid to the king, gifts were exchanged and the sacrificial reconsecration of the royal arms, soldiers, horses, and elephants took place.[9] As an essential element of the incorporative nature of the whole of the Dasara ritual, at this time all subordinate chiefs were required to be present.[10] It is notable, therefore, despite Read's comments referred to above, that there is no indication in the accounts left by British prisoners, who witnessed its celebration at Seringapatam during the years 1781–3, of either Haidar's or Tipu's attendance at the festival.[11] Furthermore, it is known for certain that they were not present on at least two occasions. In 1782 Haidar was away fighting in the Carnatic, and in 1785 Tipu was planning to engage the Marathas in battle, as Panganuri says, 'on the anniversary of the Dasara feast'.[12]

It was suggested by one of the prisoners, who left a detailed description of the 1783 festival, that its continued performance was the result of Tipu's wish not to bring about insurrection among the people of Mysore, who greatly revered the Kartar.[13] There may well have been something of this in both Haidar's and Tipu's thinking; yet it was also an opportunity for a very clear demonstration of the true state of affairs. Most significant is the fact that the ritual was only allowed to take place at their pleasure, thus indicating their superiority over the Wodeyars. As the same writer pointed out, Dasara was the only time that the Kartar was allowed to appear in public.[14] In addition, their absence from the celebrations, and thus their failure to participate in the incorporative elements of the ritual, would again have highlighted the lack of submission on their part to the Wodeyar ruler. None of this would have been lost on those who mattered, such as the Wodeyar family, the officers of the court and army, as well as other—particularly tributary—rulers. It was doubtless not a coincidence that the perpetrators of an abortive conspiracy to overthrow Tipu, which had been inspired by the dowager rani and encouraged by the British, were executed on the final day of the festival in 1783.[15]

Tipu also used other means to express his true relationship with the Kartar. It appears that in the early years of his reign, he placed emphasis upon Haidarnagar (Bednur) as his hereditary seat. Here in May 1783, following its recapture from the British, he was crowned, with many people coming to offer *nazr*.[16] This would have avoided the impression that he was merely a usurper of the Wodeyar throne, which is how his enemies perceived him. As time went on, however, and his position became surer, he asserted his power more overtly in the face of the Wodeyars. In 1787 he destroyed the fort and palace of the old capital Mysore, using the stones of the ruins to build a new fort on a hill nearby,[17] and finally, as has been seen, he felt confident enough in 1796 to forgo any semblance of a succession on the death of the Kartar.

Looked at in this context, it can be seen how Tipu's relationship with the imprisoned Kartar, which at first sight appears inconsistent or ambiguous, was, in fact, clearly articulated—particularly through the Dasara ritual. This would have been well understood by those on the ground. That this was the case is confirmed by an artefact known as a *santanambuja* or 'progeny-lotus', which gives the genealogical succession of the Wodeyar dynasty commencing with Yadu-Raya (b. 1293), and which is held in the collection of the Jagmohan Palace in Mysore. Made of brass, the lotus was commissioned by Krishna Raja Wodeyar III in 1860s. As well as listing earlier rulers and giving details of the birth, accession, pious acts and literary works of Krishna Raja III, the text mentions Haidar 'Ali ('Nawab Hyder Khan') as the 'general' of the earlier Kartars. His victories are described at such places as Chitaldrug and, most interestingly, Bednur, which is referred to as 'Nagar' (the name given to the town by Haidar), and it tells of his receipt of the title Nawab. That Tipu's reign was not viewed in the same light as Haidar's is indicated by the complete absence of the former's name from the lotus. While the fiction of Haidar's subordination to the Wodeyars could be creditably maintained, it appears Tipu's could not. His omission from the dynastic history suggests an inability to come to terms with his position as ruler of Mysore, and speaks volumes about his success in asserting his independence and eclipsing the Wodeyars entirely.[18]

THE MUGHALS

Despite the decline in the fortunes of the Mughals during the eighteenth century, the figure of the emperor was still regarded as the source of authority and legitimacy by all would-be rulers on the subcontinent, whatever their religious affiliation. As a gift from God, his position was held to be divinely ordained,[19] and as the *shahanshah* or 'king of kings', he was 'the highest manifestation of sovereignty, the court of final appeal, for Muslims an earthly successor to aspects of the authority of the Prophet Muhammad'[20]—a caliph, in other words. In the early nineteenth century, Delhi was still referred to as the *dar ul-khilafat*—the capital or royal residence—of the king of kings.[21] Even though rising powers such as the Sikhs and the Marathas developed their own sense of identity, with the former deriving their authority from the *Guru Granth Sahib* and the latter drawing upon Hindu terminology and symbols to express their rule, they still sought the legitimizing authority of Mughal sovereignty through the emperor's *sanad*.[22] Indeed, it has been argued that, with the absence of any new paramount power at this time, the ambitions of regional rulers who sought such authority actually acted as a stimulus, providing 'continued nourishment to the symbols of imperial authority'.[23]

The Wodeyar ruler of Mysore had sought the imprimatur of the imperial power in the late seventeenth century. In or about 1699, Chikkadevaraja (r. 1673–1704) despatched an embassy to Emperor Aurangzeb at Ahmadnagar. Rao believes the reasons for the mission were twofold. On the one hand Chikkadevaraja feared an invasion by the Mughal forces, who were pushing southwards, and wished to conciliate the emperor; on the other he aimed to increase his stature in the eyes of local poligars who were jealous of certain victories he had recently enjoyed.[24] The Mysore *wakil* presented lavish gifts to Aurangzeb, who was favourable impressed, and in the light of assistance he had received from Chikkadevaraja against the Marathas, the emperor awarded the ruler of Mysore the title Raja-Jagadev (King of the World), the right to use certain insignia and other honours, as well as a seal engraved in Persian script 'Raja-Chikkadevaraj-Muhammad-Shayi'. He also sent him rich presents and a latter acknowledging his right to hold darbar 'seated on the "celebrated throne of the Pandavas." '[25] The embassy returned to Seringa-patam in 1700 amid great pomp, with the honours and insignia being paraded through the streets.[26] Shortly afterwards, it seems, Chikkadevaraja made changes within his administration along the lines of the Mughal system, insti-tuting a structure of eighteen departments.[27]

From the mid-eighteenth century Mughal authority in the south was repre-sented by the Nizam of Hyderabad, in his capacity, inherited from Nizam ul-Mulk, as *subadar* of the Deccan. However, as a result of various wars and the interference of the British on behalf of Nawab Muhammad 'Ali Walajah of Arcot, the situation in the Carnatic was a great deal more complicated. Both Haidar and Muhammad 'Ali laid claim to this area, with the Nizam reportedly granting it to the former in 1766, the same year in which the British secured a *sanad* from the emperor in the name of Muhammad 'Ali. In each case large sums of money were apparently offered by the protagonists in order to secure the *sanad*s.[28] This was not the first acknowledgment by the Nizam of Haidar's growing power. In 1761 Haidar had received from Basalat Jang, the brother of Nizam 'Ali, in addition to standards and flags, the *suba* of Sira and Hos-kote, as a reward for assistance against the Marathas.[29] Following his capture of Bednur in 1763 he offered *nazr* to the Nizam and in return obtained *sanad*s for that district as well as that of Sira. At the same time he is said to have received a *mansab* of 7,000 horse, a *khil'at* or robe of honour, the *mahi-maratib* (fish standard), the right to use the *naubat* or kettledrum, a fringed palanquin, and the title Bahadur.[30] However, all this and the later *sanad* in 1766 availed him nothing as, in 1768, during the first Anglo–Mysore war, a treaty between the Nizam, on the one hand, and the British government of Madras and the Nawab of Arcot, on the other, revoked all *sanad*s granted to Haidar by the *ṣubadār* of the Deccan.[31]

By the late 1770s Haidar felt secure enough to challenge the Nizam's authority and despatched to Delhi a 'grand embassy', along with two lakh rupees, to seek the 'Hyderabad' *ṣubadāri*—essentially the territory of the Nizam.[32] Needless to say, this act of great presumption was viewed with a certain anxiety by such people as Muhammad 'Ali and the Marathas.[33] The

Nizam pretended to be unconcerned by this development, assuring the Nawab of Arcot that it was most unlikely that Haidar would seek such a *sanad*.[34] Although the Marathas believed that the emperor had viewed Haidar's request sympathetically and had promised to grant his request (Muhammad 'Ali believed it was conditional upon a payment of ten lakh rupees), nothing seems to have come of it. The Marathas reported that the Nizam was said to have been 'enraged at these transactions'.[35]

Haidar's main wish, however, seems to have been to secure the nawabship of the Carnatic, either in his name or in Tipu's. He appears to have felt his claim was legitimate as the result of a marriage alliance which he had formed in the late 1760s with a claimant to the position. The circumstances of the alliance are not entirely clear but reportedly had the Nizam's blessing.[36] Following the battle of Pollilur, and having conquered a large part of Muhammad 'Ali's territory, it is said that in 1780 Haidar asserted his right and proclaimed Tipu Nawab of the Carnatic.[37] There is no evidence, though, that this proclamation was supported in other quarters or that it was approved by the Nizam. Nor did Haidar's death in 1782 put an end to the matter, with Tipu seeking to consolidate his claim the following year by arranging for the French to petition Shah 'Alam on his behalf. They offered twelve lakh rupees in an attempt to secure the emperor's *sanad* but as a result of pressure from the British the petition failed.[38] Instead, the emperor awarded him the title 'Umdat ul-Mulk Mubarak ud-Daulat Tipu Sultan [Fath?] 'Ali Khan Bahadur Hizabr Jang Fidwi Shah 'Alam Padshah Ghazi', along with other honours such as palanquins, *khil'ats*, the *mahi-maratib*, and the *naubat*.[39] The title itself emphasized Tipu's subordination to the Padshah: 'Pillar of the Empire Blessed of the State Tipu Sultan [Fath] 'Ali Khan Hero Lion of War Devoted of Shah 'Alam Padshah Ghazi'.

The above would suggest that to those concerned the emperor was still the unchallenged fount of authority and legitimacy. Yet it is clear that his actual situation in Delhi was well understood. Years of factional infighting, attacks and incursions by the Marathas, the Persian Nadir Shah, and the Afghans under Ahmad Shah, had left his position weakened. This culminated in his dependence, first upon Madhaji Scindia, whose assistance he sought in 1785, and then the British. The state of affairs on the subcontinent during the mid-eighteenth century had been succinctly expressed by the chronicler of the Nawabs of Arcot,[40] and the Nizam, too, held no illusions about the emperor's real power. His reasons for not believing that Haidar had sought the *ṣūbadāri* of the Deccan were said to have been that Shah 'Alam was 'bereft of authority', his ministers 'covetous', their only object being 'to amass wealth'. 'A *farman* obtained in these circumstances', he reportedly stated, 'would not be much of an acquisition to Haidar as it would carry neither men nor money with it.'[41]

THE BREAK WITH THE EMPEROR

That the Mughal emperor was no longer regarded as 'strong' is further suggested by Tipu Sultan's actions following his failure to obtain the *sanad* for the nawabship of the Carnatic. Ceasing to press his claims in Delhi, the Mysore ruler instead took a number of steps aimed at asserting his independence from the imperial power. Each of these was deeply symbolic in nature and would have been clearly understood by those who observed them.

In addition to the possession of a *sanad*, subordination to the emperor was expressed on the subcontinent in the minting of coins and, in the case of Muslims, in the recitation of the *khutba* or Friday sermon, both of which acknowledged imperial authority. On his defeat and subjection in 1636 by Emperor Shah Jahan, for example, the Qutb Shahi ruler of the Deccani kingdom of Golconda was forced to strike Mughal gold *muhrs* and silver rupees from dies supplied by the imperial mint.[42] The minting of coins had a ritual significance, being 'a statement to the society at large' in terms of legitimacy.[43] In medieval India,

In places where men did not print, these stamped moneys obtruding into every Bazar constituted the most effective manifestoes and proclamations human ingenuity could have devised: readily multiplied, they were individually the easiest and most naturally transported of all official documents.[44]

The style of the coinage issued was central to its legitimizing role. Certain elements were included on the coin which gave it legitimacy and underlined the stability and power of the issuing regime, such as titles and honours of the incumbent ruler, pictorial motifs associated either with the dynasty or with kingship, names of the significant ancestors of the present king, images of tutelary divinities, as well as invocations for their protection. While powerful rulers could issue coins in their own right, weak or aspiring rulers were more likely to use the well-known symbols, titles, and style of the coins of a higher authority, gaining legitimacy by association. Once established, however, and secure in their power, these rulers might have felt able to assert their independence by issuing new coins and establishing their own style.[45]

This progression can be seen in the development of the *sikka* or coinage of Haidar 'Ali and his son. Haidar's earliest coins, as well as the initial letter— *he hutti*—of his name, displayed images of Siva, Parvati, and Visnu. Furthermore, he sometimes used Kannada as well as Arabic numerals in the design.[46]

It is believed that he had copied the Siva and Parvati image on his gold coins from those of the Keladi rulers of Ikkeri (later of Bednur).[47] In the final two years of his reign he felt confident enough to place on some of his copper coins the recognizably royal motif of the elephant. The use of this emblem of royalty on coins in the south had a long history, being shown on 'Gajapati' pagodas, which possibly had their origins in the ancient Ganga dynasty. It is also thought to have been used by Vijayanagara rulers as well as being prevalent in Wodeyar Mysore.[48] Most notable, though, is the fact that despite this tentative step towards the assertion of royalty, Haidar never included a regnal year on any of his coins.[49]

On Tipu's official assumption of power in 1783 he issued a few coins from the mints of Haidarnagar (referred to as Nagar) and Seringapatam. In 1788, the number of mints in the kingdom was increased to eight and by 1789 there were eleven operating throughout the realm. However, by 1792, as a result of the war and the ensuing loss of territory, the mints at Calicut, Feroke, Dindigul, Gurramkonda, and Dharar had passed out of Mysore's control. By the tenth year of Tipu's reign the mints at Seringapatam, Nagar, and Gooty solely remained in operation.[50] Most interestingly, the only mint to produce coins during every year of his reign was that of Nagar or Bednur, again suggesting the importance of this town in the consolidation of both Haidar's and Tipu's ambitions.[51]

Whereas Haidar had been cautious in the designs of his coins, straying little from those of his predecessors, Tipu did away with the Hindu figures, retaining only Haidar's initial and the elephant, and adopted a style which was predominantly Islamic. His gold and silver coins he named after caliphs, saints, and Imams, while those in copper he named after stars.[52] In addition, some of the coins had stylized *babri*, or tiger-stripe patterns, and representations of Tipu's flag with a sun in the centre.[53] On many of his gold and silver coins appeared the following text: on the obverse, 'The religion of Ahmad [Muhammad] is illumined in the world by the victory of Haidar'; and on the reverse, 'He is the Sultan, the Unique, the Just'.[54] Most significant of all, a date of accession or *julus* was shown on many of his gold and silver coins, as well as a regnal year. While this information hardly ever appeared on his copper coins, the elephant always did.[55] Nowhere was there any reference to the Mughal Emperor Shah 'Alam. This omission was noted by Charles Malet, the Resident at Poona, who wrote that 'the mark of royalty assumed by him in his coin is in the word Jeloos, or Era of his reign, all the Rajahs and independent Princes of Hindoostan still using that of the Mogul'.[56]

In the presentation of *nazr*, the offering from an inferior to a superior, the important role of coinage in the expression of legitimacy was underlined.[57]

Following receipt of the emperor's gifts mentioned above, in June 1785, Tipu responded by forwarding to Shah 'Alam *nazr* consisting of 121 gold *muhrs*. In his letter to the emperor, whom he addressed as Badshah, no reference was made to the omission of the imperial name.[58] However, in an accompanying letter to the chief eunuch and minister at Delhi, whom he asked to present the *nazr* on his behalf, he wrote:

But, inasmuch as the gold and silver coins, stamped with the names of the rulers of the age, contravene the prescriptions of our liturgy, I have on this account, devised and coined, and caused to be circulated, a new and superior kind of gold *Mohr*, in which the names of God, of the Holy Prophet, and of the august Prince of Sanctity and of Sages [Ali], are introduced. Of this new coinage is my *Nuzr* to his Majesty composed . . .[59]

The emperor, unsurprisingly, was not amused, and in August 1786, in response to a command that the imperial name should be reinstated on the coins, Tipu wrote to his *wakil*s in Delhi that they should convey the following to 'the Presence':

that the newly struck gold *Mohr*s were sent by us merely for the purpose of ascertaining the pleasure of his Majesty concerning them; which being now known to us, we have, in conformity with the royal commands, inserted his Majesty's blessed name in the new coin.[60]

Despite these assurances, there is no evidence that the changes were made and Tipu's coins continued to be minted without the acknowledgements of imperial authority.[61]

While the issuing of new coins was the first step by a ruler in asserting independence, it was also important that the coins gain acceptance, without which they had no value as an expression of legitimacy.[62] The Nizam of Hyderabad, for example, threatened by his Mysore neighbour's aggressive stance and assertion of power, prohibited the use of Tipu's currency in the Deccan.[63] One test of the acceptance of a ruler's coins is whether they were valued enough to be hoarded. Coins on the subcontinent never become obsolete, being used in jewellery, for example, as well as in worship and in offerings to deities. The great treasury hoards of Indian rulers, which contained archaic and apparently obsolete coinage, suggest 'attitudes toward ancient coins [which] seem rather to approach the mystical sense of manifest power, of special magic attaching to things of great age and of auspicious association'.[64] In this context, the large number of both Haidar's and Tipu's coins which have been found in collections in various parts of south India, including in at least one temple treasury, shows that their *sikka* was accepted and considered auspicious enough, to be hoarded.[65]

As well as issuing coins which did not carry Shah 'Alam's name, Tipu took other steps to distance himself from the Mughal emperor. His next action was to dispatch from Seringapatam in November 1785 an embassy to the Ottoman Sultan Abdul Hamid I in Istanbul.[66] Consisting of his *wakil*s Ghulam 'Ali Khan, Shah Nurullah Khan, Ja'far Khan and Lutf 'Ali Khan, as well as a large supporting retinue, the mission set sail from the port of Tadri on the Malabar coast on 9 March 1786, arriving in Istanbul in September the following year. It was to be away four years, finally returning to Tipu's camp near the Travancore lines in January 1790. The embassy carried with it several instructions relating to the establishment of trading relations with the Ottoman empire, the strengthening and setting up of trade links with Oman and Persia, and the securing of military assistance from the Sultan against the British. Most pertinent to this study, though, they were also instructed to seek the Ottoman ruler's confirmation, in his role as Caliph, of the legitimacy of Tipu's claims and his rule of Mysore.[67]

That Tipu should seek this authority was not as innovative as it might first appear. Prior to the establishment of the Mughal empire, several Muslim rulers on the subcontinent—such as Iltutmish and Mahmud of Ghazna, for example, as well Muhammad bin Tughlaq, Firuz Shah Tughlaq, and the founder of the Bahmanij dynasty, Muhammad I—had sought the sanction of first the Abbasid Caliphs and later, following their destruction by the Mongols in 1258, of the Fatimid Caliphs of Egypt.[68] From the time of Akbar, however, relations between the Mughal emperor and the Ottoman Sultan, who had by then taken on the role of Caliph, had become strained, although some attempt at reconciliation was made by Shah Jahan. Much of this antipathy had its roots in the perceived presumption by the Ottoman ruler of his Indian counterpart's claims to be the sole source of legitimacy on the subcontinent and the *shahanshah*.[69] Nonetheless, the Ottoman Sultan was still revered by Muslims in India; as the protector of the holy places of Islam he was regarded as an important model for Indian rulers, with many maintaining embassies at Istanbul.[70] Muhammad 'Ali, the Nawab of Arcot, for example, had applied for and received *sanad*s allowing him to spread mats at the Ka'ba and the Prophet's Mosque at Medina.[71] In the Muslim world, such *sanad*s were highly regarded as marks of rank and honour.[72] Tipu, then, in applying for the Ottoman Caliph's sanction to his rule, was merely exercising some ingenuity by drawing upon a recognizable Islamic tradition which had become superseded in the region but which nevertheless retained much credibility.

The return in 1790 of Tipu's *wakil*s was recorded by Panganuri, who noted that they brought 'a letter from the king of Rome and various jewels'.[73] A British newswriter reported that Tipu had obtained from Istanbul the title of king (probably Padshah), the permission to mint coins and to have the *khutba* read in his name.[74] Even though one might question the details, it is clear that the Ottoman Sultan supported Tipu's claim to legitimacy. Following receipt of the *farman*, the Mysore ruler ordered an Arabic inscription set up over all gates: 'the Shadow of the Most Gracious God Tipu Badshah Ghazi: may God ever bless with prosperity his land and realm'.[75] Charles Malet was well aware of the significance of the embassy's mission. Although he believed (apparently incorrectly) that Ghulam 'Ali Khan and his fellow emissaries had been ill-received by the Ottoman court, he wrote:

whether it really was so, or was not so, is very little to the purpose, if Tippoo has management enough to impose a contrary belief on the world: of this belief he will make his own life, and people will begin to consider his usurped title of king as derived from an authority held respectable among Mahommedans.[76]

The above events would seem to confirm that the possession of a significant *sanad* was integral to legitimacy on the subcontinent, yet it appears that Tipu regarded the Caliph's sanction more as the icing on the cake, so to speak, than an essential ingredient of his plans at home. Certainly he did not consider it necessary to await the return of his embassy before taking further steps to proclaim his independence from Delhi. Some time during 1786, Tipu ordered the recitation of the *khutba* to be made in his name rather than that of the Mughal emperor.[77] Just as the issuing of *sikka* was a declaration in public, so was the recitation of the *khutba* a declaration before God.[78] Described as a 'formulaic expression of political authority over the Muslim community set within the congregational sermon',[79] the *khutba* was a development of the original version which had been read by the first Caliph Abu Bakr.[80] The Sunni form acknowledged the four Caliphs, while the Shi'a emphasized the superiority of 'Ali and the twelve Imams, with the form in which it was read expressing the religious affiliation of the ruler. In Bijapur, for example, in 1590, Sultan Ibrahim II, who had been educated as a Hanafi Sunni, ordered the confinement of all *khatib*s who recited the Shi'a version, which earlier had been acceptable.[81] When acknowledging Shi'a affiliations, the rulers of both Bijapur and Golconda included in the *khutba*, as their symbolic suzerain, the name of Isma'il I of Persia and his successors. Following the Mughal conquest of Golconda, the Qutb Shahi ruler was forced to replace this with that of Shah Jahan.[82]

The recitation of the *khutba* in the name of an aspiring ruler demonstrated acceptance by the local Muslim community, in particular the 'ulama. In Awadh, for example, this was not achieved until 1819, with the rise in power of loyal Shi'a 'ulama.[83] In Mysore there appears to have been some initial resistance to Tipu's order that his name be inserted in the *khutba* in place of Shah 'Alam's. Qutbuddin Khan, responsible for its implementation in the town of Adoni, sought clarification of the issue. As with the matter of the coinage, Tipu again cited religious injunction to explain the change, at the same time clearly enunciating his view of the situation in Delhi:

The case is this. The first thing in the *Khutbah* is the praise of God; the next, the praise of the prophet (on whom be the blessing and peace of God); and after this [should follow] the name of such prince of the faith [*sultan-i din*], as, being a [true] protector of the Mahommedan religion, keeps in view, on all occasions [i.e. in every respect], the honour and interest of Islam, and exerts himself for its increase and diffusion. To introduce the names of such, and to offer up prayers for them in the *Khutbah*, is among the [most] indispensable duties. As to those ideots [sic], who at this time introduce the name of Shah Allum into the *Khutbah*, they act through ignorance; since the real condition of the abovementioned is this: he is actually enslaved, and a mere cypher; being the servant of Saindeah [sic], at the monthly wages of fifteen thousand *rupees*. Such being the case, to pronounce the name of a dependent of infidels, in reciting the *khutbah*, is a manifest sin, and repugnant to the laws [usages] of the Muselmany faith. For these reasons it is written, that the *Khuteeb* of that place [Adoni] must be directed to introduce our name constantly in the *Khutbah*.[84]

The *khatib* of Adoni's reaction to this order is not known, but the Qazi of Seringapatam, Ghulam Ahmad, had no difficulty with the change. Of the *Mu'aiyid ul-Mujahidin* by Zein ul-Abidin Shastari, which is composed of *khutbas* one extant version is known to have been copied by the Qazi in AH 1207/1793.[85]

Tipu's letter to Qutbuddin Khan would suggest that he believed that the Mughal emperor's subservient position in Delhi diminished his role as head of the Muslim community in India and that he had forfeited the right to receive the respect and loyalty of that community. Yet he did not completely sever links. In his conflict with the Marathas during 1786, for example, he was prepared to seek the assistance of Shah 'Alam 'his Majesty (the Shadow of the Divinity), who is the chief of the viceregents of Mahommed', in a bid to unite the Muslims of the subcontinent against the infidel.[86] Tipu Sultan was, in fact, a realist. He knew that the Mughal emperor still commanded reverence but was also aware that his actual power was diminished. When it suited him, Tipu was prepared to call upon the imperial authority, knowing at the same time, however, that he was also free to challenge that authority without fear of retribution.

TITLES

The assumption and conferring of *alqab* or titles by rulers in India was strictly governed by etiquette and underlined the hierarchy of the court. Their incorrect use or omission, in correspondence, for instance 'constitute(d) a capital offence against good manners in the East'.[87] Under the Mughals, the awarding of titles to inferiors was solely in the hands of the emperor, with the *zat* rank of a *mansabdar*, for example, determining the style and limit of his honorifics.[88] At the time of his coronation, the emperor himself would assume a suitably grand appellation which was then inscribed upon his seal. Thus, the son of Jahangir, Prince Khurram, on ascending the throne, became 'Sahib-i Qiran-i Sani Shahabuddin-i Muhammad Shah Jahan Badshah-i Ghazi' ('The Second Timur Meteor of the Faith of Muhammad Shah Jahan Badshah Warrior of the Faith').[89] The titles frequently emphasized the emperor's superiority, greatness, and universal rule, usually included Ghazi—warrior in defence of Islam—with the most significant being that of Padshah.[90]

The use of this last title had Turkic origins, having been adopted by Babur, who wrote, 'People had styled Timur Beg's descendants Mirza, even when they were ruling . . . now I ordered that people should style me as *Padshah*.'[91] The term itself referred to sovereignty, meaning 'emperor' or 'king', and emphasized protection and stability. Abul Fazl gave the following definition:

for *pad* signifies stability and possession, and *shah* means origin, lord. A king is, therefore, the origin of stability and possession. If royalty did not exist, the storm of strife would never subside, nor selfish ambition disappear.[92]

An early nineteenth-century writer listed the necessary attributes of a Padshah as 'justice, politics, vigor, munificence and bravery, supported by pomp, dignity, and bearing.'[93] Another Islamic royal title was *zill-i ilahi*, Shadow of God, which was frequently used in association with Padshah. Furthermore, the latter term was acknowledged by non-Muslims and absorbed into local languages. A Kannada Wodeyar inscription of 1648 describes the 'Adil Shahi ruler of Bijapur as 'Patsaha of Vijeyapura'.[94]

Aspiring rulers adopted such titles cautiously, only doing so when their position became secure. The situation of the 'Adil Shahi rulers of Bijapur is a case in point. During the reign of Akbar, the Mughals had impinged little upon the state and 'Ali 'Adil Shah claimed to be *zill-i ilahi*. His successor, Ibrahim 'Adil Shah II, did not do so, most probably because by this time Bijapur had been forced to admit subordination to both Akbar and Jahangir. When Muhammad 'Adil Shah, his successor, again took up the title, he incurred the wrath of Shah Jahan.[95] The adoption of certain styles of title, therefore, was another method, along with the issuing of coins and the form of the *khutba*, of asserting independence. For example, when the Maratha chief Sivaji was crowned in 1674, he adopted overtly Hindu symbols, and rather than Padshah assumed the title of Chhatrapati (lord of the umbrella). The Nawab of Awadh, too, in the early nineteenth century, felt secure enough to claim to be *zill-i ilahi*, and in 1819, when Ghazi ud-Din Haidar finally claimed sovereignty and asserted his independence from the Mughals, he adopted the title Padshah.[96]

As might be expected, Haidar 'Ali's grander titles conformed more to Wodeyar conventions. The first title he received was Bahadur, or hero, which was given to him by Nanjaraja for services rendered.[97] He was also entitled to the appellation Nawab (viceregent/deputy), although accounts differ about who granted him this honour.[98] Both of these are Indo–Persian in origin and both are found in Kannada inscriptions referring to Haidar from 1761 onwards.[99] However, two grants, dated 1767, to 'Saidu Muhammad Akal Shah Khadri', both in Kannada, give titles which are redolent of those of the Wodeyar ruler: 'rajadhiraja raja-paramesvara praudha-pratapa vira-narapati the Mara[ja] Navab Haidar Ali Khan Bahadur' ('supreme ruler great lord valiant renowned in arms hero lord of men the Maharaja Nawab Haidar 'Ali Khan Bahadur').[100] These two grants also make claims to universal kingship and the *Hyder-Nama* states that Haidar could use the title 'Mahamandaladhipati', that is to say 'king or emperor ruling over a great *mandala*', since he ruled over a kingdom whose circumference was 480 miles.[101] Outside the realm, the attitude of rival powers towards Haidar's titles is interesting. Throughout most of his reign, to the British, the Marathas, and the Nawab of Arcot, for example, he was merely Haidar Naik, but by the 1780s they seem to have come to terms with his status and were prepared to refer to him as Nawab Haidar 'Ali Khan.[102]

The titles Nawab and Bahadur were also used by Tipu in the early years following his father's death.[103] However, in 1784 we find him styled, in a Persian inscription on the tomb of a *pirzada*, '*adil-i sultan*', '*shah-i islam*' and '*sultan-i din*', or 'the sultan of justice', 'the king of Islam' and 'the sultan of the faith'.[104] By 1786 he had begun using the appellation Padshah. By this time also he was using the epithet 'Shadow of God'.[105] While Tipu could without difficulty introduce such changes within his realm, it was a different matter when dealing with external powers, who were more inclined to refer to him merely as 'Fath 'Ali' or 'Tipu Naik', and on occasions 'Nawab'.[106] In early 1787 he attempted to persuade the Marathas to sign a peace treaty in which he was acknowledged as Padshah. Charles Malet's informant in the Maratha camp wrote to him:

I had almost forgot to mention that there has been an altercation about Tipu's titles, as he seems to insist upon being acknowledged and titled the Padsha of the Deccan. This circumstance is thought to be the cause of the army remaining here this long, as the point is referred to Poona.[107]

The Peshwa, not unnaturally, refused to accept Tipu's right to such a grand title, consenting only to address him as Nawab Tipu Sultan Fath 'Ali Khan.[108]

A *hukmnama* issued by Tipu in about 1787 shows that by this time his assertion of universal sovereignty was complete. This document provides detailed instructions to the *chawushan* or heralds on the procedure to be followed at the palace both at the time of lighting the lamps in the evening and when saluting the Padshah. On lighting up, the heralds were to pronounce:

> May the splendour of the Lamp of Government of the Sultaun last forever
> May all the Kings of the Age petition to salute him
> Emperor of the Earth may your glory be eternal
> The people of the Earth stand to salute you
> Before the Palace of the Emperor every evening great and small rub the earth with their foreheads
> Like the New Moon
> May the Lamp of State [. . .] be forever resplendent in the Royal pavilion![109]

The salute to the Padshah himself was equally grand, consisting of a long list of epithets, including 'Protector of Kings', 'Ornament of the World', 'Refuge of the Faith', and 'the Incomparable of the Age'. The conclusion of the salute was a verse in praise of the Prophet. Such epithets were also used in inscriptions and as forms of address in correspondence.[110]

As we have seen, to proclaim oneself Padshah and to be acknowledged as such were two different things. As one would expect, within Tipu's closest circle—his family and courtiers, for instance—and the army, the title was adopted and accepted.[111] There appears also to have been a more general acceptance within the kingdom, although this may have varied from region to region.[112] Documents and information collected by Captain Colin Mackenzie seem to confirm this. The *Life of Hyder*, for example, a Kannada text, refers to Haidar as the 'Bahadur' and Tipu as the 'Sultan', with both the Mughal and the Ottoman emperors, as well as the ruler of Persia, being acknowledged as 'Badshah'.[113] In a historical work relating to the ceded territories, although the earlier rulers of Bijapur and Golconda receive the epithet 'Badshah', again Tipu is the 'Sultan' and Haidar the 'Bahadur'.[114] However, in material relating to the governors of Penukonda, dated 1800, Tipu is 'Tipu Sultan Padshah' and Haidar 'Nabob Hyder Ally Khan'.[115] Acceptance of the title does appear to have been more than superficial, though. In early 1800, at

Vellore, Charlotte Clive, daughter of the second Lord Clive, was introduced to one of Tipu's sons, Muinuddin, who she wrote was the heir apparent and thus referred to by the Muslims as the Padshah.[116]

HEREDITARY CLAIMS

Significant ancestry and respectable genealogies were also important to aspiring rulers. Once in power, emphasis was placed upon legitimacy derived from inherited authority. It will be recalled that *sikka* or coinage often displayed references to important ancestors as well as symbols of sovereignty. The Mughal emperors, for example, constantly underlined their descent from Timur. This is beautifully illustrated in a miniature from an album made for Shah Jahan in 1653. The painting shows Timur seated on a dais in the company of both Babur, the founder of the Mughal dynasty in India, and his son Humayun, with the three rulers literally surrounded by royal motifs. Also in the picture, at the bottom to the left and right, stand a Hindu Rajput and a Muslim Turk, the 'pillars' of the Mughal throne. In its rich symbolism, this group portrait is 'a political statement of legitimacy' par excellence.[117]

In the same way, Tipu Sultan based his claims to legitimacy in his inheritance from Haidar 'Ali, with one of the epithets of his government being '*Sarkar-i Haidari*'.[118] His great seal included the names of both his father and his grandfather and, as seen, he continued the practice of using the initial letter of his father's name as an heraldic device. As well as appearing on his gold and silver coins, for example, it decorated his weapons and was used as a brand on animals.[119] Through Haidar's family, on both his father's and his mother's side, Tipu claimed Quraish descent. Haidar's mother was a member of the group of Muslims of Arab origin known as Nawayats, who traced their roots to Nazarbin-Kanana, the progenitor of the family of the Prophet. Thought to have settled on the Konkan coast during the thirteenth century, these élite, mainly Shafi'i Muslims, found patronage under the 'Adil Shahis of Bijapur as merchants and government officials. The early Nawabs of Arcot were also members of this group.[120]

Haidar's father, Fath Muhammad, on the other hand, was a grandson of Sheikh Wali Muhammad, a pious man who was said to have settled in Gulbarga during he reign of Muhammad 'Adil Shah of Bijapur (1626–56). He attached himself to the dargah of Gisudaraz, where he married his son, Muhammad 'Ali, to the daughter one of the servants of the shrine.[121] This association with the dargah at Gulbarga, already referred to above, was a significant one; rulers of 'dubious background' frequently claimed such links to bolster their claims to legitimacy.[122] The tombs of Haidar's father and his family at Kolar are still revered, with '*urs* festivals being celebrated on the anniversary of the deaths of Fath Muhammad and his two wives, one of them Haidar's mother.[123] On its march away from Seringapatam in 1792, the army escorting the hostage princes halted at Kolar to allow the children to pay their respects at the shrine.[124]

Territorial claims also were seen to be inherited. During the negotiations for the Treaty of Seringapatam in 1792, Tipu's *wakils* Ghulam 'Ali Khan and 'Ali Reza Khan, emphasized their master's unwillingness to part with territory which he regarded as his 'ancient hereditary dominions'.[125] He was particularly unwilling to give up Sira, and his emissaries requested that he be allowed to keep Gurramkonda, as it 'was one of the earliest annexations of Hyder to the ancient Mysore state'. In addition, the tomb of Mir Sahib, Tipu's uncle, was located near the fort.[126] As well as basing his claims on his inheritance from Haidar, it is clear that by this time the Mysore ruler saw himself as a legitimate successor to the Wodeyar Kartars. During the same negotiations he also objected to giving up any part of his dominions 'which had formed the ancient dependency of the Raiye of Seringapatam'.[127] Possibly to formalize this aspect of his rule, at some time during his reign he ordered a history of the Wodeyar rulers to be produced in Kannada, giving in particular an account of their territories.[128] In 1798, a Persian translation was also made at his direction of a Kannada work entitled *Nasabnama-i Rajaha-i Maisur*, which gives a short account of the succession of the rulers of both Mysore and Nagar (Bednur), concluding with Haidar 'Ali.[129]

During the 1780s, then, Tipu Sultan's actions reflected his growing confidence and power. Failing to obtain the authority of the Mughal emperor to legitimize his position, he nevertheless felt secure enough to sever almost entirely his links with Delhi. By issuing coins that did not carry the name of Shah 'Alam, by replacing the emperor's name in the *khutba* with his own, and by adopting the appellation of Padshah, he directly challenged the accepted hierarchy of power on the subcontinent. Realizing the importance and value of significant *sanad*s in the acknowledgement of legitimacy, he applied for and received the sanction of an authority long recognized within Islamic tradition, namely the Ottoman Sultan in his role as Caliph. At the same time, by taking these steps the ruler of Mysore expressed not only his independence from Delhi but also the overtly Islamic nature of his rule. Furthermore, the true position at home was underlined in his relationship with the incumbent Wodeyar Kartar. Accordingly, the celebration of the Dasara festival, far from representing ambiguity, in reality was another means through which Tipu's power was displayed.

NOTES AND REFERENCES

1. See for example, C. Hayavadana Rao, *History of Mysore (AD 1399–1799)*, 3 vols, Bangalore, 1943–6, vol. 2, p. 928; Narendra Krishna Sinha, *Haidar Ali*, 4th edn, Calcutta, 1969, p. 223; Mark Wilks, *Historical Sketches of South Indian History from the Earliest Times to the Last Muhammadan Dynasty*, 4 vols, New Delhi, 1980, first published 1817, vol. 4, p. 605.

2. Intelligence received from Col. Read, 27 Jan. 1790, *Various Notices*, Mackenzie General, 46. Read did however believe that this in fact occurred, ibid., also Read to Major General Campbell, 30 Jan. 1789, ibid.

3. In Telugu-speaking areas the festival was referred to as Mahanavami, in Kannada, Dasara, and in Tamil, Navaratri. Carol Appadurai Breckenridge, 'From Protector to Litigant—Changing Relations Between Hindu Temples and the Raja of Ramnad', *Indian Economic and Social History Review*, 14, 1 (1977), p. 88.

4. Burton Stein, 'Mahanavami: Medieval and Modern Kingly Ritual in South India', Bardwell L. Smith (ed.), *Essays on Gupta Culture*, Delhi, 1983, p. 78. Also see C. Hayadavana Rao, *The Dasara in Mysore: Its Origin and Significance*, Bangalore, 1936; B. Ramakrishna Rao, 'The Dasara Celebrations in Mysore', *Quarterly Journal of the Mythic Society*, 11, 4 (1921), pp. 301–11.

5. Stein, 'Mahanavami', p. 80.

6. Ibid.

7. Nicholas B. Dirks, *The Hollow Crown: Ethnohistory of an Indian Kingdom*, Cambridge, 1987, pp. 166–7.

8. Ibid., p. 167.

9. Stein, 'Mahanavami', p. 80. C.H. Rao writes that the performance of this festival in a religious manner by ksatriyas is to 'preserve their skills in the use of warlike weapons and to retain unimpaired their martial fervour'. Since weapons are the emblems of Durga as the personification of *sakti*, they are worshipped during the festival. *Dasara*, p. 51.

10. See Stein's discussion, following Hocart's view of the king as ritual performer, of the subordination of all gods and all chiefs to the king, 'Mahanavami', pp. 85–7.

11. *Memoirs of the War in Asia from 1780 to 1784. Including a Narrative of the Imprisonment and Sufferings of Our Officers and Soldiers, by an Officer of Colonel Baillie's Detachment*, 2nd edn, London, 1789, pp. 49, 131–4; Cromwell Massy, *Diary Kept While a Prisoner at Seringapatam*, Bangalore, 1876, pp. 11, 26, 40.

12. Massy, *Diary*, p. 26; Ram Chandra Rao, 'Panganuri', *Memoirs of Hyder and Tippoo, Rulers of Seringapatam, Written in the Mahratta Language*, tr. C.P. Brown, Madras, 1849, p. 38.

13. *Memoirs of the War in Asia*, p. 132.

14. Ibid., p. 49.

15. Massy, *Diary*, p. 40. Mohibbul Hasan, *History of Tipu Sultan*, 2nd edn, Calcutta, 1971, p. 327.

16. Panganuri, *Memoirs*, p. 35; J.R. Henderson, *The Coins of Haidar Ali and Tipu Sultan*, Madras, 1921, p. 13; *Life of Hyder*, tr. from Kannada, Mackenzie Translations,

V/9, f. 74a. *Nazr* (literally 'vow') was a presentation frequently made in coin of the realm from a subordinate to his superior. By an extraordinary coincidence, the date of Tipu's enthronement at Haidarnagar—4 May—was also the date of his death.

17. Panganuri, *Memoirs*, p. 39; Francis Buchanan, *Journey from Madras through the Countries of Mysore, Canara and Malabar*, 3 vols, London, 1801, vol. 1, pp. 67–8. Tipu named the new fort Nazrabad, Henderson, *Coins*, p. 8.

18. On the progeny-lotus see *MAR* (1918), pp. 62–3 and Pl. x.

19. See Zahiruddin Malik, 'Persian Historiography in India during the Eighteenth Century', Mohibbul Hasan (ed.), *Historians of Medieval India*, Meerut, 1982, p. 156.

20. C.A. Bayly, 'Indian Society and the Making of the British Empire', *The New Cambridge History of India*, 2.1, Cambridge, 1988, p. 13.

21. Meer Hussein Ali Khan Kirmani, *The History of Hydur Naik otherwise styled Shums ul Moolk, Ameer ud Dowla, Nawaub Hyder Ali Khan Bahadoor, Hyder Jung; Nawab of the Karnatic Balaghaut*, tr. W. Miles, London, 1842, p. 54. For a study of the declining fortunes of the city, as seen through the eyes of its poets, see Ishrat Haque, *Glimpses of Mughal Society and Culture: A Study Based on Urdu Literature in the 2nd Half of the 18th Century*, New Delhi, 1992.

22. Bayly, *Indian Society*, p. 15.

23. Muzaffar Alam, *The Crisis of Empire in Mughal North India: Awadh and the Punjab, 1707–48*, Delhi, 1986, pp. 54–5. One could argue that by this stage the figure of the Mughal emperor had much in common with that of the Japanese, who as a ritual sovereign rarely held actual power, See Harold Bolitho, 'Japanese Kingship', Ian Mabbot (ed.), *Patterns of Kingship and Authority in Traditional Asia*, London and Sydney, 1985, pp. 24–43.

24. Rao, *History*, 1, pp. 318–19.

25. Ibid., p. 319.

26. Ibid., pp. 319–20.

27. Ibid., pp. 355–8. It appears that the Keladi rulers of Ikkeri were also under Mughal influence, adopting the Mughal system of assessment for revenue collection. *EC*, 8, p. 15; see also Ins. Sb. 266.

28. Nawab of Arcot to Governor-General, *Calendar of Persian Correspondence Being Letters Which Passed Between Some of the Company's Servants and Indian Notables and Rulers*, 11 vols, Calcutta and New Delhi, 1914–69, vol. 2, Suppl. to Letter 4. See also Panganuri, *Memoirs*, p. 14.

29. *MAR* (1930), p. 86; M.M.D.L.T., *Haidar Ali and Revolution in India (The History of Hyder Shah Alias Hyder Ali Khan Bahadur)*, Delhi, 1988, rpt, of 1848 ed. p. 79. De la Tour wrote that these honours came from the emperor but Wilks believed that Basalat Jang had no authority to give them. *Sketches*, 2, p. 491.

30. 'Characters', *Asiatic Annual Register*, 2, London, 1801, pp. 6–7; Rao *History*, 2, p. 487. Rao says he also received *sanads* for Sunda, Seringapatam, Chuddapah, Kurnool, and Karnatak, p. 488. See also 'Characters', *Asiatic Annual Register*, 2, p. 1.

31. For the text of the treaty, see C.U. Aitchison, *Treaties, Engagements and Sanads Relating to India and Neighbouring Countries*, 4th edn, vol. 9, Calcutta, 1909, pp. 28–34; see also *CPC*, 5, p. 414.

32. Panganuri, *Memoirs*, p. 28; Rao, *History*, 3, pp. 297–8.

33. Nawab of Arcot to his *wakil* at Nizam's court, 23 Sept. 1778, *CPC*, 5, Letter 1756/4; Communication between two Maratha officials, n.d. *CPC*, 6, p. 33.

34. *Wakil* to Nizam's court to Muhammad 'Ali, *CPC*, 5, Letter 1756/5.

35. Communication between two Maratha officials, received 21 Feb. 1781, *CPC*, 6, p. 33.

36. John Kennaway, *Journal; August 1781–25 July 1783*, MSS Eur. C. 156, ff. 21a–b; M.M.D.L.T., *Haidar Ali*, pp. 211–15; Rao, *History*, 3, pp. 31–2, 346; Wilks, *Sketches*, 2, pp. 687–8.

37. Innes Munro, *A Narrative of the Military Operations on the Coromandel Coast Against the Combined Forces of the French, Dutch and Hyder Ally Cawn from the year 1780 to the peace of 1784*, London, 1789, p. 176.

38. *CPC*, 6, Letter nos. 83, 299, 843–5, 914; 7, pp. 105–6.

39. David Price, *Memoirs of the Early Life and Service of a Field Officer on the Retired List of the Indian Army*, London, 1839, p. 432. Panganuri, *Memoirs*, p. 37; *Life of Hyder*, Mackenzie Translations. V/9, f. 77a.

40. 'Great commotion happened in the government of Shahjahanabad also on account of the domination of ungrateful amirs. That is, Ahmad Shah Padshah was blinded and thrown in prison, and some others from among that family came to the throne. Thus the Padshah was helpless in the hands of the amirs who argued among themselves and seated on the throne whomsoever they liked. . . . In these circumstances every one of the neighbouring rulers bound the waist of his independence, and Hindustan was thus broken among the kings of the provinces into which as empire it had been divided. The Mahrattas, who were no better than zamindars, found themselves rulers over great tracts of the kingdom. In like manner Salabat Jang, after attaining the authority over the Deccan, beat the drum of his fame and held authority without any hindrance. The French attained strength to do what they liked. Burhan Ibn Hasan, *Tuzak-i-Walajahi*, Pt. 2, S. Muhammad Husayn Nainar, *Sources of the History of the Nawwabs of the Carnatic*, Madras, 1939, vol. 2, pp. 144–5.

41. Jagjiwan Das to Nawab of Arcot, *CPC*, 6, Letter no 1756/5. See also Stewart Gordon, 'Legitimacy and Loyalty in Some Successor States of the Eighteenth Century', J.F. Richards, ed., *Kingship and Authority in South Asia*, 2nd edn, Madison, 1981, pp. 288–90, on the efficacy of Mughal *sanads* in the eighteenth century.

42. J.F. Richards, *Mughal Administration in Golconda*, Oxford, 1975, p. 35.

43. John S. Deyell and R.E. Frykenberg, 'Sovereignty and the "SIKKA" under the Company Raj: Minting Prerogative and Imperial Legitimacy in India', *Indian Economic and Social History Review*, 19.1 (1982), p. 4.

44. S.H. Hodiyala cited ibid.

45. Deyell and Frykenberg, 'Sovereignty', p. 9. See Michael H. Fisher, 'The Imperial Coronation of 1819: Awadh, the British and the Mughals', *Modern Asian Studies*, 19, 2 (1985), pp. 254–5, where he discusses the issuing of new coinage by the Nawab of Awadh in 1818.

46. Henderson, *Coins*, p. 1.

47. *MAR* (1913), p. 53.

48. Henderson, *Coins*, pp. 1, 24; *MAR* (1929), p. 34. See also Henderson, p. 27, for a reference to an elephant coin of the Nawab of the Carnatic.

49. Henderson, *Coins*, p. 13.
50. Ibid., pp. 8–9. Henderson's work includes a list of all the mints, with their old and new names, as well as a map.
51. Ibid., p. 62.
52. Ibid., pp. 13–15.
53. Examples can be found in ibid., passim. On the *babri* design, see chap. six below.
54. Ibid., p. 16 and passim; see also Charles Malet to Governor-General, 3 July 1787, *Malet Papers*, OIOC MSS Eur. F. 149/2.
55. Henderson, *Coins*, pp. vii, 13, 96. The difference between the copper and gold/silver coins was no doubt because the former would have circulated predominantly amongst the poorer of Tipu's subjects who would probably have been illiterate. The more valuable coins would have been viewed by those who could read, including people outside his realm.
56. Charles Malet to Governor-General, 3 July 1787, *Malet Papers*, OIOC MSS Eur. F. 149/2.
57. Deyell and Frykenberg, 'Sovereignty', p. 4.
58. William Kirkpatrick, *Select Letters of Tippoo Sultan to Various Public Functionaries*, London, 1811, Letter 71. Kirkpatrick wrote that the letter was 'remarkably deficient in the forms of respect, invariably observed in all addresses to the Emperor of Hindostan . . . from those acknowledging him as their sovereign.' Ibid., p. 92. *Padshah* was frequently spelt *badshah* in India. Bernard Lewis claims that this was the result of the former having indecent associations in that region. *Political Language of Islam*, Chicago and London, 1988, p. 57, note 30.
59. Kirkpatrick, *Letters*, Letter 72.
60. Ibid., Letter 333.
61. It is interesting to note that coins exist from the reign of Krishna Raja Wodeyar III, who was placed on the throne by the British following Tipu's death, which bear the name of Emperor Shah' Alam and the regnal year 65. *MAR* (1941), pp. 112–13.
62. Fisher, 'Imperial Coronation', p. 258.
63. Intelligence received from Colonel Read, 17 January 1790, *Various Notices*, Mackenzie General, 46. In a letter to the French in 1787, the Nizam had referred to Tipu as his 'servant and enemy', emphasizing that *he* was the Mughal emperor's representative and Tipu ('this villain') merely his vassal. Intelligence received from Pondicherry, 1 September 1787, Foreign Department. Secret. Cons. 10.
64. Deyell and Frykenberg, 'Sovereignty', pp. 5–6.
65. For descriptions of some of these collections, see *MAR* (1911), pp. 57, 59; (1912), p. 65; (1924), p. 113; (1944), p. 35; (1946–56), pp. 16, 19.
66. Tipu had earlier sent a *wakil*, Osman Khan, to Istanbul, Wilks says in 1784, to find out if an embassy would be favourably received. *Sketches*, 4, p. 361. See also Khwaja Abdul Qadir, *Waqai-i Manazil-i Rum: Diary of a Journey to Constantinople*, Mohibbul Hasan, ed. [Persian], New York, 1968, p. 39.
67. 'Introduction', *Waqai*, p. 1.
68. Deyell and Frykenberg, 'Sovereignty', p. 3 and note 5; Hasan, *History*, p. 128; see also Aziz Ahmad, *Studies in Islamic Culture In the Indian Environment*, Oxford, 1964, pp. 3–11; and Pirzada Muhammad Husain, 'Coronation of Muhammadan

Sovereigns', *Journal of the Panjab Historical Society*, 2 (1912), pp. 145–7. See also Lewis, *Political Language of Islam*, pp. 48–9. On the early history of the Calihate, see S.A.A. Rizvi, 'Kingship in Islam: Universalism through the Caliphate', Mabbett (ed.), *Patterns of Kingship and Authority in Traditional Asia*, pp. 108–30.

69. Ahmad, *Studies*, pp. 28–9, 33–4, 37–9, 44–5.

70. C.A. Bayly, 'The Origins of Swadeshi (Home Industry): Cloth and Indian Society, 1700–1930', Arjun Appadurai (ed.), *The Social Life of Things: Commodities in Cultural Perspective*, Cambridge, 1986, pp. 305–6; Husain, 'Coronation', p. 147; I.H. Qureshi, 'The Purpose of Tipu Sultan's Embassy to Constantinople', *Journal of Indian History*, 24 (1945), p. 84.

71. Muhammad Yousuf Kokan, *Arabic and Persian in Carnatic 1710–1960*, Madras, 1974, p. 91.

72. Susan Bayly, *Saints, Goddesses and Kings: Muslims and Christians in South Indian Society 1700–1900*, Cambridge, 1989, p. 172.

73. Panganuri, *Memoirs*, p. 42. The Ottoman ruler was referred to as the Sultan of *Rum* (Rome).

74. Qureshi, 'Tipu Sultan's Embassy', pp. 83–4.

75. Panganuri, *Memoirs*, p. 42 and note 4; *Life of Hyder*, Mackenzie Translations, V/9, ff 42b–43a.

76. Journal, 23 Oct. 1787, *Malet Papers*, OIOC MSS Eur. F. 149/3.

77. Wilks wrote in a latter that the order was made on 24 Jan. 1786 '. . . if my information is correct'. Mark Wilks to William Kirkpatrick, 25 Nov. 1809, *Kirkpatrick Papers*, OIOC MSS Eur. F. 228/21.

78. Deyell and Frykenberg, 'Sovereignty', p. 4.

79. Richards, *Kingship and Authority*, p. ix.

80. Husain, 'Coronation', pp. 144 ff.

81. Richard Maxwell Eaton, *Sufis of Bijapur 1300–1700. Social Role of Sufis in Medieval India*, Princeton, 1978, p. 29.

82. Iftikhar Ahmad Ghauri, 'Kingship in the Sultanates of Bijapur and Golconda' *Islamic Culture*, 46 (1972), p. 48; Ahmad, *Studies*, pp. 51–3; Richards, *Mughal Administration in Golconda*, pp. 35–6.

83. Richards, *Kingship and Authority*, p. ix; J.R.I. Cole, *Roots of North Indian Shi'ism in Iran and Iraq. Religion and State in Awadh, 1722–1859*, Berkeley, 1988, pp. 50, 176.

84. Kirkpatrick, *Letters*, Letter 331.

85. M. Hidayet Hosain, 'The Library of Tipu Sultan (AH 1197–1214/AD 1782–1799)', *Islamic Culture*, 14. 2 (1940), p. 145.

86. Kirkpatrick, *Letters*, Letter 334.

87. Charles Malet to Governor of Fort St. George, 10 April 1787, *Malet Papers*, OIOC, MSS Eur. F. 149/2.

88. Richards, *Mughal Administration in Golconda*, pp. 76–7.

89. Husain, 'Coronation', p. 149.

90. Muhammad Azhar Ansari, *Social Life of the Mughal Emperors (1526–1707)*, Allahabad and New Delhi, 1974, p. 106. See ibid., note 9 for the titles of Babur, Humayun, Akbar, Jahangir, and Aurangzeb.

91. Cited ibid. See also Iqtidar Alam Khan, 'The Turko-Mongol Theory of Kingship', *Medieval India: A Miscellany*, vol. 2, Bombay, 1972, p. 10 note .

92. Abul Fazl-i 'Allami, *A 'in-i Akbari*, tr. H. Blochmann, D.C. Phillott, ed., 2nd edn, vol. 1, Calcutta, 1939, p. 2.

93. Fisher, 'Imperial Coronation', p. 254 note 36. Also *A Clash of Cultures: Awadh, the British and the Mughals*, Riverdale, 1987, p. 125, note 27.

94. *EC*, 5, p. xxxv; Ins. Cn. 158, 165.

95. Ghauri, 'Kingship', p. 42.

96. Richards, *Mughal Administration in Golconda*, p. 44; Cole, *Roots*, p. 192; Fisher, 'Imperial Coronation', p. 263. For discussion of the response to Ghazi ud-din's actions, see Fisher, *Clash of Cultures*, pp. 146–50; also 'Imperial Coronation', pp. 272–4. Given Tipu's actions, Fisher is clearly incorrect when he states that the Nawab of Awadh was the first of the regional rulers to deny Mughal sovereignty. *Clash of Cultures*, p. 9, 'Imperial Coronation', p. 242.

97. The exact date is not clear but it appears to have been following the siege of Tiruchirappalli in the early 1750s. *MAR* (1930), p. 82. See also Kirmani, *History of Hydur*, p. 49, although see above with regard to Haidar's receiving the title from the Nizam following the capture of Bednur.

98. Panganuri claims it was the Kartar and Nanjaraya in 1758, following victories over the Marathas, *Memoirs*, p. 6; Peixote says it was Basalat Jang at the time of awarding Haidar the *suba*s of Sira and Hoskote, *History of the Navab Hyder Ali Khan Bahador*, C.P. Brown (ed.), MSS Eur. D. 295, 2, f. 2.

99. *MAR*, (1914), pp. 17, 50; *EC*, 9, Ins, Ch., 166; 12 Ins. Mi. 18.

100. *EC*. 9 Ins. Cn. 114. The titles in Ins. Cn. 18 vary slightly. For an example of Wodeyar titles, see *EC*. 12, Ins. T. 112.

101. *MAR* (1930), p. 101.

102. See, for example, *CPC*, 2, passim; Draft treaty between Madhaji Scindia and the British, *CPC*, 6, p. 71.

103. A *sanad* in Kannada dated Sept. 1783 gives his title as 'Navaba Tipu Sultan Bahadaravaru', *MAR* (1938), pp. 123–5; and a temple grant, also in Kannada and dated 1785, styles him 'Navab Tipu Sultan, emperor of justice', *EC*, 3 Ins Sr. 77. See also Henry Oakes, *An Authentic Narrative of the Treatment of the English who were Taken Prisoners on the Reduction of Bednore by Tippoo Saib*, London, 1785, p. 78 and *passim*, Price, *Memoirs*, pp. 108, 214.

104. *EC*, 11, Ins. Cd. 19.

105. Ibid., 10, Ins. Kl, 119. Wilks believed that Tipu proclaimed himself Padshah at the same time that he ordered the *khutba* to be read in his name, that is on 24 Jan. 1786. Mark Wilks to William Kirkpatrick, 25 Nov. 1809, *Kirkpatrick Papers*, OIOC MSS Eur. F. 228/21. Given the use of the title in the above inscription which is dated 1786, Hasan is incorrect in saying that Tipu did not proclaim himself Padshah until 1787, following the Treaty of Gajendragad, *History*, pp. 110–11.

106. See, for example, *CPC*, 6, p. 338; 7, pp. 149, 185, 9, pp. 20, 136. See also Price *Memoirs*, p. 301; Charles Malet to Governor-General, 3 June 1787, *Malet Papers*, OIOC MSS Eur. F. 149/2.

107. L.A. Yoon to Charles Malet, 14 March 1787, *Malet Papers*, OIOC MSS Eur. F. 149/2. This was the Treaty of Gajendragad referred to above.

108. Yoon to Malet, 30 March 1787, ibid.

109. Translation of *Hukmnama* dated 1216 Mauludi era, *Kirkpatrick Papers*, OIOC MSS Eur. E. 228/43. On the lamp metaphor, see chapter six.

110. See for example, *MAR* (1912), p. 58; *EC* 10, Ins. 119; '*arzdasht* from Tipu's *wakils* to the Peshwa, 1799', *Kirkpatrick Papers*, OIOC MSS Eur. F. 228/40; 'Chronicle' *Asiatic Annual Register*, 1, 2nd edn, London, 1801, pp. 160–1, 178–9, 182. Tipu's attitude towards bestowing titles on his own men is not clear. It is generally thought that he was not in the practice of doing so, although the British formed the view that he had conferred the title Nawab on some of his principal men. Charles Malet to Governor-General, 7 July 1786, *Malet Papers*, OIOC MSS Eur. F. 149/1 (Malet's information was based on the report of an escaped British prisoner from Mysore). Edward Moore, *A Narrative of the Operations of Captain Little's Detachment and of the Mahratta Army Commanded by Puseram Bhow*, London, 1794, p. 38. See also Kirkpatrick, *Letters*, pp. 354–5; Sunil Chander, From a Pre-Colonial order to a Princely State: Hyderabad in Transition c. 1748–1865, PhD dissertation, University of Cambridge, 1987, pp. 74–5.

111. Panganuri, *Memoirs*, p. 38; Prince Gholam Muhammad, *Extract from Capt. Colin Mackenzie's Work Regarding the Dominions of the Late Tippoo Sultan*, Calcutta, 1854, p. 6.

112. Intelligence from Alexander Read, 27 Jan. 1790. *Various Notices*, Mackenzie General, 46. Read's informant in Mysore referred to Tipu as 'the Badshah'.

113. *Life of Hyder*, Mackenzie Translations, V/9.

114. *Hindoo Collections. Head of History Containing Papers relating to that Part of the Carnatic Ballaghaat included in the Tract forming the Ceded Districts*, Mackenzie General, XI, *passim*.

115. *List of the Succession of the Governors of Penucconda Kasbah*, Mackenzie General, XI, f. 139a.

116. Charlotte Florentia Clive, *Journal of a Voyage to the East Indies and during a residence there a Tour through the Mysore and Tanjore countries &c. &c. and the return to England*, OIOC WD 4235, entry for 16 March 1800. Her mother Lady Clive, believed that the heir apparent was Muizuddin. Ibid. It is interesting to note that Kirmani did not style Tipu 'Padshah', but reverted to the title awarded him by Shah 'Alam referred to above, *History of Hydur*, p. xxii.

117. The portrait is reproduced and described in Toby Falk (ed.), *Treasures of Islam*, Bristol, 1985, pl. 152, p. 173.

118. See ch. 1; also *CPC*, 11, p. 233.

119. Moor, *Narrative*, p. 467; Henderson, *Coins*, p. ix; Mildred Archer *et al*, *Treasures from India: The Clive Collection at Powis Castle*, London, 1987, pp. 46–7, 64–5; Kirkpatrick, *Letters*, App. B, p. vii note 9.

120. Alex. A. Pais, 'The Navayats: A Account of their History and their Customs', *Quarterly Journal of the Mythic Society*, 10 1. (1919), pp. 41–58; Bayly, *Saints*, pp. 97, 100; Kirmani emphasized Haidar's regard for his Nawayat origins and his support for other members of that group. *History of Hydur*, pp. 285–7; see also *Anecdotes of the Southern Courts*, Mackenzie General 43/3, f. 233.

121. Kirmani, *History of Hydur*, pp. 1 ff. A genealogy of Haidar given in a work entitled

Karnama-i Haidari also mentions a link with the shrine of the popular saint Khwaja Muinuddin Chisti at Ajmer. M.M.D.L.T., *Haidar Ali*, App. A, p. 426.

122. Bayly, *Saints*, p. 183.
123. *MAR* (1930), p. 21, Pl. v.
124. *March from before Seringapatam by the Grand Army Commencing 26 March 1792*, OIOC, MSS Eur. A. 34.
125. Kennaway, *Narrative*, Mackenzie General, 61, pp. 31–2.
126. Ibid., p. 216.
127. Ibid., p. 40.
128. Tr. of a Kannada work *The Account of the Mysore and Seringapatam Rajahs*, Mackenzie Translations, V/15, f. 105a.
129. Three copies at least of this work are extant. They are held by the British Library, the Royal Asiatic Society in London and the Asiatic Society in Calcutta: references Ethé 514, Catalogue no. 199 & Per. MS. 86 respectively. It is not clear whether this is the same work as that just mentioned, but see also Rao, *History*, 3, pp. 991–2, who refers to a work on the succession of the Mysore rulers which was removed from the Kartar's library and later written into a book by order of Tipu.

11

Being *Jangli*: The Politics
of Wildness*

AJAY SKARIA

In the early nineteenth century, some Bhils raided Maratha villages in the Khandesh region of western India, and carried away several cattle. A Peshwa official reported that 'respectable people were sent to the Bhils to tell them that it would be well if they ceased opposing the peasants and were loyal to the state'. The Bhils then retorted: 'We are kings of the forest, our ways are different, do you not worry your head with them.'[1]

Involved in incidents such as these—and they are legion in records of the late eighteenth and early nineteenth centuries—is a postulating of difference from each other both by groups such as Bhils and by 'respectable people' such as the Marathas. As scholars, many of us have struggled in various ways to represent this difference. What makes the problem a charged one is that it involves an understanding of not only the identities of those whose 'ways are different', but also that of the 'respectable people'—those who constituted what is conventionally regarded as the mainstream of eighteenth- and nine-teenth-century Indian societies. And what makes the problem especially acute is the disintegration, over the last two decades, of the paradigm within which we formerly conceived of this difference—the colonial paradigm which posited a distinction between castes and tribes and which ranked them on an evolutionary scale, seeing the tribes as primitive and the castes as more advanced.[2] Nor is it adequate to do what many of us have done—shear the distinction of its evolutionary connotations and refigure it instead in terms of power, treating the tribes (or other similar communities) as always already

*Ajay Skaria, 'Being *Jangli*: The Politics of Wildness', *Studies in History*, XIV, 1998, 193–215.

subaltern groups; as victims successively of pre-colonial and colonial im-
perialisms. Such an operation accepts the basic terms of the colonial distinction,
even if it inverts the valences.

More interesting in this context are the possibilities opened up by the
revisionist historiography of the eighteenth and early nineteenth century,
which has challenged the older view of the period as a time of chaos and decline; an uninteresting hiatus between the Mughal and British empires. This
historiography has indicated that it was rather a time of immense ferment and
change, when a variety of post-Mughal state forms consolidated themselves,
and existing identities were transformed in significant ways. It has stressed
the centrality of apparent chaos in the growth and sustenance of settled agriculture, arguing that practices formerly regarded as disruptive, such as raids,
were often part of the construction of large centralized states; that regions
regarded as peripheral, such as the forested tracts, were tied into complex networks that strengthened trade and settled agriculture; that marauding bands
were not simply disruptive but also formed part of the armies of Mughal successor states, and so on.[3]

In other words, by problematizing decline, by foregrounding the complex
and plural processes glossed over in the earlier disregard of 'marginal' areas,
this historiography makes an effort to abandon the older emphasis on a difference between tribes and castes, and to focus instead on the ties and linkages
between groups like Bhils and the more centralized powers. Its departure lies
in this move away from the criteria of growth and decline and its stress instead
on interdependence. But this is a hesitant departure, perhaps not bold enough.
For in understanding interdependence, it shares with the older historiography the criteria by which to gauge societies. For both, the privileged criteria
are those of growth, loosely understood as a dynamism in trade, agriculture,
industry or state formation that leads in the direction of modernity. The transformations it has wrought in our understanding have principally been
because, instead of focusing on empires or even states, it has correlated a complex range of factors—including trade, urbanization, commercialization, degrees and forms of cultural activity, and the changing power relationships
amongst various social groups—to discern dynamism in many areas and
periods of 'decline' or chaos. Here, then, raids, pastoralism, forest communities,
and unsettled powers are significant most of all for the ways in which they fit
or feed into narratives about settled agriculture, greater commercialization,
indigenous capitalism, and more effectively centralized states—into narratives,
should one say, about the roots of the modernities that we inhabit.[4]

Perhaps this is why, in thinking of areas such as those where Bhils were

dominant, both the revisionist and the older historiography share the metaphor, implicit or explicit, of an inner frontier. In the Indian context, the inner
frontier has been depicted as part of a ragged and oscillating edge just beyond
the effective political control of the centralized states.[5] Both approaches
differ of course in the way they interpret the inner frontier—with one seeing
it as a source of disruption and the other as interdependent with the centralized
states for which it provided many resources—but they agree on its existence.
From such a perspective, colonial intervention can be seen as taming the inner
frontier, as the fruition of those tendencies towards the growth of large
centralized states that were already inherent in the eighteenth century, as the
almost inevitable completion of the task of subordinating communities like
Bhils.[6] The story becomes a pan-Indian one of the gradual erosion of local
decentralized systems of rule; at best, the assertions by Bhil chiefs about their
different ways or wildness represents the underlife of displaced marginal
groups.

The explanatory power of such narratives often seems undeniable.
Nevertheless, as what follows will suggest, they run the risk of being whig-
gish, of privileging those differences which were to become important after
the consolidation of colonial rule, of deploying categories—such as growth—
that are strictly anachronistic in relation to eighteenth- or early nineteenth-
century western India. When we read the period in terms of growth, we trans-
late the period into the concerns generated by the episteme of our own times;
in the period itself, growth did not exist.

If not growth, what? In this article, I would like to try and take the emphasis
on interdependence in a somewhat different direction by focusing on a distinctive politics; a politics around wildness and its antinomies. It was in terms
of such a politics that communities in eighteenth- and early nineteenth-century western India thought of the interdependence and difference amongst
them. I shall explore this politics by focusing on Dangs in western India, a
densely forested place, often described as *jangal,* a word which can be
translated for the present as forests or wild lands. The Dangis were largely
Bhils, Koknis, Varlis, and Chodhris—all communities currently classed
amongst the Scheduled Tribes of India, and formerly described by the British
as 'wild tribes'. Even before the British came up with this phrase, these communities were often referred to by surrounding communities, and sometimes
described themselves, as *jangli* or wild. Sometimes, they were also called and
described themselves as *janglijati*—the 'wild castes' or 'forest castes'.

Of course, 'wildness' is a loaded word. In the conventional modern opposition between wildness and civilization, wildness usually signifies what

comes before civilization or is outside civilization; it is the pre-discursive element that is refigured by civilization. Here, civilization is valorized and ascriptions of wildness to communities have justified much violence and oppression against them. Even primivist thought, where that which is designated as wild is celebrated, is in effect an ethnocentrism masquerading as anti-ethnocentrism. Because of this complex history, we have been suspicious of ascriptions of wildness or claims to them. We fear that by taking discourses of wildness seriously, we might at best collude with the celebration of origins and authenticity, and at worst participate in domination over that which has been designated as wild. So, with few exceptions, our focus has principally been on dismantling claims to wildness. Elsewhere, I devoted a lot of energy to peeling away any insinuations of wildness that the actions of Dangis may have carried—to showing that the Dangis were, if in a different manner, quite civilized.[7]

It now seems to me, however, that as much is lost as is gained in the process of dismantling ascriptions of wildness. What I missed out on, most of all, was a politics of wildness which, despite what may seem like striking resemblances to and prefigurations of the modern opposition between civilization and wildness, operated from a completely different order and paradigm. In the late eighteenth and early nineteenth century, when Dangs was *jangal* and Dangis *jangli*, the *jangal* and the *jangli* were in an antinomian or agonistic relationship with dominant values in surrounding plains societies. Here, being *jangli* was not about some chronologically prior state of nature, some prediscursive base which civilization transcended and overcame; wildness had no relation to time or evolution, nor even was it the Other of civilization. Efforts by Maratha officials to control raids or Bhils took place within a paradigm that was very different from the colonial one which succeeded it; these could never be about extirpating or subordinating wildness in the way the latter were to be. Rather, the efforts to control wildness took place in the same semantic and conceptual field as the practices of wildness themselves. In this sense, this article suggests that wildness and its antinomies provided a crucial medium for thinking social and political power in the late eighteenth and early nineteenth centuries, and perhaps earlier.[8]

By focusing on this politics of wildness, perhaps we can move away from the anachronistic strategy of understanding this period through narratives of growth, whether economic or civilizational. Perhaps, by abandoning the accompanying implicit metaphors of inner frontiers, we can more seriously engage with the far-reaching implications of what much recent scholarship has pointed out: that groups like Bhil chiefs were often as powerful in times of 'peace' as in those of 'disturbance'; that the Maratha 'peace' which extended settled agriculture was not simply about the suppression of Bhil power but rather about its recognition in a particular way; that an increase in raids did not necessarily signify a decline of Maratha power; that banditry was often inseparable from kingship; that raids and settled agriculture did represent two very different strategies, but it was not unusual for the same chief to resort to both in different regions, or even in the same region at the same time.[9]

More research is required to ascertain when this way of understanding wildness was constituted, or what was involved in the enactment by plains powers of its antinomies. Quite evidently, this understanding was quite different from that prevalent in ancient Indian texts in which, as Francis Zimmerman has pointed out, *jangal* referred to a particular kind of wildness—that of dry lands which were particularly suited for agriculture: 'Salubrious, fertile and peopled by Aryas, the jungle is the soil of Brahminity.' Indeed, 'in ancient India, all the values of civilization lay on the side of the jungle. The *jangala* incorporated land that was cultivated, healthy, and open to Aryan colonization.[10] The antinomies to this wildness are also clearly quite different from those explored by Romila Thapar in her classic essay.[11] The politics of wildness described in this article is not about some quintessentially Indian perspective; rather, in ways that remain to be understood, it was the product of a particular historical moment; perhaps even of the same moment in the seventeenth and eighteenth centuries which saw the emergence of regional powers to a new prominence.

RAIDS AND KINGSHIP

Two major Maratha powers shared frontiers with the several Bhil chiefs of the Dangs. To its south-east lay the Peshwa-controlled region of Khandesh; to its north lay the Gaekwadi-controlled region of Gujarat. In the late eighteenth and early nineteenth centuries, Bhil chiefs often raided both regions; they were drawn on for support by rival Maratha factions; and their employment of Makranis or professional soldiers was a source of tension for the Maratha powers. Sometimes these raids became very extensive, as during the time between 1750 and 1753, when internal rebellions, drought, and war combined to weaken the Peshwa's authority over Khandesh. During this period, we know, raids by Bhil chiefs from the hills increased, and large tracts of cultivated areas were abandoned. But the Peshwa's control was later re-established through forces sent in to crush the rebellion and put down the chiefs amongst Bhils who were raiding.[12]

A more profound challenge to the authority of the Peshwai state in Khandesh came in the late eighteenth and early nineteenth centuries. This was in part a fall out of disputes amongst Maratha chiefs, the Ahmadnagar Nizam and, indirectly, colonial involvement with the Maratha states. The conflicts eventually led to the virtual extinction of the Peshwa's authority by the British in 1803, and its formal extinction in 1818. In Khandesh, raids by Pindaris, or irregular unpaid troops maintained by various Maratha chiefs, increased dramatically in the 1790s, as did Bhil raids. In 1802, Khandesh was ravaged by the army of the Maratha chief Yeshwantrao Holkar, and this was followed by the famine of 1803–4, which resulted in many cultivators migrating to Gujarat. With the authority of the Peshwas at Poona under siege because of other conflicts, they could not spare resources to bring it back under control as had been done in the 1750s. So raids by Bhils and Pindaris on villages continued with snowballing effect. By the time Khandesh came under British rule in 1818, only around 1,836 of the 3,492 former villages were populated, and the sites of 97 villages could not even be remembered.[13] Raids continued for almost one more decade, but they were slowly, and almost completely, halted by colonial initiatives; settled agriculture became extensive, and the population of Khandesh increased dramatically.

How should we understand such *dhad*s or raids by Bhils? *Dhad*s were more common in bad years, when the monsoon was poor. They were often conducted around May or June, the time of the year when foodstocks were lowest.[14] The large spoils that could be secured during a raid underscore its importance for subsistence. When Jararsinh Raja of Ghadvi, one of the largest Dangi powers, attacked the village Kushwao in 1809, his men conducted an unexceptionally thorough sacking. They took away 77 bullocks, 106 cows, 55 calves, 11 female buffaloes, 54 brass and copper pots, 50 pieces of clothing, nine blankets, 19 iron ploughs, 65 axes, several ornaments, a good deal of grain, and other things, worth altogether around Rs 1,500.[15] Since Bhils did not have any taboos on eating beef, looted cattle were often killed and consumed at celebratory feasts after a raid.[16]

The spoils were distributed so widely as to make a difference to the subsistence of a significant proportion of the population. The group under Jararsinh had over 200 Bhils, and it was not exceptionally large.[17] The first rough population survey in 1859 (when the population may have been higher than in 1809) placed the Dangi population at 10,344 persons with 3,040 adult males. Of this, 1,178 were reported to be Bhils while around 1,714 were reported to be Koknis.[18] Even if the entire male population could be potentially drawn on (and not, as is more reasonable to assume, largely Bhils) for an attack, the raiders would have represented over 6 per cent of the total male population of the 1850s!

But an answer that explains raids only with reference to peculiarities of subsistence for forest-based communities is at best partial. After all, most Koknis and Varlis, the two other major communities of Dangs, did not resort to raids despite bad seasons. Also, raids often took place despite good monsoons, and sometimes despite more than adequate resources for cultivation: an early British official despatched to retaliate against some raiders remarked with some surprise that their area was 'well-inhabited, and the population for Bheels are rich'.[19]

Raids or *dhad* are best understood as particular claims to power, rather than being driven by subsistence needs alone. Sometimes, a *dhad* could be a political act meant to repudiate or challenge other chiefs. In 1828, when Silput Raja, Jararsinh's descendant in Ghadvi, attacked Garkhedi village along the frontiers of the Dangs, he did so because he had a dispute with the figure who held the village in *jagir*. Besides, the *patil* or headman of the village had killed two of his Bhils.[20] Similarly, another attack in 1822 on some Khandesh villages was directed against the British who, Silput felt, had challenged his authority.[21] So raids could be about demonstrating a raja's authority, or responding appropriately to challenges to that authority.

At other times, a raid could be a demand by raiders for their *hak*s or dues, especially for *giras hak*s. Literally, *giras* meant a mouthful or share, and symbolized the right to an amount as a due from a village. In eighteenth- and early nineteenth-century western India, *giras* was a pervasive and central feature of forest polities, and its payment was to continue in an ossified form well into the twentieth century.[22] The recipients of these payments were often known as *girasia*s, and near Udaipur there was a caste by that name which was entitled to *giras* payments. The Bhumia forest Naiks of Malwa and central India, the Vasava and other *mewa*s or hill chiefs of Rajpipla and Baroda, the Bhil chiefs around Khandesh and the Nizam of Hyderabad's territories—all of them claimed *giras* amongst their other *hak*s.[23] Raids were very important in sustaining or creating claims to *giras hak*s, and the sovereignty it implied. In 1825, for example, the followers of the Ghadvi chief Silput attacked Raipur village, prevented reaping or *mahua*-collection for some time, but eventually went away without taking anything.[24] Here, the raid was a means of ensuring payment of *giras* or other *hak*s, a sort of shot across the prow.

Within the Dangs, raids and *giras* were also important for the maintenance of authority and power of chiefs. Kingship was very widely shared within the Dangs amongst the *bhauband* or brotherhood of chiefs. As I argue at length in my *Hybrid Histories*, all Bhil men were considered rajas in some senses: they were all exempt, for example, from land revenue. Even when more restrictively understood, kingship was so widely shared that several of the most powerful *bhauband* had as much authority as the figure who was considered to be the principal chief. In this context, it is striking that *giras* was widely distributed. In 1828, Silput Raja of Ghadvi, and his uncle Khem Raja, were the chief recipients of Gaekwadi *giras*. But separate and independent payments were also made by Gaekwadi officials to at least six Naiks of the Ghadvi *bhauband*. By receiving *giras* directly this way from the Gaekwads, the *bhauband* asserted the distinctiveness of their authority from that of the principal chief, in this case Silput. Of the Rs 760 paid to Silput, he retained only Rs 300, distributed Rs 40 amongst his three sons and two brothers, Rs 51 to Khem's soldiers, and Rs 270 to thirty-six other persons connected with Silput raja.[25] In distributing the amount he received, Silput created allegiances and hierarchies; those who accepted money acknowledged their alliance with Silput.

Similarly, cattle and other spoils secured during raids were an important resource, and to distribute them was to make valuable gifts. A good deal of Silput Raja's authority was based on what was described as his liberality and bravery, which had made many young chiefs his followers.[26] Maybe that was why when Silput was forced in 1829 to restore cattle he and his men had carried away from a village, he preferred to send his own cattle rather than collect back what had already been distributed. To do so could have rendered him 'highly unpopular'.[27]

Authority could be extended considerably through the *giras* claims that raids sustained. Sometimes, in fact, a claim to authority and chieftancy could be constructed virtually from scratch through raids. One of the most spectacular cases of this sort occurred in the Rajpipla region to the north of the Dangs, where a minor Vasava chief, Kuver Vasava, emerged through raids as a major figure by the early nineteenth century. In Khandesh, during the early nineteenth century, similarly, many Bhil watchmen consolidated their authority through raids and emerged as important chiefs.[28] Though we know of no such dramatic cases in Dangs, Silput certainly increased his authority significantly through the distribution of *giras* and spoils from raids.[29] Being a raja thus involved raiding in order to create the resources to distribute amongst followers.

THE WILDNESS OF RAIDING

In emphasizing how raids were linked to political authority, my effort is to suggest that the wildness which raids epitomized was involved in the construction of political power itself. But what has been said so far could also be interpreted more restrictively: as implying that raids were simply the means to an end, or that raids occurred only when a system of paying *giras* collapsed. Thus, raids could continue to be cast as rational activities, and Dangis as rational actors trying to maximize their interests. Maybe we need to go further still, and understand how raiding was inextricably part of the enactment of wildness by Bhil men. In this sense, the affirmation of raiding, however infrequent it may have been as an actual activity, was very central to Bhil identities.

This may seem a deeply questionably statement to make, almost subscribing to colonial stereotypes. In colonial writings, it is often claimed that Bhils considered themselves 'Mahadev's thiefs', and described themselves as such.[30] Colonial officials picked on this Bhil assertion, of course, because it fitted in well with their own notions of the religiosity of vocations in India, and because many of them disapprovingly saw Bhils as natural plunderers. Quite rightly, these and similar descriptions have been shown to be part of a deeply questionable colonial understanding.

But to reject this colonial understanding is not to rule out the possibility that many Bhils may have, in very different ways, affirmed the wildness of raiding. Ballads celebrating raids were known and sung in the Dangs till around the early twentieth century. We now have no access to these songs; however, some similar songs recorded in the late nineteenth or early twentieth centuries amongst the Bhils of central India are known. One song tells of how the Bhil chief Damor Lal came to Sakalia village and became its *palavi* [chief of *pal* or village]. Then he sent a spy to gather intelligence of the country. The scout spied on the village Varundi and saw a number of white cows in the *gundara* (relatively open place in the forest where cattle taken out for grazing are conducted at noon) and gray buffaloes enjoying themselves in the *dobana*s (pits of mire and water). He returned and informed Damor Lal. Then the Damor *palavi* beat a drum to assemble his men. A large host of Bhils assembled and started on the raid. They crossed the river Mahiyari and plundered Varundi, seizing the white cows from the *gundara*s, and the buffaloes in the *dobana*s. After plundering and beating the villagers, they crossed the Mahiyari, and returned to Sakalia. They brought liquor of all sorts, drank it in cups of gold and silver and made merry.[31]

Several of these motifs are staple ones, repeated in most songs: there are always white cows in *gundara*s and gray buffaloes in *dobana*s, the *palavi* always beats a drum, and at the end of it all liquor is always served in cups of gold and silver. And, invariably, there is a central figure, a Damor Lal, whose feats the song celebrates. In the Dangs, some of these equivalents of Damor Lal were actual ancestors: there were celebratory songs till recently about raids by Silput Raja and Aundya Raja. Thus, the very act of leading raids was crucial to imagining a raja, his bravery and his daring. To rule, in other words, was to raid.

More broadly, the songs suggest how closely raiding, with its emphasis on wildness, was connected to being a Bhil man, and especially to wielding power. Oral traditions now often stress how kings or chiefs were expected to be particularly active in raids. As for the songs, not only do they celebrate raiding as an activity, but all those causes for raids that we have seen—scarcity, authority, *giras*, shared sovereignty—are absent from them; the only reason to raid appears to be the enactment of the raid itself.[32] This celebratory element marked raids in the nineteenth century too; we know that raids were followed by long celebrations at which alcohol flowed freely. And when Bhil men described themselves as Mahadev's thiefs, they were possibly not claiming a religiously sanctioned vocation; rather, they were refusing to reduce their actions to instrumental causes. That refusal was also, of course, a particularly loaded allegory, for Mahadev was another name for Siva. As Shulman has observed in his article on South Indian bandits and kings, 'Siva, the antinomian deity par excellence, is at his best not far removed from a bandit. . . . Siva remains unpredictable, delightfully mischevious, entirely unbound by conventions or properties.'[33] Nor was this politics of wildness affirmed only by Dangi ruling chiefs. Participation in raids and its politics of wildness was yet another way in which ordinary Bhil men enacted their claims to be rajas.

The widespread influence of this politics may also throw light on a paradoxical matter. Both in the Dangs and in surrounding areas, narrators of oral traditions repeatedly mention how, formerly, many communities—Koknis, Warlis, Naikras, Gamits, Valvis, and Chodhris amongst others—were called Bhils, and referred to themselves as such. Once alerted to this custom, we can find implicit parallels to it in nineteenth century archival sources. The occasional reference in records to 'Gamit Bhils', 'Dhanka Bhils', or 'Kokni Bhils' can now be seen as the result not of ill-informed transcription by colonial officials but of persons describing themselves as such.[34] Yet there is something profoundly counter-intuitive about all of this, for it flies in the face of much that we have learnt to regard as 'natural' about caste. Formerly, it was common to talk of Sanskritization (the adoption of Brahman values) or Rajputization (the adoption of Kshatriya values) as two related ways by which lower castes claimed higher status. Now, such talk would rightly be regarded as far too simplistic, for lower castes were often appropriating upper caste values to challenge Brahmans and Rajputs, rather than simply adopting these values. Nevertheless, it is still taken as axiomatic that castes make claims to ritually higher status.

It is this commonsensical assumption that is undermined by claims to be Bhil. Jatis like Gamits, Chodhris, Valvis, or Koknis were ritually superior to Bhils, and in many contexts they stressed this superiority. Thus, Koknis did not eat beef though Bhils did; Bhils accepted most prepared food from Koknis, but the latter refused to accept food from Bhils. Given all this, by calling themselves Bhil, Koknis were accepting a lower caste position which they rejected in other contexts. Why should they have done this? Perhaps because of the distinctive politics of wildness. Bhils were the single largest forest community in western India. This made the very name 'Bhil' a ready marker of difference, covering all groups in the region which pursued those lifestyles and forms of political power of which Bhils were considered paradigmatic. In describing themselves as 'Kokni Bhils', Koknis laid claim to the political power of being *jangli* or wild.

SHARED SOVEREIGNTIES, OR THE ANTINOMIES OF WILDNESS

But what did this politics of wildness mean outside the Dangs, or for those powers and people involved in relations with the Dangs? To the expanding Maratha powers, did it appear as an irritant that had to be put down? Were these regions inner frontiers—areas that should be subordinated and brought under control so that settled agriculture and trade could expand? Should we see these practices of wildness as a marginal discourse; as the underside of the pre-colonial expansion of centralized states?

It is tempting, of course, to think of eighteenth- and early nineteenth-century centralized states such as those of the Marathas as successfully adopting measures to control and subordinate forest polities such as those represented by the Bhil chiefs. And there seems to be much material to support such a view. In the territories of central India held by the Maratha successor state of the Holkars, for example, Ahilyabai Holkar is believed to have successfully adopted a series of measures which curbed raids and extended settled cultivation. There were efforts to follow a similar policy in the Peshwa-controlled regions of Khandesh. Here, Maratha officials sought to control raids, primarily through agreements with the chiefs that granted them rights to collect dues from passes they controlled, and through a recognition of their rights in Maratha villages. In 1789–90, after the fort of Kanhera had been captured back from some Khandesh Bhil chiefs, an agreement was arrived at by which these Bhils agreed to leave their forest and hill residences and settle down in plains villages and perform the duties of *jagalias* or watchmen. While doing such duty, they were to use only arrows, and not carry swords or guns. They were to wear around their necks a packet bearing the seal of the sarkar, and those not wearing such a packet were to be punished. In return, all existing Bhil *hak*s or rights would be protected.[35] Another mode of control involved setting up a chain of armed outposts along the foothills at times when Bhil raids were particularly high, as for example between Ajanta and Kasarbari in Khandesh between 1776–7. These outposts, as well as other additional soldiers, were financed by a *Bhil-patti* or Bhil-tax, levied on the inhabitants of the area in addition to other land revenue. Measures could be tougher too. Bhils in general were prohibited from living in the plains around Ajanta in the late eighteenth century after they were suspected of helping hill Bhils in raids. Severe punishments were meted out to those Bhils suspected of being involved in raids.

But perhaps this is too hasty. Looking more closely at the local politics of Dangi relationships with Gaekwads and surrounding communities, I would like to suggest that rather than being the Other of the latter (as Dangs and Dangis were to become later), there was an antinomian relationship between the two—a relationship which required deep affinities for the very working of its oppositions (the antinomian, after all, requires the law even as it remains heterogeneous to it). Originally, lieutenants of the Peshwa, the Gaekwads had by the mid-eighteenth century established the independent successor state of Baroda, to a significant extent with the help of Bhil chiefs. The initial base of the Gaekwadi kingdom had been at Songadh, a fort–town not very far from the northern frontiers of the Dangs. Eighteenth century Gaekwadi commanders had maintained close ties with Bhil rajas and Naiks in the Songadh and the Dangs area. As the Gaekwads consolidated their hold over large tracts of Gujarat, they moved their capital to the town of Baroda, further away to the north. But Songadh continued to be an important fort, and Gaekwadi influence in the Dangs continued to increase. Since around the late eighteenth century, there had been the sharing of fees collected from timber *naka*s or toll stations located in the villages with at least two major Dangi chiefs, those of Ghadvi and Dherbavti.[36] In the 1820s, the Ghadvi chief Silput Raja received around Rs 5,000 annually from fees at such *naka*s; Gaekwadi officials received a similar amount.[37] Another indicator of Gaekwadi influence was the approximately fifty-two villages that were co-shared with the Dangi chiefs.[38] In these villages, revenue from agriculture was divided between Gaekwadi officials and the Dangi chiefs, each collecting their portion directly from the cultivator.

The key figures in extending Gaekwadi influence were two: the *killedar*s or fort commandants, and the revenue farmer or *ijaradar*. Stewart Gordon has noted the general importance of hill-forts in maintaining Maratha dominance.[39] The *killedar* of the fort of Songadh, above the north-western tip of the Dangs, played a major role in the acquisition of co-shared villages along the northern tracts of the Dangs; he also handled the distribution of *giras* payments. Officials based at Songadh had already, by the early nineteenth century, established a thana or outpost at Malangdev village in the northern Dangs, and taken over several villages around it.[40] The *killedar* also often doubled as the *ijaradar* or revenue farmer for the area, or worked closely with the revenue farmer. Revenue farming was a technique regularly adopted by Maratha polities for dealing with 'unsettled' areas along the frontiers of forest polities.[41] The *killedar*'s involvement in struggles for authority amongst the chiefs further increased his influence. An important turning point was the struggle around 1799. According to records, a Ghadvi chief, Udesinh, was killed by the Kadmal chief Godoo Raja with whom the former's wife was staying after leaving Fatehsinh. Udesinh's son, Janak Raja, approached the Songadh *killedar* for assistance against Godoo Raja. He was given a loan of Rs 900 to raise fighting men to fight on condition that the Gaekwadi flag would fly at Ghadvi village.[42] From around 1800, then, a Gaekwadi *sowar* or mounted force came every year to the Dangs around Dussehra, carrying a fresh Gaekwadi flag. The Ghadvi chief 'was presented with a horse, a saddle, and a shawl in recognition of his authority, and the flag hoisted at Ghadvi.'[43]

But it would be hasty to conclude from all of this that the *killedar*s and *ijaradar*s were the spearheads for Maratha expansion in a region, engineering the growth of a centralized Maratha state. If Gaekwadi officials did not meet the demands of Bhil chiefs, the latter could retaliate and hold back dues.[44] More important than this point (which remains embedded in the logic of instrumental rationality), for both Bhil chiefs and for Gaekwadi officials, ties were not about the extension or creation of an exclusive sovereignty; they were, rather, about creating alliances and shared sovereignties. What was involved in shared sovereignties becomes clearer when we explore the ways in which *killedar*s and *ijaradar*s dealt with raids and *giras*. By the late nineteenth century, both British and Gaekwadi officials were often to think of *giras* as a 'species of blackmail' paid to Bhil chiefs to avert raids on Gaekwadi territory.[45] The censorious tone of such descriptions chimes in perfectly with the view of raids as the surfacing of raw power when the rule of law broke down, as the violation of the exclusive sovereignty of the British or Gaekwads over a particular village. But this kind of censoriousness was possible only after the consolidation of narratives that privileged growth; it was not how they had appeared formerly. For, in the late eighteenth and early nineteenth century, *giras* was above all a claim to shared sovereignty with surrounding powers. Thus, payments were associated with specific villages, often situated at considerable distance from the Dangs. Kuswao, which the Ghadvi chief Jararsinh raided in 1809, was near Buhari, at least a day's march from the Dangs.[46] The claim to sovereignty involved in *giras* emerges even more clearly from the *hak*s of *bhet* and *sirpav* which accompanied its payment. *Sirpav* (literally, head to toes) was the dress that Gaekwadi officials or village representatives gave the Dangi chiefs along with *giras*: Here, the *sirpav* was the acknowledgment of an explicit claim to authority over the village by the Dangi rajas and naiks.[47] It was also a symbol of alliance: amongst the Marathas, the Peshwa held a *sirpav* ceremony after Dussehra, where the army assembled at a designated place, and he distributed special dresses amongst its commanders, who in turn gave him a vow of loyalty.[48] *Bhet*, a word which translated literally as 'gift', was usually a small sum which accompanied *giras*, and was again an explicit acknowledgement of authority.[49] The raja of Ghadvi received annually a *bhet* of Re 1 from Kejban village, and every person in the village contributed two pice towards this amount.[50]

There were also fluctuations in *giras* payments to Ghadvi. The Ghadvi chiefs received around Rs 1,400 annually around 1799–1801, an amount which fell by half during the ensuing decade before rising again to Rs 1,400 by 1814. By 1828, they were getting barely half that amount again.[51] It is tempting to read these fluctuations as directly in proportion to the power of the chiefs. Ghadvi was quite powerful till around 1799–1800, when the slaying of Fatehsinh Raja by the Kadmal *bhauband* led to a period of disputes. The rise of *giras* payments again by around 1814 may have been due to the power of Jarasinh Raja, a figure who looms large in oral traditions as a powerful chief. The decline after that could have been due to the consolidation of Gaekwadi power which accompanied the British takeover, as we shall see.

Yet, such a reading may be misplaced: a case of our already presumed narratives of growth causing us to read too much into scanty data. Such a reading still implicitly presumes that *giras* payments were extortions; a cloak for raw power, paid only because the chiefs would otherwise have raided the villages in question. And on closer attention it is clear that a direct correlation between *giras* payments and the power of either the chiefs or Gaekwadi officials did not obtain. Gaekwadi officials were not interested in a systematic or complete repudiation of *giras* dues when they increased their power relative to Dangi Bhil chiefs. Rather, it was only by distributing *giras* and similar dues that *killedars* and *ijaradars* created the authority and alliances that they needed.

Nowhere, possibly, is the distance between the understanding of *giras* as an instrumental register of the power of Dangi chiefs, on the one hand, and as an enactment of shared sovereignty brought out more clearly than in disputes after 1828 over Gaekwadi *giras* payments. That year, British officials in Khandesh claimed that Gaekwadi irregularity in *giras* payments was one major cause of Dangi raids. They proposed that they take over the Gaekwadi *giras* payments, make them from the British treasury at Khandesh, and charge the amount to the Gaekwads. Gaekwadi officials fiercely opposed this measure, for such a transfer threatened the most vital means by which *ijaradars* and *killedar*s made alliances and extended their authority. Nevertheless, the British ignored Baroda's protests and took over *giras* payments. Then even more bizarre events unfolded; bizarre at least from any perspective that sees giras as a payment made because of the weakness of Gaekwadi powers. The *killedar* at Songadh took to paying *giras* clandestinely a second time—at considerable financial loss to Baroda—in order to keep up direct relations with the chiefs! Far from being an amount reluctantly paid because of their weakness, Baroda officials evidently considered the distribution of *giras* very important to the construction of shared sovereignties.[52]

Similarly, to figures like the *killedar*s or *ijaradar*s, raids were a very complex matter because of their association with shared sovereignties; they were not to be regarded with straightforward hostility merely because they hindered settled cultivation. True, the *killedar*s often pursued measures to halt raids by the Bhil chiefs on to their territory. Though expeditions into the Dangs were difficult because the forests were so dense, and malaria so rampant, counter-raids on the border villages of the Bhil chiefs were sometimes carried out and local cattle seized in retaliation.[53] They tried to bring raiding chiefs to negotiation by restricting their access to merchants outside the Dangs, or by drawing on their ties with other Bhil chiefs to put pressure on raiders. These sometimes resulted in Bhil chiefs offering either cattle or village grants in compensation.[54]

Nevertheless, they also actively encouraged raids by Bhils on rivals. Cattle raided from Peshwa, and later British-controlled Khandesh were, we know, sometimes sold at a market near Salher (on the eastern frontiers of the Dangs, where another important Gaekwadi fort was located) in Gaekwadi territory with the full encouragement of Gaekwadi officials. Looted villagers from Khandesh would even visit Salher and pay a ransom to get the cattle back. Fifty-eight of the cattle taken from Kuswao were later restored this way.[55] We do not know whether Gaekwadi officials themselves participated in Bhil raids on the former's rivals. But certainly, in the late eighteenth century, many Bhil attacks on villages in Khandesh were connected to disputes amongst Maratha chiefs in Khandesh, with rival groups jostling for the support of Bhil chiefs for their activities.[56]

Even raids on Gaekwadi territory were not necessarily met with unconditional hostility. From the 1820s onwards, British officials complained regularly of the *killedar*s' 'vacillating and mutable . . . policy' where all 'crime' from cattle-lifting to murder was 'alike visited with the extremes of punishment, or overlooked altogether'.[57] What the British did not realize was that Baroda officials' attitudes were an acknowledgment of the political rather than criminal nature of the *dhad*, its connection with *giras*, and shared sovereignties. So a *dhad* usually called not for retaliation but for a renegotiation of shared sovereignty.

In these senses, it is doubtful whether the agreements that Maratha official in Khandesh and elsewhere reached with the Bhil chiefs in the eighteenth and early nineteenth centuries, or the severe punishments meted out to raiding Bhils, were the indices of Bhil subordination in the manner that they are often presumed to be. I do not, of course, wish to deny that many Bhil chiefs were subordinated, and that considerable extension of Maratha power took place—such a denial would be quite untenable. I wish only to draw attention to the distinctive forms of domination—to the point that the agreements effectively acknowledged the substantial sovereignty of Bhil chiefs in these regions, and attempted to engineer on that basis a very contingent consensus to pursue strategies promoting settled agriculture and other Maratha concerns. Put another way, subordination occurred within the semantic and conceptual field of shared sovereignties, with all the antinomies that its forms of domination involved. It was only within this field that raids could be a legitimate form of political power, even if one not always wielded by 'respectable people'. Within the apparently similar but radically different colonial notion of exclusive sovereignties which was to succeed it, raids could only be blackmail—the thin glove over the brute force which prevailed when the rule of law failed. It is because of this enormous gulf separating two apparently similar ways of relating to Bhil chiefs that it is inadequate to see Maratha powers as making Bhils subordinate to a centralized state. When we do this, we speak from the vantage point of our exclusive sovereignties; we see shared sovereignties as a weakness or inadequacy of power that will give way logically and historically in the fullness of time to exclusive sovereignties.

THE AFFINITIES OF WILDNESS

All this is very well, but what did raids mean for regions and peoples who were raided? The answer—hardship, desertion, and desolation—often seems so straightforward and so agreed upon both by historians and contemporary chroniclers that the question itself is rarely seen as even worth posing. True enough, quite apart from the substantial and very real bloodshed and violence, the plunder of cattle, grain, and utensils could entirely impoverish a village household, and even drive it below already tenuous margins of subsistence. Many people, maybe even the bulk of cultivators, abandoned their villages and moved to places where they could continue with cultivation as before. This was what happened to Khandesh in the late eighteenth and early nineteenth centuries.

But from a perspective less committed to growth, it is possible to tease out several meanings that are suppressed or minimized in depictions of desertion and/desolation. First, desolation did not mean that all villages were deserted. Several villages brokered their own peace with the raiding chiefs when the political authority of figures like the Peshwa failed. In the Khandesh region, for example, some *patils* or headmen reached agreements of this sort with the chiefs of Amala, paying *giras* directly. As a result, cultivation continued in these regions across the early nineteenth century.[58] Second, in addition to this continuation of cultivation, at least a significant proportion of those from both these villages and deserted ones voted with their feet to join the raiders. Amongst them often were the plains Bhils. The plains Bhils, as colonial records designated these people, had an ambiguous relation with the plains villages in which they lived, and in which they were possibly quite numerous. In normal times, they served as *jagalias* or watchmen in these villages. In this position, they were responsible for securing information about potential raids. Sometimes, however, they supplied information to the raiders—they were often the spies of the sort mentioned in the song. Given their links with both sides, it is understandable that so often they should have selected to move to the hills, take up cultivation or other forms of subsistence there, and join the raiders.[59]

Third, in villages that had been deserted, forests—always nearby in the late eighteenth or early nineteenth centuries—quickly re-established themselves. In the twenty years that they lay relatively fallow, many villages in Khandesh were overrun with forests. This sort of desolation simply meant the emergence of a different complex of subsistence modes. Sometimes Bhils moved in near the area they raided, especially if there already were a significant number of Bhils around. In 1804, for example, some Bhils from Ghadvi moved into the Gaekwadi village of Raigadh in this way, and used it as a base for further raids.[60] These villages usually remained without a permanent population, but became part of an area used for gathering, hunting, fishing, or even cultivation. The whole of Navapur *taluka* was virtually resettled this way in the late-eighteenth and early nineteenth centuries, with its demographic profile changing so dramatically that Bhils became the principal community of the region.[61] So, desolation in late-eighteenth and early-nineteenth century western India can be rethought as the creation of areas where forest communities and forest polities were dominant.

Finally, and most importantly, even a sharp distinction between the plains of Khandesh or Gujarat and forested or hilly areas such as the Dangs may not be too helpful. There was a profound overlap between Dangi enactments of wildness and those of surrounding plains communities. As I argue at length in my book, the ways in which Dangis thought of themselves as *jangli* or wild—in relation to forests, masculinity, femininity, modes of livelihood, raids and *giras*, amongst other things—had significant resonances in surrounding plains communities rather than simply being opposed to the practices of these communities; being *jangli* was about having an agonistic relationship with surrounding plains societies. Consider for now only the affinities and similarities with the raids and *giras* of forest polities. Like *giras*, the famous Maratha revenue claim *chauth* was about shared sovereignty and the construction of kingship; moreover, it was sustained through raids.[62] Besides, *giras* itself was very important not only in the forest polities but in the plains of central and south Gujarat, especially in the Ahmedabad, Kheda, Bharuch, and Surat regions. In early nineteenth-century Bharuch, a prosperous region of Gujarat for which we have Rajkumar Han's suggestive study, the *girasias* claimed a fourth or a third share of the revenue, and held nearly half the land under cultivation. If their dues were not paid to them, they were likely to raid villages and collect these amounts.[63] In 1776, they held in Bharuch over 56,000 bighas of land, which yielded a revenue of Rs 1.2 lakh annually. Amongst the *girasias* were 124 Rajputs, eighty-one Muslims, and twenty-two Kolis.[64] Around Ahmedabad, virtually the whole parganas of Dhanduka, Ranpur and Gogha, except for the chief towns, were under their control. The Gaekwads had a separate Giras Department to look after the various claims to it made all over their territories. Similarly, raids and plundering affected not just areas close to forest polities but agricultural and urban centres across the subcontinent. 'Near Ahmadabad, Burhanpur, Agra, Delhi, Lahore, and many other cities, thieves and robbers come in force by night or day like open enemies', Pelsaert wrote.[65] What Shulman suggests for South India—that raids and other activities of bandits were celebrated, and regarded as having close affinities with kingship—may well be true of other parts of India too.[66]

Surely some of these affinities may have been because plains powers had to depend on alliances with Bhils or taking to the forests during disputes with the Peshwa or other Maratha chiefs. To cite only one of the most famous examples, the founder of the Baroda dynasty, Pilaji Gaekwad, rose to pre-eminence through his alliances with the Bhils and Kolis. His early ties were with the (Bhil?) Raja of Rajpipla, who controlled the fort of Songadh near the Dangs.[67] Songadh, we saw, was later to be Pilaji's first capital. Even in later decades, after the Gaekwadi capital was shifted to Baroda, Songadh remained an important base, and many Gamits, at the time a *janglijati*, joined Gaekwadi army service, eventually settling down in distant parts of north Gujarat. Given this kind of backdrop, it is not surprising that the Ghadvi chief Silput Raja should have remarked on one occasion that 'he looked to the Guicowar as his brother'; Gaekwadi officials were to acquiesce and maybe even participate in this language.[68] Being *jangli* was thus not in conflict with being Gaekwad; it was integral to the relationships that Gaekwadi officials sustained.

The role of forest polities was even greater in the small kingdoms of western and central India—those like Chhota Udepur, Baria, or Lunavada in south-east Gujarat, Boodawal and Peint towards Maharashtra, or Jura and Oghna towards Rajasthan. Most of these small kingdoms were as deeply involved in discourses of wildness as in the power of larger centralized states. Some of these had been established by Rajput adventurers between the fourteenth and the sixteenth centuries, others by Bhil chiefs who had become much more powerful than their rivals. They often had strong alliances with plains powers; the kingdoms of Boodawal and Peint held grants from plains powers for their lands on condition of their controlling Bhil raids on to the plains.[69] At the same time, a considerable degree of the power of little kingdoms too was derived from their alliances with forest polities. In the Mughal period, for example, the Surgana *deshmukh* and the Dangi chiefs rebelled together; at one time, Dangs and the *deshmukh's* territories were together called *bandi mulak*, or rebel lands.[70] During coronations, a Bhil chief often played a crucial role, seating the new king on the throne; an indicator of the centrality of wildness in these little kingdoms.[71]

Even an identity as Bhils was sometimes adopted by or ascribed to the more upper caste Rajputs in forested and hilly regions. About the rajas of Vansda, for example, there was some confusion as to whether they were Bhil or Rajput chiefs.[72] Though often simply because of colonial ignorance, such confusion shows how thin the line between Rajput and Bhil was in many forested areas. As one official noted in the early nineteenth century, Rajput chiefs were quite willing to marry into powerful Bhil lineages.[73] Claiming and participating in the wildness of being Bhil, then, was not something that only *janglijati*s like Koknis did—even Rajputs were fascinated by, and claimed involvement in, enactments of wildness. In certain contexts and situations, the discourse of wildness may have been as influential as those around Brahman or Rajput values.

In pointing to these affinities, I do not wish to deny the distance between the politics of wildness and its antinomies. Bhil chiefs were certainly less committed to settled agriculture than eighteenth-century Maratha officials, and Peshwa officials shared a considerable hostility to Bhils. If nothing else, the widespread Bhil contempt and antipathy for Brahmans would have been difficult to take for a Brahman dominated state. Even in many smaller Rajput states, there were signs of a distancing from Bhils in the late eighteenth century, with some Rajput chiefs trying to exclude Bhils from the coronation ceremonies with which they had been formerly associated.[74] My point is much more modest: that because these antinomies operated within the same semantic and conceptual field as the practices of wildness, slippages between wildness to its antinomies were both possible and often occurred, and that the politics of wildness was in this sense a crucial way of enacting power.

THE EMERGENCE OF GROWTH

With the consolidation of British rule in the region after 1818, new categories developed.[75] Amongst those which firmed up by the mid-nineteenth century was the distinction between castes and tribes, with the castes being considered relatively civilized and the tribes wild. The colonial state in Khandesh and Gujarat turned its attention to extinguishing raids by groups like Bhils, and reducing their power. What may seem striking about these developments at first glance is the affinities with pre-colonial developments. After all, it was largely those communities who had been thought of as wild formerly that now came to be called tribes; the early colonial state too was not acting very differently from its Maratha predecessors, even if it was more successful. To emphasize continuities in this manner would be in keeping with the spirit of the revisionist historiography of the eighteenth- and early nineteenth-century, which has tracked such affinities across a range of themes—religious conflict, trade, state formation practices of information, or the development of capital.

But perhaps we are sometimes misled by the persistence of what seems like the same practices into overlooking the profound transformations in the semantic and conceptual fields within which these practices occur. Consider the changing meaning of the wild and the civilized. Formerly, wildness and its antinomies had provided, in themselves, a way to enact identities and power. Now, the language of wildness persisted, but it was no longer antinomic; it was rather about an Other; one that was apprehended through a distinctive referent—time. It was through time that wildness was placed in relation to the civilized; wildness was before and inferior to civilization; the wild was now transmuted into the primitive. This incorporation of time as not merely a static backdrop but a dynamic element, itself providing a principle of transformation, made possible not only the emergence of the evolutionary thought within which the tribe-caste continuum was posited; it also made possible the birth of that medium—growth—within which we now routinely think, unconscious of the anachronism of doing so, of earlier societies. Now, clans were expected to grow into states and then empires; tribes into castes; and hunting into pastoralism into agriculture into industry. Within this evolutionary emphasis on growth, the areas inhabited by the tribes could be envisioned as an inner frontier, as that which resisted growth.

Thinking within the ubiquitous medium of growth, colonial officials dealt in two ways with wildness—ways that despite their apparent opposition shared a great affinity, and even perhaps called forth each other. There was, on the one hand, the civilizing mission, with its tasks of bringing the wild into the time of the civilized: officials halted raids, forcibly extinguished mobility, imposed settled agriculture, and refashioned kingship to make it more civilized. Colonial forestry too was often cast as a project of taming wilderness and civilizing it. On the other hand, there was primitivism, with its celebration of wildness. Thus, the Kiplingesque Anglo-Indian jungle, a space of the exotic, opposed to the baseness of Indian civilization; thus also the nobility of the wild tribes, quite like the noble Englishman. What both shared was an obsession with evolutionary time as growth: one sought to foster it under hot-house conditions, and the other to turn it back. What both also shared was an emphasis on the inner frontier: one sought to tame and erase it, the other to strengthen and complete it. On the existence and ubiquity of growth and the inner frontier, both were agreed.

By the mid-nineteenth century, settled agriculture, centralized state power and trade came to be emphasized and construed in ways that systematically marginalized wildness. Indian communities also affirmed this colonial opposition between wildness and civilization, so similar and yet so fundamentally different. Increasingly, there was a rejection of wildness. In the process, both in plains and forest communities, identities and gender relations were remade extensively. Wildness came to be associated with marginality, social and ritual inferiority, and political powerlessness; often, amongst forest communities, it was now invoked as part of an oppositional subaltern discourse.

In a very different way, wildness was to remain crucial in the twentieth century.[76] As nationalist thought developed, there emerged a primitivism which celebrated tribes as natural beings, spontaneous, free and uninhibitedly masculine—possessing some of the qualities needed for a struggle against the British. But that primitivism was also underwritten by a profound marginalization of the 'tribes'. As natural beings, they could at best rebel without knowing why. The knowing mind belonged to the nationalist élite. Indeed, no future was envisaged for the tribal in post-colonial India. The wildness of the tribal epitomized Indian backwardness; this backwardness had to be overcome for the nation to become modern, or simply for the nation to become. In all of this, there was a profound irony. The *jangal* and *jangli*, once central to kingship and authority, had become the negativities through which the civilizing processes of colonialism and nationalism defined themselves in the age of modernity. The wildness of *jangal* and the *jangli* had come to be contained within Kiplingesque exoticism or caste-tribe sociologism.

ABBREVIATIONS

Coll.	Collector
DBD	*Dangs Boundary Dispute*
DCR	Dangs Collectorate Records
DDR	Dangs District Records
DN	Daftar Number
FN	File Number
GoB	Goverment of Bombay
GSAB	Gujarat State Archives, Baroda
HPO	Huzur Political Office
IOL	India Office Library
Kh.	Khandesh
MSAB	Maharashtra State Archives, Bombay
MSAP	Maharashtra State Archives, Poona
PD	Political Department
PDD	Political Department Diaries
PSD	Political and Secret Department
RR	Residency Records.

NOTES AND REFERENCES

1. G.S. Sardesai, *Selections from the Peshwa Daftar*, Bombay, Government Central Press, 1930–4, vol. 41, p. 40, quoted in Sumit Guha, 'Forest Polities and Agrarian Empires: The Khandesh Bhils, *c.* 1750–1850', *Indian Economic and Social History Review* (henceforth *IESHR*), vol. 33:2, 1996.

2. The scholarly literature on colonial understanding of castes and tribes, or the distinction between them, is by now quite extensive. But see especially Sanjay Nigam, 'Disciplining and policing the 'criminals by birth' (2 parts), *IESHR*, vol. 27: 2 and 3, 1990, pp. 131–64 and pp. 257–87, and Nandini Sundar, 'The Dreaded Danteshwari: Annals of Alleged Sacrifice', *IESHR*, vol. 32:3, 1995, pp. 345–74; and my 'Shades of Wildness: Tribe, Caste and Gender in Western India', *Journal of Asian Studies*, vol. 56:3, Aug. 1977, pp. 726–45.

3. This revisionist perspective, now quite widely accepted, has been articulated most insightfully, of course, in C.A. Bayly's brilliant books, *Indian Society and the Making*

of the British Empire, Cambridge, 1988, and *Rulers, Townsmen and Bazaars: North Indian Society in the Age of British Expansion, 1770–1870*, Cambridge, 1983.

4. Steven Feirman has recently reminded us of how pervasive such narratives are in even some of the finest pieces of contemporary history-writing. See his 'Africa in History: The End of Universal Narratives', in Gyan Prakash (ed.) *After Colonialism: Imperial Histories and Postcolonial Displacements*, Princeton, New Jersey, 1995, pp. 40–65.

5. J.C. Heesterman, *The Inner Conflict of Tradition*, Chicago, 1985, p. 170; André Wink, *Land and Sovereignty in India: Agrarian Society and Politics Under the Eighteenth-Century Maratha Svarajya*, Cambridge, 1986, p. 197; C.A. Bayly, *Indian Society and the Making of the British Empire*, pp. 30–2.

6. Heesterman, for instance, describes the 1857 rebellion as 'a chaotic resurgence of the inner frontier', ibid., p. 176; see also his discussion on p. 174. This metaphor, and the privileging of settled agrarian regions, pervades most of the literature cited in fn. 1 above, including my 'A Forest Polity in Western India: The Dangs, 1800s–1920s', PhD dissertation, Department of History, University of Cambridge, 1992.

7. Skaria, op. cit.

8. I make this argument in greater detail in my *Hybrid Histories: Forests, Frontiers and Wildness in Western India*, Delhi, 1999. For a discussion of wildness which makes similar points, see K. Sivaramakrishnan, 'Wild Landscapes and the Politics of Memory in West Bengal', unpublished paper.

9. Much recent work has emphasized the complex relationships of interdependence between forest polities and centralized powers in the seventeenth and eighteenth centuries, showing how the latter too were involved in raiding and plunder as a form of tax collection. In the context of western India, Sumit Guha's thought-provoking work is especially important. See his 'Lords of the Land versus Kings of the Forest: Conflict and Collaboration in Peninsular India, *c.* 1500–1981', unpublished paper, 1995; and id., 'Forest polities and agrarian empires'; Wink, *Land and Sovereignty*; and Stewart Gordon, *Marathas, Marauders and State Formation in Eighteenth Century*, Delhi, 1994. For work on similar themes in other parts of the Indian subcontinent, see Bayly, *Indian Society and the Making of the British Empire*; Chetan Singh, 'Conformity and Conflict: Tribes and the Agrarian System of Mughal India', *IESHR*, vol. 25:3, 1988, pp. 319–40; and id. 'Forests, Pastoralists and Agrarian Society in Mughal India', in David Arnold and Ramachandra Guha (eds), *Nature, Culture, Imperialism: Essays on the Environmental History of South Asia*, Delhi, 1994, pp. 21–48.

10. Francis Zimmerman, *The Jungle and the Aroma of Meats: An Ecological Theme in Hindu Medicine*, Berkeley, 1987, pp. viii, 18. Michael Dove has criticized Zimmerman's reading in ' "Jungle" in Nature and Culture', in Ramachandra Guha (ed.), *Social Ecology*, Delhi, 1994, pp. 90–115, but his criticisms are vitiated by an ecological determinism.

11. Romila Thapar, 'The Image of the Barbarian in Early India', *Comparative Studies in Society and History*, vol. 13, 1971, pp. 408–36.

12. For valuable accounts of Maratha relations with forest polities such as Bhils in the eighteenth century, see B.A. Saletore's 'The Bhils of Maharashtra', *New Indian Antiquary* (henceforth *NIA*), 1938–9, vol. 1, pp. 323–36, and id., 'Relations Between

the Girassias and the Marathas', *NIA*, Extra Series I, 1939; Gordon, *The Marathas, 1600–1818*, Cambridge, 1993, p. 108ff.

13. For accounts see A.M. Deshpande, *John Briggs in Maharashtra: A Study of District Administration Under Early British Rule*, New Delhi, 1987, p. 124; Government of Bombay, *Gazetteer of the Bombay Presidency*, vol. 16, Nasik, Bombay, 1883, p. 193f.

14. Rigby to Robertson, 14 Aug. 1823, GSAB.DDR.DN 1.FN 1. Graham to Blanc, 25 March 1839, GSAB DDR.DN 1.FN 3.

15. List of things taken from Kuswao, *MSAB.PDD.351 (11)*. See Rigby to Briggs, 20 May 1821, GSAB.DDR.DN 1.FN 1. Briggs to Chaplin, 13 June 1822, op. cit. Statement of Nathu Patil and Sivaji Balaji, n.d., MSAB.PD. 1829, vol. 8/332.

16. Statement of Nathu Patil and Sivaji Balaji, n.d., MSAB.PD.1829, vol. 8/332.

17. Morrison to Keith, n.d., MSAB.PDD.351(11); Briggs to Chaplin, 13 June 1822, GSAB.DDR.DN1.FN1; see also MSAB.PD.1829, vol. 8/332.

18. Population tables, GSAB.DDR.DN 2.FN 9.

19. Rigby to Briggs, 18 June 1822, GSAB.DDR.DN 1.FN 1.

20. Coll., Kh., to Chief Secy., 19 Sept. 1828, GSAB.DDR.DN 1.FN 1.

21. Silput and Khem to Rigby, n.d., MSAB.PSD.1822, vol. 7/69.

22. So widespread was the payment of *giras* in the nineteenth century that the Gaekwads had a separate department to deal with it. See the Giras department papers at the Gujarat State Archives, Baroda.

23. See Maya Unnithan, 'Constructing Difference: Social Categories and Girahya Women, Kingship and Resources in South Rajasthan', PhD dissertation, Department of Anthropology, University of Cambridge, 1991, pp. 42–55 for a broad account of *girasia* history.

24. Rigby to Silput, 21 May 1825, GSAB.DDR.DN 1.FN 2.

25. Statement of Nathu Patil and Sivaji Balaji, n.d. MSAB.PD.1829, vol. 8/32.

26. Rigby to Briggs, 30 July 1822, GSAB.DDR.DN 1.FN 1.

27. Giberne to Newnham, 16 Oct. 1828, MSAB.PSD.1828, vol. 29/320. See also Rigby to Briggs, 2 July 1822, GSAB.DDR.DN 1.FN 1.

28. See the letters from Briggs to Elphinstone, 24 Sept. 1818. MSAP.Dec.Com. vol. 172. no. 212; 19 Nov. 1818, MSAP.Dec. Com. vol. 173, no. 292; 8 Jan. 1819, MSAP.Dec.Com, vol. 174. no. 367. See also Arvind Deshpande, *John Briggs in Maharashtra*, Chap. 3; A.K. Prasad, *The Bhils of Khandesh Under the British East India Company*, New Delhi, 1991, Chap. 2.

29. Rigby to Briggs, 30 July 1822, GSAB.DDR.DN 1.FN 1.

30. John Malcolm, 'Essay on Bhils', *Transactions of the Royal Asiatic Society of Great Britain and Ireland*, vol. 1, 1827, p. 89.

31. IOL, Luard Mss, Central India Songs, Mss Hindi D1 (27), Folio 31.

32. See the songs in the IOL, Luard Mss as well as those reproduced in T.H. Hendley, 'An Account of the Maiwar Bhils', *Journal of the Asiatic Society of Bengal*, vol. 4, 1875.

33. David Shulman, 'On South Indian Bandits and Kings', *IESHR*, vol. 17:3, 1980, pp. 290–1. See also J.F. Richards and V.N. Rao, 'Banditry in Mughal India: Historical and Folk Perceptions', *IESHR*, vol. 18: 1, 1980.

34. DCR.DN 1.FN 4Uc.

35. This paragraph is based on Saletore, 'The Bhils of Western India', and Guha, 'Forest Polities and Agrarian Empires'.

36. Report of a march through Dangs, March, 1867, GSAB.DDR.DN. 3.FN 12.

37. Rigby to Robertson, 30 Oct. 1825, GSAB.RR.DN 144.FN 719.

38. See Diwan, Huzur Kacheri to Resident, Baroda, 18 Dec. 1903, GSAB.HPO (Pol.). Section 214.1A.SN 3 for a list of all the co-shared Gaekwadi villages.

39. Gordon, 'Forts and Social Control in the Maratha State', in his *Marathas, Marauders and State Formation.*

40. DBD, I, p. 106ff.

41. André Wink, 'Maratha Revenue Farming', *Modern Asian Studies*, vol. 17: 4, 1983; see also his *Land and Sovereignty in India*, pp. 339–52.

42. Coll., Kh., to Secy., GoB, 13 March 1871, MSAB.PD.1871. vol. 56. Comp. 578; see also the evidence of Budea Naik, GSAB.RR.DN 141.FN 710. Records mention the name of the chief as Udesinh rather than Fatehsinh, but this is possibly a mistake, since oral traditions are quite unanimous about Fatehsinh being the person who was killed.

43. Coll., Kh., to Secy., GoB, 13 March 1871 MSAB.PD.1871. vol. 56. Comp. 578; Ashburner to Secy., GoB, 12 April 1871, GSAB.RR.DN 141.FN 700.

44. Amrut Rav to Silput and Khem, n.d., no. 4, GSAB.DDR.DN 1.FN 3.

45. Boyd to Secy., GoB, 9 June 1830 GSAB.DDR.DN 1.FN 3; and T. Madhav Rao, Diwan, Baroda, to The Agent to the Governor General, Baroda, 18 July 1881, *Selections from the Records of the Baroda Government, No. X, vol. 1, Dang Case*, Baroda, 1891, GSAB. *Section 8. Daftar 4. Anukram 43.*

46. Morrisson to Keith, 11 Jan. 1810, MSAB.PDD.351(11).

47. GSAB.DDR.DN .FN 2.

48. Gordon, *The Marathas*, p. 181f.

49. See MSAB.PD.1855. vol. 36.Comp. 577.

50. DBD, II, p. 153.

51. Graham to Coll., Kh., 8 July 1828. GSAB.DDR.DN 1.FN 2; Hodges to Norriss, 14 July 1829, op. cit.

52. See the correspondence in GSAB.DDR.DN 1.FN 2; GSAB.DDR.DN 1.FN 3.

53. See, for example, DBD, II, p. 18.

54. Bell to Resident, Baroda, 25 July 1845, GSAB.RR.FN 122.DN 609; Appaji Rav to Silput, n.d., No. 5, GSAB.DDR.DN 1.FN 3; Mansfield to Secy., GoB, 24 July 1855, MSAB.PD.1855. vol. 37. Comp. 123.

55. John Briggs to Resident, Baroda, 14 July 1821, MSAB.PSD.1820, vol. 4/8; List of things taken from Kuswao, MSAB.PD.351(11). See also statement of Nathu Patil and Sivali Bajali, MSAB.PD.1829, vol. 8/332.

56. Saletore gives several examples of this. See his 'The Bhils of Maharashtra', and also his 'Relations between the Girassias and the Marathas'.

57. Rigby to Robertson, 14 Aug. 1823, GSAB.DDR.DN 1.FN 1.

58. Rigby(?) to Briggs, 28 Nov. 1819, DCR.DN. 1.FN 4Uc.

59. Briggs to Ephinstone, 8 Jan. 1819, MSAP.Dec.Com. vol. 174.

60. Maharawal Raisinhji, Vansda Raja, to J. Morrison, recd. 16 June 1804, MSAB.SPD.158 (16).

61. David Hardiman, 'Small Dam Systems of the Sahayadris', in Arnold and Guha (eds), *Nature, Culture, Imperialism*, p. 205f.

62. Gordon, *The Marathas*, p. 76.

63. Raj Kumar Hans, 'Agrarian Economy of Broach District During the First Hall of the

Nineteenth Century', PhD dissertation, Department of History, M.S. University, Baroda, 1987, p. 62ff.

64. Raj Kumar Hans, 'The Grasia Chiefs and the British Power in the Beginning of Nineteenth Century Gujarat', *Proceedings of the Indian History Congress*, Waltair, 1979.

65. Wink, *Land and Sovereignty*, p. 197.

66. Shulman, 'On South Indian Bandits and Kings', *IESHR*, vol. 17:3, 1980, pp. 283–306.

67. Wink, *Land and Sovereignty*, p. 117.

68. GSAB.DDR.DN 1.FN 2.

69. Briggs to Elphinstone, 24 Oct. 1818, no. 212, MSAP.Dec.Com. vol 172.

70. Morriss to Mansfield, 15 April 1854, GSAB.DDR.DN 2.FN 7.

71. The practice of Bhils participating in the coronation of Rajput chiefs is noted in John Malcolm, 'Essay on Bhils', *Transactions of the Royal Asiatic Society of Great Britain and Ireland*, vol. 1, 1827, pp. 68–9 and in Russell and Hira Lal, *Tribes and Castes*, vol. 1, p. 280.

72. DCR.DN 1.FN 4Uc.

73. Central Provinces Ethnographic Survey, *Draft Articles on Forest Tribes*, 3rd series, Allahabad, 1911, p. 46.

74. Malcolm, 'Essay on Bhils'.

75. The arguments in this section are elaborated in detail in my *Hybrid Histories*.

76. I thank Ranajit Guha for an e-mail discussion which made the points in this paragraph clearer.

12

Tributary State*

DAVID LUDDEN

Like the human landscape, transformed by labours on the frontier after 1300, the regional order that emerged in the late sixteenth century and matured thereafter would have seemed unfamiliar to a visitor from the medieval Pandya court. Nature had not changed. The monsoons continued to bestow their most luxurious bounty on the Tirunelveli wet zone, where Brahman and Vellala villages flourished, gods enjoyed devotion, and kings reaped honour. But like the farmers who ploughed fields north and south of the Tambraparni River valley, the kings who ruled at Madurai were not of the Pandya fold. Pandya kings would have viewed the Nayaka dynasty, firmly entrenched in the capital city by 1600, as foreigners whose legitimacy as rulers derived not from ancient, indigenous roots, nor from the natural loyalties of Pandya peoples, but from sheer military force. The Nayakas themselves had no illusions about their ancestry. They had come from the Telugu-speaking lands north of the medieval Tamil *mandalams*, and, conquering under the umbrella of Vijayanagar imperial authority, had established their sovereignty at Madurai, putting an end in the process to the myth of Pandya royal authority that had survived the last effective Pandya king by two centuries. Nayaka charisma rose from the ritual supremacy of their capital and from their ability to patronize temples and Brahmans; this feature of the Nayaka state the Pandya kings would have recognized. But because the Nayaka realm was so much more socially diverse and politically complex than its Pandya predecessor in Tirunelveli, the new regional order rested squarely on the shoulders of military men. The army relied in turn on payments of tribute from royal subjects, especially peasants and traders who, being protected by Nayaka arms, generated increasing stores of wealth to support the warrior state. Regional order,

*David Ludden, 'Tributary State', in *Peasant History in South India*, Princeton, 1985, pp. 68–100.

defined and stabilized under the Pandya kings above all by ritual activity in religious networks, now became integrated anew by tributary transactions in state networks. Participating in this tributary state, the peasantry expanded its access to opportunities for market exchange and, during the eighteenth century, made that series of critical decisions which founded British rule.

WARRIOR RULE

As the Vijayanagar empire collapsed, Nayaka armies reunited the Tirunelveli region through victories in a war that spanned the sixteenth century. The founder of the Nayaka dynasty, Visvanatha, commanded a Vijayanagar army that came south in 1529. He battled a shifting alliance of Pandyas and Maravas, which fought him to a standstill in 1543 after six months of inconclusive war, and beat his forces as late as 1547. On his death, in 1564, his son claimed independence from Vijayanagar, and, despite continued resistance, set up a stable Nayaka authority system by century's end that remained intact until 1736. Its capital was first at Madurai and later, as Nayaka power expanded, at Tiruchirapalli (Trichnopoly) further north, in the Chola country.[1]

The Nayakas consummated a process begun by the Cholas, merging Chola and Pandya *mandalams*. They also continued what the later Pandyas had begun, setting up a clear-cut hierarchy of urban centres to embody the relations of subordination in their new domain. These urban centres, moreover, reflect an increased urban concentration and lifestyle for the regional ruling élite, whose authority rose much higher above its local roots than did that of their Pandya predecessors. Nayakas raised Madurai to new heights of grandeur, tore down inadequate Pandya fortifications, erected new walls, and encased the city in stone. They added new walls and internal buildings to the royal temple of Sri Minakshi–Sundaresvara, in the heart of the city. Madurai was reborn: a transcendent political and ceremonial centre that incorporated in its aura all lesser powers in the Nayaka realm.[2]

Endowed with the combined military might, ceremonial splendour, and political authority of Madurai, but on a lesser scale, Tirunelveli town became the southern provincial capital. Here stood the largest fort in the south, at Palayamkottai; the central temple, Nellaiyappa Koil; and the governor, known as the delavoy (literally, 'commander'). Ariyanatha Mudaliar, a Vellala from Tondaimandalam, the first delavoy, rose through the Vijayanagar ranks to become a minister and general under his childhood friend Visvanatha Nayaka, with whom he rode south to command armies that subdued the Tirunelveli countryside.[3] The governorship became a perpetual patrimony in his family, and hence part of the family name, Medai Delavoy Mudaliar. In their mansion astride the Nellaiyappa Koil, in the heart of their capital, the Medai Delavoy Mudaliars became one of the richest and most powerful families in the region and remained so for centuries.

Under the delavoy's authority lay two distinct political realms, one in the old Pandya territories, and one in the sub-regions commanded by Telugu and Marava chiefs. In the first, a series of officers and official transactions linked the delavoy directly to the wealth and loyalty of irrigated communities. In the second, the Nayakas by necessity recognized numerous sub-regional chiefs as junior partners or 'little kings' atop territorial segments of the Nayaka domain. Each little king received an appropriate title as the defender of one of seventy-two bastions of Madurai; each, based in his fortress town (*palayam*), was called a *palayakkaran*, or in Anglo-Indian usage, a poligar. The Nayaka system thus made use of a principle also at work in the contemporaneous Mughal empire that remained in effect into the twentieth century, wherein some lands were seen to be ruled directly by the crown—in Anglo-Indian terms sarcar or circar lands—and others were understood to be under the control of lesser royal authorities. But as we have seen, this principle also had an indigenous, Pandya legacy, for warrior chiefs had always been under Pandya kings more prominent outside the wet-zone political core of the realm than they were within it.

Ironically, though more complex than the Pandya system, the Nayaka state remains more unknown because of the relative dearth of inscriptions. We do know that it contained many more people and a greater diversity of communities than the Pandya state. To achieve order, the Nayakas developed many more specialized official positions and an elaborate state ceremonial language to articulate hierarchy among officers. One account, for instance, tells how the delavoy's son 'was accustomed to go out every night in public procession around the town, seated in a lofty howdah, on the back of an elephant, clothed in rich, perfumed dress, covered with ornaments, with numerous lights, musicians, dancers, and other usual accompaniments of such spectacles', and how the Nayaka himself, worried that such display overstepped the boy's status, rode on horse all the way from Madurai to observe, and, in the end, to grant his approval.[4] Another story tells that the Medai Delavoy Mudaliar family gained its full name because the governor would receive poligars into his presence only when seated on a high platform (*medai*).[5] We can, then, imagine Nayakas atop a hierarchy of authority that stretched from Madurai to Tirunelveli, thence to sub-regional centres and to localities, whereas Pandyas had sat at the centre of a vast set of more equal political relationships. The Nayaka system seems to have had less need for permanent stone records, which had served under the Pandyas to bridge infrequent exertions of royal authority. Now, as tribute flowed up and authority down the official hierarchy with more regularity, records of transactions became ephemeral, recorded only on palm leaves that turned to dust over the years. A new state order thus changed the character of historical records, as it had under early Pandya dynasties and would again after 1800.

Despite the dearth of records, it seems clear that a tension-ridden series of speculative revenue contracts channelled tribute from Tirunelveli localities to Tirunelveli town and to Madurai with some regularity after 1600. B.A. Saletore, in fact, argues that such a system had been in place in parts of south India by the thirteenth century. Its theory was simple, expressed in a passage from the *Sukraniti*: 'Having determined the land revenue of a village, the king should receive it from one rich man in advance, or [receive a], guarantee [for its payment] . . . by monthly or periodic installments.'[6] At each level of state hierarchy, political stature depended in principle and practice on one's ability to advance money up the hierarchy in anticipation of collection from below. Officials had not only to be rich in relation to others in their sphere of influence, but had to maintain their stature by constant patronage and at least the possibility of coercion. The character of ties that bound together these layers of tribute differed markedly between circar and poligar domains.

Poligars ruled little kingdoms, which varied in size from the tiny Sennalkudi, Kollankondan, Urkadu, and Kadalkudi, to the vast Ettaiyapuram, Panchalamkottai, Sivagiri, and Chokkampatti (Maps 15 and 16).[7] Though larger ones contained a greater number of segments, and though Marava and Telugu domains may have been organized slightly differently, in general poligar domains were defined by territorial segments linked hierarchically by caste status and military rank. Marava sub-jatis and their component kinship branches (*kilai*) settled in compact areas, part of their strategy for defence and caste dominance. The 1823 census shows each sub-jati concentrated in a separate village in areas outside the Marava core domain in the northern mixed zone; and research on Marava settlement patterns done in this century shows that, in the Marava core domain, *kilai*s are concentrated in the same way.[8] Within settlements, Marava families today rank themselves by their patrilineal proximity to one dominant chief. S. Kathirvel has shown this ranking system to have organized Marava protection services in the eighteenth century, when a chief in each village negotiated with clients for protection, collected payments, and dispersed the rewards to families under his command.[9] In core settlement areas, however, village *kilai*s bunched together into localities of sub-jati dominance, and poligars grew up as rulers of land dominated by their own sub-jati. In 1823, twelve of twenty-one Marava poligar domains (then called zamindaris) were populated by only one sub-jati; in three others one sub-jati's numerical preponderance was overwhelming; and, in six others, though two (but no more) sub-jatis were more or less equal in size, that of the poligar most likely dominated as a result of conquest.[10]

Telugu jatis also concentrated themselves spatially. Sub-jati territories thus probably constituted segments of political order in their domains. Overlapping this caste polity, however, Telugus, and perhaps Maravas, too, set up a military and administrative apparatus that employed a number of castes, linking the poligar to each village in his realm. In Ettaiyapuram's domain, for instance, the poligar divided his territory among his kinsmen and other subsidiary chiefs, called *servaikkaran*, who owed military allegiance and tribute, and who demanded the same from village headmen under their control.[11] Needless to say, everyone accepted violence as a legitimate means to establish authority in poligar territory, and struggles by those below to resist demands from above were constant features of order itself. To the end of the seventeenth century, however, records do not indicate any major challenge directed against the topmost link to the chain of authority, that between poligars and the delavoy.

In circar territory, mostly the core Pandya *nadu*s controlled locally by the Vellala–Brahman alliance, the Nayaka system depended on a different set of political relations. New military élites did not attempt to undermine old Pandya local leaders. On the contrary, Nayakas and their agents endowed temples and founded new *brahmadeya*s with unprecedented generosity.[12] Tribute collectors were sub-regional authorities with material and ritual resources under Nayaka protection and patronage. At first these were mostly military men, come to power in the Vijayanagar period; but after 1564 more and more they were Brahman immigrants, many Telugus, favoured agents in the new regime, who received land grants in addition to official titles. Under them and beside them in irrigated localities, wealthy landowners constituted the final and critical link in the chain of Nayaka authority, and profited accordingly. At each level in the chain, of course, orderly transmission of tribute and honour could be backed up with force, if necessary, by troops at Palayamkottai. But routine authority rested upon officials' skill in generating for themselves local influence, by tying themselves into transactional webs in and around irrigated communities. They became patrons, protectors, and arbiters. Their names now adorn villages and irrigation works, to suggest their activity as investors in agriculture and water management. They appear in inscriptions most often as donors to temples. But they must have been active in local grain markets too, for, as we will soon see, revenue collections 'in kind' were in fact highly commercialized wherever paddy was grown. As commercial actors, officials were probably foci of saving and lending as an expanding cash nexus developed around irrigated communities during the Nayaka years.

By paying tribute, villagers and merchants obtained protection, their leaders attained stature as intermediaries, and they were left alone by state officials to manage internal affairs. The segmented character of the regional order thus remained intact even as the central power and wealth of state officers increased under the Nayaka regime. Like poligars, Muslim merchants at Kayalpatnam were authorized to control their commercial domain in the port city in return for orderly tribute payments. Artisans, shepherds, fishermen, washermen, and other groups paid through their caste headmen.[13] Such payments entitled headmen to collect from members of their groups. Local leaders thus had good reasons to accept and support the tribute system, and to placate Nayaka agents from Tirunelveli—even competing agents, whose rival claims might raise the cost of protection at times. European merchants were but another such group of tribute payers. Despite Portuguese conversions of Parava fishermen on the coast, and despite battles between Portuguese and Dutch merchants, these overseas foreigners did not attract animosity from the Nayakas, who were content to leave the coastal tract under the control of the merchants.[14] The Portuguese controlled, according to one account, 'the entire civil and criminal jurisdiction of the fishery coast . . . and all the dues and taxes including the valuable revenue arising from the pearl fishery'. Dutch and Portuguese warriors fought constantly on the coast during the mid-1600s, taking whole towns and villages from one another without provoking Nayaka interference. Having won, the Dutch then proceeded to cement treaties of protective alliance; like the Portuguese before them, they covered their bets by paying for protection to whoever in the segmented Nayaka state system could help assure their safety.[15]

Thus, the Nayaka regime was fertile ground for the growth of militant merchant power. Unfortunately, the structure of the regime did not generate records to document the rising volume of market exchange and commodity production that certainly occurred during the seventeenth- and early eighteenth-century sway of the Nayakas at Madurai. Long-term trends, however, indicate the process by which market networks rose to increasing prominence in peasant life before the mid-1700s. We have seen that waves of warrior and peasant migration after 1300 subdued tribes that commanded stretches of dry land between medieval agricultural cores in the Tamil country. Those tribes and their conquerors settled down to farming. They populated communities on the land between irrigated core zones, and dispersed techniques of dry farming and warfare throughout the peninsula. They thus increased the diversity of crops grown in regions like Tirunelveli and shortened the distances between communities that produced complementary products for exchange. Even as they established conditions for multiple circuits of local trade, their skills as warriors also increased the purchasing power of fighting men. Because they consolidated their control of territory with militant caste and kinship organization, their subsequent integration into a regional order demanded long years of warfare and a powerful Nayaka standing army, supported by allied poligar forces. To sustain this armed state apparatus required constant expenditure on ceremonial splendour and on military muscle. Revenue for these purposes came partly from plunder and occasional tribute, but more importantly from regular tribute payments that became tantamount to taxation on agriculture and trade. Collected by layers of intermediaries between localities and the capital, most of this taxation never reached Madurai, but stayed instead in local official hands to be spent on local and sub-regional state operations. As the state demanded more tribute, it protected trade and producers who generated more profits to tax. Population growth and burgeoning towns housing state officials, traders, and temples amid widening circuits of commerce lowered transaction and transport costs well below medieval levels.

The volume of sea trade also increased. First the Portuguese and then the Dutch, both established on the Tirunelveli coast and in nearby Sri Lanka, stimulated exports, brought precious metals, and acquired provisions for their own troops and ships.[16] Such coastal settlements of European traders dotted the whole of the Indian peninsula by the eighteenth century, and they clearly had their greatest effect on localities very near the sea, within a few days' bullock walk. Political disruption in the 1700s made this proximity even more important.[17] The Tirunelveli wet zone was in a favoured position to benefit from the region's position at the tip of India, a critical juncture for Indian Ocean traders and a prize for competing European seaborne entrepreneurs.[18] Protected by the Nayakas, and with abundant water to grow the rice to feed towns, the wet zone and especially the Tambraparni bustled with opportunities for profit. Forest products travelled along the river valley to ports. Rice moved between villages and towns. Artisans congregated in major centres for weaving the cloth demanded by export merchants.[19] Here, craft producers could supply the demand from inland urban élites and European markets at the same time. Merchants, moneychangers, and moneylenders could facilitate state tribute payments and European financial needs. Commercial activity generated more wealth for the state to tax. As a result, a complex web of intersecting state and market interests developed during the seventeenth and early eighteenth centuries in the Tirunelveli wet zone. Centuries of migration, settlement, and peasant productive labour provided a base from which inland state and overseas market trends could after 1600 make market networks ever more significant for village livelihoods. State wealth depended on trade, and commercially active locals depended on state protection.

REVENUE TRANSACTIONS

The Nayaka state crumbled after 1740, forcing difficult decisions upon the peasantry and creating the environment from which emerged a British colonial regime. We shall turn to the colonial transition shortly, but to understand eighteenth-century events we must dissect the webs of state finance that contending powers fought to control after 1740. For though the Nayakas disappeared and their revenue system was distorted and racked by violent competition among contenders for regional authority, it nevertheless survived through the eighteenth century, when accounts compiled by East India Company officers reveal its working principles. From the top of the regional state to the bottom—from Madurai to Tirunelveli town to sub-regional centres to villages—state officials granted patronage, protection, and titles to office, passing down authority to arbitrate disputes and to exert legitimate force. Upward passed payments of tribute that expressed subordination and inclusion in the realm: payments in homage, service, goods, and cash. Each node in the transactional chain involved tense negotiations and at least potential conflict. Those below were better able to collect from producers and thus to transmit revenues upward in the chain of authority. Those above held higher state authority and more coercive power. Lower-level authorities, to maintain themselves in this system, had to protect their local powers from all threats, and higher officials did not have the means to bypass local leaders. Reflecting this political fact, investigations in circar villages concluded in 1789, 1802, and 1804, that village accountants routinely reduced their tax obligations by under-reporting village cultivated acreage. No comprehensive survey of total cropped area had ever been accomplished in Tirunelveli before 1800.[20]

Segmented politically, the regional order was built of many tiny domains of revenue collection. By 1800, virtually every imaginable productive asset and social group was assessed for tax purposes. A list compiled in 1823 shows thirty standard taxes in addition to land tax, transit duties, protection fees, and levies on houses, streets, and fields.[21] Centuries of increase in the money supply accompanied diversification of coinage. In 1800, thirty-two types of silver and gold coins circulated in Tirunelveli. Clipped and debased to alter their value from place to place and time to time, they were minted as far afield as Surat, Porto-Novo, Tanjavur, Travancore, Arcot, and Madras. Grain and land measures also varied locally. Each circuit of villages could thus truly report to early nineteenth-century investigators its own traditions of revenue payment.[22]

But certain key principles unified the tributary revenue system. Most importantly, tax assessments were made in kind on field crops and converted into cash by standardized means that show widespread appreciation for the relative market value of crops. Irrigated land—*nanjai* (or *nunjah*, in Anglo-Indian parlance)—was assessed perhaps twenty times higher than dry land, *punjai* (or *punjah*).[23] *Nanjai* revenues were, moreover, collected using procedures that enabled officials to profit from price fluctuations in the paddy market. Low, even nominal, *punjai* revenues were collected from villagers only in cash, according to soil type, which provided a surrogate measure of land productivity. Garden land, watered by wells, was assessed at very high cash rates, reflecting the high value of garden produce and its perishability, which prohibited official commitment to its marketing.[24] The Tamil categories for land use thus took on new commercial meanings. *Nanjai* comprised irrigated land, whose characteristic crop was paddy; and, because of paddy's market value, *nanjai* also meant land assessed by state officials in kind, so that the state might profit from sales of its share of the crop, the *melvaram*. *Punjai* meant unirrigated land, which by definition grew dry crops, like millets; and, because of millets' low market value, *punjai* also meant land assessed at very low rates, in cash collected directly by village leaders and paid to state officials. Very high-value garden land paid suitably high cash rates, which became part of the meaning of garden land and of the wells that watered their valuable crops.

A second set of conventions distinguished poligar from circar land. Poligar land was mostly dry, and poligar territories were tightly organized, militant caste domains. Economically poor, they would surely have seemed to Nayaka officers politically impenetrable. Like all dry parts of the region, these lands would have produced some garden crops, salt, salt fish, palmyra products, cotton, cattle, oil seeds, and pulses, which generated some cash income for villagers. Small deposits of iron ore and small smelting works near the hills, basket weaving, carpentry, jewelry, pottery, and peddling—all generated petty profits. But poligars and their local followers fought hard over revenue from these sources. Since the kings at Madurai did, however, provide a focal point for order among poligars, tribute payments were essential, and these would most likely have been paid—first to poligars, then by poligars—in the form of ceremonial gifts, ritual homage, and above all military service instead of cash. This was one key rule of the regional regime under the Nayakas that did change dramatically after 1740, when cash was increasingly demanded from poligars, to the distress of many, as we shall see shortly.

Dry lands and poligar domains were thus for the Nayakas a critical military base but not a lucrative source of revenue. The state relied on revenue from irrigated villages. Early nineteenth-century records indicate the extent of that dependence. In 1820, about 20 per cent of all Tirunelveli land—irrigated land—provided 85 per cent of all state revenue from field crops. Most revenue from trade, crafts, and other sources would have also come from riverine locales, where urban occupations concentrated. At the same time, of course, much of the state's income would have been spent in these same irrigated milieus. As for poligar tribute, even after 1801, when it had increased dramatically over the 1700 level, poligar tribute, or *peshcash*, as it was called, contributed only one-sixth of the regional state revenue, though poligar lands held one-third of the Tirunelveli population and more than one-third of its land.[25]

The critical set of state financial transactions centred on paddy fields. Revenue officers made a thorough account of procedures in Settur village in 1796 (Table 1). The *qanungo*, a local revenue official, supervised the division of the grain heap on the threshing floor; he made deductions from the gross produce to pay village watchmen, overseers, labourers who had reaped and threshed the crop, ploughmen, and workers who bailed water from the tank to nourish the crops when water ran low. In addition, he made a deduction for the village *maniyam*—village management fees— in turn divided among the landowners, village servants, and an unspecified group of *maniyamdars*, probably landholders who managed village external affairs. Finally, cultivators and government divided the remainder, the *qanungo*'s fee being taken from the landowner's share. Government agents in turn charged for protection (*kaval*) and took one-quarter of the fees paid for labour supervision (*kankanam*), some of which they must have provided.

Where paddy crops were unpredictable because of poor irrigation, this on-the-spot division of the grain heap seems to have been standard practice. The procedure for settling the annual revenue account (*jamabandy*) was more complex when good irrigation, regular crops, and established grain markets prevailed, that is, in the wet zone. Here revenue assessment and collection by division of the crop, which East India Company men called 'amani', began before the harvest, when calculations were made on palm-leaf manuscripts, as the crop ripened in the fields. Arriving on the spot at a sufficiently late date in the growing season, state agents estimated the gross produce in a village, and set an estimated *melvaram*, with contractual provisions for deviations

Table 1. The Division of the Crop at Settur Village, 1796

	% of Harvest
Cultivators' Share (kudivaram)	
½ net produce (after deductions)	36%
minus *qanungo*'s fees	–1%
plus share of village *maniyam*	4%
	39%
Government's Share (melvaram)	
½ net produce (after deductions)	36%
protection (*kaval*) fees	7%
¼ of supervision (*kankanam*) fees	.1%
½ of *qanungo*'s fees	.4%
	43.5%
Service Fees	
Qanungo	.4%
Labour Supervisors	.5%
Reapers and Threshers	4%
Ploughmen	4%
Waterers (for bailing from tank)	.1%
Village Maniyamdars	6%
	15%
Total	97.5%

Source: PBR, IOL, 19 March 1798, pp. 2175–90.

in the actual harvest. From this point on, procedures for *kar* and *pisanam* harvests differed. Most valuable in the market, kar paddy, harvested from September to November, usually as a second crop, could not be assured in most years, and would be divided in the grain heap, as in the Settur model. The official received only grain as tax payment. For the *pisanam* crop, however, reaped from January to April throughout the mixed and wet zones, government agents would compute the estimated cash value of the *melvaram*, using an official local harvest price, known as the *jamabandy* price, for each village. The leading landowners would be responsible for paying the land revenue: on the principle contained in the *Sukraniti* and quoted above, they would advance three-fifths of the value of the *melvaram* grain in cash. They had also to provide some security for the remaining two-fifths of the *melvaram* as a condition for official permission to reap the crop. Threats to obstruct the harvest or to abscond with the grain became useful levers for revenue agents as the crop neared maturity. Then, having collected their due at harvest time in money and grain, government agents sold paddy throughout the coming

months to generate the state's needed cash revenue. As for any grain merchant, security for stores of paddy against robbers and embezzling hired
hands was always costly and troublesome.[26]

The paddy market thus transformed grain into government revenue.
Speculating in the market became a key to official power at all levels of the
state. Assured of grain to sell during the predictable rise in prices between
May and November, agents with access to *melvaram* grain stores could use
government grain for the personal profits they needed to remain viable
intermediaries in the revenue system. Profits would be especially high when
a poor *kar* followed a good *pisanam* season, which would accelerate rising
prices after September. But any average year would provide ample income,
as we can see reflected in paddy seasonal price trends.

There exist no minute price data before 1800, and no regional data in detail
until the late nineteenth century, when information was gathered as part of
administrative modernization discussed in the next chapter. Price levels
would, of course, have been much higher during the decades after 1875, and
local prices would have then become much more uniform than before the
building of the railway. But monthly prices from 1875 to 1893, recorded in
the *Statistical Atlas of Madras Presidency for F. 1350*, still reflected seasonal
ups and downs characteristic of much earlier times, caused by the rhythm of
the monsoon and of agricultural production through the year. Relative average prices, in short, from one season to the next, would not have changed their
course of movement from the eighteenth to the late nineteenth century,
though, as I will argue in Chapter Five, improvements in transport and in irrigation would probably have made late nineteenth-century relative seasonal
prices more consistent over space and time. This said, the late nineteenth-
century price data show that the chances for making more than a 5 per cent
return on sales of paddy bought at March–April prices reached a high of 80
per cent in July and August. After that chances declined to 55 per cent in
November, because both wet and dry crop harvests would lower the value of
pisanam crops in storage. Though bad *kar* conditions or dry-land drought
could generate high profits from sales of stored grain, such profits would be
a gamble on the monsoon, and losses from rodents, rot, and theft would increase over time. Consequently, in the eighteenth century, any paddy left in
government stores as late as November or December might have to be sold
at a loss, barring poor autumn weather.

With their hands on the grain store and their eyes on local prices,
eighteenth-century local officials were key actors in the grain market, buying and selling grain on private and public accounts to boost their own and
government income. In addition, of course, their grain had to feed soldiers

stationed nearby (and resident permanently in the fort at Palayamkottai). Local agents were by no means disinterested bureaucrats. Even under the Nayakas, and certainly by the late 1700s, the distinction between 'public' and 'private' did exist, but more as a gray area for discretionary judgement than as a sharp line. State income depended upon local officials' ability to make advances in anticipation of land revenues, and to buy and sell *melvaram* grain in response to local prices. This was not a system that could be managed by bureaucrats from a distance, and attempts to work it bureaucratically did not work. In 1807, a British collector in Tirunelveli had to wait for approval from Madras to lower official selling prices after a bumper harvest in September and October; the month delay meant rotted grain in storage and lost revenue.[27]

In the net of transactions that produced state income, there was no clear division between private and public, or economic and political power. During the 1700s, and probably before, each officer at each level of state authority contracted what the British called 'leases' with the officer above, paying in advance to be authorized to collect, in turn, from below. At the pinnacle of the system in Tirunelveli, the delavoy remained one of the richest and most powerful men in the region; his family owned fifty-two villages in the mid-nineteenth century, clearly the winnings of many generations' dealing in grain, land, and revenue contracts.[28]

Swarms of moneyed men worked the middle rungs of the revenue chain; they varied in wealth from renters of a few villages to bidders for whole sub-regions. The Company received twenty bids for the entire Tirunelveli revenue in 1790, indicating that others had risen to the delavoy's financial level.[29] Many sub-regional renters would have been grain merchants like Muttuswamy Nayaka, who operated in Tirunelveli town and became one of its largest wholesalers by his success as revenue contractor and securer.[30] At the base of the system were key families whose intimate control of the grain heap, village credit, and local know-how constituted the primary links in the revenue chain. These families had intimate knowledge of the harvest, *melvaram* accounts, *jamabandy* prices, market fluctuation, and official personnel. In fact, they did much local selling of *melvaram* grain.[31] The base of the state financial system was thus built inside agricultural communities, and this, more than any other level of the system, survived intact into the nineteenth century.

VILLAGES

By working the land, building caste alliances, moving and settling in villages and towns, and making lasting arrangements to define order among unequals, the people who produced wealth from Tirunelveli soil had developed three major styles of community life by the later days of Nayaka rule. One community type characterized each agricultural zone in the plains, though the mixed zone did contain communities characteristic of the dry zone, and vice versa. Each community type, in turn, defined a local subculture that was spread throughout each agricultural zone. Thus for simplicity I will refer to wet, dry, and mixed communities as types that define local order in each zone, though in fact this convention simplifies the historical and geographical situation somewhat. By this simplification, we can more clearly follow events as the community level from the founding through the evolution of British rule.

The Dry Zone

Over the centuries during which communities in the parched terrain north and south of the Tambraparni developed, land was abundant and labour scarce. Little fixed capital was required for agriculture; the most important items were bullocks, ploughs, and wells. Survival risks were high, but anyone with family labour could find land to cultivate for at least a meagre subsistence. Calories produced per acre could not be raised simply by adding more labour without additional water, but there was plenty of land over which the population could spread thinly over generations. Many dry zone peasant families belonged to castes for whom moving in search of land into Tirunelveli remains today a living oral tradition: Shanars, Maravas, and Vadugas, whose ancestors settled the dry frontier in pioneer communities. Their life depended on the skills of hardy peasant households, who sought to command within close reach all the essentials for existence. Inter-family cooperation within jatis generated occupationally diverse and locally dominant peasant castes. Shanars were cultivators, merchants, priests, and warriors. Maravas were farmers, fighters, hunters, and priests. Vaduga cultivators fought for their land, worked the soil, and served priestly functions, too.[32] A farming jati in the dry zone became self-sufficient by necessity.

With open space all around, no single caste could control access to land in the dry zone, where dominance depended on close control of labour power by means of kinship, caste, patronage, and coercion. Even dominant caste élites remained cultivators, and even the richest non-cultivating landowner would have poor peasant relatives closeby. Because landowning, work in the fields, and dominance all went together, getting one's hands dirty in raising crops conferred relatively high status in the dry-zone cultural economy. Any caste could and would work the land. The 1823 census shows that despite its low population density, the dry zone's villages often had as many resident jatis as did villages in the wet zone; and most of these jatis would have tilled to survive. As a result, caste status did not become rigidly tied to specific roles in the production process, and did not play a dominant role in determining access to the means of production. The biggest landowner and the landless labourers in a village could be of the same caste.

By the same token, very low-caste families, such as untouchable Pallas and Pariahs, could in the dry zone set themselves up as relatively independent peasant households, giving their very low status in the regional caste system much less degraded social content here than in the wet zone. British officials noted this phenomenon in the nineteenth century, when they endeavoured to induce all 'labouring castes' to perform road work for wages, and discovered that dry-zone untouchables did not consider themselves mere labourers at others' command. Because they would not volunteer, and because they were not at the command of village high-caste families, Company officers had to use force to put them into road gangs, under the justification that all untouchable castes were of the same status, whatever their local circumstance.[33] (Such coercion was surely not unique to the nineteenth century, and perhaps was convenient during temple and tank construction over the centuries.)

Within dry-zone villages, inequality in control over productive resources seems to have arisen from several factors that could combine to create indomitable village magnates, or could conflict with one another to form competing factions led by powerful families with opposing sets of clients. Numerical size and physical vitality varied among families; fixed capital assets such as bulls, ploughs, and wells, would enable some families to live more independently than others, and perhaps to rise as local patrons.[34] One means to acquire such assets became ever more important: access to networks of trade and credit. In pursuit of wealth, moreover, some families were better connected than others, endowed with superior status in kin and caste networks. Among Shanars, the distinction between tree-climbing Shanars and landowning or merchant Nadars, and among Maravas, the importance for rank of lineal proximity to dominant chiefs represent two styles of ascribed inequality that could come to correspond substantially to material differences. The most critical factor, often combined with at least one of the other sources of local superiority, involved hereditary village offices, which remained the preserve of important families. These were the local legacy of state networks built under the Pandyas and subsequent rulers. These offices were especially important in the dry-zone community power structure: the headman (*nattanmaikkaran*), vested with highest authority (*anmai*); the accountant (*karnam* or *kanakkuppillai*), who recorded state revenue obligations; and the watchman (*kavalkaran*), protector and enforcer. Headmen almost always came from the locally dominant peasant caste, and were the primary link between local and sub-regional authorities. They paid village taxes to their superiors and were thereby authorized to collect from villagers by whatever means they saw fit.[35] Outside the Vaduga-dominated north-east, accountants took the caste epithet 'Pillai' as a rule, and may indeed have become an occupationally distinct jati, using this epithet that usually denotes Vellala status.[36] In either case, headmen and accountants commonly came from different castes, it appears; because both were powerful officers, this could provide the basis for factional feuds. Outside Telugu poligar domains, Maravas everywhere monopolized the position of watchman, and built thereby caste networks as specialists in protection. The powers of village officers, therefore, could in some instances be exerted in combination—most commonly, one imagines, when they faced together an outside threat; or could conflict with one another if, for instance, contending officers should compete for the same prize.

Officers commanded sizable grants of tax-free (*inam*) land to support their position in the community. That grants of land had been the preferred mode for compensating village officers in the dry zone before 1800 became clear to early nineteenth-century observers. By contrast, outside the dry zone, salaries for village officers in cash and/or kind were the rule, and most *inam* land was enjoyed by temples or Brahman families.[37] A register of all *inam* land compiled in the 1870s as part of a government effort to abolish all tax-free holdings reveals that even then dry-zone village officer landholding remained considerable. In a sample of 111 villages from that register, 44 headmen each held 22 acres, on average; 56 accountants held 17 acres; and 37 watchmen held 10 acres each—after decades of administrative effort to write such perquisites off the books.[38] This indicates how powerful these officers remained after 1800, a subject for further discussion in Chapter Four. Reflecting the scale of accountants' land wealth in the early 1800s, a British collector reported in 1817 that 'they in some few cases cultivate it themselves, or with hired labourers, but by far the greatest portion of the land is cultivated for them by the cultivating inhabitants of the village.'[39]

Dry-zone communities thus evolved in such a way that upon the brink of British rule there existed within them no structural correspondence between caste and class. Inequality operated within an environment in which it was difficult for any stratum to rise much above any other in village society. Ties that bound patrons to clients often included kinship and caste, and the few most powerful families in a community would be, more often than not, families with village office, relatively large landholdings, and some valuable fixed agricultural assets. These families would compose the inner core of the local

power structure. At times united, when war between chiefs meant war between villages, families also engaged in local power struggles to do battle
inside communities. Arms for battle were almost as important as arms for cultivation, and, in this rugged domain, survival demanded close cooperation
among close kin, who depended upon one another. In villages more distant
from one another than those in the wet zone, people in the dry zone nonetheless had ties that wove them into sub-regional realms: above all, ties of
caste dominion. They lived in a hard world of stiff competition and locally
tight sub-jati solidarity.

The Wet Zone

Irrigated land in the semi-arid south is scarce and highly prized; it exists only
as a result of intense labour, embodied in walls and ditches of earth and stone,
and expended in the drudgery of seasons in the paddy fields. Irrigation produces sufficient wealth to sustain not only people who labour standing in
water but concentrations of people whose work comprises management and
related tasks, as well as many who do no agricultural work at all. In the Tamil
country, irrigated agriculture developed under the Vellala–Brahman alliance,
through which high-caste landowners brought under their control land,
labour, and water; established their status in the agrarian system as a whole;
and developed technical skills to expand the irrigation economy, all at the
same time. The local order of wet-zone life does not seem to have undergone
major structural change after the fall of the Pandyas. New groups pursued
their interests in communities without disrupting the working logic of land
and labour relations.

It appears that irrigating peasant farmers pooled their resources within the
ur assemblies from very early times. Certainly by the days of *brahmadeya*
grants, it had become customary for any irrigated village to be owned by a
group of family shareholders, each endowed with a portion (*pakam*) of the
village's collective assets expressed as a fixed number of shares (*pangu*s).
Inscriptions record so many transactions between *ur* and *brahmadeya*
assemblies that their internal organization must have been quite similar, for
epigraphy would surely reflect any radical differences between them in the
nature of rights to land. Nineteenth-century reports also stress that Vellala and
Brahman landowning collectivities worked in exactly the same way, except
in matters of caste ritual custom.[40] We can thus suppose that landowning
patterns looked the same in both, though we have inscriptional evidence
primarily for *brahmadeyas*. Original *brahmadeya* grants (the only available
ones date from the thirteenth to the seventeenth centuries) all present similar

pictures.[41] In each, the land involved is described and its boundaries defined. This most often meant grouping several existing settlements; all the resources within the area are assigned to a set number of Brahmans in a fixed number of shares. The grant does not specify the land of any family or individual; land is for the group as a whole. It does not distinguish cultivated from uncultivated, irrigated from unirrigated land. It does not, as we saw in Chapter One, even distinguish payments in grain.

To own land thus meant to be a member of a family in a group of shareholders; and to own not soil itself but all the varied resources involved in one's family share. The land was not conceived as a clump of earth distinct from the social relations that made it productive, or indeed distinct from the trees and water and surrounding scrub that all fit together into the production process. Perhaps, as a result, the most basic word for land in Tamil, *kani*, also means a particular measure of land (fixed in the 1800s at 1.32 acres), as well as any hereditary right whether to land, office, or other resources.[42] To illustrate the meanings of *kani*, service caste families in wet communities, possessed a right (*kani*) to a share (*pangu*) of the village harvest as payment for services in the village throughout the year. Family members would each also have a claim to a share (*pangu*) in family assets, showing that one set of related terms in Tamil can indicate analogous rights within different kinds of collectivity. Owning land within a community of farmers on irrigated land was understood to be analogous to membership within a family.

Under the aegis of Muslim authority in the Tamil country, after 1750, the Arabic term *miras* came into vogue as a translation for the Tamil term *kani* in the sense of 'hereditary right'. A court case from 1849, for instance, describes the *miras* or *kani* right enjoyed by the headmen among the Palla workers of Tentirupperi village: 'fees received in grain or otherwise by the parties recognized as the heads of the Palla caste in compensation for services rendered by them in procuring labourers for repairs of irrigation and other purposes beneficial to government and to the village community in general'.[43] A similar position of headman for service castes seems to have existed for washermen, barbers, and others who might be needed by high-caste patrons for emergency services at any time. Thus, among service as well as landowning castes, *kani* or *miras* indicates a right of resource control by virtue of group membership. But by far the most comprehensive and powerful of all *kani* or *mirasi* rights were those that embraced irrigated villages as wholes. Families who possessed (in Tamil, literally 'controlled') shares in the village were *kaniyatchikkaran*; in the Anglo–Indian official lexicon they became known as *mirasidars*.

As in a family, how to define who would be inside and who outside the group within which shares were held became a key to community order. The ideal, most restrictive criterion for membership in a *mirasidar* collectivity would be direct lineal descent from an original shareholder. As late as the nineteenth century, some families claimed this status, and received in recognition special honours, and favourable tax rates.[44] Yet even in the early Pandya period, complex resource transactions in the local economy required broader criteria for entitlement to community assets. Mortgages, sales, loans, and gifts of *pangu*s were the transactional basis for *brahmadeya*s, royal income, temple finance, and irrigation development. The ritualized exchange relations that supported temple worship and Brahman communities—described in the previous chapter—effectively defined criteria for entitlement both wide enough to include all exchanges necessary to develop irrigation and narrow enough to keep paddy culture in the hands of a coherent caste alliance, the core Pandya élite.

By patronizing temples and Brahmans, Vellalas established themselves as a status group identifiable by regional dominance and ritual stature, so that ritual became the vehicle for alliances across kinship and territorial divisions. By shared participation in this ritual system, the Pandya peasant élite directed investments from royalty into irrigated communities, laid the basis for inter-village cooperation necessary for extensive development of irrigation, and set the criteria for *pangu* transactions outside the original village collectivity. All these were functionally significant elements in marshalling resources for irrigated agriculture, and the system worked extremely well. Inter-village cooperation (and, as we will see, conflict) would have been continual features of production routine, because drainage tied villages together over the lay of the land. Moreover, outsider investments in village agriculture were critical inputs at many points in the life cycle of tanks, channels, and dams, especially after floods or breaches in walls. Because expanding paddy culture meant trading in grain and speculating on future returns from investment in irrigation, communities had always to be open to exchange transactions in rights to land. The ritual complex established an institutional means whereby outsiders could obtain rights to village resources even as they venerated *mirasidar*s.

Court records show that by the nineteenth century it was possible for high castes other than Vellalas and Brahmans to own shares. Shareholding communities of more than one caste were not rare by then.[45] I have not found evidence to indicate that this mixing of castes among shareholders occurred before 1800; it might have. As a rule, restricting membership in *mirasidar* collectivities to people within the fold of the Vellala–Brahman alliance would have controlled productive exchange in these communities during the centuries before 1800. The ritual system that made this possible also enhanced *mirasi-dar* command of their workforce, to which we turn shortly. Reinforced by symbols of caste status and ritual honour, this community order proved extremely effective, and spread wherever irrigation spread in the Tamil country; it dominated the whole of the wet zone and scattered throughout the mixed zone.

Within a *mirasidar* community, a *pangu* constituted a family's right to a collection of resources, and represented a mix of individual and collective control over productive assets. One share would consist of one set fraction of the community's total assets. It could include payments from non-shareholders who paid for access to village land; payments from cultivators of land in which the shareholders had invested; produce from bits of land farmed by the shareholder's family or by labourers; access to trees, grazing land, and woods; claims on the labour of village servants; and rights to water. A *pangu* also embodied responsibility: to provide a share of capital and/or labour for irrigation building or repair; to pay a share of the state revenue demand and other costs incurred by the village as a whole; and to work within the established traditions of a specific shareholding community. It seems that individuals could invest their own assets, raise the value of their shares, and manage some capital assets independently of the group—in addition, of course, to buying, selling, and mortgaging whole or divided shares. Such enterprise may lie behind the fivefold rise in the value of one *pangu* between 1773 and 1837.[46] At the same time, however, it is recorded that many communities rotated specific fields among shareholders from time to time, a practice that generated numerous court cases in the nineteenth century, but how generally this occurred before 1800 records do not say.[47] A variety of local customs to accommodate family with community needs must have prevailed. In any local arrangement, the complex of individual and group rights—including people inside and outside the shareholding group—would have been staggering. The first European ever to observe ownership at work in irrigated communities reported that all the various claims had been recorded in village accounts.[48] But registers notwithstanding, these communities were rife with opportunities for conflict among closely interconnected cultivating families.

Because water flows downhill, conflicts of interest would have flowed across boundaries between irrigated communities. Along the Tambraparni, channels flowed through fields in many villages. If one took too much water, those downstream might not get enough. If channels clogged with silt because of neglect in one village, villages downstream would be deprived of their just due. Even a small tank might serve more than one village; and tanks built in a series so that one overflowed into another would forge bonds of inter-dependence among their respective villages. If one tank broke, it would release a flood to break the one below. A single tank in disrepair might affect one group of users of its water more than others, because uneven silting might clog one outlet more than another. Thus irrigation gives rise to many disputes over individual and small-group responsibility for collective and larger-group resources. If my fields do not get enough water, why should I pay as much for repairs as someone better supplied with irrigation? If you do not uphold your end of our collective bargain, why should I support your rights to water? Why should I pay for work on irrigation that will not benefit me directly at all? Within and between irrigation communities disputes would have been constant, heated, and in need of speedy, firm solution, so that paddy production could proceed and expand.

With conflict resolution a constant necessity, shareholders do not seem to have hesitated to take disputes outside their community for arbitration, and inter-community squabbles naturally required an authority outside of but respected by many distinct shareholding assemblies. Officers of the state undoubtedly served this role. Temple managers, poligars, and *sabha*s with extended authority over extended *brahmadeya*s were also in positions to do so. Certainly *mirasidar*s had no qualms about using the courts set up by the East India Company. Every kind of dispute imaginable—within families, castes, and shareholding communities, and between individuals and groups in separate villages—was rushed for resolution to the judges. In the six years from 1801 to 1806, the Zillah Court in Tirunelveli town heard 1,767 cases, almost all concerning property rights in *mirasidar* villages along the banks of the Tambraparni.[49] Thirty years later a collector reported that arbitration and adjudication were a continual burden for his staff and for the courts, because these villagers had no tradition of authoritative councils—panchayats—on account of their factional and conflict-ridden character.[50] Some sources of conflict were, of course, born of the nineteenth century, as we see in the next few chapters. But the need for authoritative decisions to resolve disputes within the production process was not: it was built into irrigated agriculture, and it became especially pronounced as a system of tanks and channels extended over time to involve many separate communities along the Tambraparni valley.

Power within communities centred on the most resourceful *mirasidar*s, for though the villages were collective entities, they were anything but egalitarian. Most recorded *brahmadeya* grants distributed shares unevenly at the outset. In one grant a Brahman was given six shares and another three shares, whereas thirty-six others were given one share each.[51] Family fortunes over generations aggravated initial inequalities; the village of Vasudevanallur was typical of recorded cases, where in 1849 two Brahmans, 4 per cent of the shareholders, owned 25 per cent of all shares, and nine Brahmans, 18 per cent of all shareholders, owned fully 57 per cent of the village.[52] Share distribution aside, the value of assets within shares would differ sharply, especially in the absence of a smoothly running system of land rotation among shares, and it is hard to envision rotation working so as to eliminate inequality. Fields farthest from the source of local irrigation were at a natural disadvantage, as were fields on high ground. In a collective situation, politics would also have played a powerful role in family fortunes. Individual families could usurp resources traditionally attached to shares, and then fight to keep them, either locally or by the favour of some higher authority. Again, a considerable number of court cases record such activity after 1800. But even before that, it seems that factions in villages were formed around families recognized as leaders in the community, who would have had many advantages in struggles occurring in that area between individual family and collective community assets. The heads of these families served, in the 1700s, as revenue contractors. In charge of village tax payments, they were dubbed 'leading shareholders' or 'head *mirasidars*' by early nineteenth-century East India Company administrators.[53]

Unlike the situation in the dry zone, village office did not become a base for power in the wet zone in the centuries before 1800. Remember that Pandya inscriptions do not record local chiefs resident in the wet zone but only in peripheral parts of the Pandya realm. There developed no tradition of wet-zone village headmen; their functions were served rather by leading *mirasidars*. Accountants and watchmen did not enjoy substantial tax-free landholdings; they relied rather on shares of the harvest from *mirasidars*, whose servants they were understood to be.[54] The status thus worked in and through village *mirasidar* bodies, whose power in the political economy of rice farming was supported from Pandya to British times. Furthermore, as the most highly educated, the highest in caste status, and the most socially mobile strata in the region as a whole, landed Brahmans and Vellalas became core personnel in sub-regional networks of state and market activity. *Mirasidars* became official revenue contractors and merchants; indeed, *mirasidars* were the government in the wet zone, not only at the village level; they and their caste stratum peers comprised the sub-regional ruling class.

Mirasidar wealth, education, and cultural refinement depended on freedom from work in the fields. Over centuries, landowning in wet communities became more and more detached from agricultural labour, and landed families could thus turn their minds toward more exalted achievement. Pre-medieval peasants had probably worked their own irrigated fields, but under the Pandyas this would have become increasingly rare. As the infrastructure of irrigated agricultural developed, fixed capital—in tanks, channels, dams, and fields—rose in value relative to labour.[55] Population growth and Pandya conquests generated numbers of cultivators excluded from rights to irrigated land; and more intense cultivation made work more continual, both in the fields and in irrigation building and repair. As Brahmans became the cultural model of élite behaviour and style among dominant peasants, not putting one's hands in the mud would have become a mark of entitlement to élite status. To own land in a village came to mean overseeing its productive use, forseeing its productive potential, and seeing that irrigation works were built, repaired, and managed properly. All of this meant supervising the labour of others. In the light of these features of landowning among medieval paddy farmers, it is suggestive that the word for land and land right, *kani*, is derived from the verb 'to see'.

Exactly how Vellalas and Brahmans obtained client cultivators to labour for them remains unclear. Pandya wars with tribal chiefs probably procured workers from the defeated populations, because both major landless labourer castes—Pallas and Pariahs—boast even today distant martial traditions, and some families from these castes maintained themselves as independent cultivators outside the wet zone, as we have seen. One of the Mackenzie Manuscripts records an oral tradition in which the Pallas are said to be 'mountain people' who settled in the plains.[56] This change of milieu might have been forced on them by wars with Pandya armies, although, on the other hand, primitive cultivators from the hills or plains might have voluntarily exchanged their precarious independence for better-fed subservient status in irrigated villages. The nutritional security of wet land has induced independent landowners to forfeit ownership for irrigation on their land; many such cases appear in the nineteenth century.[57] For those with only labour to barter, client status might have seemed a tolerable price to pay for a position, however lowly, in the wet-zone economy. Deals of this sort would have been struck, no doubt, in conditions of dire necessity, during droughts and wars that hit hardest outside the wet zone. In command of water from the Ghats, Brahmans and Vellalas were in a strong position to establish themselves as non-labouring landed élites.

Labouring client cultivators, of course, entered the caste system at the very lowest stratum. They traded subsistence for untouchability in each generation. Their lowliness found expression in public behaviour directed toward them— in temples, fields, housing locations, and on roads.[58] Labour itself became lowly in the cultural economy of irrigated agriculture. The physical lowness (*pallam*) of fields and channels (*pallakkal*) embodied the lowliness of fieldworkers, known as *pallakkudi*—low people—Pallas. Ritual pollution, associated with untouchable work, reinforced the desire of landowners to escape field labour, and at the same time limited the social and economic mobility of field hands, reinforcing their dependence on high-caste landowners.

Probably long before the nineteenth century, and most certainly by then, Pallas performed almost all the most gruelling work in paddy cultivation in Tirunelveli. Labour organization reflected the variety of jobs that Pallas had to perform. Building and repairing irrigation works were gang jobs for men, who dug, hauled, and piled dirt and rock. Gangs would also have built roads, temples, and other buildings. Groups of a few men would plough, manure, and thresh, whereas groups of women planted, transplanted, weeded, harvested, and hauled to both threshing floor and storage. Men worked mostly with stone and earth, women with seed and grain. Small-group tasks could be done on a field-by-field basis, each *mirasidar* contracting for work individually. But at peak points in the production cycle, as during the weeks when *kar* harvest and *pisanam* sowing occurred simultaneously in a village, coordinated work would have been necessary. Finally, drying, storing, measuring, and carting grain were jobs for individual workers, which merged with domestic chores like sweeping, cleaning cattle stalls, and running errands for *mirasidar* households.

A variety of labour relations organized the performance of these varied jobs. Though the mix of *mirasidar* collective and individual labour management would have varied according to the distribution of land among shareholders and the degree of village cooperation, in general it seems that agricultural labour operations were organized through dyadic contracts between *mirasidars*, either as families or as a community, and various client labouring households. Some client cultivators would have had their own stock and sufficient labour to cultivate as sharecroppers. Some would have worked for a daily grain wage, paid seasonally or by the task. Some would have worked for only one household and other families for the village as a whole.[59] Gang labour, however, would be demanded by *mirasidars* of labouring caste groups as a whole. As we saw in the village of Tentirupperi, a Palla headman would be charged to raise work gangs when needed, and would receive special status by his position.[60] In some villages, the Palla headman might have organized the entire production process, working for one large absentee landowner or upon temple land, a situation that seems to underlie the seventeenth-century Tamil folk drama, *Mukkudal Pallu*, whose hero, as headman, seems to have had considerable skill and some social status.[61]

Over the centuries, a spectrum of bonds thus developed between landowners and cultivators. Tenancy was, of course, widespread. Vellalas and lower non-Brahman families often became tenants themselves, working land with their own or hired labour. Tenancy contracts before 1800 probably followed a pattern standard thereafter, when tenant obligations varied according to the quality of irrigation and the respective contributions to production costs of landlord and tenant. Sharecropping seems to have been most common on less well irrigated land; the share (*varam*) of the crop paid to the landowner would increase, the more adequate the water supply. This arrangement would spread the risk of a bad season, and reward the landowner for providing good irrigation, which he would be responsible to maintain. On the very best irrigated land, where sufficient water for paddy was certain, landowners could demand a fixed grain rent, called *pattam*, which also prevailed on temple lands and elsewhere when landowners did not supervise the division of the grain heap. Tenants of all kinds paid more when landowners supplied bulls, ploughs, manure, seed, or other items; or when they provided advances of grain for food.[62]

The poorer the tenant, therefore, the more he would rely upon *mirasidar* capital and food advances; and hence the more dependent his position. The very poorest clients, of whom the Pallas clearly composed the majority, could at best establish themselves as share-croppers or as fixed-rent tenants. Without capital or crops by which to repay debts, they would have had to repay with family labour. With nothing to barter for food but their toil, many Palla families because perpetually bonded to *mirasidar* families or to whole *mirasidar* villages. Rights to the labour of Pallas became an asset like any other for shareholders; one that could be bought and sold, given as dowry, and attached to plots of land, an integral part of the soil.[63] When they observed this bondage, British observers called it slavery, though its origins and internal dynamics were quite different from the Mediterranean and trans-Atlantic slaveries that informed their use of the term.[64]

Thus the wet community evolved as a highly stratified social milieu where access to the means of production was thoroughly identified with caste status. In stark contrast with the dry zone, the wet zone was not a land of rustic warrior–peasants, but of two distinct peasant strata: one owned land but did not labour; the other laboured without owning even, in many cases, rights to its own labour power. Here our standard notion of 'peasant' does not seem to fit at all. Yet in its management and cultivation, the farm remained a family affair, albeit tied into a strong community order. Farms were small; they were worked with pre-modern technology; they were worked as a way of life, not as a business for profit. Farmers were, moreover, subject to taxation by ruling élites. Many peasant attributes thus apply to farmers within wet communities, though they comprised two strata, indeed two classes, defined objectively by relative access to the means of production, and subjectively by their caste identity. The élite stratum was a peasant élite, who lived on farms in farming communities, yet had become long before the 1700s refined, educated, and socially mobile. From these families came many of the region's most powerful, learned, and able people in the arts, literature, business, and government.

Mirasidar high culture made the village itself the home of Tamil erudition and classical Sanskrit wisdom. These were peasants of a very special sort; perhaps unique in the degree to which they combined attributes normally assigned either to rustic family farmers or to urban élite intellectuals. They were country folk with wide horizons, who needed protection and arbitration from ruling authorities, and upon whom rulers in turn depended to establish the economic and ideological foundation for any stable regime.

The Mixed Zone

The contrast between wet and dry communities demonstrates that peasant living standards, wealth, political power, and social status came to depend not on caste status above all, as a conventional image of traditional India would suggest, but rather on family access to agricultural assets within a specific milieu. These assets included symbolic resources—caste status, temple honours, official titles, and cash—among which status was seemingly most predictive of material status, including as it did reference to one's kin group and appropriateness for honours and titles. Yet caste ranking did not predict family material stature across agricultural zones. Lower down the scale than Brahmans and Vellalas, Telugu and Marava peasant–warriors nevertheless commanded the dry zone and its resources; even Shanars held sway in stretches of the south-east. Lowest of all, the Pallas and Pariahs who farmed their own land in the north lived more independently than their wet-zone counterparts could ever have done. Comparing wet and dry communities, caste status by itself predicts peasant living conditions only where it became equated historically with the ownership of fixed capital, that is, in irrigated communities; here caste strata became so dominant politically because the wet zone provided the financial base for regional states, and rulers supported the Vellala–Brahman alliance. Within any community, families varied in stature within castes according to their control of capital valued in their specific milieu. To own a well in the wet zone meant little compared to what it would mean in a dry-zone village. Everywhere the value of land as capital depended on its water supply.

Vellalas and Brahmans became a formidable élite in the Tamil country because during the days of the Cholas and Pandyas they seized the land best supplied with drainage. After 1300, the states they built crumbled, but their capital retained and increased its value. They developed the social and material technology to extend and intensify paddy cultivation, protected and patronized by rulers whose realms depended on their water. Over time they commanded contiguous stretches of the infrastructure for irrigation in the northern coastal plains in Tanjavur and in Tirunelveli. From their extended networks of tanks, channels, dams, and fields, built bit by bit, one paddy crop at a time, grew the symbolic assets and social prestige of *mirasidar* élites.

That Brahman and Vellala élites would not have become such a prominent force in Tamil civilization without control of the Tamil country's best drainage becomes clear when we compare the position of wet and mixed-zone *mirasidars* in Tirunelveli. Though, as descendants of the Pandya élite, *mirasidars* attained élite status wherever they commanded drainage irrigation, their position relied on the quality of that irrigation. Accordingly, *mirasidar* stature remained over the centuries much less secure in the more isolated, less well watered irrigated villages of the mixed zone. The shifting fortunes of the goddess at Srivilliputtur, previously described, indicate the ups and downs of royal patronage for localities in this tract, especially when compared with the vast endowments enjoyed by the gods at Ambasamudram and Tirunelveli town. Following the demise of the Pandya dynasty, pockets of Pandya élite control and tank irrigation in the mixed zone were surrounded by dry-farming migrant peasant settlements. In search of land, water, and power came Maravas, Telugus, and Shanars, a new and threatening set of political interests to be reckoned with.

Evidence from nineteenth-century court cases and revenue records, discussed in Chapter Six, indicates that Vellala *mirasidars* tended to work land with their own hands more often in the mixed than in the wet zone; and in the mixed zone there were many non-*mirasidar* Vellalas who worked as tenants on Brahman *mirasidar* dry lands. Here, too, the relative productive power of dry and wet land was the reverse of that in the wet zone, not only because the soil was often better, especially in the north, but because the irrigation was often much worse. As a result, dry land surrounding irrigated villages became a much more important asset for *mirasidar* communities. On these dry lands, peasant households from various castes could set up dry-crop production, independent of any need for capital assets, that is, irrigation, under *mirasidar* control. Yet over these same dry lands *mirasidars* staked their claim, justified by their Pandya élite status and compelled by the value of this land as a potential source of income to supplement precarious irrigated agriculture. The fragmented character of mixed-zone irrigation meant that *mirasidar* kinsmen had nowhere to expand irrigation and hence to develop capital assets in agriculture. Instead they sought political domain over dry land, so as to gain thereby regular payments from dry cultivators established in the category of tenants. Thus the Tenkasi Pandyas, after the fall of Madurai, in the 1300s, rapidly established a bevy of new *brahmadeyas*, whose grants included payments from subordinate dry-land farmers.[65]

Faced with competition for dry land between Pandya élites and peasant farmers, the kings at Madurai, officials at Tirunelveli, and even poligars would have in principle favoured *mirasidars*, especially Brahmans, by the cultural logic of kingship itself. Though kings, large and small, could not have actually enforced sanctions with much regularity, there did seem to emerge a lasting, if tension-ridden, custom, based on this principle, in many communities throughout the mixed zone. Dry-land farmers would pay a cash fee annually for the privilege of farming land within a *mirasidar* village domain. The fee, called *swamibhogam*, proclaims in its very name its justification: it means roughly 'gift for the lord'.[66] That this fee continued to be customary into the nineteenth century testifies to the fact that state authorities continued to patronize the Pandya élite in their dealings with the mixed zone. *Mirasidars* remained in place as preferred state agents and revenue intermediaries in circar lands through the eighteenth century.[67]

Poligar lands may well have been different. Maravas assumed strong positions throughout the mixed zone. Marava chiefs controlled some good wet land in places, and became forceful protectors as well. In the north, Marava *kaval* chiefs and poligars seem to have respected the sanctity of *mirasidar* villages in general, even as they collected protection fees over the course of Nayaka rule. The fact that nineteenth-century records show no surviving custom of *swamibhogam* payments from Marava farmers to *mirasidars* may indicate either that Marava poligars never recognized *mirasidar* claims or that the custom went into disuse during political disruption after 1740.[68] Whatever the case, mixed-zone *mirasidars* from the north to the south were much more vulnerable to harsh political winds than their wet-zone counterparts, and winds blew hard after the fall of the Nayakas.

DECISIONS

Every second century after 800 brought trauma to people in Madurai city and forced critical decisions on people throughout the Tirunelveli region. Again, in the eighteenth century, the capital broke open with war, as it had in the tenth, twelfth, fourteenth, and sixteenth centuries. Again armies vied for the throne. When the Nayakas disappeared as the pinnacle of authority in the regional system of tributary payments, competition ensued that altered the rules of political negotiations throughout the countryside. The region broke into its constituent political regions, each the scene for distinct styles of conflict and accommodation that would gradually move villages at the tip of India into the embrace of British East India Company Raj.

Shocks to the Nayakas began in 1670, when troops from Mysore occupied north-western Nayaka territory, far north of Madurai. Losses then followed in rapid succession: Maratha armies from the Deccan took Tanjavur in 1674; the Marava Raja of Ramanathapuram declared his autonomy; and Dutch merchants recognized the raja's authority on the coast, with treaties and tribute, declaring him to be 'the protector of Tuticoryn and Kayalpatam', and paying to him what had formerly been given to Madurai.[69] By 1694, the Mughal emperor, Aurangzeb, had conquered much of the peninsula and his governor, the nawab of Arcot, demanded tribute from the Nayakas, after which the nawab and others took turns conquering Madurai. The city changed hands at least ten times between 1732 and 1755, and four times in 1752 alone.

A petition of 1754 demonstrates the insecurity felt by political actors in this treacherous scene. Submitted to the British East India Company governor in Madras, it claims to represent the wishes of poligars at large, but is signed by only one, Nama Nayaka, and indicates that political transactions were at this time very far-flung in the Tamil country. Nama Nayaka requests Company help in the effort to reestablish a strong centre of order at Madurai, where the Nayaka had lost battles to forces that he hoped would succumb to an army of allied English and nawabi soldiers. The poligar moans that he and his peers are 'in a very bad circumstance having no ruler to command us', having 'had no king for these twenty years past'. He expresses their willingness 'to pay tribute to the nawab according as it was customary' and promises that he would 'endeavour to deserve his honour's favour.' His motives are clear. Strong rulers at Madurai 'will settle the country'.[70] Disruption adversely affected many, including poligars, for it turned the terms of political negotiations in favour of the physically stronger contenders whose ambitions might be kept in check by a strong centre. As it happened, troops under allied Company and nawabi command seized Madurai in 1755, and held it for the rest of the century; but, like the first Nayakas, they had to fight a shifting set of military alliances in the region for fifty years to accumulate sufficient power for settling the country.[71]

Disorder, however, also created opportunities, whose pursuit perhaps prolonged the transition to a new regime and certainly changed the rules of tribute payment in the countryside. Local Marava *kaval* chiefs began 'acting like poligars' by collecting tribute from stretches of circar territory. Revenue agents used arms to press villagers for more of the grain heap. Poligars raided each others' land and took protection money from peasants and merchants wherever they could.[72] The price of protection rose, and early nineteenth-century inquiries indicate that people who needed protection paid dearly for it.[73] Oral accounts in the Mackenzie Manuscripts show that demands on poligars thrust deeper into their pockets. Company records show that the small and relatively weak poligar of Settur paid an annual mean *peshcash* of 1,554 strings of cash (*chukram*s) in the 1740s, but 2,524 *chukram*s in the 1770s, and 5,375 in the 1790s. Settur paid more frequently, too: in six years during the 1740s and nine during the 1790s.[74] These payments went to captains of armies from Madurai, who collected what they could according to the force they could bring to bear. Madurai's revenue rose 50 per cent above the 1744–1801 average during the regional command of Yusuf Khan, who toured Tirunelveli with a powerful army, and fell to a pittance during the height of poligar resistance to the Madurai regime.[75] Poligars in turn gathered in all they could, as did local revenue agents in circar land. After 1750, a variety of cesses that had not been collected before seem to have become routine: one a percentage commission charged by agents on the village revenue demand; another, called *desakaval*, a protection fee collected by poligars in circar territory, which was said to account for up to 40 per cent of some poligar revenue.[76]

Competing warriors fought for the fruits of agricultural and commercial labour, and clearly siphoned off funds that might have been used in productive investment, such as irrigation building and repair; this diversion retarded growth in water control. But all was not chaos and decay. Temple building, it seems, surged ahead; new temple construction grew fastest precisely where poligar competition and resistance were most intense, in the north-eastern domains of Ettaiyapuram and Panchalamkurichi poligars, and where *kaval* chiefs collided in the south. Warriors thus invested in temples to convert tribute into ritual honour. It is striking, therefore, that recorded temple construction did not increase in Marava poligar lands, perhaps because these Marava little kings were too impoverished and embattled for such investments, or perhaps because their handiwork did not survive.[77]

Some commercial investors also thrived. Because most fighting took place far from the Tambraparni, where Tirunelveli town, under the protection of Company and nawabi troops, was never seriously threatened, wet-zone paddy traders could seek high prices for their goods among hungry warriors.[78] The poligar of Panchalamkurichi contracted with boatmen and grain dealers near the Tambraparni delta to supply his troops, and merchants who supplied the Palayamkottai garrison made spectacular profits in collusion with local officials. Monied men with liquid assets to unload financed military competitors at all levels. The nawab sank in debt to Company employees. The delavoy owed huge sums to the Madras banker through whom he paid tribute to the nawab.[79] Moneylenders, called sowcars, paid poligar tribute and perhaps payrolls: 'Most of the sowcars of the Southern Provinces have open accounts with the Poligars, and are in the habit of frequent dealings with them. For management of their concerns they have Gomastahs, etc. established in the Pollams to wait on the spot to receive the produce of different crops that may be assigned to the liquidation of their demands.'[80]

Politically astute and well-connected people in positions to collect, transmit, store, and promise payments in cash and kind inserted themselves into profitable niches amid the turmoil. As the nawab's power grew after 1740, so did the number of Muslim names listed in accounts of revenue contractors, though the Medai delavoy continued as top regional contractor for many years and the East India Company itself assumed this position from 1783 to 1791. At the base of the tribute system, local contractors still came from the ranks of the established élite: they were mostly Vellalas, according to an account in 1793, when a list of major contractors in the region shows fourteen Vellalas, three Muslims, and one Chetti.[81]

The resolution of struggles over regional authority progressed in stages that probably parallel the trend two centuries before, during the sixteenth-century founding of the Nayaka dynasty. The armies of the new ruling power first seized control of the capital cites, Madurai and Tirunelveli. From this base they garnered the revenues of nearby irrigated villages, the most prosperous in the realm, and, in Tirunelveli, extended their protection over the whole of the invaluable wet zone. The strategic location of the central city, its temple, its fort, and its merchants served the forces of the nawab and the East India Company well, as it had the later Pandyas and the Nayakas. Revered, protected, and patronized by regional rulers for a thousand years, wet-zone agrarian interests looked to Tirunelveli and Madurai for support, and paid their tribute in return. They seem to have been won over to the new regime as early as the 1750s, disputes over the level of revenue exactions notwithstanding. For wet-zone élites, decisions did not revolve around a central moral question of loyalty to their king—or so it appears—but on question of self-preservation and loyalty to a system of regional order that paid due respect to themselves.

Peasants and poligars outside the wet zone expressed entirely different interests and evaluations of the eighteenth-century situation in their political decisions to fight to defend or to expand their territorial and tribute-collecting power in the face of new claimants to regional authority. Village leaders and their chiefs struggled to form alliances that would better their position. As the Company brought superior force to bear, many poligars, like Ettaiyapuram, felt blows that propelled them toward an alliance with the Company and the nawab. Poligar support—gained chiefly with Company victories in the field, though Nama Nayaka's letter indicates that some supporters awaited Company commanders when they first arrived in Madurai—turned the military balance of power slowly toward the nawab and his Company protectors. By the late 1790s, only the poligar of Panchalamkurichi, Kattabomman Nayaka, kept his men in the field. After long and valiant years of war, Kattabomman's men finally succumbed to allied poligar, nawabi, and Company forces in 1801. Thus over the decades, critical decisions about who among competing claimants would merit payments of tribute from villagers in the region produced the foundations for a new regime.

CONVENTIONS

All terms in italics are Tamil terms in transliteration, without diacritics. To make this book more accessible, I have used as few Tamil terms as possible and all of these are nouns critical to my presentation with no English equivalents. Such terms appear in italics. All Tamil terms appear in the glossary with full diacritics and *Tamil Lexicon* definitions. English or Anglo-India terms are substituted for Tamil terms wherever possible, their equivalence having been indicated by juxtaposition, with parentheses, on first citation. Anglo-Indian terms also appear in the glossary, with definitions and derivations where known.

Proper names are not italicized. Place names are spelled as most widely recognized today, personal names as spelled by the people themselves. Capitalization has been kept to a minimum by reserving it for proper names for people, places, and institutions. Official titles are not capitalized except when they have become part of a person's name. 'Tirunelveli' always denotes the territory called Tinnevelly District from 1801 to 1911, or its headquarters town, according to context.

Fasli years are fiscal years. F. 1260 began May 1, 1850 and ended April 30, 1851. For simplicity, I often locate events in *fasli* years in calendar years. One lakh is 100,000.

ABBREVIATIONS

References to archival sources appear in a form designed for ready reference: by series, volume, date, page, and location. This convention is necessary because a given document series may appear in more than one place with different volume and page numbers. During the East India Company period, district collector's correspondence was usually penned about one month before it was entered into the Board of Revenue Proceedings, so that TCR and PBR dates differ; the first dates its composition in district headquarters and the second its consideration by the Board of Revenue.

Annual revenue reports for fiscal years are cited in the notes simply as 'Jamabandy Reports', with their respective *fasli* dates; full citations appear only in the bibliography. Like some other British period records, Jamabandy Reports appear in Board of Revenue volumes both in the India Office Library and Records, London, and in the Tamil Nadu Archives, Madras; but their appended revenue accounts, with cultivation data, are preserved only in the Tamil Nadu Archives. I cite only the records I have used, though they may exist in more than one series and in more than one place.

Epigraphical Sources

SII   Government of India, Archaeological Survey, *South Indian Inscriptions*

TAS   Government of Travancore, *Travancore Archaeological Series*

Government Records

A.S.   appeal suit

F.   *fasli* year

G.O.   government order

IOL   India Office Library and Records

O.S.   original suit

PBR   Proceedings of the Board of Revenue

S.A.   special appeal suit

TCO   Tirunelveli Collectorate Office

TCR   Tinnevelly District Collectorate Records

TDCR Transferred District Court Records

TNA   Tamil Nadu Archives

court case number

NOTES AND REFERENCES

1. R. Satyanatha Aiyer, *History of the Nayaks of Madurai*, Madras, 1924, chap. 2; A. Krishnaswami, *The Tamil Country under Vijayanagar*, Annamalainagar, 1964, pp. 196–216; William Taylor, *Oriental Historical Manuscripts*, Madras, 1835, 'History of the Carnatic Governors Who Ruled over the Pandya Mandalam'; K. Rajayyan, *Rise and Fall of the Poligars of Tamilnadu*, Madras, 1974, and *History of Madurai, ARE*, 1940 1: 300–9, and p. II, p. 252–3.

2. Susan Lewandowski, 'Changing Form and Function in the Ceremonial and the Colonial Port City in India', *MAS*, 11:2 (1977), pp. 183–212; Rangacharya, 'History of the Naik Kingdom', *IA*, 44, April 1915, pp. 59–66, 69–73. Carol A. Breckenridge, 'Sri Minakshi Sunderasvaran Temple Worships and Endowments in South India', Ph.D. dissertation, Wisconsin, 1976, chap. 1; Dennis Hudson, 'Siva, Minakshi, Vishnu: Reflections on a Popular Myth in Madurai', *IESHR*, 14:1 (1977), pp. 107–18.

3. K. Appadurai, *Talavay Ariyanatha Mutaliyar*, Madras, 1950, Taylor, *Oriental Historical Manuscripts*, 2: pp. 113–16.

4. Taylor, *Oriental Historical Manuscripts*, 2: p. 215.

5. S. Kathirvel, 'History of the Maravars, 1700–1802', Ph.D dissertation, Madras, pp. 46, 96–7. Also William Taylor, *A Catalogue Raisonée of Oriental Manuscripts in the Library of the (Late) College, Fort St. George*, 3 vols, Madras, 1857 62, 3, pp. 356–60; T.V. Mahalingam, *Mackenzie Manuscripts: Summaries of the Manuscripts in the Mackenzie Collection*, 2 vols, Madras, 1972–6. 1: 167ft; R. Satyanatha Aiyer, *History of the Nayaks of Madurai*, Oxford, 1924, pp. 246–8.

6. Saletore, *Social and Political Life*, 1: pp. 208, 210, 215.

7. For histories of particular little kingdoms, see Nicholas B. Dirks, 'Little Kingdoms of South India: Political Authority and Social Relations in the Southern Tamil Country',

Ph.D. dissertation, Chicago, 1981 and 'The Pasts of a Palaiyakarar: Ethnohistory of a South Indian Little King', *JAS*, 41: 4 (1982), 655–83; Pamela Price, 'Resources and Rule in Zamindari South India, 1802–1903: Sivagangai and Ramnad as Little Kingdoms under the Raj, Ph.D. dissertation, Wisconsin, 1979.

8. About 15 per cent of all villages listed in the '1823 Census' in Nellaiyambalam, Shermadevi, and Brahmadesam *taluks* had more than one Marava sub-jati in residence. On *kilais* and sub-jatis today, see Louis Dumont, 'The Distribution of Some Maravar Sub-Castes', in Bala Ratnam, *Anthropology on the March*, Madras, 1963, pp. 299–301, and *Hierarchy and Marriage Alliance in South Indian Kinship*, London, 1957, pp. 17–18.

9. Kathirvel, 'History of the Maravas', pp. 27–40.

10. Dumont, 'Distribution of Some Maravar Sub-Castes', pp. 305–6. The six are Chokkampatti, Uttumalai, Auvudiapuram, Pariyur, Naduvakurichi, and Vandai.

11. Pate, *Gazetteer*, p. 373; Rangacharya, 'History of the Naik Kingdom', *IA*, 43, July 1914, pp. 135–7; O.S. #5, Tinnevelly Zillah Court, 1851, Transferred District Court records, Bundle 92, TNA (hereafter court records will be cited in this format: O.S. #5, 1851, Zillah Court, TDCR, 92).

12. For example, T.A. Gopinath Rao, 'The Krishnapuram Plates of Sadasivaraya, Saka Samvat 1489', *EI*, 9 (1907–8), 328–41.

13. H.R. Pate, *District Gazetteer: Tinnevelly District*, Madras, 1917, pp. 98–9. This latter practice is still visible in early nineteenth-century records.

14. Clarence Maloney, 'The Paratavar: 2000 Years of Cultural Dynamics of a Tamil Caste', *MI*, 48: 3 (1969), 224–40. Robert Caldwell, *A Political and General History of the District of Tinnevelly*, Madras, 1881, p. 71. C.R. De Silva, 'The Portugese and Pearl Fishing off South India and Sri Lanka,' *SA*, NS 1:1 (1978), 14–28.

15. Caldwell, *History*, pp. 70–83; Satyanatha Aiyer, *History of the Nayaks*, pp. 90–1; *Selections from the Dutch Records of the Government of Ceylon*, no. 5, 'Memoir of Jan Shroeder, Governor of Ceylon, delivered to . . . Lubbert Van Ech on March 17, 1762, trans. E. Riemers, Colombo, 1946, pp. 33–47. The major treaties were signed in 1669, 1685, 1690, and 1711.

16. Frank Perlin, 'Proto-industrialization and Pre-colonial South Asia', *PP*, 98 (1983), 30–95, emphasizes connections between overseas trade and inland economic life through monetary circulation. For South Indian coastal commercialization in this period, see A.I. Chicherov, *Indian Economic Development in the 16th–18th Centuries: Outline History of Crafts and Trade*, Moscow, 1971; and articles by L.B. Alaev in Tapan Raychaudhuri and Irfan Habib (eds), *The Cambridge Economic History of India*, vol. 1, *c. 1200–c. 1750*, Cambridge, 1982, pp. 226–34, 315–24.

17. Joseph E. Schwartzberg (ed.), *Historical Atlas of South Asia*, Chicago, 1978, pp. 49–50. See also Ashin Das Gupta, 'Trade and Politics in Eighteenth Century India', in D.S. Richards, (ed.), *Islam and the Trade of Asia*, Philadelphia, 1970, pp. 181–214, and his article in Raychaudhuri and Habib (eds), *Cambridge Economic History*, 1: 407–33.

18. Holden Furber, *Rival Empires of Trade in the Orient, 1600–1800*, Minneapolis, 1976.

19. The '1823 Census' shows concentrations of artisans, especially weavers, in towns in the wet zone and on the road from Tenkasi to Madurai. The largest concentrations were not at the coastal export centres, of which Tuticoryn was the most important.

Aggregations of weavers were largest in the vicinities of Ambasamudram and Tirunelveli towns, where rice, patronage, and inland demand were strong and protection secure.

20. PBR, IOL, 19 March 1798, pp. 2142–53. TCR, TNA, vol. 3598, 1803, pp. 45–51, 200–7; PBR, TNA, 11 July 1803, vol. 351, pp. 7408–40; S. Lushington, *Report Regarding the Tinnevelly Poligars and Sequestered Pollams, 1799–1800*, Tinnevelly, 1916, TCR, TNA, p. 12.
21. See the '1823 Census', 'Sources From which Revenues Derive'.
22. TCR, TNA, vol. 3587, 1807, pp. 120–5, and vol. 3582, 1807, pp. 267–9. In 1830, sources list 586 different rates of assessment for land classified as irrigated but planted with dry crops and 928 rates for land irrigated with well water. In 1835, government taxed irrigated land at 146 different rates, and, in 1855, dry land at 497 rates. All this diversity in rates can be attributed to pre-1800 tax procedures, which were highly localized and generated distinct local revenue traditions, carried over into the nineteenth century by Company officials as a matter of course (se Chap. Four). Jamabandy Report F. 1239; TCR, TNA, vol. 7971, 1843, pp. 229–68; Pate, *Gazetteer*, pp. 286, 288.
23. Lushington, *Report Regarding the Tinnevelly Poligars*, p. 9.
24. PBR, IOL, 19 March 1798, pp. 2142–53; M. Hodgson, 'Report on the Province of Tinnevelly', 24 Sept. 1804, TCR, TNA (hereafter: Hodgson, 'Report of 1804').
25. Jamabandy Report F. 1238; A.J. Stuart, *Manual of the Tinnevelly District*, Madras, 1876, pp. 161, 182, 194.
26. James Hepburn, *Collector's Report on the Triennial Lease*, Tinnevelly, n.d., TCR, TNA; Hodgson, 'Report of 1804'.
27. TCR, TNA, vol. 3582, 1807, pp. 58–60; PBR, TNA, 2 Feb. 1807, vol. 439, p. 879.
28. O.S. #1, 1851, Zillah Court, TDCR, 91.
29. TCR, TNA, vol. 3641B, pp. 7–14.
30. PBR, TNA 21 May 1812, vol. 571, pp. 5163–4.
31. Hepburn, *Collector's Report*; Hodgson, 'Report of 1804'; Jamabandy Report F. 1217.
32. Pate, *Gazetteer*, p. 338; Robert Caldwell, *The Tinnevelly Shanares. A Sketch of their Religion and their Moral Condition and Characteristics as a Caste*, Madras, 1849; Kathirvel, 'History of the Maravas', p. 17; K. Ramachandran, 'Vadamalaipuram, Ramnad District', in Slater (ed.), *Some South Indian Villages*, Madras, 1918, p. 32.
33. TCR, TNA, vol. 7983, pp. 68–70. PBR, TNA, 9 Nov. 1829, vol. 1213, pp. 12326–8; *Selections from the Records of Madras Government*, vol. 6, 'Correspondence Relative to Proposals for Organizing a Permanent Corps of Coolies', Madras, 1855, pp. 2–10.
34. For family cycles as a source of local stratification, see Max Weber, *General Economic History*, New York, 1927, pp. 8–9; Daniel Thorner, Basil Kerblay, and R.E.F. Smith (ed.), *Theory of Peasant Economy*, Homewood, Ill., 1966.
35. TCR, TCO, 'Ettaiyapuram Received, 1869–1878', letter to the Collector dated 20 Feb. 1874.
36. PBR, TNA, 27 April 1812, vol. 569, pp. 4210–83.
37. Ibid.
38. Computed from *Settlement Registers. Descriptive Memoirs of Tinnevelly District*, dated 1873–1877, TNA, produced during survey and settlement operations (see

below, Chap. Four). The sample villages were in Srivilliputtur and Ottapidaram *taluks*. For details, see David Ludden, 'Agrarian Organization in Tinnevelly District, AD 800–1900', Ph.D. dissertation, Pennsylvania, 1978, p. 167. On the subject of *inams* under the Raj, see R.E. Frykenberg (ed.), *Land Tenure and Peasant in South Asia*, New Delhi, 1977, pp. 37–80.

39. PBR, TNA, 10 March 1817, vol. 747, pp. 3046–60.

40. S. Lushington, 'Settlement Report, 29 Dec. 1800' rpt. in W.H. Bayley and W. Hudleston (eds), *Papers on Mirasi Right Selected from the Records of the Madras Government*, Madras, 1862, pp. 77–84.

41. See Chap. One, note 63.

42. Hodgson, 'Report on 1804', as quoted in Bayley and Hudleston, *Papers on Mirasi Right*, p. 106. H.H. Wilson, *A Glossary of Judicial and Revenue Terms*, London, 1855, rpt. edn, Bombay, 1968, p. 342.

43. A.S. #10, 1849, Auxilliary with Zillah Court, TDCR, 17.

44. A.T. Arundel, 'Settlement of Srivilliputtu', 18 March 1878, in *Papers Related to the Settlement of Tinnevelly*, TCR, TNA, p. 248.

45. TCR, TNA, vol. 7977, 1849, pp. 163–76; A.S. #108, 1848, Zillah Court, TDCR, 91; PBR, TNA, 2 Jan. 1822, vol. 934, pp. 279–91; A.S. #3, 1834, Auxilliary Court, TDCR, 4.

46. A.S. #43, 1840, Aixilliary Court, TDCR, 65. The share concerned is from Nettur, on the banks of the Chittar, where the share was valued at Rs 603 in 1773–6, Rs 1,590 in 1816, and Rs 3,254 in 1837. Prices fluctuated without comparable increase in this period (Fig. 5).

47. H.J. Stokes, 'The Custom of "Kareiyid" or Periodic Redistribution of Land in Tanjor', *IA*, 3 (1874), 65–9.

48. Bayley and Hudleston, *Papers on Mirasi Right*, pp. 78–9.

49. 'List of Records Showing the Nature and Volume of Suits in the Tinnevelly Adalat Court', Catalogue to TDCR, TNR.

50. TCR, TNA, vol. 7967, 1837, pp. 118–19.

51. H. Krishna Shastri, 'The Kuniyur Plates at the Time of Vengata II: Saka Samvat 1556', *EI*, 3 (1844–5), 236–58,.pp. 255–7.

52. TCR, TNA, vol. 7977, 1849, pp. 163–76.

53. James Hepburn, *Collector's Report on the Decennial Lease*, 5 Dec. 1812, Tinnevelly, n.d., TCR, TNA; Jamabandy Report F. 1235. 'Leading Mirasidars' also received separate enumeration in the '1823 Census'.

54. TCR, TNA, vol. 3582, 1807, p. 285. PBR, TNA, 27 April 1812, vol. 569, pp. 4210–83.

55. For data on increase in the capital component of production with new irrigation today, see Edward J. Clay, 'Equity and Productivity Effects of a Package of Technical Innovations and Changes in Social Institutions', *IJAE*, 30:4 (1975), 74–87. For increasing labour demand in irrigated agriculture in Tamil Nadu, see Z.W.B. Zacharias, *Studies in the Economics of Farm Management in Madras*, Delhi, 1954–57, 1: 110–16 and 2: 137–58.

56. *Idangai valangai jatiyar varalaru*, Mackenzie Manuscripts, Madras Oriental Manuscripts Library MS No. R-1572, cited in Burton Stein, *Peasant State and Society in Medieval South India*, Delhi, 1980, p. 184.

57. For examples, see TCR, TNA, vol. 7971, 1843, pp. 292–316, 321–40; and TCR, TNA, vol. 7977, 1849, pp. 163–79.

58. See Ernst Wiegt, 'Der Trockene Sudosten Indiens: Mensch und Wirtschaft im Tambraparni Tal', *Geographische Rundshau*, 20: 11, (Nov. 1968), pp. 405–14; Kathleen Gough, 'Caste in a Tanjore Village', in E.R. Leach, *Aspects of Caste in South India, Ceylon and Northwest Pakistan*, Cambridge, 1971, pp. 11–60. See below, Chap. Six.

59. Hepburn, *Collector's Report on the Decennial Lease*, pp. 9–10; W. Robinson, *Minute on the Proposed Settlement of Tinnevelly*, 1868, TCR, TNA, pp. 3, 14; O.S. #1, 1851, Zillah Court, TDCR, 91.

60. A.S. #10, 1849, Auxilliary with Zillah Court, TDCR, 17; A.S. #3, 1817, Zillah Adalat Court, TDCR, 75; A.S. #126, 1851, Auxilliary Court, TDCR, 17.

61. *Mukkudal Pallu*, ed. N. Setukumaran, Madras, 1973.

62. V. Krishnan, 'Tambraparni Ryot (A Study of the Rural Economy of the Tirunelveli District)', Gokhale Prize Award Thesis, University of Madras, 1931.

63. Lushington, 'Report', in Bayley and Hudleston, *Papers on Mirasi Right*, pp. 78–9. See also the sale deed, ibid., app. 4, ix–xxxiv. For 'rights in persons', see Suzanne Miers and Igor Kopytoff (eds), *Slavery in Africa*, Madison, 1977, pp. 7–11.

64. For British attitudes and legislation, see Benedicte Hiejle, 'Slavery and Agricultural Bondage in South India in the Nineteenth Century', *SEHR*, 15:1–2 (1967), 71–126. The study of bonded labour in pre-modern agriculture is still underdeveloped. For general approaches and comparisons, see Miers and Kopytoff, *Slavery in Africa*, and Orlando Patterson, *Slavery and Social Death*, Cambridge, 1982. For an economist's line of attack, see Robert J. Evans, Jr., 'Some Notes on Coerced Labor', *JEH*, 30:4 (1970), 861–6. For a spatial approach, see Carol A. Smith, 'Exchange Systems and the Spatial Distribution of Élites: The Organization of Stratification in Agrarian Societies' in Carol A. Smith (ed.), *Regional Analysis*, 2, New York: 1976, 326–33. For a case study stressing cultural forces in the political economy of servitude, see Gyan Prakash, 'Production and the Reproduction of Bondage: Kamias and Maliks in South Bihar, India, *c.* 1300–1930, Ph D dissertation, Pennsylvania, 1984.

65. *TAS*, vol. 1, no. 6, pp. 43–4, 52, 61–88, 89–94, 106–14, 133–46.

66. This is my rough translation of an Anglo-Indian term that was part of common official vocabulary in nineteenth-century Tirunelveli. See Chaps. Four and Six, and Glossary, below.

67. For instance, the case of Tippanampatti, whose history is sketched in O.S. #41, 1828, Auxilliary Court, TDCR, 2.

68. To be more precise, I have not found cases in which such claims were contested in court or before revenue officers in the nineteenth century. This does not prove that no such claims survived, but it is suggestive, given the number and wide distribution of cases contesting *swamibhogam*. See Ch. Six.

69. Satyanatha Aiyer, *History of the Nayaks*, gives details. Also, see S. Thananjayaraja-singham, *A Critical Study of a Seventeenth Century Tamil Document Relating to a Commercial Treaty*, Peradeniya, 1968, p. 7, lines 229–30, and p. 18; and Price, 'Resources and Rule', p. 5.

70. Rajayyan, *Rise and Fall of the Poligars*, pp. 42–3.

71. For war stories, see Rajayyan, *History of Madurai*, and Caldwell, *History*.

72. Kathirvel, 'History of the Maravas', pp. 124–5, quoting a report from the Collector of Poligar Peshcash, 23 June 1892; S. Lushington, 'Settlement Report of 28 May 1802', TCR, TNA, pp. 2–3; Caldwell, *History*, Chap. Five; *Selections from the Dutch Records*, pp. 42–7; PBR, IOL, 21 Oct. 1793, pp. 6860–9; Caldwell, *History*; and Kathirvel, 'History of the Maravas'.

73. Hodgson, 'Report of 1804', parags 5–6. Thomas Munro criticized this view: A.J. Arbuthnot, *Major General Sir Thomas Munro*, London, 1881, I: 248.

74. Rajayyan, *Rise and Fall*, p. 26; Taylor, *Catalogue*, 3: 355–63. TCR, TNA, vol. 3583, 1808, pp. 309–11. The Company lowered Chokkampatti's revenue demand in 1787–97, presumably in the belief that it had been raised beyond the poligar's ability to pay; and, perhaps, to keep his people away from the Company's opposition. PBR, IOL, 21 Oct. 1793, pp. 6869–902. Nevertheless, Chokkampatti remained a problem for years to come: see Chaps. Four and Six, below.

75. S. Lushington, 'Settlement Report of 28 May 1802'. An abstract of this report appears in 'The Fifth Report of the Select Committee of the House of Commons on the Affairs of the East India Company', *Parliamentary Papers, East Indies*, rpt. Irish University Press, Shannon, 1969, vol. 3.

76. K. Rajayyan, *Administration and Society in the Carnatic (1701–1801)*, Tirupati, 1966, pp. 43–55; Caldwell, *History*, p. 104; Rajayyan, *Rise and Fall*, pp. 16–17; S. Lushington, 'Report on Desacaval', 16 Oct. 1800, PBR, TNA, vol. 264, pp. 8764–811.

77. These conclusions are based on *taluk* temple data summarized in Ludden, 'Agrarian Organization', Table 8, p. 147. Note that the 1961 census data on temples only considers major temples still in use in 1961. It is possible that a decline in Marava fortunes after 1800 (see Chap. Five) allowed for the decay of working temples. It is also possible, though unlikely, that temples were destroyed in warfare.

78. Caldwell's *History* has the most detailed battle narratives.

79. Madras Government, Foreign Department Sundries, TNA, 'Mr Hodgson's Report on the Dutch Settlements, dated 23 March 1818', App. B, 'Extract from a letter from Mr Irwin, dated 28 April 1783', p. 7; also Jamabandy Report F. 1217. John Gurney, 'The Debts of the Nawab of Arcot', Ph D dissertation, Oxford, 1968; see also Jamabandy Report F. 1245. PBR, IOL, 23 Sept. 1793, pp. 5815–19. Also PBR, IOL, 25 Sept. 1793, pp. 956–70, and PBR, IOL, 8 Aug. 1793, pp. 4882–9.

80. Lushington, 'Settlement Report of 28 May 1802'.

81. PBR, IOL, 13 June 1793, pp. 3196–205; TCR, TNA, vol. 3641B, 1790, pp. 35–6; PBR, TNA, 17 May 1831, vol. 1280, pp. 2914–17.

PART III

THE EUROPEAN INTRUSION

13

Introduction: The Twilight of Mughal Bengal*

ABDUL MAJED KHAN

INTRODUCTION

In a public letter of 25 November 1791 the government of Lord Cornwallis reported from Calcutta to the Directors of the East India Company in London,

We are much concerned to advise you of the decease of the Nabob Mahomed Reza Khan . . .

His honourable character, his regard to the English for a long period of time, and the services he had rendered in Bengal are testified upon the records of this Government and well known to the Company in England. His public and private worth equally made him an object of esteem, and they entitle his memory to respect.[1]

Such was the obituary notice of a man who had been a vital part of Bengal's history for over thirty years and witness to its history for nearly half a century. He had observed the irremediable decline of two empires, that of the Safavids in the land of his birth, Iran, and that of the Mughals in India, the land of his adoption. He had participated in the events which led to the eclipse of the Nawabs and to the rise of the English East India Company in Bengal. He had been the agent of the Company, the defender of the Nizamat, and had been a leading figure throughout what may be called the Anglo-Mughal phase in Bengal's history. That phase was brought to an end on 1 January 1791 with Cornwallis's abolition of the office of Naib Nazim and the final transfer of the Sadar Nizamat Adalat. Nine months later, having worked almost to the end

---

*Abdul Majed Khan, 'Introduction: The Twilight of Mughal Bengal', in *The Transition in Bengal, 1756–1775: A Study of Saiyid Muhammad Reza Khan*, Cambridge, 1969, pp. 1–16.

upon cases which had been awaiting his decision before Cornwallis's regulations were passed, Reza Khan died. It is the purpose of this book to study afresh the important, formative period of Reza Khan's career, down to the year 1775, and to reconsider his part in the events which shaped the pattern of British rule in Bengal.

To understand Reza Khan's career, and indeed to understand events in Bengal between 1756 and 1775 it is necessary, in the first place, to forgo the benefits of hindsight. To Reza Khan, as to every Indian of his day, this period was not that in which the British Indian Empire was founded, it was a phase in the long history of the Timurid empire. The overriding reality was that Bengal was Mughal. The reigning prince was named on the coin and in the Khutba and thus enjoyed the two prerogatives of sovereignty. He might be a tool in the hands of a minister; his mandates might be evaded or disregarded, nevertheless he was deemed 'the sole fountainhead of honour', and 'every outward mark of respect, every profession of allegiance, continued to be paid to the person who filled the throne of the house of Timour'.[2] Moreover no usurper, however, daring, felt able to outrage the general feeling by treating the emperor's name with disrespect: Nadir Shah sacked Delhi, but acknowledged Muhammad Shah as emperor; the Abdali invaded India repeatedly, but did not subvert Timurid sovereignty. Bolts may have been right in thinking in 1772 that 'if the youngest writer in the service had been sent with the authority of the Company to our Shah Allum, it was certain that his Majesty would have granted away the remainder of his empire . . .',[3] but it was also true that the Mughal grant was necessary, however obtained. Reza Khan had lived in Mughal Delhi as a boy and in Mughal Bengal under the still vigorous and effective rule of Alivardi Khan as a young man. On the issue of Timurid sovereignty he remained unyielding to his dying day, and no account of his relationship with Warren Hastings and the Company is intelligible if this is forgotten.

It is also necessary to consider what the nature of the Anglo–Mughal relationship was when Reza Khan came to Bengal, and the character it took after Plassey, if the Khan's behaviour is to be understood correctly. Before 1756, as Ghulam Husain noted, the English were known in Bengal 'only as merchants'.[4] The Mughal rulers and nobles were not unaware of the military abilities of the Europeans; mercenary Portuguese, Dutch, French, and English had long served in the imperial armies, especially in the artillery. During the Maratha invasion of 1742 Alivardi had sought the cooperation of the three European nations in Bengal, the Dutch, French and English,[5] and in 1744 he again asked the English for the loan of the services of thirty or forty Europeans to command his troops as 'his people were not trained up to the use of firearms' as the Europeans were.[6] Again, from Drake's narrative, it appears that the Nawab Siraj-ud-daulah's army, when it captured Calcutta in June 1756, contained several Europeans and Indo-Portuguese.[7] The latter may have been connected with the contingent which Murshid Quli Khan had recruited through the Portuguese padre at Bandel.[8] It is also known that the Bengal nawabs continued to maintain Christian troops, most probably Portuguese, at Chittagong right down to 1760–1 when the district was handed over to the English.[9]

The fact remains that for a century the English appeared in Mughal Bengal as traders, and that contact with them had been mostly indirect. In their negotiations for the acquisition of the three villages of Kalikata, Sutanuti, and Govindapur in 1698 from Azim us Shan, in those for the acquisition of further privileges from Farukh siyar in 1717, and in the political conspiracies of 1757 and 1760, the negotiators most extensively used had been Armenians, Christian by religion and Persian in culture.[10] In more normal times the Company had been represented in the Bengal Subahdar's court by native *vakils* or agents, usually Hindu, and these would treat with the Nawab's *mutasaddis*, secretaries or clerks, also usually Hindus. Only on very rare and important occasions did the Nawab himself grant interviews to the *vakils*, whose highest level of access was normally to the Rai-Rayan (a Hindu minister heading the revenue department) or to the Naib or deputy.[11]

This was only natural, for the military aristocrats of the imperial or provincial courts did not hold merchants in any high regard: they were useful subjects to be protected but not to be cultivated on the social level. Merchants did upgrade themselves by turning soldier or administrator. Mir Jumla for example, a merchant in origin, ended as one of the greatest Mughal generals, the conqueror of Assam.[12] But the reverse process did not take place, though a prince or noble might engage in commercial transactions as an extension of political power.[13] The Nawabs long maintained a virtual monopoly, exercised through selected favourites, of the trade in salt, betelnut, opium and saltpetre, or of the trade to Assam by way of Rangamati, while the Faujdars of Sylhet and Chittagong, by virtue of their office, enjoyed certain exclusive trade privileges within their respective jurisdictions.[14] The presence of an English merchant company in Bengal, however considerable its trade, could not disturb the picture of Bengal as a Mughal Subah.

Moreover, the pattern was not, in its essentials, broken even when the English returned to Calcutta in January 1757 at the head of forces from Madras. Admiral Watson of His Britannic Majesty's navy, and Colonel Clive, commander of the Company's forces were military leaders who could be recognized by and admitted to a Mughal society of military aristocrats. Their attack upon Hugli *bandar* or port on 9 January 1757 and their plundering of the merchants of that city[15] called forth a protest from Siraj-ud-daulah that the English were acting 'not like merchants', but simultaneously the Nawab declared to Clive, 'I know you are a soldier and as such I should chuse to be your friend'.[16] Clive had struck the right note, both by his victories and by bringing a letter of commendation from the Nawab of Arcot and demanding in another to be regarded as an officer of the King of England who, as he told Jagat Seth, was not 'inferior in power to the Padsha [or Mughal Emperor] himself'.[17] And with an intuitive understanding of the Indian attitudes he had appealed directly to the Nawab Siraj-ud-daulah, declaring 'I esteem your excellency in the place of my father and mother, and myself as your son, and should think myself happy to lay down my life for the preservation of yours'.[18]

Colonel Clive, Admiral Watson, and Major Killpatrick, known to the Indians then by their Mughal titles respectively as Sabut Jang (Firm in War), Dilir Jang (Courageous in War), and Dilawar Jang (Courageous in War)[19] were acceptable as soldiers, men of rank. They had also a claim to acceptance because they were Christians. The Nawab, in his letters to Clive, could appeal for his due regard to the treaty relationship between them on this ground: 'After having made peace to begin war again no religion can justify. The Marathas have no Books of God, yet are just to their contracts. You have the Book of God, if you are not just to your contracts it will be astonishing and unaccountable.'[20] The fact that Clive and his fellow countrymen were people of the Book in itself gave them a status superior to that of the heathen natives.[21] However, it was Clive's soldierly virtues and his professions of filial attachment which made him a particular object of regard. To the Nawab, and his nobles, Clive was one of their sort, a soldier and a nobleman, who would appreciate the gift of two leopards 'extremely good at catching deer', because he doubtless shared their own taste for hunting.[22] By 30 March 1757, Clive could report with satisfaction to the Nawab of Arcot that 'the Nawab in this country respects us'.[23] The respect was paid to the soldier, not to the merchants of the Company. 'Tell Roger Drake' not to 'disturb our affairs', Siraj-ud-daulah wrote to Clive on 10 March 1757, in a tone which showed scant respect to one who was constitutionally Clive's superior in Bengal.[24] In the same letter, again, Siraj-ud-daulah had asked Clive to 'send Dilher Jung [the Major] that I may speak my mind to him and send him back to you'.[25] The Nawab was greatly annoyed at Drake's correspondence with Manikchand— he was Siraj-ud-daulah's governor of Calcutta during occupation in 1756— and complained, 'I have delivered to Mr Watts the three Lack of rupees and I will finish the rest of the business in ten or twelve days, then why should Roger Drake write these letters privately'.[26] Even William Watts enjoyed a better status in the eyes of the Nawab. The reason was not merely the Nawab's disgust with Drake for causing trouble, but also the fact that irrespective of his official position (as Second of the Calcutta Council holding the chiefship of Kasimbazar) he was the accredited agent of Clive at Murshidabad Watts was all the more welcome because he had brought with him a contingent of artillery troops, one officer, one sergeant, one corporal and fifteen privates,[27] for which the Nawab had sent an urgent request to Clive. 'I desire that when you dispatch Mr Watts to Muxadabad', the Nawab had written to Clive on 14 February 1757, 'you will send 25 artillerymen with him for my service'.[28] Clive had readily complied with the Nawab's request, offering politely to pay for the troops himself. Watts could have no better way of creating a favourable impression at the city. While Clive and the Nawab corresponded direct or through Watts, Company business at the Durbar continued as before through a *vakil*.

The development of this new relationship between the Nawab and the English commanders was cut short, of course, by the development of a conspiracy at Murshidabad against Siraj-ud-daulah. As a new element introduced through Watts into the political life of Murshidabad, the English also became, for the first time, involved in it. The Anglo–Mughal relationship entered a new stage of development.

The newness was not in the origin of the conspiracy, but lay in the direction of its development. Soon after his accession to the *masnad* in 1756 the Nawab had faced a conspiracy at Murshidabad and a revolt at Purnea. Mir Jafar then urged Shaukat Jang to fight the Nawab, assuring him that several commanders and grandees at Murshidabad, including himself, looked upon Shaukat Jang 'as their only resource against the growing and daily cruelties of Seradj-ed-doulah's',[29] almost in the same way as a conspiracy headed by Haji Ahmad, grandfather-in-law of Reza Khan, had invited Alivardi to rise against Sarfaraz Khan on the latter's accession in 1739.[30] Siraj-ud-daulah had better success in 1756 against Shaukat Jang than Sarfaraz had against Alivardi in 1740. One reason for Siraj-ud-daulah's success had been his tighter grip over his capital, for all thoughts of getting rid of the Nawab, says William Watts in his memoirs, 'availed little, since the attempt was equally difficult and dangerous; and failing in it sure to be attended with sudden and certain destruction'.[31] In the conspiracy of 1757, however, there was, for the conspirators, 'one way to move, or rather to lessen the risk; and this also was easily discovered. It was procuring the countenance and assistance of the English'.[32] The English were no longer merely merchants of Kasimbazar, cut off from the social and political life of Murshidabad, as they had been only the previous year; they were now in Murshidabad, enjoying the friendship of the Nawab and, what is more, being courted by the latter for military assistance against the threatened invasion of the Abdali. The recapture of Calcutta by Sabut Jang and Dilir Jang,[33] and the forcing of the treaty of Alinagar[34] in February did not, to the Murshidabad nobles, mean anything more than emergence of powerful rivals of Siraj-ud-daulah, and to be courted against the latter.[35] The presence of Watts at Murshidabad was an additional advantage, and to make use of this, one of the enemies of the Nawab, Khuda Yar Khan, took the first move and 'sent several messages to Mr Watts'.[36] By 26 April 1757, Watts had reported a message also from Mir Jafar two days earlier saying that if the English were 'content' Rahim Khan, Rai Durlabh, Bahadur Ali Khan, and others 'are ready and willing to join their force, seize the Nabob and set up another person that may be approv'd of'.[37] A revolution began but it was not yet clear who was to replace Siraj-ud-daulah.

The determination of this matter came ultimately to lie in the hands of the English. The Fort St George Council had already advised the Fort William Council on 13 October 1756 'to effect a junction with any powers in the provinces of Bengal that may be dissatisfied with the violences of the Nawab's government, or that may have pretensions to the nawabship . . .'[38] On 23 April 1757, the Calcutta Council directed Clive to sound out the 'great people' at the Durbar and 'learn how they stand affected with respect to a revolution'.[39] By 1 May the Select Committee had received information of a conspiracy at Murshidabad and they spoke of themselves as allies, for they thought that with a revolution 'it would be a great error in politics to remain idle and unconcerned spectators of an event, wherein by engaging as allies to the person designed to be set up we may benefit our employers and the community very considerably . . .'[40] But a further consultation on 12 May shows that they were quite ready to act as principals, for they then seriously considered whether the Marathas should be supported before finally deciding upon the 'project of establishing Mier Jaffier in the Subaship if it can be any means be effected'.[41] Even later, when the determination of Mir Jafar seemed in doubt only a week before the battle of Plassey, Clive was putting up for consideration the notion of bringing in the Birbhum Raja, the Marathas, or even Ghazi ud din Khan, after the rains.[42]

The conspirators at Murshidabad, before Plassey, scarcely appreciated the nature of the English power which they were calling to their assistance. Mir Jafar, an immigrant into Bengal during Shuja Khan's time, was an almost uneducated soldier,[43] accepted into the ruling aristocracy because of his noble birth—he was a Najafi Arab Saiyid—and then because he had married Shah Khanum, Alivardi's half-sister. He was no politician[44] and unlike Alivardi whose name, Mahabat Jang, he later took for himself, Mir Jafar was never able to act as principal. (He had twice before been involved in conspiracies, one led by Ataullah Khan, Reza Khan's father-in-law, in 1747, and the other when Shaukat Jang had revolted in Purnea in 1756.[45] Even now he does not seem at first to have aimed personally at the *masnad*. In settling terms with the English he depended entirely on Rai Durlabh—Ghulam Husain states positively that the agreement was concluded in Mir Jafar's name by Raja Durlabhram[46]—and Scrafton reported on 30 November 1758 that 'the Nabob had only a cypher treaty and even that is lost'.[47] The pivotal figure in the conspiracy appears to have been Rai Durlabh, eldest son of Raja Janaki Ram, brought up and ushered into the military aristocracy by assignment of an army command and, on his failure as deputy governor of Orissa, made the Nizamat Diwan,[48] the job of *mutasaddi*, which fitted him. Rai Durlabh had been warned that 'if we [the English] were once permitted to march this way we should not quit Muxadabad these 3 years',[49] and it was he who objected to the lavish monetary promises in the treaty drafted at Calcutta, saying 'where shall he and Meer Jaffier be able to raise such a sum as two crores and a half in a month's time . . .'[50] However, he was silenced by the promise of five per cent for all that he could get for the English. Mir Jafar was made to sign an obligation without the least idea of its implications, and the manoeuvre was an achievement of Watts, for he knew that Mir Jafar was a 'tool in the hands of Roydulub'.[51] When, at last, on 24 June 1757, the day following Clive's victory at Plassey, Mir Jafar received a message of congratulation from the real victor, expressing a 'hope to have the honor of proclaiming you Nabob'[52] the new Nawab could only recognize Clive as the maker of his fortune.

It was only natural, for Mir Jafar had been used to serving the *masnad* for nearly thirty years, never even dreaming, perhaps, of ascending to it himself. He was very grateful to Clive personally and gratefulness soon developed into fondness for the brave young soldier. Clive, for his part, addressed Mir Jafar in terms of personal devotion: 'Whenever I write to your excellency it is the same as if I was writing to my father. Such regard and friendship as a son has for his father such have I for your excellency, and whenever I have any favour to request it is for your excellency's advantage.'[53] It is important not to lose sight of the nature of the Anglo–Mughal relationship immediately after the battle of Plassey. Clive was serving the interests of the Company, even of Britain, but to Mir Jafar government meant personal government, and his approach to Clive was also personal. The Nawab did not know the Company and felt no obligation to it: it was Clive to whom he felt and expressed his gratitude. This was understood, moreover, by the Company's servants in Bengal, and that was why, when Drake departed in June 1758, Watts, Manningham, and Becher who had been appointed governors by rotation, in a joint minute resigned their post, which was unanimously offered to Clive.[54]

The Nawab did know a few Englishmen besides Clive, some of them quite well, but even these, Watts, Amyatt, and Manningham, were seen rather as agents of Clive than of the Company. Again, Hastings gained the Nawab's confidence as Clive's man and at Clive's commendation. On 18 August 1759 Hastings acknowledged this in a letter to Clive. He wrote saying that the Nawab 'knew no body amongst the English but yourself to whom he had every obligation and that nothing but his friendship for you restrained him from retaliating the many insults which he pretended to have received from the English'.[55] He went on, 'I am much obliged to you for the desire you are pleased to express to maintain my influence at the Durbar, which (though not on this occasion) I fear will shortly fall very low indeed. It is (I own with great concern I learn) that your resolution is fixed to return this season to Europe.'[56] Curious though it may appear, the Nawab does not appear to have understood that the Company was not an individual but an impersonal and corporate body of merchants. When Clive was about to go home, early in 1760, Mir Jafar sent with him seven packets of curiosities for his ally, Clive's master in London, and with them a letter addressed as though to some individual chief or ruler. The letter, in Warren Hastings's translation, reads:

After particulars of my earnest desire to see you w[hich] w[oul]d prove of ye [the] greatest advantage to me: which exceeds anything yt [that] could be written or spoke, I proceed to address myself to your heart ye repository of friendship.

The lights of my eyes, dearer yn [than] my life, the Nawab Zobdut ool Mulk Maye-nodowla Sabut Jang Bahadr [Clive] is departing for his own country. But his conti-nuance in Bengal was in every respect satisfactory. It is my perpetual wish that the return of the [. . . .?] light of my eyes above mentioned may happen very speedily; because I call him my son though I esteem him more yn a son. A separation from him is most afflicting to me. If you dispatch him speedily, to these parts and grant me ye happiness of seeing him again, it will be a real obligation.[57]

The wording of the Nawab's letter also serves as a reminder that to Mir Jafar and to his contemporary Indians (except perhaps a few merchants of Calcutta, Madras, or Bombay) Clive was no Englishman as we might under-stand the term, but Nawab Sabut Jang Bahadur. Clive had been inducted into the Mughal system under this title by the Nawab of Arcot,[58] as the Armenian Khojah Gregory had been transformed into Gurghin Khan by the Nawab of Bengal. Before he left Bengal in 1760 Clive was a full-blown *mansabdar* with the rank of six thousand *zat* and five thousand horse,[59] and the title of Zubdat ul Mulk conferred by the Mughal Emperor. The title, particularly that of Nawab, indicated that he was placed at par with the Mughal nobility, and above that of nobles of non-Mughal and Indian origin who, irrespective of whether they were Hindus or Muslims, bore the title of Raja.[60] After Clive, all the governors of Fort William (except Holwell) and principal officers of the Company's army and civil service were similarly granted Mughal titles, and so included within the imperial system.[61] Of the months immediately preceding Plassey, Watts commented in his Memoirs that the nobles at Murshidabad 'were persuaded they could merit very much from the Company's servants, by laying open his [the Nawab's] secrets, and thereby shewing them, what these people thought they did not least suspect, the danger to which they stood exposed'. After Plassey the acceptance of Englishmen into the Mughal system became even more complete. By January 1759 Clive had also been offered the Diwani of Bengal from Delhi.[62] Room had been found in the past for all nationalities in the imperial service; there was no reason why the English should not be found a place.

Clive, though more considerate towards Mir Jafar than many of his countrymen, could yet urge William Pitt, on 7 January 1759, to consider the possibility of establishing a British dominion in Bengal, arguing that 'Mussulmans are so little influenced by gratitude' that the Nawab would doubtless 'break with us' whenever his interest would require it.[63] The Mughal attitude however was that a working partnership was perfectly possible. This is perhaps best illustrated by the conditions which a number of Mughal chiefs proposed to Major Munro in 1764 as the basis of agreement to be signed by the English in the name of Jesus and Mary.[64] The first article of the proposed agreement ran, 'The Company should in every respect regard as its own the honour and reputation of the Moghals who are strangers in this country and make them its confederates in every business'. Other articles laid down that 'whatever Moghals whether Iranis or Turanis come to offer their services should be received on the aforesaid terms' and that 'should anyone be desirous of returning to his own country . . . he should be discharged in peace'.[65] This was the political climate of Bengal when Reza Khan first came to prominence, and, sharing with the Nawabs and other Mughal leaders an absolute ignorance of English attitudes and objectives, the Khan, like the Nawabs, seems to have aimed at a sort of Anglo–Mughal rule within the framework of Timurid sovereignty.

Reza Khan, coming into Timurid India from outside, was accepted into the ruling community, was granted office and *jagir*,[66] and in return accepted the Mughal pattern of government as right and proper. Alivardi provided the example of what a Nawab should be. Haji Ahmad, Alivardi's brother and Reza Khan's grandfather-in-law, and Nawazish Muhammad Khan who headed the civil administration of Bengal under the Nawabs Shuja Khan and Alivardi Khan, provided him with his yardstick or ideal as an administrator.[67]

As Naib at Murshidabad,[68] Reza Khan was to work in conjunction with the English towards the model which these men had provided. What the Alivardian traditions in Bengal were, Reza Khan has set out in his own words.

The ryots [cultivators] tho not rich, were content. The Zamindars and Talookdars were father and friend of the people. They maintained a proper police and were accountable for every branch of it. Complaints were readily heard and justice administered. The lands were well cultivated and the Zemindars and Talookdars found their interest in encouraging it and promoting an increase of inhabitants. If either fell off, a supervisor was sent to assist the Zemindar and relieve the people.

Rents were proportioned to the value of produce of land and newcomers were assisted with utensils . . .[69]

As for revenue,

in former times there was none determined, the landlords gave a present or tribute to the sovereign. In the reign of King Akbar the revenues were settled and increased under his successors, but still the general interest was considered. The people were not oppressed. The Zemindars and Talookdars being men of property paid their rents duly and were honoured and encouraged. If they failed Amils were sent, not to dispossess them, but to inquire into the causes of their default and to relieve them.[70]

For collection of revenue

the Kistbund[y] or rent was settled yearly, viz. upon the first of April [the Bengali month of Baisakh which begins in April].

The Zemindars and Talookdars received rent for inhabited places monthly and for corn grounds at the time of harvest.

They made their own payments 6/16 at the end of the first half year and 10/16 at that of the latter. But a monthly examination was made by the officers of government, respecting the state of farms, probable prospects of collecting rents or reasonable grounds for raising them.

As a result, the Khan declared, in Alivardi's Bengal

ballances were formerly very uncommon; whenever they arose, inquiry was made into their causes. If they appeared reasonable the rent was lowered and the deficiency was remitted. If not, it was charged to and recovered from the Zemindars.

Reza Khan also describes the traditional government policy towards trade and manufacture. He says

the workmen made [goods] of their own accord, and sold to whomsoever they pleased. Merchants of all nations bought and sold without hindrance. The trading people were rich and consumption immense. There was then a great export of the produce of the country and a vast influx of specie. The governing power never interfered in trade, but encouraged the merchants and redressed every grievance;

and bankers then

were a numerous and useful body. The people trusted their property readily in their hands and in return their assistance enabled the landholder to make good his engagement to government and rendered remittance easy and promoted cultivation.

He likewise sets out the pattern of judicial administration, recording that

in this country justice has been administered to the people agreeable to the ancient established laws. There are books in which laws are clearly expressed and set forth.[71]

Two courts were appointed—viz. the Adawlut Alia or King's court for criminal matters etc. The sentence of this court was presented to the Nabob who examined the proceedings, consulted the judges, and confirmed or rejected it. The Khalsa decided all disputes relating to property, land, debts etc. But an appeal lay to the Sudder or city where cause was ultimately determined. These Khalsa courts were held essential towards a due collection of the revenue. [And] they were established in the several districts of Dacca, Poorania [Purnea], Silhet [Sylhet]. Rajemahal, Rangpur, Boglepore [Bhagalpur] and Hougley [Hugli].[72]

Reza Khan also had a clear picture of the nature of landed property in Bengal and of the reciprocal duties of the ruler and the ruled which appears to be based on the traditions to which he was heir. He states,

The Zemindars and Talookdars are masters of their own lands. The Prince may punish them but cannot dispossess them. Their rights are hereditary. Princes have no immediate property in lands. They even purchased ground to erect mosques and buryal places.

The Prince is to receive the revenues of the state, to make such laws and regulations only as are consistent with justice; to study the general good of the country, and to cherish all his subjects.

The Zemidars and Talookdars are to protect, encourage and comfort the ryots and others under them and it is the duty of them all to pay their rents faithfully and to give obedience to the laws.

Finally, he sums up the whole tradition by describing what he believed to be the essence of the ruler's duty. It was

To issue such orders and regulations only as are consistent with the customs and manners of the country;

To enforce obedience thereto in the officers of the state as well as in the people;

To protect and encourage manufacturers, merchants, bankers and all ranks of people;

To hear and decide all complaints impartially and without delay;

To pay attention to the local customs of the several Mahals or districts in settling their Bundobust and mode of collection;

To obtain a constant communication of all events and observation of consequence in every part of the province.[73]

Reza Khan's whole career as Naib at Murshidabad can be seen as an attempt to hold as far as possible to his traditional ideal of government, to protect the old Mughal ordering of society against the changes and encroachments which the English sought to impose. Or, to put it another way, his constant aim, especially in the period which forms the subject of this study, was to persuade his English masters to accept Mughal ideals and practices as their own.

ABBREVIATIONS

Add. MSS.	Additional Manuscripts, British Museum
BPC	Bengal Public Consultations (Reference by date)
BSC	Bengal Secret and Military Consultations (Reference by date)
CDR	*Chittagong District Records* (a Bengal Government publication)
Considerations	*Considerations on Indian Affairs.* By W. Bolts
CPC	*Calendar of Persian Correspondence* (usually followed by vol. no. and entry no.)
DUHB	*History of Bengal*, published by Dacca University, vol. II
Fifth Report	*The Fifth Report from the Select Committee of the House of Commons on the Affairs of the East India Company, 28 July 1812* as edited by W.K. Firminger and published in 3 volumes in 1917
I.O.	India Office Library.
I.O.R.	India Office Records.
Letter to Court	Letters received by the Directors from Bengal
Malcolm, *Clive*	*The Life of Robert, Lord Clive.* By J. Malcolm
Orme MSS.	Robert Orme's collections (O.V. and India volumes) at the India Office Library
Seir	*Seir Mutaqherin* by S. Ghulam Hussain Khan. (The reference are to the English version).

NOTES AND REFERENCES

1. India Office Records (or I.O.R.), Bengal Letters Received, vol. 30, pp. 481–2.
2. J. Malcolm, *The Life of Robert, Lord Clive*, I, pp. 402–3.
3. W. Bolts, *Considerations on Indian Affairs*, p. 31.

4. Ghulam Husain Khan Tabatabai, *Seir Mutaqherin* (or *Seir*) (English tr.), ii, p. 220.
5. Bengal Public Consultations (or BPC), 29 July 1742. The English did not participate then as it was thought 'not for the Company's interest' to do so.
6. BPC, 16 Nov. 1744. The request did not receive any better response.
7. See S.C. Hill, *Bengal in 1756–1757*, vol. i, app. 66. Attempts were made through priests to detach them from fighting for the 'Moors'.
8. See Orme MSS. (I.O.), *India*, ix, p. 2166 ff.
9. W.K. Firminger, *Chittagong District Records* (or *CDR*), i, p. 150.
10. Such as Khojah Sarhad, Khojah Petruse and Khojah Gregory.
11. The Naib (usually a near relation of the Nawab) headed the administration.
12. Mir Jumla was a seventeenth-century example (*DUHB*, ii, pp. 339–50). One more recent example was Mir Habib, 'for sometime a peddling broker at Hooghly' (F. Gladwin, *Transactions in Bengal*, p. 141).
13. Instances being the viceroys Shaista Khan and Azim us Shan (*DUHB*, ii, pp. 373–5).
14. J. Reed's letter, 17 Dec. 1770 (see *Proceedings of the Murshidabad Council of Revenue*, or *MP*, 20 Dec. 1770).
15. This attack was undertaken according to a resolution of a Council of War dated 30 Sept. 1756 'to attack Hughley or any other Moors town or to take reprizals in the river on any other Moors vessels' (see *Home Miscellaneous Series* (I.O.) (or *H.M.S.*, 95; p. 85), the hardest hit among the merchants being Khwaja Wajid, called the Fakhr ut tujar (*H.M.S.*, 193; pp. 14, 20).
16. Siraj-ud-daulah to Clive, 1 Feb. 1757, *H.M.S.*, 193; p. 27.
17. Clive to Jagat Seth, 21 Jan. 1757, *H.M.S.*, 193; p. 17.
18. Clive to Siraj-ud-daulah, 3 Feb. 1757, *H.M.S.*, 193; p. 30.
19. Clive was known in India as Sabut Jang (correctly Sabit Jang), a title which was conferred on him by the Nawab of Arcot (Malcolm, *Clive*, i, pp. 400–1). Ghulam Husain referred to Watson as Admiral Dilir Jang Bahadur (*Seir*, ii, p. 225) while the Major is referred to as 'Dilher Jung' in the Nawab's letter to Clive dated 10 March 1757 (*H.M.S.*, 193; p. 65). A list giving the Mughal names and titles of some of the early English officials of the Company in Bengal is given on pp. xii–xiii.
20. Siraj-ud-daulah to Clive, 19 Feb. 1757, *H.M.S.*, 193; p. 56.
21. Hafiz ullah Khan, eldest son of Sarfaraz Khan appealed to Clive for protection 'for the prophet Jesus's sake' (recd. 19 July 1757, *H.M.S.*, 193; p. 80).
22. Siraj-ud-daulah to Clive, 24 March 1757, *H.M.S.*, 193; p. 88.
23. *H.M.S.*, 193; p. 80.
24. *H.M.S.*, 193; pp. 64–5.
25. Siraj-ud-daulah to Clive, 10 March 1757, *H.M.S.*, 193; pp. 64–5. Major Killpatrick was meant.
26. Ibid. Drake had written to Manikchand urging the early return of goods plundered in Calcutta by the Burdwan *mutasaddis* and servants, adding 'Don't look on this as a trifling thing below your notice' (*H.M.S.*, 193; p. 65).
27. Clive to Siraj-ud-daulah, 16 Feb. 1757, *H.M.S.*, 193; p. 57.
28. Siraj-ud-daulah to Clive, 14 Feb. 1757, *H.M.S.*, 193; p. 57.
29. *Seir*, ii, p. 196.
30. Gladwin, *Transactions in Bengal*, pp. 154–5.
31. W. Watts, *Memoirs of the Revolution in Bengal*, p. 76.
32. Ibid.

33. That is, Clive and Watson.

34. This was the name given to Calcutta.

35. There was no sense of alarm. Similar was the reaction of the Mughals in Oudh, after Plassey. Omar Quli Khan, Mir Jafar's agent, wrote: 'your reputation is lost by the Frengees [Christians] having beat you; therefore they all cry out they are no soldiers in Bengal' (*H.M.S.*, 193; pp. 201–2).

36. Watts, *Memoirs*, p. 76.

37. Watts's letter, 26 April. BSC, 1 May 1757.

38. S.C. Hill, *Bengal in 1756–1757*, I, pp. 239–40.

39. Consultations and proceedings of the Bengal Select Committee, 23 April 1757.

40. BSC, 1 May 1757.

41. BSC, 12 May 1757.

42. BSC, 23 June 1757.

43. A.C. Roy, *The Career of Mir Jafar Khan (1757–1765)*, p. 2.

44. It is interesting to note Umichand's assessment of Mir Jafar. He told Robert Gregory on 15 Feb. 1758 that 'the present Nabob Meir Mohamed Jaffier would not keep the Government long that he was a soldier and not fit to govern' (Gregory's letter, 16 Feb. BSC, 18 Feb. 1758). He proved correct.

45. *Seir*, II, pp. 24–5, 196.

46. *Seir*, II, pp. 237–8.

47. Luke Scrafton to Hastings, 30 Nov. 1758 (Add. MSS. 29132, f. 52). Walsh and Scrafton had been introduced to Siraj-ud-daulah by Clive as 'a relation of mine and another person' on 3 Feb. 1757 (*H.M.S.*, 193; p. 30). Though Scrafton belonged to Dacca establishment, at Clive's request the Select Committee had posted him to Murshidabd to assist'Watts (BSC, 28 April 1757).

48. *Seir*, II, pp. 117–18. He was opposed to Siraj-ud-daulah because the latter had raised a Kashmiri Hindu, Rai Mohan Lal, to the post he once held.

49. Watts's letter to Clive, 6 June. BSC, 11 June 1757.

50. Watts to Clive, 3 June 1757. *H.M.S.*, 808; p. 57.

51. Ibid.

52. *H.M.S.*, 193; p. 165.

53. Clive to Mir Jafar, 15 July 1757. *H.M.S.*, 193; p. 180.

54. Joint minute of Watts, Charles Manningham and Richard Becher, BPC, 26 June 1758.

55. Warren Hastings, Resident at Murshidabad to Clive, 18 Aug. 1759 (Add. MSS. 29096, f. 169.).

56. Ibid.

57. See Warren Hastings Papers, Add. MSS. 29096, ff. 215–16.

58. Malcolm, *Clive*, I, pp. 400–1.

59. Ibid., p. 405. Malcolm makes a mistake. *Zat* means rank.

60. Two current examples were Raja Asad uz Zaman Khan of Birbhum and his kinsman, Raja Kamgar Khan, of Narhat Semai in south Bihar.

61. A list mentioning some of them is given on pp. xii–xiii.

62. Clive to William Pitt, 7 Jan. 1759. Quoted: G.W. Forrest, *The Life of Lord Clive*, II, p. 412.

63. Ibid.

64. *Calendar of Persian Correspondence* (or *CPC*), vol. I, nos. 2416, 2418.

65. *CPC*, I, no. 2423.
66. It may be interesting to observe that, though it would have been none too difficult for him to acquire a zamindari, the Khan could never think of acquiring one, due perhaps to his inability to shake off his sense of identity with the ruling community. A zamindar, however powerful, was after all a subject of the Mughals whose invariable maxim, Ghulam Husain says, was to 'keep them low' (*Seir*, III, p. 181). India, Reza Khan maintained, was a Dar ul Harb (Reza Khan's note, Francis MSS. (I.O.) Eur. E13, p. 417). He obviously shared the current notion of the Muslim rulers in India, to whom it was not strictly a Dar ul Islam—a Muslim homeland. Muslims living in Hindustan (that is, north India) did so, according to the same notion, as rulers or as sojourners only. A *jagir*, however insecure, like an office under government, conferred a more dignified status.
67. The Naib, assisted by the Hindu chief of the Khalsa, the Rai-Rayan and the Jagat Seth, acting as government banker, had administered the country since Shuja Khan's time. This model was adopted by Clive.
68. Reza Khan's designation underwent several changes.
69. Reza Khan's note, Feb. 1775 (Francis MSS. (I.O.) Eur. E 28, pp. 345–56).
70. Ibid.
71. By 'books' the Khan was obviously referring to the Quran and the Sunna or traditions of Islam, as also to the Fiqh literature, particularly of the Hanafi school.
72. Reza Khan's note, Feb. 1775 (Francis MSS. (I.O.) Eur. E 28, pp. 345- 56).
73. Ibid.

14

Prospective: Aristocracy, Finance and Empire, 1688–1850*

P.J. Cain and A.G. Hopkins

S tarting points have origins which lie beyond the antecedents chosen to define them. A plausible case could be made for beginning this study in the late sixteenth century, as this would encompass the Elizabethan explorers, the foundation of the East India Company, and the establishment of the first colonies in the New World. In taking the Glorious Revolution as our point of departure instead, we do not intend to minimize the importance of these events; to suggest that our argument is incompatible with them, or indeed to claim that 1688 was itself a cataclysmic year in the making of imperial history. We do, however, wish to argue that the Revolution brought together and lent impetus to forces that left a deep imprint not only on domestic history, as is well known, but also on the character and course of colonial development— a proposition that is less well appreciated. By taking this additional step, we hope to establish a systematic connection between British and imperial history from the outset of our study; by tracing the evolution of this relationship, we hope to show how one phase in the history of the empire dissolved into another in the nineteenth century.

HISTORIOGRAPHICAL PERSPECTIVES

To reach this point we need first to define our position with respect to the existing historiography. As far as Britain is concerned, this means choosing between interpretations which emphasise the persistence of an ancien regime

*P.J. Cain and A.G. Hopkins, from 'Prospective: Aristocracy, Finance and Empire, 1688–1850', in *British Imperialism: Innovation and Expansion 1688–1914*, London, 1993, pp. 53–71, 84–94.

dominated by an oligarchy of landowners from 1688, or even from 1660, down to 1832 or even beyond, and those which emphasize evidence of change as demonstrated, variously, by the Revolution of 1688, the Hanoverian succession, the rise of a 'polite and commercial' middle class, the growth of an impolite radicalism, the American and French Revolutions and, finally, industrialization.[1] Our contribution to this wide-ranging but also highly specialized debate can be only a modest one. It appears to us that the boundaries of discussion have been drawn too narrowly around political, constitutional, and ideological issues, and have not fully incorporated the results of recent research into economic history, even where reference is made to the Industrial Revolution. Our purpose in including this dimension, however, is not to renovate an argument about industrialization but to emphasize the continuing importance of agriculture and the significance of innovations in finance and commercial services. In claiming that these innovations made headway because they were compatible with the 'traditional' social order, we shall indicate how an argument for change can be combined with one emphasizing continuity without, we hope, collapsing the case into generalities.

The imperial perspective also needs to be brought into focus. At present, the mainland colonies are the only part of the empire to appear either prominently or regularly in the controversy over the direction taken by eighteenth-century Britain, principally because constitutional issues carried contemporary debate over political rights and duties across the Atlantic. The empire as a whole, however, does not feature systematically in the discussion, and its role is often pared down to the point at which near-sighted observers might begin to doubt its existence.[2] This anomaly has persisted despite the fact that Britain's presence abroad was substantially enlarged in the course of the eighteenth century. Territorial advances were made in India and in the North American settlements that were to become Canada; the West Indies rose to head the list of Britain's trading partners; commercial ties with the mainland colonies increased down to the War of Independence, survived the creation of the United States, and prospered thereafter. Imperial assertiveness was neither dimmed by the loss of the American colonies nor extinguished by the resumption of peace in 1815 after the long war with France. Colonies of settlement were promoted in New South Wales from the 1780s, in the Cape after the turn of the century, and in New Zealand from the 1840s. During and after the French Wars a chain of naval bases, some within the empire and others outside it, was established to police the ocean routes and to create points of entry into tropical Africa, South America, the Persian Gulf, south-east Asia, and the Far East. Forceful diplomacy, occasionally accompanied by house-breaking, continued to be used to bend the world overseas to Britain's will and reached a new peak of intensity with the exercise of Palmerston's muscular authority during the 1830s and 1840s.

The omission of these sizeable developments from serious consideration of the course of British history after 1688 is to some extent the result of an excess of specialization that affects all fields of historical study. But it can also be explained by the fact that imperial historians themselves have long been unsure about what role to assign the empire in the evolution of the mother country. Despite the creation of what is now a voluminous and impressive body of literature, no general interpretation of the eighteenth-century empire has succeeded either in commanding acceptance or in generating the creative dissent needed to inspire a superior alternative.[3] Imperial historians have themselves become divided by a common empire: specialists on North America have devised one set of controversies and dates; those working on India have evolved another. The outcome of these separate inquiries, valuable though it is, has contributed more to an understanding of the history of the states that arose from the debris of empire, whether British or Mughal, than to an awareness of a common imperial purpose. In these circumstances, it is easy to draw the conclusion that no common purpose and no significant unity existed, and thereby to make a virtue out of what, on closer inspection, might be a weakness in historical analysis.

There was a time when this problem appeared to have a satisfactory solution. On the assumption that the history of the empire was defined by events affecting its constitutional standing, it was acceptable for the *Cambridge History of the British Empire* to regard the creation of the United States as marking the termination of the 'old' empire.[4] However, as it became apparent that this criterion excluded too much that was relevant to an understanding of the realities of imperial relations and international power alike, increasing attention was paid to influences other than those defined by constitutional considerations. The weightiest statement of the revisionist case was presented in Vincent Harlow's *The Founding of the Second British Empire, 1763–1793*, which sought to reduce the importance attached to 1783 and to suggest that the real turning point in Britain's imperial relations occurred with the successful conclusion of the Seven Years' War 20 years earlier in 1763.[5] This date symbolized both the achievement of British naval supremacy and the emergence of new expansionist forces based on incipient industrialization and characterized by a quest for markets and raw materials rather than for territorial possession. Harlow's argument thus contained elements of the idea of informal empire that Gallagher and Robinson applied to the mid-Victorian period.[6] In effect, Harlow's interpretation created what might be called the long nineteenth century, whereby 1763 became the starting point for the industrial-based, free-trading imperialism that was to prevail until the neo-mercantilist policies of rival powers disrupted it at the close of the nineteenth century.

Had this interpretation held, historians of empire would have a thesis to offer the wider world. However, it is generally accepted that Harlow's argument created more difficulties than it could resolve. Important though it was, Britain's success in 1763 signified neither her ascendancy as a naval power nor the elimination of the French challenge. Harlow's emphasis on the part played by the process of industrialization is also at variance with current assessments of the chronology of the Industrial Revolution, which have moved the turning point forward to the close of the eighteenth century rather than back to 1763. Similarly, in underlining the significance of early experiments with free trade, Harlow was left with the problem that protectionism remained in place until well into the nineteenth century. This difficulty entailed another: in stressing the shift of policy towards trade rather than dominion, Harlow was unable to account adequately for Britain's continuing expansion within the formal empire in British North America, the West Indies, and India, while his idea that there was a 'swing to the east' following the loss of the mainland colonies minimized the enduring importance of economic ties with the United States as well as with the Atlantic economy generally.

These weaknesses have yet to be overcome either within the liberal tradition of scholarship or outside it.[7] Indeed, as far as imperial history is concerned, the contribution made by those opposed to 'bourgeois' scholarship has proved to be disappointingly conventional. André Gunder Frank, for example, claimed that the Industrial Revolution 'began with the year 1760', and that the last quarter of the eighteenth century marked the transition from mercantile to industrial capitalism.[8] Wallerstein's treatment is far more detailed, but the result falls into a familiar pattern. He, too, distinguishes between mercantile capitalism, which occupied the 'long' seventeenth century (1600–1750), and industrial capitalism which predominated thereafter. The point of transition is symbolized by the year 1763, which saw 'the victory of certain segments of the world bourgeoisie, who were rooted in England, with the aid of the British state'.[9] But this date, as we have seen, had already been selected by Harlow and been criticized subsequently, and Wallerstein is unable to substantiate his additional claim that the bourgeoisie rose (finally) to power in the mid-eighteenth century. If, today, historians of all persuasions are more likely to halt in 1776 or 1783, it is not because the conventional case for doing so is convincing but because the alternatives are even less persuasive; and one result of this decision is that the period between 1783 and 1815 is covered imperfectly or not at all.[10]

It should be evident by now that we cannot simply present a summary of an acceptable interpretation of eighteenth-century imperialism because it does not lie readily to hand; if we adopt any of the existing approaches we are likely to drive through signs warning of the hazards surrounding concepts such as mercantilism, free trade, and the Industrial Revolution. The problem is to devise a route that offers a plausible way of connecting the history of Britain to the history of the empire. There are, no doubt, a number of possibilities. But the one that appears to us to have the greatest explanatory power is that which begins by focusing on the structure of authority installed by the Revolution of 1688 and its attendant property rights, rewards and sanctions, and views imperialism as an attempt to export the Revolution Settlement (and hence to entrench it at home) by creating compliant satellites overseas. Domestic and imperial developments were joined in various ways, but none was more pervasive than the bond created by finance. As the financial revolution underwrote the new regime at home, so it helped to fund settlement, export-production, and trade overseas; the evolution of the credit and revenue-raising system provides a means of tracing not only the fortunes of the revolution settlement itself but of the empire as well.

THE FINANCIAL REVOLUTION: PRIVATE INTERESTS AND PUBLIC VIRTUES

The period 1688–1850 owes its unity to the economic and political dominance of a reconstructed and commercially progressive aristocracy which derived its power from land. Agriculture remained the most important economic activity for the greater part of the period, whether measured by its share of national income, its contribution to employment, or by its ability to generate large fortunes.[11] In 1790, no less than three-quarters of all agricultural land was owned by no more than 4,000–5,000 aristocrats and gentry, who presided over a series of innovations which raised productivity, increased incomes from rents, and helped to lift land values.[12] Down to the 1760s the prosperity of agriculture, especially in the south-east, was boosted by foreign demand, which drew grain exports out of the country; thereafter, the growth of the domestic market ensured that investment in agriculture remained high and that farm incomes stayed buoyant.[13] Throughout the eighteenth century, purchasing power derived from agricultural rents and wages formed the basis of consumer demand for both domestic manufacturers and imports, including colonial products.[14] As we shall see, the dominance of agriculture was not seriously questioned until the 1820s; even so, its decline was protracted and became irreversible only with the measures opening Britain to free trade at the close of the 1840s.

As the landed interest threw off the last traces of feudalism, eliminating the threat not of a rising bourgeoisie but of conservative farmers, so too its representatives increased their grip on the levers of power in the aftermath of the Civil War. Following the Revolution of 1688, the magnates consolidated their political authority as they consolidated their estates.[15] These 'great oaks', as Burke called them, shaded the country because they possessed, in land, a form of wealth that also carried the supreme badge of authority, being permanent, prestigious, and allowing time for the affairs of state. In dominating parliament, the landed interest also gathered together the main lines of authority, notably the legal system, public expenditure, and defence, which joined the seat of government in London to the most distant provinces. The control exercised by the peerage over the House of Commons remained undisturbed before 1832 and was only slowly eroded thereafter, while its dominance of the executive lasted well beyond 1850.[16] Social exclusiveness was maintained by in-group marriage, ideological cohesion was demonstrated by a commitment to the Church of England, and cultural homogeneity was shaped by the public schools, whose pupils, 'the glory of their country' in Defoe's judgement, were set apart from their contemporaries, 'the mere outsides of gentlemen', who were educated by other means.[17] None of this is to suggest, even in a summary as compressed as this, that the country was run by an oligarchy which became somnolent because it was allowed to rest undisturbed: opposition sprang from different quarters and was sometimes powerful enough to trouble the repose of the most complacent members of the government. But opposition that was Tory or urban middle class in origin remained within constitutional limits, at least after 1745; and, when radical protest broke the bounds of law and convention, it was brought under control.[18] At such moments, the instinct of self-preservation sharpened the quality of political judgement and caused property-owners to sink their differences in their common interest.

The most important development outside agriculture in the eighteenth century was the financial revolution of the 1690s centred on the foundation of the Bank of England and the creation of the national debt.[19] These innovations were linked to wider developments within the financial sector; the recoinage of 1697 and the establishment, thereafter, of a de facto gold standard; the evolution of specialized merchant banks in the City; the growth of a market in mortgages; the increasing use of bills of exchange to settle domestic and international obligations; the rise of the stock exchange; the development of marine and fire insurance; and the appearance of a financial press.[20] The early eighteenth century saw the expansion of the East India Company and the South Sea Company, the two great companies whose shares formed a sizeable part of the stock market, the growth of Lloyds as the international centre of underwriting, and the formation of new insurance companies, such as the Sun Fire Office (1708) and the Exchange Assurance Company (1720).[21] The external effects of these innovations were felt, in turn, on other activities in the service sector. Improvements in credit and commercial services boosted the shipping industry, promoted overseas trade, and assisted the balance of payments by generating invisible earnings.[22] The expansion of overseas commerce encouraged the rise of large mercantile firms whose size enabled them to mobilize the capital and credit needed for long-distance trade.[23] As the eighteenth century witnessed the consolidation of large estates and their perpetuation through the male line, so it saw the growth of a merchant oligarchy and its 'entailment' through commercial dynasties. It was during this period, too, that non-commercial branches of the service sector were expanded and defined. Official employment, especially in new or reformed departments, such as the Board of Trade and the Treasury, became associated with a concept of public duty that was the hallmark of gentility and was handed on, often from father to son, while in the private sector a number of prominent occupations acquired the status of professions and their members became acknowledged as gentlemen.[24]

All of these developments came together in London, and gave further impetus to the growth of what was already a large and expanding urban centre.[25] The great institutions which supported the financial revolution, and indeed the Glorious Revolution too, were based in the City, where they benefited from the externalities generated by geographical proximity and overlapping functions. As the leading port, London itself was already distinguished by the wealth and cosmopolitan character of its merchant community, and was well placed to launch new ventures overseas. London's manufactures also came to reflect the expansion of the financial and service sector: older industries, such as silk and cloth, lost ground to foreign and provincial competitors, but new industries, ranging from sugar-processing to the production of high-quality furniture, arose to meet the needs of the country's most important concentration of wealthy consumers as well as its largest mass market.[26] No other town experienced such a striking development of consumer-oriented industries that relied so heavily on wealth derived ultimately from overseas trade and government expenditure; and no other town evolved such refined gradations of status as were found among London's service class of gentlemen's gentlemen, superior shopkeepers, clerks, and the semi-employed attendants of the great and the pretenders to greatness.

This is not to say that London was unique: recent work on provincial towns as well as the long-established record of outports, such as Liverpool, Bristol, and Glasgow, indicates that both the financial revolution and the élite-consumer tastes that accompanied it spread beyond the metropolis in the course of the eighteenth century.[27] but imitation flattered the power of the centre rather than diluted it: London remained outstanding not only in its size but also in the qualitative differences that separated so many of its functions from those of even the largest provincial towns. There was only one Bank of England, one Lloyds, and one national debt, and they were all found in London. Moreover, the City was distinguished from the outset by its close involvement with government finance and by its pronounced overseas orientation. The long-term capital market, as it emerged in London, was already separated from the rest of the country; provincial needs were met by local credit networks.[28] If the supremacy of the metropole was underpinned by powerful economic causes, it owed much of its distinction to the fact that London was the capital as well as the main port. The proximity of the City to parliament, to the departments of state, and to the court provided opportunities for gaining access to information and for influencing policy that simply did not exist elsewhere. Provincial business could compete at the same level only by relocating its headquarters in London, as happened increasingly after 1850.

The causes of the financial revolution cannot be examined here in any detail. But it is clear that the preconditions had long been present in the shape of the City's merchants and goldsmiths, its cosmopolitan connections, and its already extensive international trade. By the late seventeenth century, it was apparent, too, that dear money had placed Britain at a disadvantage in her struggle with the Dutch, and that improved credit was a vital part of her defence strategy—which included overseas expansion.[29] A further perception, which was to be realized fully in the course of the next three centuries, was that invisible earnings had an important contribution to make to the balance of payments, especially at a time when commodity exports (in this case woollen textiles) were experiencing difficulties in overseas markets.[30] However, no fundamental revolution was possible before 1688 because James II's pro-French and pro-Catholic policies frightened the predominantly Protestant bankers and investors whose support it required. The gentlemanly revolution of 1688 removed this fear by installing not just a new monarch but a new type of monarchy. The financial independence of the crown was destroyed: to secure an adequate income the king was compelled to govern through parliament and thus to acknowledge the political dominance of the landed interest.[31] The price that had to be paid was participation in the continental wars of the new ruler and his successors, and it was the demand for war finance after 1688 that precipitated the expansion of the national debt.

The distinctiveness of these innovations also needs to be emphasized. The extensive literature on economic growth defines 'early start' and 'late start' countries almost exclusively with reference to the development and spread of industry. What has still to be fully appreciated is the extent of Britain's lead in the area of finance and commercial services, and the degree to which it set her apart from her rivals, as well as the role of these activities in the history of economic development.[32] The suggestion that Britain was about a century ahead of France in evolving modern financial institutions[33] is supported by recent detailed research on public finance and monetary policy.[34] Both the form taken by the public debt and its management were far more advanced in Britain than they were in France. During the final conflict between the two powers from 1793 to 1815, Britain was able to borrow extensively and efficiently because investors had confidence that their money would be returned, whereas France was forced to rely much more heavily on taxation because creditors were unimpressed by the government's record in honouring its obligations. Moreover, confidence in sterling enabled Britain to leave the gold standard in 1797 and adopt an emergency monetary policy without provoking a flight from the currency. What part this difference played in the outcome of the wars is impossible to say, but its existence needs to be stressed, not least because superior credit facilities in helping to make Britain an international power, had given her a considerable stake to defend, as well as the means of doing so.

If the developments that flowed from the financial revolution seem recognizably modern, so they were. Contemporaries were universally impressed and often greatly disturbed by the far-reaching implications of the financial revolution, and their reactions gave rise to a debate that still echoes today in discussions of Britain's economic problems. Swift's alarm at the rise of the moneyed interest led him to argue that financiers had encouraged the flow of capital abroad to the detriment of the country's real interests, which lay in preserving the value of productive investments in agriculture:

I have known some People such ill Computers as to imagine the many Millions in Stocks and Annuities are so much real Wealth in the Nation; whereas every Farthing of it is entirely lost to us, scattered in Holland, Germany and Spain.[35]

Defoe drew attention to another recurring feature of the debate, and one that also struck Hobson nearly two centuries later: the division between a highland, pastoral and industrial north and west and a lowland, arable, and commercial south and east.[36] In making this distinction, Defoe also underlined London's special function as a centre of finance and commercial services. His aim, however, was not to attack the capital, but rather to defend the role of services in maximizing employment and adding value to economic activities. As these contrasting interpretations suggest, the rise of the moneyed interest was the subject of one of the principal controversies of the eighteenth century.[37] To some observers, the new financiers were patriots whose expertise in organizing low-cost credit funded the defence of the realm, overseas expansion, and domestic employment. To others, they were upstarts who threatened to undermine the established social order by importing 'avarice' into a world that depended on 'virtue' to guarantee good government. As Bolingbroke, the most eminent of the City's critics in the early eighteenth century, put it: 'the landed men are the true owners of our political vessel; the moneyed men, as such are but passengers in it'.[38] The question of ownership was indeed central because the activities of the moneyed interest created new forms of property, essentially paper instruments representing financial claims and obligations, that appeared to be insubstantial but were in practice powerful and invasive. The national debt became a particular focus of attention partly because it was readily identifiable and partly because it continued to expand throughout the century. On one view, the debt saved Britain from defeat at the hands of France; on another, it subverted the kingdom from within by attracting capital away from agriculture, by advancing representatives of the City to positions of privilege previously held exclusively by the landed interest, and by threatening the nation with bankruptcy. Not surprisingly, the debate joined by Swift and Defoe was carried on by Hume, Smith, and Burke later in the century and by Southey and his contemporaries in the 1820s.[39]

However, the debate was being resolved even as it was being continued. As the eighteenth century advanced, the new financial institutions and services took root, and leading members of the moneyed interest were accepted into the inner circles of political and social influence.[40] The economic argument for incorporating the City was compelling because its expertise was vital to financing the wars that were the price of upholding the Revolution Settlement.[41] The national debt was also directly profitable to the small minority who could afford to invest in it—mainly substantial bankers, merchants and landowners, most of whom lived in London or the Home Counties (or had a residence there).[42] The growing integration of land and finance was symbolized by the action of the Earl of Bath, reputedly one of the wealthiest magnates in the country, who lent his weight in 1737 to a successful move to prevent a reduction in the interest paid on the national debt because his wife's considerable capital was invested in government stock.[43] In addition, the debt helped to fund the patronage system, which gave light work to many potentially idle hands, especially younger sons of landed families. In 1726 about one-quarter of the peerage held government or court office, and in the second half of the century it became increasingly acceptable for the younger sons of aristocrats to take posts in the colonies, including placements arranged by the East India Company.[44] Outside the national debt, important connections between the country's large landowners and the City were formed by apprenticing younger sons to the leading merchant houses, especially those involved in the prestigious import and export trades,[45] and by the growth of the mortgage market, which developed rapidly as mortgages became the recognized means of obtaining credit on the security of land.[46] In these ways, the fortunes of the magnates who made the Revolution of 1688, and the merchant bankers who underwrote it became increasingly entwined both in the definition of the national interest and in matters of personal finance.

Social integration was necessarily a gradual process, but it was greatly helped by affinities in the lifestyles of leading City figures and magnates at their meeting points in London, and by the subsequent gentrification of new money through the purchase of land, intermarriage and the acquisition of titles.[47] This process led to the assimilation of recent immigrants, such as Jacob Houblon, who founded a City dynasty, bought a country estate, and finally entered parliament during the reign of George II—who was also, of course, a member of a successful immigrant family.[48] It assisted established banking families, too, such as the Hoares, who gained impetus from the financial revolution, married into the English and Irish peerage, and thereafter combined broad acres with service to the City and to the crown.[49] Old money also prospered from new opportunities: Henry Lascelles came from a family of Yorkshire landowners, but he made his own fortune from colonial trade (principally imports from Barbados), entered parliament, and at his death in 1753 was worth an estimated £284,000 in land, the national debt, and loans to planters in the West Indies.[50] His son, Edwin, became a baron in 1796, and his grandson became Earl (and Viscount) Harewood in 1812.[51] By the close of the eighteenth century, the principle of the national debt had won general acceptance, though there was continuing concern about its size, and the avarice that Bolingbroke had associated with the moneyed interest had become virtuous in public service and in enhancing the private wealth of the magnates who managed the country. Bankers became gentlemen not least because gentlemen needed bankers.

Manufacturers were already important and familiar figures on the landscape in 1688, and their role expanded thereafter, as is well known. The woollen industry made a sizeable contribution to domestic employment, export earnings and state revenues in the eighteenth century, and the cotton industry performed a similar function, on an even larger scale, in the nineteenth century. At the same time, it must also be acknowledged, in the light of recent research, that industrialization was a much slower process than was once thought: it now seems unlikely that there was a marked upward shift in the contribution made by manufacturing to national output in the 1740s; the spurt of the 1780s was confined largely to cotton goods; it was not until the 1820s that the quantitative weight of new industries imposed itself on the economy as a whole.[52] Only then did investment in industry become significantly larger than in agriculture; even so, the greater part of manufacturing output still came from small-scale traditional (often household) units of production. Given the persistence of low productivity in so much of the manufacturing sector, it ought not to be surprising to find that industrial producers were content to shelter behind protectionist barriers for most of the period under review.[53] Even in branches of industry where productivity was growing impressively, such as cotton goods, the risks associated with new manufacturing techniques inspired a high degree of caution with respect to free trade.[54] Moreover, productivity gains in manufacturing still had to be realized in rising sales; and, as the home market became saturated, manufacturers found themselves relying increasingly on the worldwide system of distribution organized and financed from London.[55]

The success of the new industrial forces was therefore highly qualified, even in 1850. The number of large fortunes amassed by industrialists did not compare with those derived from land and from the financial and service sector.[56] Moreover, manufacturers did not make money in acceptable ways, and were not considered to be suitable candidates for entry into what Hume called 'that middling rank of men who are the best and finest basis of public liberty'.[57] In the eighteenth century, members of the banking and mercantile élite gained a degree of social approval for their activities that was 'not accorded to the captains of industry, whose profit-making inhibited the pursuit of pleasure, and whose petty bourgeois origins created formidable social barriers'.[58] It is true that sections of the landed interest benefited as producers from connections with industry, most obviously by supplying wool to textile manufacturers or by leasing mineral rights; but in general they used the capital they raised in London to improve their estates, and few landed magnates derived much of their income from investment in manufacturing, even in the nineteenth century.[59] Successful bankers and merchants were also disinclined to involve themselves in manufacturing, and showed a consistent preference for investments in urban property and country estates.[60] Indeed, there is evidence to suggest that landowners responded to the rise of the new industries by distancing themselves from them at the close of the eighteenth century, while merchants who expanded their operations were more likely to move into banking, shipping, and allied services than into manufacturing.[61]

Industry's direct political influence also remained limited, even after the constitutional reforms of 1832. This was partly because the Bounderbys of the Midlands and the north of England (as they were increasingly portrayed by spokesmen in the south) had neither the time nor the social connections to shape national policy, and partly because they were rarely able to present a united front when they decided to make the attempt. A General Chamber of Manufacturers was formed in 1785, but its one great success—aborting Pitt's Anglo–Irish treaty—was motivated by timid protectionism rather than bourgeois self-confidence; and divisions among manufacturers on the issue of freer trade destroyed their unity in the following year, when the Anglo–French commercial treaty was negotiated, and led to the demise of the Chamber in 1787.[62] Thereafter, it proved impossible to pull the manufacturing interest together, except on an ad hoc basis, until the 1830s, and even then unity tended to follow the business cycle in emerging at times of slump and dissolving with the return of prosperity.

An alliance between land and money was firmly in place, well before the economic and political consequences of industrialization compelled attention. When the new industries eventually made their presence felt, their importance in generating income from overseas trade and in creating employment was widely acknowledged in government circles. But their representatives never took control of policy: they were claimants among others whose interests had to be balanced and mediated, not a force whose time had finally come; and, as far as international policy was concerned, their claims fitted into government priorities rather than challenged them. To adapt a phrase, the industrial bourgeoisie played an evolutionary part, at least in the period down to 1850.

EXPORTING THE REVOLUTION SETTLEMENT

In the most general terms, the empire created before the mid-nineteenth century represented the extension abroad of the institutions and principles entrenched at home by the Revolution of 1688. The export version of the new order was compelled to adjust to the conditions it encountered overseas, but it remained a recognizable reflection of its domestic self. Indeed, the various crises of empire helped to define the profile of the gentlemanly order in Britain more clearly both by revealing and by determining the limits of its flexibility.

The imprint of the landed interest was felt most obviously in the colonies of settlement, especially in the New World, which was the most important growth area for British trade and influence in the eighteenth century. The planters in the West Indies and the gentry in the mainland colonies saw themselves as being Britons and wanted to remain so.[63] If they distanced themselves from some aspects of the emerging British way of life, they also espoused gentlemanly ideals, succumbed to the 'irresistible lure' of London,[64] and employed the rhetoric of the 'country' opposition to express their dissent and their preferences.[65] Even in regions where white settlement was unimportant, such as India, extensions of imperial control were accompanied by systematic attempts to establish property rights in land, and the new rulers instinctively looked to indigenous landholders to provide steady support for civil order.[66] In settled and non-settled parts of the empire alike, the patronage system provided employment for the younger sons of magnates and gentry, and endowed authority with a military bearing and a paternal style that survived long after 1850.[67] The influence of the City and the newer forces thrown up by the financial revolution was very evident too, especially in the impetus given to overseas trade by improved credit facilities, by the expansion of the mercantile marine, powerfully supported by the Navigation Acts, and by advanced forms of commercial capitalism, such as the East India Company, with its close links with Westminister and its predominantly City-based investors.[68] Overseas expansion was backed by other important interest groups: manufacturers who needed a vent for their surplus products, export merchants who handled their goods, and import merchants and their associates who dealt with the re-export trades.[69] Expansion abroad also conferred indirect benefits on the home government, which gained from enlarged customs revenues, on the landed interest, which in consequence enjoyed favourable tax treatment, and on investors in the national debt, whose returns rose when borrowing and interest rates increased.[70]

The pursuit of what Adam Smith termed 'opulence' merged with the interests of defence to produce Britain's long-serving 'Blue Water' policy.[71] Since Britain could not hope to control continental Europe and felt herself to be threatened by the emergence of any large single power there, she capitalized on her geographical location and her comparative advantage in services by building up her naval power instead. The Navigation Acts, as we have seen, boosted British shipping, which in turn fostered both trade and defence. This policy commended itself because it was cheap, and hence kept taxation within acceptable bounds and avoided the need for a standing army, which was a highly sensitive option on political grounds as well as a costly one. By commanding the seas, Britain hoped to prevent France from blockading her trade with the continent and to frustrate any attempt at invasion. By the middle of the eighteenth century, these calculations had already been made and acted on. In the 1750s, Pitt was well aware that the threat of invasion endangered both financial and political stability. He observed that 'paper credit may be invaded in Kent', and anticipated the 'consternation that would spread through the City, when the noble, artificial yet vulnerable fabric of public credit should crumble in their hands'.[72] However, Britain's focus on naval defence did not mean that she was isolated from the continent. On the contrary, both diplomacy and money were devoted to the task of creating allies in Europe, especially among the smaller states that were conscious of their vulnerability in the face of larger neighbours. But the balance of advantage lay in the blue water and overseas; and one of the consequences of this decision was to elevate the standing of those who supported it, so that in time they became defenders of the national interest and not merely advocates of sectional advantage.

The most striking commercial results of the Blue Water strategy in the eighteenth century can be seen in the changing direction of British trade.[73] Continental Europe's share of Britain's home-produced exports fell from 82 per cent in 1700–1 to 40 per cent in 1772–3, while imports from Europe declined from 68 per cent of the total to 47 per cent during the same period. Over a rather longer term, Europe's share of Britain's total overseas trade dropped from 74 per cent in 1713–17 to 33 per cent in 1803–7.[74] This fundamental reorientation of British commerce was prompted by two considerations. In the first place, it seems likely that down to the third quarter of the century Britain's foreign trade was propelled primarily by import-led demand, especially for new colonial products, such as sugar, tea and tobacco, and was driven by rising incomes in London and south-east England, which in turn derived from wealth generated from arable farming and from finance and services.[75] The second influence was the difficulty of increasing sales of manufactured goods (chiefly woollens) in Europe and the need, consequently, to prise open new markets elsewhere. These were found chiefly in the mainland colonies, where competition was limited, rather than in Asia, where British goods were unable to make headway against local substitutes.[76]

The import bill was met partly by pushing manufactures into new corners of the world, and partly by capturing the re-export trade, that is by selling colonial products in continental Europe. The re-export trades made a notable additional to Britain's own exports: they accounted for about one-third of the value of all exports during the first three-quarters of the eighteenth century and played a vital part in closing the gap that would otherwise have opened up in Britain's visible trade balance. Britain's competitive advantage in the transactions sector thus made it possible for her to solve the formidable problems posed by the limited competitiveness of woollen textiles and by the array of protectionist barriers that hampered access to the major markets on her door-step in continental Europe, and also to dominate the rapidly expanding trade in overseas products. In doing so, she forged a chain of multilateral links that spanned the world and enabled a system of compensating balances to function long before the better-known settlements pattern of the nineteenth century came into being.[77] Even as the Industrial Revolution was beginning, Britain was already becoming the warehouse and shop-window of the world.

With the development of the cotton industry from the 1780s, Britain finally had a product that gave her a competitive edge in major markets, and exports became a powerful 'engine of growth' of national income for the first time.[78] The rate of export expansion rose steeply, and the ratio of exports to national income doubled between 1783 and 1801, when it reached 18 per cent. Cotton products accounted for about 53 per cent of the increase in total export values between 1784–6 and 1814–16. By 1804–6, cotton goods were responsible for no less than 42 per cent of the value of total exports, and in 1807 more than two-thirds of the value of the cotton industry's output was exported. The main markets were found outside the empire, in Western Europe and the United States, and after 1806 (when Napoleon's blockade closed much of Europe to British exports) in Latin America. However, these impressive developments did not signal the 'triumph of industry' or even the triumph of one particular industry. By the close of the eighteenth century, Europe and the United States had already reached the peak of their relative importance as markets for British cotton goods, and early in the new century manufacturers were again seeking new outlets for their products.

After 1815, despite the resumption of peace, exports failed to act as an engine of growth, as they had done after 1780. The volume of exports increased rapidly between 1815 and 1850, but values grew much more slowly as productivity gains reduced manufacturing costs and cut export prices. But falling prices did not enable Britain to hold on to her share of major markets: exports of cotton goods lost ground in Europe and the United States, where import-substitution aided by protection severely limited the prospects of foreign suppliers. Consequently, as we noted earlier, the cotton industry suffered from bouts of excess capacity and from reduced profit margins during the 1820s and 1830s.[79] Exports of other finished goods, notably woollens and metal products, did increase in Europe and the United States; but the overall tendency, even at this early date, was for Britain to become a supplier of semi-finished manufactures, such as yarn, to her rivals (especially those in Europe), thus aiding their industrialization.

The inadequate rate of growth of exports, combined with rising demand for imports (fuelled by increased population), caused the trade gap to widen, especially in the late 1830s and early 1840s. Since income from shipping services increased only slowly, a trade-plus-services gap also appeared.[80] From the mid-1820s Britain depended upon rapidly increasing returns on foreign investments in Europe, North America, and the Middle East to provide a small current-account surplus and to hold imports of raw materials at a level that would maintain domestic employment. In the period after 1815 the City therefore began to assume a fully international role and to perform a key function in balancing Britain's payments. During this period, too, London's finance and commercial services continued to play a vital part in creating markets for Britain's staple exports and in securing the resources needed as inputs into industry. In the case of exports, for example, no less than four-fifths of the increase in values that occurred between 1816–20 and 1838–42 arose from sales to new markets in Asia, Latin America and Africa.[81]

We turn, finally, to the ways in which the impulses we have described so far, in shaping British history and the course of overseas trade, also shaped the history of the empire. The installation in 1688 of a cohesive government, whose supporters had seen instability and were determined to avoid it, expressed itself in centralizing tendencies that aimed at bringing all the outer provinces under closer central control. Scotland was incorporated by the Act of Union in 1707, the Welsh, who were already incorporated, were subjected to renewed Anglicizing influences, and Ireland was placed under the management of an Anglo–Irish, Protestant gentry.[82] Further afield, the mainland colonies came under firmer direction from the Board of Trade and from a new generation of military governors, and were integrated more closely with the developing Atlantic economy managed from London.[83]

Whether or not this flurry of activity was followed by a period of 'salutory neglect' is a matter of dispute.[84] It is equally plausible to suggest that, once the initial institutional changes had been made, Britain's main interest lay in developing trade and increasing revenues, and that this priority is not captured by measures of administrative activity. However, the failure of overseas trade to grow at a pace that met the expectations of powerful mercantile lobbies in London helped to push Walpole into war with Spain between 1739 and 1748; and the Seven Years' War that followed in 1756 witnessed the further development of an ideology of aggressive commercial expansion.[85] When the war came to an end in 1763, France had been driven out of Canada and India, and Britain had emerged as a major colonial and commercial power. In the course of this struggle, Britain had tightened her hold on the colonies in order to secure her defences. After the war, as the costs of victory began to be counted, she extended her grip in searching for ways of balancing the budget and servicing the national debt. This quest led to increased revenue demands both at home, as we have seen, and in the colonies, where it was accompanied by a spirit of assertiveness that was one of the legacies of military success.[86] Since Britain's fiscal problems were not offset by domestic economic growth or by foreign trade during the 1760s and 1770s,[87] there was some anxiety about her ability to maintain the level of re-exports needed to settle the import bill, and at moments of crisis doubts were also expressed about her creditworthiness.[88] It is against this background that Britain's changing relations with India and her mainland colonies in the third quarter of the century can best be approached.

Until the mid-eighteenth century, Britain's interests in India were represented by the East India Company and associated private traders, and were almost exclusively commercial.[89] From the 1720s, however, the Company's trade in its main spheres of activity in western India and Bengal began to run into difficulties. The problem stemmed principally from the dislocation caused by the break-up of the Mughal empire, but was compounded by competition from French companies and by military costs incurred during the conflict with France in the middle of the century. The attempt to resolve these problems, by restructuring trade relations to improve profitability and by using local revenues to subsidize the Company's activities, produced two important initiatives. The first, prompted by Clive's enterprise, led in 1757 to the Battle of Plassey, which delivered Bengal into British hands and a fortune into his own.[90] The second resulted in 1759 in the capture of Surat, which gave Britain a commanding position on the west coast.[91] The British government's interest in these advances was aroused by a desire to annex some of the Company's gains for its own budgetary needs:[92] 'Plassey plunder' did not fund the Industrial Revolution, as was once supposed, but it did enable Britain to indigenize the national debt by purchasing foreign (especially Dutch) holdings.[93] Thereafter, the quest for revenues to pay for military costs became a permanent one, and it greatly distorted the Company's commercial operations. As the East India Company began to generate debts and not just revenues in the 1770s, the British government found itself drawn further into the task of controlling the Company's administration and, in this way, of managing India too.[94]

Britain was not pulled into India simply by a breakdown of 'law and order'. The decline of central authority disrupted existing relations, but it did not lead to anarchy and it spawned a cluster of independent and semi-independent states whose ambitions sometimes cut across Britain's own purposes. Nor was Britain's advance the product of new industrial forces at home. The role of private traders expanded in the second half of the century, but their interest lay in selling Indian rather than British manufactures.[95] It is more plausible, we suggest, to view the move into India as being the result of competition between two military-fiscal organisations, one represented by the Mughals and their successor states and the other by the Company and the British government.[96] Both sides sought revenues to bolster trading profits, and both became involved in territorial expansion as a result. The outcome was strongly influenced by the military resources that the two were able to mobilise, and this in turn depended largely upon finance. The key decisions in this respect were made by local merchant bankers, who stood at the point of intersection between British and Indian commercial and political systems. In the end, the British were able to present themselves as the side likely to succeed, if not deserving of success: they won the support of the 'great moneyed men' of Surat before capturing the port;[97] and the balance of advantage in Bengal tilted in the Company's direction when local financiers deserted the nawab in 1757 and jeopardised his control of provincial treasuries.[98] Clive's actions were not directed from London; but they cannot be understood unless they are placed in the broader context of the financial revolution, the expansionist forces that it generated, and the problems these forces experienced on distant frontiers, where credit lines were fully stretched and where the junctions made with representatives of indigenous financial and fiscal systems were a necessary precondition of commercial success.

ABBREVIATIONS

Am. Hist. Rev.	*American Historical Review*
Bus. Hist. Rev.	*Business History Review*
Econ. Hist. Rev.	*Economic History Review*
Econ. Jour.	*Economic Journal*
Eng. His. Rev.	*English Historical Review*
Expl. Econ. Hist.	*Explorations in Economic History*
Hist. Jour	*Historical Journal*
Hist. Research	*Historical Research*
Internat. His. Rev.	*International History Review*
Jour. Econ. Hist.	*Journal of Economic History*
Jour. Imp. and Comm. Hist.	*Journal of Imperial and Commonwealth History*
Jour. Interdisc. Hist.	*Journal of Interdisciplinary History*
Jour. Mod. Hist.	*Journal of Modern History*
Mod. Asian Stud.	*Modern Asian Studies*
PP	Parliamentary Papers
Trans. Royal Hist. Soc.	*Transactions of the Royal Historical Society*

NOTES AND REFERENCES

1. The continuity thesis has been restated by J.C.D. Clark, *English Society, 1688–1832: Ideology, Social Structure and Political Practice during the Ancien' Regime*, Cambridge, 1985. Statements of the alternative view are too numerous to be listed, but for the one quoted here (and for further references), see Paul Langford, *A Polite and Commercial People: England, 1727–1783*, Oxford, 1989.

2. See Philip Lawson, 'The Missing Link: the Imperial Dimension in Understanding Hanoverian Britain', *Hist. Jour.*, 29 (1986), and the agenda drawn up by J.G.A. Pocock, 'British History: a Plea for a New Subject', *Am. Hist. Rev.*, 87 (1982).

3. See the judgements of I.K. Steele, 'The Empire and Provincial Élites: An Interpretation of Some Recent Writings on the English Atlantic, 1675–1740', in Peter Marshall and Glyn Williams, (eds), *The British Atlantic Empire Before the American Revolution* (1980), p. 2, and Peter Marshall, 'The British Empire in the Age of the American Revolution', in William M. Fowler and Wallace Coyle, (eds), *The American Revolution: Changing Perspectives*, Boston, Mass., 1979, p. 193.

4. J. Holland Rose, A.P. Newton, and E.A. Benians, (eds), *The Old Empire From the Beginnings to 1783*, Cambridge, 1929. See also Sir Reginald Coupland, *The British Empire After the American Revolution*, 1930.

5. Vol. I, *Discovery and Revolution*, Oxford, 1952, and vol. II, *New Continents and Changing Values*, Oxford, 1964. The discussion that follows draws especially on vol. I, pp. 1–11, 147–8, 154, 158, and 647, and vol. II, pp. 1–3, 259, 782–6, and 792–3, and on two valuable guides: Peter Marshall, 'The First and Second Empires: A Question of Demarcation', *History*, 44 (1964), and Ronald Hyam, 'British Imperial Expansion in the Late Eighteenth Century', *Hist. Jour.*, 10 (1967). There is also a perceptive review of vol. I by Richard Pares in *Eng. Hist. Rev.*, LXVIII (1953).

6. J. Gallagher and R.E. Robinson, 'The Imperialism of Free Trade', *Econ. Hist. Rev.*, 2nd ser., VI (1953).

7. Starting points other than that advanced by Harlow have been put forward: 1748 is one; the 'middle of the eighteenth century' is another. But these suggestions have not been accompanied by a thesis encompassing the 'first' empire as a whole. Harlow's argument therefore deserves to retain its place in the historiography of the eighteenth-century empire, despite the fact that it now has few advocates.

8. *Dependent Accumulation and Underdevelopment* (1978), pp. 72–3 and the discussion of periodization on pp. 7–10.

9. Immanuel Wallerstein, *The Modern World System*, vol. II, *Mercantilism and the Consolidation of the European World Economy, 1600–1750*, New York, 1980, p. 258 and the discussion of the periodization on pp. 2–9.

10. A recent exception, which should encourage imperial historians to look more closely at this neglected period, is C.A. Bayly, *Imperial Meridian: The British Empire and the World, 1780–1830*, Cambridge, 1989.

11. We follow here N.F.R. Crafts, 'British Economic Growth, 1700–1831: a Review of the Evidence', *Econ. Hist. Rev.*, 2nd ser. XXXVI (1983); id. 'British Industrialization in an International Context', *Jour. Interdisc. Hist.*, 19 (1989); and C.H. Feinstein,

'Capital Formation in Great Britain', in Peter Mathias and N.M. Postan, (eds), *The Cambridge Economic History of Europe*, Cambridge, 1978, VII, pt. 1.

12. J.V. Beckett, 'The Pattern of Landownership in England and Wales, 1660–1880', *Econ. Hist. Rev.*, 2nd ser. XXXVII (1984); J.R. Wordie, 'Rent Movements and the English Tenant Farmer, 1700–1839', *Research in Economic History*, 6 (1981); P.K. O'Brien, 'Quelle a été exactement la contribution de l'aristocratie britannique au progrès de l'agriculture entre 1688 et 1789?', *Annales*, 42 (1987).

13. A.H. John, 'The Course of Agricultural Change, 1660–1760', in L.S. Pressnell (ed.), *Studies in the Industrial Revolution Presented to T.S. Ashton* (1960), pp. 125, 130–2; and for the stimulus provided by the corn bounties, id., 'English Agricultural Improvement and Grain Exports, 1660–1765', in D.C. Coleman and A.H. John, (eds), *Trade, Government and Economy in Pre-Industrial England: Essays Presented to F.J. Fisher*, 1976, pp. 48–50.

14. Patrick O'Brien, 'Agriculture and the Home Market for English Industry', *Eng. Hist. Rev.* (c. 1985).

15. See, for example, John Cannon (ed.), *The Whig Ascendancy*, 1981; G.E. Mingay, *English Landed Society in the Eighteenth Century*, 1963, pp. 10–11, 111–13.

16. M.W. McCahil, *Order and Equipoise: The Peerage and the House of Lords, 1783–1806*, 1978; J. Slack, 'The House of Lords and Parliamentary Patronage in Great Britain, 1802–32', *Hist. Jour.*, 23 (1980); John Cannon, *Aristocratic Century: The Peerage of Eighteenth-Century England*, Cambridge, 1984; Ellis Archer Wasson, 'The House of Commons, 1660–1945: Parliamentary Families and the Political Élite', *Eng. Hist. Rev.*, CVI (1991).

17. Quoted in Cannon, *Aristocratic Century*, p. 39.

18. See, for example, Linda Colley, *In Defiance of Oligarchy: The Tory Party, 1714–60*, Cambridge, 1982; id., 'Eighteenth-Century Radicalism Before Wilkes', *Trans. Royal Hist. Soc.* 31 (1981); John Stevenson, *Popular Disturbances in England, 1700–1870*, 1979; and John Brewer, 'English Radicalism in the Reign of George III', in J.G.A. Pocock (ed.), *Three British Revolutions*, Princeton, NJ, 1980. The constituencies and the towns are dealt with by Frank O'Gorman, *Voters, Patrons and Parties: The Unreformed Electorate of Hanoverian England, 1734–1832*, Oxford, 1989, and Nicholas Rogers, *Whigs and Cities: Popular Politics in the Age of Walpole and Pitt*, Oxford, 1989.

19. Our thinking on this subject, and on the period as a whole, owes a great deal to two very different but complementary books: P.G.M. Dickson, *The Financial Revolution in England: A Study in the Development of Public Credit, 1688–1756*, 1967, and J.G.A. Pocock, *The Machiavellian Moment: The Florentine Contribution to the Atlantic Republican Tradition*, Princeton, NJ, 1975. See also, id., 'The Machiavellian Moment Revisited: a Study in History and Ideology', *Jour. Mod. Hist.*, 53 (1981); id., *Virtue, Commerce, and History*, Cambridge, 1985; and Julian Hoppit, 'Attitudes to Credit in Britain, 1680–1790', *Hist. Jour.*, 33 (1990).

20. A.E. Feaveryear, *The Pound Sterling: A History of English Money* (2nd edn 1963), pp. 154–7; J. Sperling, 'The International Payments Mechanisms in the Seventeenth and Eighteenth Centuries', *Econ. Hist. Rev.*, 2nd ser. XIV (1962); D.M. Joslin, 'London Private Bankers, 1720–1785', *Econ. Hist. Rev.*, 2nd ser. VII (1954), pp. 175–9, 184; Dickson, *Financial Revolution*, pp. 225–8, 493, 505–6, and Chap. 20; Larry Neal,

'The Rise of a Financial Press: London and Amsterdam, 1681–1810', *Bus. Hist.*, 30 (1988). Recent Research drawing attention to the importance of the service sector in the eighteenth century is summarized by N.F.R. Crafts, *British Economic Growth During the Industrial Revolution*, Oxford, 1985, pp. 12–13, 16–17.

21. Dickson, *Financial Revolution*, Chap. 16; P.G.M. Dickson, *The Sun Insurance Office, 1710–1960* (1960); B.E. Supple, *The Royal Exchange Assurance: A History of British Insurance, 1720–1970*, Cambridge, 1970; A.H. John, 'Insurance Investment and the London Money Market of the Eighteenth Century', *Economica*, 20 (1953).

22. Ralph Davis, *The Rise of the English Shipping Industry in the Seventeenth and Eighteenth Centuries* (2nd edn, 1972), pp. 389–90; Simon Ville, 'Michael Henley and Son, London Shipowners, 1775–1830: With Special Reference to War Experience', PhD thesis, London University, 1983.

23. Jacob M. Price, 'What Did Merchants Do? Reflections on British Overseas Trade, 1660–1790', *Jour. Econ. Hist.*, 49 (1989), pp. 273, 278–82.

24. John Brewer, *The Sinews of Power: War, Money and the English State, 1688–1783*, 1989, Chap. 3 (which also discusses the relationship between public service and patronage), Geoffrey Holmes, *Augustan England: Professions, State, and Society, 1680–1730*, 1982. Our formulation (see also Chap. 1) suggests that some occupations in the private sector were compatible with gentlemanly status and therefore refines the contrast drawn by Brewer, *Sinews of Power*, p. 206.

25. E.A. Wrigley, 'A Simple Model of London's Importance in Changing English Society and Economy, 1650–1750', *Past and Present*, 37 (1967), and the pioneering studies by F.J. Fisher now gathered together in *London and the English Economy, 1500–1800*, 1990. For the concentration of wealth and service-sector employments see James Alexander, 'The Economic Structure of the City of London at the End of the Seventeenth Century', *Urban History Yearbook* (1989); L.D. Schwartz, 'Social Class and Social Geography: the Middle Class in London at the End of the Eighteenth Century', *Social History*, (1982); and John A. James, 'Personal Wealth Distribution in Late Eighteenth-Century Britain', *Econ. Hist. Rev.*, 2nd ser. XLI (1988).

26. A.E. Musson, 'The British Industrial Revolution', *History*, 67 (1982), pp. 257–8. See also Neil McKendrick, John Brewer, and J.H. Plumb, *The Birth of a Consumer Society*, 1982, though the precise date of birth is open to discussion, as the title of Joan Thirsk's study of the seventeenth century suggests: *Economy, Policy and Projects: The Development of a Consumer Society in Early Modern England*, Oxford, 1978.

27. See, for example, P.J. Corfield, *The Impact of English Towns, 1700–1800*, Oxford, 1982; Peter Borsay, *The English Urban Renaissance: Culture and Society in the Provincial Town, 1660–1770*, Oxford, 1989; and the important essay by J.A. Chartres, 'Cities and Towns, Farmers and Economic Change in the Eighteenth Century', *Hist. Research*, 64 (1991).

28. Peter Mathias, *The Transformation of England*, 1979, pp. 91–4; B.L. Anderson, 'Provincial Aspects of the Financial Revolution of the Eighteenth Century', *Bus. Hist.*, 11 (1969), pp. 11–12; and id., 'Money and the Structure of Credit in the Eighteenth Century', *Bus. Hist.*, 12, 1970.

29. Dickson, *Financial Revolution*, pp. 4–6, 304–5.

30. Davis, *Rise of the English Shipping Industry*, p. 300; Dickson, *Financial Revolution*, pp. 304–5. It ought to be noted here that 'mercantilist' writers were well aware of the

importance of invisible items in the balance of payments: see Jacob Viner, *Studies in the Theory of International Trade*, 1937, pp. 13–15.

31. Clayton Roberts, 'The Constitutional Significance of the Financial Settlement of 1690', *Hist. Jour.*, 20 (1977).

32. This subject has been put on the agenda of historical inquiry by Patrick O'Brien and Caglar Keyder, *Economic Growth in Britain and France, 1780–1914*, 1978. Contemporaries were well aware of the disparity: François Crouzet, 'The Sources of England's Wealth: Some French Views in the Eighteenth Century' in P.L. Cottrell and D.H. Aldcroft, (eds), *Shipping, Trade and Commerce: Essays in Memory of Ralph Davis*, Leicester, 1981, pp. 71–2.

33. Charles P. Kindleberger, 'Financial Institutions and Economic Development: A Comparison of Great Britain and France in the Eighteenth and Nineteenth Centuries', *Expl. Econ. Hist.*, 21, 1984.

34. D. Weir, 'Tontines, Public Finance and Revolution in France and England, 1688–1789', *Jour. Econ. Hist.*, 49 (1989); Michael D. Border and Eugene N. White, 'A Tale of Two Currencies: British and French Finance During the Napoleonic Wars', *Jour. Econ. Hist.*, 51, 1991; and a source that might easily be overlooked in this connection, Gilbert Faccarello and Philippe Steiner, (eds), 'La pensée économique pendant la révolution française', *Economies et sociétés*, 13 (1990), pt. 4.

35. *The Conduct of the Allies* (1711), quoted in Dickson, *Financial Revolution*, p. 26.

36. Peter Earle, 'The Economics of Stability: the Views of Daniel Defoe', in Coleman and John, *Trade, Government and Economy*, pp. 277–8; and id., *The World of Daniel Defoe*, 1976, pt. 3.

37. In addition to the references given in n. 19, there is a particularly valuable set of essays in J.G.A. Pocock (ed.), *Three British Revolutions: 1641, 1688, 1776*, Princeton, NJ, 1980.

38. Quoted in Donald Winch, *Adam Smith's Politics*, Cambridge, 1978, p. 123. Isaac Kramnick, *Bolingbroke and his Circle*, Cambridge, Mass., 1968, has provoked methodological criticism but remains the classic statement.

39. Pocock, *Virtue, Commerce, and History*; Winch, *Adam Smith's Politics*; David Eastwood, 'Robert Southey and the Intellectual Origins of Romantic Conservatism', *Eng. Hist. Rev.*, CIV (1989).

40. For a broad survey of these tendencies, see P.J. Corfield, 'Class by Name and Number in Eighteenth-Century Britain', *History*, 78 (1987).

41. For one example see Larry Neal, 'Interpreting Power and Profit in Economic History: A Case Study of the Seven Years War', *Jour. Econ. Hist.*, 37 (1977).

42. This remained the case right down to 1815. See Dickson, *Financial Revolution*, pp. 58–9, 285, 295, 297–8, 302; Alice Carter, *Getting, Spending and Investing in Early Modern Times*, Assen, The Netherlands, 1975, pp. 19, 66–75, 136–7; also J.R. Ward, *The Finance of Canal Building in Eighteenth-Century England*, Oxford, 1974, pp. 140–2, 171–2. For the very similar composition of the original subscribers to the Bank of England, see Dickson, *Financial Revolution*, p. 256.

43. R.S. Neale, 'The Bourgeoisie, Historically, has Played a Most Important Part', in Eugene Kamenka and R.S. Neale, (eds), *Feudalism, Capitalism and Beyond*, 1975, p. 90.

44. Mingay, *English Landed Society*, pp. 71–6; P.J. Marshall, *East India Fortunes: The British in Bengal in the Eighteenth Century*, 1976, pp. 9–14.

45. Richard Grassby, 'Social Mobility and Business Enterprise in Seventeenth-Century England', in Donald Pennington and Keith Thomas, (eds), *Puritans and Revolutionaries: Essays in Seventeenth-Century History Presented to Christopher Hill*, Oxford, 1978, pp. 355–7, 365–6, 378–9. The direct connection with trade may have declined in the course of the eighteenth century as more attractive openings arose in public service, but at the highest levels ties between land and trade remained close, especially in London: Nicholas Rogers, 'Money, Land and Lineage: the Big Bourgeoisie of Hanoverian London', *Soc. Hist.*, 4 (1970), pp. 444–4.

46. Dickson, *Financial Revolution*, pp. 5–7; Neale, 'The Bourgeoisie', p. 98.

47. Dickson, *Financial Revolution*, p. 282; Carter, *Getting, Spending*, p. 106; Rogers, 'Money, Land and Lineage', pp. 444–7; G.C.A. Clay, 'The English Land Market, 1660–1770: the Role of the Moneyed Purchasers'. We are grateful to Dr Clay for allowing us to cite his unpublished paper. As F.M.L. Thompson points out, the purchase of a country estate did not necessarily mean that the new owner left the town or his business: 'Desirable Properties: the Town and Country Connection in British Society Since the Late Eighteenth Century', *Hist. Research*, 64 (1991).

48. Derek Jarrett, 'The Myth of "Patriotism" in Eighteenth-Century English Politics', in J.H. Bromley and E.H. Kossman, (eds), *Britain and the Netherlands*, vol. 5, The Hague, 1975, p. 124. For the background, see Daniel Statt, 'The City of London and the Controversy over Immigration, 1600–1722', *Hist. Jour.*, 33 (1990).

49. G.C.A. Clay, 'Henry Hoare, Banker, and the Building of the Stourhead Estate'. We are grateful to Dr Clay for allowing us to cite his unpublished paper on this subject.

50. Richard Pares, 'A London West India Merchant House', in id., *The Historian's Business*, Oxford, 1961.

51. Thereafter, the family was prominent in public service, especially the army. Its eminence was crowned in 1922, when the 6th earl married Princess Mary, the only daughter of George V.

52. Crafts, *British Economic Growth*; id., 'British Industrialization'; C.K. Harley, 'British Industrialisation before 1841: Evidence of Slower Growth during the Industrial Revolution', *Jour. Econ. Hist.*, 42 (1982). Peter H. Lindert, 'Remodelling British Economic History', *Jour. Econ. Hist.*, 43 (1983).

53. Contemporary views are discussed by Michael Kammen, *Empire and Interest: The American Colonies and the Politics of Mercantilism*, Philadelphia, Pa, 1970.

54. Mathias, *Transformation*, pp. 23, 31; D.J. Jeremy, 'Damming the Flood: British Government Attempts to Check the Outflow of Technicians and Machinery, 1780–1843', *Bus. Hist. Rev.*, 51 (1977); Douglas Farnie, *The English Cotton Industry and the World Market, 1815–96*, Oxford, 1979, p. 97. On the benefits of protection to special interests see, for example, N.B. Harte, 'The Rise of Protection and the English Linen Industry, 1690–1790', in N.B. Harte and K.G. Ponting, (eds), *Textile History and Economic History*, Manchester, 1973.

55. S.D. Chapman, 'British Marketing Enterprise: The Changing Role of Merchants, Manufacturers and Financiers, 1700–1860', *Bus. Hist. Rev.*, 53 (1979).

56. W.D. Rubinstein, 'The Victorian Middle Classes: Wealth, Occupation, and Geography',

Econ. Hist. Rev., 2nd ser. xxx (1977); id., 'Wealth, Élites, and the Class Structure of Modern Britain', *Past and Present*, 76 (1977). Information on the eighteenth century is less systematic, but see, for example, Brewer, *Sinews of Power*, pp. 208–9.

57. Quoted in Thomas A. Horne, *The Social Thought of Bernard Mandeville*, 1978, p. 95. See also Winch, *Adam Smith's Politics*, p. 99.

58. Rogers, 'Money, Land, and Lineage', p. 453.

59. Dickson, *Financial Revolution*, p. 203; Mingay, *English Landed Society*, pp. 197–8; David Spring, 'English Landowners and Nineteenth-Century Industrialisation', in J.T. Ward and R.G. Wilson, (eds), *Land and Industry: The Landed Estate and the Industrial Revolution*, Newton Abbot, 1971, pp. 39–42, 51–3.

60. See n. 44. Also John, 'Insurance Investment', p. 157; Joslin, 'London Private Bankers', p. 185; Thompson, 'Desirable Properties'.

61. François Crouzet, *The First Industrialists: The Problem of Origins*, Cambridge, 1985, pp. 68, 77, 80–4; Michael W. McCahill, 'Peers, Patronage and the Industrial Revolution, 1760–1800', *Jour. Brit. Stud.*, 16 (1976); David Spring, 'English Landowners', pp. 51–2.

62. On the General Chamber see Donald Read, *The English Provinces, 1760–1960: A Study in Influence* (1964), pp. 22–3. However, in scoring their success it seems likely that the manufacturers were manipulated by Pitt's opponents, who supplied the Chamber with alarming and possibly misleading information about the proposed Irish treaty. See J. Ehrman, *The Younger Pitt: The Years of Acclaim*, 1969, pp. 207–9; and Harlow, *Founding of the Second British Empire*, i, p. 608.

63. See Nicholas Canny and Anthony Padgen, (eds), *Colonial Identity in the Atlantic World, 1500–1800*, Princeton, NJ, 1987; Carl Bridge, P.J. Marshall and Glyndwr Williams, 'Introduction: a "British" Empire', *Internat. Hist. Rev.*, 12 (1990).

64. Richard L. Bushman, 'American High-Style and Vernacular Cultures', in Jack P. Greene and J.R. Pole, (eds), *Colonial British America: Essays in the New History of the Early Modern Era*, Baltimore, Md, 1984, p. 367.

65. Richard Pares, *A West India Fortune*, 1950; idem, *Merchants and Planters*, Cambridge, 1960; Tamara P. Thornton, *Cultivating Gentlemen: The Meaning of Country Life Among the Boston Élite, 1785–1860*, New Haven, Conn., 1989; and Pocock, *Three British Revolutions*, 'Introduction', and Chs. 8, 10 and 11.

66. For two contrasting cases see Rajat Ray and Ratna Ray, 'Zamindars and Jotedars: A Study of Rural Politics in Bengal', *Mod. Asian Stud.*, 9 (1975); and Neil Rabitoy, 'System v Expediency: The Reality of Land Revenue Administration in the Bombay Presidency, 1812–1820', *Mod. Asian Stud.*, 9 (1975).

67. Stephen S. Webb, *The Governors-General: The English Army and the Definition of Empire, 1569–1681*, Chapel Hill, NC, 1979, Paul David Nelson, *William Tryon and the Course of Empire: A Life in British Imperial Service*, Chapel Hill, NC, 1990; Marshall, *East India Fortunes*, pp. 9–14; Bayly, *Imperial Meridian*, pp. 133–6.

68. The Navigation Acts were reinforced in 1696 and the East India Company, founded in 1600, was restructured in 1708. On the capitalist qualities of the Company, see K.N. Chaudhuri, *The Trading World of Asia and the English East India Company, 1660–1760*, Cambridge, 1978, and Hoh-cheung Mui and Lorna H. Mui, *The Management of Monopoly: A Study of the English East India Company's Conduct of its Tea*

Monopoly, 1784–1833, Vancouver, 1984. Complementary views are expressed in Leonard Blussé and Femme Gastra, (eds), *Companies and Trade: Essays in Overseas Trading Companies During the Ancien Regime*, The Hague, 1981. The investors have been analysed by H.V. Bowen, 'Investment and Empire in the Later Eighteenth Century: East India Stockholding, 1756–1791', *Econ. Hist. Rev.*, 2nd ser. XLII (1989). While Dr Bowen is in agreement with the main direction of our argument, he questions (pp. 195–6) our claim that gentlemanly capitalism was a 'formidable mixture of the venerable and the new' on the grounds that there were few landowners among the East India Company's stockholders. We accept his evidence but not his conclusion. Our claim does not depend on showing that landowners were stockholders in the Company, but on a broader set of connections arising from the financial revolution and the increased degree of social integration that it encouraged—as we have suggested earlier in this chapter.

69. On mercantile lobbies, see Brewer, *Sinews of Power*, pp. 169, 231–49. We acknowledge that there is a gap in the literature at this point: there is no study of the eighteenth century to match the detailed work undertaken on the seventeenth century by Robert Brenner, *Merchants and Revolution: Commercial Change and Political Conflict in the London Merchant Community, 1550–1660*, Princeton, NJ, 1992, and on the turn of the century by D.W. Jones, *War and Economy in the Age of William III and Marlborough*, Oxford, 1988.

70. Consumers, especially but not exclusively in London and the south-east, also benefited from the increased availability (at steadily falling prices) of imports of colonial products.

71. See Richard Pares, 'American Versus Continental Warfare, 1739–63', in id., *The Historian's Business*, Oxford, 1961; W.A. Speck, 'The International and Imperial Context', in Jack P. Greene and J.R. Pole, (eds), *Colonial British America: Essay in the New History of the Early Modern Era*, Baltimore, Md, 1984; Daniel A. Baugh, 'Great Britain's "Blue Water" Policy', *Internat. Hist. Rev.*, 10 (1988); and, for a view that extends beyond strategic considerations, J.S. Bromley, 'Britain and Europe in the Eighteenth Century', *History*, 66 (1981).

72. Quoted in Pares, 'American Versus Continental Warfare', p. 144. See also ibid., pp. 140–3.

73. The trade data summarized in the following five paragraphs derive principally from: Ralph Davis, 'English Foreign Trade, 1700–1774', in W.E. Minchinton (ed.), *The Growth of English Overseas Trade in the Seventeenth and Eighteenth Centuries* (1969); id., *The Industrial Revolution and British Overseas Trade*, Leicester, 1979; François Crouzet, 'Toward an Export Economy: British Exports During the Industrial Revolution', *Expl. in Econ. Hist.*, 17 (1980); Jacob M. Price, 'New Time Series for Scotland's and Britain's Trade with the Thirteen Colonies and State, 1740–1791', *William & Mary Quarterly*, 32 (1975); and Crafts, 'British Economic Growth', A slightly fuller commentary is given in P.J. Cain and A.G. Hopkins, 'The Political Economy of British Expansion Overseas, 1750–1914', *Econ. Hist. Rev.*, 2nd ser. XXXIII (1980), pp. 470–8. Additional references will therefore be given selectively.

74. Seymour Drescher, *Econocide: British Slavery in the Era of Abolition*, Pittsburgh, Pa, 1977, p. 20.

75. On import-led growth, see F.J. Fisher, 'London as an Engine of Growth', in J.S. Bromley and E.H. Kossmann, (eds), *Britain and the Netherlands*, 6, 1971; and Davis, 'English Foreign Trade', p. 108.

76. Chaudhuri, *Trading World*, Chaps. 10–11.

77. See Davis, *Industrial Revolution*, pp. 53–61, 73, 85; and the neglected study by C.J. French, 'The Trade and Shipping of the Port of London, 1700–1776', PhD thesis, Exeter University, 1980, Chap. 2. By the middle of the eighteenth century contemporary writers had distinguished between the balance of trade and the balance of payments, and soon afterwards David Hume published his celebrated analysis, 'Of the Balance of Trade', in his *Essays and Treatises on Several Subjects*, vol. 1 (1772). At the close of the century, Paine made a characteristically scathing reference to the 'motley amphibious-charactered thing called the balance of trade', which, he said, was deployed to deceive members of parliament whose understanding of 'fox-hunting and the game laws' was somewhat ahead of their knowledge of economics. See Paine, *Complete Works*, p. 492.

78. Crouzet, 'Toward an Export Economy'.

79. See pp. 80–4.

80. Cain and Hopkins, 'Political Economy', p. 475.

81. Calculated from A.H. Imlah, *Economic Elements in the Pax Britannica: Studies in British Foreign Trade in the Nineteenth Century*, New York, 1958, Table 12.

82. For a recent survey, see J.C.D. Clark, 'English History's Forgotten Context: Scotland, Ireland, Wales', *Hist. Jour.*, 32 (1989).

83. I.K. Steele, *The Politics of Colonial Policy: The Board of Trade in Colonial Administration, 1696–1720*, Oxford, 1968; Webb, *The Governors–General*; and, for colonial reactions to first royal absolutism and then Whig oligarchy, the essays by Murrin and Lovejoy in Pocock, *The British Revolutions*.

84. James A. Henretta, *'Salutory Neglect': Colonial Administration Under the Duke of Newcaste*, Princeton, NJ, 1972; and the commentary in Speck, 'The International and Imperial Context'.

85. For a summary and further references, see Brewer, *Sinews of Power*, pp. 173–8, and H.T. Dickinson, *Walpole and the Whig Supremacy*, 1973, ch. 6 and pp. 105–6, 135–7.

86. On the mood of assertiveness that took hold in the 1760s, see P.J. Marshall, 'Empire and Authority in the later Eighteenth Century', *Jour. Imp. and Comm. Hist.*, 15 (1987); and for the perception (by others) that Britain was the main threat to peace and stability after 1763, see H.M. Scott, *British Foreign Policy in the Age of the American Revolution*, Oxford, 1990.

87. For the abysmal performance of Britain's exports during this period, see Crouzet, 'Toward an Export Economy', p. 52.

88. For example, Riley, *International Government Finance*, pp. 123–5.

89. The detailed literature has now been brought together in two complementary studies: P.J. Marshall, *Bengal: The British Bridgehead. Eastern India, 1740–1828*, Cambridge, 1987, and C.A. Bayly, *Indian Society and the Making of the British Empire*, Cambridge, 1988. We should like to express our debt to Prof. Marshall for the comments and advice he has generously supplied over many years on the subject of British interests in India in the eighteenth century.

90. We are aware that we are over-compressing an episode that began rather than ended with Plassey, which was more of a coup than a battle. Subsequent developments culminated in the more important military engagement at Buxar in 1764. On Clive, see Huw V. Bowen, 'Lord Clive and Speculation in East India Company Stock, 1766', *Hist. Jour.*, 30 (1987). We are grateful to Dr Bowen for discussing these and related issues; we hope that any differences that remain are those of perspective rather than of substance.

91. Lakshmi Subramanian, 'Capital and Crowd in a Declining Asian Port City: the Anglo-Bania Order and the Surat Riots of 1795', *Mod. Asian Stud.*, 19 (1985), relates the problems of the 1790s to commercial and financial difficulties that first surfaced in the middle of the century. On the subsequent shift of influence from Surat to Bombay, see Pamela Nightingale, *Trade and Empire in Western India, 1784–1806*, Cambridge, 1970.

92. Huw V. Bowen, 'A Question of Sovereignty: the Bengal Land Revenue Issue, 1765–67', *Jour. Imp. and Comm. Hist.*, 16 (1988).

93. Marshall, *East India Fortunes*, p. 256; Davis, *The Industrial Revolution*, pp. 55–6.

94. The principal measures were the Regulating Act of 1773, Pitt's India Act of 1784, and the Charter Act of 1793. The political background to the first of these measures has now been reappraised by H.V. Bowen, *Revenue and Reform: the Indian Problem in British Politics, 1757–1773*, Cambridge, 1991.

95. See, for example, P.J. Marshall, 'Economic and Political Expansion: the Case of Oudh', *Mod. Asian Stud.*, 9 (1975); and Anthony Webster, 'British Export Interests in Bengal and Imperial Expansion in South-East Asia, 1780–1824: The Origins of the Straits Settlements', in Barbara Ingham and Colin Simmons, (eds), *Development Studies and Colonial Policy*, 1987.

96. On the Mughal empire as a patronage state that was ceasing to deliver, see Richard B. Barnett, *North India Between Empires: Awadh, The Mughals and the British, 1720–1801*, Berkeley, Calif., 1980.

97. The relative power of the Company and the banias (and much else of consequence) is debated by Lakshmi Subramanian, 'Banias and the British: The Role of Indigenous Credit in the Process of Imperial Expansion in Western India in the Second Half of the Eighteenth Century', *Mod. Asian Stud.*, 21 (1987), and Michelguglielmo Torri, 'Trapped Inside the Colonial Order: the Hindu Bankers of Surat and their Business World during the Second Half of the Eighteenth Century', *Mod. Asian Stud.*, 25 (1991). See also Subramanian's reply in ibid.

98. We base ourselves here on J.D. Nichol's important study, 'The British in India, 1740–1763: A Study in Imperial Expansion into Bengal', PhD thesis, Cambridge University, 1976, pp. 62–75, chaps. 3–4, and pp. 163–71. There is a published discussion of these issues, but it is at a rather general level and does not include an assessment of Nichol's research: Karen Leonard, 'The Great Firm Theory of the Decline of the Mughal Empire', *Comp. Stud. in Soc. and Hist.*, 21 (1979); J.F. Richards, 'Mughal State Finance and the Pre-Modern World Economy', ibid. 73 (1981); and Leonard's reply in ibid.

PART IV
THE NEW BRITISH ORDER

15

The Agrarian Economy
and the Dynamics of Commercial
Transactions*

B ehind all the developments in rural society were the rhythms of economic
life, especially those of the manner, channels, and agencies for the consumption and distribution of food. Apart from its importance for the physical
survival of people, economic transactions and exchange in agricultural
produce had a critical bearing on the structure and organization of internal
markets,[1] the modes, methods, and formation of mercantile activity, and the
relationships between the merchants and the producers. Equally critical were
the factors of demand and prices in shaping the dynamics of local trade and
in influencing the spatial directions of the flow of commodities. These separate questions, when combined together, give us a typology of agrarian com-
mercialism, and it is to this construction that we now turn.

BENGAL'S ECONOMY AND THE FACTOR
OF DEMAND

The influence of town demand had a clear effect on local trade in agricultural
produce. Contemporary observers talked eloquently of the increase in
Calcutta's population throughout the century.[2] Dhaka had about 4,50,000
people living within its environs in 1765[3] and continued to be thickly peopled
later on.[4] In 1757, Murshidabad was declared as 'one of the richest cities in
the world'[5] and, in 1764, Robert Clive described the city of Murshidabad as

*Rajat Datta, 'The Agrarian Economy and the Dynamics of Commercial Transactions,
in *Society, Economy and Market: Commercialization in Rural Bengal, c. 1760–1800*,
Delhi, 2000.

'extensive, populous and rich as the city of London, with this difference that there are individuals in the first possessing infinitely greater property than in the last [named] city'.[6]

Apart from these premier cities, there were other towns which were positioned at medium levels of consumption and had their combined effect on trade. Bhagwangola, near Murshidabad, handling about 18 million maunds of grain in the 1760s[7] was one such centre. Azimganj in Hughli was another, having grown during the early eighteenth century as a centre of the grain trade between Murshidabad and southern Bengal: 'being one of the first gunges and established under a powerful patronage, it was invested with extensive controul [sic]' was how it was described in 1773.[8] Then there were the towns like Katwa and Kalna in western Bengal which, along with Calcutta, redistributed grain from the eastern parts of Bengal (like Jessore) to other parts of Bengal and Bihar.[9] Chinsura, a prosperous trading settlement, was 'thickly interspersed with houses and small gardens' in 1778,[10] whereas Chittagong was described as a 'very large and extensive town' in 1789.[11]

The demand for food generated by these towns exerted a crucial influence on the direction and movement of local trade. The average monthly consumption of common quality rice in Calcutta was 2,50,000 maunds in the 1780s.[12] Murshidabad needed more than 1,30,000 maunds of rice and 57,000 maunds of paddy for its sustenance in the 1790s.[13] Towns lower down the scale needed proportionate amounts of food. Unfortunately, these needs cannot be worked out even in the most tentative fashion because of the scarcity of relevant statistical information. Quantitative data of the amounts of money involved in the purchase of food and other items of consumption are equally scarce. However, the evidence indicates that the amount of foodgrains available for merchants from different localities for catering to town demand and for exports outside the province (referred to as the 'exportable surplus' in our sources) seldom exceeded 20 per cent of the gross agricultural output under normal circumstances.[14] The remaining portion, excluding 6 to 8 per cent retained as seed stock,[15] was consumed in the countryside.

Unfortunately, how much of this remaining produce entered the rural market, or how much of it was directly consumed within the household, and the proportion of both in the overall structure of rural consumption cannot be worked out due to the limitations of the evidence. A contemporary calculation valued the annual turnover of rice, both traded and untraded, at 43.8 million maunds in 1791.[16] If we see this in relation to the fact that the combined annual consumption of rice in Calcutta and Murshidabad was 4.56 million maunds (based on the data of monthly consumption given earlier), then there is a very strong indication that rural demand was indeed exerting an extremely dynamic influence on the movement of marketed rice in our period. It would perhaps not be incorrect to suggest that this demand probably accounted for 70 to 80 per cent of the local trade in rice.

The idea that most of Bengal was an interlinked chain of 'innumerable villages' interspersed with a few towns was originally put forward by James Rennell in 1765.[17] The same theme recurs when W. Hamilton, writing in 1828, says: 'villages from 100 to 500 inhabitants are astonishingly numerous, and in some parts form a continued chain of many miles along the bank of rivers'.[18] The absence of area statistics for this period does not allow us to estimate the number of villages in all areas of the province, or account for their spatial distribution. Table 1 gives the data available.

Obviously, clusters of villages would tend to be greater in areas closer to important commercial and administrative centres, but the spatial distribution of these villages does suggest a continuous, and often densely packed, chain constituting most parts of Bengal's countryside. Area figures given by Rennell and the data available in Table 1 show the spatial distribution of villages in our period as shown in Table 2.

Table 1. Estimates of Villages in Different Districts of Bengal

Year	District	Number of villages
1760	Burdwan	8,000
1765	Birbhum	6,000
1771	Birbhum	4,500
1772	Nadia	3,499*
1774	Hijli	579
1778	Mahisadal	438
1778	24-Parganas	3,124
1778	Hughli	579
1778	Purnea	5,350
1778	Rajshahi	16,132
1788	Midnapur	4,303
1788	Jalasore	1,891
1788	Badakhal	1,200

Note: *Indicates the severity of the famine of 1769–70 in this district.

Sources: John Johnstone, Letter to the Proprietors of the East India Stock, London, 1776, p. 6; R.K. Gupta, 1977; 47; B.M. Add. MS, 29076, fol. 11; Add. MS 29087, fols. 58, 97, 119; Add. MS 29088, fols. 108, 116–22; IOR, BRP, P/70/49, 15 Dec. 1788; ibid., P/70/48, 7 Nov. 1788.

Table 2. Spatial Distribution of Villages

District	Village: square mile ratio
Burdwan	1: 0.64
Birbhum	1: 1.16
Midnapur	1: 1.14
Purnea	1: 0.96
Rajshahi	1: 0.80
Nadia	1: 0.91
Jessore	1: 1.71

Source: James Rennell, *Bengal Atlas: Containing Maps of the Theatre of War and Commerce on that Side of Hindostan*, London, 1781, p. 53 and Table 34.

Population data for these villages are practically non-existent, though Johnstone's estimate does give us an average of 50 persons per village in Burdwan in the 1760s.[19] Relatively large villages could have more than 250 households around Murshidabad,[20] whereas in relatively less developed districts like Commilla 'the average is less than 10 persons [per] village'.[21] The crucial fact about these villages is that they jointly accounted for about 70 per cent of the agricultural product available for internal consumption. An interesting example of this phenomenon is provided by the rice of the spring harvest (*aus dhan*). It was generally recognized that this rice was intrinsically of an inferior quality than the one produced in winter (*aman*) and was consumed by the 'lowest and poorer classes'.[22] Rice of this kind would presumably have featured prominently in a system of natural exchange; yet the grain merchants made it a point to purchase the *aus* crop from the cultivators *before* they could dispose of their surpluses independently in local markets.[23] Since the so-called 'coarsest grains' were sown in the *aus* season, the intervention of the merchants here indicates the existence of an exchange economy in the province.

The important bearing this system of exchange had on the working of the provincial economy would come sharpest in focus under conditions of dearth. Witness for instance the following description of the state of the food-market during the dearth of 1791: 'The bazaars have hitherto been sufficiently well supplied to answer the immediate wants of the inhabitants; but the alarm of an approaching scarcity is now become so universal that *the poorer sort of people* will shortly experience considerable distress, as *the price of grain* and the difficulty of procuring it, *even for money*, is daily increasing.'[24] In an earlier drought (in 1774), the peasants of Burdwan complained that: 'Our condition is most miserable, for though there is grain in the hands of the

Merchants ... they have leagued together to keep the price up and we are perishing with hunger. If we *cannot procure food even with money*, how is possible for us to stay in the District?[25] These descriptions underscore the fact the money-bazaar-market nexus determined the availability of food in the countryside as it did in the towns.

Who were the consumers? Large and intermediate towns exclusively depended on the arrival of traded rice for their sustenance. The social organization in the urban areas was complex and was based on a hierarchy of occupational groups and standards of living; therefore the structure of demand in these centres was correspondingly complex.

With regard to rural demand, the evidence is less definitive. A detailed list of houses, compiled in 1775, in *tarf* Rangamati, *chakla* Murshidabad is of interest.[26] Out of a total of 256 households, *chasis* (cultivators) accounted for 101, that is 39.45 per cent, of the total. The rest were as detailed in Table 3.

Table 3: Professional Groups in Rangamati, 1775

Profession	Number of households	% of total
Putwa, those who breed silkworms	22	8.59
Tanti (cotton weavers)	6	2.34
Carpenters	3	1.17
Smiths	2	0.78
Barbers	1	0.39
Dokandars (shopkeepers)	2	0.78
Teli (oilpressers)	5	1.95
Widows	3	1.17
Fishmongers	7	2.73
Manjhi (boatmen)	1	0.39
Goala (milkmen)	17	6.64
Coolies	22	8.59
Chassars (silk weavers)	3	1.17
Officials	33	12.89
Mendicants	13	5.08
Bamboo cutters	3	1.17
Moochi (shoemaker)	1	0.39
Moodi (grocer)	1	0.39
Baori caste	8	3.12
Filature worker	1	0.39
Unspecified	4	1.56
Total	158	61.68

Source: WBSA, PCR Murshidabad, vol. 7, 15 Feb. 1776.

This evidence reveals a high concentration of non-agricultural occupations in rural society. Pure artisans, that is, those who were completely separated from any form of agricultural production accounted for 27 per cent of the households; officials comprised a sizeable 12.89 per cent. This suggests quite strongly that an overwhelming number of people in rural society, at least 50 per cent, depended substantially on the market for their subsistence requirements. Significantly, therefore, this *tarf* had two grocery shops plus a *haat* with thirteen shops divided as follows:

Moodis (grocers)	3
Cowri shops	3
Shroffs (money-changers)	2
Tobacconist	1
Carpenter	1
Widows	2
Pashari (general provisioner)	1

A survey made by Robert Kyd of the village of Sibpur, on the western bank of the Hughli, showed that in 1791 out of a total of 419 Hindu households in that village, pure agriculturist, *chasis*, comprised 106 households thus accounting for 37.23 per cent of the residents.[27] The rest were divided in the fashion as shown in Table 4.

Thus, in Sibpur, a purely non-agricultural population of artisans constituted 15.5 per cent of the households. A further 21.72 per cent were fishermen, the nature of whose occupation made them net consumers of food. Added to this was a substantial—20.51 per cent—upper caste rural gentry who would

Table 4. Professional Groups in Sibpur, 1791

Professionals	Number of households	% of total
Brahmins	65	15.51
Vaidya or physicians	3	0.71
Kayasthas	18	4.29
Moira or confectioners	10	2.39
Kasari or brass makers	2	0.48
Milkmen	4	0.95
Chootor or carpenter	14	3.34
Soonar or goldsmith	3	0.71
Teli or oilmen	6	1.43
Tantee or weavers	26	6.20
Bania or shopkeepers	27	6.44
Jallia or fishermen	91	21.72

Source: IOL, MS, Eur. F. 95, fol. 64.

generate a systematic demand for the relatively luxury end of the market. In all, more than half of Sibpur's population depended upon the market for subsistence; of this the dependence of the artisans and the fishermen was the most critical, and it is perhaps no accident that 6.44 per cent of the population in that village was that of the bania.

The high concentration of a food-dependent population in rural Bengal as demonstrated by the case of Rangamati and Sibpur are not isolated cases. According to Buchanan, there were 1,00,809 houses of artisans in Rangpur. In addition were the categories shown in Table 5.

A contemporary estimate computed that the all-Bengal average of members per household was of 5.5 persons.[28] This would give us a population of 5,54,450 artisans in Rangpur alone at the turn of the century: a concentration of nearly 207 artisans per square mile of territory.[29]

The patterns of consumption are also indicative. Table 6 gives the annual consumption of various items by a 'Hindoo family in Respectable Circumstances' in Buldacaul in eastern Bengal surveyed by commissioner J. Paterson in 1789.

Paterson additionally noted that a 'Mussullman family in similar circumstances differs from the Hindoo in the addition of onions and garlick to their food and less pawn [betel-leaf] being consumed. They are less expensive in their clothes, ornaments and utensils [and] the expenses of a Mussulman for religious ceremonies are not so great as those of the Hindoos.'[30]

On the other hand, the expenditure of an artisan in somewhat comfortable circumstances in maintaining a family of six persons in Rangpur is shown in Table 7. Finally, the consumption patterns of a 'common artificer' are detailed in Table 8. Buchanan's data also show that different ranks of people in Rangpur spent on food in fashion as shown in Table 9.

The fact that expenditures on food were inversely proportional to an individual's economic station in life is perhaps a strong statement in favour of the argument that overwhelming numbers in Bengal were dependent on the

Table 5. Professional Groups in Rangpur, c. 1808

Professional groups	Number
Kolu or Oil Mills	3,254
Distilleries	27
Badyakar or common musicians	2,660
Notis or dancing girls	79
Kirtaniyas, those who sing the praises of different Gods	578

Source: Buchanan, 'Survey of Ronggoppur', Statistical Tables, Table 39.

Table 6. Consumption Patterns of the Rural Gentry
in Eastern Bengal, 1789

Item	Value (Rs)	% of total
Rice	199.65	33.18
Salt	8.25	1.37
Oil	27.38	4.55
Turmeric	1.37	0.23
Pepper	2.81	0.47
Ginger	1.37	0.23
Dhania (coriander)	1.37	0.23
Paan (betel-leaf)	5.69	0.94
Betel-nut	5.50	0.91
Tobacco	4.56	0.76
Gur (Molasses)	22.81	3.79
Fish	17.06	2.83
Vegetables	17.06	2.83
Firewood	0.75	0.12
Chunam (lime)	0.75	0.12
Clothing	48	7.98
Bedding	29.25	4.86
Utensils and Ornaments	208	34.57
Total	601.63	

Source: IOR, BRC, P/51/40, 15 July 1789.

Table 7. Patterns of Consumption of an Artisan in Comfortable
Circumstances, Rangpur, c. 1807

Item	Annual value (Rs)	% of total
Rice	32.25	48.59
Pulse	1.5	2.26
Salt	4.5	6.78
Mustard oil	8.25	12.43
Onions, garlic, capsicum and turmeric	1.12	1.69
Fish	5.25	7.91
Vegetables	3.00	4.52
Betel with spices	6.00	9.04
Molasses or gur	3.75	5.65
Tobacoo	0.75	1.13
Total	66.37	

Source: F. Buchanan, 'Statistical Tables of Ronggoppur', IOL. MS Eur. G. 11.

Table 8. Patterns of Consumption of a common Artisan:
Rangpur, *c.* 1807

Item	Annual value (Rs)	% of total
Rice	22.5	84.43
Pulse	0.22	0.82
Salt	0.75	2.81
Oil	1.01	3.79
Fish, vegetable, turmeric and capsicum	1.2	4.5
Betel-leaf and nuts	0.75	2.8
Tobacco	0.23	0.86
Total	26.65	

Source: F. Buchanan, 'Statistical Tables of Ronggoppur', IOL, MS, Eur. G. 11.

Table 9: Patterns of Food Consumption in Rangpur, *c.* 1807

Category	Total annual expenses (Rs)	Expense on food (Rs)	% of total
First Class	4,095.13	658.81	16.09
Second Class	1,443.37	354.87	24.59
Third Class	447.12	195.62	43.75
Fourth Class	168.44	84.75	50.31
Fifth Class	65.01	45	69.22
Sixth Class	32	27	84.37
Seventh Class	25.75	21.37	82.99

Source: F. Buchanan, 'Statistical Tables', Table 39.

market for their subsistence. Coarse rice and salt were items which even people at the lowest levels of income, such as a 'man who labours for others in the field'[31] or a 'wretched boatman' in Bengal's numerous rivers and creeks[32] had to purchase on a continuous basis. In Rangpur, such people never used fish nor vegetables in their diet, but there were occasional purchases of pulses, oil, tobacco and betel-leaf.[33] The significance of such high clusters of people depending on local networks of exchange for their subsistence and other requirements is heightened when we consider the fact that the worst brunt of the famine of 1769–70 was borne by the rural artisan: 'the number of *consumers* who suffered by that calamity was greater in proportion, than that of the cultivators of grain'.[34] The mortality among this group is said to have accounted for 25 per cent (in Purnea) and 50 per cent (in Malda) of the total deaths which occurred in that catastrophe.[35]

With regard to the demand for agricultural produce in general, the fragmentary bits of evidence which are available may perhaps allow the following purely tentative reconstruction. J. Paterson, Commissioner at Commilla, calculated that in 1791 a 'Hindoo family in respectable circumstances' consisting of 16 persons, including dependants, spent roughly Rs 333.50 per year on food.[36] This would give us an annual per capita consumption of Rs 20.54. This figure closely approximates to the evidence from Rangpur where F. Buchanan's estimate of the domestic consumption of 'seven ranks' of people in 1807 gives a crude per capita consumption average of Rs 21.02 a year.[37] The population of Bengal and Bihar in 1790 was stated to be 22 million,[38] of which 12 million may have been the share of Bengal.[39] Multiplying the latter figure by the lower rate of Rs 20.54, we arrive at a purely tentative sum of Rs 246.8 million annually being spent on food in the province.

An estimate such as this will be open to a wide range of criticisms and all of them may perhaps be valid. This estimate does not take into account the regional variations in consumption. It assumes a fixed pattern of consumption for all social strata, it does not discuss consumption expenditures over time, and fails to relate these expenditures to the price situation—these are perhaps just a few objections which can reasonably be anticipated. The estimate I have made is *purely tentative* and is an attempt to indicate the money involved in the annual demand for agricultural produce. The other reason is to draw attention to the fact that such large amounts could not have emerged from consumption in towns alone.

THE REGIONAL FOOD MARKET: SOME EVIDENCE OF PRICE MOVEMENTS

One major indication of an integrated provincial market would be the behaviour of prices of food across the region. In this connection, M.M. Postan's study of the medieval British economy provides helpful insights into the working of a pre-modern market. It is essentially characterized by wide fluctuations in prices and in the flow of commodities from season to season and from locality to locality, as well as by the seasonality of the consumers. 'Grains were at their cheapest in the early autumn, i.e. immediately after the harvest had been gathered, since the villagers then had some grain of their own to eat. But they almost invariably rose in summer, since by that time many villagers had exhausted their own grain supplies and swelled the ranks of the buyers.' Incidentally, the 'narrowness' of the market 'merely widened the amplitude of fluctuations [of price]', and that 'prices would not have risen or fallen as sharply as they did had buyers and sellers been more numerous, the volume of commodities larger, and the access to imported food easier'.[40]

On the basis of the above typology, an integrated market, therefore, would exhibit opposite tendencies. Prices would not show such wide amplitude of fluctuations (at least not under normal climate conditions), though a seasonal price-swing would be naturally built into the movement of prices. In other words, prices would tend to be lower immediately after the harvest and rise subsequently, not because of the impermanence of consumers but as a normal trend from season to season. In addition, a permanency of 'pure' consumers would generate a palpable demand for a basket of goods and services with a large number of buyers ensuring commodity transactions of a particular order. Further, a well-oiled machinery of trade in foodgrain would exist and importation of food both to meet exigencies and on a regular basis would be possible without any or much internal barriers. Finally, with regard to the significance of a secular price-trend, one can argue, following Labrousse, that 'as opposed to short term convulsive movements . . . a more extended and progressive price rise . . . spells expansion and prosperity, [while] a [sustained] decline denotes economic recession'.[41]

A recent study of the integration of the early modern grain market in Scotland[42] makes the following pertinent observations regarding the indices of market integration:

Most recent work relating price movements to market conditions has been predicated on the assumption that the degree to which prices in different markets fluctuate in unison reflects to the extent which those markets were associated or integrated. . . . As knowledge and trade flow more freely and unity of marketing is achieved over a number of previously disconnected markets, so any local imbalance of the effective supply would be transmitted throughout the wider marketing region. Grain movements would seek to address such imbalances and price movements in one area would naturally come to be reflected by price movements elsewhere in the enlarged market region.

Specific indicators of such market integration as suggested in this study are: an increased synchronicity of price movements of a particular grain in different regions and a concomitant decrease in the synchronicity of price movements of different grains within a single region. A third possible consequence of market integration 'would be a decrease in the volatility with which individual grain prices fluctuated from year to year'.[43]

While there is no doubt that market integration would mean increased synchronicity of price over different regions largely because of the nature of demand and the networks of local trade, a continuing volatility of individual grain prices would not necessarily cut into this integration. Grain prices were initially determined by the state of the current harvest which was in turn influenced by prevailing climatic conditions. As the latter variable was beyond the control of human agency, the amplitude of price fluctuation would continue notwithstanding a high degree of market integration. Under such conditions the inelasticity of demand would be the oil and local trade, the motor of this integrative process. As has been shown below, merchants would be the principal beneficiaries of the volatility of spot prices. Gibson and Smout also suggest that market integration results in a better access to food from outside, especially in case of localized crises of subsistence. This eliminates the need for substitution in grain consumption (that is switching to locally available lower grade crops) as would happen in an incompletely integrated market. 'As market integration proceeded there would be less need for such substitution, and grain prices within a single market would tend to move more independently of one another.'[44]

Figure 1 charts the movements of two basic commodities, fine and common rice, and of wheat in lower Bengal between 1700 and 1800 on the basis of the Chinsura series provided by G. Herklotts (in *Gleanings in Science*, vol. 1) in January 1829.[45] Figure 2 provides the prices of coarse rice of the *aman* and *aus* harvests in the district of Birbhum between 1784 and 1813 on the basis of the series of prices provided by W.B. Bayley in the *Asiatick Researches* (1816).[46] Both these figure are unequivocal about the synchronicity of prices.

The reason for such symmetry was to be in all likelihood the inelasticity of demand for rice in the countryside. The fact that nearly a quarter of Bengal's society, especially rural society, depended on the ebb and flow of commodities in the market is eloquent testimony to the pull of a regional demand. The impermanence or uncertainty of consumption imposing a deleterious impact on prices was thus not a problem in the economy. Naturally, demand influenced the movement of agricultural prices. In this, the demand for the most basic necessities, especially foodgrains, tended to exert an extremely powerful effect on the movement of prices because of its intrinsic inelasticity owing to the increase in the numbers of those who did not produce their own food, either because they lived in the cities, or belonged to the rural consumption-élite or comprised those peasants who had little or inadequate agricultural land and had to rely on wages earned as sharecroppers or agricultural labourers. Since consumption behaviour was a function of income, lower wage-earners would tend to consume coarser (that is inferior) grains within a region, thereby explaining the symmetry of price movements of rice especially as they are reflected in Figure 1.

The behaviour of the economy to such a buoyant demand for food is also apparent from the discussion of prices in Chapter 1 which shows that the steady secular increase in the prices of agricultural produce through the eighteenth century was accompanied by a positively correlated response of the production system which took the form of an expansion of the agricultural frontier.

Figure 3 compares the prices of common rice over the century from the series compiled by Akhtar Hussain for Bengal and the series provided for lower Bengal (Chinsura) by Herklotts. This figure demonstrates the striking concordance of prices between the Bengal averages, that is the prices which the Company paid in order to buy food chiefly for its garrisons and those prevailing in lower Bengal. This impression is buttressed by Figures 4 and 5 which separately show the actual price lines, quinquennial moving averages and the linear trends of the two series. The conclusion that there was a secular rise in the prices of agricultural goods is inescapable.

Prices of other agricultural products also rose in a similar fashion. Figure 6 gives the prices and their linear trends of two commodities, clarified butter and mustard oil, from the Chinsura series. Figure 7 charts the prices and linear trends of clarified butter and mustard oil in the city of Calcutta between 1754 and 1800 on the basis of the data provided by W.B. Bayley.

The price data show certain important trends. First, they reveal a generalized rise in the prices of all agricultural commodities. Second, there was a fairly continuous rise in the rural prices of rice, and this feature is of great significance in understanding the developments in the provincial economy. In this context, Figure 8, which compares the prices of common rice in different districts with those prevailing at Calcutta for years when such comparative data are available, certainly allows the conclusion that it is for the first time in Bengal's history that we can speak of a provincial market integrated by uniform price-trends. That the economy was price sensitive is also highlighted by the fact that a rise in the price in some districts would immediately push up prices in far-flung areas. This aspect of price behaviour comes into sharper relief during times of dearth and famine. This I discuss in Chapter 5.

On the whole, it is the synchronicity of prices of different agricultural products which is the clearest indicator of market integration. In this connection, Figure 9, which shows the movement of *aman* rice prices in Burdwan and Birbhum between 1784 and 1813, is a clear illustration of the symmetry of prices in two contiguous districts of Bengal.

Finally, agricultural prices exerted a grave influence on the prices of other commodities and on the living standards of both the agricultural and non-agricultural population, a point which requires further elucidation.

An inter-sectoral interdependency of prices, whereby the oscillation in one sector influenced prices in another, seems to have been a well-established feature of Bengal's agrarian economy. Naturally, therefore, price movements influenced incomes in the different sectors of production. A rise in the price of rice or paddy meant that 'the ryotts are obliged to sell the produce of their lands dearer than formerly' while the manufacturers 'paying more than formerly for the materials & for the necessaries of life are unable to subsist without increasing the price of their goods'.[47] H.T. Colebrooke (writing in 1793) observed that the price of grain had the greatest influence on the prices of other commodities in the market.[48] The high price of cotton in 1789 was being blamed 'upon the famine [1788] which increased the value of corn'.[49] 'Should a degree of scarcity raise the price of grain above the average rate, it falls heavily on the manufacturer',[50] and an 'exorbitant encrease [sic] on the rate of the necessaries of life renders the ordinary allowances for labour insufficient'[51] are statements which clearly indicate the economic influence exerted by the state of agricultural prices on the conditions of practically every harvest-dependent social strata in Bengal. The people who were most affected by the state of agricultural prices were presumably the poorer-peasants having insufficient lands at their disposal, the rural and urban labourers, and those artisans who depended exclusively on the market for their subsistence. A study of the weavers in the employment of the East India Company shows that a rise in food prices was fraught with severe consequences since these artisans had to pay more to buy food for their subsistence, but were themselves unable to raise the prices of their products.[52]

That the prices of non-agricultural products had risen prodigiously during the course of the late eighteenth century appears an undeniable fact. For instance, the market price of silk-cocoons apparently increased by more than 50 per cent within the space of one year between 1770 and 1771,[53] while there was a short-run slump in the prices of paddy and other 'inferior variety of grains' in many districts between 1771 and 1773.[54] Whatever relief this may have provided for the artisans was clearly to be short-lived, as 1773–4 and 1775 were once again years of dearth caused by bad harvests. As rice prices rose, the prices of raw materials and of the finished-good tended to rise proportionately. Thus by 1789: 'The unusual rise in the prices of the two principal articles so necessary to the weavers, Rice and Cotton, has created an encrease [sic] in the price of cloths at the Markets beyond what was ever known, and introduced a practice of reducing the number of threads of the warp, which has debased the cloths in their texture.'[55]

Another aspect, vital to the structure of local trade in food-grains, was the nature of the price differential prevailing between town and country. Table 10 sets the widely scattered evidence regarding this in a somewhat comprehensible fashion.

Table 10. Price Differentials Between Town and Country
(*Rs per maund*)

Year	Place	Price in towns	Price in country
1773	Chittagong	0.62	0.55
1774	Chittagong	0.61	0.54
1775	Chittagong	0.62	0.56
1774	Burdwan	1.43	0.80
1775	Murshidabad	1.31	0.52
1788	Dinajpur	1.17	1.06
1789	Dhaka	0.68	0.53
1791	Birbhum	1.54	1.06
1792	Birbhum	1.40	1.05
1794	Dhaka	0.80	0.57
1791	Calcutta	1.38	1.14
1792	Calcutta	1.82	1.25
1792	Calcutta	0.94	0.44

Source: IOR, BRC,P/49/44, 11 Dec. 1773, 10 Jan. 1774; P/49/47, 22 Aug. 1774; P/49/50, 28 Jan. 1775; P/51/21, 4 June 1788; P/51/50, 28 Oct. 1789; P/52/37, 23 Nov. 1791; P/52/42, 9 March 1792; P/52/44, 4 May 1792; P/52/45, 1 June 1792; Rajat Datta, 'Merchants and Peasants', p. 389.

Thus Bengal prices show an integrated economy undergoing a fairly noticeable rise in the rural prices of food, and this fact was important in shaping merchant–peasant linkages. In other words, the nature of price differentials between town and country, coupled with the rise in country prices had significant socio–economic implications. As will be discussed subsequently, they provided a new direction to local trade in agricultural produce, not just in terms of movement of food, but also with regard to the social relationships which emerged in the countryside in this period.

MARKETS AND THE STATE

The importance of an orderly system of markets in the overall movement of local trade and the connection between trade and revenue was recognized both by the Nizamat and the East India Company. Murshid Quli Khan, the first really powerful Nazim of the province, seems to have made it his avowed policy to intervene in the movement of grain from the countryside to the towns only during periods of food shortages in an attempt to restrict monopolies by the grain merchants.[56] Apart from the tax motive, such intervention by the regional state was also guided by the immediate expedient of keeping supply lines open to towns under the threat of scarcity. Price regulations and control by the Nizamat was an exercise in redirecting the movement of the agricultural surplus from the countryside to the towns during years of scanty harvests. In normal agricultural years, the relative balance between supply and demand was allowed to regulate both the amount of staples flowing into the towns and the prices at which these were sold. The *nirkh* (price rates) in the bazaars of the early eighteenth century signified 'the prices which the vendors generally regulated on their own', which were then confirmed by the official seal of the market supervisor (*daroga-i-bazaar*).[57]

The Nizamat's attitude towards the market under normal economic circumstances was guided by its own perception of mercantile activity and by the social milieu in which these markets were formed and functioned. The state's attitude to mercantile activity is perhaps evident from Alivardi Khan's assertion that the 'merchants are the Kingdom's benefactors; their imports and exports are an advantage to all men. . . '.[58] It was this attitude, held by the Nazims in general, which probably resulted in their farming the trade of 'the several articles which constitute the internal commerce of Bengal and Bihar' to the local merchants: 'such commerce seems to have consisted principally, if not exclusively, in commodities of the natural produce, or manufactures, of these provinces' wrote Henry Vansittart (in 1762) about the state of internal commerce under the Nizamat.[59] Such an arrangement seems to have been mutually acceptable to both parties involved in the venture. For the state it was certainly considered financially viable;[60] so was it for the merchants.

Thus, in Bishnupur the betel-leaf (paan) merchants had in the past the 'exclusive privilege vested in them of vending all the betel produced in Bishnupur or brought from other districts [thereby becoming] purchasers at their own prices & vendors at what rates they please'.[61] The betel-leaf trade at Dhaka was similarly situated. The farmer of this trade (paan *mahal*) purchased zones of exclusive trade from the state and 'no other person could bring any betel leaf from the moffusul and if anyone attempted it, the farmer attached the leaf, as his property, by virtue of his engagements with the government'.[62] These exclusive rights of trade were not limited to a high-value article like betel. The Nizamat era seems to have seen the formation of such rights in practically all types of commercial activity, even at the lowest rung of the market (the *haat*) at the village level. At Nadia, petty retailers of rice and paddy paid special monetary gifts (*salami*) to the zamindar for the exclusive privilege of selling rice at the *haat*; there were *salami*s paid for acquiring similar rights over retailing salt, over gathering shells for making lime (*chunam*), for weighing and measuring commodities being brought for sale at the *haats* (*kayali*), and even for the sale of firewood to cremate the dead in the village.[63]

The other factor which influenced the state's attitude towards markets was the social origins of such places in Bengal. What mattered here were not merely the larger markets in towns like Dhaka and Murshidabad, but the whole range of small and intermediate markets (*haats* and bazaars) which were linked in a pervasive commercial network. As discussed in Chapter 3, some of these smaller centres of redistribution were created partly by the family members of the Nazims and by their officials. In greater part however, they were the products of zamindari initiative. A census of the number of markets in Burdwan in 1790 showed that the rajas actually owned 7 *ganjs*, 1 bazaar, and 16 *haats*. Of these, Raja Tejchand had established 9; Trilok Chand, 11, and Kirti Chand, 4.[64] Of the 42 *haats* in pargana Buluah in 1795, 39 belonged to zamindars 'in regular succession' while the remaining three were 'dwattar'.[65] In Dhaka, several 'petty bazars' were established by holders of revenue-free lands, and the profits from such markets were 'employed in defraying the expences of different Musjids [mosques] & Takoor Baris [temples] & for performance of religious ceremonies'.[66] It is, therefore, not surprising that the zamindars persisted in claiming from the Company 'an equal right in rents arising from gunges and bazaars' as late as 1790,[67] when the entire political equation had changed in the province.

The Nizamat implicitly recognized the importance of mercantile activity and of an articulated network of markets to the regional economy. An illustrative example of how commercial considerations shaped the attitudes of the potentates of the state can be given from the case of liquor manufacturing and retailing in the environs of Murshidabad. Here, 38 out of 80 shops selling high grade liquor, 28 out of 53 shops retailing toddy, and 62 out of the 139 shops dealing in opium in 1790 were owned by Nawab Mubarak-ud-daulah and his family.[68] Given the fact that the 'vend of liquor is extensive in towns',[69] ownership of retailing outlets provided supplementary income for the town élites, thereby showing the extent to which the upper crust had become integrated with the commercial network. Further down the social scale we find merchants, even at the *haat* level, willing to pay a tax (even a bribe) in exchange for acquisition of exclusive privileges of trading even in basic staples like rice.

But there were still major barriers in the way of a regionally integrated market in the first half of the century. The fact that merchants, and even petty vendors at the *haat* level, were able to carve out petty domains of privileged trade, and that zamindars and other landed proprietors were the prime agents for the establishment of these markets jointly militated against the development of an unfettered system of markets in the province. The reason for this zamindar/*byapari* combination was largely due to the state's internal need to balance the two social strata in order to ensure its own stability[70] in the midst of a prosperous economic situation. However, the overall outcome of such an arrangement seems to have been a combination of two developments: (*a*) a proliferation of zamindari *chowkis* (outposts) to collect tolls at various rates dictated by the financial predilections of an individual zamindar;[71] and (*b*) continuous conflicts between merchants and zamindars, and between zamindars and other landed proprietors, over the rate of tolls, over market jurisdictions and the movement of commodities. These conflicts often assumed violent proportions and could even disrupt marketing networks in the short run.[72]

The post-1757 era saw the state and markets interacting along significantly restructured lines because of the changing political and commercial situations in Bengal which necessitated a closer control over internal markets than that which had prevailed under the previous regime. After 1757, state intervention assumed the apparently contradictory forms of rigorous control in the marketing of some commodities and a relatively striking non-interference in the movement of others. The pressures of a world market meant that commodities like textiles and opium (and later indigo) were to be rigorously controlled at all levels including production. After 1772, salt was added to the list of official monopolies, not so much for its overseas value as for its being lucrative in the internal trade of the province.[73]

For trade in other commodities, especially that in agricultural produce, the Company's attitude was one of ensuring 'fair trade',[74] which entailed the dissolution of the restraints not only of the type inherited from the Nizamat, but also of the type fostered by the Company's own officials in the form of the Society of Trade. The latter task was tackled by the administrative exercise of prohibiting the private trade of its officials from 1771 onwards, and by attempting to place severe restrictions on profiteering and hoarding of grain during times of scarcity.[75] The former job occupied a major portion of its official business, especially after the disastrous famine of 1769–70. With regard to the internal barriers to the movement of trade, the Company's attitude was that *chowkis* were inimical to fair trade and to the honest trader as these, and the tolls levied there, meant that merchants were 'too frequently and . . . unnecessarily subjected to the exercise of authority' other than the Company's, and that too many transit duties tended to push up prices beyond any reasonably accepted standards. The logical step from this type of reasoning was that the *chowkis* had to be abolished and duties had to be streamlined so that prices 'of manufactures and of the necessaries of life' could be brought down.[76] Implicit also was the need to display the Company's newly acquired political power. 'A market is a place', wrote Vansittart in 1778, ' where authority must be exercised to regulate the weights and scales, to preserve order and to afford protection to the persons who frequent it. . . .'[77]

The first major step in the realization of the Company's aims came in 1773 when:

(1) all duties levied upon grain 'in its transportation from the country' were abolished;

(2) duties on trade in agricultural produce were henceforth to be collected 'only at the capital towns whither it is brought for consumption', and the management of such duties was to be under five customs houses to be established and stationed at Calcutta, Hughli, Murshidabad, Dhaka, and Patna;

(3) 'all road duties [*rahdari*] whether by land or water exacted antecedent' to the regulations of 1773 were to be made null and void;

(4) 'all the inferior types of chokies [*chowkis*]' over all types of trade routes were to be dismantled in a phased manner; and

(5) the right of the local merchant to be 'at liberty to carry his merchandize where ever he thinks proper for sale' was to be ensured.[78]

The thrust of these regulations seems to have had an immediate impact, at least on the movement of trade to the towns. For example, the general levies made on zamindari piers (*ghat chowkis*) between Murshidabad and Calcutta declined from a previous (in 1756) range of Rs 4 to Re 1 to a high of Rs 3 and a low of Re 0.12 in 1774.[79]

The control exercised by the zamindars and *talluqdars* over markets was not easy to tackle. The main reason for this was the continuing resistance of these people to any state interference in what they considered to be their hereditary and ancient rights.[80] The problems in this regard were many, thereby showing the complexities involved in state intervention in a sphere it considered a pure economic institution but which was in reality a distinct form of agrarian property. Markets were established by 'zemindars, talookdars and every denomination of rent free holders'[81] with a view to their income, but like all things privately owned, these were often sold to a host of buyers which created major problems in the way of the state's plans for outright dispossession. For instance, a detailed survey of markets situated around the town of Murshidabad in 1793 showed that 23 of the 32 markets situated in its proximity had changed hands within the past fifty years.[82] The buyers of such places, according to John Shore, were 'proprietors', and dispossessing such a person would amount to taking 'away his whole property from him; and this in Bengal would excite clamour and discontent in the proprietors'.[83] The apparent explosiveness of the situation forced the Company to drag its feet till about 1790 when the first major steps were taken to bring the landed proprietors to heel. The option of outright dispossession was hotly debated in the Board of Revenue, but was finally shelved. In order to circumvent the 'clamour and discontent', the state took a close look at the pattern of ownership and the structure of taxes and duties (*sair jihat*) in these market places, established a major difference between the two, and decided to continue one and abolish another.

What the Board of Revenue did was to make a separation between rents collected in these markets and taxes collected on trade. Rents were designated as 'any collections made . . . as a consideration for the use of grounds, shops and other buildings belonging to landholder', whereas taxes were deemed to be those levied as a 'duty on commodities' and on transit of goods. A landholder's right to collect rent was considered his 'private right' and therefore not to be interfered with, but the right to tax was construed as the 'exclusive right of government'.[84] Thus, on 20 July 1790, landholders were prohibited from all involvement in the collection of *sair jihat* in lieu of a fixed compensation, and henceforth 'no proprietor of land [would] be admitted to any participation thereof, or be entitled to make any claims on that count'.[85]

The Company's intrusion had a major impact on the state of Bengal's internal market. It led to that crucial bit of state intervention necessary for the final crystallization of an integrated market for agricultural produce in Bengal, thereby bringing to a culmination the processes already set in motion under the Nizamat.[86] The Regulations of 1773 were able to free the merchant from the clutches of zamindari outposts and toll-stations, at least in the commercially important areas of the province. The merchants were quick to react. Almost immediately they resorted to establishing '*private gunges* for the reception of all goods brought to the market by themselves and others' and were reportedly busy turning out from 'their golahs [granaries] and landing places the sircars [officials] and kyalls [weighmen] who are employed by the [Company's] Customs House'.[87] For the merchants, this jurisdictional redistribution actually served to expand their direct control over the internal market, both over the networks in them and over their spatial distribution.

The countryside of Bengal underwent a proliferation of such 'private gunges'. By the 1770s Calcutta was definitely undergoing an increase in 'various kinds of hauts and bazars',[88] which, in some quarters (like the police) was seen as a 'great public nuisance . . . by the general exposure of provisions of all kinds in the highways and the innumerable shops and sheds erected thereon'.[89] In the 1780s, 24-Parganas, situated south of Calcutta, was seeing an 'extension of hauts and bazars . . . by which old hauts are destroyed and new ones constructed'[90] and by 1792 this district had 144 markets of which *haats* numbered 100.[91] In 1790 Jessore was served by a chain of 225 *haats*,[92] and Burdwan had 17 *ganjs* and 345 *haats* in the same year.[93] The figure in Table 11 give some indication of the increase in the numbers of market-places in some districts of Bengal during our period.

The scale with which markets in Bengal appear to have expanded in this period was almost spectacular. A comparison with China is revealing. The Ch'ing period, which was characterized by an expansion of trade and the growth of 'periodic markets',[94] was undergoing a general 'accretion of markets'. For instance, in Szechwan the number of standard markets increased from 4 in 1622 to 13 in 1875.[95] Compare this to the fact that in Dhaka district alone there were 536 markets (*haats*, bazaars, and *ganjs*) in 1765; these had increased to 650 in 1791 (see Table 12). Obviously, areas previously deficient in markets were now brought under their purview. This facilitated peasant–market integration which, as is being argued here, was one of the distinctive developments in the eighteenth century. Skinner sees the proliferation of marketing centres in Ch'ing China as the 'intensification of the rural landscape'. In China this meant an increase in the volume of trade in an average market

Table 11. Number of Market-places in Selected Districts

District	Year	No. of markets	Year	No. of markets
Dhaka	c. 1765	536	1791	650
Jessore	c. 1778	69	1790	225
Rangpur	c. 1770	321	c. 1807	591
Dinajpur	c. 1770	206	c. 1807	635

Source: Taylor, *A Sketch of the Topography and Statistics of Dacca*, p. 203; BR Misc., IOR, P/89/37, 27 July 1791; BM, Add. MS 29088, fol. 150.

Table 12. Volume of Local Trade in Food-grains

Year	District	Trade in grain (% of total)
1771	Jalalpur	56.22
1779	Pagladanga[96]	62.37
c. 1807	Dinajpur	67.9
c. 1807	Rangpur	49.64

Source: Rajat Datta, 'Merchants and Peasants', p. 145; IOR, CCR, P/67/76, 12 March 1779; Martin, *Eastern India*, vol. 3, app. F; F. Buchanan, 'Statistical Tables of Ronggoppur', IOL, MS Eur. G. 11, Table 38.

day at already existing markets and/or an absolute increase in the number of fixed market days.[97] Considering the phenomenal expansion in Bengal, it seems likely that these features would be present here; and indeed they were. Apart from the *ganj*s, which were fixed daily markets, the *haat*s—the periodic (usually weekly) village market—in rural Bengal were beginning to be assembled every alternate day in certain localities.[98] Even in low-lying areas prone to inundation and floods by the seasonal overflowing of its rivers, markets were held 'for four & sometimes in some places for six months of the year on board of boats'.[99]

COMMERCIAL PROFILE OF LOCAL MARKETING NETWORKS

One aspect, crucial to the movement of local trade in Bengal was that many of the local marketing systems (*haat*, bazaar, and *ganj*) had become specialized agencies for the circulation of food and other items of immediate consumption. Bhagwangola, the main centre feeding Murshidabad handled about 18 million maunds of rice per year in the 1760s.[100] Large markets (*ganj*s) in Calcutta, like Baitakhana and Sovabazar, derived their tax revenue chiefly from the rice and paddy brought there for sale.[101] Similar patterns can be seen even in those areas where large towns did not exist. Purnea's annual trade in grain was worth 2 million maunds; single parganas in Dhaka circulated about 1.8 million maunds of paddy and rice a year; and individual *haat*s (village markets) in Bakarganj handled on an average 3,50,000 maunds of rice and 1,20,000 maunds of paddy a year.[102]

Estimates of the share realized by agricultural produce in the total amount of local trade are few, but those available for rice and paddy do strongly suggest that these were remarkably high (see Table 12).

Commercial dealings in these markets seem to have been quite buoyant in the period between 1760 and 1800, both in terms of the frequency of transactions and in terms of the social participation in them. In Jessore, 'every pergunnah and village have established bazars and hauts. Several of the villagers keep shops in them, while others hold them at their houses'.[103] The *moodie*s (grocers) of Calcutta traded in bazaars and from their own houses, while the *tahbazari*s[104] went to markets during the day, 'exposed their goods on stalls, or in temporary shops outside the established market', and returned home at night, only to arrive the next day 'with no other intention than to vend their articles which are usually of a perishable nature and must be sold within the day. . . .'.[105] In Dhaka, the *haat*s assembled twice or thrice a week, those in the city were open daily, and the main items of trade consisted of 'agricultural produce and of native manufactures'.[106]

These markets catered for a variety of local needs, both of commodities and services. A purely rural market supplying a few villages (*tarf*) of Rangamati (with a total of 256 houses in 1776) had 13 shops which included 4 grocers, 1 tobacconist, 3 dealers in cowries, and 2 money-changers (*sarrafs*).[107] A market established in early 1778, about '760 cubits away' from the big Sovabazar of Calcutta, had, by 1779, 54 shops comprising 39 *tahbazaris*, 9 *moodies*, 3 fishmongers, and 3 sellers of 'threads and blankets'.[108] A bazaar in Sutanuti (established in 1777) had, by December 1778, managed to attract a sizeable number of 101 permanent shops and 731 *tahbazaris* vending their goods in the open;[109] 6 new shops were added to this market in 1779, of which one was that of a *sarraf*.[110]

The apparent vibrancy in these markets can be explained partly by the exercise of the Company's political will in freeing the markets from the traditional social control of the landholders and partly by the significance of town demand. The *haats* of Jessore, for instance, seem to have proliferated in the 1780s, precisely at a time when its estuarine marshes were being reclaimed; and these markets functioned as a chain of feeder lines between the Sunderbans and Calcutta, which along with Katwa and Kalna formed the three consumption and redistribution centres in western Bengal.[111] But equal emphasis must also be given to the place occupied by rural demand in this situation. It is perhaps significant that Tippera, commonly recognized as having one of the most inhospitable terrains in its hilly parts, had 'upwards of 300 hauts' in 1790,[112] and Sylhet had 'no fewer than six hundred gunges and bazars' in the same year.[113] The flood prone area of Contai had *haats* where, apart from the usual trade in agricultural produce, 'small quantities of thread, coarse weaving cloth, mats made of split bamboos, brass and tutenag plates, *koddalies* [spades], plough shares, and ruts for winding thread' were sold at regular intervals.[114] In Rajshahi *haats* took to boats during peaks of monsoon flooding.[115] These examples reinforce the argument that there was a widely pervasive structure of rural demand. It is no accident, therefore, that the grain *byaparis* based in towns would often be found sending their surplus stocks, ostensibly kept to meet town demand, back into the countryside at the slightest available opportunity.

A SOCIAL PROFILE OF THE BYAPARI

Trade in agricultural produce was the task of a specialized community of merchants at all levels of the tiered markets in Bengal. At the *ganjs* and bazaars, there existed the 'principal' or 'capital' merchant, variously called the *goldar* (*golahdar* or owner of granaries), *aratadar* (wholesaler) and the *bhusi mahajan* (wealth in grain), depending on the colloquialisms of different areas.[116]

Below them existed a wide range of petty traders who usually traded with their stocks, but also functioned as part of an extensive network of commercial dealings created by the town-based merchants. The *farias* (pedlars) of Bakarganj[117] and the *paikar* and *baladiya* of Purnea[118] are examples of such lower groups of traders who, while functioning independently at one level, also combined the role of middlemen for some other, and obviously bigger, merchant. This would make the structure of local trading networks more of a multiform set of exchange relationships between a number of differentiated partners rather than a 'pyramidal structure' with an easily identifiable base and apex.[119] Multifarious relations of exchange would explain the function of the itinerant traders, like the ones in Birbhum who were merchants 'not residing but trading in the *zillah* [district] through agents in grain' in 1796.[120] Such relationships would also explain the existence of the bara *byaparis* of Rangpur who came on boats 'partly loaded with salt and other commodities and partly with cash' and made their purchases of 'grain, tobacco, oil and sugar', which were in turn sold to other merchants trading in the bigger centres.[121] In Dinajpur, the principal grain *byaparis* were stationed in Rajnagar (the main grain mart of the district) and traded through a wide range of commission agents (*gomasthas*) who made spot purchases and then transported the grain to Rajnagar for onward distribution.[122]

Such mercantile linkages also gave rise to various circuits of exchange between a whole set of merchants depending upon the nature of an individual's operations. In Jessore, for instance, *golahdars* sold to *bhashaneah* (river based) traders, who in turn dealt with petty retailers making spot purchases, but these retailers would often make spot purchases directly from the *golahdars* as well from the 'occasional vendors in the Bazars'.[123] We also come across a whole range of shopkeepers (*dokandars*) of Birbhum who were 'all retailers of grain' and dealt with the wholesale merchant who resided in the *zilla* and the itinerant trader who was usually non-resident.[124] Then there were the *tahbazaris* who, as in Calcutta, traded in open spaces outside an established bazaar mostly in items of immediate consumption. In Rangpur, Buchanan provides evidence for the existence of 17 specialized retailing outlets ranging from the grocer (*moodi*) to the dealer in unbleached cloths (*kaporiya*).[125] The existence and the apparent proliferation of such trading networks indicate the speed with which the circuits of exchange were completed in the local markets.

Who were the traders in agricultural produce? Data for reconstructing the social profile of the entire range of merchants in this sector are scarce. There is some evidence, however, for analysing the social origins of the 'principal' traders in the following tentative fashion. Buchanan lists merchants from Benares, presumably of the Khatri caste, and Gosains of north India as the richest merchants in Rangpur at the turn of the century.[126] In Dinajpur, the principal trader was the family-based concern of Bhoj Raj, an Oswal merchant from Rajasthan.[127] The single longest piece of evidence so far available of these merchants comes from the letters of R.P. Pott, the comptroller of government customs at Murshidabad, who (in 1787) described 'the whole body of grain beparis' in Murshidabad as being composed of 'four tribes', these being 'coyer, buccali, ouzineah and moorchak'.[128]

D.H. Curly makes an orthographical study of these names and then suggests that 'coyer' (*kaya*) refers to the merchants from Rajasthan, 'buccali' (*baqqali*) points to a traditional group of grain merchants common in all parts of north India, 'ouzineah' (*ujjaini*) alludes to merchants native to Ujjain and 'moorchak' (*murcha*) was the name of a merchant group trading with Murshidabad on the Jalangi river. Curly further suggests that these names do not refer to specific caste groups but rather to a set of regional identities and occupational positions; and that the *kaya* and *baqqal* probably represent a split between the Marwari and Bengali merchants.[129] A list of merchants trading in Rangpur in 1770, shows a dominance of banias or *baniks* (*saha, pal, seth*, and *poddar*),[130] while similar caste-names (*pal, saha, sheel*, and *addi*) figure prominently among the principal grain traders in Calcutta's Sovabazar in 1787.[131] Of a total of 45,835 maunds of grain allegedly withheld from the markets of Midnapur during the famine of 1788, grain *mahajans*, or *baniks* figure prominently as responsible for controlling 37,710 maunds; the rest (8,125 maunds) was held back by the zamindars and *chaudhuri*s.[132]

The overall weight of the evidence shows that wholesale trading in foodstuffs was the function of a specialized social community, the *banik* or *bania*,[133] and it is quite likely that it was in a process of transition from previously occupational groups into a distinct social caste in the eighteenth century. H. Sanyal's study of the Sadgops (an agricultural caste in south-west Bengal) and the *teli*s (oil-pressers) documents the social movement of groups from occupational categories to specific castes or sub-castes in agrarian society from the seventeenth century.[134] His study perhaps lends credibility to the view I propose of the grain merchants coalescing into a specific caste during the period under review.

MERCANTILE STRATEGIES: CREATION OF INTERMEDIARIES AND CIRCUMVENTING STATE CONTROL

Crucial to the principal traders were the links they could establish between their trading headquarters and the supply bases, and the manner in which they did so is of central importance to the ways in which they exercised their control over markets. In essence, what the merchants did was to establish a chain of intermediate dealing agents, the *gomastha* and the *paikar*. They traded with loaned capital for a commission, buying up from the *haat*s as well as directly from the peasants.[135] The reason why these agents had easier access to the peasants' threshing floor was due to their ownership of pack oxen which facilitated their movements in the *muffassal*.[136] These agents were also instrumental in forwarding seed advances to the needy *raiyat* on behalf of the superior trader.[137]

*Gomastha*s and *paikar*s purchased directly from the cultivators, and these purchases were made both at the latter's house and at the *haat*.[138] The *paikar*s took small advances from the non-resident merchant (in Purnea these advances ranged from anything between Re 1 and Rs 30 at a time),[139] gave 'ample security for the money' and made their purchases 'at a rate sufficiently moderate to admit of the pykars selling of it at the gunge price without loss to himself'.[140] The *kaya* and *baqqali* merchants of Murshidabad had their kinsmen stationed in the principal markets of Dinajpur;[141] so did the non-resident merchants purchasing their grain in Rangpur[142] and in Birbhum.[143] But the networks did not stop at this. Big traders also entered into ties with other social groups not belonging to the same caste or kin. The *baladiya*s considered to be of a lower caste were the *paikar*s of the grain merchants of Rangpur[144] and Purnea.[145]

The establishment of these trading intermediaries represents the growth of interlinked capital in Bengal's countryside; a type of capital whose main concentration was in towns, and which, by a process of internal division, became fragmented into numerous clusters. Yet, in essence, these clusters were only the other face of a centralized deployment of capital. That the management of capital was centralized is apparent from the way in which these different merchants functioned. The Murshidabad-based merchants, divided as they were into four major groups, managed their affairs under the leadership of a head who was appointed by the group. Each 'tribe', writes Comptroller Pott, 'has a head who manages the business in Murshidabad for the collective body'.[146] What these so-called 'tribes' did was to form tightly-knit groups (*dala*) under the leadership of a *paramanik* or *dalapati* (the 'head' in Pott's language) who regulated the activities of its members spread out over an extensive catchment area. The Dinajpur merchants did so by having regular meetings (*baithak*) with their *dalapati* in Murshidabad where they formulated general principles and regulations in mutual consultation.[147] The importance of their trading concerns meant that restrictions on commercial and social dealings on the basis of caste could not be rigidly enforced. Other castes had to be incorporated in the wider network of the *dala*; even those considered low in the caste hierarchy were brought into its ambit as, for example, the *baladiya*s of Purnea and the *sahu* or *teli* merchants in Rangpur.[148]

All these factors resulted in a honeycomb of intermediate agents who were crucial to the control these merchants could exercise over markets. Close control over supply lines from the *muffassal* and an overriding profit motive were two inter-related considerations for any trader and these intermediaries were one way in which such aspirations could be realized.

Another crucial factor in merchant operations was the manipulation of agricultural prices. The price mechanism comprised two elements: the prices in the urban centres or in towns and the prices in the countryside.[149] The latter sphere determined what the merchants considered their price of procurement. The other aspect of the price situation (to which I have already drawn attention) was its apparent volatile nature, even during relatively normal agricultural years. Famines, or near-famines, and harvest failures exerted further destabilizing effects on prices.

To circumvent the problem of oscillating prices and to ensure remunerative returns at both ends of the trading scale were some of the principal concerns of these merchants. Any interference in this sphere was viewed with immediate hostility which even the Company realized much to its chagrin, especially during times of scarcity. Thus, in August 1774, when an 'unusual drought' was looming large and prices had risen to 'an alarming height' in the city of Murshidabad, boats loaded with rice at Bhagwangola would not proceed to the city as the *byapari*s 'were in hopes that the price would still rise, particularly if the unfavourable weather should continue. . .'.[150] During the widespread flood-induced famine of 1787, merchants continued to send rice to Calcutta from the already deficient places like Sylhet, Dinajpur, Dhaka and Rajshahi: 'the famine has already raised the price of rice considerably and the merchants continue daily increasing it by exportation'.[151] An attempt was made to place an embargo on exports from Rangpur by the Collector D.H. MacDowall, but the *byapari*s continued sending their stocks to Murshidabad, to be re-routed to Calcutta, saying that 'we have never sold grain at Rungpore, and from selling here great loss will accrue to us. . .'.[152] In fact, even Warren Hastings was forced to deregulate prices and suspend *ganj* duties to coax merchants to bring rice to Calcutta in 1784 (a year of a partial famine) as 'they were deter'd from bringing it to market because they were obliged to sell it at an arbitrary valuation'.[153]

Governmental efforts to meet this problem head-on met with less success than had been anticipated. They simply could not break through the mercantile web and deal directly with the cultivators. Merchants bought all the surplus grain available at the slightest suspicion of state interference. 'The mahajans having by some means obtained information of Government's intention are endeavouring to purchase up all the grain of the country in the expectation of making their own terms', wrote the collector of Tirhut in February 1795.[154] In Sylhet, attempts to keep the state's involvement in the purchases of grain under wraps failed in October 1794 as 'the rice merchants forming an idea that the government are in want of grain store it up to enhance the price and thereby distress the District'.[155] State buying in Purnea was similarly troubled. The collector there wrote in dismay that his attempts to purchase 10,000 maunds had increased the spot price of rice 'by one-fourth the next market day', whereas 50 merchants could purchase 20,000 maunds in one day '*without any enhancement of price*'.[156]

This covert resistance by the grain merchants made the Company reverse its policy initiated in 1794, to buy directly from the producers at regulated prices and to stockpile in 'public granaries'.[157] This resistance forced them to make purchases 'by private arrangements with grain merchants and other persons in such manner as may appear best calculated to procure grain at the cheapest rate',[158] even though it was universally known that the 'mohajons always sell at a higher price than what can be purchased from the ryotts'.[159]

MERCHANTS, PRICE CONTROL, AND PROFITS

Having circumscribed the interference of the state in agricultural prices, the merchants set about determining these themselves. It was commonly accepted that the sale prices in towns and *ganj*s were determined by the merchants themselves,[160] presumably in their periodic *baithak*s. The merchants of Calcutta, who purchased grain from the ones trading from Murshidabad and Dhaka, frequently complained that coming to agreeable sale prices between these groups was difficult because of the interference of the Company in Calcutta's bazaars; their logic clearly being that prices had to be negotiated between the traders themselves, and that the merchants would trade wherever they received a better price: 'more will be brought to the market if the merchants are permitted to sell [at] what price they please', said the *byapari*s of Calcutta to John Shore in February 1788.[161]

Apart from manipulating prices during times of scarcity (discussed later), these merchants also took advantage of the seasonal flow of the principal riverine systems upon which the larger towns depended on their supplies of food from long distances. The following description pertaining to the supplies of food to Calcutta in 1791 is extremely revealing:

The times when rice becomes most scarce and dear are in a month or two after the communication between the Great River [i.e. the Ganges] by means of the Gelingee, Cossembuzar and Sooty Rivers, with the river Hoogly are stopt [sic], and become unnavigable, even for small craft, which usually happens by the end of November, or early in December, and continues to the end of May, or beginning of June, when these channels of conveyance again are opened, and become navigable; from which it appears that all communication with the upper provinces, and the importation of grain from these parts are shut up, for about six months in a year. This therefore is the season when rice usually becomes dear, not because a real dearth or scarcity reigns, but that here in Calcutta, and the province of Bengal, the corn-merchants in wholesale and retail raise the price of their grain; and this they always do from December to June when the communication with the upper country is open again.[162]

It was precisely the determination of 'the price they please' which made the merchants hostile to state intervention, as I have just shown. At another level, it caused them to chart out numerous strategies in order to control prices and supplies as well as to ride the numerous price crests and troughs. These strategies were designed to control the source of all trade: the peasant. One such agency was the chain of intermediaries who made spot purchases from the *raiyat* houses as well from the *haat*s. This was complemented by the ownership of storehouses (*golahs*) at various places capable of storing up to 5,000 maunds of rice or paddy for more than five years without damage, and by the possession of those crucial modes of transportation which the *raiyat* lacked.[163]

The *gomastha* and *paikar* both purchased whatever surplus was available and forestalled competition, thus enabling particular merchants to emerge as pre-emptive buyers in their own trading regions. The *golahs* enabled the merchants to tide over seasonal variations in agricultural prices between the time of ploughing and sowing (when prices were at their highest and grain was sold or advanced as seed loans) and harvests (when prices ebbed and grain was purchased). These *golahs* also enabled them to even out any disadvantages which may otherwise have arisen from unseasonal price oscillations created by an intermixture of good and bad agricultural years. In good years, when grain prices dropped sharply, the merchants would buy up, store in their *golahs*, and release in both directions (town and country) in bad years brought about by crop failures.[164] The *gomasthas* were under strict instructions to cease making spot purchases (usually done immediately after the harvest) if they felt that the prices were not low enough, or that the peasants were bargaining for better terms.[165] The producers faced major problems if this ever materialized as it would immediately jeopardize the payment of revenue to the state in cash since 'without the assistance of the merchants, the ryotts suffer the greatest distress to liquidate the demand for rent upon them'.[166] This pressure forced the cultivators to suffer an enforced reduction of price in order to appease the merchant. It is therefore hardly surprising that the *raiyat*s were often 'obliged to dispose of their grain on any terms, for one third, often for half less, than the customary market price'.[167]

Profits from trade seem to have emerged from three levels. At the first level were those profits which accrued from the act of selling in the towns. At the second level we can see those profits which emerged while purchasing grain from peasants, and at the third level were the super-profits which merchants made during times of scarcity. The first two levels were ever present in any type of transaction,[168] whereas the third was periodic but immense nevertheless.

Contemporary notions that average rates of profit from selling grain in towns ranged from 15 to 20 per cent under normal circumstances[169] may have been a conservative estimate as the following figures show.[170]

Year	Sale of rice in	% of profit
1775	Murshidabad	52.6
1794	Dhaka	42.8
1794	Calcutta	77.7

Trade with the towns was not a profitable venture in grain alone. Betel-leaf merchants of Dhaka, who had carved petty monopolies of their own, had an extremely lucrative trade going precisely because of the price differentials which prevailed between the town and the *muffassal*: 'the difference between the price at which paun is sold in the city of Dacca, and the rate at which it is purchased, probably within three miles of the town, is frequently one thousand per cent' was how the profit from this trade was described by W. Douglas, the collector of Dhaka in October 1789.[171]

Such profits could emerge because of the prevailing modes of procurement which forced the peasant to remain at the lowest rung of the price mechanism prevailing in the countryside,[172] and it was here that we see the second level of profit in operation. The fact that peasants were coerced into selling at prices below a third or even half the 'customary market price' perhaps indicates the techniques of pricing strategies adopted by the merchants. In fact, the data available shows that the extent of under-pricing the producer could be higher than half the prevailing market prices at the village level.[173]

At the third level (during years of scarcity) the merchants made profits ranging from 150 to 200 per cent by manipulating the prices between town and country. Famines were boon years for these merchants in another way: these were also the years when villages became gross importers of food and profits ranging from 40 to 20 per cent were easily made by sending grain to

Year	Locality	Produce	% profit in procurement
1777	Burdwan	Rice	88.6
1777	Dinajpur	Rice	66.6
1794	Murshidabad	Paddy	75
1794	Murshidabad	Rice	44.4
1794	Purnea	Paddy	33.3

the *muffassal*,[174] but these were much below the advantages arising from trading with towns during such years.[175]

MERCHANTS AND THE AGRARIAN ECONOMY

As it is quite evident, the connections between the grain merchants and agricultural production were caused by a combination of factors in the late eighteenth century. Briefly stated, the linkages seem to have arisen out of a buoyant demand for food both in the towns and in the countryside, rising agricultural prices and a recurrence of famines and semi-famine situations which plagued the province from 1769 onwards (discussed in Chapter 5). These situations made it imperative for traders to keep a tight control over lines of supply which they did in two ways: (*a*) by the creation of a wide network of trading intermediaries (*paikar* and *gomastha*) scattered over an extensive catchment area; and (*b*) by the formulation of strategies designed to control the peasants' freedom of choice in the market. An analysis of the latter provides a picture of mercantile penetration in agricultural production.

There is some evidence to suggest that the grain *byapari* had started getting involved in the process of agricultural reclamation as a device to ensure steady supplies in the long-run. Evidence for merchants providing advances of money, through their agents, to cultivators wanting to reclaim wastes or cultivate their own lands 'to be repaid in kind at the time of cutting the crops' is available from Jessore. Such advances seem to have become endemic here, as can be seen from the description of such annual advances as 'the *invariable mode*, and the Ryotts having no other means of obtaining seed, rely upon their respective merchants, the whole of their profits arising from their lands, having been applied solely to the discharge of other debts, and their own subsistence'.[176]

In Rangpur, merchants could also be seen participating directly in production, that is, organizing production with the use of sharecroppers, apparently in a widely prevalent fashion.[177]

The merchants' participation in agricultural production was guided not only by their long-term interests as merchants, but also by certain constraints on Bengal's peasant economy and society which forced the producers to reach out to external agencies to fulfil crucial production requirements. One such constraint was the shortage of material resources in the hands of the 'inferior ryott' or the 'poorer class of ryotts'. Lack of resources made small peasant production vulnerable to any unbalancing forces, and the periodic incursions of famines and partial crop failures made this vulnerability chronic. It was precisely this susceptibility, caused by persistent shortage of working capital and the uncertainties of production, which enabled merchants to enter the realm of production by a combination of subsistence and production loans.

Consumption loans were taken by the peasants for a variety of reasons, the chief of which appears to have been to tide over particularly bad agricultural years. In Birbhum, 'money borrowed by the ryotts assumes such a variety of shapes that I [the collector] am at a loss what term to give it. Generally however [a loan] corresponds with the exigencies of a borrower.'[178] Interest on such loans ranged from 24 to 36 per cent per annum depending on the dictates of the creditor.[179] In the context of a persistent shortage of the means of livelihood and productive resources, these subsistence loans were the first steps in what subsequently would become a vicious cycle.[180] Once a loan was incurred, a series of good harvests in continuous succession would be the only way in which households could circumvent the prospects of prolonged indebtedness. Alternating cycles of good and bad agricultural years, because of the impact these had on the prices of their produce and their incomes, tended to drive peasant households further into arrears so that finally they were confronted by a seemingly insurmountable wall of debt servicing as well as a range of creditors. 'His debts annually accumulating, the ryott becomes enslaved to his creditor,' wrote Henry Colebrooke about the situation in Purnea.[181] Subsistence loans also provided one lever by which merchants could get a grip on the end produce antecedent to any interference in production.

Consumption loans were often accompanied by production loans, and it seems probable that loans of the latter type tended to predominate. The 'annual practice of the beparris to advance to the poorer class of ryotts a sufficient quantity of grain to sow their lands to be repaid in kind at the time of cutting their crops' had become the 'invariable mode' in Jessore by the later 1780s.[182] Half the standing crop of Burdwan in October 1794[183] and 'one half of the whole cultivation' of Dinajpur in 1807[184] were estimated to be the product of production loans. The cultivators of Purnea were 'accustomed to loans from the principal merchants which, however oppressive are absolutely necessary to them as they are unable to maintain cultivation unless they receive such assistance'.[185]

In Rangpur, where the general level of indebtedness was said to be lower than in its neighbouring district of Dinajpur, loans for the production of grain had nevertheless grown into a 'ruinous system' by the turn of the century.[186] Production loans were given as advance payments much before the commencement of the agricultural season, or as our sources describe 'long before the crops of the poorer ryotts are fit to gather'.[187] Writing in 1772, James Stuart commented that 'large sums of money are yearly lent out to the ocupyers [sic] of the lands in order to advance the improvements of the soil. The interest exacted for such loans is exorbitant because the repayment of capital is precarious.'[188]

Bengal had two major agricultural seasons, the *aman* (winter) and the *aus* (spring), and loans were contracted on both occasions. The winter rice harvest was considered of greater market value 'bearing a higher price and sought after by all'[189] and was, therefore, a prime area of merchant intervention. The seedlings for this harvest were universally sown in the Bengali month of *assar* (June–July) and reaped in *agrahan* (November–December). Advances on this crop were made in the months of *pous* or *magh* (December to February) and the repayments were made in the subsequent month of *agrahan*, thereby completing a yearly cycle of loans and repayments.[190] For the *aus* (spring) crop, merchant strategies were twofold: *gomasthas* (commission agents) would be sent to the villages '*to purchase it from the ryotts before they could dispose of their surplus crops*';[191] alternatively, advances to the cultivator were made in the month of *assin* (September–October), six months before sowing in the month of *baisakh* (April–May), to be repaid next *assin*, immediately after the harvest in the month of *bhadro* (August–September).[192] The timing of these loans was critical as any delay, even by a month, could lessen the amount of interest in the annual cycle of advances and repayments. Thus a 'man who shall make advances in Bhadoon expects and obtains a greater increase than the man who makes his advances in Assin and in this manner the increase is lessened as the time approaches for cutting the grain', wrote a contemporary observer in October 1794 in relation to the system of advances for the *aus* crop.[193]

Such loans were not limited to the cultivation of rice alone. Almost all major agricultural products were tilled under varying degrees of advance contracts. As discussed in Chapter 1, betel-leaf in eastern Bengal, and sugarcane in Birbhum were based on such arrangements with merchants, who then sent refined sugar to Calcutta. Tobacco grown in Nadia and Rangpur was partly financed by merchants of Calcutta, Dhaka and Murshidabad, and the rest was purchased by their agents on the spot. Ginger produced in Rangpur was sold immediately by the farmers to merchants as 'the whole is paid for in advance'.[194]

How did these loans operate? The terms on which such loans were given were elaborately laid down. First, the peasant contracting for these loans was not given any written document; the whole episode was conducted on a 'verbal basis'.[195] Second, he was to receive a maximum of two-thirds of the value contracted for as advance and the 'balance at the delivery of grain and at the rate that may first be established in the pergunnah after the reaping is over';[196] but the proportion of the total loan being given in advance depended upon the type of rice being cultivated. Peasants cultivating *aman* rice could hope to get up to half the amount in advance while those cultivating the intrinsically inferior *aus* grain had to be satisfied with a quarter.[197] Third, the terms of the agreement had to be faithfully 'observed and abided' by the borrower as he was 'under penalty of making good every loss that may occur [to the lender] from the non-payment, in addition to the amount being returned with interest'.[198]

Regarding modes of repayment, it appears that the interest charged on such loans was higher than what was demanded on loans of immediate subsistence. The available evidence suggests that these were to be repaid in kind at rates ranging from 38 to 50 per cent,[199] which would make the interest on such loans one and a half times greater than on loans for consumption. Moreover, the price mechanism under which such loans were given was crucial as well as additionally profitable for the merchants. These advances were made six months before the commencement of the sowing season, when prices were at their highest in the seasonal swing. Repayment had to be made immediately after the harvest—'settlement of account takes place as soon as the crops come in',[200] at a time when prices were at their lowest, thereby making the cultivator part with a larger portion of the produce while making adjustments for the seasonal price variation. The loans 'are made in the season when grain is dearest and repaid when the price is lowest'.[201] Peasants could stand to lose between '2 annas per rupee'[202] (or 12.5 per cent) and 25 per cent in real terms while making these adjustments.[203] 'The cultivators, of necessity, have to bear with all this,' remarked an Indian observer of agrarian matters in this period.[204]

These loans symbolize the intrusion of merchant capital into the very core of Bengal's economy; they also provide the point of reference for studying the dynamics of social domination over the processes of agricultural production. These loans were the 'usual and long standing custom'[205] between the merchant and the peasant all over Bengal, which meant that, apart from debt servicing, the cultivators were tied to the merchant 'in preference to bringing grain to the market'.[206] It is, therefore, hardly surprising that the trader could often procure supplies 'without making purchases with ready money.[207] The fact that the peasants of pargana Burdwan could declare unequivocally in the midst of a bad agricultural season that 'it is only because of the merchants that we have the means of purchasing our subsistence and preserving our lives' clearly shows the grip of merchant capital in rural Bengal.[208] The power inherent in a relationship of this kind is apparent from the fact that when merchants decided to call in, or discontinue such loans, the peasants were immediately 'obliged to dispose of their grain on any terms'[209] to appease the merchants as without their financial assistance 'the Ryotts suffer the greatest distress'.[210]

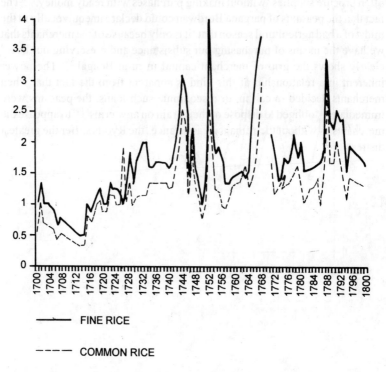

FINE RICE

COMMON RICE

FIGURE 1. FOOD GRAIN PRICES IN LOWER BENGAL, 1700–1800
(Rs per maund)

Source: G. Herklotts, 'Prices in Lower Bengal', *Gleanings in Science*, vol. 1,
January 1829
Note: Famine prices excluded

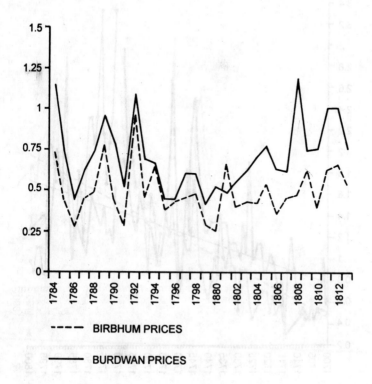

- - - - BIRBHUM PRICES

——— BURDWAN PRICES

FIGURE 2. COMPARATIVE RICE PRICES IN BIRBHUM, 1784–1813, COARSE RICE (*Rs per maund*)

Source: W. B. Bayley, 'Statistical View', *Asiatick Researches*, vol. 12, 1816.

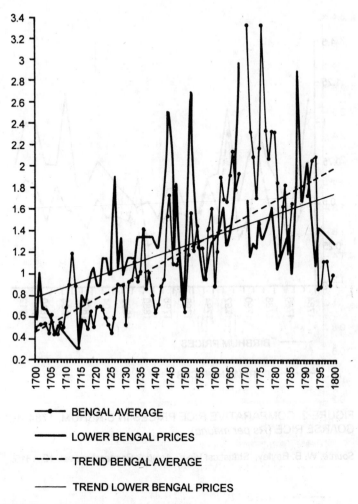

FIGURE 3. COMPARATIVE RICE PRICES IN BENGAL, 1700–1800:
COMMON RICE (*Rs per maund*).

Source: G. Herklotts, 'Prices in Lower Bengal'; Hussain, 'A Quantitative Study',
pp.368–9.
Note: Famine prices excluded.

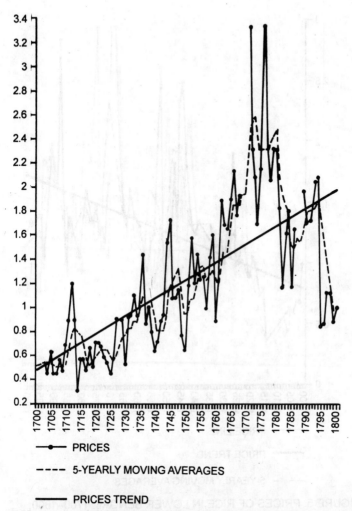

- ● - PRICES

- - - - 5-YEARLY MOVING AVERAGES

——— PRICES TREND

FIGURE 4. PRICES OF RICE IN BENGAL, 1700–1800, PRICE LINE,
TREND AND MOVING AVERAGES OF COMMON RICE
(*Rs per maund*)

Source: G. Herklotts, Prices in Lower Bengal'; Hussain, 'A Quantitative Study',
pp. 368-9.

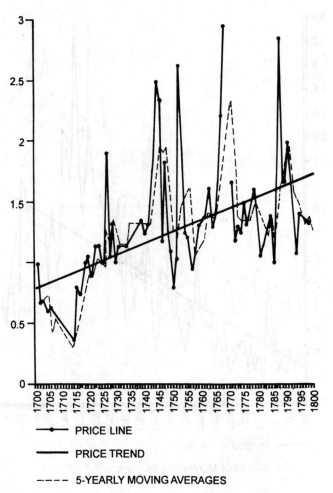

FIGURE 5. PRICES OF RICE IN LOWER BENGAL, 1700–1800,
PRICE LINE, TREND AND MOVING AVERAGES OF COMMON RICE
(*Rs per maund*).

Source: G. Herklotts, 'Prices in Lower Bengal'; Hussain, 'A Quantitative Study',
pp.368–9.

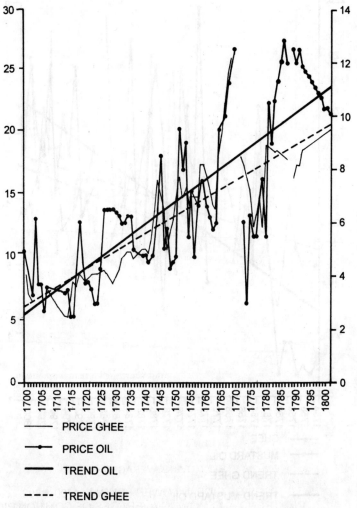

FIGURE 6. PRICES OF OIL AND GHEE IN LOWER BENGAL, 1700–1800 (*Rs per maund*)

Source: G. Herklotts, 'Price in Lower Bengal'.
Note: Famine prices excluded.

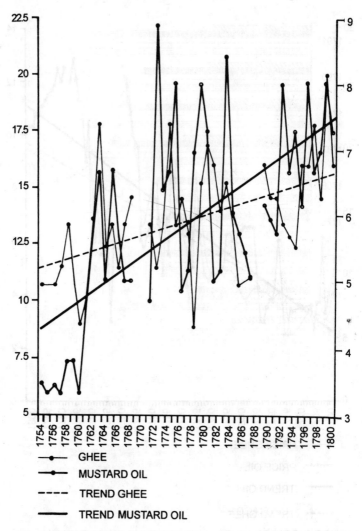

FIGURE 7. MUSTARD OIL AND GHEE PRICES IN CALCUTTA, 1754–1800 (*Rs per maund*)

Source: Bayley, 'Statistical View', *Asiatick Research*, vol. 12, 1816, pp. 560–1.
Note: Famine prices excluded.

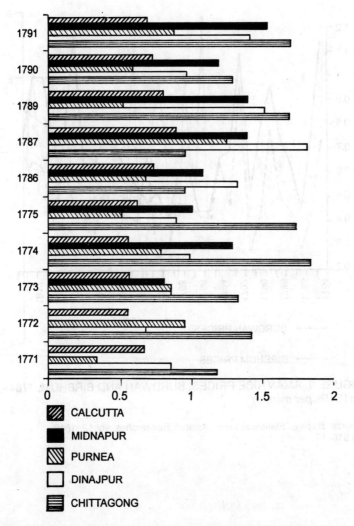

FIGURE 8. PRICES OF ORDINARY RICE IN BENGAL DISTRICTS
(*Rs per maund*).

Source: Bayley, 'Statistical View', *Asiatick Researches*, vol.12, 1816, pp.560–1;
IOR, BRC, P/59/42 to P/52/40; WBSA, Grain, vol.1, 17 Oct.1794 and WBSA,
PCR, Dinajpur, vols. 4 and 6; Appendix to Proceedings.
Note: Famine prices excluded.

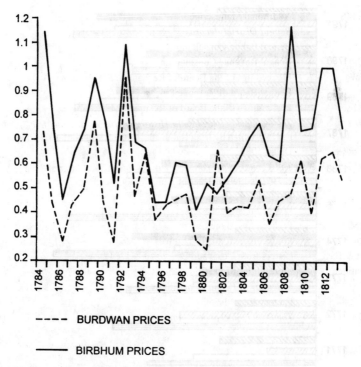

---- BURDWAN PRICES

—— BIRBHUM PRICES

FIGURE 9. *AMAN* RICE PRICES, BURDWAN AND BIRBHUM, 1784–1813 (*Rs per maund*)

Source: Bayley, 'Statistical View', *Asiatick Researches*, vol.12, 1816, pp.516–17.

ABBREVIATIONS

Add. MS	Additional Manuscripts
BDR	*Bengal District Records*
BPC	Bengal Public Consultations
BRC	Bengal Revenue Consultations
BRFW	Proceedings of the Board of Revenue at Fort William
BRP	Bengal Board of Revenue Proceedings
BR Misc	Proceedings of the Board of Revenue (Miscellaneous)
CEHI 1	*The Cambridge Economic History of India, Volume 1, c. 1200–c. 1750*, edited by Irfan Habib and Tapan Raychaudhuri, Indian rpt., Delhi, 1984
CEHI 2	*The Cambridge Economic History of India, Volume 2, c. 1757–c. 1970*, edited by Dharma Kumar with Meghnad Desai, Indian rpt., Delhi, 1984.
CCR	Proceedings of the Calcutta Committee of Revenue
CCRM	Proceedings of the Controlling Council of Revenue at Murshidabad
Circuit	Proceedings of the Committees of Circuit
Coast & Bay	Letters from Coast and Bay
Committee	Proceedings of the Controlling Committee of Revenue
CPC	*Calendar of Persian Correspondence*, Calcutta, various dates
FR	Factory Records
FR-2	*The Fifth Report of the Affairs of the East India Company, Volume II*, edited by W.K. Firminger, Calcutta, 1917
Grain	Proceedings of the Board of Revenue, Grain Branch
JPS	*Journal of Peasant Studies*
HM	Home Miscellaneous
IESHR	*The Indian Economic and Social History Review*
IOL/IOR	India Office Library/Records
Khalsa	Proceedings of the Board of Revenue, Khalsa Branch
LCB	Letter Copy Book of the Resident at the Durbar
MS/MSS	Manuscripts
WBDR, ns	*West Bengal District Records, New Series*, Calcutta, various dates
WBSA	West Bengal State Archives

NOTES AND REFERENCES

1. This question is particularly important in the context of eighteenth-century Bengal because the writing of economic history has hitherto been overwhelmingly concerned with Bengal's relations with the world market, or with the marketing structures and strategies for the high-profile commodities like textiles, opium and indigo.
2. P.J. Marshall, *East Indian Fortunes: the British in Bengal in the Eighteenth Century*, Oxford, 1977, p. 24.

3. IOR, HM, vol. 465, p. 146.
4. Rajat Datta, 'Merchant and Peasants: A Study of the Structure of Local Trade in Grain in Late Eighteenth-Century Bengal', IESHR vol. 23, no. 4, Oct–Dec. 1986, p. 287.
5. IOL, Francis, MS Eur. E. 12, fol. 250.
6. Robert Clive, *An Address to the Proprietors of the East India Stock*, London 1764 (IOL, *Tracts*, vol. 113) p. 19.
7. J.Z. Holwell, *Interesting Historical Events Relative to Bengal and the Empire of Indostan*, pt 1, London, 1765, p. 194.
8. IOR, BRC, P/49/38, 23 March 1773.
9. Ibid., P/51/20, 7 May 1788.
10. IOR, CCR, P/67/70, 30 April 1778.
11. IOR, BRP, P/71/70, 29 June 1789.
12. IOR, BRC, P/51/17, 4 March 1788.
13. Ibid., P/52/50, 19 Oct. 1792.
14. Rajat Datta, 'Merchants and Peasants', p. 148.
15. H.T. Colebrooke, *Remarks on the Husbandry and Internal Commerce of Bengal*, Calcutta, 1793; also F. Buchanan, 'Statistical Tables of Ronggoppur', IOL, MS Eur. G. 11, Table 40.
16. IOR, HM, vol. 434, 28 February 1791, p. 647.
17. Ibid., vol. 765, p. 146.
18. Cited in P.J. Marshall, *Bengal the British Bridgehead: Eastern India 1740–1828*, Cambridge, 1987, p. 151.
19. *Letter to the Proprietors of East India Stock*, London, 1776, p. 6.
20. WBSA, PCR, Murshidabad, vol. 8, 15 Feb. 1776.
21. IOR, BRP, P/70/48, 7 Nov. 1788.
22. WBSA, Grain, vol. 1, 17 Oct. 1794.
23. Ibid., 29 Oct. 1794.
24. IOR, BRC, P/52/27, 23 Nov. 1791; emphasis added.
25. Ibid., P/49/47, 30 Aug. 1774; emphasis added.
26. WBSA, PCR, Murshidabad, vol. 7, 15 Feb. 1776.
27. IOL, MS Eur. F. 95, fol. 64.
28. W.B. Bailey, 'Statistical View of the Population of Burdwan &ca.', *Asiatick Researches*, vol. 12, 1816, pp. 557–8.
29. Rangpur's area was 2,679 square miles according to James Rennell (*Bengal Atlas, Containing Maps of the Theatre of War and Commerce on that side of Hindoostan*, London, 1781, p. 53).
30. IOR, BRC, P/51/40, 15 July 1789.
31. IOR, BRC, P/51/40, 3 April 1789.
32. See Indrani Ray, 'Journey to Kasimbazar and Murshidabad: Observations of a French Visitor to Bengal in 1743', *Bengal Past and Present*, vol. C, pt II, no. 191, July–Dec. 1981, p. 56.
33. F. Buchanan, 'Statistical Tables of Ronggoppur'.
34. 'Memoir by Sir George Campbell on the Famines which Affected Bengal in the Last Century', in J.C. Geddes, *Administrative Experience Recorded in Former Famines*, Calcutta, 1874, p. 421; emphasis added.

35. See chap. 5.

36. IOR, BRC, P/51/12, 19 Oct. 1787.

37. In Rangpur the 'seven ranks' of people in society having a total of 66 persons, including dependents and servants, spent a combined sum of Rs 1,387.43 a year on food (F. Buchanan, 'Statistical Tables of Ronggoppur', IOL, MS Eur. G. 11, Tables 38, 39; hereafter, 'Ronggoppur'). These figures pertain to predominantly rural populations, patterns of consumption in cities would differ as large numbers of wealthy people residing there would tend to spend more on different types of food.

38. W. Tennant, *Indian Recreation*, 3 vols, Calcutta, 1804–8, 2, p. 2.

39. IOR, HM, vol. 434, George Smith to Henry Dundas, 28 Feb. 1791, p. 647.

40. M.M. Postan, *The Medieval Economy and Society: An Economic History of Britain in the Middle Ages*, 1975, p. 265.

41. C.E. Labrousse, 'Economic Fluctuations and the Individual', in M. Aymard and H. Mukhia (eds), *French Studies in History, Vol. 1: The Inheritance*, Delhi, 1989, p. 271.

42. A.J.S. Gibson and T.C. Smout, 'Regional prices and market regions: the evolution of the early modern Scottish grain market', *Economic History Review*, vol. 48, no. 2, pp. 258ff.

43. Ibid., pp. 260–1.

44. Ibid., p. 261.

45. I have used Akhtar Hussain's interpolations for the gaps in Heklotts's data. A part of this series is reproduced by Brij Narain, *Indian Economic Life: Past and Present*, Lahore, 1929. Brij Narain has given details only of rice prices whereas Herklotts gives the prices of a basket of major agricultural products.

46. Figures 5 also highlights the fact that notwithstanding the long-term provincial trend of a secular rise in price, there was a short-slump in prices just prior to the Permanent Settlement. This price trend is also revealed in Figure 13 which compares the prices of *aman* rice in the districts of Burdwan and Birbhum between 1784 and 1813. Though prices seem to have recovered around the turn of the century, the price slump was the unfavourable conjuncture amidst which the Permanent Settlement was introduced, the implications of which are beyond the prurview of this discussion. The synchronicity of the inter-district and inter-harvest price lines despite the temporary sharpness of the slump clearly indicates the relative inelasticity of rural demand.

47. IOR, HM, vol. 206, p. 149.

48. *Remarks*, p. 67.

49. IOR, BRP, P/71/9, 15 May, 1789.

50. IOR, BRC, P/51/22, 15 Aug. 1788.

51. IOR, HM, vol. 393, 6 Nov. 1788, p. 121.

52. Hamida Hossain, *The Company Weavers of Bengal: The East India Company and the Organization of Textile Production in Bengal*, 1750–1813, Delhi, 1980, pp. 9–11.

53. IOR, HM, vol. 769, 22 Aug. 1771, p. 361.

54. See WBSA, CCRM, vol. 3, 25 Jan. 1771; WBSA, Circuit at Purnea, 2 Feb. to 9 Feb. 1771, p. 8; IOR, BRC, P/49/40, 26 June 1773; ibid., P/49/46, 31 May 1774.

55. 'Report of Commercial Occurrences', 6 Aug. 1789, IOR, HM, vol. 393, pp. 254–5.

56. Francis Gladwin, *A Narrative of the Transactions in Bengal*, Calcutta, 1788, p. 122; also cf IOR, BPC, P/1/10, 15 Jan. 1733 and ibid., P/1/26, 19 Nov. 1757.

57. IOR, BRP, P/70/44, 11 July 1788; emphasis added.

58. Alivardi Khan to Barwell, 9 Jan. 1749, IOR, HM, vol. 804, p. 61.

59. Ibid., vol. 92, 15 Dec. 1762, p. 32; emphasis Vansittart's.

60. Ibid., p. 30.

61. IOR, BRP, P/71/23, 25 March 1790.

62. IOR, BRC, P/51/50, 24 Oct. 1789; emphasis added.

63. IOR, BR Misc., P/89/36, 13 May 1790.

64. IOR, BRC, P/52/16, 9 July 1790.

65. IOR, BR Misc., P/89/42, 29 May 1795.

66. Ibid., P/81/36, 13 May 1790.

67. Ibid., P/52/9, 9 April 1790.

68. IOR, BR Misc., P/89/36, 29 Oct. 1790.

69. Ibid., 7 May 1790.

70. See Philip Calkins, 'The Formation of Regionally Oriented Ruling Group in Bengal', *Journal of Asian Studies*, vol. 29, no. 4, Aug. 1970 pp. 799–806; Marshall, *Bridgehead*, pp. 63–4 and J. McLane, *Land and Local Kingship in Eighteenth Century Bengal*, Cambridge, 1993, for the political necessities facing the Nizamat.

71. For example in the crucial trade route between Calcutta and Murshidabad there were 18 *chowkis* (K.M. Mohsin, *A Bengal District in Transition: Murshidabad, 1765–1794*, Dhaka, 1973, p. 104).

72. Rajat Datta, 'Merchants and Peasants', p. 395.

73. See A.M. Serajuddin, 'The Salt Monopoly of the East India Company's Government in Bengal', *Journal of the Economic and Social History of the Orient*, vol. 21, pt 3, Oct. 1978; Balai Barui, *The Salt Industry of Bengal, 1757–1800: A Study in the Interaction of British Monopoly Control and Indigenous Enterprise*, Calcutta, 1985; P.J. Marshall, *Bridgehead*, pp. 111–12.

74. Minute of Warren Hastings, 9 March 1773; IOR, HM, vol. 217, p. 29.

75. Marshall, *East Indian Fortunes*, p. 243; Rajat Datta, 'Merchants and Peasants', p. 380.

76. Ibid., pp. 28–9; also cf IOR, BRC, P/49/38, p. 836, 1032.

77. Minute of Henry Vansittart, 16 Dec. 1778, IOR, CCR, P/67/72; emphasis added.

78. 'Regulations for the Future Establishments and Regulation of Duties of the Country Government, March 1773', IOR, HM, vol. 217, pp. 44–9; also BRC, IOR, P/49/38, 23 March 1773.

79. Compare K.K. Datta, *Studies in the History of the Bengal Suba*, Calcutta, 1936, pp. 159–60; and WBSA, PCR, Murshidabad, vol. 2, 20 June 1774.

80. For the opposition of the zamindars in Burdwan, IOR, BRC, P/52/9, 9 April 1790; in Jessore, ibid., P/52/14, 24 June 1790; and in Nadia, IOR, BRP, P/70/32, 28 Aug. 1787.

81. IOR, BRC, P/52/12, 28 May 1790.

82. Ibid., 15 May 1793.

83. John Shore in *FR 2*, p. 493.

84. IOR, BRC, P/52/13, 11 June 1790.
85. Ibid., P/53/1, p. 475.
86. This is in complete contrast to the assertion made by A.K. Bagchi that British rule completely 'disrupted' the 'network of markets' which were 'oriented towards domestic exchange' and 'failed often to compensate for this disruption' ('Markets, Market Failures and Transformation', in B. Stein and S. Subrahmanyam (eds), *Institutions and Economic Change in South Asia*, Delhi, 1996, pp. 51–2).
87. IOR, BRC, P/49/38, 19 Feb. 1773; emphasis added.
88. IOR, CCR, P/67/72, 16 Dec. 1778.
89. Ibid., P/67/62, 13 May 1776.
90. IOR, BRP, P/70/271, 8 May 1787.
91. IOR, BR, Misc., P/89/37, 27 June 1792.
92. Ibid., P/89/36, 5 July 1790.
93. IOR, BRC, P/52/16, 9 July 1790.
94. Rawski, *Agricultural Change and Peasant Economy in South China*, Cambridge, Mass., 1972, p. 69.
95. W.G. Skinner, 'Marketing and Social Structure in Rural China', *Journal of Asian Studies*, vol. 25, no. 2, pt 2, Feb. 1965, p.195.
96. This was a market in close proximity to Calcutta and handled the grain arriving from the 24-Parganas.
97. Skinner, 'Marketing and Social Structure', p. 196.
98. John Taylor, *Sketch of the Topography and Statistics of Dacca*, Calcutta, 1840, p. 294.
99. IOR, BR, Misc., P/89/36, 15 Sept. 1776; emphasis added.
100. Rajat Datta, 'Merchants and Peasants', p. 145.
101. IOR, CCR, P/68/8, 3 Sept. 1781.
102. Rajat Datta, 'Merchants and Peasants', p. 145.
103. IOR, BRP, P/71/25, 28 May 1790.
104. Literally below the market: a name given to the itinerant petty-pedlars in the bazaars.
105. IOR, CCR, P/67/72, 16 Sept. 1778; emphasis added.
106. Taylor, *Dacca*, p. 294.
107. WBSA, PCR, Murshidabad, vol. 8, 15 Feb. 1776.
108. IOR, CCR, P/67/65, 24 Jan. 1779.
109. IOR, BRC, P/50/13, 22 Dec. 1778.
110. Ibid., P/50/18, 27 July 1779.
111. Ibid., P/51/7, 26 Feb. 1788.
112. Ibid., P/52/19, 7 Sept. 1790.
113. Ibid., P/52/13, 8 May 1790.
114. IOR, BR Misc., P/89/41, 15 April 1794.
115. See n. 101.
116. For a discussion of the hierarchy of markets and merchants in neighbouring Bihar, see Kumkum Banerjee, 'Grain Traders and the East India Company: Patna and its Hinterland in the Late Eighteenth and Early Nineteenth Centuries', *IESHR*, vol. 23, no. 4, Oct.–Dec. 1986.
117. H. Beveridge, *The District of Bakarganj, Its History and Statistics*, Calcutta, 1876, p. 282.

118. WBSA, Grain, vol. 1, 17 Oct. 1794; also Buchanan-Hamilton, *Purnea*, pp. 695–6.
119. K. Banerjee ('Grain Traders and the East India Company') views local trade as a pyramidal structure.
120. *WBDR, ns, Birbhum*, p. 64.
121. F. Buchanan, 'Survey of Ronggoppur', IOL, MS, Eur. D. 75, fol. 85.
122. WBSA, Board of Revenue, Judicial Branch, 2 June to 30 Aug. 1790, 14 July 1790; WBSA, Grain, vol. 1, 15 Oct. 1794.
123. IOR, BR Misc., P/89/40, 20 Jan. 1795.
124. *WBDR, ns, Birbhum*, 4 June 1796, p. 64.
125. IOL, MS Eur. D. 75, fols. pp. 83–4.
126. Ibid., fol. 87.
127. M. Martin, *The History, Topography and Statistics of Eastern India*, 3 vols, Delhi, 1976, vol. 2, p. 759.
128. IOR, BRP, P/70/35, 27 Sept. 1787, letter dated 19 Nov. 1787; emphasis added.
129. 'Rulers and Merchants in Late Eighteenth Century Bengal', D Phil thesis, University of Chicago, 1980, pp. 24–5.
130. K.M. Mohsin, *Murshidabad*, pp. 24–5.
131. IOR, BRP, P/70/40, 18 April 1787.
132. IOR, BRC, P/51/21, 2 July 1788.
133. 'Dealers in the necessaries of life are of the same cast or tribe and connected with each other', and this was seen as a important reason for enabling 'them to form combinations against the public with greater facility than in other countries' (IOR, BRC, P/52/26, 21 Oct. 1791).
134. H. Sanyal, 'Continuities of Social Mobility in Traditional and Modern Society: Two Case Studies of Caste Mobility in India', *Journal of Asian Studies*, Feb. 1971.
135. See WBSA, Grain, vol. 1, 17 Oct. 1794 for Burdwan: 18 Oct. 1794 for Jessore; 10 Oct. 1794 for Bakarganj; 15 Oct. 1794 for Dinajpur; 17 Oct. 1794 for Purnea; 10 Nov. 1794 for Tippera.
136. Kumkum Banerjee ('Grain Traders and the East India Company', p. 408), following Buchanan-Hamilton, says that the *paikars* of Purnea did not use oxen, considered sacred beasts, as they were men of pure birth. Evidence to the contrary is however available. The *paikars* of Purnea 'from keeping a number of cattle are enabled to go some distance into the country and purchase the grain immediately as it is harvested from the cultivator . . .' says a report from the collector of Purnea in Oct. 1794 (WBSA, Grain, vol. 1, 17 Oct. 1794).
137. Rajat Datta, 'Merchants and Peasants', pp. 396–7, 399.
138. Beveridge, *Bakarganj*, p. 282; *BDR, Dinajpur, vol. 2*, 3 June, p. 231.
139. WBSA, Grain, vol. 1, 17 Oct. 1794.
140. Ibid.
141. WBSA, Board of Revenue: Judicial Branch, 2 June–30 Aug. 1790, 14 July 1790.
142. IOL, MS, Eur. D. 75, fol. 84.
143. *WBDR, ns, Birbhum*, p. 64.
144. Ibid., fol. 88.
145. Buchanan-Hamilton, *An Account of the District of Purnea*, Calcutta, 1928, p. 528.
146. IOR, BRP, P/70/35, 27 Nov. 1787; emphasis added.
147. Martin, *Eastern India*, vol. 2 p. 758.

148. IOL, MS, Eur. D. 75, fol. 84.

149. 'In distant parganas, far removed from proper means of transport and market towns, grain sells considerably cheaper, the price rising in places more contiguous to marts of grain' (WBSA, Grain, vol. 1, 31 Oct. 1794).

150. IOR, BRC, P/49/51, 13 Feb. 1775.

151. Ibid., 9 Aug. 1787.

152. Ibid., P/51/9, 21 July 1787.

153. 'Abstract of an Examination of Several Grain Merchants in Calcutta', Sir John Shore to Council, 1 Feb. 1788, in ibid., P/51/7.

154. WBSA, Grain, vol. 3, 14 Feb. 1795.

155. Ibid., vol. 1, 19 Oct. 1794.

156. Ibid., 31 Oct. 1794; emphasis added.

157. Ibid., p. 2.

158. Ibid., p. 147.

159. Ibid., 29 Oct. 1794.

160. IOR, BRC, P/50/30, 5 Jan. 17811; IOR, BRP, P/70/40, 1 April 1788; ibid., P/70/44, 20 Aug. 1788; Taylor, Dacca, p. 296.

161. IOR, BRC, P/51/17, 1 Feb. 1788.

162. Ibid., P/52/28, 1 March 1791; emphasis added.

163. Rajat Datta, 'Merchants and Peasants', pp. 400–1.

164. Ibid., pp. 395, 399–400.

165. WBSA, Grain, vol. 1, 17 Oct. 1794.

166. IOR, BRP, P/71/30, arzi of the Raja of Burdwan, 31 July 1790.

167. IOR, CCR, P/68/7, 4 May 1781; emphasis added.

168. In fact the distinction between the first and second levels of profits is largely formal in an effort to show the various channels which contributed to the making of mercantile profit. In actual operation these two levels were intertwined in a complex fashion, and it was level two (profits made from underpricing the peasant) which actually determined the range of profits which could be made in level one.

169. CPC, vol. 8, letter no. 158, 12 Feb. 1788.

170. Calculated from Rajat Datta, 'Merchants and Peasants', p. 389.

171. IOR, BRC, P/57/50, 24 Oct. 1789; emphasis added.

172. Also cf Rajat Datta, 'Merchants and Peasants', pp. 397–8.

173. Ibid., p. 398.

174. Ibid., pp. 389–90.

175. This relative disadvantage would perhaps explain the higher relative mortality in primarily rural areas (like Purnea, for instance) during the famine of 1769–70.

176. IOR, BRC, P/51/20, T. Henckell to Board, 7 May 1788; emphasis added.

177. IOL, MS Eur. D. 75, fol. 103.

178. IOR, BRP, P/790/35, 6 Nov. 1787.

179. IOR, BRC, P/49/38, 15 Dec. 1772; IOR, BRP, P/70/35, 13 Nov. 1787.

180. 'Once begun, a chronic cycle of indebtedness tends to reproduce itself. Prior debt prevents saving after the harvest, because the creditor calls in his loan, and means

456   THE EIGHTEENTH CENTURY IN INDIAN HISTORY

of personal and productive consumption will consequently be likely to run short again before the next harvest' (H. Friedmann, 'Household Production and the National Economy: Concepts for the Analysis of Agrarian Formations', *JPS*, vol. 7, no. 2, Feb. 1980, p. 172).

181. IOR, BRP, P/71/26, 18 June 1790.
182. IOR, BRC, P/51/20, 7 May 1788.
183. WBSA, Grain, vol. 1, 17 Oct. 1794.
184. M. Martin, *Eastern India*, vol. 3, p. 906.
185. IOR, BRP, P/71/25, 26 May 1790.
186. IOL, MS Eur. D. 75, vol. 2, book 4, fol. 84.
187. WBSA, Grain, vol. 1, 17 Oct. 1794.
188. 'Memoirs of the Coinage in Bengal', IOR, HM, vol. 62, p. 46.
189. WBSA, Grain, vol. 1, 17 Oct. 1794.
190. Ibid., 29 Oct. 1794.
191. Ibid., emphasis added.
192. Ibid., 17 Oct. 1794; also IOR, BRC, P/51/21, 29 Jan. 1788.
193. WBSA, Grain, vol. 1, 17 Oct. 1794.
194. IOL, MS Eur. D. 75, vol. 2, book 2, fol. 16.
195. IOR, BRP, P/71/26, 18 June 1790.
196. WBSA, Grain, vol. 1, 22 Oct. 1794.
197. IOR, BRP, P/71/26, 18 Oct. 1790.
198. WBSA, Grain, vol. 1, 22 Oct. 1794.
199. Rajat Datta, 'Merchants and Peasants', p. 159.
200. IOR, BRC, P/51/29, 29 Jan. 1788.
201. IOR, BRP, P/71/26, 26 April 1790.
202. IOR, BRC, P/51/21, 29 Jan. 1788.
203. IOL, MS Eur. D. 75, vol. 2, book 4, fol. 84.
204. *Risala-i-Zira'at* (tr. Harbans Mukhia, *Perspectives on Medieval History*, Delhi, 1993), sect. vii.
205. IOR, BRC, P/51/21, 14 June 1788.
206. Ibid.
207. IOL, MS Eur. D. 75, vol. 2, book 4, fol. 84.
208. IOR, BRC, P/49/37, 30 Aug. 1774; emphasis added.
209. IOR, CCR, P/68/7, 4 May 1781.
210. IOR, BRP, P/71/20, 11 Oct. 1790.

Notes on Contributors

P.J. Marshall retired as Rhodes Professor of Imperial History, King's College, University of London.

Frank Perlin was formerly of the Erasmus University, Rotterdam.

The late *Burton Stein* was Professorial Research Associate, School of Oriental and African Studies, University of London.

The late *M. Athar Ali* was Professor of History, Aligarh Muslim University.

Irfan Habib was formerly Professor of History and Co-ordinator of the Centre of Advanced Study, Aligarh Muslim University.

B.S. Cohn retired as Professor of Anthropology and South Asian History, University of Chicago.

C.A. Bayly is Vere Harmsworth Professor of Imperial and Naval History, University of Cambridge.

Muzaffar Alam is Professor in the Departments of History and South Asian Languages and Civilizations, University of Chicago.

Susan Bayly is University Lecturer in Social Anthropology, University of Cambridge.

Stewart Gordon is Research Fellow at the Center for South Asian Studies, University of Michigan.

John F. Richards is Professor of History, Duke University.

Kate Brittlebank is Vice-Chancellor's Postdoctoral Fellow in the School of History, University of New South Wales.

Ajay Skaria is Professor in the Department of History, University of Minnesota.

David Ludden is Professor of History and South Asian Regional Studies, University of Pennsylvania.

The late *Abdul Majed Khan* was formerly of the Victoria University, Wellington, New Zealand.

P.J. Cain is Research Professor in the Department of History, Sheffield Hallam University.

A.G. Hopkins is Professor of History, University of Texas at Austin.

Rajat Datta is Professor at the Centre for Historical Studies, Jawaharlal Nehru University, New Delhi.